Phobias

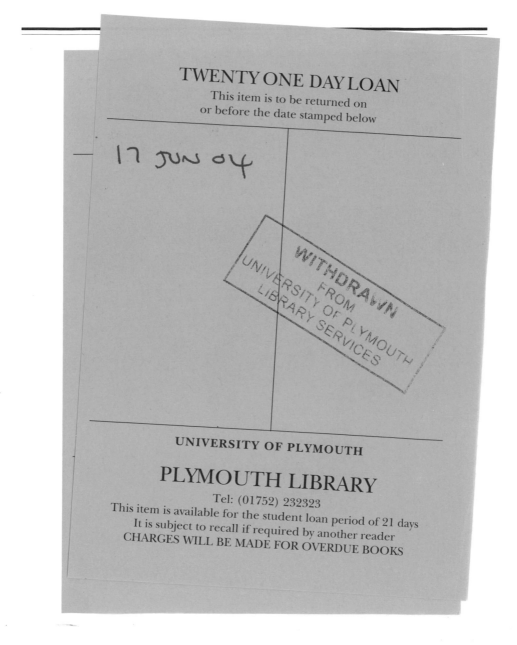

Phobias
A Handbook of Theory, Research and Treatment

Edited by
Graham C.L. Davey
University of Sussex, Brighton, UK

JOHN WILEY & SONS
Chichester · New York · Weinheim · Brisbane · Singapore · Toronto

Copyright © 1997 by John Wiley & Sons Ltd,
Baffins Lane, Chichester,
West Sussex PO19 1UD, England

National   01243 779777
International   (+44) 1243 779777
e-mail (for orders and customer service enquiries): cs-books@wiley.co.uk
Visit our Home Page on http://www.wiley.co.uk
or http://www.wiley.com

Reprinted June 1998
Published in paperback October 1999

Other Wiley Editorial Offices

John Wiley & Sons, Inc., 605 Third Avenue,
New York, NY 10158-0012, USA

VCH Verlagsgesellschaft mbH,
Pappelallee 3, 0-69469 Weinheim,
Germany

Jacaranda Wiley Ltd, 33 Park Road, Milton,
Queensland 4064, Australia

John Wiley & Sons (Asia) Pte Ltd, 2 Clementi Loop #02-01,
Jin Xing Distripark, Singapore 129809

John Wiley & Sons (Canada) Ltd, 22 Worcester Road,
Rexdale, Ontario M9W 1L1, Canada

Library of Congress Cataloging-in-Publication Data

Phobias: a handbook of theory, research and treatment / edited by
Graham C.L. Davey.
p.   cm.
Includes bibliographical references and index.
ISBN 0-471-96983-4 (cloth: alk. paper)
1. Phobias—Handbooks, manuals, etc.   I. Davey, Graham.
RC535.P486   1997
616.85′225—dc20   96-32895
CIP

British Library Cataloguing in Publication Data

A catalogue record for this book is available from the British Library

ISBN 0-471-96983-4 (hbk)✔
~~0-471-49220~~-5 (pbk)

Typeset in 10/12pt Times by Best-set Typesetter Ltd., Hong Kong
Printed and bound in Great Britain by Bookcraft (Bath) Ltd
This book is printed on acid-free paper responsibly manufactured from sustainable forestation,
for which at least two trees are planted for each one used for paper production.

Contents

About the Editor

Graham Davey is professor of psychology at The University of Sussex, Brighton, UK. His current research interests include the application of conditioning models to the understanding of anxiety disorders and investigation of the cognitive processes involved in worrying, and he has published scientific articles on these topics in international journals. He has written two text books on conditioning and learning, and has either edited or co-edited four other academic texts on conditioning theory and its applications. He was until recently an honorary editor of *The Psychologist* and is currently a member of the Council of the British Psychological Society.

Contributors

Arnoud Arntz, Department of Psychology, University of Limburg, PO Box 616, 6200 MD Maastricht, The Netherlands

Catherine M. Cameron, Psychology Group, School of Cognitive and Computing Sciences, University of Sussex, Falmer, Brighton BN1 9QR, UK

Tim F. Chapman, Box 13/NYSPI, 722 West 168th St., New York, NY10032, *and* Rutgers University, New Brunswick, NJ, USA

David M. Clark, Department of Psychiatry, University of Oxford, Warneford Hospital, Headington, Oxford OX3 7JX, UK

Michelle G. Craske, Department of Psychology, University of California, Los Angeles, 405 Hilgrad Avenue, Los Angeles, CA 90024-1563, USA

Graham C.L. Davey, Psychology Group, School of Cognitive & Computing Sciences, University of Sussex, Falmer, Brighton BN1 9QH, UK

Peter J. de Jong, Department of Psychology, University of Limburg, PO Box 616, 6200 Maastricht, The Netherlands

Ann Hackmann, Department of Psychiatry, University of Oxford, Warneford Hospital, Headington, Oxford OX3 7JX, UK

Louis P. Hagopian, The Kennedy Krieger Institute, Johns Hopkins University School of Medicine, Baltimore, MA 21218, USA

Peter Hayward, Department of Psychology, Institute of Psychiatry, De Crespigny Park, Denmark Hill, London SE5 8AF, UK

Kerstin Hellström, Department of Psychiatry, University of Uppsala, POB 256, 75105 Uppsala, Sweden

Gerry Kent, Department of Psychiatry, Sheffield Centre for Health and Related Research, University of Sheffield, Regent Court, 30 Regent St., Sheffield S1 4DA, UK

Neville J. King, Faculty of Education, Monash University, Wellington Rd., Clayton, Victoria 3168, Australia

Klaus Kuch, Smythe Pain Clinic, Toronto General Hospital, 3-640 Bell wing, 200 Elizabeth St., Toronto, Canada M5G 2C4

Richard J. McNally, Department of Psychology, Harvard University, William James Hall, 33 Kirkland Street, Cambridge, MA 02138, USA

Ross Menzies, Department of Behavioural Sciences, Faculty of Health Sciences, University of Sydney, PO Box 170, Lidcombe, N.S.W., 2141, Australia

Harald Merckelbach, Department of Psychology, University of Limburg, PO Box 616, 6200 Maastricht, The Netherlands

Arne Öhman, Department of Clinical Neuroscience, Karolinska Institute, Karolinska Hospital, S-171 76 Stockholm, Sweden

Tom Ollendick, Department of Psychology, Virginia Polytechnic & State University, Blacksburg, VA 24061-0436 USA

Lars-Göran Öst, Department of Psychology, University of Stockholm, S-106 91, Stockholm, Sweden

S.J. Rachman, Department of Psychology, The University of British Columbia, 2136 West Mall, Vancouver, British Columbia, Canada V6T 1Z4

Melissa K. Rowe, Department of Psychology, University of California at Los Angeles, 405 Hilgard Avenue, Los Angeles, CA 90024-1563, USA

Paul M. Salkovskis, Department of Psychiatry, University of Oxford, Warneford Hospital, Headington, Oxford OX3 7JX, UK

Susan J. Thorpe, Department of Psychiatry, University of Oxford, Warneford Hospital, Headington, Oxford OX3 7JX, UK

Jane Wardle, Department of Psychology, Institute of Psychiatry, De Crespigny Park, Denmark Hill, London SE5 8AF, UK

Adrian Wells, Department of Psychiatry & Behavioural Sciences, University of Manchester, Rawnsley Building, Manchester Royal Infirmary, Oxford Road, Manchester MI3 9WL, UK

Preface

The word "phobia" comes from the Greek word φοβος, meaning fear or terror, and is derived from Phobos, the god who was thought to provoke fear and terror in the enemies of the Greeks. The term phobia has come to cover a wide variety of fears and anxieties, but is used in clinical practice to denote inappropriate fears to relatively specific stimuli or events. What is fascinating about phobias is that we all know of at least one person who suffers some kind of phobia—whether it be something as common and yet seemingly as irrational as a spider phobia or as problematic, yet perhaps more understandable, as a dental phobia. Recent epidemiological studies have indicated that the life-time prevalence rates for clinically diagnosable phobias is between 11 and 12% (Epidemiologic Catchment Area [ECA] Study, Robins & Regier, 1991; National Comorbidity Survey (NCS), Kessler et al., 1994) and that specific phobias represent the most common psychiatric disorder amongst those studied in these surveys. What is more, these surveys have shown that phobic symptoms in general are exceptionally common, with around 60% of the population experiencing "unreasonable fear" of an event or situation at some point in their lives.

While phobias are currently acknowledged as being particularly common across all cultures and ethnic and socio-economic groupings, it is only rarely that specific fears and phobias are mentioned in historical writings and documents. Thorpe & Salkovskis (Chapter 4) recount how during the Middle Ages phobias were considered to be out of the domain of science and were seen as manifestations of evil spirits. Common phobias at the time appeared, not surprisingly, to be plague phobia and syphilophobia, with the first mention of spider phobia also being recorded. During the eighteenth and nineteenth century phobias came more within the domain of science and medicine, and many attempts were made to classify fears and phobias, their causes became linked more to psychical rather than demonic factors, and initial attempts at therapeutic treatment were explored. More recently, the study of phobias has been highlighted by Freud's analysis of "Little Hans'" horse phobia, and Watson & Rayner's attempt to deliberately induce a phobia of his pet rat in 8-month-old "Little Albert". These studies provoked a significant amount of critical analysis which did little to cast much light on the aetiological origins of phobias and served mostly to project these studies into psychological folklore, where they are now frequently misquoted and misunderstood.

Research on the aetiology, maintenance and treatment of phobias began to gather pace in the late 1960s and early 1970s, with Seligman's theory of the biological preparedness of phobias and the development of a range of exposure-based therapies arguably being the most significant contributions during this period. The 1980s and 1990s have seen an increasing understanding of the role of cognitive factors in the aetiology and maintenance of phobias, and such developments have indicated that phobic responding is far from non-cognitive and may well be maintained by a network of consciously available beliefs about the phobic stimulus and interactions with that stimulus. Thus, phobias may not be as non-cognitive and irrational as popular belief would seem to imply.

One of the most recent important changes that is relevant to our conceptions of phobias is the change to the diagnostic criteria for clinical phobias found in DSM-IV (American Psychiatric Association, 1994). First, this entailed the diagnostic category changing from "simple phobia" to "specific phobia"—the former name clearly implied a sense of mildness which belies the distress, suffering and disruption caused by a phobia of clinically diagnosable proportions. The current DSM-IV definition of a specific phobia is:

1. Marked and persistent fear that is excessive or unreasonable, cued by the presence or anticipation of a specific object or situation (e.g. flying, heights, animals, receiving an injection, seeing blood).
2. Exposure to the phobic stimulus almost invariably provokes an immediate anxiety response, which may take the form of situationally bound or situationally predisposed panic attack. Note: In children, the anxiety may be expressed by crying, tantrums, freezing or clinging.
3. The person recognizes that the fear is excessive or unreasonable. Note: In children, this feature may be absent.
4. The phobic situation(s) is avoided or else is endured with intense anxiety or distress.
5. The avoidance, anxious anticipation, or distress in the feared situation(s) interferes significantly with the person's normal routine, occupation, or (academic) functioning or social activities or relationships, or there is marked distress about having the phobia.
6. In individuals under 18 years, the duration is at least 6 months.
7. The anxiety, panic attacks or phobic avoidance associated with the specific object or situation are not better accounted for by another mental disorder, such as obsessive–compulsive disorder (e.g. fear of dirt in someone with an obsession about contamination), post-traumatic stress disorder (e.g. avoidance of stimuli associated with a severe stressor), separation anxiety disorder (e.g. avoidance of school), social phobia (e.g. avoidance of social situations

because of fear of embarrassment), panic disorder with agoraphobia, or agoraphobia without history of panic disorder.

The changes from DSM-III-R to DSM-IV have emphasized: (a) that a panic attack may be a specific form of response to interaction with the phobic stimulus or event; and (b) that anticipatory anxiety is a central feature of the phobic syndrome. This has in turn led to greater research interest in those factors which maintain anticipatory anxiety, and to an interest in the aetiology of specific phobias rather than phobic responding in general.

Since the earliest studies of phobias it has been apparent that fear and phobic responding attaches more readily to some stimuli and situations than others. Social phobia aside, epidemiological studies have indicated that fear of insects and small animals is the most common category of phobic fears (reported in 46% of all individuals who report any phobic fears), with heights, water, public transport, storms, closed spaces (claustrophobia), tunnels, and crowds the next most prominent (ECA study, 1984; see Chapter 20). However, despite the fact that there is an uneven distribution of phobias across stimuli and events, phobic symptoms can attach to almost any specific object or event. There are numerous anecdotal accounts of severe phobic reactions to stimuli such as chocolate, plants, individual vegetables, cotton wool, etc., and some of these more common atypical phobias are described in Chapter 10.

However, more than anything else, this handbook acknowledges three important developments in our understanding of phobias that have taken place in recent years. First, it now seems clear that underlying different phobias may be quite different aetiological mechanisms. Whereas earlier theorists had attempted to explain phobic acquisition in terms of a single underlying mechanism or process (such as Pavlovian conditioning), this now seems inappropriate. To be sure, some phobias do appear to be acquired as a result of specific traumatic experiences with the phobic stimulus (e.g. dental phobias, dog phobias), but such experiences are rarely found in the aetiologies of others (e.g. spider and snake phobia, water phobia, height phobia) (see Chapter 4). Some phobias appear to be associated with dispositional factors, such as increased disgust sensitivity (e.g. fear of animals such as snakes, spiders, insects, rats, mice etc., fear of blood or injury) whereas others do not (e.g. social phobia) (see Chapter 16). This has led to more detailed understanding of specific phobic conditions, and hence to the development of treatment packages specifically geared towards individual phobias. Second, recent years have seen substantial refinements in the psychological treatments available for specific phobias. These treatment programmes are detailed yet take very little time to apply, and have good to excellent long-term effectiveness (see Chapter 12). Thirdly, study of the role of cognitive factors in psychopathology has been prominent in the investigation of psychological disorders for many years now, but it has only recently assumed an importance in research into phobias. This volume reflects the importance that cognitive analyses have acquired in the understanding of phobic responding, especially how dysfunctional beliefs about the consequences of phobic encounters can maintain phobic responding (Chapter 18), the role that cognitive factors now play in contemporary conditioning models of phobias (Chapter 15), and how cognitive models have begun to challenge the supposed importance of biologically based theories of the uneven distribution of phobias (Chapter 16).

Graham C.L. Davey
Brighton, 1996

REFERENCES

Kessler, R.C., McGonagle, K., Zhao, S., Nelson, C., Hughes, M., Eschelemann, S., Wittchen, H-U. & Kendler, K.S. (1994). Lifetime and 12-month prevalence of DSM-III-R psychiatric disorders in the United States: results from the National Comorbidity Survey. *Archives of General Psychiatry*, **51**, 8–19.

Robins, L.N. & Regier, D.A. (eds). *Psychiatric Disorders in America: the Epidemiologic Catchment Area Study*. New York: Free Press.

Section I

The Nature and Description of Prevalent Phobias

Chapter 1

Social Phobia: a Cognitive Approach

Adrian Wells
*Department of Psychiatry and Behavioural
Sciences, University of Manchester, Manchester, UK
and*
David M. Clark
Department of Psychiatry, University of Oxford, Oxford, UK

Imagine, for a moment that you have to present a speech, and that your whole worth depends on a faultless, fluent and relaxed performance. Your whole self-image and the image that others hold of you rests on a smooth performance. A show of anxiety or lack of fluency of speech is all that it would take to shatter your self-esteem. For safety's sake you take care in selecting your words, conceal your shakiness and avoid eye contact. You watch yourself and the audience watches you and each move is scrutinized and judged seemingly by them and actually by you. When the ordeal is over you're troubled by thoughts of how you felt. The thoughts reverberate for hours or days.

This anecdote presents a description of key cognitive–behavioural responses in social phobia. In this chapter we present an overview of the nature of social phobia and illustrate the nature and significance of these factors with reference to a specific cognitive model. Evidence for the model and its implications for designing specific cognitive–behavioural treatment techniques is discussed.

THE NATURE AND DIAGNOSIS OF SOCIAL PHOBIA

The essential feature of social phobia is fear of one or more situations in which one may be seen to behave in a way that is humiliating or embarrassing. Humiliating or embarrassing events include displaying visible anxiety symptoms, or

Phobias—A Handbook of Theory, Research and Treatment. Edited by G.C.L. Davey.
© 1997 John Wiley & Sons Ltd.

performing inadequately (e.g. DSM-III-R, American Psychiatric Association, 1987; DSM IV, American Psychiatric Association, 1994). Exposure to such situations is either avoided or endured with considerable distress. Two subtypes of social phobia are differentiated in DSM-III-R and DSM-IV: specific, and generalized subtypes. Specific social phobia concerns fear of a circumscribed situation, such as making a formal speech in public, signing one's name in front of others or eating in public. Individuals with multiple or more broad-based fears, such as fear of most types of social contact with other people, are classified as generalized social phobics.

Social anxiety is likely to be widespread within the general population. The variables differentiating normal social anxiety from social phobia are probably degree of impairment and the extent of avoidance. Bryant & Trower (1974) found that 10% of a sample of 223 students had difficulties in social situations. Arkowitz et al. (1978) reported that almost one-third of male and female college students report anxiety about dating. The prevalence rates for social phobia in males and females appears equal (Amies, Gelder & Shaw, 1983) in most studies of clinic populations, but there is a suggestion from epidemiological studies that it is somewhat more common in women in the community as a whole (Chapman, Mannuzza & Fyer, 1995; see Chapter ••). The age of onset of social phobia is usually between 15 and 20 years (Liebowitz et al., 1985; Turner et al., 1986).

Social Phobia and Avoidant Personality

The inclusion of a generalized subtype of social phobia in DSM-III-R and DSM IV (only a specific form was identified in DSM-III; American Psychiatric Association, 1980) has produced considerable overlap between criteria for this subtype and criteria for avoidant personality disorder (APD). Avoidant personality disorder (APD) is described as a "pervasive pattern of inhibition, feelings of inadequacy, and hypersensitivity to negative evaluation that begins by early adulthood and is present in a variety of contexts" (DSM-IV, p. 662). All of the seven criteria set out for the diagnosis of APD refer to social interaction factors. The issue arising from this overlap concerns whether or not independent diagnoses of social phobia or APD are useful. Holt, Heimberg & Hope (1992) classified social phobics as specific and generalized subtypes, with or without additional diagnoses of APD. Comparison on a number of measures suggested that generalized social phobics were more depressed, more anxious and showed greater fear of negative evaluation than specific social phobics. Differences between generalized social phobics with or without APD were less prevalent. Patients with APD were rated as more severe by clinicians, had higher scores on the social avoidance and distress scale (Watson & Friend, 1969) and had higher social anxiety ratings. These data suggest that social phobia with APD is a more severe problem. Holt, Heimburg & Hope (1992) suggest than an additional diagnosis of APD may simply identify a severe subgroup of social phobics.

MODELS OF SOCIAL PHOBIA

Cognitive models of social phobia have conceptualized the problem in terms of beliefs and cognitive processes that interfere with social performance, and thereby perpetuate the social phobic's anxiety. Beck, Emery & Greenberg (1985) propose that the social phobic is hypersensitive to signals from other people regarding personal acceptability, and autonomic arousal symptoms activate fears concerning the possibility of failed performance. The fear of failed or diminished performance is responsible for maintaining anxiety that is associated with exposure to the phobic situation. Moreover, this fear may actually lead to problems with performance, and the individual is motivated to avoid such problems. Hartman (1983) advanced a cognitive model of social phobia founded on the premise that socially anxious individuals engage in too much self-focused processing in social situations, and this interferes with satisfactory social functioning. Hartman (1983) proposed that a negative sense of the self combines with self-monitoring in producing anxiety. Furthermore, self-monitoring may interfere with the development of more favourable self-concepts by inhibiting attention to corrective information.

Hope, Gansler & Heimberg (1989), drawing heavily on empirical work with analogue populations, also argue that self-focused attention and its consequences are involved in the maintenance of social phobia. When entering a social situation, the social phobic's increased physiological arousal increases self-focus. This interferes with task performance if the individual has a low expectancy of success, and may in addition lead to negative feedback from others. Self-focus increases the probability of internal attributions and thus, even if no negative feedback is encountered, the social phobic is more likely to make internal attributions for neutral or ambiguous feedback. Positive feedback, in contrast, may be discounted by attributing it to an external cause. These attributional and self-focusing effects are considered to play an important role in the maintenance of social phobia.

Although Hartman (1983), and Hope, Gansler & Heimberg (1989) propose a pivotal role of self-focused attention in the maintenance of social phobia. Self-focus is a feature of most emotional disorders (Ingram, 1990; Wells & Matthews, 1994; 1996). Moreover, Wells & Matthews (1994) suggest that self-focused attention tendencies are a marker for the presence of a dysfunctional self-referent processing configuration that predisposes to emotional disorder. The mechanisms linking self-focus to social phobia in the Hartman and Hope et al. models are mechanisms that are also likely to operate in other disorders. Nevertheless, as discussed in the next section, self-focused processing may be linked to particular appraisals that are more specific to social phobia.

Cognitive Themes

Dysfunctional cognitive processes in the form of elevated self-focused attention and internal attributions have been implicated in the maintenance of social phobia. Cognitive approaches have given differential emphasis to cognitions reflecting themes of negative evaluation by others and cognitions focused on negative self-evaluations in the generation and maintenance of the problem. Studies assessing the frequency of negative self-statements converge on the finding that both high socially anxious analogue samples and social phobic patients report greater negative self-statements than low socially anxious samples (Cacioppo, Glass & Merluzzi, 1979; Beidel, Turner & Dancu, 1985; Dodge et al., 1988).

The cognitive model assumes that social phobics interpret social situations in a more threatening fashion than non-social phobics. Stopa (1995) used modified versions of the Ambiguous Events Questionnaire developed by Butler and Mathews (1983) to investigate this assertion. Social phobics, other anxiety disorder patients and non-patient controls completed two questionnaires. One questionnaire contained ambiguous social situations (e.g. "You have visitors round for a meal and they leave sooner than expected") and ambiguous non-social situations (e.g. "A letter marked urgent arrives at your home"). Social phobics were significantly more likely to choose negative interpretations of the ambiguous social situations than either other anxious patients or non-patient controls, but did not differ from these two groups in their interpretation of non-social ambiguous situations. The second questionnaire contained mildly negative social events (e.g. "You have been talking to someone for a while and it becomes clear that they're not really interested in what you're saying") and was used to assess catastrophic interpretations. Consistent with the cognitive model, social phobics were more likely to choose catastrophic interpretations of mildly negative social events (e.g. "It means I am a boring person") than other anxious patients or non-patient controls.

Investigations of thoughts in actual social situations using various thought listing procedures have produced results consistent with the questionnaire data on hypothetical social situations. Stopa & Clark (1993) reported an experiment in which social phobics, other anxious patients, and non-patient controls were asked to have a brief conversation with an attractive, female stooge. The stooge was instructed to behave in a reserved but not unfriendly manner. After the conversation subjects listed their thoughts and gave ratings of the extent to which they had shown a variety of positive and negative behaviours. Independent assessors rated the same behaviours. Analysis of the thoughts data revealed that social phobics reported more negative self-evaluative thoughts than both the other anxious patients and the non-patient controls.

Although social phobics show greater negative evaluations of their own performance in social situations, it is important to establish whether these evaluations are accurate. The cognitive approach suggests that social phobics' negative evaluations of their performance are at least partly distorted. To investigate this,

Stopa & Clark (1993) compared self and observer ratings of performance follow-ing a conversation with a stooge. When compared to the observers' ratings, social phobics underestimated their performance while other anxiety disorder patients and non-patient controls were relatively accurate. Other investigators have also found that high socially anxious individuals underestimate their performance (Rapee & Lim, 1992) and overestimate how anxious they appear to others (Bruch et al., 1989; McEwan & Devins, 1983).

EFFICACY OF TREATMENT

Treatment approaches to social phobia can be broadly classed as social skills training approaches, exposure-based treatments, and combined cognitive–behavioural treatments.

Interventions based on social skills training are founded on the principle that social anxiety is a consequence of a deficit in the skills needed for effective social performance. The aim of therapy is the provision of verbal and non-verbal communication skills through modelling, behavioural rehearsal, corrective feed-back and social reinforcement. In an early evaluation of social skills training Marzillier, Lambert & Kellet (1976) allocated patients to social skills training, systematic desensitization, or a no treatment control group. Both treatments were associated with improvements. However, the treatments did not produce significantly greater improvements than those observed in the no-treatment group. Trower et al. (1978) examined the relative effectiveness of social skills training and systematic desensitization in social phobics that they classified as either "socially phobic" or "socially inadequate". These classifications were made on the basis that the individual's problem was either predominantly anxiety or lack of social skills. Social phobic patients reported anxiety reduction with both types of treatment but showed little change in the quality of their social behav-iour. Socially inadequate patients showed the greatest improvement with social skills training. Ost, Jerremalm & Johansson (1981) divided their patients into "behavioural reactors" (subjects displaying inadequate social behaviour but a relative absence of cardiovascular arousal during a social interaction) or "physi-ological reactors" (subjects with adequate social skills but with cardiovascular arousal), in comparing the effects of social skills training with applied relaxation. Both treatments were effective, but social skills training produced greater changes for behavioural reactors, whilst applied relaxation was more effective for the physiological reactors. Several other studies have sought to examine the effectiveness of social skills training but these studies have not included control groups, and they have shown that social skills training does not produce signifi-cantly different levels of change compared to other treatments. The effectiveness of these procedures therefore cannot be unambiguously tied to treatment itself and may be linked to factors, such as passage of time, etc. (see Heimberg, 1989, for a more detailed review).

The research on exposure therapy as a treatment for social phobia has re-

vealed that although it is effective when compared to no treatment (Butler
et al., 1984), it has limitations. In particular, a sizeable proportion of
patients either fail to respond or show only partial improvement. For example,
Mattick & Peters (1988) found that at the end of treatment only 30% of
exposure-treated patients had achieved high endstate function and 47% felt
they were still in need of treatment. Similar figures are reported by Butler et al.
(1984).

Although exposure appears to reduce social anxiety and avoidance (e.g.
Alstrom et al., 1984; Butler et al., 1984; Emmelkamp et al., 1985; Mattick &
Peters, 1988) it produces only modest effects. Moreover, changes in cognitive
measures of irrational beliefs following exposure (Emmelkamp et al., 1985),
and fear of negative evaluation (Mattick, Peters & Clarke, 1989) are small.
The modest effects obtained with exposure may be due to small or inconsistent
cognitive change obtained with this treatment. Clark & Wells (1995) propose
that more effective treatment depends on cognitive change of greater
magnitude.

Cognitive-based treatments have tended to use versions of rational emotive
therapy (e.g. Kanter & Goldfried, 1979), self-instructional training (e.g.
Jerremalm, Jansson & Öst, 1986), or combinations of exposure and self-control
techniques such as anxiety management (Butler et al., 1984). Several investigators have devised and evaluated cognitive–behavioural treatments for social
phobia. These treatments differ in emphasis, but all of them use a mixture of
cognitive and behavioral procedures to help patients modify their negative
beliefs about their performance in social situations and about the way their
behaviour is evaluated by others. Heimberg et al. (1990) found that a cognitive–
behavioural group treatment was superior to an equally credible placebo psychological intervention, and a follow-up study suggested that differences between
the groups were still evident 5 years after treatment termination (Heimberg et al.,
1993). Mattick & Peters (1988) compared cognitive restructuring and exposure
with exposure alone, and found that the combined condition was more effective
than exposure alone on measures of end-state functioning and avoidance. In
addition, correlational analysis showed that treatment-induced changes in a cognitive variable (fear of negative evaluation) was a significant predictor of improvement in both treatments. A subsequent study (Mattick, Peters & Clarke,
1989) replicated these results and also found that cognitive restructuring alone
(without exposure) was somewhat less effective than combined treatment. In
both studies, the gains patients made during combined treatment were maintained or enhanced at 3-month follow-up. Finally, Heimberg et al. (1994) recently
reported the results of a multi-site comparison between cognitive–behavioural
group treatment, phenelzine, placebo medication, and placebo psychological
treatment. At the end of active treatment, cognitive–behavioural therapy and
phenelzine were both superior to the two placebo conditions. The proportion of
patients who were classified as improved was similar in the two active treatments,
but phenelzine was superior to cognitive–behavioural treatment on some asses-

sor ratings. At 1-year follow-up, cognitive–behavioural therapy patients had maintained their gains, whereas 50% of phenelzine patients relapsed. As a consequence, cognitive–behavioural therapy was superior to phenelzine at follow-up. Taken together, these studies indicate that cognitive–behavioural treatment is effective in social phobia and superior to exposure alone. Immediate response to phenelzine is similar, or maybe slightly better, than cognitive–behavioural therapy, but cognitive–behavioural therapy is superior to phenelzine in the long term. These data suggest that it may be valuable to examine treatments that combine phenelzine with cognitive therapy. More specifically, as Wells & Matthews (1994) suggest, pharmacotherapy could be combined with cognitive therapy in a way that facilitates cognitive change. For example, in social phobia phenelzine could be used to increase compliance with exposure and enhance the social phobics in-situation attentional strategies aimed at disconfirming negative appraisals.

In summary, treatment outcome data demonstrates that interventions using exposure are effective in reducing anxiety and avoidance in social phobia. However, the degree of cognitive change in exposure treatments is modest. Some studies shown that cognitive–behavioural treatments are more effective than exposure. It is likely that improved outcomes would result from a specific cognitive model of social phobia that expresses the interrelationship between causal mechanisms underlying problem maintenance. We now consider the detailed specifications of such a model.

A COGNITIVE MODEL

Drawing on several cognitive literatures, on extensive clinical work, and based on a self-regulatory information processing model of emotional disorder (Wells & Matthews, 1994), Clark & Wells (1995) advanced a comprehensive cognitive model of social phobia. In the model, the social phobic is motivated to present a favourable impression of the self but is insecure in his/her ability to do so in particular situations. The insecurity is a manifestation of negative self-focused processing, and is linked to "safety behaviours" intended to protect self-esteem and avert negative judgements of others. Paradoxically, some of these safety behaviours inflame problematic symptoms and increase the likelihood of poor performance. Anxiety symptoms and the negative consequences of safety behaviours fuel self-consciousness and reinforce distorted impressions of the self. Three phases of distorted processing are distinguished. Dysfunctional processing occurs in the phobic situation; it occurs in advance of the situation as apprehension and rumination, and after leaving the situation distorted processing is likely to continue as a "post mortem". In the post mortem the social phobic goes over the situation, contemplating what happened, what should have happened and what the consequences might be. Thus, three stages of processing can be distinguished in social phobia; an anticipatory processing phase, an in-situation

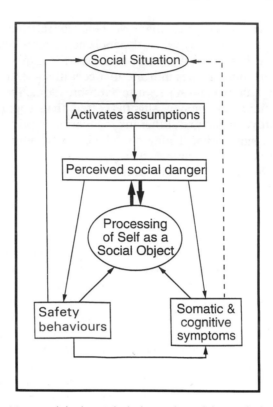

Figure 1.1   A cognitive model of social phobia (adapted from Clark & Wells, 1995)

processing phase, and a post mortem. The most significant phase of processing in problem maintenance is the in-situation phase. A model of this phase is presented in Figure 1.1.

In the figure, dysfunctional assumptions and beliefs render the individual vulnerable to the range of cognitive and behavioural factors that maintain social phobia. Three types of information are conceptualized at this schema level: core self-beliefs, conditional assumptions, and rigid rules for social performance. The pattern of the onset of social phobia may be linked to the particular types of schema that exist. For example, some individuals have rigid rules for governing their social behaviour, such as: "one should never show signs of anxiety; I must always sound fluent and intelligent; I must have something interesting to say". These people may function perfectly well until they encounter an event that leads to an important failure in meeting these standards. Following a "critical incident" of this type, social situations are perceived as more dangerous since they have the potential to lead to further instances of "failed performance". Instances of "failed performance" contribute to negative self-processing, as an important requirement for the maintenance of a positive sense of self has not been met. In other cases, conditional assumptions predispose to self-focused dysfunctional processing central to social phobia. Conditional assumptions are explicit representations of the consequences of performing or not performing in a particular way. Examples are: "If I'm quiet people will think I'm boring"; "If people see me shake they'll think I'm stupid"; "If I show I'm anxious people will think I'm a failure/incompetent"; "If I get my words wrong no one will take me seriously". Finally, negative self-beliefs in the form of unconditional statements about the self are also linked to vulnerability. These represent the superordinate self-view. In social phobia these beliefs centre on the self as a social object, and are activated in social situations rather than being chronically activated. When not in anxiety-provoking situations these constructs are less believable, although they become compelling when a social stressor is encountered. Examples of these beliefs are: "I'm weird"; "I'm boring"; "I'm different"; "I'm unintelligent"; "I'm stupid". These core beliefs resemble the content of schemas in disorders such as depression. However, the model predicts a difference in the schemas of social phobia and of depression. In social phobia the belief is held strongly for specific problematic social situations, whilst in depression the belief is less situationally specific. One possible explanation for this difference is that the depressive belief is more closely associated with a general private self-concept, and is prone to activation in a wide range of non-social as well as social situations, whereas the social phobic belief is more closely associated with the public self-concept and is prone to activation in a narrow range of particular social situations.

Schemas of the type discussed render the individual vulnerable to appraising social situations as potentially dangerous. Three further processes are involved in the maintenance of social phobia: processing of the self as a social object; safety behaviours; and cognitive and somatic anxiety symptoms.

PROCESSING OF THE SELF AS A SOCIAL OBJECT

When the social phobic enters an anxiety-provoking social situation there is a shift in the individual's focus of attention. Given that social phobia has been equated with fear of negative evaluation, one might predict that the social phobic shifts attention to monitoring and appraising other people's reactions. If correct, this assertion would be concordant with findings in other anxiety disorders demonstrating selective attention to threat-related stimuli. However, the present model asserts that a crucial process in social phobia is negative self-processing. It is predicted, therefore, that social phobics show a shift in attention in social situations characterized by intensified self-focused attention. This reduces the attention available for processing external information such as feedback from other people. Wells & Matthews (1996, 1994) suggest that self-focused processing is a consciously mediated strategy that in some instances is a component of self-regulation and safety behaviours. However, in other instances the self is rendered more perceptually salient by increased anxiety symptoms. It is difficult for the social phobic to disengage attention from such influences when their schemas

signal the personal importance of symptoms and their regulation for social
well-being.

The shift in attention that follows from initial danger appraisals is experienced
as an increase in self-consciousness in which the individual usually reports that
he/she "feels more conspicuous" or "feels as if he/she is the centre of attention".
A more detailed analysis of the contents of self-consciousness reveals that the
social phobic often has an impression of how he/she thinks he/she appears to
others when anxious. This occurs as a "felt sense" or as an image. As an example
of a felt sense, the social phobic might say: "My shaking feels so bad it must look
bad"; or "It feels as if everyone is looking at me". When images constitute self-
processing they typically occur from a particular vantage point in which the social
phobic sees him/herself as if outside of the body looking back at the self. This
"observer perspective" in self-image usually contains distorted representations of
the observability of anxiety and performance symptoms. Social phobics use
interoceptive information to construct an impression of how they think they
appear to others. For example, an individual notices that he/she feels hot and is
perspiring, and based on this felt sense constructs an image of how this looks to
others. Typically, symptoms are much less apparent than their representation in
the observer image. Social phobics mistakenly assume that because they feel
uncomfortable they must look uncomfortable and abnormal.

The distorted observer self-image and other negative appraisals are maintained by self-focused processing, avoidance and safety behaviours, and the fact
that social situations rarely provide unambiguous feedback of how we are perceived by others. Even when positive information about the self in social situations is available, the social phobic is unlikely to process it because of diversion
of attention to self-processing rather than external processing.

Table 1.1   Negative beliefs and associated safety behaviours in a sample of four social
phobics

Negative belief	Safety behaviour
"I'll get my words wrong and be unable to speak"	Rehearse sentences mentally before saying them. Try to remember what I've said. Try to speak clearly, speak quickly, ask question, don't talk about myself
"I'll sweat profusely and people will stare"	Wear cool clothes, wear white, drink cool drinks, keep jacket on, wear a T-shirt beneath clothes. Use antiperspirant several times a day
"I'll shake and spill my drink"	Avoid using cups and saucers, grip cups with both hands, drink when no- one is watching, hold arms rigid, rest elbows on table
"I'll go red and everyone will notice"	Hide face with hands, pull hair over face, cover-up with make-up, avoid eye-contact, try not to attract attention, keep still, say little, try to keep occupied, distract myself

SAFETY BEHAVIOURS AND AVOIDANCE

Safety behaviours are strategies that are intended to avert feared catastrophes. One of the most complete forms of catastrophe prevention is avoidance of social situations. By avoiding anxiety-provoking social situations, the social phobic eliminates the risk of failed performance and its appraised consequences. Unfortunately, avoidance leads to diminished opportunities to disconfirm negative appraisals and it thus maintains fear. When avoidance is not possible the socially phobic situation is endured and the individual practises "safety behaviours" (Salkovskis, 1991; Wells et al., 1995) aimed at reducing the risk of social failure and humiliation. Safety behaviours vary in form but are logically linked to negative appraisals. For example, the belief that shaking is observable or will get "out of control" is linked to responses aimed at concealing shaking, such as when drinking, doing so when others are not looking, or maintaining control by gripping objects tightly, and moving slowly. Fears concerning sweating are associated with concealment strategies such as wearing light-coloured clothes, wearing additional layers of clothing, and prevention strategies such as restricting oneself to cold drinks and sitting by open windows. A range of safety behaviours reported by four patients with different social concerns is presented in Table 1.1 for illustrative purposes.

Why Are Avoidance and Safety Behaviours Problematic?

There are four mechanisms by which safety behaviours maintain distorted thinking in social phobia: (a) exacerbation of symptoms; (b) prevention of disconfirmation; (c) maintenance of self-attention; (d) contamination of the social situation.

Safety behaviours directly exacerbate feared bodily sensations. Use of behavioural control strategies such as tightening muscles to prevent tremor impedes movement and contributes to feelings of loss of control and clumsiness. Wearing additional clothing to conceal sweating increases body temperature and contributes to sweating. Concentrating on correctly pronouncing words can disrupt verbal fluency and increases the likelihood of mispronunciation. Monitoring and regulating one's behavioural responses in social situations imparts extra cognitive load. The social phobic who mentally rehearses and/or covertly censors their sentences before articulating them constructs a divided attention situation, in which attention to an interaction partner's conversation and self-monitoring compete in a way that leads to detriments in social performance.

Safety behaviours also support an *attributional bias* that interferes with the disconfirmation of negative appraisals and beliefs. The non-occurrence of feared outcomes, such as rejection by others, is attributed to the use of the safety behaviour rather than to the fact that the outcome is unlikely. Avoidance, in the form of complete failure to enter feared situations, eliminates a potential opportunity to acquire disconfirmatory information.

Safety behaviours maintain attention on the self and use up processing capacity that should be directed at disconfirmatory processing, such as determining the true responses of other people. Finally, safety behaviours contaminate the social situation and are often more noticeable than the symptoms they are designed to conceal, and more disruptive than the feared catastrophe they are intended to prevent. Other people appraise safety behaviours as a sign of aloofness or disinterest by the social phobic. For example, a social phobic who conceals self-appraised shortcomings by continuously deflecting the topic of conversation away from the self is likely to be seen as aloof or disinterested in other people, rather than appraised as anxious or inadequate.

COGNITIVE AND SOMATIC SYMPTOMS

The present model imparts an important role to anxiety symptoms in the maintenance of dysfunction. These symptoms engage attention and are disruptive for social performance. However, their disruptive and problematic status is largely determined by their interaction with social self-processing. More specifically, it is the individual's interpretation of the social significance of symptoms that maintains and exacerbates danger appraisals. Arousal symptoms are interpreted as a sign of impending failure to meet acceptable standards of social performance, with catastrophic consequences in terms of loss of status, loss of self-worth, rejection or humiliation. Because of the appraised social dangers associated with arousal symptoms, individuals become hypervigilant for early signs of symptoms. This hypervigilance serves to increase the subjective intensity of bodily and cognitive symptoms and may actually activate the unwanted somatic or cognitive event.

We have seen how the content of the observer perspective on the self is based on interoception. As symptom intensity increases, due in part to paradoxical effects of safety behaviours, increased danger appraisals and hypervigilance, the content of the public self-image is adversely affected. The role of public self-appraisal of symptoms in the generation of anxiety in social phobia is clear when we consider that the presence of a symptom evokes anxiety predominantly when the social phobic is in a social context or is appraising the social implications of his/her symptoms. If symptoms such as sweating, blushing or trembling occur when alone and the processing of their social significance is inactive they are unlikely to elicit high anxiety.

Feedback Cycles

The model we have presented consists of four key feedback cycles involved in the maintenance of the dysfunctional self-focused processing configuration. First, processing of the public self can serve to increase or decrease danger appraisals depending on the nature of the self-appraisals made. Second, safety behaviours maintain negative self-beliefs by interfering with attention to corrective information, and by preventing exposure to "difficult" situations. Third, anxious symptoms fuel construction of distorted self-appraisals, and fourth, safety behaviours can contaminate the social situation and negatively bias the appraisals of others. Because of the existence of several feedback loops, individuals may show a predominance of particular types of feedback within the system. Thus, the formulation of individual cases based on the model gives differential emphasis to particular feedback mechanisms. However, the central drive for the disorder is provided by dysfunctional processing of the self as a social object.

ANTICIPATORY AND POST-MORTEM PROCESSING

Two further cognitive processes that play a role in maintaining social phobia in the present model are: *anticipatory processing* and the *"post mortem"*. These factors bias thinking and have an influence on anxiety and mood.

Social phobics often report considerable anticipatory anxiety. Prior to a social event, they review in detail what they think might happen, and ways that they might deal with particular problems. As they start to think about the situation, they become anxious and their thoughts tend to become dominated by negative recollections and predictions. If these ruminations do not lead to complete avoidance of the situation, they are likely to cause the phobic to enter the situation in a pre-activated self-focused processing mode.

The social phobic's negative thoughts and distress do not necessarily cease on leaving or escaping from a social situation. Because of the nature of social situations and the nature of the social phobic's processing in situations, the social phobic is unlikely to have received or processed signs of social approval. As a result, the interaction is reviewed in detail and the phobic's anxious feelings and negative self-perception figure highly in this process. This "post mortem" of the event may be motivated by the perceived need to take reparative action and plan ways of managing the situation more effectively in the future. It may also be an attempt to reduce uncertainty about the observable impression that the phobic has presented to others. Unfortunately, the post mortem is dominated by the social phobic's negative self-perception, and the interaction is likely to be seen as more negative than it really was.

EMPIRICAL SUPPORT FOR THE MODEL

The model that we have outlined synthesizes concepts from previous cognitive formulations with unique self-focused processing characteristics of the Wells & Matthews (1994) self-referent executive function (S-REF) model of vulnerability to emotional dysfunction. Evidence from several sources is supportive of the behavioural and cognitive constructs in the model. Three central hypotheses and supportive data will be considered here:

Hypothesis 1: Social Phobics Show Attentional Bias Towards Self-focused Processing and Diminished Attention to External Social Cues

The concept of heightened self-focus in social anxiety is well known. Evidence supporting a link between self-focused attention and social anxiety has a long tradition in the self-consciousness literature (Buss, 1980; Fenigstein, Scheier & Buss, 1975). For example, Fenigstein, Scheier & Buss (1975) suggest that public self-consciousness, the tendency to focus attention on the observable aspects of the self, is a necessary antecedent of social anxiety, but whether or not anxiety is caused depends on the nature of evaluation of the self as a social object.

Experimental work generally confirms the view that self-focus is associated with social anxiety. Fenigstein, Scheier & Buss (1975) report significant positive correlations between public self-consciousness and social anxiety. Other studies show a relationship, albeit of smaller magnitude, between private self-consciousness and social anxiety (Hope & Heimberg, 1988; Darvill, Johnson & Danko, 1992). Private self-consciousness (Fenigstein, Scheier & Buss, 1975) is a construct of dispositional attention to internal (e.g. feelings, thoughts) aspects of self.

The association between private self-consciousness and social anxiety is consistent with the assertion that an important source of information concerning the self is derived from interoception in social situations. Johansson & Öst (1982) investigated awareness of heart-rate changes in social phobics and controls in social situations. Social phobics were particularly accurate in estimating their heart-rate changes, suggesting an enhanced awareness of interoceptive information.

Whilst these theoretical and empirical data support enhanced self-focused processing as a feature of attentional bias in social phobia, the importance of these data for modelling processes specific to social phobia is questionable. Self-focused attention is a characteristic of most types of emotional dysfunction (Wells & Matthews, 1994). However, the nature of this type of processing in social phobia differs from that in other disorders, such as panic or obsessional states. In social phobia, self-focused processing represents a shift of attention away from the phobic stimulus (i.e. other people), whilst in panic disorder or obsessional states self-focus represents a focus on the feared stimulus (i.e. bodily sensations or intrusive thoughts). If we accept that social phobics fear scrutiny and negative evaluation by others, focus on the phobic stimulus requires attention to the reactions of others, rather than attention to the self. Building on the model of self-regulation in emotional disorder advanced by Wells & Matthews (1994), the social phobia model (Clark & Wells, 1995) accounts for this apparent discrepancy by re-defining the social phobic's fear. Social phobics fear not only other people's reaction to the self, but also potential failure to meet personal goals for publicly acceptable performance. Failure to meet these goals, which could lead to disapproval of others, is profoundly threatening because it undermines one's positive sense of self. This redefinition implies that self-focus does constitute attending to the feared stimulus, namely an impression of the extent to which the social phobic is meeting self-presentational goals. Information signalling anxious arousal and disruption of performance that becomes more amenable through self-focus leads to the creation of a situational public self-image that falls short of goals, leading to diminished confidence in performance and anxiety.

If social phobics are self-focusing in social situations, it is reasonable to assume that they should show diminished attention to social cues. However, the direction of biased attention is likely to be affected by the type of stimulus material used. The literature on attentional bias in anxiety disorders shows a robust effect in filtering and Stroop test paradigms. For example, patients with generalized anxiety, specific phobias and post-traumatic stress disorder show biased attention for emotion-related stimuli (for review, see Wells & Matthews, 1994). The results for social phobia present a somewhat more mixed picture. When word stimuli are used in a Stroop, socially anxious subjects show increased colour-naming times for social threat words, but not for physical threat words (Hope et al., 1990; Mattia, Heimberg & Hope, 1993). In studies using variants of the dot-probe task designed by MacLeod, Mathews & Tata (1986), conflicting results have been found, depending on the nature of the test stimuli. In the original dot-probe task, physical threat and neural word pairs were presented simultaneously, one at the upper and one at the lower position on a computer screen, for 500 msec. Subjects were asked to name the upper word and then respond as quickly as possible to a dot probe which appeared in the location of one of the words after the display of words was terminated. By examining the effect of word type on probe reaction time it was possible to determine if the subject's attention shifted away or towards the word. In a similar paradigm using social threat words, Asmundson & Stein (1994) showed that, compared to non-patient controls, social phobics were quicker at responding to dots that followed social threat words (e.g. foolish) than dots following either neutral or physical threat words. These data suggest that social phobics show attentional bias for social threat stimuli, rather than diminished attention to social stimuli as predicted by the model. However, to interpret this effect it is necessary to determine the nature of the effect measured by these tasks. Word stimuli are not the types of stimuli that social phobics normally find problematic; it is likely that bias for negative social words reflects the content of social phobics' mental pre-occupation with negative self-evaluation, rather than reflecting the type of attentional bias activated in threatening social situations. In a preliminary study, Clark & Yuen (1994) used positive and negative faces in place of words in a dot-probe paradigm. Faces more closely resemble the types of stimuli that social phobics encounter. Subjects with high fear of negative evaluation scores, as measured by the Fear of Negative Evaluation (FNE) Scale (Watson & Friend, 1969), were slower at locating the dot if it appeared in the location where the negative face had been than if it appeared in the location occupied by the neutral face. Subjects low in FNE showed no difference in reaction times for the two locations.

Studies of memory also provide partial support for the claim of diminished external attention in social anxiety. If social phobics fail to attend to features of the external social environment, they should show poorer memory for details of the situation. Kimble & Zehr (1982), Daly, Vangelisti & Lawrence (1989) and Hope, Heimberg & Klein (1990) all found that, compared to low socially anxious subjects, high socially anxious subjects had poorer memory for the details of a recent social interaction. However, Stopa & Clark (1993), using a slightly different methodology, failed to replicate this effect.

Several studies have suggested that social phobics' belief that others are evaluating them negatively is not based on detailed information about others' responses to them. Stopa & Clark (1993) found that social phobics reported more negative self-evaluative thoughts (e.g. "I'm boring") than controls during a conversation with a stooge, but did not report more negative thoughts which explicitly mentioned evaluation by the stooge (e.g. "She thinks I'm boring"). Winton, Clark & Edelman (1995) investigated accuracy in detecting negative emotion in briefly presented slides of different emotional expressions. Slides of negative and neutral facial expressions were presented for 60 ms, followed by a pattern mask. Students scoring high on FNE (Watson & Friend, 1969) correctly identified more negative facial expressions than low-FNE students, but a signal detection analysis revealed that this was due to a negative response bias. That is to say, high-FNE students were more likely to rate a briefly presented face as negative in the absence of having abstracted more affective information from the face. These data suggest that when social phobics encounter other people they extract little information from them.

In conclusion, the hypothesis that social phobics show self-focused processing in social situations gains substantial support. The concept of attentional bias away from social stimuli is partially supported. The detection of attentional avoidance is probably dependent on the types of test stimuli used. Negative social word stimuli attract attention, whilst negative faces are associated with attentional avoidance. Initial results are promising but further empirical demonstrations of attentional avoidance of phobic stimuli are required to confirm the bias hypothesis.

Hypothesis 2: Social Phobics Construct a Negative Impression of Themselves from an Observer Perspective

Several studies have demonstrated that socially anxious subjects overestimate the observability of their anxiety responses in social situations. McEwan & Devins (1983) showed that socially anxious undergraduates over-rated the observability of behavioural signs of anxiety presented on a checklist, compared to ratings made of them by a peer who knew them well. Low socially anxious subjects, in contrast, made ratings that were in agreement with the peer. In a different study, Bruch et al. (1989; Study 2) asked shy and non-shy subjects to interact with an opposite sex partner. Subjects and confederates were asked to rate the degree to which "nervous behaviours" of the subject were noticeable during the conversation. Instructions directed subjects to think back over the conversation and to rate on a scale ranging from 5 (very noticeable) to 1 (not at all noticeable) the degree to which 14 different behaviours were visible to the other person. Confederates completed the same measure, but the instructions emphasized that they rated the noticeability of the subjects behaviours from their own perspective. Compared with non-shy subjects, the shy subjects believed that they displayed a greater number of noticeable signs of anxiety than were actually noticed by the interaction partner. Interestingly, men in contrast to women were more likely to exaggerate how noticeable their nervousness was to a confederate. Bruch et al. (1989) attempted to explore the source of exaggerated appraisals of noticeability by correlating heart-rate change during interaction, and frequency of negative thoughts with the discrepancy between subject and confederate noticeability rating. Whilst heart-rate change was not significantly correlated with the discrepancy, negative thoughts did show a significant positive association with discrepancy. These results are consistent with the cognitive model to the extent that overestimates of the observability of anxiety reflects negative self-processing from an observer perspective.

Wells, Clark & Ahmad (1995) set out to test directly the hypothesis that social phobics construct an impression of themselves from an observer perspective. A group of 12 individuals meeting DSM-III-R criteria for social phobia were compared with 12 age- and sex-matched non-anxious controls. Subjects were asked to recall and image a recent social situation in which they felt anxious, and a non-social situation. The two imagery instructions were presented in a counterbalanced within-subjects design. After each instruction subjects were asked to rate the extent to which their image was from an "observer perspective" or a "field perspective". The observer perspective was defined as standing outside of themselves looking back at themselves as someone else would see them. The field perspective was defined as looking out through their own eyes from their original position being able to see the things happening around them. Social phobics were significantly different from normals in their perspective for social memories but not non-social memories. In the case of social memories, the social phobics showed a clear observer perspective, whilst the non-anxious subjects showed a field perspective. For the non-social memory, both groups of subjects showed the same field perspective.

In summary, the available data is consistent with the hypothesis that social phobics overestimate the observability of their anxiousness in social situations, and they tend to construct an image of themselves from an observer perspective when recalling social encounters.

Hypothesis 3: In-situation Safety Behaviours Impede Exposure Effects in Modifying Anxiety and Beliefs

A central prediction of the present model is that safety behaviours maintain anxiety and belief in negative appraisals concerning the self in social situations.

Wells, Clark, Salkovskis, Ludgate, Mackmann & Gelder (1995) tested this prediction by asking social phobics to enter a feared social situation for a specified
period of time under conditions involving no manipulation of safety behaviours,
and under conditions of intentional abandonment of safety behaviours. Subjects
were instructed under both conditions that the exercise would help them overcome anxiety. The effect of these two manipulations on anxiety during the
situation, and on belief in negative appraisals was assessed. All subjects met
DSM-III-R criteria for social phobia, and credibility of the two manipulations did
not differ significantly. Exposure plus abandonment of safety behaviours produced significantly greater reductions in anxiety and belief in negative appraisals
than exposure alone.

TOWARDS A COMPREHENSIVE COGNITIVE THERAPY

The model that we have outlined presents a number of specific predictions
concerning the implementation of effective cognitive–behavioural treatment
strategies. Unlike existing cognitive–behavioural approaches that have tended to
combine cognitive and behavioural strategies to enhance self-control of anxiety
and social skills, the present approach argues that most social phobics do not have
a skills deficit, and suggests that teaching anxiety management skills should not
be a long-term strategy. The goal of treatment should be the modification of
dysfunctional self-appraisals and beliefs. The model suggests an optimal pathway
for this type of change. Wells (1997) and Wells & Clark (in preparation) propose
a particular sequence to treatment: initially this involves development of an
idiosyncratic formulation of problem maintenance based on the model; this is
followed by selling the model through the use of behavioural experiments that
increase and decrease safety behaviours and self-focus during analogue phobic
situations. The aim of these experiments is to illustrate the links between use of
safety behaviours, increased self-focus, and disruption of social performance. The
next step involves exposure experiments for homework, in which subjects are
encouraged to reorient their attention away from the self and toward the processing of others in the environment. This cognitive re-configuration is an important
prerequisite to the processing of disconfirmatory information. Individuals are
encouraged to drop safety behaviours, whilst "interrogating" the environment
for signs of disconfirmatory information. Subsequent stages of treatment consist
of challenging the distorted public image of the self. A powerful means of
accomplishing this is with audio or video feedback. The social phobic is asked to
engage in a feared activity (e.g. talking in front of a group of people, drinking
from cups and saucers) and is videotaped whilst doing so. The next step is to elicit
the patients' impression of themselves during the exercise, focusing on the way
they think they looked (the observer perspective). With a detailed impression in
mind they are asked to view the videotape and compare the actual image of

themselves with the subjective image they have generated. Other methods for correcting the distorted public self-image include questioning the evidence for believing the self-generated impression, listing counter-evidence, and using replacement accurate images of the self when the dysfunctional impression becomes activated.

An important component of treatment consists of testing patients' predictions concerning the feared consequences of particular types of behaviour using behavioural experiments. For example, a person who fears getting his/her words wrong or leaving silences in conversation is asked to practise deliberately getting words wrong and leaving gaps in sentences, to test out other people's reactions. Similarly, an individual who predicts that the sight of them sweating in social situations will lead them to be the centre of attention, would be encouraged to dampen a shirt they are wearing and enter a social situation, whilst determining other people's level of reaction.

Cognitive therapy also works with dysfunctional assumptions and beliefs. Overly narrow assumptions concerning the boundaries of permissable social behaviour are broadened by paradoxical procedures involving increased risk-taking. These techniques are intended to increase the individuals "band-width" of behaviours believed to be acceptable. For example, the individual may deliberately draw other people's attention to his/her anxiety, or deliberately shake and spill drinks in restaurants, or disagree with friends.

Anticipatory processing and the post-mortem is specifically targeted in treatment. Anticipatory processing primes the social phobic to process negative self-focused information in the situation or culminates in avoidance. The post-mortem does not contain information capable of disconfirming the patient's fears, but incubates fears and is likely to contribute to a sense of subjective failure. The advantages and disadvantages of anticipatory processing and the post-mortem are discussed in detail. The aim is to establish that it is predominantly disadvantageous to think in this way. The social phobic is then asked to ban these activities. Other strategies that are useful in assisting the suspension of such processing include attempts to shift from an observer to a field perspective during the post mortem, and the recounting of information that is inconsistent with the dysfunctional self-image. Because the patient has not encoded information about the environment during the phobic encounter, disconfirmatory information is not available during the post mortem and a shift to the field perspective is therefore difficult. These problems are highlighted as evidence for the unhelpful and distorted nature of the post mortem. During the course of treatment, information on actual features of social situations should become increasingly available. As more realistic and positive information becomes accessible the patient may be asked to complete a positive data log aimed at modifying underlying negative beliefs.

COMPARISON OF MODELS

Hartman (1983) suggested that socially anxious individuals are preoccupied with their physiological arousal, ongoing performance and other people's appraisals of them as incompetent, nervous or inadequate. This preoccupation leads to a reduced ability to experience others in social situations. Based on this approach, a treatment method termed "other-centred" therapy has been devised (e.g. Hartman, 1986), in which clients are trained to be more attentive to other people during social discourse as a means of developing improved control over affective experience. Initially, clients are asked to rehearse skills of attending to others, in particular the observation of non-verbal behaviours. Listening skills are practised through various exercises and the program culminates with the practise of "responding" skills. The cognitive model of social anxiety that we have presented bears some similarity to the central concept of Hartman's model. However, there are several important differences. First, the present model provides a detailed analysis of the content of self-focused processing, and the types of belief and assumptions that predispose to that state. Second, it links an individual's behavioural responses to the maintenance of dysfunction through several causal pathways. Thus, the model comprises a series of specific and detailed feedback mechanisms involved in problem maintenance. Third, the model highlights the role of contamination of the social situation resulting from the social phobic's safety behaviours. Both approaches emphasize an attentional bias toward self-focused processing that prevents processing of information capable of correcting faulty appraisals; both models assume that self-focus intensifies the experience of certain arousal symptoms. However, the current model identifies safety behaviours as contributors to symptom severity. Treatment specifications differ markedly between the models. Whilst Hartman (1986) advocates the use of other-focused training to moderate symptoms, our model asserts that external other-focused processing is an important prerequisite for disconfirmatory processing. Thus, the principle aim is not symptom management but to reorient processing so that corrective information can be effectively processed. In this respect the reorientation of attention is aimed at challenging specific appraisals and beliefs. A danger with attention modification strategies aimed at symptom control is that they may become additional safety behaviours. Ideally, social phobics should be ultimately encouraged to *exhibit* anxious symptoms, as a means of evaluating the true consequences of experiencing them.

Finally, a number of other models suggest that social phobics are hyperattentive to negative feedback from others. However, it is difficult to unify concepts of heightened self-focus with increased attention to external situational feedback within the same model. The present model resolves this problem by emphasizing that social phobics make inferences about their social performance based on public self-processing. Moreover, safety behaviours tend to support orientation away from processing others (e.g. gaze aversion), supporting attentional bias away from others. Whilst social phobics are concerned with themes of negative evaluation by others, the presence of such evaluation is usually inferred from self-focused processing rather than from external processing.

SUMMARY AND CONCLUSION

Social phobia is a common and disabling disorder. Cognitive–behavioural therapy is the leading empirically validated psychological intervention. Existing treatment programs have been shown to have specific effects, but a sizeable proportion of patients fail to obtain substantial benefits. In an attempt to overcome this problem we have proposed a new model of processes involved in the maintenance of social phobia. The model builds on previous work on the role of self-focused attention in social anxiety. It is suggested that social phobia is maintained by reduced attention to external social cues, safety behaviours, enhanced self-focused attention, and the use of interoceptive information to construct an impression of the self as a social object.

A review of the literature provides encouraging preliminary support for the model, but further research is required. The central clinical implication of the model is that it suggests a new way of treating social phobics within a cognitive–behavioural framework. In particular, it emphasizes the need to conceptualize and modify a range of maintenance cycles. Moreover, treatment techniques should be geared towards generating a more realistic and stable sense of the self as a social object. This will typically involve extensive exposure to situations in conjunction with carefully selected manipulations that augment disconfirmatory processing and produce changes in self-appraisals, assumptions and beliefs.

REFERENCES

Alstrom, J.E., Nordlund, C.L., Persson, G., Harding, N. & Ljungqvist, C. (1984). Effects of four treatment methods on social phobia patients not suitable for insight-oriented psychotherapy. *Acta Psychiatrica Scandinavica*, **70**, 97–110.

Amies, P.L., Gelder, N.G. & Shaw, P.N. (1983). Social phobia: a comparative clinical study. *British Journal of Psychiatry*, **142**, 174–179.

American Psychiatric Association (1980). *Diagnostic and Statistical Manual of Mental Disorders*, 3rd edn. Washington, DC: American Psychiatric Association.

American Psychiatric Association (1987). *Diagnostic and Statistical Manual of Mental Disorders*, 3rd edn (revised). Washington, DC: American Psychiatric Association.

American Psychiatric Association (1994). *Diagnostic and Statistical Manual of Mental Disorders*, 4th edn. Washington, DC: American Psychiatric Association.

Arkowitz, H., Hinton, R., Perl, J. & Himadi, W. (1978). Treatment strategies for dating anxiety in college men based on real-life practice. *Counselling Psychologist*, **7**, 41–46.

Asmundson, G.J.G. & Stein, M.B. (1994). Selective attention for social threat in patients with generalized social phobia: evaluation using a dot-probe paradigm. *Journal of Anxiety Disorders*, **8**, 107–117.

Beck, A.T., Emery, G. & Greenberg, R.L. (1985). *Anxiety Disorders and Phobias: a Cognitive Perspective*. New York: Basic Books.

Beidel, D.C., Turner, S.M. & Dancu, C.V. (1985). Physiological, cognitive and behavioural aspects of social anxiety. *Behaviour Research and Therapy*, **23**, 109–117.

Bruch, B.A., Gorsky, J.M., Collins, T.M. & Berger, P.A. (1989). Shyness and sociability re-examined: a multi-component analysis. *Journal of Personality and Social Psychology*, **57**, 904–915.

Bryant, B. & Trower, P.E. (1974). Social difficulty in a student sample. *British Journal of Educational Psychology*, **44**, 13–21.

Buss, A.H. (1980). Self-consciousness and social anxiety. San Francisco, CA: Freeman.

Butler, G. & Mathews, A. (1983). Cognitive processes in anxiety. *Advances in Behaviour Research and Therapy*, **5**, 51–62.

Butler, G., Cullington, A., Munby, M., Amies, P. & Gelder, M. (1984). Exposure and anxiety management in the treatment of social phobia. *Journal of Consulting and Clinical Psychology*, **52**, 642–650.

Cacioppo, J.T., Glass, C.R. & Merluzzi, T.B. (1979). Self-statements and self-evaluation: a cognitive response analysis of heterosocial anxiety. *Cognitive Therapy and Research*, **3**, 249–262.

Chapman, T.F., Mannuzza, S. & Fyer, A.J. (1995). Epidemiology and family studies of social phobia. In R.G. Heimberg, M. Liebowitz, D. Hope & F. Schneier (eds), *Social Phobia: Diagnosis, Assessment and Treatment*. New York: Guilford.

Clark, D.M. & Wells, A. (1995). A cognitive model of social phobia. In R.G. Heimberg, M. Liebowitz, D. Hope & F. Schneier (eds), *Social Phobia: Diagnosis, Assessment and Treatment*. New York: Guilford.

Clark, D.M. & Yuen, P.K. (1994). Social anxiety and attentional bias away from negative faces. Manuscript in preparation.

Daly, J.A., Vangelisti, A.L. & Lawrence, S.G. (1989). Self-focused attention and public speaking anxiety. *Personality and Individual Differences*, **10**, 903–913.

Darvill, T.J., Johnson, R.C. & Danko, G.P. (1992). Personality correlates of public and private self-consciousness. *Personality and Individual Differences*, **13**, 383–384.

Dodge, C.S., Hope, D.A., Heimberg, R.G. & Becker, R.E. (1988). Evaluation of the social interaction self-statement test with a social phobic population. *Cognitive Therapy and Research*, **12**, 211–222.

Emmelkamp, P.M.G., Mersch, P.P., Vissia, E. & van de Helm, M. (1985). Social phobia: a comparative evaluation of cognitive and behavioural interventions. *Behaviour Research and Therapy*, **23**, 365–369.

Fenigstein, A., Scheier, N.F. & Buss, A.H. (1975). Public and private self-consciousness: assessment and theory. *Journal of Consulting and Clinical Psychology*, **43**, 522–527.

Hartman, L.M. (1983). A meta-cognitive model of social anxiety: implications for treatment. *Clinical Psychology Review*, **3**, 435–456.

Hartman, L.M. (1986). Social anxiety, problem drinking and ·slef-awareness. In L.M. Hartman & K.R. Blankstein (eds), *Perception of Self in Emotional Disorder and Psychotherapy*. New York: Plenum.

Heimberg, R.G. (1989). Cognitive and behavioural treatments for social phobia: a critical analysis. *Clinical Psychology Review*, **9**, 107–128.

Heimberg, R.G., Dodge, C.S., Hope, D.A., Kennedy, C.R. & Zollo, L.J. (1990). Cognitive behavioural group treatment for social phobia: comparison with a credible placebo control. *Cognitive Therapy and Research*, **14**, 1–23.

Heimberg, R.G., Salzman, D.G., Holt, C.S. & Blendell, K.A. (1993). Cognitive behavioural group treatment for social phobia: effectiveness at five-year follow-up. *Cognitive Therapy and Research*, **14**, 1–23.

Heimberg, R.G., Juster, H.R., Brown, E.G., Holly, C., Makris, G.S., Leung, A.W., Schneier, F.R., Gilow, A. & Liebowitz, M.R. (1994). Cognitive–behavioural and pharmacological treatment of social phobia. Paper presented at the 128th Annual Meeting of the Association for the Advancement of Behaviour Therapy, San Diego.

Holt, C.S., Heimberg, R.G. & Hope, D.A. (1992). Avoidant personality disorder and the generalised sub-type of social phobia. *Journal of Abnormal Psychology*, **101**, 318–325.

Hope, D.A., Gansler, A.D. & Heimberg, R.G. (1989). Attentional focus and causal attributions in social phobia: implications from social psychology. *Clinical Psychology Review*, **9**, 49–60.

Hope, D.A. & Heimberg, R.G. (1988). Public and private self-consciousness and social anxiety *Journal of Personality Assessment*, **52**, 629–639.

Hope, D.A., Heimberg, R.G. & Klein, J.F. (1990). Social anxiety and the result of interpersonal feedback. *Journal of Cognitive Psychotherapy*, **4**, 185–195.

Hope, D.A., Rapee, R.N., Heimberg, R.G. & Dombeck, N.J. (1990). Representations of the self in social phobia: vulnerability to social threat. *Cognitive Therapy and Research*, **14**, 177–189.

Ingram, R.E. (1990). Self-focused attention in clinical disorders: review and a conceptual model. *Psychological Bulletin*, **107**, 156–176.

Jerremalm, A., Jansson, L. & Öst, L.G. (1986). Cognitive and physiological reactivity and the effects of different behavioural methods in the treatment of social phobia. *Behaviour Research and Therapy*, **24**, 171–180.

Johannson, J. & Öst, L.G. (1982). Perception of autonomic reactions and actual heart rate in phobic patients *Journal of Behavioural Assessment*, **4**, 133–143.

Kanter, N.J. & Goldfried, M.R. (1979). Relative effectiveness of rational restructuring and self-control desensitisation in the reduction of interpersonal anxiety. *Behaviour Therapy*, **10**, 472–490.

Kimble, C.E. & Zehr, H.D. (1982). Self-consciousness, information load, self-presentation, and memory in a social situation. *Journal of Social Psychology*, **118**, 39–46.

Liebowitz, M.R., Gorman, J.M., Fyer, A.J. & Klein, D.F. (1985). Social phobia: review of a neglected anxiety disorder. *Archives of General Psychiatry*, **42**, 729–736.

McEwan, K.L. & Devins, G.M. (1983). Is increased arousal in social anxiety noticed by others? *Journal of Abnormal Psychology*, **92**, 417–421.

MacLeod, C., Mathews, A. & Tata, P. (1986). Attentional bias in emotional disorders. *Journal of Abnormal Psychology*, **95**, 15–20.

Marzillier, J.S., Lambert, C. & Kellett, J. (1976). A controlled evaluation of social skills training for socially inadequate psychiatric patients. *Behaviour Research and Therapy*, **14**, 225–238.

Mattia, J.I., Heimberg, R.G. & Hope, D.A. (1993). The revised Stroop colour-naming task in social phobics. *Behaviour Research and Therapy*, **31**, 305–313.

Mattick, R.P. & Peters, L. (1988). Treatment of severe social phobia: effects of guided exposure with and without cognitive restructuring. *Journal of Consulting and Clinical Psychology*, **56**, 251–260.

Mattick, R.P., Peters, L. & Clarke, J.C. (1989). Exposure and cognitive restructuring for social phobia: a controlled study. *Behavior therapy*, **20**, 3–23.

Öst L.G., Jerremalm, A. & Johansson, J. (1981). Individual response patterns and the effects of different behavioural methods in the treatment of social phobia. *Behaviour Research and Therapy*, **19**, 1–16.

Rapee, R.M. & Lim, L. (1992). Discrepancy between self and observer ratings of performance in social phobics. *Journal of Abnormal Psychology*, **181**, 728–731.

Salkovskis, P.M. (1991). The importance of behaviour in the maintenance of anxiety and panic: a cognitive account. *Behavioural Psychotherapy*, **19**, 6–19.

Stopa, L. (1995). Cognitive Processes in Social Phobia. Unpublished DPhil thesis, University of Oxford.

Stopa, L. & Clark, D.M. (1993). Cognitive processes in social phobia. *Behaviour Research and Therapy*, **31**, 255–267.

Trower, P., Yardley, K., Bryant, B. & Shaw, P. (1978). The treatment of social failure: a comparison of anxiety reduction and skills acquisition procedures on two social problems. *Behaviour Modification*, **2**, 41–60.

Turner, S.M., Beidel, D.C., Dancu, C.V. & Keys, D.J. (1986). Psychopathology of social phobia and comparison to avoidant personality disorder. *Journal of Abnormal Psychology*, **95**, 389–394.

Watson, D. & Friend, R. (1969). Measurement of social evaluative anxiety. *Journal of Consulting and Clinical Psychology*, **33**, 448–457.

Wells A. (1997). *Cognitive Therapy of Anxiety Disorders: A Practise Manual and Conceptual Guide*. Chichester, UK: Wiley.

Wells, A., Clark, D.M., Salkovskis, P., Ludgate, J., Hackmann, A. & Gelder, M. (1995). Social phobia: the role of in-situation safety behaviours in maintaining anxiety and negative beliefs. *Behavior Therapy*, **26**, 153–161.

Wells, A., Clark, D.M. & Ahmad, S. (1995). How do I look with my mind's eye: perspective-taking in social phobic imagery. Paper presented at the annual conference of the British Association of Behavioural and Cognitive Psychotherapy, Southampton, September.

Wells, A. & Clark, D.M. (in preparation). Cognitive Therapy of Social Phobia: a Treatment Manual.

Wells, A. & Matthews, G. (1994). *Attention and Emotion: a Clinical Perspective*. Hove, UK: Erlbaum.

Wells, A. & Matthews, G. (1996). Modelling cognition in emotional disorder: the SREF model. *Behavior Research and Therapy*, **34**, 881–888.

Winton, E., Clark, D.M. & Edelman, R.J. (1995). Social anxiety, fear of negative evaluation and the detection of negative emotion in others. *Behaviour Research and Therapy*, **33**, 193–196.

Chapter 2

Agoraphobia

Paul M. Salkovskis
and
Ann Hackmann
Department of Psychiatry, University of Oxford, Oxford, UK

DEFINITIONS OF AGORAPHOBIA AND SOME ASSOCIATED PROBLEMS

The term "agoraphobia" in ICD-10 refers to an interrelated and overlapping cluster of phobias embracing fears of leaving home, fear of entering shops, crowds and public places, or travelling alone in trains, buses or aeroplanes. The lack of an immediately available exit is a key feature, and many sufferers are terrified by the thought of collapsing or being left helpless in public. As in all psychological problems, the specific pattern of fears is idiosyncratic. For example, some agoraphobics are afraid of relatively deserted places, others feel less anxious if it is dark; some feel more comfortable if accompanied by their young children, others feel more afraid in these circumstances.

Over the past 15 years it has been suggested that agoraphobia may not exist as a distinct clinical entity, but that it develops as a complication of panic disorder (Klein, 1981). It is certainly true that panic attacks are characteristic of a large subgroup of agoraphobic patients. However, the evidence seems to be that this association is characteristic of patient samples seen in the clinic rather than reflecting the epidemiology of the problem itself. Unfortunately, a failure to recognize this sampling bias has become self-perpetuating through the current classification system. DSM-III (American Psychiatric Association, 1980) gave panic a central place in anxiety disorders, particularly agoraphobia. DSM-IV (American Psychiatric Association, 1995) currently recognizes two types of agoraphobia: with and without panic. The diagnosis of *panic disorder with agoraphobia* requires:

Phobias—A Handbook of Theory, Research and Treatment. Edited by G.C.L. Davey.
© 1997 John Wiley & Sons Ltd.

1. Recurrent unexpected panic attacks; *and*
2. At least one of the attacks has been followed by 1 month (or more) of one (or more) of the following:
    (a) Persistent concern about having additional attacks.
    (b) Worry about the implications of the attack or its consequences (e.g. losing control, having a heart attack, "going crazy").
    (c) A significant change in behaviour related to the attacks; *and*
3. The presence of agoraphobia as defined below.

It has to be established that the panic attacks are not due to the direct physiological effects of a substance (e.g. a drug of abuse, a medication) or a general medical condition (e.g. hyperthyroidism). It is also important (and, in many instances, difficult) to establish that the panic attacks are not better accounted for by the phobic aspect of another mental disorder.

The diagnostic criteria for *agoraphobia without history of panic disorder* are similar, except that the criteria require that the presence of agoraphobia is related to fear of developing panic-like symptoms (e.g. dizziness or diarrhoea), rather than full-blown panic attacks.

According to DSM-IV, agoraphobia "is not a codable disorder"; this means that, within this framework, agoraphobia exists only in relation to the presence or absence of full-blown panic disorder (i.e. the specific disorder in which the agoraphobia occurs is coded, that is, either *panic disorder with agoraphobia* or *agoraphobia without history of panic disorder*). DSM-IV nonetheless does define agoraphobia as:

1. Anxiety about being in places or situations from which escape might be difficult (or embarrassing) or in which help may not be available in the event of having an unexpected or situationally predisposed panic attack or panic-like symptoms. Agoraphobic fears typically involve characteristic clusters of situations that include: being outside the home alone; being in a crowd or standing in a line; being on a bridge; and travelling in a bus, train or automobile. (If the avoidance is limited to one or only a few specific situations, specific phobia is suggested as an alternative diagnosis, or social phobia if the avoidance is limited to social situations.)
2. The situations are avoided (e.g. travel is restricted) or else are endured with marked distress or with anxiety about having a panic attack or panic-like symptoms, or require the presence of a companion.
3. The anxiety or phobic avoidance is not better accounted for by another mental disorder (as above).

Note that, even when the diagnosis is of agoraphobia without a history of panic attacks, there is a requirement for the "presence of agoraphobia related to fear of developing panic-like symptoms (e.g. dizziness or diarrhoea)". This means that a peculiarity of the diagnostic criteria is that agoraphobia without panic or panic-like symptoms does not exist as a definable disorder. The diagnostic criteria therefore ensure that there will, by definition, be an association between panic and agoraphobia. This calls into doubt the validity of the conclusion of many writers that panic attacks are the *cause* of agoraphobia (Barlow, 1988; Klein, Ross & Cohen, 1987; Rachman, 1990; Thyer, 1986; Thyer & Himle, 1985). Although it is recognized in the present chapter that panic and panic-like symptoms are important for (and *often* central to) the experience of a substantial proportion of agoraphobics, the attribution of all agoraphobia to panic and panic-related symptoms may be premature; it is certainly not properly substantiated, and there are reasons to doubt such an extreme conclusion.

It has been demonstrated that panic attacks are prevalent in all other anxiety disorders (Barlow et al., 1985). A number of studies have also shown that panic also occurs relatively frequently in non-clinical subjects (Margraf & Ehlers, 1988; Norton, Dorward & Cox, 1986; Norton et al., 1985). The most telling data are those that show that agoraphobia without panic attacks is much more common in samples from the general population. Angst & Dobler-Mikola (1986) found a 1-year prevalence rate for agoraphobia without panic as 1.6%, compared to 0.7% for panic disorder with agoraphobia. In the ECA (Epidemiological Catchment Area) study, Weissman et al. (1986) found a lifetime prevalence for agoraphobia without panic of 1.4–6.6% compared to that of agoraphobia with panic symptoms of 1.7–2.6%. In the Munich study, Wittchen (1986) found that 50% of agoraphobics in the community had never experienced a panic-like state or panic disorder.

A possible conclusion is that clinical researchers have been unduly influenced by an over-representation of panic with agoraphobia in the clinic (i.e. amongst the patients seen by clinicians and referred for research studies). Rather than reflecting actual prevalence, this pattern may reflect influences on help-seeking behaviour. Boyd (1986) analysed data from the ECA study across a range of diagnoses, and found that people with panic disorder were more likely to seek help for their problem than those with any other psychiatric diagnoses (including schizophrenia). The high prevalence of panic, both in other anxiety disorders and in affective disorders as noted by Barlow (1988; Barlow & Craske, 1988; Barlow et al., 1985) has been proposed as a factor influencing the decision of these other groups to seek professional help (Barlow, 1988). Boyd (1986) suggests that the strong element of somatic sensations and fears of associated catastrophes might account for the decision to seek medical consultation. Work by Katon (Katon, 1984; Katon et al., 1987) supports this view. He noted that early presentation of panic to primary care physicians focused almost exclusively on somatic symptoms (Katon et al., 1987), and that physical causes were initially attributed in 89% of a sample of panic cases; misdiagnoses persisted "for months or even years" (although exact figures are not given). A further important implication is that research samples may over-represent panic-associated agoraphobia, resulting in a tendency to assume that panic or panic-like symptoms are an invariant and primary feature of agoraphobia.

This view is particularly favoured by biological researchers, who insist that panic is a biological abnormality and the primary phenomenon, relegating agoraphobia to the status of a secondary psychological phenomenon (Gorman et al.,

1989). There is a danger that this medical-model view may obscure important psychological research which suggests a more normalizing account of anxiety problems (Salkovskis, 1996). The assumption that panic is best understood as a biological or neurological abnormality is also under challenge (Clark, 1986). These considerations mean that the diagnostic criteria need to be considered with great caution. Those conducting research may consider the use of additional or alternative operational definitions of agoraphobia, relaxing the criteria in definable ways (e.g. not requiring the presence of panic-like symptoms) or tightening them (e.g. requiring a specified number of panic attacks in a given period, such as the 3 weeks prior to assessment).

DEFINING AGORAPHOBIA WITHOUT DIAGNOSING THE PATIENT: AGORAPHOBIA AS MOTIVATED AVOIDANCE

There is no doubt that avoidance is a key feature of agoraphobia. A simple way to begin to unravel the links between agoraphobia and other problems such as panic is to conceptualize it as motivated avoidance. In agoraphobia, the avoidance is of situations which involve being away from safety, most commonly embodied by the person's home (or other trusted helper's homes) and its extension by other "safe" objects (e.g. the person's car). This does not necessarily mean that the person is free of anxiety when at home, but that they feel relatively safer there than in other situations. The fear in agoraphobic situations revolves around not being able to leave the situation for a safer one (or not being able to do so without embarrassment). This distinguishes agoraphobia from problems in which other types of phobic avoidance predominate, because the person does not exclusively avoid (or endure with considerable anxiety) situations where they are likely to be negatively evaluated (as in social phobia), or to be in a confined space (as in claustrophobia), or avoid because of some other type of anxiety, such as obsessive–compulsive disorder (OCD) or post-traumatic stress disorder (PTSD). However, fear of these other types of situations may be present in many people suffering from agoraphobia, as is it perfectly possible to experience multiple fears of this type.

Such a view has the merit of considering agoraphobic avoidance as a distinct psychological phenomenon (with much in common with other types of avoidance) rather than as a symptom of some other diagnosis. According to this view, people develop a pattern of avoidance of particular situations because these situations have become associated with unpleasant experiences (or the expectation of unpleasant experiences). These associations may be historical (and may therefore be relatively inaccessible to current introspection), or may be more recent and vivid. This helps make sense of why panic attacks are neither necessary nor sufficient for the experience of agoraphobia, but why there is such a strong association. Other types of anticipated unpleasant experience which can

lead to an agoraphobic pattern of behaviour include epileptic attacks, inconti-
nence and irritable bowel (i.e. episodes where the person believes they are in
danger of losing control over their bowels). Agoraphobia can develop in the
elderly, who fear falling and breaking their bones. This way of viewing agoraphobic avoidance has the further advantage of normalizing the behaviour. Avoidance as a reaction to the *perceived* possibility of physical or social threat is, of
course, an understandable reaction.

Within this framework, panic is the single commonest factor associated with
agoraphobia. This then raises the important question of why only some people
develop agoraphobia when they experience panic attacks (the same question
clearly applies to irritable bowel problems, epilepsy and other associated features; for understandable reasons research has tended to focus on the association
with panic). The second question concerns those people who have no panic or
"panic-like symptoms" associated with their agoraphobia. There are several ways
in which a tendency to avoid particular situations may result in actual avoidance
behaviour amounting to agoraphobia. Persons may be particularly strongly motivated because their fear of agoraphobic situations is especially intense (as is
usually the case when panic is present or anticipated) or they may believe they
are particularly vulnerable to even relatively small amounts of fear, perhaps
because they underestimate their ability to cope either with the agoraphobic
situation or their own emotional reactions. Before a more detailed analysis of
theories of agoraphobia, clinical factors thought to be meaningfully correlated
with agoraphobia will be considered in order to evaluate the extent to which
these inform the notion of motivated avoidance.

FACTORS ASSOCIATED WITH AGORAPHOBIA

A commonly held view is that agoraphobics may show two basic dispositional
qualities: dependence on others, and a tendency to cope with difficulties by using
avoidance as a coping stratagem (e.g. Andrews, 1966; McGennis, Nolan &
Hartman, 1977; Shafer, 1976). Andrews suggests that this may be due to maternal
overprotection. Mathews, Gelder & Johnston (1981) reviewed the evidence for
this theory. The seven studies considered gave equivocal results, although several
did find evidence of overprotection, dependency and somewhat unstable and
more "anomalous" families (with more adopted children, etc.). Mathews, Gelder
& Johnston conclude that few properly conducted studies have been done, but
that there is some suggestive evidence of dependence as a pre-existing trait.
Reich, Noyes & Troughton (1987) compared subjects who had panic disorder
with varying amounts of agoraphobic avoidance, and found that about 40% of
subjects with some (as opposed to no) phobic avoidance met criteria for dependent personality disorder, although it was not possible to determine whether the
dependent behaviour was primary or whether it was secondary to the agoraphobia. Kleiner & Marshall (1987) reported a high degree of dependent behaviour in
agoraphobics, prior to the onset of the phobia, and Borden & Geller (1981), in

their review, suggested that dependent personality traits are a key feature of agoraphobia.

There is some evidence that people who go on to develop agoraphobia may have been premorbidly more fearful of being out and about in the world. A history of school phobia is more common in agoraphobics than in panic disorder patients without agoraphobia, and the relatives of agoraphobics are more likely to suffer from school phobia or agoraphobia (Deltito et al., 1986; Gittelman-Klein & Klein, 1984). Renneberg, Chambless & Gracely (1992) studied the incidence of DSM-IIIR Axis II personality disorders in a large group of agoraphobics, and found that 56% of the sample had at least one personality disorder, of which avoidant personality was the single most frequent disorder. They also note that personality disorders seem more common in agoraphobics than in individuals with panic disorder (see also Friedman, Shear & Frances, 1987; Green & Curtis, 1988). These results are difficult to interpret, however, as agoraphobic behaviour overlaps with the diagnostic criteria for avoidant personality disorder; it is therefore possible that any association found between agoraphobia and avoidant personality may be the result of criterion contamination.

Chambless & Goldstein (1982) report that agoraphobic patients show low scores on the Bernreuter Inventory of Self-sufficiency (although they also note that it incorporates items to do with activities to be done alone, again suggesting possible criterion contamination). Buglass et al. (1977) reported no extra premorbid dependency in agoraphobics than in a matched group of normals, but found more conflict over dependency on the mother in the agoraphobic group. They may have contaminated their results by excluding those agoraphobics with marked dependency. Torgersen (1979) studied a small group of monozygotic twins of patients with agoraphobia. He found that the agoraphobic twins were more likely to have been dependent, self-doubting and suggestible on a personality inventory, and to report having been like that since childhood. They were also likely to have been the second twin, and the smaller one. Chambless & Goldstein (1982) report two other studies of assertiveness in agoraphobics. In one they found that the agoraphobics were less assertive than simple phobics on therapist ratings, and in the other they found that they were less assertive on assertion inventories at intake than a group of college students, and more anxious about assertion. Rapee & Murrell (1988) also found that very avoidant individuals scored higher on the Neuroticism scale of the Eysenck Personality Questionnaire and lower on a measure of assertiveness than minimally avoidant subjects with panic disorder. Clum & Knowles (1991) review this type of data in an attempt to relate it to why some people with panic disorder become avoidant.

Most studies report a higher percentage of women in groups of agoraphobic patients than in groups with panic disorder without avoidance (Wittchen, 1986; Chambless, 1985). This has led to the stereotyped notion of the typical agoraphobic as a housebound housewife. Chambless (1985) does, however, point out that of her sample of 378 agoraphobics, 64 were men and only 52% were currently married, so that this description fitted less than half of the patients. There has, however, been considerable interest in the relationship between gender and avoidance in patients with agoraphobia. There has been speculation that, where the roles adopted are more "traditional", it is easier and more acceptable for women to become housebound than men, and for men to use alcohol as an alternative coping strategy. The stereotypical female gender role is also associated with traits of dependency and unassertiveness, both found to be prominent in agoraphobics. This literature is reviewed in detail by Chambless (1985).

A number of studies indicate that greater degrees of depression are associated with more severe avoidance in agoraphobia (Sanderson & Barlow, 1986; Klosko et al., 1986; Telch et al., 1989; Vitaliano et al., 1987). This finding was not replicated in several other studies (e.g. Thyer et al., 1985; Rapee & Murrell, 1988). Aronson & Logue (1987) reported a reliable difference between panic disorder (PD) and panic disorder with agoraphobia (PDA), such that depression was more likely in individuals who later developed avoidance, and McNally & Lorenz (1987) found that in a group of PDA patients depression predicted a resurgence of avoidance. The association between depression and avoidance may be conceptualized within the theoretical framework of learned helplessness and attributional style, if it is found that PD patients with avoidance have weaker beliefs in their own ability to cope with stress. Klosko et al. (1986), who showed that panic disorder patients with avoidance were more likely to attribute negative events to stable and global factors, and Telch et al. (1989) showed that panic disorder patients with avoidance were likely to rate their ability to cope with panic as lower than patients with panic disorder without avoidance.

Several studies indicate that there is very little difference between the thoughts of possible physical consequences of bodily sensations (or in the extent to which they fear them) in people suffering from panic with agoraphobia, as opposed to panic patients with minimal avoidance. The main difference observed is a greater fear of dizziness, and a higher frequency and belief in thoughts of fainting amongst the agoraphobics (Salkovskis, 1990; Telch et al., 1989). In the study by Telch et al. the more avoidant group showed much higher scores on scales reflecting fears of loss of mental control, or social ridicule. These results echo those of other studies that have found that agoraphobics tend to have more social evaluative concerns than patients with panic disorder (Pollard & Cox, 1988; de Ruiter & Garssen, 1989; Meldrum, Pollard & Fraunhoffer, 1989). In the study by Telch et al. (1989) agoraphobics were found to have less perceived self-efficacy relating to dealing with panic than other panic patients. Hoffart (1995) has also shown that low scores on a measure of perceived self-efficacy predict situational avoidance more strongly than other measures, including a measure of catastrophic beliefs about the symptoms of panic.

THEORIES OF AGORAPHOBIA

Psychodynamic Accounts of Agoraphobia

The term "agoraphobia" was first used by Westphal (1871) to describe anxiety that appeared in a predictable way in empty streets, in crowded rooms or when walking across open spaces, and was alleviated by the presence of a companion.

In an earlier description, Benedikt (1870) suggested that the central symptom was dizziness rather than anxiety, and thought it might be due to a disorder of the eye muscles. A further contemporary account by Cordes (1871) highlighted the importance of what we would now recognize as cognitive factors, making the important observation that anxiety is based on the ideas in the patient's mind and is not provoked in an automatic way by stimuli in the environment.

These accounts of phenomenology were followed by theoretical speculations. Freud's earliest writing about agoraphobia (Freud, 1895) concerned the notion that such patients had a fear of walking in the streets lest it led to sexual temptation, the idea of which had been repressed. In 1926 he wrote about anxiety, suggesting it was often due to missing some loved person, but he did not extend this theory to agoraphobia. Other writers have hypothesized that the fear of leaving home could be linked to unconscious hostile wishes, which could be enacted on their families whilst they were absent (Deutsch, 1929; Weiss, 1964). Quite recent psychoanalytic reviews (e.g. Compton, 1992) still give prominence to these ideas about the condition. Phobic avoidance is seen as serving the patient's needs, whilst the real motive remains unconscious because of the mechanisms of displacement and repression. Some of the possible underlying motives are aggressive, sexual and dependency needs. Weiss (1964) relates agoraphobia to regression and unresolved dependency needs. Arieti (1979) has argued that the root of the problem lies in global interpersonal fears which the agoraphobic finds can be reduced to definite concrete physical fears, and thus avoided.

A variation on the theme of unconscious motivation is the theory that agoraphobia may be one way in which individuals may attempt to cope with an unsatisfactory marriage. There are a number of clinical papers with anecdotal accounts suggesting that the marriages of agoraphobics tend to be pathological. These are reviewed by Hafner (1982). However, there are few properly controlled studies using comparison groups. Agulnik (1970) and Buglass et al. (1977) found no abnormalities in the husbands of agoraphobics, either at interview or in objective measures of personality and symptoms. However, Hafner (1982) suggests that careful perusal of the data of Buglass et al. indicates some discrepancies between the accounts of agoraphobics and their husbands, suggestive of a degree of denial in the husbands' accounts of their "normal" lives. Also, their wives experienced them as less sympathetic than they reported themselves. Poor psychosexual functioning has been observed in agoraphobics (Marks & Gelder, 1965; Roberts, 1964), but also in severe anxiety (Winokur & Holeman, 1963). Sexual difficulties may well be secondary to anxiety, since Buglass et al. found that the sexual problems began at the same time or after the development of agoraphobia.

Hand & Lamontagne (1976) observed exacerbation of marital problems after group exposure in six of the 14 agoraphobics with chronic marital problems (out of a total of 21 married agoraphobics who had received treatment). Hafner's own studies (1977a,b) systematically looked at 30 agoraphobics and their husbands, and felt that there were probably two overlapping groups, with different patterns of relationship, and that the most hostile husbands tended to deteriorate when their wives were showing most improvement. In contrast, Bland & Hallam (1980) found that phobia removal led to a reduction in the spouse's dissatisfaction with the patient. They also found a relationship between level of marital satisfaction and response to treatment. Similarly Hudson (1974), Milton & Hafner (1979) and Hafner (1977a) found that patients with unsatisfactory marriages were likely to improve less with treatment, and were more likely to relapse. Emmelkamp & van der Hout (1983) found that agoraphobics who complained more about their husbands did less well in therapy. None of the above findings about the relationship between outcome and marital satisfaction imply a causal relationship between agoraphobia and marital state. Both could be related to another variable, such as high levels of neuroticism.

Separation Anxiety

Another theory which has been seriously considered by many, and particularly by Bowlby, is that panic and agoraphobia have something to do with separation anxiety. It has been suggested that this type of anxiety has a usefulness from an evolutionary point of view, as it keeps the young close to their protectors. Bowlby and others have studied young children's reactions to separation, and observed its damaging consequences. Bowlby's own work (1969, 1973) has led him to suggest that people with agoraphobia or school refusal may be those whose childhoods have been characterized by anxious attachment and the lack of a secure base.

There are some studies which support the view that agoraphobia is more common in those with a history of separation anxiety. For example, in a community study of women at heightened risk for neurotic disorders, Silove et al. (1995) found that women with a history of panic disorder with agoraphobia had statistically higher scores on a retrospective measure of early separation anxiety than women with generalized anxiety or other phobic disorders. The results were not accounted for by higher levels of neuroticism or General Health Questionnaire (GHQ) scores. Deltito et al. (1986) found a significant difference between panic disorder patients with and without agoraphobia, in that while there was a 60% incidence of previous school phobia among the agoraphobics, there was not a single case among the patients with panic disorder without a history of agoraphobia. Berg (1976) found in an uncontrolled study that 7% of the offspring (aged 7–15 years) of agoraphobics (and 14% of the 11–15 year olds) were school phobics, although the same group (Berg, Butler & Pritchard, 1974), had reported no more psychiatric problems in the parents of school phobics than in the parents of a normal control group. Gittelman-Klein & Klein (1984) also report that 50% of their agoraphobic sample had a history of school phobia, in comparison with 27% of a group with specific phobics. Tearnan, Telch & Keefe (1984) report that, in a subgroup of agoraphobics, the first occurrence of agoraphobia was preceded by separation experiences, although this is only one of a range of previous stresses noted.

A review by Margraf, Ehlers & Roth (1986) found that the literature does not indicate an increased frequency of actual separations from parents, such as permanent or long-term separations from parents before the age of 15, or death of a parent (Berg, Butler & Pritchard, 1974; Solyom et al., 1974; Buglass et al., 1977). Parental death has also not been found to be a selective precursor to either panic disorder or agoraphobia in a study by Thyer, Himle & Fischer (1988). Some of the studies reviewed by Margraf, Ehlers & Roth (1986) also found no evidence of signs of anxiety during shorter separations from the mother in the childhoods of agoraphobics. Margraf, Ehlers & Roth conclude appropriately that the evidence is very equivocal, probably because the studies done have been almost entirely based on retrospective reporting.

Biological/Epidemiological Theory

Von Korff & Eaton (1989) discuss panic disorder with and without agoraphobia as a sequenced and staged problem. The sequence proposed is based on that suggested by Klein, Ross & Cohen (1987), and runs as follows:

1. Occurrence of panic attacks.
2. Cognitive appraisal of symptoms as harmful.
3. Sensitization to symptoms.
4. Development of avoidance.

These stages are said to represent different phases in the development of a disease. Agoraphobia is thus said to represent a later stage of panic disorder. However, the evidence supporting this epidemiologically-based view is scanty and, in some instances, contradictory. Thyer et al. (1985) found that panic disorder patients had a (non-significantly) *longer* duration of disorder compared to agoraphobics. The disease-stage model would predict a significantly shorter duration. There are other quite striking differences in the histories of those with panic disorder without avoidance and those with severe agoraphobia. For example, it has been shown that agoraphobics tend to have an earlier mean age of onset (Wittchen, 1988; Deltito et al., 1986), a history more often characterized by school phobia (Deltito et al., 1986; Gittelman-Klein & Klein, 1984) and relatives who tend to have a higher incidence of school phobia or agoraphobia than patients who have panic disorder without avoidance. Another difference between the groups is that agoraphobia is much more common amongst women than men, whilst panic disorder is somewhat more evenly distributed among the sexes, although still more common in women (Wittchen, 1986). Salkovskis (1988b) suggests that the data is consistent with two possibilities; either that there are important idiosyncratic individual differences involved in the reaction to anxiety and panic, or that there may be a difference in severity, with agoraphobia with panic representing the more severe variant (rather than a later stage).

A further shortcoming of the disease-stage model is the implication of a passive relationship between panic and avoidance, such that avoidance is caused by panic. There is a considerable amount of data supporting Marks' (1987a,b) assertion that a functional relationship exists between agoraphobia and panic and vice versa; not least is the demonstration that exposure treatments not only reduce avoidance but also ameliorate panic attacks (Marks et al., 1983; see also review in Michelson, 1988). There is a requirement for detailed longitudinal studies if such issues are to be resolved (Klein, Ross & Cohen, 1987; Marks, 1987a).

Biological Theory: Klein's View

Klein (1980, 1981; Klein & Klein, 1988, 1989a) argues that several findings indicate a qualitative distinction between panic anxiety and anticipatory or phobic anxiety. These are (a) the apparently spontaneous nature of some panic attacks; (b) the observation that panic but not anticipatory anxiety responds to antidepressant medication (Sheehan, 1982), and that panic does not respond to phenothiazines or (as shown later) benzodiazepines; (c) the finding that panic disorder with agoraphobia patients have experienced more separation anxiety and school "phobia" (50%) than mixed psychiatric controls who were not diagnosed as suffering from panic disorder (27%) (Klein, 1964; Gittelman-Klein & Klein, 1984); (d) the finding that sodium lactate frequently precipitates panic attacks in panic disorder patients but does not do so as frequently in non-clinical control subjects or socially anxious patients (Liebowitz et al., 1984, 1985; Pitts & McClure, 1967); (e) evidence of familial (possibly genetic) component in panic; particularly the higher concordance rate for panic in monozygotic as compared to dizygotic twins (Crowe et al., 1980; Torgersen, 1983).

Klein regards the mechanism involved in panic as similar to that in epilepsy, with uncontrolled discharges of activity in the "bio-behavioural anxiety system" producing semi-random bursts of panic. This is said to happen because a normally stabilizing negative feedback loop has become converted to a pathological positive feedback loop, possibly as a result of sensitizing separation experiences during childhood. All other panic-related phenomena follow on from these bursts of pathological activity, including agoraphobia (Klein, Ross & Cohen, 1987).

Klein's position has been criticized as being too vague, especially in terms of the failure to specify the exact nature of the disordered mechanism (Rachman, 1990). The hypothesis is in grave danger of simply referring to there being "something wrong or peculiar with panic patients" (Klein, personal communication). Klein & Klein (1989b) suggest that the specific mechanism may involve an evolutionarily evolved central alarm mechanism which functions in relation to separation anxiety or impending asphyxia. There have been a variety of critiques of the evidential basis of Klein's theory; these are fully discussed in Clark (1988), Margraf, Ehlers & Roth (1986), Rachman (1990) and Barlow (1988). The main points at issue are:

1. The degree of spontaneity of panic, even early attacks, is debatable; in the
    longer term, work such as that reported by Faravelli (1985), Finlay-Jones &
    Brown (1981), Pollard, Pollard & Corn (1989), and reviewed in Roy-Byrne &
    Uhde (1988), indicates that threat-related life events tend to precede the
    onset of panic. In more acute terms, there is evidence that specific episodes of
    panic are usually preceded by identifiable stimuli such as bodily sensations
    and frightening thoughts (Beck, Laude & Bonhert, 1974; Hibbert, 1984).
    These interview studies have received support both from studies using 24
    hour ambulatory psychophysiological monitoring (reviewed in Freeman,
    1989) and from work using telemetry and computer-based *in situ* question-
    naires (Taylor, Fried & Kenardy, 1990).
2. It is not clear whether or not the effectiveness of drug treatments such as
    imipramine is *independent* of the self-exposure instructions which accompany
    pharmacological treatment. The effectiveness of such instructions on their
    own and combined with pharmacological treatments has been the subject of
    much investigation. At present, there is some evidence that the effects of
    imipramine and self-exposure instructions might be synergistic (Telch,
    Tearnan & Taylor, 1983).
3. The evidence for a familial component is potentially stronger than the other
    evidence for the biological hypothesis (Kendler et al., 1987). However, there
    are some distinct oddities in the concordance data which are difficult to make
    sense of from the standpoint of a genetic diathesis for the occurrence of panic
    attacks. For example, groups of relatives who should show similar genetic
    risk have been shown to have widely differing rates of panic and other
    anxiety disorders. Dizygotic twins were shown by Torgersen (1983) to have
    lower rates than for non-twin siblings, and concordance between siblings is
    less than between parents and children (Moran & Andrews, 1985). Barlow
    (1988, pp. 172–174) suggests that the evidence on heritability of anxiety is
    most consistent with the hypothesis that what is inherited is the *trait* of
    anxiety (often described as emotionality, nervousness or neuroticism). He
    argues that studies reporting a difference between heritability for panic
    disorder and other anxiety disorders have not controlled for the fact that all
    panic disorder subjects are generally anxious, or for different levels of sever-
    ity which are inherent in the structure of the DSM-III diagnostic rules. When
    severity of disorder is taken into account, Barlow points out that the different
    anxiety disorders appear to be equally heritable.

The Neuroanatomical Hypothesis

A group of researchers from Klein's centre suggested a "neuroanatomical hypothesis", which they described as being inspired by his work (Gorman et al.,
1989). This detailed and complex hypothesis takes Klein's basic assertions as its
starting point, but attempts both to make the position more explicit and to
identify the neuroanatomical basis of the components of the hypothesis. The

paper also makes some attempt to incorporate cognitive–behavioural findings, arguing that it is not useful to specify whether panic is "a behavioural–cognitive disease" or "a biological disease", and that it should be regarded as having elements of both. By describing the basis of their hypothesis in this way, they misconstrue the basis of the debate, which is not biological vs. psychological, but disease vs. non-disease (Rachman, 1990).

The neuroanatomical hypothesis proposes that:

> There are three distinct components of the illness panic disorder—the acute panic attack, anticipatory anxiety and phobic avoidance. These three clinical phenomena arise from excitation of three distinct neuroanatomical locations, respectively: the brainstem, limbic lobe and prefrontal cortex. Reciprocal innervation among nuclei in these three centres explains the genesis of the disease and its clinical fluctuations over time (Gorman et al., 1989, p. 149).

Like Klein's view, the model proposed is a disease-stage one, with acute panic being the *necessary* first stage, followed by the development of anticipatory anxiety and agoraphobic avoidance. The problems already described for this type of approach also apply here. The problem of the development of agoraphobia without preceding panic attacks is acknowledged (Gorman et al., 1989, p. 149) but not dealt with, except by suggesting that "phobic avoidance and anticipatory anxiety could conceivably be maintained without the induction of panic if only these reciprocal pathways between prefrontal cortex and limbic areas were involved" (Gorman et al., 1989, p. 156). Gorman et al. specify that the complexity of the hypothesis mean that a great many experiments will be required to validate or disprove the model; they also argue in their conclusion that, because the disorder is complex and involves so many facets, it requires a complex theory to account for it. Perhaps the principal problem with this position is the fact that they do *not* specify any differential predictions *vis-à-vis* alternative hypotheses, relying instead on a proposed synthesis which incorporates alternative accounts ("combined rather than opposed", p. 158). However, they do insist on the basic assumption of "the neural circuits of the brain as the basis for pathology".

The brainstem basis of acute panic is based on the physical character of panic symptoms and the panic provocation studies discussed above in the context of Klein's theory. The suggestion is that the various panic-provoking agents produce paroxysmal brainstem activity as a result of activity in one or more specific brainstem loci. The central basis of at least one panic-provoking agent, isoproterenol, (which provokes panic at the same rate as lactate infusions; Rainey et al., 1984) is particularly hard to explain in these terms, as isoproterenol does not cross the blood–brain barrier and therefore cannot have its panic-provoking effects as a result of direct action on the brainstem.

The data cited in support of a link between the limbic system and anticipatory anxiety is somewhat more consistent, being mainly derived from the work of animal researchers such as Gray (1982). The *specific* link with panic disorder in man is more difficult to justify. Little evidence supporting such a link is presented, other than general allusions to the vulnerability of the limbic system to the generalization of spasmodic electrical activity ("kindling effects"), coupled with speculation that general anxiety associated with panic may result from such kindling effects. The importance of this system to the neuroanatomical model resides in the notion that it is through this system that non-pharmacological interventions (particularly exposure) are said to have their effects. It is difficult to see how these propositions can be evaluated directly, and whether this component of the hypothesis advances the understanding of mechanisms involved in panic attacks and their treatment.

Perhaps the most valuable aspect of Gorman et al.'s (1989) paper is that it offers specific predictions which are said to allow experimental testing of the hypothesis. These predictions generally specify the likely locus of brain activity which should accompany various forms of stimulation and treatment. The prediction which is particularly relevant to psychological hypotheses concerns treatment, specifically that cognitive–behavioural treatments will leave a core of occasional panic attacks (whilst drug treatments will not), because cognitive–behavioural therapies "exert ameliorative effects at a different 'site' of disease progression than do antipanic drugs" (p. 157). This proposition seems to have been already invalidated (Clark et al., 1994). Altogether, the hypothesis is disappointing in that it does not utilize new data and seems to explain less that Klein's original hypothesis. The attempted integration is unhelpful because it retains the basic proposition of a disease process, and because psychological factors are included in the account as phenomena secondary to the unmodified "fact" of biologically determined panic. That is, all psychological factors are considered to operate "downstream" of fundamental biological mechanisms modifying the secondary response to panic itself, with the most minimal of interactions even at this secondary level.

Behavioural Theory and the Development of the "Exposure Principle"

The main breakthrough in the understanding of phobias came with the adoption of conditioning theories. Western psychologists, notably Watson and Rayner, adopted and developed the ideas pioneered by Pavlov (see Chapter 15). Wolpe (1958) adapted this type of approach and used his modification to develop a treatment referred to as systematic desensitization; he applied this theory to both simple phobias and agoraphobia. The 1960s saw the development and application of the two-process model of the acquisition and maintenance of phobic anxiety (Rachman, 1977; Rachman, 1990). According to this hypothesis, phobic anxiety results from classical conditioning, where a formerly neutral stimulus (e.g. a crowded place) is associated with intrinsically aversive consequences or situations. Work on observational conditioning (Mineka et al., 1984) suggests the importance of vicarious learning. In this instance, the unconditioned stimulus (UCS) is defined as observing an adult showing fear (adult fear being an intrinsically aversive stimulus to the infant); this is associated with potentially phobic stimuli (conditioned stimulus, CS), such as snakes or spiders (CSs). After a few such experiences, the infant would respond to the CS with fear, even if the fearful adult were not present. This particular hypothesis of the origin of agoraphobic fears may also account for the familial aggregation of agoraphobia. Nevertheless, such fears should eventually extinguish in the absence of further conditioning experiences. The failure of at least some agoraphobia to extinguish is said to be due to both (a) the way in which avoidance behaviour prevents the occurrence of actual exposure to the feared stimuli, and (b) the way in which exposure to feared stimuli is terminated or shortened by escape behaviour (when exposure to the feared stimulus unavoidably occurs) (Rachman, 1977). In turn, the persistence of avoidance and escape behaviours is accounted for by the negative reinforcement associated with the omission or termination of anxiety ("anxiety relief").

This theory is of key clinical importance, because it dictates the way exposure to feared stimuli is conducted as part of the treatment known as "graded exposure". Agoraphobics are encouraged to go into situations which they feel able to tolerate (but which produce at least moderate levels of anxiety). A key instruction is that they should remain in the phobic situation *until their anxiety has begun to decline*. Leaving the situation when anxiety has not substantially decreased from the initial level is regarded as counterproductive (Mathews, Gelder & Johnston, 1981), having the effect of preventing fear reduction and reinforcing avoidance and escape on subsequent exposure to the stimulus. Based on this theory, graded exposure became the treatment of choice for agoraphobia (Mathews, Gelder & Johnston, 1981; Marks, 1987b). Graded exposure remained firmly grounded in its learning theory origins (e.g. Borkovec, 1982).

The Exposure Principle

Rachman pinpointed a range of problems with the fundamentals of two-process theory (see, for example, Rachman, 1977). Difficulty in resolving theoretical problems led to the adoption by some researchers, particularly Isaac Marks, of an atheoretical approach described as the "exposure principle", detaching the effectiveness of treatment from underlying theory. The basic assumption seems to be that previous research had clearly identified the fundamental change process (exposure), obviating the need for any further theoretical development. No attempt is made to understand why exposure works (and therefore how it could be done more effectively). An unfortunate result of this abandonment of theory is that research from this perspective focused on seeking to minimize the therapeutic input required to bring about anxiety reduction. For example, Marks et al. obtained equivalent results when therapeutic instructions were delivered by a therapist, a computer programme or a self-help book. O'Sullivan et al. used telephone contact compared with face-to-face therapist instruction. Research into the effectiveness of such variants of delivery systems are, at best, complementary to work intended to improve the effectiveness of the treatments which are being delivered. They cannot be a substitute for such development work, at least until treatments are shown to be fully effective for the majority of sufferers.

At worst, the degree of improvement may be unnecessarily reduced, leading to treatments which are cheaper and statistically effective but at the cost of reduced levels of clinical change and stagnation of further refinements of treatment. This point is illustrated by work by Öst, Salkovskis & Hellström (1991), who showed that Marks' type of self-help treatment in specific phobias was associated with significant reductions in phobic anxiety, but that almost none of the patients achieved high endstate functioning. The comparison therapist-delivered cognitive–behavioural package, with less exposure time, produced substantially more change in phobic anxiety and resulted in high endstate functioning in 70% of those treated (using conservative criteria).

Rachman and colleagues (de Silva & Rachman, 1984; Rachman et al., 1986) have attempted the most direct test of two-process theory (and of the clinical procedures arising from them). If phobic anxiety persists because of avoidance behaviour preventing exposure and the rapid termination of any exposure which takes place by escape behaviour whenever exposure to the feared stimulus un-avoidably occurs, then uninterrupted exposure should produce fear reduction, whilst encouraging escape should not. Subjects were told to enter the feared situation and either (a) to remain until their anxiety declined (as in exposure-based treatments) or (b) to leave when their anxiety rose to 70 on a 100-point scale (as is hypothesized to normally occur in untreated agoraphobics). Unfortunately, the manipulation did not fully succeed, and escape was rare. Both groups showed anxiety reduction. There was, however, some evidence that the *second* (escape) group may have shown a tendency to experience greater anxiety reduction, an apparently paradoxical finding. Although methodological considerations limit the conclusiveness of these studies (the subjects allowed to "escape" seldom did so), they are nonetheless difficult to account for in terms of purely behavioural accounts. Rachman suggests that perceived control over the possibility of panic may have been responsible for the effects observed (Rachman, 1990; Sanderson, Rapee & Barlow, 1989). However, this explanation does not deal with the issue of why the perception of control over escape in a clinical experiment should have produced an anxiety-reducing effect compared to the usual situation experienced by these agoraphobic patients. Under normal circumstances, agoraphobics constantly remind themselves that they are able to escape, and much of their behaviour in phobic situations is designed to ensure that possibility remains open to them. They not only watch their escape route to ensure that it is clear, but also often choose to escape. In the experimental situation it might be expected that there was a certain amount of social pressure not to escape, which may have resulted in *lower* perception of control.

Barlow's Model: False Alarms and Learned Alarms

Barlow's model is particularly interesting and useful because it is presented in the context of a major monograph in which Barlow attempts to develop an overarching theory relevant to all anxiety disorders and to synthesize conditioning, neurobiological and psychosocial factors. Panic is again seen as a defining problem. The model bears some resemblance to the neuroanatomical hypothesis in that it is a disease-stage model with an emphasis on concepts of malfunctioning subsystems. Unlike most of the other psychological models of panic, Barlow's specifically proposes a qualitative distinction between panic and other forms of anxiety. The basis for the model concerns a "complex biopsychosocial process", involving the interaction between:

> ... an ancient alarm system, crucial for survival, with inappropriate and maladaptive learning and subsequent cognitive and affective complications (Barlow, 1988, p. 209).

Thus, a biological (evolutionarily relevant) alarm system is postulated; this primitive system is designed to react to actual danger with a set of energizing responses, termed a "true alarm"; such responses prepare the organism to react in appropriate ways to threat, and is therefore associated with "action tendencies", which are either escape/flight, freezing/immobility or aggression/attack. However, under conditions of non-focal threat and consequent generalized hyperarousal (for example, during a period following a major threat-related life event), biologically (genetically) vulnerable individuals become prone to spontaneous discharges of the alarm system. Specifically, "false alarms" (panic attacks experienced at the outset of development of panic disorder) are said to "spike off" from a stress response in such vulnerable individuals. That is, generalized anxiety increases under stress and forms a kind of platform which puts the alarm system on a hair-trigger and makes the sparking off of an alarm-type response particularly likely. This initial occurrence of spontaneous panic as "false alarms" (which are said to be characteristic of non-clinical panickers) may, in turn, become conditioned interoceptive stimuli if a false alarm was associated with such stimuli. The formation of such conditioned associations is particularly likely if the association occurs in a situation where the ability to carry through "action tendencies" is blocked). This conditioning process then results in the occurrence of "learned alarms". For panic disorder to result, there is a further crucial step, however. Anxious expectation over the occurrence of negative events or subsequent "alarms" must develop, and is said to be "a crucial psychological vulnerability", possibly arising as a result of a "pre-existing disposition to focus anxiety specifically on somatic events". This tendency would make such individuals "exquisitely sensitive to false alarms". Agoraphobia, avoidance and cognitive symptoms follow on in a relatively passive way, although this is not made more explicit than already described, except as a diagram in which these are depicted as a noninteracting end-point of the sequence. The lack of emphasis of cognitive factors in the theory contrasts markedly with Barlow & Cerny's (1988) and Rapee & Barlow's (1989) description of treatment, which includes a major component of cognitive intervention.

Barlow does not himself suggest any specific predictions from this model, neither does he differentiate it in this way from other hypotheses. However, he does state that "there should be enough coherence within the theory to enable investigators to design research protocols that result in confirmation or disconfirmation (Barlow, 1988, p. 209). Both agoraphobic avoidance and cognitive factors are regarded as relatively passive "downstream" consequences of a response to the experience of physiological sensations previously associated with excessive arousal. Cognition is thus seen as consequent on a biologically initiated sequence. The effectiveness of cognitive treatments (including Barlow's own panic control training) are difficult to reconcile with this view.

Goldstein's & Chambless Model of Agoraphobia

Goldstein & Chambless (1978) proposed that agoraphobia is based on a fear of fear, rather than a fear of places (see also Chambless & Gracely, 1989). They distinguish between complex and simple agoraphobia: in the latter, panic attacks can be precipitated in a fairly straightforward way by experiencing symptoms in public places which are in fact due to the effects of drugs, physical illness, past trauma, etc, and not realizing their true cause. However, the majority of agoraphobics are said to suffer from complex agoraphobia. They suggest that the roots of this type of agoraphobia lie in childhood, so that many agoraphobics lacked the sort of secure base as children which facilitates independence. It is argued that their clinical work reveals that many of them were reared in homes where their parents either overprotected them, or gave them too much responsibility within the home, or were overcritical or unpredictable, or they felt threatened by the threat of separation from one or both parents, or they were sexually abused (Goldstein & Stainback, 1991). Many patients report suffering in more than one of these ways. This lack of a secure base, in the absence of truly supportive parents, is thought to lead to a tendency to deny, suppress or avoid painful feelings, rather than to acknowledge their true causes, since the problems posed by such problems appear insoluble. This leads to chronic anxiety, coupled with a lack of self-sufficiency, non-assertiveness, trouble functioning independently, a great fear of being alone, and an exaggerated sense of their own destructive power, should they express angry feelings.

It is hypothesized that such personality characteristics make it difficult to handle conflict effectively. When under stress, such as that associated with leaving home, the tendency to suppress or deny emotions and avoid conflict can lead to anxiety and depression, which in turn may culminate in a series of panic attacks, and thence (since the avoidant style of dealing with stress makes it difficult for the agoraphobic to realize that the cause lies in his/her personal relationships) a conditioned fear of the bodily sensations of stress. Such fears lead in turn to catastrophic thoughts of illness, loss of control and death, a spreading pattern of avoidance and a conditioned fear of certain places. This is then thought to lead to an isolated, fear-dominated lifestyle which further increases interpersonal stress, anxiety and depression. The whole process can then become part of a vicious circle.

Goldstein & Chambless call their therapy (designed to combat these factors) systematic eclectic therapy, aiming to treat the whole person, using modern psychoanalytic techniques, Gestalt techniques and behaviour therapy.

Beck and the Oxford Group: Threat and Safety-seeking

Influenced by Chambless & Goldstein's concept of fear of fear, the Oxford cognitive therapy research group views agoraphobic avoidance not only as a consequence of threat appraisal but also as an important factor in maintaining the threat beliefs (and therefore anxiety) (Clark, 1988; Salkovskis, 1988b, 1991; Salkovskis, Clark & Gelder, 1996). Thus, the cognitive theory is predicated on the assumption that the proximal cause of anxiety is threat appraisal, and that anxiety-related behaviours are directly related to such appraisals.

Threat Appraisals

Based in the work of Beck (1976) and Beck Emery & Greenberg (1985), the cognitive hypothesis proposes that anxiety occurs as a result of the appraisals of the person's situation as threatening. In any particular situation, the negative appraisals made are the result of persons' pre-existing beliefs and assumptions about the situation they find themselves in. These beliefs may be very generalized (e.g. "The world is a very dangerous place; bad things could happen to me unexpectedly at any time"), anxiety-specific (e.g. "I must not allow myself to become anxious, otherwise I am in danger of totally losing control") or specific to particular symptoms (e.g. "If I feel faint, this means that I could pass out at any moment"). Because the person holds such beliefs, particular stimuli or situations are appraised in a relatively more threatening way, as indicating some kind of imminent danger. The intensity of threat appraisal is related to at least four interacting factors in the following way:

$$\text{Anxiety} \propto \frac{\text{Perceived likelihood of danger} \times \text{perceived "cost" or awfulness of danger}}{\text{Perceived coping ability} + \text{perceived rescue factors}}$$

Clearly, anxiety in a given situation may be inappropriately elevated if, because of his/her pre-existing assumptions, the person *overestimates* the probability of danger and/or the awfulness of that danger were it to happen, or if he/she *underestimates* his/her ability to cope if the threat were to happen, and/or the extent to which factors external to his/her own efforts would help him/her. Distorted beliefs about probability of threat and the awfulness of that threat appear to interact and synergize, whereas the two potentially anxiety-reducing factors appear to be additive. This model helps in understanding the range of ways in which a wide range of apparently unconnected pre-existing negative beliefs may contribute to the experience of anxiety. For example, a person may believe that feeling faint means he/she is likely to pass out, that passing out will result in totally unbearable humiliation, that he/she is so incompetent that he/she will be unable to cope with this humiliation and will be taken to a mental hospital and locked up, and that no-one will try to help or even understand. Although panic attacks and panic-like symptoms are likely to activate this type of appraisal, other patterns of beliefs can also have the same effects. An example would be the person who chronically underestimates his/her ability to cope in any unusual or unexpected situation.

In cognitive therapy for panic disorder the importance of high levels of perceived probability has tended to be emphasized, probably because the awfulness of many of the feared catastrophes appears to be self-evident. In agoraphobia it is suggested that there may also be major distortions in the cost, coping and rescue factors, which would therefore need to be dealt with as part of therapy. The literature indicates that, whilst agoraphobics differ very little from panic patients in their catastrophic interpretations of the physical consequences of bodily sensations (Telch et al., 1989; Salkovskis, 1990), the avoidant group show greater fear of loss of mental control or social ridicule (Telch et al., 1989) and have more social evaluative concerns (Pollard & Cox, 1988; Meldrum, Pollard & Fraunhoffer, 1989; de Ruiter & Garssen, 1989). These fears are less obviously catastrophic. That is, for some people, fainting would be a minor inconvenience. It is suggested that, for some agoraphobics, to faint would mean not only passing out but being mocked or scorned by people around them, to be taken to a mental hospital and confined there indefinitely, and so on.

These factors may play a role in the development of the disorder. If one is socially anxious and develops panic attacks, this will enhance reluctance to enter situations in which one will be under scrutiny if a panic attack occurs. This feature of embarrassment is mentioned in the DSM-IV definition of agoraphobia. The other fear mentioned is that help may not be available in the event of a panic attack, which may seem paradoxical in public places. However, there are beliefs which could make one less optimistic about getting help in such a situation. One would be a lack of trust that others would be willing to help, and another would be a lack of confidence in one's own ability to cope with the situation, or get help. These have been common themes in our work, and also in the literature on factors associated with agoraphobia, where it has been found that the more avoidant panic disorder patients tend to have more dependency issues and less confidence in their own self-efficacy premorbidly.

Maintenance of Threat Beliefs

For most (but probably not all[1]) agoraphobics, their negative appraisals of agoraphobic situations are not justified, in the sense that they (objectively) do not pass out, have a heart attack, lose control, go insane and so on. At least three factors

---

[1] This is less clear when the focus of appraisal is on coping, being emotional, trembling, showing anxiety and so on.

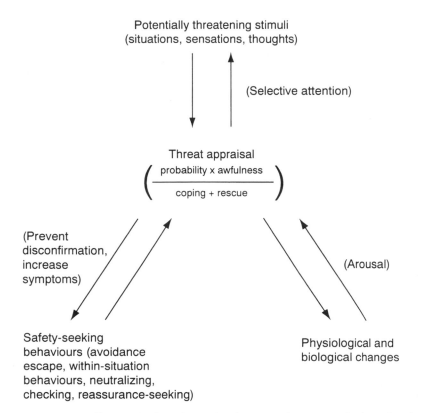

Potentially threatening stimuli
(situations, sensations, thoughts)

(Selective attention)

Threat appraisal

$$\left(\frac{\text{probability x awfulness}}{\text{coping + rescue}} \right)$$

(Prevent disconfirmation, increase symptoms)

(Arousal)

Safety-seeking behaviours (avoidance escape, within-situation behaviours, neutralizing, checking, reassurance-seeking)

Physiological and biological changes

Figure 2.1 Diagram illustrating the relationship between threat appraisals and maintaining factors in anxiety disorders (from Salkovskis, 1996, *Frontiers of Cognitive Therapy*, Guilford Press with permission)

have been identified as contributing to the persistence of these negative beliefs. These are: (a) physiological arousal; (b) selective attention and (c) safety-seeking behaviours. These are illustrated in Figure 2.1.

Physiological arousal

The best known of these is the feedback loop which occurs in panic attacks. As outlined above, panic (or panic-like symptoms) is seen as an important way in which agoraphobic avoidance can develop. The basic cognitive hypothesis of panic (Clark, 1986, 1988; Salkovskis & Clark, 1986; Salkovskis, 1988a; Beck, 1988) has been developed, based on initial work by Clark (1979) and Beck, Emery & Greenberg (1985). It is hypothesized that patients with recurring panic attacks have *an enduring tendency* to misinterpret certain bodily sensations as a sign of imminent disaster. Acute panic results from the misinterpretation of bodily or mental sensations as signs of imminent personal disaster. The anxiety engendered by the misinterpretation of sensations produces an increase in sensations, which in turn feed back to the catastrophic misinterpretation, rapidly culminating in a full-blown panic attack, as illustrated in Figure 2.1. Thus, accord-ing to the cognitive hypothesis, panic occurs only if sensations are misinterpreted; patients who experience repeated panic attacks are particularly vulnerable to making such misinterpretations by virtue of a pre-existing set of beliefs. A variety of things may trigger off the panic vicious circle in the first instance; it may be triggered by anxiety from general stress, by the anxiety of entering a situation where panic previously occurred, by a sensation from an unrelated source, such as a hangover or too much coffee, by a frightening thought, and so on. It is important to note that the whole process of panic generation can occur within a few seconds, as the person responds physically and psychologically to what seems, at that time, to be a profound threat to his/her safety.

For example, a patient may interpret palpitations and a racing heart as a sign that he/she is having a heart attack. This misinterpretation in turn results in intense anxiety and thus the sensations associated with physiological arousal, including palpitations and tachycardia, perhaps also dizziness and precordial pain. This increase in intensity and range of symptoms appears to confirm the original misinterpretation, further increasing anxiety and symptoms and so on, rapidly culminating in an acute panic attack.

A wide range of symptoms can give rise to misinterpretations, but the cogni-tive hypothesis proposes that these are particularly likely to be sensations which can result from autonomic or central nervous system responses to anxiety itself, given the immediate nature of the feedback loop. A further factor in the readi-ness to misinterpret bodily sensations should be the extent to which the person has available any innocuous alternative explanations of the intense and wide-ranging sensations associated with panic attacks. For example, if someone were to notice his/her heart racing, being short of breath, feeling dizzy and found he/she was sweating a great deal immediately after running to catch a train, misinter-pretation is unlikely. The same sensations experienced without any obvious cause would, at best, be bewildering and, at worst, be taken as a sign of serious illness.

The catastrophic beliefs specified by the cognitive hypothesis account for the intensity of anxiety and the associated physical symptoms, insofar as the anxiety reaction experienced would not be considered abnormal if occurring in the context of a truly life-threatening situation. Typically, patients express very strong beliefs in the possibility of feared disaster *during the attacks themselves*, although in the clinician's office (when the symptoms are not present and a trusted individual is) patients will report that they do not, at that time, feel convinced that the disasters would happen. The apparent unexpectedness or "spontaneousness" of some panic attacks can also be accounted for; although the panic may start with a mild (and often normal) physical sensation, if such a sensation triggers off the thoughts of disaster and hence a panic, the originating sensation may then be lost in the surge of much more intense, anxiety-generated symptoms which follow. Often, there is no specific explanation for the triggering symptom; it was simply one of the many ordinary physical fluctuations which most people experience every day.

The misinterpretations made by individual patients are based on aspects of their experience, such as the person's previous experience (direct or vicarious) of symptoms and their meaning. For each patient, there tends to be an internally consistent and logical link between the sensations experienced during panic and the particular interpretations made. The link between particular sensations and interpretations are frequently based on conventional wisdom and "common sense", so that the links are immediately obvious (e.g. shortness of breath interpreted as a sign that the patient is about to stop breathing), although the links may not always be so clear. In many agoraphobic patients, an excessively negative misinterpretation of bodily sensations will be a potent maintaining process; the negative interpretation may be of imminent catastrophe, which would partially explain the strong association with panic attacks, or may be of "panic-like symptoms", such as feelings of dizziness interpreted as a sign of an impending epileptic fit, or gastrointestinal disturbance interpreted as a sign of impending diarrhoea.

The cognitive theory of anxiety in general and panic in particular partially accounts for why some agoraphobics become anxious in agoraphobic situations; they do so because they believe themselves to be in danger of harm in that situation; as described above, agoraphobic behaviour is then easily understood as motivated avoidance. That is, agoraphobics are motivated to avoid situations where they believe harm may occur if they do not leave. However, one of the virtues of the cognitive theory is that it assumes an internal logic to emotional problems. How then to account for the persistence of anxiety and avoidance in the face of apparent repeated disconfirmation of the person's belief that they are in imminent danger? This brings us to a consideration of the reciprocal relationship between threat beliefs and avoidance behaviours. This is the second key maintaining factor.

Avoidance Behaviour

A variety of researchers have attempted to conceptualize the relationship between fear, anxiety and avoidance. Rachman has carried out an influential series of experiments in which he examines the relationship between predicted fear and actual fear in subjects repeatedly confronting aversive events (summarized in Rachman & Bichard, 1988). The basic paradigm used involved asking student volunteers, previously identified as claustrophobic, to repeatedly enter a very small enclosed space; in the course of experimental sessions, they are asked to rate anxiety and a range of other variables, particularly their expectation of anxiety prior to entering the enclosed space. Using this paradigm, it was found that anxious subjects were consistently more likely to over-predict than under-predict the fear associated with phobic situations, and overpredictions were particularly likely to follow underpredictions. Reductions in fear were most likely after overpredictions, but there was evidence of an inherent bias towards overprediction of aversive events, including both anxiety provocation and pain (Rachman & Bichard, 1988). Rachman (1990, Chapter 17) proposes that, if agoraphobics show the same type of tendency as people with other types of fear to overpredict, then avoidance behaviour may be a product of overprediction. Rachman goes on to suggest that, in agoraphobia as in claustrophobia, the occurrence and intensity of panic attacks will form the basis of predictions of fear. He also suggests that the anticipation of fear may itself provoke *situational* panic attacks, and that the occurrence of such panic in turn affects subsequent avoidance. Although this view is consistent with clinical observations of agoraphobics' pessimism regarding the impact of exposure, despite repeated positive experiences of anxiety reduction (and reluctance to continue or repeat exposure sessions), more direct evaluation is required if overpredictions are to be regarded as a key factor in the maintenance of avoidance behaviour (Rachman, 1990). An important consideration is whether it is anxiety that is being avoided, or if the avoidance of panic patients may not take a more specifically cognitive form.

The cognitive hypothesis proposes a specific set of links, both between panic and avoidance and *vice versa*. If panic patients fear imminent disasters because of their misinterpretation of bodily sensations, their behaviour should be logically related to the avoidance of the feared catastrophes, rather than of anxiety *per se*. This means that avoidance behaviour would be meaningful but idiosyncratic, both to the individual and to attacks involving specific types of misinterpretations. Situations which generate anxiety might become the focus of avoidance, but this will only become debilitating when accompanied by fears that the anxiety might lead to other, more serious consequences. Furthermore, the scope of avoidance could be regarded as broader than generally encompassed by behavioural descriptions (e.g. Marks, 1987b), with both subtle and more generalized avoidance playing a major role in the maintenance of panic attacks (Salkovskis, 1988). For example, a patient who interprets weak legs as a sign that he may collapse attempts to prevent collapse by holding on to nearby objects, tensing his legs and seeking a seat at the earliest possible opportunity. By doing so, he has a further effect; he prevents disconfirmation of his fears of collapse. The patient is unaware of the anxiety-maintaining effects of his avoidant behaviour (perhaps better described as safety-seeking behaviour). Thus, the subjective impact of his behaviour is to transform an incident which could have provided a disconfirmation of his fears into evidence *bolstering* his negative interpretation of symptoms, in the form that he has just experienced a "near miss". The situation would be interpreted as "If I had not prevented it by tensing my legs, then I would certainly have collapsed". The cognitive hypothesis predicts an internally logical match between such beliefs and behaviours during panic; for example, fears of loss of control should be associated with attempts to control oneself. (There is now evidence for such meaningful associations between within-situation safety-seeking behaviours and the catastrophic beliefs which occur within panic attacks; see Salkovskis, Clark & Gelder, 1996.)

Similar considerations can be applied to more generalized forms of actual avoidance and escape behaviour; an agoraphobic who decides not to go shopping on a particular day may conclude "It's lucky I did not go, otherwise I would have had an enormous panic; if I had panicked today, I would certainly have collapsed". Once again, avoidance has "prevented" collapse. However, these types of escape behaviours are only logically possible when the feared catastrophe has external correlates; that is, leaving a situation has only limited value as a strategy for dealing with an impending heart attack. The main usefulness of such a strategy would be in situations where social evaluative concerns predominate; removing oneself from other people is a helpful strategy, both as catastrophe avoidance and removing the person from the scrutiny of others.

As panic and avoidance become more chronic, the behaviours, involved become more habitual and awareness of the specific cognitive component of avoidance diminishes, except when directly challenged by deliberate or accidental exposure. Often patients express this as the desire to escape; for example, when asked what went through his mind in a phobic situation, a patient typically responds "I just had to get out". The cognition is readily revealed by asking what, at that time, he would have thought the worst thing that could have happened should he be unable to get out. Thus, the cognitive analysis of avoidance involves an analysis of *what the patient is avoiding* rather than just of the anxiety arousal/relief associated with the specific situation. The importance of the minutiae of anxiety-related and safety-seeking behaviour also takes on a new importance, particularly for therapy.

Safety-seeking behaviours have the subjective effect of "saving" the person from the potential catastrophe, in the sense that the person comes to believe that his/her behaviour is all that stands between him/her and the feared disaster. Thus, disconfirmation is converted to *confirmation* by the subjective experience of "a near miss". This account also helps explain the potency of graded exposure, and provides a framework to understand the difficult and unresolved issue of the difference between a *coping* response and an *avoidance* response. Furthermore, it seems likely that this account may generalize beyond panic to other anxiety problems. The key issue concerns the question of *what the person is avoiding*. If the cognitive account is correct, then avoidance responses are those behaviours which are intended to avoid *disaster*, but thereby also have the secondary effect of preventing the disconfirmation that would otherwise take place. On the other hand, coping responses are those behaviours brought to bear by a person intending to deal with *anxiety alone*, with no further fears about the consequences of the anxiety and so on. The second strategy is not catastrophe-based, and therefore will not interfere with disconfirmation; in fact, it would be expected to enhance cognitive change because the strategy is based on an alternative, non-catastrophic account of symptoms and situations.

TREATMENT OF AGORAPHOBIA

The earliest demonstrations of effective treatment came from work on systematic desensitization; within the behavioural approach, this rapidly evolved into flooding-type approaches and then graded exposure. There has been considerable debate concerning the possible mechanisms of change in exposure treatments; the main candidates are habituation/extinction or cognitive change. There is surprisingly little evidence for habituation accounts. Early accounts of cognitive change emphasized self-efficacy theory, in which the extent to which anxiety is anticipated plays a central role. Several treatments currently advocated emphasize teaching patients to control panic attacks. Whilst such treatments certainly reduce agoraphobic symptoms, panic attacks and related symptoms, there is reason to doubt the usefulness of treatment which emphasizes control. At the simplest level of analysis, such treatment is likely to result in a person who is confident that, with sufficient effort, he/she will be able to prevent a panic attack reaching its full crescendo. If treatments emphasizing panic control do have such a result, the outcome is likely to be a person who is "living on the edge", constantly vigilant for the developing panic attack (so that it can be aborted). This does seem to be the case for some people who undergo such treatment. Such an outcome could be seen as good, in the way that a good outcome for a person suffering from angina is to take medication at the outset of each attack. Whether this is necessary as a way of dealing with the problem is another question. At worst, we believe that such treatments may have the unfortunate result that panic control measures are seen as a way of averting the feared catastrophe (i.e. safety behaviours) and therefore become avoidance rather than coping behaviours. If this occurs, panic control strategies will actually maintain rather than reduce the agoraphobia. For example, a patient may come to believe that the relaxation and breathing exercises he does calm him down sufficiently to prevent him from suffering a heart attack or going insane. The fact that such strategies were taught by a therapist will only serve to reinforce his belief in their value, and therefore to ensure the continuation of his agoraphobia. Panic control measures will be effective if they result in the patient realizing that the symptoms he/she is experiencing are innocuous, and that he/she need never use the control strategies as there is nothing to fear if he/she does not.

More recent cognitive–behavioural approaches do not suffer from this drawback. Given that the cognitive theory suggests that anxiety is a direct consequence of threat appraisal, belief change is the key to improvement (see pp. 45–46 above). In a study of severe agoraphobics, Salkovskis, Clark & Hackmann (1991) demonstrated that pure cognitive strategies (focusing on verbal techniques of bringing about changes in threat beliefs without any interoceptive exposure or exposure to feared situations) were effective in reducing panic symptoms. However, such a purely cognitive approach to treatment is only of theoretical interest (to show that focused belief change can be effective). In fact, the cognitive theory outlined above suggests that more effective therapeutic interventions should involve a degree of behaviour change where the behaviour change occurs within the framework of a cognitive conceptualization, and is focused on bringing about belief change. The cognitive–behavioural theory also suggests an entirely different mechanism for the effectiveness of exposure, and one which has specific implications for the way in which treatment is conducted. It is proposed that safety-seeking behaviours are generated by threat beliefs, and in turn serve to maintain these beliefs by preventing the person from discovering that the things of which he/she is afraid do not actually happen (Salkovskis, 1988,

1991). If this is so, exposure to a particular situation will be effective to the extent to which it allows the patient to discover that the things which he/she believes might happen (and which he/she believes he/she has previously prevented by avoiding, escaping or engaging in within-situation avoidance behaviours) do not. In many instances, remaining in the feared situation for long enough will, in many instances, be sufficient to provide a disconfirmation, at least in that situation. However, this is unlikely to be so if the patient uses within-situation safety behaviours. For example, a patient may lean against a wall to stop him/herself from falling over; it is not surprising that he/she subsequently believes that leaning against the wall stopped him/her from falling over. In this instance, exposure will be relatively inefficient. If, through sufficiently long and repeated sessions in which exposure is practised, the patient does learn that he/she does not fall over in this situation, this may not generalize well to another situation where the patient has not had such practice.

Cognitive–behavioural treatment seeks to identify the beliefs which motivate generalized avoidance and escape behaviours and any within-situation safety-seeking behaviours which accompany them (Salkovskis & Clark, 1991; Clark, 1989). The patient is helped to understand the relationship between the threat beliefs and the behaviours which have prevented these beliefs from being disconfirmed. In the subsequent discussion, this understanding of the relationships between threat beliefs, anxiety and safety-seeking behaviour is used as an alternative account of the person's reactions. This alternative is presented as incompatible with the threat appraisals which have previously dominated the patient's understanding of phobic situations. This discussion is supplemented by behavioural experiments, in which the patient is helped to devise exercises which test his/her threat beliefs and which demonstrate the way in which the mechanisms involved operate. This is done both on a within- and a between-session basis. For agoraphobic patients, such behavioural experiments commonly focus on helping the person disconfirm his/her beliefs by dropping or totally reversing his/her safety-seeking behaviour.

For example, the patient who believes that, in the supermarket, his/her dizziness and wobbly legs mean that he/she is about to collapse normally leans on a trolley and keeps his/her legs tense to make sure they don't collapse. Once the patient understands how this fear could be a misinterpretation of bodily sensations which is being maintained by the safety-seeking behaviours which he/she carries out (avoiding supermarkets, leaving when anxious, leaning on the trolley and tensing the legs), an *in vivo* behavioural experiment is designed. This involves patient and therapist going into the supermarket with the explicit purpose of finding out whether it is possible to collapse. The patient starts by rating his/her belief that he/she will collapse on a 0–100 scale. A trolley is not used; once the patient begins to feel the symptoms, he/she *relaxes* his/her legs in an attempt to make them give way. Any other safety behaviours are identified at this time; the patient rapidly discovers that his/her legs do not give way, so he/she and the therapist try to identify anything they could do to *increase* the chances of collapsing, and then try this out. At the end of this session (which can often be as short as 30 minutes) a belief rating is taken for the likelihood of collapsing. What does the patient make of the exercises they have just carried out? How easy was it to bring about a collapse? Is there anything else they can do now to continue the process of disconfirmation and belief change? These interventions are embedded in an overall cognitive approach to panic and agoraphobia (Clark, 1989; Salkovskis & Clark, 1991).

Therapeutic behavioural experiments are often done in settings such as shopping centres to test interpersonal predictions. For example a therapist may pretend to faint while the patient observes from the vantage point of a nearby cafe. Does everyone ignore the person who has fainted? Or does a huge crowd gather, send for an ambulance and rush the person to hospital against their will? Our experience with behavioural experiments shows that people are usually offered exactly the amount of attention they desire in this type of situation. We have found that conducting this type of behavioural experiment not only produces a radical change in the perceived awfulness associated with a catastrophe such as fainting, but also results in an almost total abolition of the perceived probability (even when this has not been specifically targeted in the behavioural experiment).

Patients can also be asked to practice asking for directions while anxious, to test out how helpful others are, and how capable they are at getting about alone, since many of them have always been nervous of doing things alone, in contrast to patients with panic disorder without agoraphobia. A dread of being alone has been a theme for a number of our patients, and many report early memories of feeling very isolated. For example, one of our patients reported being left alone for a whole afternoon by a childminder who assumed that her aunt would be coming soon to pick her up. This had the effect of setting the scene for a life-long fear of being abandoned, and never being able to reach home alone, which re-emerged more strongly in adult life as an aspect of her agoraphobia, once her panic attacks started.

Our experience of using these techniques is that substantial and lasting changes in agoraphobic avoidance and panic can be brought about in a very short time. In an experimental test of the functional role of safety behaviours in maintaining anxiety, severely agoraphobic patients (many of whom were housebound at the beginning of the study) were randomly assigned to one of two conditions; either (a) brief exposure conducted as habituation, or (b) an equivalent period of exposure during which patients were actively encouraged to decrease safety-seeking behaviours. The decreased-safety behaviours condition resulted in the almost total abolition of anxiety in a subsequent behaviour test, while the pure exposure condition did not result in any decrease in anxiety during the behaviour test (Salkovskis, 1995). A further study is under way in which these conditions are extended from being a brief behavioural test to three sessions of treatment with reduced safety behaviours compared to habituation-based exposure. Preliminary results indicate substantial and clinically significant differences in favour of the condition in which reducing safety behaviours is used as a disconfirmation of negative beliefs occurring in the phobic situation.

CONCLUSION

A range of theories have contributed to the development of current cognitive–behavioural treatments which represent the treatment of choice for agoraphobia where panic attacks are present. Some of these theories have focused on panic as a primary phenomenon, others have been more concerned with dispositional and interpersonal variables. The diagnostic emphasis on panic and panic-like symptoms has become a potential obstacle to the investigation of factors other than those related to panic itself; it is suggested that those interested in agoraphobia should consider agoraphobia as a type of motivated avoidance, with panic as one of a number of possible motivational factors. The existence of agoraphobia without coexisting panic attacks (or panic-like symptoms) needs to be closely examined.

Two main types of treatment have been established as effective in controlled trials: exposure treatments focusing on the modification of avoidance (Mathews, Gelder & Johnston, 1981; Barlow, 1988) and cognitive treatments focusing on the modification of panic attacks (Clark et al., 1994) with and without agoraphobic avoidance. The cognitive–behavioural theory asserts the primacy of cognition, with behaviour playing a crucial role in maintaining distorted beliefs and hence anxiety. It also claims to be the next stage of a treatment development and refinement process which originated with Wolpe's development of the first demonstrably effective treatment for phobias, systematic desensitization. Validation of the theoretical and clinical claims made for cognitive–behavioural approaches to the understanding and treatment of agoraphobic avoidance requires at least two types of study to be conducted. First, experimental studies are needed to establish the importance of belief change mechanisms, as opposed to behaviour change *per se*, in the effectiveness of exposure to avoided situations. Second, treatment studies which demonstrate the relative impact of treatments which simply seek to change behaviour, as opposed to those which maximize belief change, may lead to more efficient and effective clinical interventions.

ACKNOWLEDGEMENTS

Paul Salkovskis is Wellcome Trust Senior Research Fellow in Basic Biomedical Science. Ann Hackmann is supported by a grant from the Wellcome Trust.

REFERENCES

Agulnik, P. (1970). The spouse of the agoraphobic patient. *British Journal of Psychiatry*, **117**, 59–67.

American Psychiatric Association (1980). *Diagnostic and Statistical Manual of Mental Disorders* (3rd edn). Washington, DC: American Psychiatric Association.

American Psychiatric Association (1995). *Diagnostic and Statistical Manual of Mental Disorders* (4th edn). Washington, DC: American Psychiatric Association.

Andrews, J.D.W. (1966). Psychotherapy of phobias. *Psychological Bulletin*, **66**, 455–480.
Angst, J. & Dobler-Mikola, A. (1986). Assoziarion und Depression auf syndromaler und diagnostischer Ebene. In H. Helmchen & M. Linden (eds), *Die Differenzierung yon Angst und Depression*. Berlin: Springer.
Arieti, S. (1979). New views on the psychodynamics of phobias. *American Journal of Psychotherapy*, **33**, 82–95.
Aronson, T.A. & Logue, C.M. (1987). On the longitudinal course of panic disorder: development history and predictors of phobic complications. *Comprehensive Psychiatry*, **28**, 344–355.
Barlow, D.H. (1988). *Anxiety and Its Disorders*. New York: Guilford.
Barlow, D.H. & Cerny, J. (1988) *Psychological Treatment of Panic*. New York: Guilford.
Barlow, D.H. & Craske, M.G. (1988). The phenomenology of panic. In S.J. Rachman & J. Maser (eds), *Panic: Psychological Perspectives*. Hillsdale, NJ: Erlbaum.
Barlow, D.H., Vermilyea, J., Blanchard, E.B., Vermilyea, B.B., DiNardo, P.A. & Cerny, J.A. (1985). The phenomenon of panic. *Journal of Abnormal Psychology*, **94**, 320–329.
Beck, A.T. (1976). *Cognitive Therapy and the Emotional Disorders*. New York: International University Press.
Beck, A.T. (1988). Cognitive approaches to panic disorder: theory and therapy. In S.J. Rachman & J. Maser (eds), *Panic: Psychological Perspectives* Hillsdale, NJ: Erlbaum.
Beck, A.T., Emery, G. & Greenberg, R.L. (1985). *Anxiety Disorders and Phobias*. New York: Basic Books.
Beck, A.T., Laude, R. & Bohnert, M. (1974). Ideational components of anxiety neurosis. *Archives of General Psychiatry*, **31**, 319–325.
Benedikt. (1870). Uber Platzwindel. *Allegemeine Wiener Medizinische Zeitung*, **15**, 488.
Berg, I., Butler, A. & Pritchard, J. (1974). Psychiatric illness in the mothers of school-phobic adolescents. *British Journal of Psychiatry*, **125**, 466–467.
Berg, I. (1976). School phobia in the children of agoraphobic women. *British Journal of Psychiatry*, **128**, 86–89.
Bland, K. & Hallam, R.S. (1980). Investigation of agoraphobic patients' response to exposure *in vivo* treatment in relation to marital satisfaction. Unpublished manuscript, Maudsley Hospital, London.
Borden, J.W. & Geller, E.S. (1981). Agoraphobia: appraisal of research and proposal for an integrative model. In M. Hersen, R.M. Eisler & P.M. Miller (eds), *Progress in Behaviour Modification*, **12**, 1–66. New York: Academic Press.
Borkovec, T.D. (1982). Facilitation and inhibition of functional CS exposure in the treatment of phobias. In J. Boulougouris (ed.), *Learning Theory Approaches to Psychiatry*. New York: Wiley.
Bowlby, J. (1969). Attachment and loss. In *Attachment*, vol. I. New York: Basic Books.
Bowlby, J. (1973). Attachment and loss: separation anxiety and anger. In *Attachment*, vol. II. New York: Basic Books.
Boyd, J.H. (1986). Use of mental health services for the treatment of panic disorder. *American Journal of Psychiatry*, **143**, 1569–1574.
Buglass, D., Clarke, M., Henderson, A.S., Kreitman, N. & Presley, A. (1977). A study of agoraphobic housewives. *Psychological Medicine*, **7**, 73–86.
Chambless, D. (1985). The relationship of severity of agoraphobia to associated psychopathology. *Behaviour Research and Therapy*, **23**(3), 305–310.
Chambless, D.L. & Goldstein, A.J. (1982). *Agoraphobia: Multiple Perspectives on Theory and Treatment*. New York: Wiley.
Chambless, D. & Gracely, E. (1989). Fear of fear and the anxiety disorders. *Cognitive Therapy and Research*, **13**(1), 9–20.
Clark, D.M. (1986). A cognitive approach to panic. *Behaviour Research and Therapy*, **24**, 461–470.
Clark, D.M. (1988). A cognitive model of panic. In S.J. Rachman & J. Maser (eds), *Panic: Psychological Perspectives*. Hillsdale, NJ: Erlbaum.

Clark, D.M. (1989). Anxiety states. In K. Hawton, P.M. Salkovskis & D.M. Clark (eds), *Cognitive Behaviour Therapy for Psychiatric Problems: a Practical Guide*. Oxford: Oxford University Press.

Clark, D.M., Salkovskis, P.M., Hackmann, A., Middleton, H., Anastasiades, P. & Gelder, M. (1994). A comparison of cognitive theory, applied relaxation and imipramine in the treatment of panic disorder. *British Journal of Psychiatry*, **164**, 759–769.

Compton, A. (1992). The psychoanalytic view of phobias. III. Agoraphobia and other phobias of adults. *Psychoanalytic Quarterly*, **61**(3), 400–425.

Clum, G. & Knowles. (1991). Why do some people with panic disorders become avoidant? A review. *Clinical Psychology Review*, **11**, 295–313.

Cordes, E. (1871). Die Platzangst [Agoraphobic]: Symptom einer Erschöpfungsparese. *Archiv für Psychiatrie und Nervenkrankleiten*, **3**, 521–524.

de Ruiter, C. & Garssen, B. (1989). Social anxiety and fear of bodily sensations in panic disorder and agoraphobia: a matched comparison. *Journal of Psychopathology and Behavioural Assessment*, **11**(2), 175–184.

de Silva, P. & Rachman, S.J. (1984). Does escape behaviour strengthen agoraphobic avoidance? A preliminary study. *Behaviour Research and Therapy*, **22**, 87–91.

Deutsch, H. (1929). The genesis of agoraphobia. *International Journal of Psychoanalysis*, **10**, 51–69.

Deltito, J.A., Perugi, G., Maremmani, I., Mignani, V. & Cassano, G.B. (1986). The importance of separation anxiety in the differentiation of panic disorder from agoraphobia. *Psychiatric Developments*, **3**, 227–236.

Emmelkamp, P.M.G. & van der Hout, A. (1983). Failure in treating agoraphobia. In E. Foa & P. Emmelkamp (eds), *Failures in Behavior Therapy*. New York: Wiley.

Faravelli, C. (1985). Life events preceding the onset of panic disorders. *Journal of Affective Disorders*, **9**, 103–105.

Finlay-Jones, R. & Brown, G.W. (1981). Types of stressful life event and the onset of anxiety and depressive disorders. *Psychological Medicine*, **11**, 801–815.

Freeman, R.R. (1989). Ambulatory monitoring findings on panic. In R. Baker (ed.), *Panic Disorder: Theory, Research and Therapy*. Chichester: Wiley.

Friedman, C.J., Shear, M.K. & Frances, A. (1987). DSM-III personality disorders in panic patients. *Journal of Personality Disorders*, **1**, 132–135.

Freud. (1895). Obsessions et phobias. *Revenue Neurologique*, **3** (also in Freud, S. (1952). *Gesammelte Werke*, Band I, pp. 345–355. London: Imago).

Freud, S. (1926). Inhibitions, Symptoms and Anxiety. SE20, pp. 87–174. London: Hogarth.

Gittelman-Klein, R. & Klein, D. (1984). Relationship between separation anxiety and panic and agoraphobic disorders. *Psychopathology* (suppl.), **17**, 56–65.

Goldstein, A.J. & Chambless, D.L. (1978). A re-analysis of agoraphobia. *Behavior Therapy*, **9**, 47–59.

Goldstein, A. & Stainback, B. (1991). *Overcoming Agoraphobia: Conquering Fear of the Outside World*. New York: Viking Penguin.

Gorman, J.M., Liebowitz, M.R., Fyer, A.J. & Stein, J. (1989). A neuroanatomical hypothesis for panic disorder. *American Journal of Psychiatry*, **146**, 148–161.

Gray, J.A. (1982). *The Neuropsychology of Anxiety*. New York: Oxford University Press.

Green, M. & Curtis, G. (1988). Personality disorders in panic patients. *Journal of Personality Disorders*, **2**, 303–314.

Hafner, R.J. (1977a). The husbands of agoraphobic women: assortative mating or pathogenic interaction? *British Journal of Psychiatry*, **130**, 233–239.

Hafner, R.J. (1977b). The husbands of agoraphobic women and their influence on treatment outcome. *British Journal of Psychiatry*, **131**, 289–294.

Hafner, R.J. (1982). The marital context of the agoraphobic syndrome. In D.L. Chambless & A.J. Goldstein (eds), *Agoraphobia: Multiple Perspectives on Theory and Treatment*. New York: Wiley.

Hand, I. & Lamontagne, Y. (1976). The exacerbation of interpersonal problems after rapid phobic-removal. *Psychotherapy: Theory, Research and Practice*, **13**, 405–411.

Hibbert, G.A. (1984). Ideational components of anxiety: their origin and content. *British Journal of Psychiatry*, **144**, 618–624.

Hoffart, A. (1995). Cognitive mediators of situational fear in agoraphobia. *Journal of Behaviour Therapy and Experimental Psychiatry*, **26**(4), 313–320.

Hudson, B. (1974). The families of agoraphobics treated by behaviour therapy. *British Journal of Social Work*, **4**, 51–59.

Katon, W. (1984). Panic disorder and somatization. *The American Journal of Medicine*, **77**, 101–106.

Katon, W., Vitaliano, P.P., Russo, J., Jones, M. & Anderson, K. (1987) Panic disorder: spectrum of severity and somatization. *Journal of Nervous and Mental Disease*, **175**, 12–19.

Kendler, K.S., Heath, A.C., Martin, N.G. & Eaves, L.J. (1987) Symptoms of anxiety and symptoms of depression. Same genes, different environment? *Archives of General Psychiatry*, **44**, 451.

Klein, D.F. (1964). Delineation of two-drug responsive anxiety syndromes. *Psychopharmacologia*, **5**, 397–408.

Klein, D.F. (1980). Anxiety reconceptualized. *Comprehensive Psychiatry*, **21**, 411–427.

Klein, D.F. (1981). Anxiety reconceptualized. In D.F. Klein & J. Rabkin (eds), *Anxiety: New research and Changing Concepts*. New York: Raven Press.

Klein, D.F. & Klein, H.M. (1988). The status of panic disorder. *Current Opinion in Psychiatry*, **1**, 177–183.

Klein, D.F. & Klein, H.M. (1989a). The nosology, genetics and theory of spontaneous panic and phobia. In P. Tyrer (ed.), *Psychopharmacology of Anxiety* (pp. 163–195). Oxford: Oxford University Press.

Klein, D.F. & Klein, H.M. (1989b). The definition and psychopharmacology of spontaneous panic and phobia. In P. Tyrer (ed.), *Psychopharmacology of Anxiety* (pp. 135–162). Oxford: Oxford University Press.

Klein, D.F., Ross, D.C. & Cohen, P. (1987). Panic and avoidance in agoraphobia. Application of path analysis to treatment studies. *Archives of General Psychiatry*, **44**, 377–385.

Kleiner, L. & Marshall, W. (1987). The role of interpersonal problems in the development of agoraphobic with panic attacks. *Journal of Anxiety Disorders*, **1**, 313–324.

Klosko, J.S., Shadick, R., Heimberg, R. & Barlow, D.H. (1986). The attributional styles of patients diagnosed with agoraphobia with panic attacks versus patients diagnosed with panic disorder. Paper presented at the annual meeting of the Association for the Advancement of Behaviour Therapy. Chicago, November.

Liebowitz, M.R., Fyer, A.J., Gorman, J.M., Dillon, D., Appleby, I.L., Levy, G., Anderson, S., Levitt, M., Palij, M., Davies, S.O. & Klein, D.F. (1984). Lactate provocation of panic attacks. I. Clinical and behavioural findings. *Archives of General Psychiatry*, **41**, 764–770.

Liebowitz, M.R., Fyer, A.J., Gorman, J.M., Dillon, D., Davies, S., Stein, J.M., Cohen, B.S. & Klein, D.F. (1985). Specificity of lactate infusions in social phobia versus panic disorders. *American Journal of Psychiatry*, **142**, 947–950.

Margraf, J. & Ehlers, A. (1988). Panic attacks in non-clinical subjects. In I. Hand & H.U. Wittchen (eds), *Panic and Phobias*, 2nd edn. Berlin: Springer-Verlag.

Margraf, J., Ehlers, A. & Roth, W. (1986). Biological models of panic disorder and agoraphobia: a review. *Behaviour Research and Therapy*, **24**(5), 553–567.

Marks, I. & Gelder, M. (1965). A controlled retrospective study of behaviour therapy in phobic patients. *British Journal of Psychiatry*, **111**, 561–573.

Marks, I.M. (1987a). Behavioral aspects of panic disorder. *American Journal of Psychiatry*, **144**, 1160–1165.

Marks, I.M. (1987b). *Fears, Phobias and Rituals*. New York: Oxford University Press.

Marks, I.M., Grey, S., Cohen, S.D., Hill, R., Mawson, D., Ramm, E.M. & Stern, R.S. (1983). Imipramine and brief therapist-aided exposure in agoraphobics having self exposure homework: a controlled trial. *Archives of General Psychiatry*, **40**, 153–162.

Mathews, A.M., Gelder, M. & Johnston, D.W. (1981). *Agoraphobia: Nature and treatment.* London: Tavistock.

Meldrum, D.L., Pollard, C.A. & Fraunhoffer, D. (1989). Relationship between panic cognitions and phobic avoidance in agoraphobic sub-samples. Paper presented to the Association for Advancement of Behaviour Therapy, November.

McGennis, A., Nolan, G. & Hartman, M. (1977). The role of self-help associations in agoraphobia: one year's experience with "out and about". *Irish Medical Journal*, **70**, 10–13.

McNally, R.J. & Lorenz, M. (1987). Anxiety sensitivity in agoraphobics. *Journal of Behavior Therapy and Experimental Psychiatry*, **18**, 3–11.

Michelson, L. (1988). Cognitive, behavioral and psychophysiological treatments and correlates of panic. In S. Rachman & J. Maser (eds), *Panic: Psychological Perspectives.* Hillsdale, NJ: Erlbaum.

Milton, F. & Hafner, J. (1979). The outcome of behaviour therapy for agoraphobia in relation to marital adjustment. *Archives of General Psychiatry*, **36**, 807–811.

Mineka, S., Davidson, M., Cook, M. & Keir, R. (1984). Observational conditioning of snake fear in rhesus monkeys. *Journal of Abnormal Psychology*, **93**, 355–372.

Moran, C. & Andrews, G. (1985). The familial occurrence of agoraphobia. *British Journal of Psychiatry*, **146**, 262–267.

Norton, G.R., Dorward, J. & Cox, B.J. (1986). Factors associated with panic attacks in non-clinical subjects. *Behavior Therapy*, **17**, 239–252.

Norton, G.R., Harrison, B., Hauch, J. & Rhodes, L. (1985). Characteristics of people with infrequent panic attacks. *Journal of Abnormal Psychology*, **94**, 216–221.

Öst, L.G., Salkovskis, P.M. & Hellström, K. (1991). One-session therapist-directed exposure vs. self-exposure in the treatment of spider phobia. *Behavior Therapy*, **22**(3), 407–422.

Pollard, C.A. & Cox, G.L. (1988). Social-evaluative anxiety in panic disorder and agoraphobia. *Psychological Reports*, **6**, 323–326.

Pollard, C.A., Pollard, H.J. & Corn, K.J. (1989). Panic onset and major events in the lives of agoraphobics: a test of contiguity. *Journal of Abnormal Psychology*, **98**, 318–321.

Rachman, S. (1977). The conditioning theory of fear acquisition: a critical examination. *Behaviour Research and Therapy*, **15**, 375–387.

Rachman, S.J. (1990). *Fear and Courage*, 2nd edn. New York: Freeman.

Rachman, S.J. & Bichard, S. (1988). The overprediction of fear. *Clinical Psychology Review*, **8**, 303–312.

Rachman, S.J., Craske, M., Tallman, K. & Solyom, C. (1986). Does escape behaviour strengthen agoraphobic avoidance? A replication. *Behaviour Therapy*, **17**, 366–384.

Rainey, J.M., Pohl, R.B., Williams, M., Kritter, E., Freedman, R.R. & Ettedugi, E. (1984). A comparison of lactate and isoproterenol anxiety states. *Psychopathology*, **17**, 74–82.

Rapee, R.M. & Barlow, D.H. (1989). Psychological treatment of unexpected panic attacks: cognitive/behavioural components. In R. Baker (ed.), *Panic Disorder: Theory, Research and Therapy.* Wiley: Chichester.

Rapee, R. & Murrell, E. (1988). Predictors of agoraphobic avoidance: an explanatory analysis. *Journal of Anxiety Disorders*, **2**, 203–217.

Reich, J., Noyes, R. & Troughton, E. (1987). Dependent personality disorder associated with phobic avoidance in patients with panic disorder. *American Journal of Psychiatry*, **144**, 323–326.

Renneberg, B., Chambless, D. & Gracely, E. (1992). Prevalence of SCID-diagnosed personality disorders in agoraphobic outpatients. *Journal of Anxiety Disorders*, **6**, 111–118.

Roberts, A.H. (1964). Housebound housewives: a follow-up study of a phobic anxiety state. *British Journal of Psychiatry*, **110**, 191–197.

Roy-Byrne, P.P. & Uhde, T.W. (1988). Exogenous factors in panic disorder: clinical and research implications. *Journal of Clinical Psychiatry*, **49**, 56–61.

Salkovskis, P.M. (1988a). Hyperventilation and anxiety. *Current Opinion in Psychiatry*, **1**, 76–82.

Salkovskis, P.M. (1988b). Phenomenology, assessment and the cognitive model of panic. In S.J. Rachman & J. Maser (eds), *Panic: Psychological Perspectives*. Hillsdale, NJ: Erlbaum.

Salkovskis, P.M. (1990). The Nature of and Interaction between Cognitive and Physiological Factors in Panic Attacks and Their Treatment. Unpublished PhD Thesis, University of Reading.

Salkovskis, P.M. & Clark, D.M. (1991). Cognitive therapy for panic attacks. *Journal of Cognitive Psychotherapy: an International Quarterly*, **5**(3), 215–226.

Salkovskis, P.M., Clark, D.M. & Gelder, M. (1996). Cognition–behaviour links in the persistence of panic. *Behaviour Research and Therapy*, **34**(5/6), 453–458.

Salkovskis, P.M. (1991). The importance of behaviour in the maintenance of anxiety and panic: a cognitive account. *Behavioural Psychotherapy*, **19**, 6–19.

Salkovskis, P.M. (1995). Cognitive approaches to health anxiety (hypochondriasis) and obsessional problems: some unique features and how this affects treatment. Keynote Address, World Congress of Behavioural and Cognitive Therapies, Denmark.

Salkovskis, P.M. & Clark, D.M. (1986). Cognitive and physiological processes in the maintenance and treatment of panic attacks. In I. Hand & H.U. Wittchen (eds), *Panic and Phobias*, vol. I. Berlin: Springer-Verlag.

Salkovskis, P.M., Clark, D.M. & Hackmann, A. (1991). Treatment of panic attacks using cognitive therapy without exposure to feared situations or bodily sensations. *Behaviour Research and Therapy*, **29**, 161–166.

Salkovskis, P.M. (1996). The cognitive approach to anxiety: threat beliefs, safety-seeking behaviour and the special case of health anxiety and obsessions. In P.M. Salkovskis (ed.), *Frontiers of Cognitive Therapy*. New York: Guilford.

Sanderson, W.C. & Barlow, D. (1986). A description of the sub-categories of the DSM-III revised category of panic disorder: characteristics of 100 patients with different levels of avoidance. Paper presented at the annual meeting of the Association for the Advancement of Behavior Therapy. Chicago, November.

Sanderson. W.C., Rapee, R.M. & Barlow, D.H. (1989). The influence of an illusion of control on panic attacks induced via inhalation of 5.5% carbon dioxide-enriched air. *Archives of General Psychiatry*, **46**, 157–164.

Shafer, S. (1976). Aspects of phobic illness: a study of 90 personal cases. *British Journal of Medical Psychology*, **49**, 221–236.

Sheehan, D.V. (1982). Panic attacks and phobias. *New England Journal of Medicine*, **307**, 156–158.

Silove, D., Harris, M., Morgan, A., Boyce, P., Manicavasagar, V., Hadzi-Pavolvic, D. & Wilhelm, K. (1995). Is separation anxiety a specific precursor of panic-disorder agoraphobia? *Psychological Medicine*, **25**(2), 405–411.

Solyom, L., Beck, P., Solyom, C. & Hugel, R. (1974). Some etiological factors in phobic neurosis. *Comprehensive Psychiatry Association Journal*, **19**, 60–78.

Taylor, C.B., Fried, L. & Kenardy, J. (1990). The use of a real-time computer diary for data acquisition and processing. *Behaviour Research and Therapy*, **28**, 93–97.

Tearnan, B., Telch, M. & Keefe, P. (1984). Etiology and onset of agoraphobia: a critical review. *Comprehensive Psychiatry*, **25**, 51–62.

Telch, M.J., Brouillard, M., Telch, C.F., Agras, W.S. & Taylor, C.B. (1989). Role of cognitive appraisal in panic-related avoidance. *Behaviour Research and Therapy*, **27**, 373–383.

Telch, M.J., Tearnan, B.H. & Taylor, C.B. (1983). Antidepressant medication in the treatment of agoraphobia: a critical review. *Behaviour Research and Therapy*, **21**, 505–527.

Thyer, B. (1986). Agoraphobia: a superstitious conditioning perspective. *Psychological Reports*, **58**, 95–100.

Thyer, B.A. & Himle, J. (1985). Temporal relationship between panic attack onset and phobic avoidance in agoraphobia. *Behaviour Research and Therapy*, **23**, 607.

Thyer, B., Himle, J. & Fischer, D. (1988). Is parental death a selective precursor to either panic disorder or agoraphobia? A test of the separation anxiety hypothesis. *Journal of Anxiety Disorders*, **2**(4), 333–338.

Thyer, B.A., Himle, J., Curtis, G.C., Cameron, O.G. & Neese, R.M. (1985). A comparison of panic disorder and agoraphobia with panic attacks. *Comprehensive Psychiatry*, **26**, 208–214.

Torgersen, S. (1979). The nature and origin of common phobic fears. *British Journal of Psychiatry*, **134**, 343–351.

Torgersen, S. (1983). The genetics of neurosis: the effects of sampling variation upon the twin concordance ratio. *British Journal of Psychiatry*, **142**, 126–132.

Vitaliano, P., Katon, W., Russo, J., Maiuro, R., Anderson, K. & Jones, M. (1987). Coping as an index of illness behaviour in panic disorder. *The Journal of Nervous and Mental Disease*, **175**, 78–83.

Von-Korff, M.R., Eaton, W.W. & Keyl, P. (1985). The epidemiology of panic attacks and disorder: results from three community studies. *American Journal of Epidemiology*, **122**, 970–981.

Westphal (1871). Die Agoraphobie: eine neuropathische Erschienung. *Archiv für Psychiatrie und Nervenkrankheiten*, **3**, 384–412.

Weiss, E. (1964). *Agoraphobia in the Light of Ego Psychology*. New York: Grune and Stratton.

Weissman, M.M., Leaf, P.S., Blazer, D.G., Boyd, S.H. & Florio, L. (1986). The relationship between panic disorder and agoraphobia: an epidemiological perspective. *Psychopharmacology Bulletin*, **26**, 543–545.

Wittchen, H.-U. (1986). Epidemiology of panic attacks and panic disorder. In I. Hand & H.-U. Wittchen (eds), *Panic and Phobias*. Berlin: Springer-Verlag.

Wittchen, H.-U. (1988). Natural cause and spontaneous remissions of untreated anxiety disorders: results of the Munich Follow-up Study (MFS). In I. Hand & H.-U. Wittchen (eds), *Panic and Phobias*, 2nd edn. Berlin: Springer-Verlag.

Winokur, G. & Holeman, E. (1963). Chronic anxiety neurosis: clinical and sexual aspects. *Acta Psychiatrica Scandinavica*, **39**, 384–412.

Wolpe, J. (1958). *Psychotherapy by Reciprocal Inhibition*. Stanford, CA: Stanford University Press.

Chapter 3

Blood–Injury–Injection Phobia

Lars-Göran Öst
Department of Psychology, University of Stockholm, Sweden
and
Kerstin Hellström
Department of Psychiatry, University of Uppsala, Sweden

DEFINITION AND DIAGNOSTIC CRITERIA

DSM-IV (American Psychiatric Association, 1994) classifies Blood–Injection–Injury (BII) phobia as a subtype of specific phobia. In BII phobia "the fear is cued by seeing blood or an injury or by receiving an injection or other invasive medical procedure" (American Psychiatric Association, 1994, p. 406). Furthermore, in order to fulfil this diagnosis the subject must meet the other diagnostic criteria for specific phobia. These are (in abbreviated form): B. Exposure to the phobic stimulus almost invariably provokes an immediate anxiety response; C. The person recognizes that the fear is excessive or unreasonable; D. The phobic situation is avoided or else is endured with intense anxiety; E. The avoidance, anxious anticipation or distress in the feared situation interferes significantly with the person's normal routine, occupational functioning or social activities or relationships, or there is a marked distress about having the phobia; F. In individuals under age 18 years, the duration is at least 6 months; and G. The anxiety can not be better explained by another anxiety disorder (e.g. obsessive–compulsive disorder, post-traumatic stress disorder, separation anxiety disorder, social phobia, panic disorder with agoraphobia).

One important characteristic differentiating BII phobia from all other phobias is the high prevalence of fainting (70–80%) when exposed to the phobic stimuli (Thyer, Himle & Curtis, 1985; Öst, 1992).

Phobias—A Handbook of Theory, Research and Treatment. Edited by G.C.L. Davey.
© 1997 John Wiley & Sons Ltd.

Öst (1992) compared a group of 81 primary blood phobics with 59 primary injection phobics, and found that a significantly higher proportion (69%) of blood phobics had injection phobia than the 31% of injection phobics who had blood phobia. There were few other variables that yielded significant differences between the groups, and thus it was suggested that injection phobia is a more circumscribed form, and should be subsumed under the category of blood–injury–injection phobia.

PREVALENCE

BII Phobia

The prevalence of blood–injury phobia in the general population was 3.1% in an American study by Agras, Sylvester & Oliveau (1969) and 4.5% in a Canadian female sample reported by Costello (1982). In children a mild fear of blood was present in 44% of 6–8 year-olds, while it was 27% in 9–12 year-olds (Lapouse & Monk, 1959). Miller, Barret & Hampe (1974) reported intense fear of blood–injury in 2–3% of the children they investigated.

Neale et al. (1994) investigated the prevalence of phobia for blood, needles, hospitals and illness (BNHI) in 541 monozygotic and 388 dizygotic pairs of female twins from the Virginia Twin Registry. This is a wider concept than BII phobia and the authors defined a phobia as fear accompanied by interference (minor plus major), i.e. they did not strictly follow criterion E of the DSM-IV specific phobia diagnosis. With this in mind, they reported a prevalence of 6.2%, which was reduced to 1.7% when only major interference was counted.

Kleinknecht (1994) classified a student sample (n = 933) based on their responses on the Mutilation Questionnaire (Klorman et al., 1974). The students were considered BII-phobic if they scored 19 or greater, but no diagnostic interview was done. With this caveat, the prevalence of BII phobia in this student population was 3.1%, i.e. exactly the same as found by Agras, Sylvester & Oliveau (1969).

When it comes to injection phobia, much less is known about the prevalence. Agras, Sylvester & Oliveau (1969) unfortunately did not report the proportion of patients having a phobia of injections. However, the incidence of what they called "common fear" of injections was 12% for 10- and 20 year-olds, and then it declined to 10%, 7%, 6%, and 0% for the age groups 30, 40, 50 and 60 years, respectively.

Family Prevalence of BII Phobia

In the study by Öst (1992), 61% of the blood–injury phobics had a first-degree relative with the same phobia, while this was the case for only 29% of the injection phobics. In the clinical series reported by Thyer, Himle & Curtis (1985), however, only 27% of the BI phobics said they had family members with the same phobia. The figure of 61% in our series is 2–12 times higher than for other specific phobias at our clinic; claustrophobia 5%, animal phobias 8% and dental phobia 23% (Öst, 1992).

Kleinknecht (1987) reported that in a student sample of those who *fainted* at the sight of blood or injury, 35% had a close family member who did so as well, significantly higher than the 13% reported for non-fainters. In a subsequent study (Kleinknecht, 1988) the figures were very similar (32% vs. 11%). In the study by Kleinknecht & Lenz (1989), the same difference was found, but the proportions were much higher, 66% for fainters and 41% for non-fainters.

To get a perspective on the these data, the family prevalence of specific phobia in general is instructive. Fyer et al. (1990) reported a family study on transmission of simple phobias. They found that first-degree relatives of simple phobia probands had a significantly higher risk (31%) for simple phobia, compared with relatives of never-mentally-ill controls (11%). Looking at the results from the patients' perspective, 74% of the simple phobics compared with 29% of the normal controls had at least one simple phobic relative. However, in only 13% of the patients did the relative have the same phobia as the proband, a figure quite similar to those reported by Öst (1992) above.

Fainting in Relation to BII Stimuli

Thyer, Himle & Curtis (1985) reported that 80% of their sample ($n = 15$) of blood phobics had a history of fainting. Öst (1992) found that 70% of the patients with a primary diagnosis of blood phobia ($n = 81$) and 56% of those with injection phobia ($n = 59$) had a history of fainting when confronted with phobic stimuli.

Even if a large proportion of BII phobics has a history of fainting in the phobic situation, not all of them faint, and of course not all people who faint in these situations are BII-phobic. In a series of studies on university students, Kleinknecht has investigated the prevalence of fainting at the sight of blood or injuries. Kleinknecht (1987) reported that 13% had fainted *or almost fainted*, and that this was significantly more common among females (17%) than males (7%). Furthermore, 23.5% reported having fainted in other situations, and there was a significant relationship between fainting in blood–injury and other situations. In his next study Kleinknecht (1988) found that 14.5% of the sample had fainted or almost fainted, but there was no gender difference. There was also a significant association between fainting in blood-injury situations and fainting in other situations. In the third study (Kleinknecht & Lenz, 1989) it was reported that 25% of the females and only 11% of the males had one or more fainting or near fainting episodes in response to blood stimuli, and the overall proportion was 19.3%. In the most recent study, Kleinknecht (1994) found that 30% of the sample had fainted or almost fainted in response to blood, injury or needles, and among those considered to be phobics the proportion was 64%. The latter figure is close to the 70% found by Öst (1992) and the 80% reported by Thyer, Himle & Curtis (1985). However, in these clinical studies only *actual* fainting is counted, while

Kleinknecht also included almost fainting in his studies but did not report the proportions in each category.

Fainting in Relation to Medical Procedures

It is well known that fainting occurs among blood donors to a certain extent. A review of studies on blood donor fainting (Ruetz et al., 1967) found that 4–5% of blood donors experienced vasovagal syncope. This was also the case in a study of more than 1000 Australian blood donors during a 6-year period (Beal, 1972), in which 5.1% experienced at least one vasovagal syncope. However, a study by Graham (1961) found that 17.9% of white donors fainted, but no black donors reacted as strongly.

Besides fainting during bloodletting, Marks (1988) in his review on blood–injury phobia reported that fainting is known to occur during cardiac catheterization, dentistry, prostatic palpitation during rectal examination and dilatation of the cervix, and by pneumo-encephalography. Other situations that can cause vasovagal syncope are described by Thyer, Himle & Curtis (1985); sudden emptying of the bladder, immersion of one's face in water, and anticipation of electric shock.

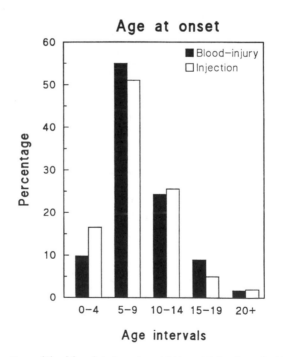

Figure 3.1 Proportion of the blood–injury (*n* = 111) and injection phobia (*n* = 64) patients with onset of their phobia in the different age intervals

AGE AT ONSET

The distributions of age at onset (Öst, unpublished data) for our sample of 111 blood–injury phobics and 64 injection phobics are shown in Figure 3.1. The distributions are very similar, with 65% of the blood phobics and 68% of the injection phobics having an onset before 10 years of age. The means are 8.5 (SD = 4.5) for blood phobia and 8.2 (SD = 4.9) for injection phobia. The series of 15 blood–injury phobics described by Thyer, Himle & Curtis (1985) had a mean of 14.1 years, with a positively skewed distribution. However, the median was 9 years, very close to the median of 8 years in our sample. Neale et al. (1994) did not give the mean age of onset for their study on female twins. However, an estimation from their graph (Neale et al., 1994, p. 330) yields a median of about 9 years of age. Thus, BII phobia usually starts in childhood or adolescence and it is very uncommon for adults to acquire this phobia.

AETIOLOGY

Genetics

As described above, there is a high proportion of blood–injury phobics who report having a close relative with the same phobia. This is consistent with the hypothesis that there is a heritable component in BII phobia. However, the high concordance rate could also be explained by vicarious learning.

Rose & Ditto (1983) investigated 250 pairs of twins answering a Fear Survey Schedule. They found that the morbid fears factor (including items about blood, injury, needles, etc.) correlated 0.46 in monozygotic (MZ) and 0.24 in dizygotic (DZ) twins. Torgersen (1979) also found higher MZ correlations for blood–injury fears than for DZ twins.

In the largest twin study on this issue, Neale et al. (1994) interviewed 1000 female pairs of twins and tested three sources of variance in liability to phobia: (a) additive genetic effects; (b) shared family or "common" environment; and (c) individual-specific environment. They found that the results were consistent with a genetic or a shared environment factor (a and b), but it was impossible to differentiate between them. The only factor that could be rejected was that of individual-specific environment. The correlations for fear of blood (MZ: 0.59; DZ: 0.08) and fear of needles (MZ: 0.49; DZ: 0.10) are also similar to the previous studies. Moreover, their data supported the hypothesis that the familial resemblance is genetic, rather than the rival hypothesis that it is environmental.

Pathways of Acquisition

Rachman (1977) described three "pathways to fear", or ways that phobias can be acquired. These have been investigated in a number of studies, primarily on various types of specific phobias (summarized by Kleinknecht, 1994), but also in social phobia and agoraphobia (Öst & Hugdahl, 1981). Öst (1991) assessed how 137 blood–injury or injection phobics attributed the onset of their phobias. The majority (52%) of the patients attributed their phobias to traumatic conditioning experiences, 24% to vicarious learning, 7% to transmission of information, while 17% could not recall the onset of their phobias. Kleinknecht (1994) has recently replicated this study in a sample of 128 students fearful of blood–injury situations. He found that 53% attributed the onset to traumatic conditioning, 16% to vicarious learning and 3% to information, while 27% could not recall the conditions of onset.

Even if these two studies, the only ones published on BII phobia, arrived at very similar results, it should be emphasized that we are assessing the subjects' memories for experiences made on average 20–22 years earlier (Öst, 1992). It is very difficult, not to say impossible, to ascertain the validity of the patients' attributions. One possibility would be to interview the parents of the patients, but it is not self-evident that they would have a more "accurate" memory of what took place, especially since they might not even have been present on the occasion. Probably the best way to obtain these data, at least from a methodological point of view, would be a longitudinal study starting with a large sample of children who are assessed frequently up to adult age.

IMPAIRMENT AND CONSEQUENCES

Criterion E for specific phobia in DSM-IV (American Psychiatric Association, 1994) states that: "The avoidance, anxious anticipation, or distress in the feared situation interferes significantly with the person's normal routine, occupational functioning, or social activities or relationships, or there is a marked distress about having the phobia". Öst (1992) reported interview data on the extent to which blood–injury and injection phobics, respectively, experienced their phobias as interfering with various aspects of their lives. The proportions of subjects who rated moderate, much, or very much interference with regard to choice of career or work was 36% of the blood phobics and 25% of the injection phobics. The corresponding proportions for leisure and social activities were 41% and 32%, respectively.

During the screening interview our patients were also asked about any consequences that the phobia had for them. In our larger sample of 111 blood–injury phobics (Öst, unpublished data), 32% said that the phobia had negative consequences concerning their career choice, work and education, 9% said that they would not be able to help other people (especially their children) should they be injured, 8% completely avoided visiting hospitals, medical check-ups etc., 8% did not go to the movies, 7% said that they were generally worried and avoided various situations, and 2% did not dare to become pregnant, while 33% stated no direct negative consequences, even if they were distressed by their phobia.

COGNITIONS

Öst (1992) found that both blood–injury phobics (70%) and injection phobics (73%) reported various negative cognitions when asked to describe what typically went through their minds and/or what they believed would happen when confronted with the phobic situation. In our larger sample of 111 blood–injury phobics (Öst, unpublished data) 81% believed they would faint, 4.5% that they would be hurt physically or die, 1.8% that they would become ill or vomit, while 12.7% did not know what would happen or had no specific cognitions about this. When the sample was divided into two subgroups based on the patients' fainting history, it turned out (as could be expected) that those with a fainting history (89%) significantly more often than those without such a history (60%) believed that they would faint when confronted with blood–injury stimuli. For the sample with injection phobia the relationship was the same, with 66% of those with a fainting history, and 26% of those without such a history fearing to faint in the phobic situation (Öst, 1992).

PHYSIOLOGICAL RESPONSE PATTERNS

When phobic patients are confronted with their phobic stimuli there is usually an increase in heart rate, blood pressure, skin conductance, etc. compared to baseline values, and if the person stays in the phobic situation there is a gradual return to baseline levels (Marks, 1987). However, in BII phobics the initial increase of blood pressure and heart rate is brief and is followed by a rapid decrease to a level significantly below baseline, and often results in the patient fainting (Foulds, 1993; Curtis & Thyer, 1983; Öst, Sterner & Lindahl, 1984; Thyer & Curtis, 1984; Wardle & Jarvis, 1981).

This reaction is illustrated by Figure 3.2, showing the blood pressure of one of our patients during the initial behavioural test. This patient is a 24-year-old female with a 14-year duration of her phobia. She does not have a fainting history, but according to the patient both her mother and a brother have BII phobia. Her baseline was stable with mean systolic and diastolic blood pressures (SBP and DBP) of 120.2 and 77.6 mmHg, respectively. During the instruction phase the SBP increased to 135 and the DBP to 84 mmHg, and after 2 minutes of watching the videotape of thoracic operations, SBP was 181 and DBP 110 mmHg. Two minutes later an extreme reduction had occurred; SBP was down to 83 and DBP to 45 mmHg. The patient fainted after 4 minutes, 8 seconds of watching the tape. During the post-baseline phase the patient did not quite reach the baseline levels; the highest values of SBP were 109 and DBP 68 mmHg.

This pattern was called *diphasic* by Graham, Kabler & Lunsford (1961) in describing fainting in blood donors, but the same descriptor has been adopted for describing the physiological responses of BII phobics, e.g. in reviews on blood–

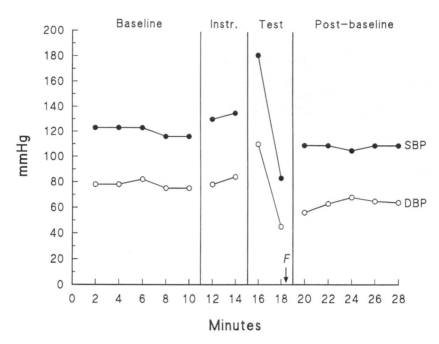

Figure 3.2 Systolic (SBP) and diastolic (DBP) blood pressure for patient 1 during the different phases of the test

injury phobia by Thyer, Himle & Curtis (1985), Marks (1988), and Page (1994). Marks (1988) proposed that the response pattern shown in BII phobics is just an exaggeration of the normal discomfort that humans display in response to blood–injury cues. Barlow (1988) suggested that the vasovagal syncope may have a survival value for the human species. Those historic ancestors who responded to injury with a large drop in blood pressure would minimize blood loss and thus be more likely to survive. However, Page (1994) points out that this account does not accommodate what is commonly seen when people sustain severe injuries and blood loss.

Furthermore, the diphasic response pattern is not necessary for fainting to occur. This is illustrated in Figure 3.3, depicting the blood pressure of another of our patients. This was also a 24-year-old female with the onset of phobia at 8 years of age. She reported having fainted 20 times in the phobic situation, and estimated the average duration of unconsciousness to 30 seconds. She also had a sister with the same phobia. Her baseline was fairly stable with SBP and DBP of 111.0 and 63.6 mmHg, respectively. During the instruction phase the blood pressure did not change. The patient fainted after watching only 25 seconds of the video-tape and at this point her SBP was 50 and DBP 30 mmHg. During the post-baseline phase the patient showed a continuous increase in her blood pressure and reached baseline levels after 10 minutes.

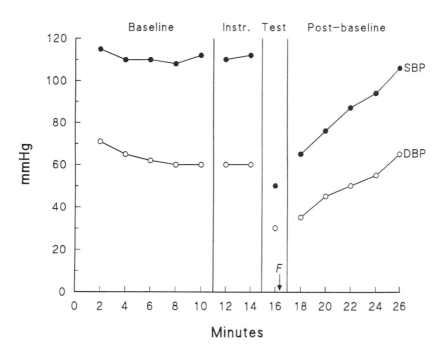

Figure 3.3 Systolic (SBP) and diastolic (DBP) blood pressure for patient 2 during the different phases of the test

Asystole

In a minority of BII patients the drop in blood pressure and heart rate results in asystole, i.e. the ECG will show no electrical activity from the heart. Cohn, Kron & Brady (1976) described a 28 year-old male with BI phobia since age 4. After 75 seconds of watching a slide of a mutilated body he had bradycardia (30 BPM) and a 3-second episode of complete cardiac asystole. Öst, Sterner & Lindahl (1984) found that of the 18 assessed patients, five (all males aged 28–44 years) who fainted during a behavioural test had at least one period of asystole of 5 seconds in duration. The "strongest" reactor had no less than 33 periods, varying in length between 2 and 9 seconds, during a 7-minute interval. Hand & Schröder (1989) described a 25-year-old male who had been BII-phobic since age 7, and reported having fainted 25 times. During a pre-treatment venipuncture he fainted and displayed an asystole of 27 seconds duration.

The literature also contains a number of cases who were not in treatment for BII phobia but reacted with asystole during various medical procedures. Herlevsen & Andersen (1987) described a case of a 33-year-old male with an asystole lasting 33 seconds. Selleger et al. (1988) reported a 36-year-old male with asystole of 28 seconds. Lipton & Forstater (1993) described a case of a 42-year-old male with asystole lasting 8 seconds.

The brief review above shows that asystole, varying in length between 3 and 33 seconds, can occur in some cases of BII phobia. Interestingly, all the cases are men, which may suggest that males have a propensity to react more strongly than females in this respect. However, there is a large void of knowledge concerning, for example, what circumstances are necessary for asystole to occur, what predictors there are for this extreme cardiac reaction, whether the electrical activity of the heart resumes spontaneously or whether active measures have to be taken, as in the reports by Herlevsen & Andersen (1987) and Lipton & Forstater (1993), etc.

Theoretical Explanations for the Response Pattern

Page (1994) provided a thorough description of various explanations in his excellent review of blood–injury phobia. Lewis (1932) was the first to describe "vasovagal syncope", suggesting that two processes are involved—cardiac slowing mediated by the vagus nerve, and a concomitant fall in blood pressure. Later, Weissler et al. (1957) proposed that limited venous inflow to the heart plays a significant role in the restriction of cardiac output, and Engel (1962) that the hypotension appeared to be caused by active sympathethic vasodilation in the skeletal musculature. From these early descriptions it was suggested that the vasovagal syncope involves an initial increase in arousal followed by a marked decrease.

Graham, Kabler & Lunsford (1961) gave the following account for the "diphasic" response pattern in fainting blood donors: "The first phase is a reflection of anxiety, while the second phase begins with the sudden cessation of anxiety. It is suggested that physiologically the faint reflects the action of the reflex mechanism activated by the first phase, and left suddenly unopposed" (p. 506). They suggested that during the first phase there is a massive sympathetic arousal, which to some degree is counterbalanced by parasympathetic activity. Then this homeostasis ceases abruptly (when the person has reached the point of "no return" and need not be anxious any more), leaving the parasympathetic activity unopposed, which eventually leads to fainting.

However, this account does not fit the self-rated anxiety obtained from BI phobics. There is the initial anxiety increase, but the decrease does not seem to occur; if anything, the anxiety continues to rise or at least to stay at the same level (e.g. Curtis & Thyer, 1983). Engel (1978) suggested that the vasovagal syncope consists of a diphasic reaction comprising a fight–flight and a conservation–withdrawal response. Vingerhoets (1984) had the same description of the two phases but, based on biochemical assessment, he stated that the first phase was mediated via the orbital frontal cortex and the amygdala, while the second was mediated by the pituitary–adrenal axis. Page (1994) pointed to the possibility that hyperventilation, besides the reduction in blood pressure, could contribute to the prodrome of vasovagal syncope. However, this is based only on a case study by Foulds (1993), in which breathing was not assessed, and data on fainting blood donors by Ruetz et al. (1967), showing that fainters showed a decrease in P_{CO_2} values.

Page (1994) also speculated about a similarity between fainting and disgust sensitivity. He posited that: "When the (parasympathetic) processes underlying disgust combine with a homeostatic increase in parasympathetic activity (which counteracts the sympathetically mediated fight-or-flight response), the joint effect may produce a pattern of vascular and vagal responding responsible for fainting" (p. 452). Page acknowledged that this explanation is speculative but that it leads to a number of testable predictions that research in this area should test in future studies.

In conclusion, there remains a lot of research to be done on BII phobia in order to understand fully the psychology, physiology and biochemistry of this specific phobia.

ASSESSMENT

Diagnostic Interview

In order to diagnose BII phobia, a screening interview using a structured schedule like the Anxiety Disorders Interview Schedule-IV (ADIS-IV; Brown, DiNardo & Barlow, 1994) is recommended. This has a section for specific phobia which is structured according to the subtypes of specific phobias in DSM-IV, i.e. animal, natural environment, blood–injection–injury, situational and other types. The specific questions asked for BII concern the individual's fear and avoidance regarding blood from minor cut, receiving injections, and having blood drawn. Furthermore, these are asked first regarding the individual him/herself and second, concerning witnessing others in these situations. Subsequent questions concern, for example, what the patients believe will happen in the situation, if they experience anxiety when entering the feared situation, to what extent the fear interferes with the their lives, and when and how the fear began causing distress for the patients.

In order not to miss a potentional BII phobia, the assessor should ask the person about somatic reactions when confronted with these types of stimuli. If the patient reports dizziness, lightheadedness, feeling faint, sweating and/or fainting or almost fainting, there is a high chance that the individual is BII-phobic. Patients with panic disorder (with or without agoraphobia) may report similar symptoms but they very rarely faint in a panic attack. BII phobics, on the other hand, very rarely report panic attacks in their phobic situations.

Criterion C, "The person recognizes that the fear is excessive and unreasonable" of the DSM-IV specific phobia, is not included in ADIS-IV. This is also a bit problematic in BII phobia. As described above, 81% of our sample believed that they would faint when confronted with BII stimuli, and 73% actually had fainted in these situations, on average 11 times (Öst, 1992). In this respect BII phobics differ from, for example, panic disorder patients, who fear that a certain catastrophe, will happen (Clark, 1986; Westling & Öst, 1993), but this has never occurred. What is "excessive or unreasonable" in BII phobics is perhaps what they fear will happen after the fainting has occurred. Unfortunately, no systematic data have been published on this issue.

Behavioural Test

In order to assess the BII phobic's behavioural, physiological and cognitive reactions when confronted with the phobic stimuli, a behavioural test should be used. For blood–injury phobics it is difficult, not to say impossible, to subject them to real-life confrontations with blood–injury stimuli, e.g. witnessing accidents or surgery. In our research (Öst, Sterner & Lindahl, 1984; Öst et al., 1984; Öst, Sterner & Fellenius, 1989; Öst, Fellenius & Sterner, 1991; Hellström, Fellenius & Öst, 1995) we have used a 30-minute silent colour video-tape consisting of four thoracic operations. The test starts with a 10-minute baseline, prior to which the patient is instructed that this is done to obtain a reliable measure of their heart rate and blood pressure. After the baseline an instruction period (4 minutes) follows, during which the patient is told about the video-tape and its content. The patient is instructed to watch the TV screen all the time; he/she is not allowed to close his/her eyes or to look away. However, if watching becomes unendurable the patient can stop the tape by using the remote control. After the 4-minute instruction period the tape is started and is shown until 30 minutes have elapsed or the patient stops the tape, either actively or passively by closing the eyes, looking away or fainting. Then follows a 10-minute post-baseline phase.

The patient's heart rate is measured continuously during the test phases, while blood pressure is assessed every 2 minutes, since it takes 30–40 sec to inflate the cuff and let the air out. Simultaneously with the blood pressure assessments the patient rates (0–10 scale) the degree of anxiety/discomfort experienced at that moment. Once the test is completed the patient also answers a scale concerning thoughts that went through his/her mind during the test.

When using the above behavioural test in our treatment studies we have used an exclusion criterion; any patient who is able to watch the film for more than 20 min is not considered a sufficiently severe case to participate in the study. However, the validity of this test is uncertain and we have no data on this issue, since they are difficult to ascertain. What we know, however, is that 26% of the patients (across our treatment studies) who fulfilled the diagnostic criteria failed this behavioural criterion. The clinical impression is that a majority of these patients reacted strongly to BII stimuli in natural situations but may not have generalized their fear to such an extent that it included film representations.

Self-report Measures

The specific fear scale used for blood–injury phobia is the Mutilation Questionnaire (MQ; Klorman et al., 1974) consisting of 30 true–false items. It has been shown to have good reliability (internal consistency 0.83) and preliminary validity data. Kleinknecht (1988) studied the relation between the MQ and fainting (in a student sample) and partialled out the fear component. MQ was found to comprise two factors; one concerned blood and injury fears in general, and the other fainting when confronted with these stimuli. In our treatment trials MQ has been used as the primary self-report measure and it has proven to be sensitive to changes after various behavioural treatments (Öst et al., 1984; Öst, Sterner & Fellenius, 1989; Öst, Fellenius & Sterner, 1991; Hellström, Fellenius & Öst, 1995). Across these four studies the mean pre-treatment scores have been reduced, with 42% at post-treatment.

For injection phobics, Öst, Hellström & Kåver (1992) developed the Injection Phobia Scale, consisting of 18 items which are rated for fear (0–4 scale) and avoidance (0–2). Preliminary psychometric data show that the scale has adequate internal consistency, concurrent validity, and is sensitive to change after treatment.

Besides these specific fear questionnaires, our BII patients filled out the Beck Anxiety Inventory (Beck et al., 1988) and the Beck Depression Inventory (Beck, 1967) to obtain measures of general anxiety and depression. Finally, they answered the Fear Survey Schedule (Wolpe & Lang, 1964) and the Fear Questionnaire (Marks & Mathews, 1979) which give measures of phobias in general. The latter has a section (five items) on BII phobia, and from the former a BII subscale comprising eight items can be constructed.

TREATMENT

As shown above, the main problem in BII phobia is the large drop in blood pressure that takes place during exposure to BI stimuli, and which eventually leads to fainting in the large majority of cases. What is needed from a therapeutic point of view is a treatment that prevents the blood pressure from dropping to such a low level, and preferably also increases the pressure, and thus prevents fainting. If the patient can learn a safe way of preventing fainting, he/she can also stay exposed to the phobic stimuli long enough for the anxiety to subside. Such a method has been developed in our clinic, and it is called applied tension. The treatment used for "pure" injection phobics without the fainting reaction is exposure *in vivo*, especially the one-session treatment evaluated by Öst, Hellström & Kåver (1992) (see Chapter 12).

Applied Tension

Based on a case study by Kozak & Montgomery (1981), Öst and his co-workers developed a treatment package specifically designed for blood–injury phobia and called it "applied tension" (AT; Öst & Sterner, 1987). This treatment method has two goals: (a) teaching the patient an effective tension technique that will increase the blood pressure; and (b) teaching the patient to recognize the very first signs of the blood pressure dropping and when and how to apply the tension technique. The original five-session format of applied tension will be described below, while the abbreviated one-session format is described in Chapter 12.

Rationale

As in any good cognitive–behavioural treatment, a detailed rationale should be given, which includes a description of the phobia, its maintaining factors, the treatment chosen to modify these and how it is supposed to work. In BI phobia the therapist should explain that the patient has learnt to associate BI stimuli with fainting or almost fainting, and that the only way to prevent fainting has been to avoid or escape from all situations having these stimuli. Furthermore, the physiological response with the drop in blood pressure, which probably leads to a drop in cerebral blood flow and eventually fainting, is described. Finally, the therapist tells the patient about the tension technique, what it is, what effect it has on the blood pressure, and how it is to be applied during and after the treatment.

Tension Technique

After receiving explanation of the rationale, the patient is instructed how to tense the gross body muscles; the arms, chest and legs. He/she should tense as much as possible for 15–20 seconds, and then release the tension and go back to normal (but not relaxing). After a pause of 30 seconds another tension period is started. As a homework assignment the patient is asked to do five cycles of tension release, which takes about 5 minutes, and to do this five times per day during the treatment period.

Application Training

During sessions 2 and 3 the patient is shown a series of 30 slides of injured people. He/she is instructed to watch the screen and scan his/her body for the very first signs of the prodromal phase of fainting. These can be idiosyncratic, e.g. a feeling of warmth around the head and neck, cold sweat in the forehead, lightheadedness, a queasy sensation in the stomach, nausea, visual and auditory changes. As soon as the patient perceives this sign he/she tells the therapist, who measures the patient's blood pressure. Directly afterwards the patient starts to tense and keep tensing on and off for as long as is necessary to abort the prodromal signs. When he/she is able to watch the slide without feeling this symptom the therapist once more measures the patient's blood pressure. Then the subsequent slides are shown and the patient repeats the same task. During session 4 the therapist takes the patient to the blood donor centre so that he/she can watch other people donate blood, and has a blood sample withdrawn in order to test if he/she is suitable as a blood donor. The fifth session takes the patient to the department of thoracic surgery to observe open heart or lung surgery. The instruction during these sessions is the same; scan the body for the first sign of the prodromal phase and apply the tension technique as long as it is needed.

Physiological Effects

The blood pressure assessments during sessions 2–3 will yield data as to whether the tension technique really is achieving what it is supposed to achieve. Öst, Fellenius & Sterner (1991) showed that during sessions 2 and 3 the subjects receiving applied tension increased their SBP with 15 and DBP with 7 mmHg on average, *while* being exposed to BI stimuli. In the subsequent study by Hellström, Fellenius & Öst (1995) the mean increases for the two applied-tension conditions (sessions 1 and 5) were SBP 21 and DBP 14 mmHg. In both these studies tension-only conditions were applied as comparison and the mean increases were SBP 18 and DBP 10 mmHg. A study by Foulds et al. (1990) showed that BI phobics could increase their heart rate an average of 12 beats/minute and cerebral blood flow velocity 4 cm/second, after just a brief practice (90 seconds) with a simpler form of tension. Thus, it can be concluded that the tension technique leads to substantial increases in blood pressure, heart rate, and probably cerebral blood flow, which serves to prevent fainting.

Treatment Outcome

The above treatment has been evaluated in three randomised outcome trials. Öst, Sterner & Fellenius (1989) found that 90% of the applied tension patients were clinically significantly improved, both at post-treatment and at 6-month follow-up. The corresponding figures in the Öst, Fellenius & Sterner (1991) study were 90% at post-treatment and 100% at 1-year follow-up; and in the Hellström, Fellenius & Öst (1995) study, 50% post-treatment and 60% at 1 year.

CONCLUSIONS

Blood–injury–injection phobia is one of the most prevalent phobias, which also can cause major problems for the affected individual, and in extreme cases can lead to a refusal of life-saving treatments, e.g. dialysis. The treatment research has yielded effective treatments both for blood–injury and pure injection phobia, but the knowledge concerning aetiology and physiological responses is still limited. The latter will hopefully change with the development of new non-invasive methods to assess sympathetic, and particularly parasympathetic, activity.

REFERENCES

Agras, S., Sylvester, D. & Oliveau, D. (1969). The epidemiology of common fear and phobia. *Comprehensive Psychiatry*, **10**, 151–156.

American Psychiatric Association (1994). *Diagnostic and Statistical Manual of Mental Disorders*, 4th edn. Washington, DC: American Psychiatric Association.
Barlow, D.H. (1988). *Anxiety and Its Disorders*. New York: Guilford.
Beal, R.W. (1972). Vasovagal reactions in blood donors. *Medical Journal of Australia*, **2**, 757–760.
Beck, A.T. (1967). *Depression: Causes and Treatment*. Philadelphia: University of Philadelphia Press.
Beck, A.T., Epstein, N., Brown, G. & Steer, R.A. (1988). An inventory for measuring clinical anxiety: psychometric properties. *Journal of Consulting and Clinical Psychology*, **56**, 893–897.
Brown, T., DiNardo, P. & Barlow, D.H. (1994). *Anxiety Disorders Interview Schedule IV (ADIS-IV)*. Albany, NY: Graywind Publications.
Clark, D.M. (1986). A cognitive approach to panic. *Behaviour Research and Therapy*, **24**, 461–470.
Cohn, C.K., Kron, R.E. & Brady, J.P. (1976). A case of blood–illness–injury phobia treated behaviorally. *Journal of Nervous and Mental Disease*, **162**, 65–68.
Costello, C.G. (1982). Fears and phobias in women: a community study. *Journal of Abnormal Psychology*, **91**, 280–286.
Curtis, G.C. & Thyer, B. (1983). Fainting on exposure to phobic stimuli. *American Journal of Psychiatry*, **140**, 771–774.
Engel, G.L. (1962). *Fainting*, 2nd edn. Springfield, IL: Charles Thomas.
Engel, G.L. (1978). Psychologic stress, vasodepressor (vasovagal) syncope, and sudden death. *Annals of Internal Medicine*, **89**, 403–412.
Foulds, J. (1993). Cerebral circulation during treatment of blood-injury phobia: a case study. *Behavioural Psychotherapy*, **21**, 137–146.
Foulds, J., Wiedmann, K., Patterson, J. & Brooks, N. (1990). The effects of muscle tension on cerebral circulation in blood-phobic and non-phobic subjects. *Behaviour Research and Therapy*, **28**, 481–486.
Fyer, A.J., Mannuzza, S., Gallops, M.S., Martin, L.Y., Aaronson, C., Gorman, J.M., Liebowitz, M.R. & Klein, D.F. (1990). Familial transmission of simple phobias and fears. *Archives of General Psychiatry*, **47**, 252–256.
Graham, D.T. (1961). Prediction of fainting in blood donors. *Circulation*, **23**, 901–906.
Graham, D.T., Kabler, J.D. & Lunsford, L. (1961). Vasovagal fainting: a diphasic response. *Psychosomatic Medicine*, **23**, 493–507.
Hand, I. & Schröder, G. (1989). Vasovagale Ohnmacht bei der Blut–Verletzungs–Katastrophen (BVK) Phobie und ihre verhaltenstherapeutische Behandlung. In I. Hand & H.-U. Wittchen (eds), *Verhaltenstherapie in der Medizin* (pp. 196–206). Berlin: Springer Verlag.
Herlevsen, P. & Andersen, P.T. (1987). Constitutional predisposition to vasovagal syncope: an additional risk factor in patients exposed to electrical injuries. *British Heart Journal*, **57**, 284–285.
Hellström, K., Fellenius, J. & Öst, L.-G. (1996). One vs. five sessions of applied tension in the treatment of blood phobia. *Behaviour Research and Therapy*, **34**, 101–112.
Kleinknecht, R.A. (1987). Vasovagal syncope and blood/injury fear. *Behaviour Research and Therapy*, **25**, 175–178.
Kleinknecht, R.A. (1988). Specificity and psychosocial correlates of blood/injury fear and fainting. *Behaviour Research and Therapy*, **26**, 303–309.
Kleinknecht, R.A. (1994). Acquisition of blood, injury, and needle fears and phobias. *Behaviour Research and Therapy*, **32**, 817–823.
Kleinknecht, R.A. & Lenz, J. (1989). Blood/injury fear, fainting and avoidance of medically related situations: a family correspondence study. *Behaviour Research and Therapy*, **27**, 537–547.
Klorman, R., Weerts, T.C., Hastings, J.C., Melamed, B.G. & Lang, P. (1974). Psychometric description of some specific-fear questionnaires. *Behavior Therapy*, **5**, 401–409.

Kozak, M.J. & Montgomery, G.K. (1981). Multimodal behavioral treatment of recurrent injury scene-elicited fainting (vasodepressor syncope). *Behavioural Psychotherapy*, **9**, 316–321.

Lewis, T. (1932). Vasovagal syncope and the carotid sinus mechanism. *British Medical Journal*, **1**, 873–876.

Lapouse, R. & Monk, M.A. (1959). Fears and worries in a representative sample of children. *American Journal of Orthopsychiatry*, **19**, 803–818.

Lipton, J.D. & Forstater, A.T. (1993). Recurrent asystole associated with vasovagal reaction during venipuncture. *Journal of Emergency Medicine*, **11**, 723–727.

Marks, I.M. (1987). *Fears, Phobias and Rituals*. Oxford, Oxford University Press.

Marks, I.M. (1988). Blood–injury phobia: a review. *American Journal of Psychiatry*, **145**, 1207–1213.

Marks, I.M. & Mathews, A.M. (1979). A brief standard self-rating for phobic patients. *Behaviour Research and Therapy*, **17**, 263–267.

Miller, L.C., Barret, C.L. & Hampe, E. (1974). Phobias of childhood. In A. Davids (ed.), *Child Personality and Psychopathology: Current Topics*, Vol. 1 (pp. 89–134). New York: Wiley.

Neale, M.C., Walters, E.E., Eaves, L.J., Kessler, R.C., Heath, A.C. & Kendler, K.S. (1994). Genetics of blood–injury fears and phobias: a population-based twin study. *American Journal of Medical Genetics*, **54**, 326–334.

Öst, L.-G. (1991). Acquisition of blood and injection phobia and anxiety response patterns in clinical patients. *Behaviour Research and Therapy*, **29**, 323–332.

Öst, L.-G. (1992). Blood and injection phobia: backdground and cognitive, physiological and behavioral variables. *Journal of Abnormal Psychology*, **101**, 68–74.

Öst, L.-G., Fellenius, J. & Sterner, U. (1991). Applied tension, exposure *in vivo*, and tension-only in the treatment of blood phobia. *Behaviour Research and Therapy*, **29**, 561–574.

Öst, L.-G., Hellström, K. & Kåver, A. (1992). One versus five sessions of exposure in the treatment of injection phobia. *Behavior Therapy*, **23**, 263–282.

Öst, L.-G. & Hugdahl, K. (1981). Acquisition of phobias and anxiety response patterns in clinical patients. *Behaviour Research and Therapy*, **19**, 439–447.

Öst, L.-G., Lindahl, I.-L., Sterner, U. & Jerremalm, A. (1984). Exposure *in vivo* vs. applied relaxation in the treatment of blood phobia. *Behaviour Research and Therapy*, **22**, 205–216.

Öst, L.-G. & Sterner, U. (1987). Applied tension: a specific behavioral method for treatment of blood phobia. *Behaviour Research and Therapy*, **25**, 25–29.

Öst, L.-G., Sterner, U. & Fellenius, J. (1989). Applied tension, applied relaxation, and the combination in the treatment of blood phobia. *Behaviour Research and Therapy*, **27**, 109–121.

Öst, L.-G., Sterner, U. & Lindahl, I.-L. (1984). Physiological responses in blood phobics. *Behaviour Research and Therapy*, **22**, 109–117.

Page, A.C. (1994). Blood–injury phobia. *Clinical Psychology Review*, **14**, 443–461.

Rachman, S. (1977). The conditioning theory of fear-acquisition: a critical examination. *Behaviour Research and Therapy*, **15**, 375–387.

Rose, R.J. & Ditto, W.B. (1983). A developmental-genetic analysis of common fears from early adolescence to early childhood. *Child Development*, **54**, 361–368.

Ruetz, P.P., Johnson, S.A., Callahan, R., Meade, R.C. & Smith, J.J. (1967). Fainting: a review of its mechanisms and a study in blood donors. *Medicine*, **46**, 363–384.

Selleger, C., Adamec, R., Morabia, A. & Zimmerman, M. (1988). Vasovagal syncope during rectosigmoidoscopy: report of a case. *PACE*, **11**, 346–348.

Thyer, B. & Curtis, G.C. (1984). On the diphasic nature of vasovagal fainting associated with blood–injury–illness phobia. *Pavlovian Journal of Biological Science*, **20**, 84–87.

Thyer, B., Himle, J. & Curtis, G.C. (1985). Blood–injury–illness phobia: a review. *Journal of Clinical Psychology*, **41**, 451–459.

Torgersen, S. (1979). The nature and origin of common phobic fears. *British Journal of Psychiatry*, **134**, 343–351.

Vingerhoets, A.J.J.M. (1984). Biochemical changes in two subjects succumbing to syncope. *Psychosomatic Medicine*, **46**, 95–103.

Wardle, J. & Jarvis, M. (1981). The paradoxical fear response to blood, injury and illness—a treatment report. *Behavioural Psychotherapy*, **9**, 13–24.

Weissler, A.M., Warren, J.V., Estes, E.H., McIntosh, H.D. & Leonard, J.J. (1957). Vasodepressor syncope: factors affecting cardiac output. *Circulation*, **15**, 875–882.

Westling, B.E. & Öst, L.-G. (1993). Relationship between panic attack symptoms and cognitions in panic disorder patients. *Journal of Anxiety Disorders*, **7**, 181–194.

Wolpe, J. & Lang, P. (1964). A fear schedule for use in behavior therapy. *Behaviour Research and Therapy*, **2**, 27–30.

Chapter 4

Animal Phobias

Susan J. Thorpe
and
Paul M. Salkovskis
Department of Psychiatry, University of Oxford, Oxford, UK

SPECIFIC PHOBIA OF ANIMALS: WHY BOTHER?

Specific phobias tend to be less disruptive and disabling, are associated with less co-morbidity and can be treated more quickly and easily than other anxiety disorders. They are however, the most prevalent of the anxiety disorders, and a significant proportion of sufferers are severely disabled by them. Because extremely effective treatments are now available, it is sometimes forgotten that the current ease of treatment has only come about as a result of intensive research over almost four decades, during which time continual therapeutic refinements have been driven by theory-driven experimental findings. Animal phobias in particular have played an important role in the evolution of these psychological theories of anxiety and of its effective treatment: behaviour therapy developed from early work almost exclusively confined to animal phobias (Jones, 1924; Wolpe, 1958), and the extension and amplification of this early work has been particularly important in the development of cognitive–behavioural treatments, which are now applied to a wide range of psychological problems (Hawton et al., 1989). Research into animal phobias continues to make a major contribution to the understanding of the nature of fear and the psychopathology of anxiety disorders.

Historical Perspective

Early accounts of animal phobias are mainly to be found in medical writings from early Greek and Roman perspectives and eighteenth- and nineteenth-century writings. During the intervening thirteen centuries (fifth to seventeenth), psycho-logical manifestations like theophobias and demonophobias were described by philosophers and theologians (as well as poets and playwrights) but were defined as out of the jurisdiction of science, being seen as manifestations of evil spirits and as evidence of an imbalance in the hierarchical order of the universe. The occa-sional mentions of phobias during this period are confined to plague phobia (Oxenbridge, 1576–1642), syphilophobia (Daniel Tyrner, 1667–1741) and in a parody of nosology by Benjamin Rush, who identified 18 specific phobias (some satirical) and who mentions spider phobia for the first time:

> the insect phobia. This disease is peculiar to the female sex. A spider—a flea—or a musqueto, alighting upon a lady's neck, has often produced an hysterical fit . . . (Rush, 1798, cited in Errera, 1962).

The word phobia was taken from the Greek word φοβοζ meaning panic-fear, terror, flight (Liddell & Scott, 1883). Phobos was a deity honoured by the Greeks as provoking fear and panic in their enemies. Until the middle of the nineteenth century the only use of the word had been for the symptom "hydrophobia", a term for rabies coined by Celsus, and it was another 75 years before the word attached itself firmly to a set of diagnostic criteria.

Hippocrates noted two of the earliest clinical descriptions of men suffering from unreasonable and pronounced fear. The first, Nicanor, would be "beset by terror" when he heard the sound of a flute at a banquet in the evening, though he could hear the sound with perfect equanimity during the day. The second, Damocles, was morbidly afraid of heights and "could not go near a precipice, or over a bridge, or beside even the shallowest ditch; and yet he could walk in the ditch itself". He also described a cat phobic. Hippocrates put these symptoms, along with other neurotic ones, under the heading of melancholia (suffering from an excess of black bile), one of the three major types of insanity. Temporary fears and terrors were assumed to be due to an overheating of the brain caused by a build-up of bile. Later physicians explained that "melancholic humour, being cold, cools the brain and the heart, seat of courage, and hence fear develops" (Semelaigne, 1869, cited in Errera, 1962).), and well into the eighteenth century phobic reactions remained associated with melancholias. However, following on from Hippocrates, Caelius Aurelianus placed phobias in with the manias (that is, specifically to do with the mind):

> . . . For mania fills the mind now with anger, now with gaiety, now sadness, now with nullity, now with the dread of petty things. As some people have told; so that they are afraid of caves at one time, and chasms at another, lest they fall into them; or there may be other things which frighten them.

Celsus was another early contributor to the field, who appears to have in-vented flooding as a therapeutic technique. Referring to a patient with hydropho-bia, his term for rabies, he recommends the proper course of action is to:

... throw the patient unawares into a water tank he has not seen before. If he cannot swim, let him sink under and drink, then lift him out; if he can swim, push him under at intervals so that he drinks his fill of water even against his will; for so his thirst and dread of water are removed at the same time (*trans.* Grieve, 1814).

After this there is little reference to such fears in medicine until the eighteenth century apart from those described above. Zilboorg (1941) suggests that this paucity of information is due to the changing role of the physician in the upheaval of changing social and cultural values. Outside the field of medicine, Descartes made a succinct analysis of idiosyncratic fear in *The Passions of the Soul*. He wrote:

... there is such a tie between our soul and body that when we once have joined any corporal action with any thought, one of them never presents itself without the other—and that they are not always the same actions which are joined to the same thoughts ... it is easy to conceive that the strange aversions of some, who cannot endure the smell of roses, the sight of a cat, or the like, come only from hence, that when they were but newly alive they were displeased with some such objects, or else had a fellow-feeling of their mother's resentment who was so distasted when she was with child; for it is certain there is an affinity between the motions of the mother and the child in her womb, so that whatsoever is displeasing to one offends the other; and the smell of roses may have caused some great headache in the child when it was in the cradle; or a cat may have affrighted it and none took notice of it, nor the child so much as remembered it; though the idea of that aversion he then had to roses or a cat remain imprinted in his brain to his life's end (Descartes, 1650, pp. 107–108).

Some of this is suggestive of later theories to do with conditioning, modelling and the importance of the mind in relation to the body.

In literature, Shakespeare had described animal phobic behaviour in *The Merchant of Venice*.

Some men there are that love not a gaping pig;
Some that are mad when they behold a cat ...

During the eighteenth and nineteenth centuries several attempts were made to understand and classify this "mania without delirium" (Pinel, 1748–1825), "partial insanity" or "monomania" (Esquirol, 1772–1840), "emotional delirium" (Morel, 1809–1873, himself a height phobic), and "lucid insanity" (Trelat, 1795–1879). Etiological theories included a dysfunction in the eye muscle (Benedikt, 1870), a poor upbringing (Trelat), stomach ailments (Benedikt) and a "morbid predisposition of the visceral ganglionic nervous system" (Morel). All agreed that hereditary factors were important (all cited in Errera, 1962).

In 1872 Westphal published his classical monograph *Die Agoraphobie*, which was an important step in the evolution of modern thinking about phobias. He made few pronouncements on their aetiology beyond suggesting a cerebral origin and noting that often the thought of the feared situation was as frightening as being in the situation itself, which presages contemporary thinking on anticipatory anxiety. He describes three male patients with the following symptoms:

> ... impossibility of walking through certain streets or squares, or possibility of so doing only with resultant dread of anxiety ...

Some information based on individual cases was therefore available to the physician before Freud began to formulate his detailed theories of the acquisition of phobia.

Prevalence

Epidemiological studies indicate that the point prevalence of *clinically* defined phobias in the general population reaches 11% in the USA and 13% in West Germany (Agras, Sylvester & Oliveau, 1969; Robins et al., 1984; Wittchen, 1986; Öst, 1987). Specific phobias form the largest part of this number and of these, 14% are animal phobias (Barlow, 1988). Within the subgroup of intense fears, as opposed to specific phobias, Agras, Sywester & Oliveau (1969) found differing prevalence rates per thousand of the general population, with intense fear of snakes being the most widespread (253 per 1000), followed by heights (120) and flying (109). The prevalence of *clinical* phobias was found to be different, with illness/injury phobia being most common (31 per 1000 of the general population), followed by storms (13), animals (11), agoraphobia (6), death (5), crowds (4) and heights (4).

There is evidence that animal phobia occurs more often in women than in men. A community survey by Bourdon et al. (1988), of 18,572 adults (of whom 10,954 were women) revealed that women had significantly higher rates of agoraphobia and specific phobia than men, but not of social phobia. The most common phobias were spiders, bugs, mice, snakes and heights, although the largest gender differences were found in the item concerning going out of the house alone (in agoraphobia) and, in specific phobia, two items: fear of animals and of storms. Chambless (1988) has suggested that two of the factors involved are female reproductive hormones and sociocultural factors such as sex-role stereotyping: it is, of course, part of the mythology of gender difference that women are afraid of harmless animals (mice or spiders usually) from which they are constantly having to be resucued by doughty males. Costello (1982) found that in a survey of the prevalence rates of fears and phobias amongst women, factors *not* associated with fears and phobias were social class, educational level completed, employment status or number of children at home. Liddell & Hart (1992) have shown that cultural changes, in the form of a wider range of threats towards women, have affected their perceptions of themselves and consequently their attitudes to some items on the fear survey schedule, mainly those items concerning personal safety in public places, rather than fear of animals. This may be taken as evidence of the importance of perception in the formulation of fear responses and of the relative unimportance of hormonal balance.

Natural History

Öst (1987) is one of a number of researchers to examine the age of onset in a variety of different types of specific phobia, compared to social phobia or agoraphobia, and has found that they are quite clearly differentiated. Age of onset is consistently the earliest in animal phobics, with a mean age of onset of 7 years, followed by blood phobics (mean age 9 years) and dental phobics (mean age 12 years). Claustrophobia was closer to agoraphobia (where age of onset is in the 20s) in onset age at 20 years, so that even within the subtype of specific phobia there are different ages of onset, with dental phobics having a later age of onset than animal phobics.

Following the onset of fear, the prevalence of animal phobia declines with age (Agras, Chapin & Oliveau, 1972), as many children lose their fear as they grow older. McNally & Steketee (1985) suggest that this may be due in part to individual differences in the toleration of anxiety in avoidance behaviour. There is little other evidence that there are particular personality traits or sensitivities which make people vulnerable to the acquisition of animal phobia.

AETIOLOGICAL THEORIES

The Psychoanalytic Theory

Freud attempted a systematic account of the development of specific phobias based on his interpretation of an animal phobia suffered by a young boy ("Little Hans"). According to Freud, phobias are a defence against the anxiety experienced when impulses formed by the id are being repressed, resulting in a displacement of the repressed feelings onto an object or situation with which it is symbolically connected. These objects or situations then become the phobic stimuli and the patient is able to avoid having to deal with the repressed conflicts by avoiding their symbolic correlates—closed spaces, cats, spiders and so on. The acquisition of a phobia is therefore seen as a displacement activity allowing avoidance of a real problem, often a childhood conflict. The most famous case quoted is that of Little Hans, a 5 year-old boy who was afraid to go out of the house (after an incident in which a horse and van fell down in the street in front of him) in case a horse bit him. He subsequently elaborated this fear and became afraid of blinkers and muzzles on the horses (but not of vans). Although Freud never saw him, in his correspondence with Hans' father the explanation he proffered was that boy's fear resulted from the repression and subsequent projection of his aggressive impulses, which were to do with hostility towards his father and sadism towards his mother. The motivation for this repression was a fear of castration, which Hans expressed overtly as a fear that his "widdler" would be cut off by his father. The blinkers and muzzles were seen as symbols for his father's eyeglasses and moustache.

There is little or no empirical evidence to support this view. The most serious challenge to the psychoanalytic theory is the effectiveness of symptomatic treatment, as for example in cognitive–behavioural therapy. A specific prediction from psychoanalytic theory is that, although such treatments might produce short-term relief, this will inevitably be followed by the appearance of new symptoms (symptom substitution), because the underlying conflict is unresolved (Breger & McGaugh, 1965). This does not appear to be the case.

Behavioural Theories

Fear of animals has formed the basis of behavioural theories of the aetiology of fear and phobias. Animals themselves, of course, were used in the formulation of the principles of conditioning as first described by Ivan Pavlov at the turn of the century. Pavlov and his group believed that any natural phenomenon could become a conditioned stimulus (CS), in any of the sensory modalities. Thus, a red light systematically paired with an electric shock will result in an animal's conditioned fear response to the red light alone. This led to the hypothesis that phobias could be regarded as having their origin in conditioned fears, with the phobic object being the CS. The best known early conditioning experiment was the anecdotal description of the case of "Little Albert" and the induction of an animal phobia (Watson & Rayner, 1920). In their experiment, every time Albert reached for a white rat (the CS) in order to play with it, Watson made a loud noise, the unconditioned stimulus (UCS), with a steel bar behind his head, giving him "a great fright", the unconditioned response (UCR). After five of these experiences, Albert became disturbed (the conditioned response, CR) by the sight of the rat (the conditioned stimulus, CS), even when the steel bar was not struck, so the fear associated with the loud noise became associated with the rat. The conditioning extended (generalized) to similar stimuli, such as cotton wool and the experimenter's white hair.

Conditioning Theory: Constraints

One problem with conditioning theory has been its concentration on conditioned phenomena in the physiological and behavioural dimensions. According to Lang (1971), "emotional behaviours are multiple system responses—verbal–cognitive, motor and physiological events—that interact through interoceptive (neural and hormonal) and exteroceptive channels of communication. All systems are controlled or influenced by brain mechanisms, but the level of the important centres of influence (cortical or subcortical, limbic or brainstem) are varied and, like the resulting behaviours, partially independent". This is sensible in the light of the crucial nature of the adaptive benefits conferred upon an individual, who is primed to be alert to possible predation by a variety of other species and who is able to be flexible in response to such threats. It is in contrast to the two-factor theory, which places the emphasis on avoidance behaviour as the consequence of a fearful response, which has itself the consequence of immediate fear reduction but also results in long-term fear maintenance. Bandura (1971) endorsed the view that changes in *each* of the three subsystems are often reflected in the others, so that someone who is bitten by a dog "can *simultaneously* produce a dislike of dogs, endow a dog with fear-arousing properties, and establish dog-avoidance behaviour", but this is not always the case. However, according to Rachman & Hodgson (1974) there can be, and often is, discordance in the subsystems and in the way they change. Lang (1971) points out that human speech is a far more refined and subtle measure of emotion than any physiological measure can be, highlighting a problem in the experimental data accrued by conditioning theorists, who concentrate on the physiological response data and ignore self-reported emotion.

Another problem with the conditioning hypothesis for the acquisition of animal phobia is that conditioning theory alone cannot account for the fact that not all people who have traumatic experiences with animals subsequently become phobic (DiNardo, Guzy & Bak, 1988) and that not all animal phobics can remember an unpleasant early experience with their phobic object. DiNardo et al. (1988) found that in a group of dog phobics, nearly two-thirds had experienced a conditioning event in which a dog featured and in over half of these incidents pain had been experienced. However, two-thirds of a non-phobic control group had undergone the same experience in the same proportion without subsequent phobic acquisition. DiNardo et al. (1988) noted that all of their dog phobics "believed that fear and physical harm were likely consequences of an encounter with a dog, while very few non-fearful subjects had such expectations ... an exaggerated expectation of harm appears to be a factor in the maintenance of fear" (p. 244). It could also be that the fear itself causes such illusory correlates between the stimuli and the likelihood of an aversive event, while also being the result of this bias.

More problematic evidence for the conditioning theory of animal phobia has come from experiments failing to induce fear in humans by conditioning (English, 1929; Thorndike, 1935; Davison, 1968). Although a majority of phobic patients in a Swedish sample (approximately 60%) attribute their phobia to a conditioning experience (Öst & Hugdahl, 1981; Öst, 1985; Hugdahl & Öst, 1985), only 50% of animal phobics in the survey attributed their phobia to a conditioning experience. Merckelbach, Arntz & de Jong (1991) found that 57% of spider phobics reported conditioning experiences, although modelling was most often reported (71%). Murray & Foote (1979) found little evidence of conditioning experiences in their 60 snake phobics and Kleinknecht (1982) found that only a quarter of tarantula-phobic subjects attributed their fear to an unpleasant experience concerning a spider.

Rachman (1977) tried to reconcile these data by suggesting that there may be at least three pathways to fear. These are: (a) direct acquisition by conditioning experience(s); (b) indirect/vicarious acquisition—direct or indirect observations of fearful people; and (c) transmission of information likely to induce fear. So, conditioning processes may be involved in the aetiology of some animal phobias, but other processes are also involved in their development, including modelling and beliefs (see below). Also the physiological, behavioural and cognitive components interact with each other and are likely to have differential effects.

Clearly, conditioning theory alone does not deal adequately with the range of mechanisms involved in the maintenance of anxiety responses. This has led to the proposal of an addition to the theory of fear acquisition, derived from the evolutionary perspective. This is known as "preparedness".

Preparedness

Seligman (1971), noting that phobias are highly resistant to extinction and are generally confined to a relatively limited set of objects which seem to be non-arbitrary, proposed that they are instances of "prepared" learning. According to preparedness theory, over the course of thousands of generations, organisms evolve *preparedness* to learn associations which are likely to enhance survival (i.e. between fear and stimuli which are dangerous in the "natural range" of the species), whilst survival-irrelevant associations are *unprepared* and associations which would have negative implications for survival are *contra-prepared* (see Chapter 16 for a fuller evaluation of this theory).

Seligman suggested that the acquisition of phobias is an example of biologically prepared learning, because the objects of phobic reactions are generally animals and situations which may have threatened humans in our historical ecological niche, first as foragers and then as hunter/gatherers. Given that this stage of our evolutionary history lasted for many hundreds of thousands of years and it is only in the last few centuries that we have been relatively removed from the natural world (and only in the West), then it is reasonable to assume that some of the evolved mechanisms in our brains may be specialized for vigilance to attack by poisonous or toothful animals. The failure of laboratory-based attempts to induce fears could therefore be attributed to the use of unprepared associations which are not adaptively significant.

Some limited evidence for preparedness theory has come from conditioning studies in which different types of stimuli were used as the CS (Öhman, Erixon & Löfberg, 1975; Öhman, 1979; Öhman, Dimberg & Öst, 1985). Galvanic skin response (GSR) proved more difficult to extinguish after it had been paired with snakes an spiders than after pairing with houses or flowers. However, these studies have concentrated on the conditioning of a physiological arousal response as measured by skin conductance, and have proven difficult to replicate. Thus the specific prediction made by Seligman that preparedness should facilitate acquisition of phobias has not been borne out by subsequent research (for a review, see McNally, 1987), and the preparedness of specific phobias does not relate to behavioural treatment outcome (de Silva, Rachman & Seligman, 1977).

A related proposition was put forward by Bennett-Levy & Marteau (1984). They examined the characteristics which are associated with humans and suggested that preparedness to fear certain animals could be a function of general fear-evoking properties and a discrepancy from the human form, so that "ugly, slimy, speedy or sudden-moving animals are experienced as less approachable and more fear-provoking than animals without these qualities" (p. 40) and that the perception of harmful properties overrode even these concerns: rats were rated the most feared stimuli because they were perceived as potentially harmful. Again, this makes sense from an evolutionary perspective.

Modelling/Observational Conditioning

Mineka and colleagues have demonstrated vicarious learning of animal phobias by observation in primates (Mineka et al., 1984; Mineka & Cook, 1986; Tomarken, Mineka & Cook, 1989; Cook & Mineka, 1989). They showed that young monkeys acquired an "intense and persistent fear of snakes" on becoming afraid after seeing adult monkeys behave fearfully towards real, toy and model snakes which were presented for 40 seconds, six times a session. Six sessions were carried out over a period of 3 weeks. Given that the sight of an intensely fearful adult is intrinsically aversive to infant monkeys, this work is an example of conditioning where the snake (CS) is associated with the sight of a fearful adult (UCS), so that the snake subsequently comes to elicit fear (CR). Mineka & Cook (1986) also explored the possibility of the transmission of an immunizing experience and found that young monkeys who had previously seen adults interacting in a non-fearful way with snakes did not subsequently become afraid when subjected to observational conditioning. This "inoculation" is likely to have the effect of reducing the likelihood of inappropriate fears being accidentally acquired to common and everyday stimuli and situations.

Evidence for preparedness in observational fear learning in primates was found by Cook & Mineka (1989). They demonstrated that primates acquired a fear of fear-relevant objects (toy snakes and toy crocodiles) but not of fear-irrelevant objects (flowers and a toy rabbit) after observational conditioning experiences. Research by Masataka (1993) has indicated that a further element in observational conditioning of fear may be to do with the effects of the experience of live, moving insects prior to being exposed to conditioning trials. Baby squirrel monkeys fed entirely upon fruit did not acquire fear of snakes, while those who had an addition of live insects to their diet *did* acquire a fear of snakes during modelling trials.

The other significant ingredient in this work was the use of *infant* primates. The acquisition of insect and animal phobias takes place in humans during early childhood, the period during which these pose the greatest potential threat (by virtue of the size and competencies of the human infant). Thus, preparedness may operate during a developmentally critical period; the greatest preparedness may be for associations where adult fear is the UCS. Clearly survival would be enhanced when fear acquisition does not require the pain of a venomous bits, and where danger information is transmitted as a result of no greater harm than mild emotional disturbance, which arises from seeing a fearful adult.

The Cognitive Paradigm

Cognitive developments within conditioning theory (e.g. Davey, 1989, 1992a,b; Mackintosh, 1983; Rescorla, 1988) invite a re-examination of Seligman's (1971) influential assertion that phobias are irrational and therefore are not subject to cognitive influences. This is especially relevant given the recent rapid development of cognitive approaches to the understanding and treatment of anxiety. The cognitive theory of emotions is based on the idea that it is not things *per se* which evoke fear, but the appraisal of those things. That is, the cognitive account of anxiety is predicated on the notion that the appraisal of threat is necessary and sufficient for the experience of anxiety (Beck, Emery & Greenberg, 1985; Salkovskis, 1991). Patients suffering from anxiety can be regarded as having acquired/learned a particular sensitivity to potential harm in situations which most others would not perceive as threatening (Beck, Emery & Greenberg, 1985; Clark, 1986). The degree of anxiety experienced in a given situation is proportional to:

$$\frac{\text{Perceived probability of danger} \times \text{Perceived awfulness}}{\text{Perceived ability to cope} + \text{Perceived rescue factors}}$$

Once a situation is perceived as threatening, several factors may operate to maintain inappropriately high levels of these belief elements. This is clear in the case of animal phobias: First, hypervigilance (or hyperattention): when a person believes themselves to be in danger from the encroachments of, for example, a bird, they constantly scan their environment for any signs of threat. This can lead to them noticing things of which they might otherwise be unaware (e.g. a shadow moving along the ground, a feather in a cushion, the inadequate security devices on a bird cage, the sound of birdsong in the morning). Once noticed, these observations reinforce the phobic's sense of threat, making it appear that they are in imminent and constant danger of being confronted with the very things that they fear most. Second, avoidance: phobics believe that escape and avoidance have prevented "the worst" from happening. Avoidance and escape responses therefore have the effect of transforming what would otherwise have been a disconfirmation of danger into a perceived "near miss", reinforcing the belief that the danger is a real one (Salkovskis, 1991, 1996; Salkovskis, Clark & Gelder, 1996). A bird phobic may keep all the windows closed, block off the chimneys and avoid going anywhere there may be birds—extremely constraining due to the universal presence of these in our cities as well as in more natural surroundings. These measures may result in fewer encounters and consequently less anxiety, which will usually reinforce the avoidance behaviours. Third, if autonomic arousal forms part of the focus of the person's fears (for example, in the phobic who believes that the anxiety of confronting a bird could kill them), anxiety can increase physiological arousal and in turn increase anxiety, forming an entry point to the vicious circle characteristic of panic attacks (Clark, 1986). Fourth, anxiety appears to produce an increase in the perceived probability of danger (Butler & Mathews, 1983) so that an encounter with a bird, for a bird phobic, will feel inevitable and immutable.

INFORMATION-PROCESSING, COGNITIVE AND PSEUDO-COGNITIVE APPROACHES

Williams et al. (1988) proposed an information-processing model of anxiety. They suggest that there are a number of operations performed in the brain which happen pre-attentively, including the "sensory registration, semantic labelling, associative spread and disambiguation of a stimulus". This is a pre-attentive stage of processing, when there is a bombardment of sensory information upon the brain's receptors which needs to be filtered and made sense of. At this stage in the processing of information, Williams et al. (1988) proposed that all information is ambiguous. The ambiguity starts to narrow when the activation of all these meanings interacts with the activation of the context. Then a dominant meaning emerges which leads to the rejection of the other possible interpretations. Williams et al. (1988) also hypothesize that a mechanism exists in *pre-conscious* processes which judges the emotional valence of the situation. This has the effect of orienting the organism towards or away from the stimulus. Williams et al. (1988) also suggest that this in effect creates a processing priority and that it is at this, still pre-attentive, stage that anxious people orientate their attention towards threatening stimuli, while non-anxious people orientate attention away from threat.

Emotion, Conditioning and Cognition

Foa & Kozak (1986) follow Lang (1984) in proposing that emotions are encoded in networks in memory that include information about stimulus features, the individual's responses (including verbal, physiological and behavioural responses) and information about the meaning of the stimulus and response features. Anxiety changes result from a modification of the threat elements that are connected to the stimulus and response elements in the structure. When the emotion experienced is fear, the network serves as a template for escape and avoidance reactions and the information includes knowledge of the dangerousness of the stimuli or responses, as well as physiological activity to do with escape. They also concur with Lang (1971) in suggesting that emotions are evoked when a "good match" is found for incoming information amongst existing memory structures. Emotion is therefore automatically called up each time there is this congruence between internal representations and external events.

Mogg, Mathews & Weinman (1987) came to a similar conclusion to Foa & Kozak (1986) in outlining a general multi-stage process which reconciles the automatic orientating response to threat with a seeming absence of memory bias. They hypothesized that anxious individuals are biased towards threat information at an early stage in the process leading to a heightened detection capability and speed of recognition. Once the stimulus is found to be potentially dangerous it may then be suppressed or avoided in some way, leading to a less efficient recall/recognition strategy. They ascribe the motivation for this to a possible reduction in the experience of feelings of anxiety, and a potential consequence of this inhibition in relation to the full processing of stimuli may be a poorer memory for such stimuli (Williams et al., 1988). Unfortunately, this does not seem sensible in the case of real animal stimuli, where it is of distinct advantage in survival terms to be aware of unexpected movement in the field of vision. Other studies using agoraphobics (Nunn, Stephenson & Whalen, 1984) and panic patients (McNally, Foa & Donnell, 1989; Norton et al., 1988) have shown evidence of such memory bias. The model suggests that, in animal phobia, the encoding of information about the actual characteristics of the animal, and the reality of its potential to cause actual bodily harm, is avoided (cognitive avoidance), resulting in weaker associations between internal representations. This automatic cognitive avoidance of the phobic object prevents the extinction of the fear response. Thus, this theory is not cognitively based, but is a direct derivation of two-process theory which happens to focus on cognitive (i.e. information-processing) *measures*. That is, the measures used in its evaluation are cognitive, but the foundations of this theory are not novel, being almost exclusively behavioural. Again, the evidence for this in animal phobics is equivocal. Due to the discrete and concrete nature of the stimuli and the fact that animals live in the real world and move autonomously in that world, then human reactions are likely to be different to real, live stimuli than to (often abstract) interoceptive cues.

McNally et al. (1989) suggested that the priority processing of anxiety-related stimuli during the process of encoding should lead to a more robust memory trace for anxiety words, with a consequent enhancement of memory retrieval. In their study, subjects showed better recall for fear-relevant stimuli which they had processed using a self-referent encoding task. Conversely, Mogg et al. (1987), using a similar self-referent processing strategy, found that anxious subjects showed poorer recognition and a trend towards poorer recall of threatening words, so the evidence for the effect of anxiety on memory has been more ambiguous. Mogg et al. (1987) found no evidence of memory bias towards threatening words in patients diagnosed as suffering from generalized anxiety disorder. Their results indicate a poorer memory for threatening words in anxious patients, leading to a reformulation of the schema theory and including some inhibitory process in anxiety which interferes with memory. As phobics respond to the object of their phobia in a way which suggests hypervigilance (being aware before anyone else of a spider in the corner, noticing shapes similar to spiders in innocuous objects where no one else would make the connection), the results would suggest that in other forms of anxiety at least, an initial orientation to threat may be connected with impaired memory functions to do with the threatening material, perhaps as a function of the cognitive correlate of behavioural avoidance, which inhibits memory. In support of this, phobics often report during treatment that they have never really looked at, for instance, a spider, indicating that an initial attentive bias may rapidly be displaced by the need to be attentive to the possible avenues of escape from the situation. Mogg et al. (1987) suggest that this "vigilance-avoidance pattern" (p. 97) at the processing level may maintain the disorder by the combination of heightened awareness for threat cues and a subsequent effort to reduce the anxiety caused by that awareness by repressing the memory of it. This is consistent with conditioning theories of panic and phobias. They also go on to state that cognitive bias is present in both depression and anxiety, but that the nature of the bias may be "fundamentally different" (p. 97) in these emotional disorders.

Memory and Phobia

Experimentation on the effect of phobic anxiety on memory has so far concentrated on using semantic or quiescent (dead) stimuli, with inconsistent and conflicting results. Given that spider phobics seem particularly afraid of the unpredictability of the movement and direction that spiders take, and that one of the characteristics most noted by both non-phobics and spider phobics in relation to spiders is "creeping/crawling" (Davey, 1992b), the logical step is to use real spiders moving in real settings to test whether any cognitive avoidance (as evinced by impaired recognition and recall memory) comes into play when the element of movement is added, enabling further conclusions to be drawn about the relationship between danger and cognitions and to bring the experimental situation closer to that experienced in real life. The use of real-life stimuli is also presumed to be more meaningful to the phobic. As fear and vigilance are part of a highly evolved survival mechanism, it does not seem to make sense for an individual to be hyperattentive to a moving threat and then to suppress the information, unless the information so suppressed is only to do with the features and characteristics of the threat object rather than the movement, and it is this which is of paramount importance, rather than extraneous information about colour and shape. If the above theorizing is taken to its logical conclusion, this would lead to a heightened attentional bias for movement and direction, along with a heightened response detection and a decrease in stimulus feature detection. If the situation is sufficiently meaningful, then this may override these other considerations. At this point it is therefore crucial that the nature of attentional processes be examined. Attention is the other process said to be involved in the functioning of fear networks.

Attention

Macleod (1987) has said that the future refinement of clinical treatments may depend on an "ability to identify the precise nature of the actual processing biases

which underlie any particular disorder" (Macleod, 1987, p. 181). He saw in the
Stroop test just such a sensitive measure. Foa & McNally (1986) and Watts et al.
(1986) reported that behaviour therapy can eliminate attentional bias in both
obsessive–compulsive disorder and spider phobia. In both cases, behaviour
therapy was spread over a number of sessions and, in the latter case, in a
subsequent avoidance test there was no significant improvement. Unfortunately,
Watts et al. (1986) have used an unconventional statistical analysis which renders
interpretation of their findings difficult. Lavy, van den Hout & Arntz (1993a,b)
used one-session treatment for spider phobia (Öst, 1989), with an elaboration
condition (where patients were encouraged to notice spider feature details) to
prevent cognitive avoidance. Before treatment, spider phobics, but not controls,
showed increased response latencies to spider words compared to control words,
both negative and neutral. After one-session treatment the decrease in the difference between response to spider words and negative/neutral in the phobic group,
as measured by an interference index, was significantly greater than in the non-
phobic group. In this study elaboration made no difference to the outcome and
the authors' conclusion was that there is no evidence to suggest that elaboration
enhances the disintegration of the fear network, although they also point out that
preventing elaboration in the spider phobics undergoing treatment was extremely difficult and not very successful. This study did not use matched untreated phobics as control subjects and this causes large baseline differences in
many of the initial measures taken which invalidate the findings. It is difficult to
assess how far the process of verbal elaboration matches the process of the
elaboration of internal representations as envisaged by Williams et al. (1988).
Thorpe & Salkovskis (1997b) tested spider phobics before and after one-session
treatment for spider phobia, or a comparable waiting period, using a spider-word
Stroop test and questionnaires in which they rated spider-relevant threat beliefs.
Compared with untreated spider phobic controls the treated phobics changed
significantly in their negative beliefs about spiders after treatment, but were no
different to the controls in their reaction time latencies to spider stimuli in the
Stroop test, indicating that it is the modification of threat beliefs which is important in changing the response to phobic stimuli. The threat-specific Stroop test
appears to be, at the very least, an ambiguous measure of fear-related cognitive
processes.

Beliefs

Traditional accounts of the aetiology of animal phobias have concentrated on the
amount of expectation of physical harm suffered by phobics. This is partly because a number of animal phobics referred for treatment have traced the onset of
their fear back to an actual physical attack (Marks, 1987; McNally & Steketee,
1985). Other, more common phobias (snake and spider in particular) have been
explained by Seligman (1971) as being "prepared" in an evolutionary sense, in
that animals potentially harmful to prehistoric people may in some way trigger

fear responses in some individuals. This has also contributed to the previously held belief in the non-cognitive nature of animal phobias, as has Öhman's (1986) suggestion that the fear may originate in the predatory defence system, which facilitates animals in escaping from predators. A combination of both factors seems likely, where animal physical characteristics call forth a range of escape responses and this leads to the formation of particular cognitions. So, these evolutionary ideas can be taken as a possible explanation for the supposed irrationality of fixed beliefs, while also suggesting the type of beliefs to be expected in phobic consciousness. The emphasis on such physicality and harm has led to an empirical concentration on the cognitions to do with harm potential and with behavioural and physiological responses. These seem to be the natural outcome of evolved predispositions, but another line of enquiry concerning coping or contamination fear should also be followed, in line with the theoretical stances outlined above. The physical nature of animal phobias has led to a concentration on physical harm to the detriment of more esoteric concerns and, in order to redress the balance of enquiry, it may be useful to divide cognitions in animal phobics in relation to their phobic object into cognitions to do with primary appraisal (beliefs about properties the object/environment may be thought to have), secondary appraisal (beliefs about coping), and beliefs about future harm (however imminent that future may be). In this way the meaning that a particular phobic object has for a phobic may become clearer and hence changeable.

Rachman & Levitt (1988) examined the relationship between predicted and actual fear experiences in phobic subjects repeatedly confronting aversive events. Claustrophobic volunteers were asked to enter a small enclosed space several times. Their anxiety levels were obtained on each occasion, particularly levels immediately before entry. Anxious subjects consistently over predicted the fear associated with their phobic situations, and these overpredictions were particularly likely to follow underpredictions. Reductions in fear were most likely to follow overpredictions, but there was evidence of an inherent bias towards the overprediction of subsequent anxiety and pain (i.e. the belief that the next time will be worse). Avoidance behaviour may follow from this tendency, based on the collation of material from past experience which then becomes part of a system of beliefs, or meaningful cognitions, which in turn lead to concomitant avoidant and fearful behaviours. This has not yet been examined in animal phobics. Hitherto, assessment of cognitions in specific phobia has come from three main sources:

1. The work by Watts & Sharrock (1984) on cohesion of constructs in spider phobia and the construction of a questionnaire incorporating measures of vigilance, preoccupation, avoidance-coping, factual knowledge and cognitive–behavioural items. Cognitions listed in the questionnaire do not access specific subjective beliefs about the nature of the specific object, or subjective beliefs about the probable consequences to the phobic person of interaction with the phobic object. They are a measure of phobic intensity as

a corollary of metacognitive constructs, rather than an exploration of the underlying cognitions from which these are derived.

2. Work carried out by two groups on the aetiology and maintenance of animal phobia. McNally & Steketee (1985) looked at a variety of animal phobics (10 snake, 4 cat, 4 bird, 2 dog, 2 spider) and examined the incidence of distressing stimulus characteristics (movement, 77%; physical appearance, 64%; sound, 27%; and touch, 23%) and feared consequences (panic, 91%; physical attack, 41%; insanity, 18%; injury while fleeing, 14%; and heart attack, 9%). The second group worked with dog phobics and also confirmed that an exaggerated expectation of harm is a factor in the maintenance of fear responses (DiNardo, Guzy & Bak, 1988; DiNardo et al., 1988). Of the cognitions to do with potential actual harm, the most prevalent appears to be concerned with fear of panic responses (although these may differ from the panic responses of panic patients, for whom panic means death, losing control and so on), followed by fear of actual physical harm, although the secondary hidden cognitions to do with the causal beliefs of this remain mysterious.

3. Work by Öst (1989) and Öst, Šalkovskis & Hellström (1991) on one-session treatment of spider phobia, which challenges the beliefs held by individual spider phobics, once they have been garnered. Salkovskis (1991) has emphasized the importance of "safety-seeking behaviours" which the anxious person believes have saved him/her from disaster, and has pointed out that the content of these cognitions provides a logical context for anxiety responses.

The Watts & Sharrock (1984) questionnaire concentrates on the operational and behavioural side of phobic responding; McNally & Steketee (1985) concentrate on cognitions derived from underlying beliefs, rather than the specific beliefs themselves, as does the DiNardo, Guzy & Bak (1988) experiment; and Öst, Salkovskis & Hellström (1991) concentrate on methodological issues and only make mention of the need to bring out and examine catastrophic thoughts, without giving specific examples other than, "I will lose control".

Conscious cognitions concerning the phobic object, stimuli, response and so on are present, specific and identifiable in animal phobics. These cognitions are meaningful at the propositional level and provide a logical framework for phobic beliefs in a similar way to that in which cognitions in panic disorder contribute to the continuance of panic attacks. The implicational meaning of a feared animal will be an emergent property arising from these propositions. If a bird phobic believes that terrible harm will follow from the sighting of a bird, whether it is in the form of having eyes pecked out or of having physiological discomfiture, it is reasonable within this framework that birds should become objects of avoidance. Similarly, it is reasonable that the same bird phobic should believe that it was only his/her safety-seeking action which prevented him/her from being harmed by the bird. Ultimately, the meaning of a bird for a bird phobic is very different to the meaning a bird has for a non-phobic, or to an ornithologist.

Thorpe & Salkovskis (1995) found that specific phobics have a range of negative beliefs about their phobic object which are identifiable and which together form a logical framework for phobic fear responses. These beliefs form an important part of the meaning which the phobic object has for the phobic person. This meaning is not only to do with the possible harm the bird/frog/spider/snake could inflict, but also involves beliefs about the phobics' ability to cope (with the bird and with themselves), subjective negative evaluations of the appearance of the bird and beliefs about the efficacy of avoidance of contact with the bird, or escape from it if such contact is unavoidable. The meaning also has emotional content, which may cause the different beliefs to cohere. The basis for this proposal lies in the finding here that negative cognitions about with harm and coping are highly correlated to feelings of fear and avoidance. This meaning may not be evident to the non-phobic observer. Salkovskis argues that:

> The rationality or irrationality of a person's beliefs to the *outside observer* is not the key issue. The degree of anxiety is proportional to the immediate personal and idiosyncratic appraisal of threat; in the case of panic attacks, the *catastrophic* nature of the misinterpretations generates spectacular levels of anxiety incomprehensible to the observer, who does not share the patient's assumptions (and bodily sensations) (Salkovskis, 1991, p. 13).

In the Thorpe & Salkovskis (1995) study, cognitions were divided into three categories—harm, coping and disgust—and these were looked at in relation to measures of phobic fear, interference in daily life, and avoidance in three groups of subjects: non-phobic controls; phobic controls (mostly animal but not spider); and spider phobics. The intensity of fear experienced by the phobics is related to the strength of negative beliefs about harm and coping, while interference and general avoidance were related only to the strength of negative beliefs about coping. Disgust beliefs appeared to be related neither to phobic fear nor to interference, neither were they related to the amount of *avoidance* of their phobic object estimated by phobics. This does not support the view that revulsion leads to avoidant behaviour, as suggested by Matchett & Davey (1991).

It would appear, then, that in animal phobics, thoughts are composed of a variety of beliefs which together contribute to the meaning the animal/insect/spider has for the phobic. These beliefs are to do with the amount of perceived harm emanating from the animal itself (possible physical harm or contamination), the amount of harm experienced by the phobic (going mad, having hysterics, paralysis, syncope) combined with a feeling of helplessness (not able to cope, feeling trapped, unable to escape). These beliefs are all closely related to levels of emotional intensity and are important in the maintenance of the phobia.

The question remains as to why otherwise normal and rational people should have extremely irrational ideas about animals which other people see as harmless or even endearing and lovable. Psychoanalysts would suggest that it is some repressed instinct or hidden childhood memory, behaviourists that it is a learned response and as such unavailable to conscious scrutiny. There is some current speculation that deficits in the cognitive processing system are such that they engender strange ideas of the type noted here, but no evidence has been conclu-

sive so far (Thorpe & Salkovskis, 1997a,b). An alternative explanation is that
these ideas are based on a high-level construction of information which is an
emergent property of underlying systemic functioning: what Teasdale (1993)
describes as the "generic, holistic" level.

Disgust

Until recently phobias have been seen as exclusively associated with the emotion
of anxiety, as opposed to other emotional responses. However, two research
groups have recently suggested an additional association between *disgust* and
animal fears and phobias. Watts (1986) was the first to suggest that spider phobics
had an element of disgust in their response to spiders, "and that it is the element
of disgust (in spider phobics) which interferes with the recall of spider words" in
a recall task (Watts, 1986, p. 299), while Matchett & Davey (1991) have made a
more specifically causal link by suggesting that some animals may become objects
of phobic avoidance by nature of their having revulsive properties to do with
disease avoidance/contamination fear. The suggestion is that there may be cognitive avoidance of disgust stimuli going on at the automatic processing level, which
interferes with the priming and elaboration of stimuli perceived to be disgusting. This helps to perpetuate the phobic response by the process of negative
reinforcement.

It has been shown that aversive conditioning is particularly effective, fast-
acting and long-lasting when the UCR is nausea (Garcia & Koelling, 1966;
Garcia, Rusiniak & Brett, 1977). Several researchers have previously proposed
that taste aversions may be of relevance in the acquisition of phobias (e.g.
Seligman, 1971; Rachman, 1978). Wolves and coyotes, for example, have taken
extreme avoidant action of lambs when those lambs have been associated with
previous sickness.

It remains difficult to see how this translates to phobia. Following an unpleasant experience after a party, people often describe an aversion to a particular
flavour of alcohol. However, few would then describe these people as phobic of,
for example, whisky, the next time they come into contact with it. It may be that
the link is between taste aversion and *avoidance* behaviour, rather than fear,
which is known to be a component in the behaviour of spider phobics in relation
to spiders and has been seen as a part of the maintenance of phobic responses.

Matchett & Davey (1991) found that measures of disgust and contamination
sensitivity were highly correlated with scores on the animal subscale of the Fear
Survey Schedule (Wolpe & Lang, 1964). In addition, disgust and contamination
sensitivity correlated with fear of animals normally considered to be fear-relevant
(as defined by Bennett-Levy & Marteau, 1984), but mostly not physically harmful
(e.g. camel, rat, eagle, spider, snake, cockroach, maggot, snake) but did not
correlate with animals considered to be physically harmful, attacking or predatory (shark, tiger, lion, bear, snake, jellyfish, wolf). However, these results were
obtained from non-phobic subjects.

There is some evidence from research into taste aversion and contamination that is consistent with the view that the disgust reaction can be acquired very easily, is associated primarily with food but is also associated with objects previously in contact with disgust-inducing stimuli which have transferred their properties to these objects. It may also be associated with contamination fear through familial or cultural transmission. Disgust may lead to avoidant behaviour; taste aversion definitely does. Rozin & Fallon (1987) suggest that there is a substantial overlap between people's perception of disgusting and dangerous objects. They also suggest that objects evoking disgust are either animals, parts of animals, the bodily products of animals (faeces, urine, mucus) or objects that have been in contact with these, which resemble them or which are associated with spoilage and decay. Watts (1986) and more recently, Davey (1992), has seen the area of disgust as potentially accounting for some aspects of the acquisition and maintenance of some animal phobias. Thorpe & Salkovskis (1995), however, showed that disgust does not appear to be related to phobic intensity, neither does exposure significantly increase disgust feelings towards spiders by spider phobics. They also found that animal phobics were significantly less likely than controls to associate their phobic object with beliefs about its disgustingness. This is due in part to the fact that the phobic disgust response seems to be different to the non-phobic disgust response: the indications are that the important features of phobic disgust are not those conventionally considered disgusting.

TREATMENTS

Treatments for animal phobias have been derived from the theories discussed above and can be grouped under the headings of psychoanalytic, behavioural and, most recently, cognitive–behavioural therapy. Drugs have not been found to be effective as treatment for animal phobias ("No psychotropic drug has been demonstrated to be effective in the treatment of simple phobias"; Fyer, 1987, p. 190). Treatments are discussed elsewhere, but it might be helpful to discuss the specialized and particular treatment of spider phobia here.

New developments have included the increasing use of cognitive change in therapy, based on the cognitive approach. The culmination of the drawing together of these ideas about anxiety reduction has led to the creation of *cognitive–behavioural therapy*. In the field of therapy for specific phobias, this has been further refined into one-session treatment for specific phobias (Öst, 1989; Öst, Salkovskis & Hellström, 1991; Thorpe & Salkovskis, 1997b). This treatment consists of exposure *in vivo* combined with modelling and with the alteration of cognitions to do with both the phobic object, responses to it, and with the coping strategies of the phobic person (behavioural and cognitive) as they pertain to fear and avoidance. Treatment consists of a combination of prolonged graded exposure, modelling and information. Therapy begins with an interview identifying the individual's responses to spiders in the areas of cognitions, physiology and behaviour. The nature of anxiety, arousal and the relation between avoidance and the maintenance of phobia is discussed and the subject's negative beliefs about spiders are identified and challenged, as are any distorted ideas concerning their own control of themselves and the predictability of their responses.

The therapist demonstrates to the spider phobic the explicit behavioural goal of the exercise, which is to able to catch spiders in a glass and to remove them. The subject practises with a glass and a piece of card until they feel confident in the use of this technique. Therapy continues with the phobic following the example of the therapist by first holding the spider in the jar, then directing the spider around a clear plastic bowl with a pen and lastly, with a finger. During this and subsequent stages the phobic's beliefs about the spider and their reactions to contact with it are closely monitored and any negative beliefs discussed and challenged. Each stage continues until the spider phobic's anxiety level has dropped to a negligible level. The final activity of each stage involves the subject manipulating the spider on the hands, having first watched the therapist. Then a larger spider is introduced and the process begins again. At all times the therapist emphasizes the way in which the spider could be controlled and its movements predicted. The session ends when the phobic can handle all the spiders with little or no anxiety, and can relax while a spider is out of sight either on the arm, the back or the head. The session is videotaped so that phobic and therapist can remind themselves of what has taken place during treatment and how much they have accomplished. They are then given instructions on how to maintain their improvement by practising, any questions are answered and they are sent home with one of the spiders in a jar, in order to keep practising while at home.

The purpose is to expose the patient to his/her feared object in a controlled way in a calm environment and enable him/her to stay in the situation until a belief in the non-occurrence of the feared consequence is assimilated. The meaning of the phobic object is thus changed and absorbed, along with an emotional change from phobic fear to a more normal reaction. The patient must continue to carry out exposure in future situations to maintain the therapeutic effects of the session, and is given the tools to do this. In contrast to the ideas about the relative importance of active and passive exposure posited by de Silva & Rachman (1981), Arntz & Lavy (1993) have shown that elaboration (or engaged exposure) did not potentiate the effects of the exposure treatment during one-session treatment with spider phobics and it is suggested that the processing of information seems to occur spontaneously when the patient is undergoing the exposure treatment. One-session treatment is not only an effective treatment: its brevity makes it a potentially important tool for research.

CONCLUSION

Animal phobias are much more complex in their aetiology than it first appears, and much more resistant to extinction than is accounted for by purely behavioural theorizing. Cognitive theories have moved away from the simple notion that merely providing contradictory information is enough to modify beliefs and therefore anxiety. They have also moved away from the idea that cognitive change in itself, as brought about by the power of logic, will be enough to change emotion. Conducting effective belief modification is a complex undertaking, even with stimuli as simple and circumscribed as that found in animal phobia. If the nature of phobic beliefs and the processes involved in their modification were better understood, then therapeutic efforts could be more precisely directed. What is required is a true paradigm shift away from the theoretical underpinnings of two-process conditioning theory (even when presented in the guise of information-processing). The contribution of belief-based cognitive theories to the treatment of other anxiety disorders is well established. Theoretical refinements of our understanding of the nature of meaning involved in emotional problems (Teasdale, 1993) and the link between beliefs and behaviour (Salkovskis, 1991; Thorpe & Salkovskis, in press), as well as a more precise evaluation of the necessary elements going towards the making of meaning, should allow yet further progress in the understanding and treatment of specific phobia in general, and animal phobia in particular.

ACKNOWLEDGEMENTS

Paul Salkovskis is Wellcome Trust Senior Research Fellow in Basic Biomedical Science. Susan Thorpe is supported by a grant from the Wellcome Trust.

REFERENCES

Agras, W.S., Sylvester, D. & Oliveau, D. (1969). The epidemiology of common fears and phobia. *Comprehensive Psychiatry*, **10**, 151–156.
Agras, W.S., Chapin, H.N. & Oliveau, D. (1972). The natural history of phobia: course and prognosis. *Archives of General Psychiatry*, **26**, 315–317.
Arntz, A. & Lavy, E. (1993). Does stimulus elaboration potentiate exposure *in vivo* treatment? Two forms of one-session treatment of spider phobia. *Behavioural Psychotherapy*, **21**, 1–12.
Bandura, A. (1971). *Principles of Behaviour Modification*. New York: Holt, Rinehart & Winston.
Barlow, D.H. (1988). *Anxiety and Its Disorders: the Nature and Treatment of Anxiety and Panic*. New York: Guildford.
Beck, A.T., Emery, G. & Grenberg (1985). *Anxiety Disorders and Phobias: a Cognitive Perspective*. New York: Basic Books.
Benedikt (1870). Uber Platzwindel. *Allgemeine Wiener Medizinische Zeitung*, **15**, 488.
Bennett-Levy, J. & Marteau, T. (1984). Fear of animals: what is prepared? *British Journal of Psychology*, **75**, 37–42.
Bourdon, K.H., Boyd, J.H., Rae, D.S. & Burns, B.J. (1988). Gender differences in phobias: results of the ECA community survey. *Journal of Anxiety Disorders*, **2**, 227–241.
Breger, L. & McGaugh, J.L. (1965). Critique and reformulation of "learning theory" approaches to psychotherapy and neurosis. *Psychological Bulletin*, **63**, 338–358.

Butler, G. & Mathews, A. (1983). Cognitive processes in anxiety. *Advances in Behaviour Research and Therapy*, **5**, 51–62.
Chambless, D.L. (1988). Gender and Phobia. Congress of the European Association for Behaviour Therapy (1987, Amsterdam). *Gedragstherapie*, **21**, 283–293.
Clark, D.M. (1986). A cognitive approach to panic. *Behaviour Research and Therapy*, **24**, 461–470.
Cook, M. & Mineka, S. (1989). Observational conditioning of fear to fear-relevant versus fear-irrelevant stimuli in rhesus monkeys. *Journal of Abnormal Psychology*, **98**, 448–459.
Costello, C.G. (1982). Fears and phobias in women: a community study. *Journal of Abnormal Psychology*, **91**, 280–286.
Davey, G.C.L. (1992a). An expectancy model of laboratory preparedness effects. *Journal of Experimental Psychology, General*, **121**, 24–40.
Davey, G.C.L. (1992b). Characteristics of individuals with fear of spiders. *Anxiety Research*, **4**, 299–314.
Davison, G.C. (1968). Systematic desensitization as a counterconditioning process. *Journal of Abnormal Psychology*, **73**, 84–90.
Descartes, R. (1650). *The Passions of the Soule*. London: Martin and Ridley.
de Silva, P., Rachman, S.J. & Seligman, M.E. (1977). Prepared phobias and obsessions: therapeutic outcome. *Behaviour Research and Therapy*, **15**, 65–77.
de Silva, P. & Rachman, S. (1981). Is exposure a necessary condition for fear reduction? *Behaviour Research and Therapy*, **19**, 227–232.
Di Nardo, P.A., Guzy, L.T. & Bak, R.M. (1988). Anxiety response patterns and etiological factors in dog-fearful and non-fearful subjects. *Behaviour Research and Therapy*, **26**, 245–242.
Di Nardo, P.A., Guzy, L.T., Jenkins, J.A., Bak, R.M., Tomasi, S.F. & Copland, M. (1988). Etiology and maintenance of dog fears. *Behaviour Research and Therapy*, **26**, 241–244.
English, H.B. (1929). Three cases of the "conditioned fear" response. *Journal of Abnormal and Social Psychology*, **24**, 221–225.
Errera, P. (1962). Some historical aspects of the concept, phobia. *The Psychiatric Quarterly*, **36**, 325–336.
Foa, E.B. & Kozak, M.J. (1986). Emotional processing of fear: exposure to corrective information. *Psychological Bulletin*, **99**, 20–35.
Foa, E.B. & McNally, R. (1986). Sensitivity to feared stimuli in obsessive-compulsives: a dichotic listening analysis. *Cognitive Therapy and Research*, **10**, 477–485.
Fyer, A. (1987). Simple phobias. In D. Klein (ed.), *Anxiety*. Basel: Karger.
Garcia, J. & Koelling, R. (1966). Relation of cue to consequence in avoidance learning. *Psychonomic Science*, **4**, 123–124.
Garcia, J., Rusiniak, K.W. & Brett, L.P. (1977). Conditioning food-illness aversions in wild animals. In H. Davis & H.M.B. Hurwitz (eds), *Operant Pavlovian Interactions*. New York: Wiley.
Grieve, J. [trans.] (1814). *Celsus, Aulus Cornelius: Of Medicine*. Edinburgh: Dickson.
Hawton, K., Salkovskis, P.M., Kirk, J. & Clark, D.M. (1989). *Cognitive Behaviour Therapy for Psychiatric Problems: A Practical Guide*. Oxford: Oxford University Press.
Hugdahl, K. & Öst, L.G. (1985). Subjectively rated physiological and cognitive symptoms in six different clinical phobias. *Personality and Individual Differences*, **2**, 175–188.
Jones, M.C. (1924). The elimination of children's fears. *Journal of Experimental Psychology*, **7**, 382–390.
Kleinknecht, R.A. (1982). The origins and remission of fear in a group of tarantula enthusiasts. *Behaviour Research and Therapy*, **20**, 437–443.
Lang, P.J. (1971). The application of psychophysiological methods to the study of psychotherapy and behaviour modification. In A.E. Bergin & S.L. Garfield (eds), *Handbook of Psychotherapy and Behaviour Change*. New York: Wiley.

Lang, P.J. (1984). Cognition in emotion: concept and action. In C.E. Izard, R.J. Zajonc & J. Kagan (eds), *Emotion, Cognition and Behaviour* (pp. 192–228). Cambridge: Cambridge University Press.

Lavy, E., van den Hout, M. & Arntz, A. (1993a). Attentional bias and spider phobia: conceptual and clinical issues. *Behaviour Research and Therapy*, **31**, 17–24.

Lavy, E., van den Hout, M. & Arntz, A. (1993b). Attentional bias and facilitated escape. *Advances in Behaviour Research and Therapy*, **15**, 279–289.

Liddell, A. & Hart, D. (1992). Comparison between FSS-II scores of two groups of university students sampled 15 years apart. *Behaviour Research and Therapy*, **30**, 125–131.

Liddell, H.G. & Scott, R. (1983). *Greek–English Lexicon*, 7th edn. New York: Harper.

Mackintosh, N.J. (1983). *Conditioning and Associative Learning*. New York: Oxford University Press.

Macleod, C. (1987). Cognitive psychology and cognitive therapy. In H. Dent (ed.), *Clinical Psychology: Research and Developments*. London: Croom Helm.

McNally, R.J. (1987). Preparedness and phobias: a review. *Psychological Bulletin*, **101**, 282–303.

McNally, R.J. & Steketee, G.S. (1985). The etiology and maintenance of severe animal phobias. *Behaviour Research and Therapy*, **23**, 431–435.

McNally, R.J., Foa, E.B. & Donnell, C.D. (1989). Memory bias for anxiety information in patients with panic disorder. *Cognition and Emotion*, **3**, 27–44.

Marks, I.M. (1987). *Fears, Phobias, and Rituals*. Oxford: Oxford University Press.

Masataka, N. (1993). Effects of experience with live insects on the development of fear of snakes in squirrel monkeys, *Saimiri scuireus*. *Animal Behaviour*, **46**, 741–746.

Matchett, G. & Davey, G.C.L. (1991). A test of a disease-avoidance model of animal phobias. *Behaviour Research and Therapy*, **29**, 91–94.

Merckelbach, H., Arntz, A. & De Jong, P. (1991). Conditioning experiences in spider phobics. *Behaviour Research and Therapy*, **29**, 333–335.

Mineka, S. & Cook, M. (1986). Immunization against the observational conditioning of snake fear in rhesus monkeys. *Journal of Abnormal Psychology*, **95**, 307–318.

Mineka, S., Davidson, M., Cook, M. & Keir, R. (1984). Observational conditioning of snake fear in rhesus monkeys. *Journal of Abnormal Psychology*, **93**, 355–372.

Mogg. K., Mathews, A. & Weinman, J. (1987). Memory bias in clinical anxiety. *Journal of Abnormal Psychology*, **96**, 94–98.

Murray, E.J. & Foote, F. (1979). The origins of fear of snakes. *Behaviour Research and Therapy*, **17**, 489–493.

Norton, G.R., Schaefer, E., Cox, B., Dorward, J. & Wozney, K. (1988). Selective memory effects in non-clinical panickers. *Journal of Anxiety Disorders*, **2**, 169–177.

Nunn, J.D., Stevenson, R.J. & Whalan, L. (1984). Selective memory effects in agoraphobic patients. *British Journal of Clinical Psychology*, **23**, 195–201.

Öhman, A. (1979). Fear relevance, autonomic conditioning and phobias: a laboratory model. In P.O. Sjödé, S. Bates & W.S. Dockens (eds), *Trends in Behaviour Therapy* (pp. 107–133). New York: Academic Press.

Öhman, A. (1986). Face the beast and fear the face: animal and social fears as prototypes for evolutionary analyses of emotion. *Psychophysiology*, **23**, 123–145.

Öhman, A., Dimberg, U. & Öst, L.G. (1985). Animal and social phobias: biological constraints on learned fear responses. In S. Reiss & R.R. Bootzin (eds), *Theoretical Issues in Behaviour Therapy* (pp. 123–175). New York: Academic Press.

Öhman, A., Erixon, G. & Löfberg, U. (1975). Phobias and preparedness: phobic versus neutral pictures as conditioned stimuli for human autonomic responses. *Journal of Abnormal Psychology*, **84**, 41–45.

Öst, L.G. (1985). Ways of acquiring phobias and outcome of behavioural treatments. *Behaviour Research and Therapy*, **23**, 683–689.

Öst, L.G. (1987). Age of onset in different phobias. *Journal of Abnormal Psychology*, **96**, 223–229.

Öst, L.G. (1989). One session treatment for specific phobias. *Behaviour Research and Therapy*, **27**, 1–7.

Öst, L.G. & Hugdahl, K. (1981). Acquisition of phobias and anxiety response patterns in clinical patients. *Behaviour Research and Therapy*, **19**, 439–447.

Öst, L.G., Salkovskis, P.M. & Hellström, K. (1991). One-session therapist-directed treatment vs. self-exposure in the treatment of spider phobia. *Behavior Therapy*, **22**, 407–422.

Rachman, S.J. (1978). *Fear and Courage*. San Francisco: W.H. Freeman & Co.

Rachman, S.J. & Hodgson, R. (1974). Synchrony and desynchrony in fear and avoidance. *Behaviour Research and Therapy*, **12**, 311–318.

Rachman, S.J. & Levitt, K. (1985). Panics and their consequences. *Behaviour Research and Therapy*, **23**, 585–600.

Rescorla, R.A. (1988). Pavlovian conditioning: it's not what you think it is. *American Psychologist*, **43**, 151–160.

Robins, L.N., Helzer, J.E., Weissam, M.M., Orvaschel, H., Gruenberg, E., Burke, J.D. & Regier, D.A. (1984). Lifetime prevalence of specific psychiatric disorders in three sites. *Archives of General Psychiatry*, **41**, 949–958.

Rozin, P. & Fallon, A.E. (1987). A perspective on disgust. *Psychological Review*, **94**, 23–41.

Salkovskis, P.M. (1991). The importance of behaviour in the maintenance of panic and anxiety. *Behavioural Psychotherapy*, **19**, 6–19.

Salkovskis, P.M. (1996). Avoidance behaviour is motivated by threat beliefs: a possible resolution of the cognitive-behaviour debate. In P. Salkovskis (ed.), *Current trends in Cognitive and Behaviour Therapy*. Chichester: W.J. Wiley & Sons.

Salkovskis, P.M., Clark, D.M. & Gelder, M.G. (1996). Cognition–behaviour links in the persistence of panic. *Behaviour Research and Therapy*, **34**, 453–458.

Seligman, M.E.P. (1971). Phobias and preparedness. *Behavior Therapy*, **2**, 307–321.

Teasdale, J.D. (1993). Emotion and two kinds of meaning: cognitive therapy and applied cognitive science. *Behaviour Research and Therapy*, **31**, 339–354.

Thorndike, E.L. (1935). *The Psychology of Wants, Interests and Attitudes*. New York: Appleton, Century.

Thorpe, S.J. & Salkovskis, P.M. (1995). Phobic beliefs: do cognitive factors play a role in specific phobias? *Behaviour Research and Therapy*, **33**, 805–816.

Thorpe, S.J. & Salkovskis, P.M. (1997a). Information processing in spider phobics: the Stroop colour-naming task may indicate strategic but not automatic attentional bias. *Behavior Research & Therapy*, **35**, 131–144.

Thorpe, S.J. & Salkovskis, P.M. (1997b). The effect of one-session treatment for spider phobia on attentional bias and beliefs. *British Journal of Clinical Psychology*, **36**.

Tomarken, J.T., Mineka, S. & Cook, M. (1989). Fear-relevant selective associations and covariation bias. *Journal of Abnormal Psychology*, **98**, 381–394.

Watson, J.B. & Rayner, R. (1920). Conditioned emotional reactions. *Journal of Experimental Psychology*, **3**, 1–4.

Watts, F.N. (1986). Cognitive processing in phobias. *Behavioural Psychotherapy*, **14**, 295–301.

Watts, F.N. & Sharrock, R. (1984). Questionnaire dimensions of spider phobia. *Bahaviour Research and Therapy*, **22**, 575–580.

Watts, F.N., Mckenna, F.P., Sharrock, R. & Trezise, L. (1986). Colour naming of phobia related words. *British Journal of Psychology*, **77**, 97–108.

Williams, J.M.G., Watts, F.N., MacLeod, C. & Mathews, A. (1988). *Cognitive Psychology and Emotional Disorders*. Chichester: Wiley.

Wittchen, H-U. (1986). Epidemiology of panic attacks and panic disorders. In I. Hand & H.-U. Wittchen (eds), *Panic and Phobias*. Berlin: Springer-Verlag.

Wolpe, J. (1958). *Psychotherapy by Reciprocal Inhibition*. Stanford, CA: Stanford University Press.
Wolpe, J. & Lang, P.J. (1964). A fear survey schedule for use in behaviour therapy. *Behaviour Research and Therapy*, **2**, 27.
Zilboorg, G. (1941). *A History of Medical Psychology*. New York: Norton.

Chapter 5

Dental Phobias

Gerry Kent
Department of Psychiatry, University of Sheffield, Sheffield, UK

INTRODUCTION

There are many reasons why the study of anxiety and phobia in the dental setting is a practically important and theoretically interesting area. On the practical side, as we shall see, dental phobias are quite common. Depending on how it is measured, 3–5% of the adult general population can be said to have debilitatingly high levels of fear of dentistry. Insofar as fear results in avoidance of professional care, an understanding of this difficulty could have many beneficial effects for patients' oral health. It is possible that a vicious circle could develop, in which fear leads to avoidance of professional dental care, leading to feelings of guilt and shame and thence to increased anxiety (Moore, Brodsgaard & Birn, 1991). On the theoretical side, the dental setting can be viewed as a "natural laboratory". Levels of state anxiety rise and fall, Pavlovian learning processes are mediated and affected by cognitive processes such as memory and perceptual biases, the effects of experience can be monitored in longitudinal studies and, although behavioural and cognitive interventions are usually effective, they are not helpful for a large minority of patients, so that it is possible to gather information about the precursors of treatment success and failure.

This chapter considers five areas of research: measurement, prevalence, aetiology, maintenance or resistance to attenuation, and factors associated with treatment efficacy. By considering these topics, strengths and weaknesses in the area are considered. One particularly important weakness is a lack of integration with concepts and ideas developed within theoretical social and cognitive psychology. This leads on to the final section, conclusions and recommendations for future research.

Phobias—A Handbook of Theory, Research and Treatment. Edited by G.C.L. Davey.
© 1997 John Wiley & Sons Ltd.

MEASUREMENT

The DSM-IV (American Psychiatric Association, 1995) indicates that an individual with dental fears ought to meet seven criteria to qualify for diagnosis of a specific phobia (see preface to Section I). In the literature on dental phobia, some of these criteria are better researched and more adequately measured than others. Whereas there are several scales designed to measure the extent of anxiety according to criteria A, B and D, only recently have criteria E and G received attention.

There are several self-report questionnaires. Perhaps the best-known and most commonly used scale is Corah's Dental Anxiety Scale or DAS (Corah, 1968), a four-item self-report questionnaire with scores ranging from 4 (low) to 20, with a score of 15 or greater indicating extreme anxiety (Corah, Gale & Illig, 1978). It is quick to complete and provides a general measure of perceived emotional arousal and physiological reactions. A scale which inquires about fears of specific aspects of the dental setting (e.g. about drilling, injections) is the Dental Fear Survey or DFS (Kleinknecht, Klepac & Alexander, 1973), which has somewhat more support in terms of validity and reliability (Moore, Berggren & Carlsson, 1991; Schuurs & Hoogstraten, 1993) than the DAS. The Dental Belief Survey is concerned with patients' beliefs about the way they are treated interpersonally by dentists, including such items as "Dentists do not really listen" and "I don't feel comfortable asking questions" (Milgrom et al., 1985). There are several other scales (Schuurs & Hoogstraten, 1993; ter Horst & De Wit, 1993) which attempt to gauge various aspects of these and other aspects of the dental situation.

Recently, there has been interest in assessing the cognitive component of dental anxiety. With the recognition that anxious dental patients experience many more negative cognitions of a catastrophic kind than low-anxiety patients (de Jongh et al., 1994; Kent & Gibbons, 1987), de Jongh et al. (1995a) have developed the Dental Cognitions Questionnaire, which contains such items as "I will panic during treatment", "Surely something will go wrong" and "Anaesthetics often do not work": patients are asked to indicate both the frequency and the believability of the statements. Not only does the frequency of such thoughts discriminate extremely well between phobic and non-phobic patients, but they contribute substantially to the variance in state anxiety.

There are also many scales which are appropriate for children, which can be completed by parents, such as the dental subscale of the Children's Fear Survey (Klingberg, 1994) or scales which are completed by children themselves. The latter include projective techniques (Klingberg & Hwang, 1994) and asking children to choose between a set a pictures which illustrate varying levels of distress (Venham, 1979).

Besides self-report questionnaires, attempts have also been made to assess the physiological aspects of dental anxiety and phobia, but as in other areas there are many conceptual difficulties in dealing with results. Several studies (Carlsson et al., 1986; Berggren & Carlsson, 1985; Harrison, Carlsson & Berggren, 1985;

Hugdhal & Öst, 1985) have shown that there is no clear correspondence between measures of physiological arousal as measured by heart-rate and skin conductance. Although Lang's (1971) three-factor model of anxiety does not require concordance between self-report, behavioural and physiological reactions, one would expect that there would be fairly consistent differences between high- and low-anxious patients, or that there would be changes on physiological indices after successful therapeutic interventions, but this has not been shown consistently (Hirschman et al., 1969; Carlsson et al., 1986).

Quality of Life

While these scales and measures attempt to assess level of anxiety according to the A, B and D DSM-IV criteria, there has been recent interest in criterion E: the effect on social relationships and activities, or what has become known as quality of life. Not only might a phobia lead to avoidance of professional care, but also to embarrassment, days off work and a degree of social isolation. Research in these areas is beginning to appear. For example, Berggren & Carlsson (1986) found that successfully treated phobics reported several areas of psychosocial improvement, including reduced alcohol intake and reduced time on sick leave and, as shown below, treatment of dental phobia can improve functioning in these areas. Berggren (1993) sent questionnaires to 109 patients who were referred for assistance to a dental anxiety clinic. Although there was no comparison group, many patients scored highly on a modified Nottingham Health Profile, with 52% indicating that their dental fear caused problems with social activities (eating out, meeting friends), 46% with going on vacation and 41% with family relationships. These types of situations, which demand interactions with other people, could be severely curtailed.

Another approach was taken by Kent (Kent et al., 1996) who designed a scale to measure the social and psychological effects of phobias. They compared the responses of patients who had been referred for anxiety difficulties with patients attending an emergency dental clinic for other difficulties. The phobic patients were more likely to endorse items which indicated social and cognitive consequences (e.g. "I feel that people will laugh at me if I tell them about my fears about dentistry" and "The need to see a dentist is constantly on my mind"), avoidance (e.g. "When walking or driving somewhere I take a route in order to avoid passing by a dentist's office", and "I become upset when I see adverts on TV about tooth decay and tooth loss") and social inhibitions (e.g. "I stop myself from smiling or I cover my mouth when I laugh", and "I am reluctant to meet new people because of the state of my teeth").

Thus it can be argued that an accurate and complete assessment of dental phobia needs to include a variety of areas. Stouthard, Hoogstraten & Mellenbergh (1995) contend that there are three facets to dental phobias; namely a *situation* facet (including the nature of the dentist–patient relationship as well as the specific fears of particular procedures, such as drilling and extractions, and preliminary aspects, such as sitting in the waiting room and making an appointment); a *time* facet (as the appointment approaches in time); and a *reaction* facet (including affect, physical reactions and cognitive intrusions). Their Dental Anxiety Inventory includes items on all three aspects of the phobia and, with development, could provide a more comprehensive assessment than other scales.

PREVALENCE

The prevalence of dental phobias is interesting in its own right, but by examining age and cultural patterns it might also be possible to identify factors which are relevant to aetiology. If prevalence rates vary across cultures, for example, it is plausible that cultural beliefs or learning processes, such as the way that dental care is delivered, may be crucial in the development of dental phobia. On the other hand, if prevalence is similar across cultures, then biological processes could be more significant.

Estimates of the prevalence of extreme levels of dental anxiety and phobia vary with the populations studied and the measures used. In several studies with a variety of populations, mean scores on the DAS range between 7 and 8 (ter Horst & De Wit, 1993; Kaufman et al., 1992). Using the criterion of scores of 15 or greater, studies have indicated a range of 3–5% (Kleinknecht, Klepac & Alexander, 1973; Moore et al., 1993; Klingberg, Berggren & Noren, 1993; Hakeberg, Berggren & Carlsson, 1992; Vassend, 1993) in unselected adult populations, but there are a few higher estimates, of up to 13% or higher (ter Horst & De Wit, 1993; Mellor, 1992). For children and adolescents, using different scales, the estimates tend to be somewhat greater at 6–7% (de Moraes et al., 1994; Klingberg, Berggren & Noren, 1993). Using self-reported avoidance to define extreme anxiety, the prevalence seems to be higher. For example, in a large representative Dutch sample, 36% reported "dread" of visiting the dentist (cited in Lindsay & Jackson, 1993).

Another reason for the interest in prevalence is its relationship with oral health. Although dental phobia can be distressing in its own right, from a purely dental point of view the interest is in its relationship with pain, carious lesions and periodontal disease. Many authors have concluded that there is an indisputable relationship between avoidance and poor oral health. There is evidence that patients with high levels of anxiety are more likely to have experienced extractions and to have more decayed surfaces and fewer fillings (Locker & Liddell, 1992; Hakeberg, Berggren & Grondahl, 1993; Bedi et al., 1992; Kaufman et al., 1992). But in fact this relationship is far from clear. It may be that some patients are anxious because of their perceptions of the poor state of their oral health, they may have become anxious because of previous extractions rather than avoidance leading to poor oral health, and there are many influences on oral health, including diet and fluoridation of toothpaste and of the water supply. It is possible that these background factors may be responsible for high anxiety or outweigh the disadvantages of poor attendance *per se*.

While it is possible to make some general observations concerning prevalence—that high levels of dental anxiety are very common in all countries studied, they are more likely in women than in men, and that they peak during early
adolescence and decline with advancing age (Liddell & Locker, 1993)—the wide
range of instruments used means that it is not possible to provide a definitive
answer with respect to prevalence. Prevalence studies using standard measures
with representative samples are still required (Vassend, 1993). In order to understand aetiological processes, it is necessary to move away from epidemiological
data towards more psychologically-based research.

AETIOLOGY

This is the area where most research has been conducted. In general, the evidence suggests that a Pavlovian conditioning model is helpful in understanding
the onset of dental phobias, but that this model needs to be adapted to include
the idea of latent inhibition, issues of perceived control, innate biological predispositions to learn anxiety responses and the nature of the dentist–patient relationship. Unfortunately, the reliance on retrospective accounts of past traumas
and experiences is exceedingly problematic for many reasons, and there is a
dearth of longitudinal research.

Negative Experiences

Pavlovian Conditioning

The notion that dental phobias are the result of a learned association between
pain and dental care received early support from Lautch (1971), who interviewed
phobic and non-phobic patients about their previous experiences. In his sample
of 34 dental phobics, all reported at least one previous traumatic experience with
dental care—usually the experience of intense pain—whereas only 10 of the 34
non-phobics could remember such an incident. Of the phobic patients who had
returned to a dentist at least once after the trauma (30 patients), all reported
further traumas but only one of the non-phobics did so, suggesting that more than
one negative experience is needed for the development of a phobia. The suggestion that dental anxiety is the result of conditioning has been supported many
times (Öst, 1987; Hugdhal & Öst, 1985; ter Horst & De Wit, 1993; Moore et al.,
1991c).

This Pavlovian model is consistent with the notion of preparedness, that
humans are innately predisposed to become anxious about some objects and
situations more readily than others (de Silva, 1988). It is possible to see a link with
dentistry in this regard. Lying on one's back with an adult placing sharp instruments in the mouth "should", in some sense, be frightening. Anxiety might be
particularly heightened if the adult is a stranger (patients often find the prospect

of joining a new practice distressing because they are concerned that the dentist will have a rough manner) or if the child is a patient (where there is a large disparity of strength). This attractive idea goes some way towards explaining the widespread prevalence of dental anxiety, why anxiety is most likely to develop before adulthood, and why it is often associated with fears about pain and mutilation.

However, it is easy to see that there are a number of difficulties with this explanation which relates conditioning processes with preparedness. One difficulty is that many people who are not highly anxious or phobic have also experienced a situation where classical conditioning could be expected to occur. In one large-scale survey, 30% of respondents reported that they had experienced "intense" or "violent" pain at some point in their dental care histories (Vassend, 1993). Conversely, some phobic patients cannot recall such an incident (Moore, Brodsgaard & Birn, 1991c). Another difficulty is that all of these studies have relied on retrospective accounts of experience, thus introducing all the cognitive and memory biases that retrospective accounts imply. For example, the timing of the request for information on previous experiences may be relevant. Many of the studies in this area have asked patients to recall incidents when they arrive for treatment or at least when they are scheduled to attend, when levels of state anxiety are high. In a study designed to explore the effect of anxious mood on recall, Kent (1989) asked patients to describe a previous visit to a dentist, but some were asked to do this just before a dental appointment, whereas others were asked to do so just afterwards. State anxiety levels were found to be related to the vividness and unpleasantness of these recollections for female patients. It is plausible that phobic patients—whose levels of state anxiety will be high—may recall more traumatic incidents partly because of their anxious mood, and not experience of incidents being responsible for mood.

A third difficulty with these studies is that phobic patients are typically asked to relate their difficulty to previous experiences. This raises issues of attribution theory, particularly the fundamental error of attributing negative events to external causes (Ross, 1977). It is possible that one individual who is already highly anxious, perhaps because of other factors or high levels of trait anxiety, will attribute their anxiety to such an event, whereas another individual who might have undergone a similar experience will not do so. In the absence of a method for objectively rating the aversiveness of an experience, attribution theory can provide an equally plausible explanation for the association between "traumatic" events and the onset of a dental phobia.

Latent Inhibition

Davey (1989) and de Jongh et al. (1995b) have added a degree of sophistication to this area by exploring the possibility that the concept of latent inhibition is relevant to this learning process. Latent inhibition refers to the hypothesis that if a conditioned stimulus (CS) (in this case a visit to the dentist) is presented alone on several occasions before it is paired with the unconditioned stimulus (UCS) (a painful or traumatic experience such as pain), then it is more difficult to condition an association between the CS and UCS than if there were no CS-alone trials prior to conditioning. Thus, according to this principle a dental patient might not acquire a phobia if he/she has a history of previous positive (or at least not negative) visits to the dentist.

Although Davey and de Jongh again relied on retrospective accounts (in both cases, studies from students), they attempted to specify the conditions under which traumatic events fail to promote the development of anxiety. They asked their samples to indicate their current levels of anxiety, their experiences of pain or trauma in the dental setting and, importantly, whether their levels of anxiety had changed over time. One group consisted of people who had always been anxious about dental treatment, a second group consisted of those who were once anxious but were now more relaxed, a third group comprised those who were once relaxed but who were now anxious, and the fourth group those who had always been relaxed. For the present purposes the important finding was that, in both studies, latent inhibition seemed to have been operating. Subjects who reported the experience of a traumatic event but who did not become anxious were more likely to have had a number of previous non-traumatic encounters. Latent inhibition was attenuated after undergoing a particularly painful experience. Like Lautch (1971), Davey found that those who had always been anxious had received two or more aversive experiences.

Clearly, a prospective study is required before such conclusions can be confirmed. In fact, one of the great weaknesses of research in dental anxiety and phobia is the almost complete lack of longitudinal data. An important exception to this is provided by Murray, Liddell & Donohue (1989). They collected data from children age 9 and then again at age 12, while monitoring their dental experiences from dental records. Children who did *not* receive invasive treatment (i.e. having an injection, having teeth filled or removed) during this time were significantly more anxious than those who had received treatment, while the anxiety of children who attended regularly and who had experienced invasive treatment did not change significantly. This result implies that exposure acts prophylactically and is again consistent with the notion of latent inhibition.

The Dentist's Role

Most of the research relating dental anxiety to experience involves encounters with pain. However, there is another thread of research which involves encounters with the dentist him/herself. Bernstein, Kleinknecht & Alexander (1979) first divided their sample of students into high- and low-fear groups. The students were then asked to write an essay describing their visits to the dentist as children. These essays were to include "the features and events associated with those visits which determine present attitudes". Forty-two per cent of the high-fear group mentioned pain during early appointments as a factor in their present feelings about dental care, compared to 17.4% of the low-fear students. While these proportions discriminated between the groups to some extent, there was still the

58% of high-fear students who did not cite pain as a factor and a sizeable minority of low-fear students who did experience pain.

This overlap was clarified by considering another factor—the perceived manner of the dentist. Half of the high-fear group mentioned negative behaviour on the part of the dentist as a factor in their present feelings, most of these not citing pain as a reason for their current feelings. The dentists were considered "impersonal", "uncaring", "uninterested" or "cold". Furthermore, of the low-fear group who had experienced pain as children, many found the dentist "careful", "patient" and "friendly". The effects of any pain seemed to have been mitigated by a caring and concerned dentist. Thus this study suggested that the dentist had an independent effect on the students' feelings (i.e. cold or uninterested behaviour was enough to make some students feel negatively about dentistry) and an interactive effect (i.e. caring and warmth could obviate the long-term effects of painful experiences).

Social Learning Theory

Besides the direct experience of aversive events, there is evidence that learning can take place in a more indirect fashion, via modelling or cultural beliefs about an association between dental care and pain. Social learning theory would suggest that children could learn that professional dental care is painful and distressing through observing parental reactions in the dentist's office or hearing about negative experiences. A number of studies have implicated the importance of parental—especially maternal—responses to dental care as an aetiological influence (Milgrom et al., 1995; ter Horst & De Wit, 1993; Corkey & Freeman, 1994; Klingberg, Berggren & Noren, 1993). However, such learning may be overridden by actual experience quite quickly (Koenigsberg & Johnson, 1972). In most cases these studies are again reliant on retrospective accounts (although actual observational studies support a link; Johnson & Baldwin, 1968), and may be more relevant for the development of moderate rather than extreme levels of anxiety. In any case, it is not possible to disentangle learning processes from biological ones in these studies: it is possible that children of anxious parents are fearful themselves, not because they had observed distress but because both children and parents share a genetic propensity to be anxious. This possibility leads on a second major explanation as to the aetiology of dental fear—the notion that there are individual differences in propensity to learn anxiety responses.

Biological Characteristics

If the conditioning approach places the cause of phobias within the experience of dental trauma, the biological approach suggests that there are individual differences in how patients react to dental care. This approach is particularly relevant to the finding that, in some patients at least, anxiety occurs in the absence of any specifiable negative experience. Some children are very anxious on their first visit. It is possible that some people will be more liable to learning anxiety responses than others. There are three types of study which support this approach—studies on temperament, studies on neuroticism and studies on specificity.

The concept of temperament is based on the work of Thomas and Chess (Thomas et al., 1963), whose studies describe the range of responses given by young children, especially when they encounter new situations. These reactions emerge at a young age and can persist for many years. Of particular relevance to this area is the notion of the "difficult child", one who tends to withdraw from and who has difficulty in adapting to novel situations. The relevance of temperament has been explored in four studies (Lochary et al., 1993; Williams et al., 1983; Liddell, 1990; Holst et al., 1993), all of which suggest that children who have difficulty in meeting unfamiliar people and coping with new situations are less likely to be able to accept routine dental care, even under sedation (Lochary et al., 1993). Associated with temperament is Eysenck's notion of neuroticism. Again, several studies (Frazer & Hampson, 1988; ter Horst & De Wit, 1993; Lautch, 1971; Klepac, Dowling & Hauge, 1982) have indicated that patients with high levels of anxiety also score highly on the N scale of the EPI or EPQ.

Taken together, the work on temperament and neuroticism would suggest that many people with high levels of dental anxiety also have a number of other unrelated anxieties and concerns. This is a central issue, since it bears upon the possibility that dental phobia can be indicative of more general psychological or psychiatric difficulties, rather than a specific difficulty. There is now growing evidence that this is often but not always the case (Alwin, Murray & Niven, 1994; Brown, Wright & McMurray, 1986; McNeil & Berryman, 1989; Corkey & Freeman, 1994; Milgrom et al., 1995; Moore et al., 1991b; Klingberg, Berggren & Noren, 1993; ter Horst & De Wit, 1993). A recent study (Roy-Bryne et al., 1994) indicated that in a sample of phobic patients 40% could be assigned another concurrent psychiatric diagnosis, such as panic disorder.

MAINTENANCE

In many respects, it is possible to see how dental phobias are maintained, due to the defining characteristic of avoidance. A decision to put off visiting a dentist would itself be reinforcing since it results in a short-term reduction of anxiety, as Mowrer (1960) would suggest. It would also explain how anxiety could increase over time, as perceptions of dentition worsens, thus increasing the likelihood of invasive treatment. However, this two-stage theory does not explain why many patients who continue to attend regularly still experience high levels of anxiety. Although anxious patients typically experience much less pain than they expect (Lindsay & Jackson, 1993; Kent & Warren, 1985), high levels of anxiety are often maintained. There are several possible reasons for this apparent paradox.

One reason is that dentistry is not consistently pain-free. One survey of dentists themselves indicated that local anaesthetics can fail in about 13% of instances (Kaufman, Weinstein & Milgrom, 1984), so that one negative experience could re-confirm an anxious patient's belief that dental treatment can be painful and thus anxiety is maintained. Lindsay & Jackson (1993) argue that the anxious patient may believe that it is less distressing to expect pain—just in case it occurs—and be pleasantly surprised if it doesn't, than to be unexpectedly hurt.

Even if all future dental appointments were pain-free, there are several reasons based in cognitive psychology which can be used to explain the maintenance of anxiety. One concerns the notion of typicality. As noted above, latent inhibition theory suggests that dental anxiety is unlikely to develop if the patient has previously experienced many pain-free appointments. In the language of cognitive heuristics, this could be seen in terms of typicality: one painful experience could be interpreted as anomalous and unlikely to recur. The converse of this is that anxiety might be maintained if pain-free experiences were seen as atypical, perhaps as a result of chance rather than because of the non-aversive nature of care itself. Kent (1986) explored this possibility by first ascertaining the discrepancy between expected pain (as ascertained before the appointment) and experienced pain (as ascertained at the end of treatment). Patients were also asked at the completion of the appointment to indicate the extent to which they believed the amount of pain they experienced was typical, through the question "How confident are you that you will experience the same amount of pain [on the next appointment] as today?". When contacted 3 months later, decreases in dental anxiety were found for patients who (a) experienced a sizeable discrepancy between expected and experienced pain, and (b) had a high level of confidence in the typicality of this discrepancy. A decrease in anxiety was less likely if the patient had low confidence. It is possible, then, that regular attendance and the experience of pain-free dentistry is slow to result in a reduction of anxiety because of the co-variation biases which can be present in phobias more generally (de Jong et al., 1995).

The common 6-month period between appointments may also contribute to the persistence of anxiety for patients who require little treatment. The "natural" exposure that regular attendance implies may not be sufficiently frequent. Studies of the effectiveness of behavioural therapies suggest that interventions are more efficacious if they are applied frequently (e.g. a few times per week over a few weeks) rather than infrequently (e.g. one or two days a month) (Marshall, Gauthier & Gordon, 1979). In cognitive terms, frequent interventions may be more efficacious in altering expectations than infrequent ones because there is less opportunity for positive experiences to be reconstructed into existing anxiety-dominated schemata.

That such schemata can serve to maintain anxiety was shown in two studies (Arntz, van Eck & Heijmans, 1990; Kent, 1985b) where patients were asked to indicate the levels of expected pain (before the appointment), their levels of experienced pain (afterwards), but were then contacted again 3 months after the appointment. On this later occasion they were asked to recall the amount of pain they had experienced at the appointment. The findings implicated the relevance of cognitive structures, since the amount of pain remembered by the anxious patients had increased over time, to become more similar to the original expected pain, while the non-anxious patients recalled their levels of experienced pain more accurately.

Clearly, there is considerable scope for future research into the reasons why anxiety is maintained, but equally important are the reasons why anxiety comes to be reduced in patients without formal interventions. Although longitudinal studies are more expensive in time and effort, they are clearly needed here, since they could provide information which could serve to inform the choice and design of therapeutic interventions, an area which is considered in the next section.

TREATMENT

A wide variety of interventions has been employed in the treatment of dental anxiety and phobia, with considerable success. With doubts about the appropriateness and safety of general anaesthesia, there has been a growing interest in the use of conscious sedation, as afforded by nitrous oxide (Roberts et al., 1979; Veerkamp et al., 1993) and the new sedative midazolam (Kupietzky & Houpt, 1995).

A wide variety of behavioural therapies has been used in dentistry, ranging from such minimal yet effective interventions as information leaflets (Jackson & Lindsay, 1995) which are probably most effective for low or moderate levels of anxiety, to much more intensive interventions which are appropriate for extreme levels of anxiety. Many of these interventions involve a traditional graded exposure approach to the dental setting, the encouragement of patient control while receiving dental treatment, and attention-focusing techniques such as hypnosis (ter Horst & De Wit, 1993; Kent, 1985a; Gokli et al., 1994; Melamed, 1979; Kent & Blinkhorn, 1991). As would be expected, they are successful in relieving anxiety for most patients (Moore et al., 1991; Smith et al., 1987), although across many studies approximately 25–35% of patients do not benefit or cannot follow through with treatment. These studies raise a number of issues, including the selection of outcome measures, the identification of variables which correlate with success or failure, and the enhancement of self-efficacy.

Outcome Measures

The most usual measures concern reductions of anxiety—either state anxiety or scores on dental anxiety scales—and/or the achievement of more regular attendance patterns. However, there is no one-to-one relationship between a reduction of measured anxiety and subsequent improvement in attendance (Schuurs, Makkes & Duivenvoorden, 1995). It can be argued that the range of outcome measures ought to be broadened to include some quality of life measures, such as reduction in embarrassment and dysphoric mood and improvements in social functioning (Moore et al., 1991). For example, there is evidence that treatment for the dental anxiety can have positive effects on a variety of psychosocial measures such as use of drugs and days off work (Berggren & Carlsson, 1986). In order to examine the latter possibility, Hakeberg & Berggren (1992) examined data from their local National Health Insurance Office in Sweden to ascertain the time spent on sick leave by successfully treated patients and by a comparison group of patients who were attending the dental hospital for difficulties not connected with anxiety. Before the intervention, the anxious patients spent a median of 15.0 days off work on sick leave in the previous year, but this was reduced to 3.0 days in the year following treatment. By contrast, there was no difference in the number of days off work by the comparison group. These results suggest that a wider range of outcome measures would be appropriate and might provide a more sophisticated view of the effects of treatment.

Correlates of Success

A second issue concerns the correlates or precursors of success or failure of treatment. Although one might expect that patients with higher levels of pre-treatment anxiety would be less likely to benefit, this has not been demonstrated (Berggren & Carlsoon, 1985). As mentioned earlier, there is evidence that many patients with dental phobia have more generalized difficulties (Roy-Bryne et al., 1994). Liddell & Locker (1994) found that elderly individuals with wide-ranging problems were more likely to carry their dental anxiety into old age than those whose anxiety was more specific. We could expect that the more specific the dental anxiety the more likely it would be that a behavioural treatment would be successful. Patients who do not benefit from traditional graduated exposure to the dental setting may "fail" because the dental anxiety would only be a manifestation of more deep-seated difficulties. This possibility was supported by Berggren & Carlsson (1985), who found that patients who were anxious about a variety of situations and objects were less likely to benefit from behavioural therapy than those whose anxiety was more specific. Liddell et al. (1994) conducted a 1–4 year follow-up of patients who completed a group behavioural programme. At that time, 70% of patients were paying regular dental visits. Those patients who were not regular attenders at follow-up reported higher scores (on the Dental Anxiety Scale) at the completion of treatment, but unfortunately measures of generalized anxiety were not taken.

Another possibility is that patients are more likely to succeed if the intervention provided is consonant with the main component of their anxiety. Within Lang's (1971) three-factor model, anxiety has cognitive, behavioural and physiological components. These can co-vary or be largely independent, varying between individuals. For example, Harrison, Carlsson & Berggren (1985) demonstrated that intra-individual correlations between various psychological assessments of dental anxiety, mood and physiological recordings are largely idiosyncratic. Some have argued that if an individual's anxiety is primarily physiologically-based, then applied relaxation methods would be most effective, while if the anxiety is primarily cognitive in nature, then such methods as self-instructional training would be more appropriate. Jerremalm, Jansson & Öst (1986) tested this hypothesis by first assessing the nature of their patients' anxiety and then randomly assigning them to a physiological or a cognitive programme. Unfortunately for the concordance hypothesis, both interventions were about equally successful and success was not associated with a match between individual response pattern and type of intervention, a conclusion supported elsewhere (Ning & Liddell, 1991).

A related possibility is that when behavioural treatments do not succeed it is because of a misdiagnosis. There has been some interest in the possibility that the difficulties of some patients who present with dental phobia might be better understood within the context of panic disorder. That is, perhaps some patients are not simply fearful of aspects of dental care, but rather of their own anxiety reactions (Weiner & Sheehan, 1990; Holst et al., 1993). If so, then cognitive–behavioural interventions which aim to help patients cope with their catastrophic ideation about the possibility of a heart attack (Clark, 1986) would be helpful.

Another issue concerns the method of delivery of the intervention. In most studies interventions have been provided on an individual basis. This may not be necessary, with group therapy being potentially at least as clinically effective and more cost-effective. Using systematic desensitization, Moore & Brodsgaard (1994) compared group vs. individual sessions for patients with extreme levels of dental anxiety. There were no significant differences in drop-out rates between the two types of intervention, but group therapy required fewer therapist hours and at the completion of treatment the group approach resulted in greater declines in anxiety levels. At a 1-year follow-up, however, patients in group therapy were less likely to have continued to visit a dentist. Moore & Brodsgaard argue that a combination of group and individual therapy might provide the advantages of group support and allow the therapist to target the needs of individuals.

Self-efficacy and Control

Related to this is the role of self-efficacy. Bandura (1982) would argue that the type of treatments used to help patients with dental anxiety are successful because they increase patients' belief that they are able to control their behaviour and affect outcomes. Thus, an intervention would be successful if perceptions of control and self-efficacy could be enhanced. There is also a large body of research in the stress literature which indicates that people are more able to cope with stressful events if they believe that they have some control over the nature and aversiveness of outcomes (Steptoe & Appels, 1989). In the dental setting, patients can experience a lack of control (partly because it is difficult to communicate needs with a mouthful of instruments) and there are several studies which indicate that providing a measure of control through stop signals (Wardle, 1983) and information (Thrash, Marr & Box, 1982) can have beneficial effects on anxiety levels.

Litt, Nye & Shafer (1993) explored the importance of self-efficacy by assigning some patients to a relaxation condition and others to a self-efficacy-enhancing condition. In the latter, the patients were given false feedback about their ability to relax: not only was the biofeedback equipment set to indicate great success in relaxing but also the experimenter emphasized their ability verbally. Measures of patients' belief in ability to cope, distress before a scheduled appointment to have a molar removed, and staff's blind ratings of distress during the appointment all indicated that the self-efficacy enhancement strategy was successful and provided additional benefits to relaxation alone.

As mentioned above, there is little evidence for the notion that attempting a match between an individual patients' response component (e.g. physiological or cognitive) and type of intervention has little advantage over random assignment. There is more support that attempting a match between coping style and intervention type is helpful. Of particular interest are designs in which individuals' desire for information or control is ascertained first and then some patients are provided with an intervention which is either consonant or not consonant with their coping style. There are a number of studies on this topic (Auerbach, Martelli & Mercuri, 1983; Baron, Logan & Hoppe, 1991; Auerbach et al., 1976) which suggest that when a patient is presented with a non-preferred coping mechanism (e.g. given more information than they require for their coping style) stress levels can increase. Law, Logan & Baron (1994) first measured patients' desire for control and their perceived coping resources and then assigned them to either a stress inoculation training (SIT) programme (which included a video which emphasized ways of controlling both emotions and the dentist's behaviour) or to a placebo condition, in which patients watched a video on local areas of interest. As predicted, SIT significantly reduced the amount of pain experienced during a subsequent dental appointment only for patients who initially reported a high desire for control coupled with low perceived control.

One area which deserves attention in this regard is the control of anxiety-provoking cognitions. Since levels of anxiety are associated with both the content of cognitions and patients' ability to control their intrusiveness (Kent & Gibbons, 1987; de Jongh et al., 1994), diminishing catastrophizing ideation and providing patients with means of controlling thoughts may be an important determinant of adjustment to dental treatment and reduction of distress (de Jongh et al., 1995a).

The Dentist–Patient Relationship

The above results suggest that aspects of the relationship between the patient and the dentist are significant. When some patients feel in control of their dentist's behaviour they are less likely to experience pain and heightened anxiety. Furthermore, some patients locate the reason for their anxiety in previous negative encounters with dentists themselves (Bernstein, Kleinknecht & Alexander, 1979). The research on temperament indicates that some patients find it more difficult to adapt to the dental setting than others, suggesting that the same individual may have more or less anxiety depending on the dentist's ability to provide a secure setting (Lochary et al., 1993), and anxious patients often make great efforts to stay with a dentist they know (Kent, 1984). In their follow-up of patients treated for high levels of anxiety, Liddell et al. (1994) found that the most successful discriminator between those who managed to attend regularly and those who didn't was perceptions of the amount of communication and information given by the practice dentist. Such findings indicate that a more detailed examination of the dentist–patient relationship may provide important information about the nature and treatment of high levels of anxiety.

In this context, it is interesting to note studies on the relationship between levels of anxiety and avoidance on the one hand and the behaviour of the dentist on the other. In a number of observational studies (Melamed et al., 1983; Weinstein et al., 1982), certain types of behaviour on the part of dentists have been shown to increase the likelihood of disruptive or anxiety-based behaviours in children. The suggestion that punitive statements and lack of warmth can exacerbate anxiety responses has been confirmed in some experimental studies (Greenbaum et al., 1993; Melamed et al., 1983) where dentists have been coached to behave in supportive or non-supportive ways. In one study, for example (Greenbaum et al., 1993), children were assigned to either a touch condition (in which the dentist gently patted the patient on the arm and provided reassuring descriptions of the treatment) or the no-touch condition (in which reassurance alone was provided). Based on analysis of video-tapes of the consultations, older children (7–10 years of age) in the touch condition were less likely to fidget in the chair and the touched children reported significantly fewer feelings of displeasure and of being dominated.

It is also interesting to note the comments of patients who have been provided with behavioural treatments for their anxiety. From a psychologist's perspective, the implementation of graded exposure and relaxation training or challenging catastrophic thinking patterns are important. From the patient's perspective, however, interventions can be conceptualized quite differently. Smith et al. (1987) asked a sample of 24 patients who successful completed a cognitive–behavioural programme about which aspects helped them to tolerate treatment. Patients indicated that a number of factors were important, including the provision of information, the time taken, perceptions of control and the dentist understanding and listening to their concerns and not treating them as "silly".

Such factors are firmly grounded in an interpersonal model of anxiety and anxiety-reduction. Perhaps it would be helpful in understanding high levels of anxiety and phobia to consider them not simply as residing within the individual or in the individual's perceptions of dental care, but more within the relationship with the dental care provider. In such a model, the behaviour of the dentist and the anxiety of the patient could be considered as equally important.

CONCLUSIONS

This brief review of the research on dental phobias makes it clear that it is an excellent area in which to conduct research which has both practical implications for the well-being of dental patients and which could be very fruitful theoretically. It also points to a number of topics that future research could explore and ways in which it could be conducted. In terms of assessment, there is a need to develop instruments which consider a wider variety of aspects of dental anxiety and phobia. In particular, there is a need for assessments which include aspects of quality of life and an exploration of the ways in which dental phobia can affect patients' lives outside of the dental setting. Some consensus on the applicability of particular assessments would also aid studies of prevalence. For the understanding of aetiology, longitudinal studies are clearly required. While there are many studies based on retrospective accounts, following patients through their dental histories is likely to the only method which could tease out issues of cause and effect. New treatment programmes which are based on cognitive–behavioural approaches and which target negative cognitions may be of special benefit.

Perhaps most of all, it is important that researchers in this area place much more emphasis on theoretical work within psychology. This would have two advantages. First, theoretical psychology could inform the choice of research problem and research design more than it has done previously. As this review makes clear, our understanding of the processes involved in the aetiology, maintenance and treatment of dental phobia has been advanced much more efficiently when conceptual issues have been addressed than when data are collected in a theoretically uninformed manner. Second, there are considerable opportunities for psychologists to extend their theories of anxiety when they are put to the test in the dental setting. Because high levels of dental anxiety are common, because patients who have this difficulty are often willing to contribute to research, and because dental care providers are willing to allow access to their patients, there is great scope for further work.

REFERENCES

Alwin, N., Murray, J.J. & Niven, N. (1994). The effect of children's dental anxiety on the behaviour of the dentist. *International Journal of Paediatric Dentistry*, **4**, 19–24.
American Psychiatric Association (1995). *Diagnostic and Statistical Manual of Mental Disorders (DSM-IV)*. Washington, DC: American Psychiatric Association.
Arntz, A., van Eck, M. & Heijmans, M. (1990). Predictions of dental pain: the fear of any expected evil is worse than the evil itself. *Behaviour Research and Therapy*, **28**, 29–41.
Auerbach, S., Kendall, P., Cuttler, H. et al. (1976). Anxiety, locus of control, type of preparatory information and adjustment to dental surgery. *Journal of Consulting and Clinical Psychology*, **44**, 809–818.
Auerbach, S., Martelli, M. & Mercuri, L. (1983). Anxiety, information, interpersonal impacts and adjustment to a stressful health care situation. *Journal of Personality and Social Psychology*, **44**, 1284–1296.

Bandura, A. (1982). Self-efficacy in human agency. *American Psychologist*, **37**, 122–147.

Baron, R.S., Logan, H. & Hoppe, S. (1991). Desired and felt control as mediators of stress in a dental setting. *Health Psychology*, **10**, 352–359.

Bedi, R., Sutcliffe, P., Barrett, N. & McConnachie, J. (1992). Dental caries experience and prevalence of children afraid of dental treatment. *Community Dentistry and Oral Epidemiology*, **20**, 368–371.

Berggren, U. (1993). Psychosocial effects associated with dental fear in adult dental patients with avoidance behaviours. *Psychology and Health*, **8**, 185–196.

Berggren, U. & Carlsson, S. (1985). Usefulness of two psychometric scales in Swedish patients with severe dental fear. *Community Dentistry and Oral Epidemiology*, **13**, 70–74.

Berggren, U. & Carlsson, S. (1986). Qualitative and quantitiative effects of treatment for dental fear and avoidance. *Anaesthesia Progress*, **33**, 9–13.

Bernstein, D., Kleinknecht, R. & Alexander, L. (1979). Antecedents of dental fear. *Journal of Public Health Dentistry*, **39**, 113–124.

Brown, D., Wright, F. & McMurray, N. (1986). Psychological and behavioural factors associated with dental anxiety in children. *Journal of Behavioral Medicine*, **9**, 213–217.

Carlsson, S., Linde, A., Berggren, U. & Harrison, J.A. (1986). Reduction of dental fear: psychophysiological correlates. *Community Dentistry and Oral Epidemiology*, **14**, 253–257.

Clark, D.M. (1986). A cognitive approach to panic. *Behaviour Research and Therapy*, **24**, 461–470.

Corah, N.L. (1968) Development of a dental anxiety scale. *Journal of Dental Research*, **48**, 596.

Corah, N.L., Gale, E. & Illig, S. (1978). Assessment of a dental anxiety scale. *Journal of the American Dental Association*, **97**, 816–819.

Corkey, B. & Freeman, R. (1994). Predictors of dental anxiety in six-year-old children: findings from a pilot study. *Journal of Dentistry for Children*, **61**, 267–271.

Davey, G. (1989). Dental phobias and anxieties: evidence for conditioning processes in the acquisition and modulation of a learned fear. *Behaviour Research and Therapy*, **27**, 51–58.

de Jong, P., van den Hout, M. & Merckelbach, H. (1995) Co-variation bias and the return of fear. *Behaviour Research and Therapy*, **33**, 211–213.

de Jongh, A., Muris, P., ter Horst, G., Van-Zuuren, F. & De Wit, C. (1994). Cognitive correlates of dental anxiety. *Journal of Dental Research*, **73**, 561–566.

de Jongh, A., Muris, N., Schoenmakers, N. & ter Horst, G. (1995a). Negative cognitions of dental phobics: reliability and validity of the dental cognitions questionnaire. *Behaviour Research and Therapy*, **33**, 507–515.

de Jongh, A., Muris, P., ter Horst, G. & Duyz, M. (1995b). Acquisition and maintenance of dental anxiety: the role of conditioning experience and cognitive factors. *Behaviour Research and Therapy*, **33**, 205–210.

de Moraes, A., Milgrom, P., Tay, K. & Costa, S. (1994). Prevalence of dental fear in Brazilian high school students in Sao Paulo state. *Community Dentistry and Oral Epidemiology*, **22**, 114–115.

de Silva, P. (1988). Phobias and preparedness: replication and extension. *Behaviour Research and Therapy*, **26**, 97–98.

Frazer, M. & Hampson, S. (1988). Some personality factors related to dental anxiety and fear of pain. *British Dental Journal*, **165**, 436–439.

Gokli, M., Wood, A.J., Mourino, A., Farrington, F. & Best, A. (1994). Hypnosis as an adjunct to the administration of local anaesthetic in pediatric patients. *Journal of Dentistry for Children*, **61**, 272–275.

Greenbaum, P., Lumley, M., Turner, C. & Melamed, B.G. (1993). Dentist's reassuring touch: effects on children's behavior. *Paediatric Dentistry*, **15**, 21–24.

Hakeberg, M. & Berggren, U. (1992). Changes in sick leave among Swedish dental patients after treatment for dental fear. *Community Dental Health*, **10**, 23–29.

Hakeberg, M., Berggren, U. & Carlsson, S. (1992). Prevalence of dental anxiety in an adult population in a major urban area in Sweden. *Community Dentistry and Oral Epidemiology*, **20**, 97–101.

Hakeberg, M., Berggren, U. & Grondahl, H. (1993). A radiographic study of dental health in adult patients with dental anxiety. *Community Dentistry and Oral Epidemiology*, **21**, 27–30.

Harrison, J.A., Carlsson, S. & Berggren, U. (1985). Research in clinical process and outcome methodology: psychophysiology, systematic desensitization and dental fear. *Journal of Behavior Therapy and Experimental Psychiatry*, **16**, 201–209.

Hirschman, R., Revland, P., Hawk, G. & Young, D. (1969). Effects of dental anxiety and phase of treatment on discomfort during dental stimulation. *Journal of Dental Research*, **48**, 444–447.

Holst, A., Hallonsten, A., Schroder, U., Ek, L. & Edlund, K. (1993). Prediction of behavior-management problems in 3-year-old children. *Scandinavian Journal of Dental Research*, **101**, 110–114.

Hugdhal, K. & Öst, L. (1985). Subjectively rated physiological and cognitive symptoms in six different clinical phobias. *Personality and Individual Differences*, **6**, 175–188.

Jackson, C. & Lindsay, S. (1995). Reducing anxiety in new dental patients by means of leaflets. *British Dental Journal*, **179**, 163–167.

Jerremalm, A., Jansson, L. & Öst, L. (1986). Individual response patterns and the effects of different behavioral methods in the treatment of dental phobia. *Behaviour Research and Therapy*, **24**, 587–596.

Johnson, R. & Baldwin, D. (1968). Relationship of maternal anxiety to the behaviour of young children undergoing dental extraction. *Journal of Dental Research*, **47**, 801–805.

Kaufman, E., Weinstein, P. & Milgrom, P. (1984). Difficulties in achieving local anesthesia. *Journal of the American Dental Association*, **108**, 205–208.

Kaufman, E., Rand, R.S., Gordon, M. & Cohen, H.S. (1992). Dental anxiety and oral health in young Israeli male adults. *Community Dental Health*, **9**, 125–132.

Kent, G. (1984). Satisfaction with dental care. *Medical Care*, **22**, 211–221.

Kent, G. (1985a). Hypnosis in dentistry. *British Journal of Experimental and Clinical Hypnosis*, **3**, 103–112.

Kent, G. (1985b). Memory of dental pain. *Pain*, **21**, 187–194.

Kent, G. (1986). The typicality of therapeutic surprises. *Behaviour Research and Therapy*, **24**, 625–628.

Kent, G. (1989). Memory of dental experiences as related to naturally occuring changes in state anxiety. *Cognition and Emotion*, **3**, 45–53.

Kent, G., Rubin, G., Getz, T. & Humphris, G. (1996). The development of a scale to measure the social and psychological effects of severe dental anxiety. *Community Dentistry and Oral Epidemiology*, **24**, 394–397.

Kent, G. & Blinkhorn, A. (1991). *The Psychology of Dental Care*. London: Wright.

Kent, G. & Gibbons, R. (1987). Self-efficacy and the control of anxious cognitions. *Journal of Behavior Therapy and Experimental Psychiatry*, **18**, 33–40.

Kent, G. & Warren, P. (1985). A study of factors associated with dental anxiety. *Journal of Dental Research*, **64**, 1316–1318.

Kleinknecht, R., Klepac, R. & Alexander. L. (1973). Origins and characteristics of fear of dentistry. *Journal of the American Dental Association*, **86**, 842–848.

Klepac, R., Dowling, J. & Hauge, G. (1982). Characteristics of clients seeking therapy for the reduction of dental avoidance: reactions to pain. *Journal of Behavior Therapy and Experimental Psychiatry*, **13**, 293–300.

Klingberg, G., Berggren, U. & Noren, J.G. (1993). Dental fear in an urban Swedish child population: prevalence and concomitant factors. *Community Dental Health*, **11**, 208–214.

Klingberg, G. (1994). Reliability and validity of the Swedish version of the Dental Subscale of the Children's Fear Survey Schedule, CFSS-DS. *Acta Odontologica Scandinavica*, **52**, 255–256.

Klingberg, G. & Hwang, C.P. (1994). Children's dental fear picture test (CDFP): a projective test for the assessment of dental fear. *Journal of Dentistry for Children*, **61**, 89–96.

Koenigsberg, S. & Johnson, R. (1972). Child behavior during sequential dental visits. *Journal of the American Dental Association*, **85**, 128–132.

Kupietzky, A. & Houpt, M. (1995). Midazolam: a review of its use for conscious sedation of children. *Pediatric Dentistry*, **15**, 237–241.

Lang, P. (1971). The application of psychophysiological methods to the study of psychotherapy and behavior modification. In A. Bergin & S. Garfield (eds), *Handbook of Psychotherapy and Behavior Change*. New York: Wiley.

Lautch, H. (1971) Dental phobia. *British Journal of Psychiatry*, **119**, 151–158.

Law, A., Logan, H. & Baron, R.S. (1994). Desire for control, felt control, and Stress Inoculation Training during dental treatment. *Journal of Personality and Social Psychology*, **67**, 926–936.

Liddell, A. (1990). Personality characteristics versus medical and dental experiences of dentally anxious children. *Journal of Behavioral Medicine*, **13**, 183–194.

Liddell, A., Di Fazio, L., Blackwood, J. & Ackerman, C. (1994). Long-term follow-up of treated dental phobics. *Behaviour Research and Therapy*, **32**, 605–610.

Liddell, A. & Locker, D. (1993). Dental anxiety in the elderly. *Psychology and Health*, **8**, 175–183.

Liddell, A. & Locker, D. (1994). Disproportionate dental anxiety in the over-50s. *Journal of Behavior Therapy and Experimental Psychiatry*, **25**, 211–216.

Lindsay, S. & Jackson, C. (1993). Fear of routine dental treatment in adults: its nature and management. *Psychology and Health*, **8**, 135–153.

Litt, M.D., Nye, C. & Shafer, D. (1993). Coping with oral surgery by self-efficacy enhancement and perceptions of control. *Journal of Dental Research*, **72**, 1237–1243.

Lochary, M., Wilson, S., Griffen, A. & Coury, D. (1993). Temperament as a predictor of behavior for conscious sedation. *Pediatric Dentistry*, **15**, 348–352.

Locker, D. & Liddell, A. (1992). Correlates of dental anxiety among older adults. *Community Dentistry and Oral Epidemiology*, **20**, 372–375.

Marshall, W.L., Gauthier, J. & Gordon, A. (1979). The current status of flooding therapy. In M. Hersen, R. Eisler & P. Miller (eds), *Progress in Behaviour Modification*, Vol. 7. New York: Academic Press.

McNeil, D. & Berryman, M. (1989). Components of dental fear in adults. *Behaviour Research and Therapy*, **27**, 233–236.

Melamed, B.G. (1979). Behavioural approaches to fear in dental settings. In M. Hersen, R. Eisler & P. Miller (eds), *Progress in Behaviour Modification*, Vol. 7 (pp. 171–203). New York: Academic Press.

Melamed, B.G., Ross, S., Courts, F., Bennett, C., Bush, J., Ronk, S., Jerrell, G. & Hill, C. (1983). Dentists' behavior management as it affects compliance and fear in pediatric patients. *Journal of the American Dental Association*, **106**, 324–330.

Mellor, A.C. (1992). Dental anxiety and attendance in the north-west of England. *Journal of Dentistry*, **20**, 207–210.

Milgrom, P., Weinstein, P., Kleinknecht, R. & Getz, T. (1985). *Treating Fearful Dental Patients: a Clinical Handbook*. Reston, VA: Reston Publishing Company.

Milgrom, P., Mancl, L., King, B. & Weinstein, P. (1995). Origins of childhood dental fear. *Behaviour Research and Therapy*, **33**, 313–319.

Moore, R., Berggren, U. & Carlsson, S. (1991). Reliability and clinical usefulness of psychometric measures in a self-referred population of odontophobics. *Community Dentistry and Oral Epidemiology*, **19**, 347–351.

Moore, R., Brodsgaard, I., Berggren, U. & Carlsson, S. (1991). Generalization of effects of dental fear treatment in a self-referred population of odontophobics. *Journal of Behavior Therapy and Experimental Psychiatry*, **22**, 243–253.

Moore, R., Brodsgaard, I. & Birn, H. (1991). Manifestations, acquisition and diagnositic categories of dental fear in a self-referred population. *Behaviour Research and Therapy*, **29**, 51–60.

Moore, R., Kirkegaard, E., Brodsgaard, I. & Scheutz, F. (1993). Prevalence and characterisitcs of dental anxiety in Danish adults. *Community Dentistry and Oral Epidemiology*, **21**, 292–296.

Moore, R. & Brodsgaard, I. (1994). Group therapy compared with individual desensitization for dental anxiety. *Community Dentistry and Oral Epidemiology*, **22**, 258–262.

Mowrer, O.H. (1960). *Learning Theory and Behavior*. New York: Wiley.

Murray, P., Liddell, A. & Donohue, J. (1989). A longitudinal study of the contribution of dental experience to dental anxiety in children between 9 and 12 years of age. *Journal of Behavioral Medicine*, **12**, 309–320.

Ning, L. & Liddell, A. (1991). The effect of concordance in the treatment of clients with dental anxiety. *Behaviour Research and Therapy*, **29**, 315–322.

Ost, L. (1987). Age of onset in different phobias. *Journal of Abnormal Psychology*, **96**, 223–229.

Roberts, G., Gibson, A., Porter, J. et al. (1979). Relative analgesia: an evaluation of safety. *British Dental Journal*, **146**, 177–182.

Ross, L. (1977). The intuitive psychologist and his shortcomings. In L. Berkowitz, (ed.), *Advances in Experimental Social Psychology*, Vol. 10. New York: Academic Press.

Roy-Bryne, P., Milgrom, P., Khoon-Mei, T., Weinstein, P. & Katon, W. (1994). Psychopathology and psychiatric diagnosis in subjects with dental phobia. *Journal of Anxiety Disorders*, **8**, 19–31.

Schuurs, A.H.B., Makkes, P.C. & Duivenvoorden, H. (1995). Attendance pattern of anxiety-treated patients: a pilot study. *Community Dentistry and Oral Epidemiology*, **20**, 221–223.

Schuurs, A.H.B. & Hoogstraten, J. (1993). Appraisal of dental anxiety and fear questionnaires: a review. *Community Dentistry and Oral Epidemiology*, **21**, 329–339.

Smith, T., Getz, T., Milgrom, P. & Weinstein, P. (1987). Evaluation of treatment at a dental fears research clinic. *Special Care in Dentistry*, **7**, 130–134.

Steptoe, A. & Appels, A. (eds) (1989). *Stress, Personal Control and Health*. Chichester: Wiley.

Stouthard, M., Hoogstraten, J. & Mellenbergh, G. (1995). A study on the convergent and discriminant validity of the dental anxiety inventory. *Behaviour Research and Therapy*, **33**, 589–595.

ter Horst, G. & De Wit, C. (1993). Review of behavioural research in dentistry, 1987–1992: dental anxiety, dentist–patient relationship, compliance and dental attendance. *International Dental Journal*, **43**, 265–278.

Thomas, A., Birch, H., Chess, S., Hertzig, M. & Korn, S. (1963). *Behavioral Individuality in Early Childhood*. London: University of London Press.

Thrash, W., Marr, J. & Box, T. (1982). Effects of continuous patient information in the dental environment. *Journal of Dental Research*, **61**, 1063–1065.

Vassend, O. (1993). Anxiety, pain and discomfort associated with dental treatment. *Behaviour Research and Therapy*, **31**, 659–666.

Veerkamp, J.S.J., Gruythuysen, R., Hoogstraten, J. & van Amerongen, W. (1993). Dental treatment of fearful children using nitrous oxide. Part 4: Anxiety after two years. *Journal of Dentistry for Children*, **60**, 372–376.

Venham, L. (1979). The effect of mother's presence on child's response to dental treatment. *Journal of Dentistry for Children*, **46**, 219–225.

Wardle, J. (1983). Psychological management of anxiety and pain during dental treatment. *Journal of Psychosomatic Research*, **27**, 399–402.

Weiner, A. & Sheehan, D. (1990). Etiology of dental anxiety: psychological trauma or CNS chemical imbalance? *General Dentistry*, **38**, 39–43.

Weinstein, P., Getz, T., Ratener, P. et al. (1982). The effect of dentist's behaviors on fear-related behaviors in children. *Journal of the American Dental Association*, **104**, 32–38.

Williams, J.M.G., Murray, J.J., Lund, C., Harkiss, B. & de Franco, A. (1983). Anxiety in the child dental clinic. *Journal of Child Psychiatry and Psychology*, **26**, 305–310.

Chapter 6

Water Phobia

Ross Menzies
Department of Behavioural Sciences,
University of Sydney, Lidcombe, NSW, Australia

Water phobia is a relatively infrequent specific phobia of adulthood that typically appears in the first 5 years of life (Menzies & Clarke, 1993a). Although its intensity often diminishes by the teenage years it can persist to become a disabling condition with refusal to bathe or shower being a prominent feature (Menzies, 1985). In severe childhood cases refusal to wash hair may lead to its removal, and the inability to bathe adequately to the need for regular bed-bath routines. Typically, it makes the acquisition of swimming-readiness skills and water-safety skills impossible. In adulthood, the inability to engage in water-related social and sporting activities is the primary symptom and the usual reason for seeking treatment. In sum, water phobia may persist from the early years of life into adulthood, where it can have a significant impact on social life. This is particularly true in countries like Australia, from where the majority of recent investigations of water phobia have come, since the majority of individuals live in coastal cities where water-related activties form a major part of social life. Drowning remains a significant cause of death of young children in Australia, and anything that delays the onset of water-safety skills in such a country is of obvious concern. Similarly, anything that restricts adults from normal social activities warrants intervention. This chapter will summarize what is currently known about the nature, prevalence, origin and treatment of water fear and phobia.

NATURE AND PREVALENCE

Without doubt, the single most frequently reported area of difficulty associated with water phobia, particularly in childhood, surrounds bathing. It is the difficulty

Phobias—A Handbook of Theory, Research and Treatment. Edited by G.C.L. Davey.
© 1997 John Wiley & Sons Ltd.

faced in bathing the anxious child that leads most parents of a water phobic to seek help. A mother of a 4-year-old phobic girl described the bathing problems associated with her daughter's water fears:

> Showers and baths have not been possible for some time. Screaming in the bath as an infant didn't seem unnatural, but it has never stopped. As she got older, she would plead for hours not to be placed in the bath. It appeared unrelated to whether or not we washed her hair, or to anything else—she just wouldn't get in the water, even when her favourite toys were there. In the end we decided to cut her hair very short and wash it in the sink only when it was absolutely necessary. She doesn't seem to mind putting her head backwards towards a sink full of water—she says it's because she can't see it.

In the adult water phobic bathing rituals may also be difficult, as a 54-year-old female described:

> I've never been able to cope with baths. I can sit in a very shallow bath, just covering my legs, if there is no shower available. But the idea of being submerged up to my chest in a deep bath is simply intolerable. On a recent holiday I tried to confront it and forced myself into a deep bath. I didn't last long—in deep water I feel like I'm slipping under all the time and I have visions of being submerged and not knowing which way is up. I know its crazy—how can you get lost in a bath?

Irrational cognitions about the dangers of water are commonplace in adult cases. An anxious adult described the basis of the fear of his fish tank:

> It started with a nightmare about a new fish in our fish tank. I dreamed that it grew and grew and finally broke through the glass when it was too big to fit in. It was huge and violent and tried to attack me as it slithered on the floor. Over the months that followed, the dream changed. There were no fish, just a large tank full of water that would spontaneously break and pour all its water out on top of me. I saw a scene like that in a movie once and it has haunted me ever since. I worry I'll drown if the water gets out. I know it would simply go all over the floor, but I can't help thinking that somehow I'd drown. I've even worried about drowning in a sink full of dishes.

Water phobia can make a variety of social activities difficult if not impossible. In addition, in cities with major arterial waterways the mobility of the sufferer can become affected:

> I can't travel on a boat—being out on a large body of water terrifies me. It just doesn't seem natural. I've never understood how they stay afloat with people on board. We lived in Manly for a time and I could never use the ferry to the city. I'd drive every day to work in the peak-hour traffic rather than get on a ferry. Needless to say, I can't swim and I don't feel comfortable even sitting on the beach. I fear the whole tide will come up suddenly and swallow up all the people. In the end we left Manly because I just couldn't use the sea-side. My husband was most upset.

How many adults suffer with water fears to this extent is not well known. In childhood, however, water phobia appears to be a particularly prevalent fear. Miller, Barrett & Hampe (1974) found that excessive fear or phobia of water was more frequently reported than phobias of spiders, insects, dogs, high places, enclosed spaces, injections, blood and 71 other concerns in their large sample of children aged 7–12. Only phobias of snakes and rats were more frequently reported. They found that 1 in 20 of the 249 children they tested had excessive or unreasonable fears of water. Menzies & Clarke (1993a), relying on parental reports of excessive water fear, found water-related anxiety in 1 in 40 of the 8000 children they examined in a large community survey of 3–10-year-olds. The difference in the frequency of water fear found in these two studies may depend on the use of parental reports by Menzies & Clarke (1993a), the small sample size of Miller, Barrett & Hampe (1974), or the different age-ranges surveyed. In addition, Menzies & Clarke's (1993a) search for water-phobic children focused on the beachside suburbs of eastern Sydney, an area where exposure to water-related activities is likely to be substantially greater than in the average population, perhaps reducing the general level of water fear. At this point, it is probably safe to suggest that the prevalence of water phobia in pre-teenage children lies between 2.5 and 5% of the population at any point in time. Unfortunately, no data exist on the frequency of the fear in adulthood.

AETIOLOGY

Given its early onset, it would seem appropriate to investigate the origins of water fear and phobia in early childhood. However, as with many other specific phobias this strategy has rarely been employed. Ollendick & King (1991) point out that, despite the fact that the majority of specific phobias are acquired in childhood, few researchers have investigated aetiological formulations with child subjects. Instead studies of the origins of phobias have tended to rely on the retrospective reports of adult patients who are asked to recall onsets that have often occurred long ago. Not surprisingly, many adult patients appear unable to recall the events surrounding early onsets (McNally & Steketee, 1985). To the present author's knowledge, there is only a single published study investigating the origins of a clinical group of childhood phobic cases (i.e. Menzies & Clarke, 1993b). Given the fact that the focus of this study was water phobia, its findings and conclusions will be examined most closely in the present chapter.

Menzies & Clarke (1993b) used parental reports of the events surrounding onset to investigate the origins of water phobia in young children. The sample comprised 50 subjects (20 female) with a mean age of 5.5 years who were taking part in a water phobia treatment study (Menzies & Clarke, 1993a) at the University of New South Wales on the east coast of Sydney, Australia. This sample had been selected from 200 initial respondents to announcements of the availability of treatment for water phobia at 55 infant and primary schools. All children who could spontaneously place their heads underwater were excluded from the study because of the low levels of their fear. The authors developed their own origins instrument, which consisted of a list of commonly reported water phobia onsets previously identified. These events covered all three of Rachman's (1977) pathways to fear (i.e. direct classical conditioning, vicarious conditioning, and information/instruction). From the list, parents were asked to indicate which option they believed to have been the most influential factor in the development of their child's water phobia.

Menzies & Clarke (1993b) reported that the majority of parents (56%) believed that their child's phobic concern had been present from their very first contact with water. None of these parents chose any of the associative alternatives as being influential in the development of their child's phobia. That is, they believed their child's concern to be unrelated to either direct experience or information/observation. While a substantial proportion of parents (26%) did report indirect conditioning episodes, only 2% of parents attributed their child's phobic concern to a direct Pavlovian conditioning episode. That is, only one parent surveyed could recall such an event in the development of her child's fear. The remaining parents (16%) had no explanation of onset, recalling no traumatic experience, but also reporting that their child had not always displayed a fear of water.

The findings of this investigation include one of the lowest rates of classical conditioning ever reported in a retrospective study of the origins of human fear. Only in studies of spider fear have lower rates of conditioning been observed (e.g. Jones & Menzies, 1995). The 2% rate of conditioning is a much lower percentage than has typically been found with clinical cases of phobia, particularly in the extensive work on the origins of phobias conducted by Öst and his colleagues at the University of Uppsala. In their series of studies, across a variety of different phobic conditions, Öst & Hugdahl have found direct conditioning to account for between 45.5 and 81.3% of clinical cases (Öst & Hugdahl, 1981, 1983, 1985). Several explanations of the marked differences between Menzies & Clarke's (1993b) report and those of Öst & Hugdahl (1981, 1983, 1985) have been previously examined in detail (see further, Menzies & Clarke, 1994). First, Menzies & Clarke's (1993b) report, as previously stated, was the first to use child subjects. Adult memories of early childhood onsets in Öst & Hugdahl's studies may have been subject to greater error than Menzies & Clarke's (1993b) study. Alternatively, the fact that Menzies & Clarke (1993b) relied on parental reports rather than on the phobics' own recall may have led to an underestimate of the rate of conditioning in their report. Menzies & Clarke (1993b) argued that the water-related experiences of young children are likely to have been closely monitored by parents. Still, it is difficult to rule out the possibility that associative, traumatic events occurred in the presence of other care-givers or guardians of which the reporting parent was unaware. It is perhaps significant that Menzies & Clarke (1993b) did not ask *both* parents to complete the origins instrument, but simply the attending parent. Third, differences between the origins instruments used across studies may account for some differences. It has been previously argued that the use of Öst & Hugdahl's (1981) *Phobic Origin Questionnaire* may lead to a significant overestimate of the frequency of classically conditioned cases (Marks, 1987; Menzies & Clarke, 1994). Menzies & Clarke (1993b, 1994, 1995) have repeatedly suggested that the two classical conditioning questions on Öst &

Hugdahl's scale fail to identify the essential ingredients of a Pavlovian conditioning procedure (e.g. presence of an independent UCS, pairing of the CS and the UCS, prior affective neutrality of the CS). Finally, differences across studies may be partly due to the nature of the different specific phobias examined in these reports. Fears of water, as well as spiders and heights, may simply not require associative learning events for acquisition to occur. This is the interpretation of the data offered by Menzies & Clarke (1993b). They suggest that fear of water can develop in the absence of any previous negative experience with the feared stimulus in essentially a non-associative way. No direct or indirect traumatic pairing is required, and neither is negative information. Although some background experiences may be necessary, relevant aversive associative learning is not.

Menzies & Clarke (1993b) are not the first to claim that fear of water may appear in childhood without prior trauma. Marks (1987) notes that as early as 1897, Stanley Hall had suggested that the first experience with water may excite fear (Marks, 1987). Menzies & Clarke's data suggests that this initial anxiety may remain and necessitate treatment many years later. Still, one needs to ask of all these non-associative accounts, why fear does not remain across the population. If our first contacts with water are experienced with fear, why does this reaction not persist in all individuals? That is, what makes water fear persistent in only some people? Several answers to this question have been offered by supporters of the non-associative position. Clarke & Jackson (1983) propose that the initial fearful response will typically diminish across time due to repeated, non-traumatic exposure to the feared object or situation (i.e. habituation). However, they suggest that poor habituators, and those who do not get the opportunity for safe exposure, will remain fearful of such stimuli from their first encounter, often appearing for treatment at a later age. Certainly, in the present author's experience, adult water phobics have typically had little childhood exposure to water-related activities. Adult water phobics tend to be raised in families with little interest in water sports and little access to water-related activities. According to the non-associative model, individual genetic differences may obviously account for some differences in the strength of water fear expressed in later life. That is, some individuals will simply be born with a strong genetic preponderance to develop a persistent water-fear reaction.

Before leaving the aetiology of water phobia, some comment should be made about the high rate of indirect learning present in Menzies & Clarke's (1993b) sample. In each of Öst & Hugdahl's (1981, 1983, 1985) examinations of phobic origins, direct conditioning episodes have been more frequently reported than observational conditioning episodes. In Menzies & Clarke's (1993b) water phobic sample, 26% reported vicarious learning experiences, while only 2% reported direct conditioning. The strong presence of indirect learning in these young children might suggest that other family members had experienced fearful encounters with water and that a familial link exists in water fear. This possibility was examined by Menzies (1985) by comparing the level of children's and parents' fears of water. Children's scores on a seven-item water phobia schedule were correlated with parents' reports of their own fears on a modified version of the instrument. A small to moderate relationship between the fear intensity of mothers and their children ($r = 0.39$) was observed, whereas no relationship between fathers' and children's fear levels was found ($r = 0.05$). Since more young children spend most time in their mothers' care, the opportunity for vicarious learning with their fathers may be reduced. Of course, vicarious conditioning is only one of the many possible explanations for a relationship between the water-fear level of mother and child. Other explanations include genetic influences, similar direct traumatic experiences, and a lack of opportunity to receive repeated non-traumatic exposure to water so that habituation may occur. This latter possibility seems particularly plausible from the perspective of the non-associative model of water fear previously described. If a mother is water-fearful, it is unlikely that she will frequent beaches or swimming pools with her young children. If they spend the majority of time in their mother's care, young children may selectively fail to habituate to fears that their mothers also share.

Unfortunately, to date, no data is available on the histories of adult water phobics. Whether or not the fear can persist into adulthood in the absence of water-related trauma is simply not known at this point. Nothing has been published on the natural history of the fear and it is possible that adult water phobics seen in clinical practice come from an essentially different population to the childhood subjects of Menzies & Clarke (1993b). Certainly the fear appears to be less frequent in adulthood, suggesting that in most individuals it passes in early years. This is not surprising from either an associative or a non-associative perspective. Whether due to extinction or habituation, the constant exposure to water or regular bathing should eliminate the fear in most individuals. Again, anecdotally, it is the present author's experience that persistent cases of water fear have been associated with a marked avoidance of bathing from the earliest years of life.

TREATMENT

The fact that water fear is most frequently observed in childhood and only rarely seen in adult phobia clinics is reflected in the treatment literature. No reports on the management of the condition in adulthood exist. In contrast, three clinical case reports, one experimental analogue and two clinical outcome studies have been published on childhood water fear. In the studies on water phobia to date, exposure-based therapies have generally been found to be effective. In each of the three clinical case studies the child's phobic concern was successfully eliminated with therapies centring on *in vivo* exposure (Bentler, 1962; Pomerantz et al., 1977; Weinstein, 1976). In two cases treatment gains were found to generalize to other situations involving water (Bentler, 1962; Pomerantz et al., 1977), and the follow-up data in each report indicated that benefits achieved appeared to be persistent (Bentler, 1962; Pomerantz et al., 1977; Weinstein, 1976).

The results of the only experimental analogue study further support the use of *in vivo* exposure in the treatment of water fear. Lewis (1974) found *in vivo* exposure to be more effective than filmed modelling (a vicarious treatment component that has been widely used). However, he also observed that the improvements obtained through *in vivo* exposure were enhanced by prior vicarious exposure. Menzies & Clarke (1993a) have questioned the relevance of these suggestions to the treatment of clinical cases of water phobia. Subjects in Lewis' (1974) study had not sought treatment but were solicited during water activities at a summer camp and displayed only mild levels of fear.

Using a small sample of water-phobic children, Ultee, Griffioen & Schellekens (1982) found *in vivo* exposure to be an effective treatment in reducing water-fear levels. Imaginal exposure, however, was found to be no more effective than a control condition. Furthermore, imaginal exposure did not increase the effectiveness of subsequent *in vivo* exposure. Again, however, this study has been criticized on methodological grounds. Ultee et al. (1982) failed to provide either generalization or follow-up data, severely limiting the conclusions that can be drawn about the efficacy of *in vivo* exposure in water phobia. Without a demonstration of the generality of the treatment benefits or their maintenance, it is difficult to confidently endorse a treatment procedure (Kazdin & Wilson, 1978).

A more recent but unpublished clinical outcome study with water-phobic children did provide adequate follow-up and generalization data. Willis (1983) obtained significant treatment gains with five brief sessions of *in vivo* exposure. The treatment gains were found to generalize to another situation involving water, and were persistent at 3-month follow-up. Contrary to the findings of Lewis (1974), however, prior vicarious exposure (filmed) did not enhance the treatment benefits obtained through *in vivo* exposure. While the success of exposure at follow-up and generalization is encouraging, the study remains unpublished.

Finally, Menzies & Clarke (1993a) compared the effectiveness of the following four conditions: (a) *in vivo* exposure plus vicarious exposure (IVVE); (b) vicarious exposure (VE); (c) *in vivo* exposure (IVE); and (d) assessment-only control. Since Willis (1983) found filmed models to be ineffective in reducing levels of fear, a live model was employed in the vicarious components of treatment. Thirty-one boys and 17 girls, ranging in age from 3 to 8 years (mean age = 5.5 years), took part in the largest study of water-phobic children published to date. Each had severe water fears. Subjects who could reportedly place their heads underwater easily and spontaneously had been eliminated from an original and larger sample, as had subjects displaying mild to moderate fear levels during an initial water avoidance test. All children received three treatment sessions which were administered individually over a 3-week period. In the exposure plus modelling condition, each subject observed a live model (the therapist) engage in progressively more intimate interactions with water for 15 minutes. The model displayed highly competent, fearless behaviour to the child who observed the model from the side of the pool. This vicarious component was followed by 15 minutes of gradual *in vivo* exposure to the water and a hierarchy of activities on a water avoidance test. The therapist entered the pool after the subject, doing no modelling but lending physical assistance when necessary, and giving praise for any activities attempted and completed by the subject. Gradual *in vivo* exposure involved the same tasks as demonstrated by the model.

In the modelling-alone condition, each subject observed the live model engage in water-related activities for 15 minutes as described above, followed by 15 minutes of exposure to other activities with the therapist. This latter component provided an interpersonal experience with the therapist of the same length and similar in content to the *in vivo* exposure phase of the combined condition, but which did not involve participation in water activities. Finally, in the exposure-alone condition, each subject observed, but did not participate in, a variety of activities demonstrated by the therapist in the large room adjacent to the pool. The demonstration lasted for 15 minutes. It provided an experience with the therapist of the same length and similar in content to the vicarious exposure phase of the combined treatment (IVVE), but which did not involve modelling of water activities. The demonstration was followed by 15 minutes of gradual *in vivo* exposure to the water as described above.

No differences were observed between the combined (IVVE) and exposure-alone (IVE) procedures at post-treatment. The *in vivo* plus vicarious exposure (IVVE) group and the exposure-alone group had experienced clinically and statistically significant gains in three short sessions. The encouraging results were shown to generalize to another testing situation. In contrast to these positive findings, the vicarious exposure (VE) condition led to no greater reduction in children's water phobia than the control condition.

It is of note that the *in vivo* exposure group (IVE) showed poorer maintenance than the combined condition (IVVE). Three months post-treatment, the IVVE group means for all four dependent variables were higher than the IVE group means. The exposure-alone condition showed a decay of therapeutic benefits on three of the four measures of water fear used. In contrast, the combined (IVVE) group had improved on all four measures.

The failure of the Menzies & Clarke's (1993a) vicarious procedure is at variance with the findings of Lewis (1974) and the earlier studies on modelling by Bandura and his colleagues (e.g. Bandura et al., 1969). However, these reports involved subjects who did not actively seek treatment and displayed only mild to moderate levels of distress. Data from analogue studies involving water-fearful children may be irrelevant to the treatment of clinical levels of water phobia. It must be remembered that with an earlier clinical sample, Willis (1983) also failed to find benefits with modelling procedures. However, given the decay of improvements observed in the exposure alone condition across the 3-month follow-up period in Menzies & Clarke's (1993a) study, the inclusion of a vicarious component in the early intervention of water phobia is recommended at this point. Even the modelling-alone condition in the Menzies & Clarke (1993a) study showed greater stability across the 3-month follow-up period than did exposure alone. What it is about modelling that seems to retard the decay of treatment benefits across time is not clear. Whether or not the effect is unique to water phobia is not known, although the present author is unaware of the finding in any other phobic type. Clearly, the reasons for the merits of the procedure in water fear need to be elucidated.

CONCLUDING COMMENTS AND FUTURE DIRECTIONS

Menzies & Clarke (1993b) have argued that initial fear displays to water are essentially an evolutionary reaction to a long-standing danger to the species. Given normal background experiences and maturation of the nervous system to an appropriate level, they suggest that most members of the species should show fear of deep water on their first encounter. The age at which this fear appears in most children is unknown, but could be simply established through tests of large numbers of pre-school children on a constant water stimulus. In any investigation of this sort the previous experiences of the subjects should be examined most closely. Is water fear modified by prior regular, exposure to deep water? Is water fear less common in children from homes with pools? Is water fear less common in children who bathe rather than shower? Is water fear less common in children from coastal areas?

The absence of any data on the aetiology or treatment of adult water phobia suggests obvious directions for future research. Is water phobia in adulthood related to the developmental fear of water observed in early childhood, or are aversive conditioning episodes required for persistent water fear to become established? Is adult water fear associated with reduced access to water-related activities in childhood? Is the onset of adult water fear consistent with the dishabituation explanation of Menzies & Clarke (1993b)? That is, does onset appear to follow traumas that are apparently unrelated to water? Finally, given the irrational danger-related cognitions that have been anecdotally reported in adult water-phobic cases, what role do outcome expectancies have in the mediation of adult water fear? Do procedures that reliably reduce danger expectancies in other fears (e.g. exposure) also do so for water fear?

Clearly, an enormous amount of basic research on water phobia in both children and adults is necessary before strong claims about the aetiology and treatment of the condition can be made. It can be hoped that such research will be forthcoming in the near future as the potential severity of the condition becomes more widely recognized. As the observations from patients given earlier in the chapter show, water phobia is a serious specific phobia that can significantly interfere with the daily life of the sufferer and his/her family.

REFERENCES

Bandura, A., Blanchard, E.B. & Ritter, B. (1969). The relative efficacy of desensitization and modeling approaches for inducing behavioral, affective and attitudinal changes. *Journal of Personality and Social Psychology*, **13**, 173–199.

Bentler, P.M. (1962). An infants phobia treated with reciprocal inhibition therapy. *Journal of Child Psychology and Psychiatry*, **3**, 185–189.

Clarke, J.C. & Jackson, J.A. (1983). *Hypnosis and Behavior Therapy: the Treatment of Anxiety and Phobias*. New York: Springer.

Jones, M.K. & Menzies, R.G. (1995). The aetiology of fear of spiders. *Anxiety, Stress and Coping*, **8**, 227–234.

Kazdin, A.E. & Wilson, G.T. (1978). Criteria for evaluating psychotherapy. *Archives of General Psychiatry*, **35**, 407–416.

Lewis, S. (1974). A comparison of behaviour therapy techniques in the reduction of fearful avoidance behaviour. *Behavior Therapy*, **5**, 648–655.

Marks, I.M. (1987). *Fears, Phobias and Rituals: Panic, Anxiety and their Disorders*. New York: Oxford University Press.

McNally, R.J. & Steketee, G.S. (1985). The aetiology and maintenance of severe animal phobias. *Behaviour Research and Therapy*, **23**, 431–435.

Menzies, R.G. (1985). The Aetiology and Treatment of Children's Water Phobia. Unpublished honours thesis, University of New South Wales, Kensington, Sydney.

Menzies, R.G. & Clarke, J.C. (1993a). A comparison of *in vivo* and vicarious exposure in the treatment of childhood water phobia. *Behaviour Research and Therapy*, **31**, 9–15.

Menzies, R.G. & Clarke, J.C. (1993b). The aetiology of childhood water phobia. *Behaviour Research and Therapy*, **31**, 499–501.

Menzies, R.G., & Clarke, J.C. (1994). Retrospective studies of the origins of phobias: a review. *Anxiety, Stress, and Coping*, **7**, 305–318.

Menzies, R.G. & Clarke, J.C. (1995). The aetiology of phobias: a non-associative account. *Clinical Psychology Review*, **15**, 23–48.

Miller, L.C., Barrett, C.L. & Hampe, E. (1974). In A. Davids (ed.), *Child Personality and Psychopathology: Current Topics*. New York: Wiley.

Ollendick, T.H. & King, N.J. (1991). Origins of childhood fears: an evaluation of Rachman's theory of fear acquisition. *Behaviour Research and Therapy*, **29**, 117–123.

Öst, L.-G. & Hugdahl, K. (1981). Acquisition of phobias and anxiety response patterns in clinical patients. *Behaviour Research and Therapy*, **19**, 439–447.

Öst, L.-G. & Hugdahl, K. (1983). Acquisition of agoraphobia, mode of onset and anxiety response patterns. *Behaviour Research and Therapy*, **21**, 623–632.

Öst, L.-G. & Hugdahl, K. (1985). Acquisition of blood and dental phobia and anxiety response patterns in clinical patients. *Behaviour Research and Therapy*, **23**, 27–34.

Pomerantz, P.B., Peterson, N.T., Marholin, D. & Stern, S. (1977). The *in vivo* elimination of a child's water phobia by a para-professional at home. *Journal of Behavior Therapy and Experimental Psychiatry*, **8**, 417–421.

Rachman, S. (1977). The conditioning theory of fear acquisition: a critical examination. *Behaviour Research and Therapy*, **15**, 375–387.

Ultee, C.A., Griffioen, D. & Schellekens, J. (1982). The reduction of anxiety in children: a comparison of the effects of systematic desensitization *in vitro* and systematic desensitization *in vivo*. *Behaviour Research and Therapy*, **20**, 61–67.

Weinstein, D.J. (1976). Imagery and relaxation with a burn patient. *Behaviour Research and Therapy*, **14**, 481.

Willis, L.M. (1983). The Aetiology, Assessment and Treatment of Children's Phobic Fear of Water. Unpublished honours thesis, University of New South Wales, Kensington, Sydney.

Chapter 7

Height Phobia

Ross Menzies
*Department of Behavioural Sciences, University of Sydney,
Lidombe, NSW, Australia*

Research on the aetiology, nature and treatment of height phobia (acrophobia) has increased dramatically in recent years with the recognition that this particular specific phobia can be extremely disabling. Acrophobic behaviour typically involves avoidance of a range of stimuli that can include ladders, lookouts, stairwells, high-rise residential and office space, bridges, lifts and plane travel. Not surprisingly, given the variety of stimuli that can be feared, acrophobic individuals are often more restricted in their movements than other specific phobics. This chapter will review what is currently known about the nature, origin and management of this condition.

PREVALENCE

Unfortunately, well conducted studies on the incidence, prevalence and distribution of the specific phobias are scarce (Weissman, 1983). Early epidemiological research suffered from various methodological flaws, yielding little accurate and useful information. For example, researchers typically used idiosyncratic definitions of the phobic disorders. Many defined phobia in terms of arbitrary scores on differing rating scales (Agras, Sylvester & Oliveau, 1969; Burns, 1980; Burns & Thorpe, 1977; Shephard et al., 1981), making comparisons between studies difficult if not impossible. This was a particular problem in research conducted prior to the widespread acceptance and use of diagnostic criteria.

Since the development of structured interviews to assess accepted criteria, reliable information on the epidemiology of phobic disorders should now be available. However, recent research has continued to neglect the individual specific phobic subtypes. Thus, while general statements about the prevalence of specific phobias can be made, less is known about the prevalence of the different specific phobic conditions. Although little is currently known about the frequency of acrophobia, the following observations can be made. Acrophobia was described as early as Hippocrates and has been claimed by some to be the most common of the simple phobias (e.g. Zutt, 1952). Several researchers admit to selecting acrophobia for study because of its relatively high prevalence in clinical populations and the associated ease of soliciting large sample sizes (e.g. Sutton-Simon & Gotfried, 1979). Burns (1980) found fear of heights to be the third most common fear in a sample of patients seen in general practice. It ranked above fears of thunder and lightning, enclosed spaces, crowds, aeroplanes and blood. Similarly, Agras, Sylvester & Oliveau (1969) reported the frequency of intense height fear to be 120 per 1000, placing it second behind snakes. Again, it ranked above many phobic concerns that have received seemingly more research attention, including fears of flying, enclosed spaces and dentistry. According to Agras, Sylvester & Oliveau (1969), it accounted for 5% of all phobics, including agoraphobics, and 2% of all phobics in treatment. With the ever-increasing number of high-rise residential and business facilities in developed cities, this latter figure may underestimate the present frequency of acrophobia in psychiatric settings. There is little doubt that most height phobics can less easily avoid phobic encounters than in the past, a situation that may lead to greater impact on the functioning of the modern acrophobic, and an increased need for professional help. In any event, what is clear from the literature is that acrophobia is one of the most significant specific phobic concerns in both the community and the clinic.

AETIOLOGY

Despite the frequency of intense height fear, until very recently acrophobia has received virtually no attention from clinical researchers. For example, it was not until 1993 that any group data on the origins of the fear in human adults was published (Menzies & Clarke, 1993). Prior to this time only anecdotal accounts of the origins of individual cases had been described in the literature. In 1995, in an extension of their 1993 analogue study, Menzies & Clarke presented the first group data on a solicited patient sample of height phobics. Since the two reports of Menzies & Clarke (1993, 1995a) are the only group studies examining the origins of height fear in human adults, they will be examined closely in this chapter.

Menzies & Clarke's (1993) initial report sought to establish a new instrument for use in retrospective human origins research and to avoid the major methodological failings of previous research (see further, Menzies & Clarke, 1994). They argued that selection of methodology and the construction of origins questionnaires in the past had too often depended on the researcher's theoretical position, and by virtue of their methodology, a variety of researchers had imposed preliminary constraints upon their possible results. This, they claimed, had most frequently occurred when investigators had begun with the assumption that *all* phobias are indebted to some traumatic experience with the object or situation and, as a result of this assumption, predisposed themselves to support a learning-based account of phobic onset by excluding non-associative modes of origin from study (e.g. Öst & Hugdahl, 1983, 1985; Rimm et al., 1977). In addition, it was argued that many researchers had equated *any* traumatic event with classical conditioning. For example, from the conditioning questions on their origins survey it is clear that Öst & Hugdahl (1981, 1983, 1985) did not require the identification of an independent unconditioned stimulus (UCS), and did not ascertain that the conditioned stimulus (CS) was affectively neutral prior to the proposed conditioning episodes. Not surprisingly, some recent reviews have suggested that Öst's methodology has led to a significant overestimate of the frequency of conditioned cases in specific phobias (e.g. Marks, 1987; Menzies & Clarke, 1994).

With these methodological inadequacies in mind, Menzies & Clarke (1993) investigated the acquisition of fear of heights in an undergraduate student sample with a new origins instrument. Their 16-page questionnaire, called simply the Origins Questionnaire (OQ), was designed to give a comprehensive picture of the history of the subject in relation to the phobic object or situation prior to the onset of their concerns. Unlike previous popular measures (e.g. Öst & Hugdahl's Phobic Origin Questionnaire, 1981), it did not require the subject to make causal attributions, but rather to simply indicate and describe any informational, vicarious, direct conditioning or other relevant events that had occurred prior to onset. The questionnaire distinguishes between subjects who claim to have always been fearful and those who, while failing to recall the beginning of their concerns, recognize an earlier non-phobic period in their lives. In addition, the open-ended nature of the questions allows for the distinction between classical conditioning events and traumatic events in which no identifiable UCS can be found. Height-fearful and non-fearful groups were formed on the basis of extreme scores to the heights item on the FSS-III (Wolpe & Lang, 1964). Subjects were then assessed with a battery of measures including: (a) the new Origins Questionnaire (OQ); (b) the Acrophobia Questionnaire (AQ; Cohen, 1977); (c) Global Assessment of Severity; (d) Self-Rating of Severity; and (e) an Origins Interview. Results obtained questioned the significance of simple associative-learning events in the acquisition of height phobia. Only 18% of fearful subjects were classified as directly conditioned cases. No differences between groups were found in the proportion of subjects who knew other height-fearful subjects, or had experienced relevant associative-learning events, or the ages at which these events had occurred. In addition, no relationships between mode of acquisition and severity or individual response patterns were obtained. Finally, strong evidence for the inter-rater reliability and construct validity of the new Origins Questionnaire (OQ) was found, with significant agreement between raters and a strong relationship between the OQ and the Origins Interview being obtained.

Given the risks of generalizing findings from student samples to clinical subjects, Menzies & Clarke (1995a) sought to replicate these findings with a group of acrophobics who had sought treatment. In addition, a more thorough examination of Rachman's (1977) hypothesized relationships between onset and response patterns was undertaken by including a behavioural test and physiological data in the second study. One-hundred-and-forty-eight subjects who sought treatment at a height phobia clinic at the University of New South Wales were given a large battery of tests. All of the measures used in Menzies & Clarke's earlier study were administered, in addition to a Behavioural Avoidance Test (BAT) that allowed for the assessment of subjective distress, negative thoughts, heart-rate, systolic blood pressure, diastolic blood pressure, and avoidance. As in their earlier investigation, more acrophobic subjects again claimed that their fear had always been present, or had arisen in a non-associative traumatic event, than were classified as directly conditioned cases. Non-associative categories accounted for 56% of subjects, compared to only 11% of subjects who were classified as cases of direct conditioning. Despite the inclusion of physiological and avoidance data, no relationships between onset, severity and individual response patterns could be found. Again, no differences between groups were found in the proportion of subjects who knew other height-fearfuls, had experienced aversive associative-learning events, or the ages at which these events had occurred.

The findings from these studies have been taken to support the non-associative account of fear acquisition that continues to attract theorists from a variety of backgrounds (e.g. Bowlby, 1975; Clarke & Jackson, 1983; Marks, 1969, 1987; Menzies & Clarke, 1995b; cf. Chapter 16). This model claims that, given maturational processes and normal background experiences, most members of the species will show fear to a set of biologically relevant stimuli on their *first* encounter (Menzies & Clarke, 1995b). No direct aversive associative-learning is required, neither is indirect learning (vicarious conditioning or information/instruction). Other evidence for the model can be found in the growing list of fears that appear to emerge in a variety of species in the absence of aversive conditioning. Separation, strangers, visual looming, eyespot patterns, various odours and novelty can produce fear in the first days of life without any prior aversive CS–UCS pairing (see further, Marks, 1987). Not only does the evidence seem to support the case for the non-associative acquisition of fear but, according to many, the "unlearned" account is a more plausible explanation than its major Darwinian opponent, namely Seligman's (1971) preparedness theory. In Seligman's account, at least one aversive associative-learning trial is required for acquisition. One learning trial, given the dangers to the individual that it may bring, is said to be one trial too many in these modern Darwinian models (e.g. Bowlby, 1975; Clarke & Jackson, 1983; Menzies & Clarke, 1995b).

Further evidence for the non-associative account of height fear comes from animal and infant studies, beginning with the work of Gibson & Walk and the now-famous "visual cliff". The visual cliff consists of a thin board laid across a large sheet of glass which is supported at varying heights above the floor. On one side of the board a sheet of patterned material is placed flush against the underside of the glass. On the other side, a sheet of the same material is laid upon the floor. The latter side thus becomes the visual cliff. Although the board width, thickness and height of the glass varied in Gibson & Walk's various studies (in order to accommodate different species), the apparatus remained, in its essentials, as described above.

In their original work with human subjects, Gibson & Walk (1960) tested 36 infants ranging in age from 6 to 14 months. The procedure began by placing the infant on the centre board. The child's mother would then call from the deep side and the shallow side alternately. *All* of the 27 infants tested who moved off the centre board crawled onto the shallow side at least once; only 3 of them ever crawled onto the deep "cliff" side (Gibson & Walk, 1960). Many infants crawled away from their mother when she called to them from the deep side. Others would pat the glass but, despite the tactual evidence that the "cliff" was in fact a solid surface, would refuse to cross it. Others simply cried (Gibson & Walk, 1960).

Findings with other terrestrial species were largely consistent and equally dramatic. Due to their early self-produced locomotion, chicks, kids and lambs could be tested on the first day of life, as soon as they could stand. *No* chick, goat or lamb tested ever stepped onto the glass on the deep side, even at 1 day old (Gibson & Walk, 1960). When lowered onto the deep side, kids and lambs would initially refuse to put their feet down. This was followed by the adoption of a posture of defence, the front legs becoming rigid and the hind legs limp. From this immobile state they would often leap in the air to the apparent safety of the centre board rather than walk on the glass. Similar findings with cats were obtained, and other researchers have extended the list to include dogs, pigs and neonatal monkeys, to name but a few. Indeed, there are few fears that appear more consistently in terrestrial animals. Unlike land-dwelling animals, aquatic species such as ducks, who have little reason to fear a perceived drop, readily cross onto the deep side (Emlen, 1963; Routtenberg & Glickman, 1964).

Walk & Gibson (1961) concluded that in a variety of terrestrial species, fear and avoidance of heights is innate and appears by the time the infant is locomotive. However, as we have been urged by more recent writers, to deny the role of experience and the environment in the development of fear is fraught with danger. Subsequent research has not surprisingly shown that certain background experiences may be necessary for the development of avoidance of the visual cliff. The most notable of these is self-produced locomotion. Despite some controversy (cf. Bertenthal & Campos, 1984; Richards & Rader, 1983), it now appears clear that previous experience of self-produced locomotion may be necessary for avoidance and fear of the visual cliff to be consistently observed. Bertenthal, Campos & Barrett (1984) report on various findings supporting this conclusion. Pre-locomotive infants $7\frac{1}{2}$ months old showed little cardiac changes indicative of fear when placed on the deep side, whereas locomotive infants of the same age showed heart-rate acceleration. Also, prelocomotive infants given locomotor experience through 40 hours in an "infant walker" showed heart-rate acceleration when placed on the deep side, whereas prelocomotor infants of the same age without "walker" experience did not.

However, it must be emphasized that while self-produced locomotion appears to be important in the development of the avoidance of the visual cliff, previous falls have been found to be unrelated and unnecessary for avoidance to occur (e.g. Scarr & Salapatek, 1970). That is, while experience seems to play a role in the emergence of this fear, it need not take the form of aversive classical conditioning. Crawling may be important in expanding the infant's perspective by increasing its encounters with new experiences, and seems to speed the emergence of spatial cognition, form extraction and social communication, as well as fear of heights (Marks, 1987).

At this point, while the data are clearly supportive of the non-associative account of height phobia, more research on human subjects is needed before strong claims can be made. It must be remembered that to date only two human retrospective studies have been conducted, and neither has used unsolicited acrophobic patients as subjects. Still, what can be claimed with some confidence is that in both human infancy and adulthood, fear of heights *can* appear in the absence of any direct aversive conditioning episodes.

TREATMENT

If one excludes studies that combine height-fearful subjects with other simple phobic types, then the number of reports available for review is dramatically reduced. Below is a brief discussion of the findings of outcome studies that have focused exclusively on the behavioural or cognitive–behavioural treatment of acrophobia.

There are three case studies in the literature on the behavioural treatment of acrophobia (Guralnick, 1973; Hall & Dietz, 1975; Schneider, 1982). First, Guralnick (1973) successfully applied a combination of imaginal systematic desensitization with visual supports, *in vivo* desensitization and behaviour-shaping in the treatment of a 21-year-old male with Down's syndrome. Prior to treatment, severe acrophobia was markedly restricting the patient's participation in general programs at a treatment centre for retardation. The behavioural intervention enabled the patient to significantly increase his involvement in these other therapeutic activities.

Schneider (1982) reported on the treatment of a single case with lens-assisted *in vivo* exposure. The 40-year-old male patient was successfully treated with *in vivo* desensitization using reverse viewing through binoculars to magnify the apparent height. Schneider argued that the technique allows effective treatment from low actual heights, and provides the opportunity to extend exposure to apparent heights greater than those normally available. It is a technique that warrants more attention than it has received in the clinical and experimental literature.

Finally, Hall & Dietz (1975) reported on the successful treatment of a 20-year-old acrophobic patient who was concurrently suffering from an ear infection. The patient's fear of heights had expanded to include driving as well as fear of sitting in college classrooms. During treatment, the authors discovered that the ear infection occasionally led to a gag reflex, and that the patient's principle concern was the possibility of choking. This latter fear seemed to underpin the other symptoms. The patient reported that his fears of heights and driving were directly related to the dangerous consequences that a gag reflex might produce in such sites. The fear in classrooms seemed to involve social embarrassment of the gag reaction. The patient was successfully treated with systematic desensitization using a hierarchy related to the gag response.

Of the group outcome studies, Schaap & Dana (1968) were the first to demonstrate the effectiveness of systematic desensitization in the treatment of fear of heights. They allocated two subjects to each of the following three conditions: (a) experimenter-administered systematic desensitization; (b) self-administered systematic desensitization; and (c) a control interview about heights. Interestingly, self-administered desensitization proved superior to the experimenter-administered condition. However, the authors noted several large individual differences in the experimenter-assisted group, which they believed may have obscured change in this condition. They warned against any firm conclusions being drawn from these results.

In the following year, Ritter reported on two outcome studies with acrophobic patients. Ritter (1969a) assigned four acrophobic subjects to each of three treatments: (a) contact desensitization; (b) contact desensitization without physical contact with the therapist; and (c) no treatment. Contact desensitization produced greater reductions in fear of heights than the other two conditions, leading Ritter to conclude that therapist contact may be a crucial therapeutic ingredient. Ritter (1969b) repeated the findings in a second study in which the first two treatments above were compared to modelling. Again, contact desensitization proved superior to the other treatments. Modelling produced no significant changes in severe acrophobic subjects.

In a further examination of contact desensitization and acrophobia, Morris & Magrath (1979) examined the contribution of therapist warmth to treatment outcome. Nineteen height-fearful volunteers were each assigned to one of the following conditions: (a) contact desensitization with a "warm" therapist; (b) contact desensitization with a "cold" therapist; and (c) a wait-list control. While both treatment groups showed greater improvement than the control condition, no consistent differences were found between the "warm" and "cold" therapist conditions. They concluded that therapist warmth did not appear to be a critical factor in contact desensitization with height-fearful subjects.

The remaining group studies examined different behavioural treatments for acrophobia. Leitenberg & Callahan (1973) examined the effects of reinforced practice (i.e. in vivo exposure plus reinforcement) on height avoidance. Eighteen subjects were randomly assigned to treatment and no-treatment conditions. Ten sessions of reinforced practice led to a significant reduction of height avoidance compared to the control condition. Although treatment effects seemed to diminish over time, subjects were still more significantly improved at 2-year follow-up than they had been at pre-treatment.

Williams, Turner & Peer (1985) allocated 38 solicited acrophobics to one of three conditions: (a) guided mastery; (b) performance desensitization; and (c) no treatment. Guided mastery led to significantly greater reductions in fear and avoidance than desensitization. Williams et al. (1985) argue that these results suggest that self-efficacy, on which the guided mastery procedure was based, may be an important mediator of treatment effects.

Marshall (1985) examined the effect of varying lengths of exposure on treatment outcome in two acrophobic studies. In both studies acrophobic patients who received brief exposures made little gain. In contrast, those subjects whose exposure sessions continued until anxiety had returned to baseline or beyond showed significant reductions in fear. The condition that led to the greatest gains involved prolonged exposure in combination with training in coping self-statements.

Finally, in their most recent therapy evaluation, Menzies & Clarke (1995c) examined the relationship of individual response patterns to cognitive–behavioural treatment outcome. Sixty acrophobic subjects were initially tested with a battery of measures including a Height Avoidance Test that allowed direct physiological (heart-rate, systolic and diastolic blood pressure), verbal–cognitive (subjective anxiety, danger expectancies), and behavioural (avoidance) assessment. Subjects were then randomly allocated to a physiologically-focused (progressive muscle relaxation), cognitively-focused (cognitive therapy), or behaviourally-focused (*in vivo* exposure) treatment. After follow-up assessment subjects were divided into physiological, cognitive and behavioural responders on the basis of their standardized pre-treatment Height Avoidance Test scores. Subjects who had been treated consonantly (i.e. with the procedure designed to target their primary response) had not experienced any greater improvement on any of the 11 outcome measures than subjects who had been treated non-consonantly. That is, at post-treatment and follow-up, no support for the treatment matching hypothesis could be found. Supplementary analyses showed that *in vivo* exposure produced significantly greater treatment benefits than relaxation or cognitive restructuring which were equally, but less, effective.

Interpreting and integrating the many and varied findings of the above studies is far harder than simply describing their results. First, different therapeutic labels for exposure-based procedures often belie identical therapeutic procedures (Clarke & Jackson, 1983). This makes the comparison of different studies more difficult than it need be. Second, a variety of methodological problems in the above studies temper any conclusions that can be drawn. Inadequate sample sizes are a problem with many of the studies. With as few as two subjects per group in some experiments (e.g. Schaap & Dana, 1968), many researchers simply had too little power to detect small treatment differences. Short duration of treatment is another problematic feature of many of the studies. In some reports the duration of therapy is not even provided (Schaap & Dana, 1968). In many others, subjects received only one or two sessions of treatment (Ritter, 1968a, 1968b; Williams, Turner & Peer, 1985), with a total treatment duration of as little as 24 minutes (Ritter, 1968a). Periods of follow-up were also too brief. With some notable exceptions (e.g. Hall & Dietz, 1975; Leitenberg & Callahan, 1973), following-up durations were generally short, often 1 month or less (e.g. Marshall, 1985; Morris & Magrath, 1979; Williams, Turner & Peer, 1985). Many studies did not include *any* follow-up assessment (e.g. Ritter, 1969a, 1969b; Schaap & Dana, 1968). Also lacking were measures of treatment integrity, credibility of treatment procedures and multiple assessments across all three response systems. In only two studies was any attempt made to assess treatment integrity (Morris & Magrath, 1979; Menzies & Clarke, 1995c). Similarly, only two studies provided a complete three-system assessment by using behavioural avoidance tests in combination with physiological assessment and measures of subjective distress (Emmelkamp & Felton, 1985; Menzies & Clarke, 1995c). Finally, some researchers relied on student samples with minimal levels of fear (e.g. Schaap & Dana, 1968), while others solicited subjects with lures of monetary reward (e.g. Leitenberg & Callahan, 1973).

In sum, methodological problems cloud the findings of these studies, making specific conclusions and recommendations about treatment in acrophobia difficult to offer. Given the failure of Menzies & Clarke (1995c) to find any treatment matching effect, and the general support for exposure-based procedures that has been consistently obtained, it is tempting to suggest that gradual exposure is all that is needed to overcome height fear, and further, that cognitive and other behavioural procedures simply prolong treatment unnecessarily. However, recent research on danger ideation in height-phobic subjects suggests that the exclusion of cognitive procedures might be premature with this particular specific phobia. This research will be summarized below.

DANGER EXPECTANCIES AND INSIGHT IN ACROPHOBIA

In several recent reports, the ability of acrophobic subjects to estimate accurately the danger in potential phobic encounters has been questioned. Three studies have found acrophobic subjects to display exaggerated beliefs about the probability of falling on height avoidance tasks involving ladders (Andrews, Freed & Teeson, 1994; Menzies & Clarke, 1995d; Menzies, in press). In addition, in two of these reports acrophobic subjects were also shown to believe that their excessive levels of anticipated anxiety were reasonable and appropriate to the demands of the task (Menzies & Clarke, 1995d; Menzies, in press). On the strength of these findings, Menzies & Clarke (1995d) have called into question the level of insight found in acrophobic cases, and the validity of insight-based diagnostic criteria for specific phobias (e.g. DSM-IV, American Psychiatric Association, 1994).

Using a large sample of acrophobic patients and a matched set of controls, Menzies & Clarke (1995d) obtained danger ratings on the ground and during a height avoidance test on a triple extension ladder. Before the test acrophobic patients: (a) gave higher estimates of the probability of falling from the ladder than did controls; (b) gave higher estimates of the injuries that would result from falling; and (c) believed their excessive levels of anticipated anxiety were more reasonable and appropriate to the demands of the situation than did normals. In addition, during the height avoidance test the differences between the two groups grew as phobic danger estimates increased, while control group estimates did not. Finally, moderate relationships were obtained between danger ratings and subsequent anxiety and avoidance.

In a recent replication and extension of this report involving several methodological refinements and the inclusion of self-efficacy ratings, Menzies (in press) has again demonstrated the potential mediating role of danger expectancies in acrophobia. When detached from the phobic stimulus, acrophobic subjects again reported higher danger estimates than did controls. Both self-efficacy and danger expectancies were found to be significantly related to ladder anxiety and avoidance. In general, both self-efficacy and danger ratings remained significantly related to anxiety and avoidance when the alternative mediator was held constant in a series of partial correlation analyses. Finally, Menzies (in press) extended these findings to other acrophobic situations using a different methodology. Modified Acrophobia Questionnaries (AQ; Cohen, 1977) were given to a small sample of acrophobic subjects and a group of controls. Subjects were asked to indicate the level of anxiety that they believed was most appropriate, or realistically warranted by, each of the 20 situations listed on the AQ. Not surprisingly, given the previous findings described above, acrophobic subjects claimed that significantly more anxiety was warranted by the AQ situations than did controls. In addition, they believed that their high levels of anticipated anxiety were more reasonable and appropriate to the demands of the 20 situations than did controls.

In sum, with several different samples of acrophobics, important differences have been found between acrophobic and control expectancies of danger. Thus, the traditional claim that acrophobic patients, like all specific phobics, have complete insight into the irrationality of their fears, appears to be in error.

FUTURE DIRECTIONS AND CONCLUDING COMMENTS

Given the moderate to high correlations between danger beliefs and anxiety and avoidance obtained in the reports of Menzies & Clarke (1995d) and Menzies (in press), this cognitive variable is a likely mediator of acrophobic phenomena. Of course, it must be remembered that the partial correlation analyses in the report of Menzies (in press) failed to establish whether danger beliefs or self-efficacy ratings represent the most likely cause of acrophobic responses. It can be argued that the most appropriate strategy in the future involves the direct manipulation of the postulated mediators in order to measure their impact on subsequent anxiety and avoidance. For example, using Menzies & Clarke's (1995d) experimental paradigm, differing instructions regarding the sturdiness of the ladder could be used across groups to manipulate directly the probability-of-falling estimates. Different thicknesses of matting on the cement below the ladder might directly manipulate estimates of potential injury. Direct manipulations of self-efficacy and other postulated mediators could also be similarly achieved. These suggested studies represent an appropriate direction for research on acrophobia to progress. In many ways, this type of research offers the most likely basis for the development of major innovations in the treatment of acrophobia, for if one of the postulated cognitive variables can be shown to mediate height-phobic behaviour, treatments might be designed with a more direct target for maximum efficacy in the future. Time will tell.

REFERENCES

Agras, S., Sylvester, D. & Oliveau, D. (1969). The epidemiology of common fears and phobias. *Comprehensive Psychiatry*, **10**, 151–156.

American Psychiatric Association (1994). *Diagnostic and Statistical Manual of Mental Disorders*, 4th edn. Washington, DC: American Psychiatric Association.

Andrews, G., Freed, S. & Teeson, M. (1994). Anticipation and proximity in phobias. *Behaviour Research and Therapy*, **32**, 161–164.

Bertenthal, B.I. & Campos, J.J. (1984). A re-examination of fear and its determinants on the visual cliff. *Psychophysiology*, **21**, 413–417.

Bertenthal, B.I., Campos, J.J. & Barrett, K.C. (1984). Self-produced locomotion: an organizer of emotional, cognitive and social development in infancy. In R. Emde & R. Harmon (eds), *Continuities and Discontinuities in Development* (pp. 175–210). New York: Plenum.

Bowlby, J. (1975). *Attachment and Loss*, Vol. 2. Harmondsworth: Penguin.

Burns, L.E. & Thorpe, G.L. (1977). Fears and clinical phobias: epidemiological aspects and the national survey of agoraphobics. *Journal of International Medical Research*, **5**(suppl. 1), 132–139.

Burns, L.E. (1980). The epidemiology of fears and phobias in general practice. *Journal of International Medical Research*, **8**(suppl. 3), 1–7.

Clarke, J.C. & Jackson, J.A. (1983). *Hypnosis and Behavior Therapy: the Treatment of Anxiety and Phobias*. New York: Springer.

Cohen, D.C. (1977). Comparisons of self-report and overt-behavioral procedures for assessing acrophobia. *Behavior Therapy*, **18**, 17–23.

Emlen, J.T. (1963). Determinants of cliff edge and escape responses in herring gull chicks. *Behaviour*, **22**, 1–15.

Emmelkamp, P.M.G. & Felton, M. (1985). The process of exposure *in vivo*: cognitive and physiological changes during treatment of acrophobia. *Behaviour Research and Therapy*, **23**, 219–223.

Gibson, E.J. & Walk, R.D. (1960). The "visual cliff". *Scientific American*, **202**(4), 64–71.

Guralnick, M.J. (1973). Behavior therapy with an acrophobic mentally retarded young adult. *Journal of Behavior Therapy and Experimental Psychiatry*, **4**, 263–265.

Hall, R.A. & Dietz, A.J. (1975). Systematic organismic desensitization. *Psychotherapy: Theory, Research and Practice*, **12**, 388–390.

Leitenberg, H. & Callahan, E.J. (1973). Reinforced practice and reduction of different kinds of fears in adults and children. *Behaviour Research and Therapy*, **11**, 19–30.

Marks, I.M. (1969). *Fears and Phobias*. London: Heinemann.

Marks, I.M. (1987). *Fears, Phobias and Rituals: Panic, Anxiety and their Disorders*. New York: Oxford University Press.

Marshall, W.L. (1985). The effects of variable exposure in flooding therapy. *Behavior Therapy*, **16**, 117–135.

Menzies, R.G. (in press). Danger expectancies, self-efficacy and insight in acrophobia. *Behaviour Research and Therapy*.

Menzies, R.G. & Clarke, J.C. (1993). The aetiology of fear of heights and its relationship to severity and individual response patterns. *Behaviour Research and Therapy*, **31**, 355–365.

Menzies, R.G. & Clarke, J.C. (1994). Retrospective studies of the origins of phobias: a review. *Anxiety, Stress and Coping*, **7**, 305–318.

Menzies, R.G. & Clarke, J.C. (1995a). The aetiology of acrophobia and its relationship to severity and individual response patterns. *Behaviour Research and Therapy*, **33**, 795–805.

Menzies, R.G. & Clarke, J.C. (1995b). The etiology of phobias: a non-associative account. *Clinical Psychology Review*, **15**, 23–48.

Menzies, R.G. & Clarke, J.C. (1995c). Individual response patterns, treatment matching, and the effects of behavioural and cognitive interventions for acrophobia. *Anxiety, Stress and Coping*, **8**, 141–160.

Menzies, R.G. & Clarke, J.C. (1995d). Danger expectancies and insight in acrophobia. *Behaviour Research and Therapy*, **33**, 215–221.

Morris, R.J. & Magrath, K.H. (1979). Contribution of therapist warmth to the contact desensitization treatment of acrophobia. *Journal of Consulting and Clinical Psychology*, **47**, 786–788.

Öst, L.-G. & Hugdahl, K. (1981). Acquisition of phobias and anxiety response patterns in clinical patients. *Behaviour Research and Therapy*, **19**, 439–447.

Öst, L.-G. & Hugdahl, K. (1983). Acquisition of agoraphobia, mode of onset and anxiety response patterns. *Behaviour Research and Therapy*, **21**, 623–632.

Öst, L.-G. & Hugdahl, K. (1985). Acquisition of blood and dental phobia and anxiety response patterns in clinical patients. *Behaviour Research and Therapy*, **23**, 27–34.

Rachman, S. (1977). The conditioning theory of fear acquisition: a critical examination. *Behaviour Research and Therapy*, **15**, 375–387.

Richards, J. & Rader, N. (1983). Affective, behavioral, and avoidance responses on the visual cliff: effects of crawling onset age, crawling experience, and testing age. *Psychophysiology*, **20**, 633–642.

Rimm, D.C., Janda, L.H., Lancaster, D.N., Nahl, M. & Dittmar, K. (1977). An exploratory investigation of the origin and maintenance of phobias. *Behaviour Research and Therapy*, **15**, 231–238.

Ritter, B. (1969a). Treatment of acrophobia with contact desensitization. *Behaviour Research and Therapy*, **7**, 41–45.

Ritter, B. (1969b). The use of contact desensitization, demonstration-plus-participation and demonstration-alone in the treatment of acrophobia. *Behaviour Research and Therapy*, **7**, 157–164.

Routtenberg, G.A. & Glickman, S.E. (1964). Visual cliff behavior in undomesticated rodents, land and aquatic turtles and cats. *Journal of Comparative and Physiological Psychology*, **58**, 143–146.

Scarr, S. & Salapatek, P. (1970). Patterns of fear development during infancy. *Merrill–Palmer Quarterly*, **16**, 53–90.

Schaap, C.M. & Dana, R.H. (1968). Experimental treatment of phobias by systematic desensitization. *Psychological Reports*, **23**, 969–970.

Schneider, J.W. (1982). Lens-assisted *in vivo* desensitization to heights. *Journal of Behavior Therapy and Experimental Psychiatry*, **13**, 333–336.

Seligman, M.E.P. (1971). Phobias and preparedness. *Behavior Therapy*, **2**, 307–320.

Shephard, M., Cooper, B., Brown, A.C. & Kalton, G. (1981). *Psychiatric Illness in General Practice*, 2nd edn. Oxford: Oxford University Press.

Sutton-Simon, K. & Gotfried, M.R. (1979). Faulty thinking patterns in two types of anxiety. *Cognitive Therapy and Research*, **3**, 193–203.

Walk, R. & Gibson, E.J. (1961). A comparative and analytic study of visual depth perception. *Psychological Monographs*, **75**(15, Whole No. 519), 1–44.

Weissman, M.M. (1983). Anxiety disorders: rates, risks and familial patterns. In A.H. Tuma & J.D. Maser (eds), *Anxiety and the Anxiety Disorders*. Hillsdale, NJ: Erlbaum.

Williams, S.L., Turner, S.M. & Peer, D.F. (1985). Guided mastery and performance desensitization treatments for severe acrophobia. *Journal of Consulting and Clinical Psychology*, **53**, 237–247.

Wolpe, J. & Lang, P.J. (1964). A fear schedule for use in behavior therapy. *Behaviour Research and Therapy*, **2**, 27–30.

Zutt, J. (1952). Uber den hohenschwindel Acrophobie: die am weitesten verbreitete Phobie. *Journal of Nervous and Mental Disease*, **116**, 789–793.

Chapter 8

Accident Phobia

Klaus Kuch
*Smythe Pain Clinic, Toronto General Hospital, and The Clarke
Institute of Psychiatry, University of Toronto, Toronto, Canada*

Accident phobia should be considered when survivors of motor vehicle accidents (MVA) fail to recover their normal travel habits and live in fear of another accident. Many accident phobics suffer from nightmares and other symptoms of post-traumatic stress disorder (PTSD). A resumption of driving for pleasure is a reliable criterion of recovery (Kuch, Swinson & Kirby, 1985). Characteristic MVA-related fears are listed in Table 1, Part 2 (Kuch, Cox & Direnfeld, 1995).

A number of clinical studies report PTSD after MVA (Burstein, 1989). Phobic anxiety may be obscured by somatic complaints and by inactivity due to pain. Depression may be a common complication of MVA (Goldberg & Gara, 1990). It may be understood as partial PTSD, as a complication of pain or as a separate condition. Common combinations of anxiety, depression and pain are "whiplash neurosis" (Hodge, 1971) and post-traumatic headache (Chibnall & Duckro, 1994; Hickling et al., 1992; Parker, 1977). Anxious MVA survivors who present with pain as a chief complaint are best understood in terms of behavioural medicine. Patients with muscle contraction headache are sensitive to stressful stimuli (Thompson & Adams, 1984) and mood disturbance may augment self-perceived disability in headache (Duckro, Chibnall & Tomazic, 1995). Anxiety and depression may augment the impact of generalized myofascial pain on daily living by 25% (Kuch et al., 1993). Psychosocial factors may exert greater influence on the decision to return to work than the extent of any orthopaedic impairment (Cornes, 1992). PTSD may present with dysfunction equal to that of severe physical handicap (Green et al., 1993).

Accident phobia seems more rational than a fear of harmless animals and may be misunderstood as a normal reaction to MVA. It is as maladaptive as any other phobia. Particularly in North America, normal life is difficult to imagine without the comforts of a car. Accident phobia interferes with normal mobility. Relatives of phobic MVA survivors offer dramatic descriptions of anxious expectation before trips and excessive startle in the car. The heart-rate reactivity of MVA survivors with full or partial PTSD (Blanchard, Hickling & Taylor, 1991; Blanchard et al., 1995b) demonstrates the degree of distress endured by phobic survivors. Many reorganise their lives to accommodate their fears, move from jobs and sell homes in order to reduce the need for driving. Discretionary travel is avoided. In severe cases, driving is restricted to essential journeys and select driving conditions. Complete driving avoidance is rare (Kuch, Cox & Direnfeld, 1995; Blanchard et al., 1995a). Phobic anxiety may persist for years, as studies of chronic populations suggest (Hickling et al., 1992; Kuch et al., 1991, 1994).

Criteria for accident phobia include criteria for specific phobia, situational type (American Psychiatric Association, 1994). The phobic situation is road traffic, which reminds the survivor of the MVA and associated injury. Driving is endured with intense distress and excessive guarding, or is avoided. Life-style is substantially altered as a result of phobia (Kuch et al., 1991, 1994; Kuch, Cox & Direnfeld, 1995). By definition, accident phobia is partial PTSD. Onset must meet DSM stressor criterion A (McNally & Saigh, 1993). Intense psychological distress in response to re-exposure and efforts to avoid feared situations are diagnostic criteria of PTSD, similar to the diagnostic criteria of specific phobias.

PREVALENCE

Motor vehicle accidents are ubiquitous and one of the most common traumatic stressors of civilian life (Norris, 1992). One survey of injured MVA survivors elicited traffic fears in 19% of respondents (Slocum, 1981), and another survey found symptoms suggestive of PTSD in roughly 10% of MVA survivors drawn from a police register (Brom, Kleber & Hoffman, 1993). In a chronic pain sample, phobias and PTSD were over three times more common in MVA survivors than in subjects with a non-vehicular onset of pain (Kuch et al., 1991). A prospective emergency room study found an acute stress syndrome in almost one-fifth of MVA survivors and fully developed PTSD in roughly 10% during the following year. One year after the MVA, 16% of car occupants and 21% of sufferers from "whiplash" experienced major effects on their ability to ride as passengers. Eleven percent of car occupants and 25% of sufferers from "whiplash" experienced major effects on their ability to operate a vehicle (Mayou, Bryant & Duthie, 1993). Accident-related phobic anxiety persisted for 4–6 years after the MVA in one-third of the respondents from a prospective study (Mayou, Simkin & Threlfall, 1991).

PTSD and phobia may be more prevalent in treatment-seeking subjects than in non-clinical samples, particularly when complaints are chronic. In two studies of acute medical treatment-seekers referred to a psychology service, close to one-third suffered from PTSD (Blanchard et al., 1994, 1995a). In three samples of subjects with chronic symptoms, close to 40% suffered from partial or full-blown PTSD (Hickling et al., 1992; Kuch et al., 1991, 1994). However, phobia appears to be more common than fully developed PTSD (Mayou et al., 1993; Kuch et al., 1991, 1994, 1995).

Gender effects on prevalence of PTSD were apparent in medical treatment-seekers referred to a psychology service (Blanchard et al., 1995) but not in emergency room subjects (Mayou, Simkin & Threlfall, 1991; Mayou, Bryant & Duthie, 1993) or subjects referred to a pain clinic because of pain (Kuch et al., 1991, 1994). This discrepancy may reflect gender effects on referral patterns. Differences in the reported prevalence of phobic anxiety between studies are due to more (Blanchard et al., 1994, 1995a) or less (Mayou, Bryant & Duthie, 1993; Kuch et al., 1991, 1994; Kuch, Swinson & Kirby, 1985; Kuch, Cox & Direnfeld, 1995) restrictive criteria for phobia. The Albany group requires almost complete driving avoidance, whereas the Toronto group requires only partial avoidance and admits driving with panic anxiety and covert avoidance expressed by excessive guarding (Blanchard & Kuch, oral discussion, Society for Post-traumatic Stress, Boston, 1995).

CAUSATION

PTSD is the only anxiety disorder where causation is assumed by definition (American Psychiatric Association, 1994). Most phobias develop in association with "false" alarms, whereas post-traumatic phobias are learned in association with "true" alarms (Barlow, 1988). The distinction between "false" and "true" is difficult when an event is alarming only to some and when subjective factors enter the equation. PTSD and related phobic anxiety are credible after catastrophic events, but as the alleged result of a "fender bender", PTSD may be viewed with incredulity. Criterion A (American Psychiatric Association, 1994) defines the characteristics of a traumatic event. Two views exist on the importance of criterion A as entrance criterion. The broad view would lessen its importance and admit all events associated with symptoms of PTSD. The narrow view would emphasize it and would admit only near-catastrophic events that are known to cause PTSD (March, 1993).

Accidents can be genuinely "alarming" even when the victim escapes without injury, and the accident must be explored in detail to determine its emotional impact (Pilowski, 1992). Prevalence (Kuch et al., 1991; Mayou, Bryant & Duthie, 1993; Blanchard et al., 1995a) and the specificity of learned fear (Kuch et al., 1994) support the theory that accident phobia and PTSD are caused at least in part by MVA. Further support comes from two additional observations. Concussion and memory loss appear to have a protective effect (Mayou, Bryant & Duthie, 1993; O'Brien, 1993). A psychophysiological stimulus–response (S–R) paradigm to audiotaped reminders of MVA has also been demonstrated (Blanchard, Hickling & Taylor, 1991) and replicated (Blanchard et al., 1995b). Heart rate reactivity is greatest in subjects with PTSD, less intense in subjects with partial PTSD and minimal in subjects without PTSD (Blanchard, Hickling & Taylor, 1991; Blanchard et al., 1995b).

Not everyone is equally "alarmed" by MVA. Severity of injury and severity of perceived threat may predict PTSD (Blanchard et al., 1995d), but the psychological reaction to a crash may depend to a greater extent on subjective perception than on objective damage (Slocum, 1981; Malt & Olafsen, 1992). Accident phobia and PTSD are associated with past psychiatric disorder, although studies differ with regard to prevalence. Three studies report a history of past anxiety disorder in between one-quarter and one-third of subjects (Kuch et al., 1991; Kuch, Cox & Direnfeld, 1995; Blanchard et al., 1995a), and of past depression in one-half of subjects (Blanchard et al., 1995a). Past trauma other than MVA was more common in subjects with PTSD than in those without PTSD (Blanchard et al., 1995c; Kuch, Cox & Direnfeld, 1995) and, according to one study, past depression predicted post-MVA depression. However, PTSD was not associated with past neuroticism and depression (Mayou, Bryant & Duthie, 1993).

Only a minority of survivors stay "alarmed" for years. Numerous and severe symptoms of acute PTSD, in particular "horrific memories", predict persistent PTSD (Mayou, Bryant & Duthie, 1993; Blanchard et al., 1995c) and another risk factor may be "victim status". Patients who had undergone surgery following traffic accidents used emotion-focused coping strategies more and task-oriented strategies less than other surgery groups (Koutsosimou, McDonald & Davey, 1996). Avoidance may perpetuate phobias and some symptoms of PTSD. In a sample of MVA survivors, avoidant coping accounted for 41% of intrusion scores on a PTSD scale (Bryant & Harvey, 1995). Persistent physical impairment may also slow remission (Mayou, Bryant & Duthie, 1993), conceivably by reducing self-exposure to traffic and by contributing to a pessimistic outlook. Litigation is also associated with non-remission according to two studies (Bryant & Harvey, 1995; Blanchard et al., 1995c), but not according to a third (Mayou, Bryant & Duthie, 1993)—whatever perpetuates distress may matter more to clinicians than original causation.

ASSESSMENT

By necessity, the stressor criterion "A" is assessed retrospectively and open to embellishment. For clinical purposes, this writer relies on a composite impression of MVA-severity including head injury, extent of injury, property damage and conduct of survivors immediately afterwards that may indicate symptoms of an acute stress disorder (American Psychiatric Association, 1994). Dissociative symptoms characteristic of acute stress disorder are sometimes mislabelled as unconsciousness (Kuch, Cox & Direnfeld, 1995).

The Accident Fear Questionnaire (AFQ) is a recently developed screening instrument that discriminates between PTSD, accident phobia and non-PTSD. Subjects with PTSD tend to score highest, followed by "accident phobics", followed by subjects with neither diagnosis. This order of severity was preserved in a study assessing reliability and validity after subjects with major depression had been removed from the analysis. Pain was not associated with phobic avoidance ratings. Lacking effects from depression and from pain suggest that the AFQ is a specific measure of MVA-related phobic avoidance. Table 8.1, Part 1 presents "yes" vs. "no" responses to supplemental items 1–10 of the AFQ and results of χ^2 analyses. Table 1, Part 2 presents scores of phobic avoidance items 11–20, total AFQ scores and results of one-way analyses of variance (ANOVA) (Kuch, Cox & Direnfeld, 1995).

Jointly with fear, pain and depression questionnaires, the AFQ may facilitate rapid diagnostic screening of MVA survivors with chronic symptoms. The AFQ may also identify targets for exposure therapy and provide behavioural outcome measures. Avoidance items may be verified by interviews of eyewitnesses who had an opportunity to observe the survivor's driving habits. Frequently, these eyewitness accounts are more revealing than the victim's self-report. Assessors and therapists can also "road-test" their clients, with a third party at the wheel who is acceptable to the client.

The differential diagnosis of accident phobia includes agoraphobia, common driving phobia and adjustment disorder. Agoraphobia may have its onset after loss events (Favarelli & Pallanti, 1989). Loss events are both similiar and subtly distinct from the more "alarming" stressor criterion A for PTSD. Common driving phobia is related to unexpected panic while driving a car and unrelated to MVA. Driving phobics avoid freeways, overpasses, bridges and tunnels. This writer believes that common driving phobia expresses a fear of losing control over the car in the event of a panic attack. Accident phobics, however, prefer the control that goes with being in the driver's seat (Kuch, et al., 1994; Kuch, Cox & Direnfeld, 1995). Ehlers et al. (1994) noted unexpected panic at the onset in 50% of their subjects and diagnosed panic disorder and/or agoraphobia in close to one-third. Munjack (1984) reported similar findings on the basis of a telephone survey. Forty per cent of his subjects attributed their fear to uncued panic on the highway. In both studies, only 15–20% of phobic subjects attributed the onset of their driving fear to MVA.

TREATMENT

Behavioural management is promising (McCaffrey & Fairbank, 1985; Kuch, Swinson & Kirby, 1985; Kuch, 1989; Taylor & Koch, 1995), but to date no controlled studies have been published. Cognitive preparation may be required before exposure therapy can be implemented. Cognitive preparation includes reappraisal of victim status to survivor status, acceptance of normal risk-taking and a definition of what constitutes safe driving. Without preparation it may be unrealistic to expect extensive self-exposure to traffic and extinction of excessive guarding. Imaginary exposure elicits a strong emotional response in some subjects and this may predict a favourable outcome (Kuch, Cox & Direnfeld, 1995). Imagery may be enhanced by audiotaped reminders of the MVA (Blanchard,

Table 8.1 AFQ comparisons between MVA survivors with PTSD, accident phobia, and neither diagnosis

Part 1
Patients with:

Items	PTSD n	PTSD (A) Reporting positive (%)	Accident phobia n	Accident phobia (B) Reporting positive (%)	Neither A nor B n	Neither A nor B (C) Reporting positive (%)	Significant[a]	X^2
1. During the accident, did you fear for your life?	12	66.7	14	71.4	28	21.4	9.89*	(B > C)
2. During the accident, did you see anyone injured or killed?	11	45.5	14	21.4	28	17.9	ns	
3. During the accident, did you lose consciousness?	12	33.3	14	42.9	27	18.5	ns	
4. Do you have nightmares about the accident?	12	91.7	14	78.6	27	18.5	18.37** 13.97**	(A > C) (B > C)
5. Are you nervous before trips?	12	100.0	14	78.6	27	33.3	14.86**	(A > C)
6. Do you easily get upset in the car?	12	100.0	14	85.7	27	40.7	12.06**	(A > C)
7. Do you tell the driver what to do?	12	91.7	14	71.4	27	37.0	9.98*	(A > C)
8. Do you drive less than you used to?	11	100.0	14	92.3	28	60.7	ns	
9. Do you expect another accident soon?	12	58.3	14	42.9	25	4.0	14.12** 9.20*	(A > C) (B > C)
10. Would most people feel after an accident the way you do?	12	75.0	13	100.0	19	84.2	ns	

Part 2
Patients with:

Items	PTSD	(A) Reporting positive (%)		Accident phobia	(B) Reporting positive (%)		Neither A nor B	(C) Reporting positive (%)		F-value	Significant[a] post-hoc
	n			n			n				
Since your accident, do you avoid[b]:											
11. Driving as a passenger	12	4.42	1.88	14	2.93	1.50	28	0.82	1.28	27.23***	A > C, B > C
12. Driving yourself	11	5.91	2.74	14	4.07	2.56	27	2.33	2.54	7.85*	A > C
13. Riding in a particular seat	11	5.36	2.58	14	2.21	2.29	28	1.39	2.67	9.57**	A > B, A > C
14. Driving on certain roads	11	5.91	2.17	14	4.36	2.50	27	1.22	1.95	22.04***	A > C, B > C
15. Riding with certain drivers	12	5.67	2.87	14	4.43	2.38	28	2.21	2.82	7.71*	A > C
16. Driving in certain weather conditions	12	6.17	2.52	14	5.43	2.62	28	2.36	2.41	12.97***	A > C, B > C
17. Hearing news of accidents	12	6.33	1.87	14	2.79	2.49	28	1.04	1.86	28.39***	A > B, AC
18. Seeing wounds and injuries	12	6.83	1.75	14	3.50	3.18	28	1.61	2.87	15.16***	A > C
19. Crossing streets alone	12	3.83	2.41	14	1.64	2.31	28	0.43	1.23	14.35***	A > C
20. Riding a bus or streetcar	12	3.92	2.15	14	2.64	3.10	28	1.25	2.59	ns	
Total AFQ Score	12	54.44	11.36	14	34.00	14.77	28	14.66	12.46	41.83***	A > B, B > C, A > C

[b]0 = would not avoid it; 2 = sometimes avoid it; 5 = often avoid it; 8 = always avoid it.
$* p < 0.05$; $** p < 0.01$; $*** p < 0.001$; $**** p < 0.0001$; [a]adjusted for Bonferroni level of significance $p < 0.0005$.
Reprinted from Kuch, Cox & Direnfeld, 1995, copyright ©1990 by kind permission from Elsevier Science Ltd, The Boulevard, Langford Lane, Kidlington OX5 1GB, UK.

Hickling & Taylor, 1991; Blanchard et al., 1995b). Safe driving requires skill and a steady hand. Therefore, desensitization to the role of passenger should precede desensitization to the role of driver. Patients are instructed to pay close and prolonged attention to traffic while "accepting whatever will be". Some patients dread most being chauffeured with their eyes closed and thus being prevented from checking traffic. Interpersonal conflict may become apparent during exposure, particularly when driving arrangements reflect arrangements at the time of the MVA (Kuch, 1989). Desensitization may be followed by a defensive driving course. Depression, development of panic disorder and alcoholism have complicated flooding in some Vietnam veterans with PTSD (Pitman et al., 1991), but we have not encountered these complications in the treatment of accident phobia.

Accident phobia may be preventable. Some phobics recover after self-exposure instructions, and a model for early intervention may be based on the brief exposure instructions for panickers in an emergency room (Swinson et al., 1992). Further research is needed to test effects of cognitive and exposure therapy and of response prevention. We hypothesize that PTSD complicated by pain will have the worst prognosis. Accident phobia complicated by full-blown PTSD will fare somewhat better. Uncomplicated accident phobia will have the best prognosis.

REFERENCES

American Psychiatric Association (1994). *Diagnostic and Statistical Manual of Mental Disorders* (4th edn). Washington, DC: American Psychiatric Association.
Barlow, D. (1988). *Anxiety and Its Disorders*. New York: Guilford.
Blanchard, E.B., Hickling, E.J. & Taylor, A.E. (1991). The psychophysiology of motor vehicle accidents related to post-traumatic stress disorder. *Biofeedback and Self Regulation*, **16**, 449–458.
Blanchard, E.B., Hickling, E.J., Taylor, A.E., Loos, W.R. & Gerardi, R.J. (1994). Psychological morbidity associated with motor vehicle accidents. *Behaviour Research & Therapy*, **32**, 283–290.
Blanchard, E.B., Hickling, E.J., Taylor, A.E. & Loos, W.R. (1995a). Psychiatric morbidity associated with motor vehicle accidents. *Journal of Nervous and Mental Disease*, **183**, 495–504.
Blanchard, E.B., Hickling, E.J., Taylor, A.E., Loos, W.R. & Gerardi, R.J. (1995b). The psychophysiology of motor vehicle accidents related post-traumatic stress disorder. *Behavior Therapy*, **25**, 453–467.
Blanchard, E.B., Hickling, E.J., Vollmer, A.J., Loos, W.R., Buckley, T.C. & Jaccard, J. (1995c). Short-term follow-up of post-traumatic stress disorder in motor vehicle accident victims. *Behaviour Research & Therapy*, **11**, 369–377.
Blanchard, E.B., Hickling, E.J., Mitnick, N., Taylor, A.E., Loos, W.R. & Buckley, T.C. (1995d). The impact of severity of physical injury and perception of life-threat in the development of post-traumatic stress disorder in motor vehicle accident victims. *Behaviour Research and Therapy*, **33**, 529–534.
Brom, D., Kleber, R.J. & Hoffman, M.C. (1993). Victims of traffic accidents: incidence and prevention of post-traumatic stress disorder. *Journal of Clinical Psychology*, **49**, 131–140.

Burstein, A. (1989). Post-traumatic stress disorders in victims of motor vehicle accidents. *Hospital and Community Psychiatry*, **40**, 295–297.

Bryant, R.A. & Harvey, A.G. (1995). Avoidant coping style and post-traumatic stress following motor vehicle accidents. *Behaviour Research & Therapy*, **33**, 631–635.

Chibnall, J.T. & Duckro, P.N. (1994). Post-traumatic stress disorder in chronic post-traumatic headache patients. *Headache*, **34**, 357–361.

Cornes, P. (1992). Return to work of road accident victims claiming compensation for personal injury. *British Journal of Accident Surgery*, **23**, 256–260.

Duckro, P.N., Chibnall, J.T. & Tomazic, T.J. (1995). Anger, depression and disability: a path analysis of relationships in a sample of post-traumatic headache patients. *Headache*, **35**, 7–9.

Ehlers, A., Hofmann, S.G., Herda, C.A. & Roth, W.T. (1994). Clinical characteristics of driving phobia. *Journal of Anxiety Disorders*, **8**, 323–339.

Faravelli, C. & Pallanti, S. (1989). Recent life events and panic disorder. *American Journal of Psychiatry*, **146**, 622–626.

Green, M.M., McFarlane, A.C., Hunter, C.E. & Griggs, W.M. (1993). Undiagnosed post-traumatic stress disorder following road vehicle accidents. *Medical Journal of Australia*, **158**, 529–534.

Goldberg, L. & Gara, M.A. (1990). A typology of psychiatric reactions to motor vehicle accidents. *Psychopathology*, **23**, 15–20.

Hickling, J.E. & Blanchard, E.B., Silverman, D.J. & Schwarz S.P. (1992). Motor vehicle accidents, headaches and post-traumatic stress disorder: assessment findings in a consecutive series. *Journal of Anxiety Disorders*, **6**, 285–291.

Hodge, J.R. (1971). The whiplash neurosis. *Psychosomatics*, **12**, 245–249.

Koutsosimou, M., McDonald, A.S. & Davey, G.C.L. (1996). Coping and psychopathology in surgery patients: a comparison of accident patients with other surgery patients (manuscript under review).

Kuch, K., Swinson, R.P. & Kirby, M. (1985). Post-traumatic stress disorder after car accidents. *Canadian Journal of Psychiatry*, **30**, 426–427.

Kuch, K. (1989). A treatment for post-traumatic phobias and PTSD after car accidents. In P.A. Keller & S.R. Heyman (eds), *Innovations in Clinical Practice: a Source Book*, Vol. 8. Sarasota, FL: Professional Resource Exchange.

Kuch, K., Evans, R.J., Watson, P.C., Bubela, C. & Cox, B.J. (1991). Road vehicle accidents and phobia in 60 patients with fibromyalgia. *Journal of Anxiety Disorders*, **5**, 273–280.

Kuch, K., Cox, B.J., Evans, R.J., Watson, P.C. & Bubela, C. (1993). To what extent do anxiety and depression interact with chronic pain? *Canadian Journal of Psychiatry*, **38**, 36–38.

Kuch, K., Cox, B.J., Evans, R.J. & Shulman, I. (1994). Phobias, panic and pain in 55 survivors of road vehicle accidents. *Journal of Anxiety Disorders*, **8**, 181–187.

Kuch, K., Cox, B.J. & Direnfeld, D. (1995). A brief self-rating scale for PTSD after road vehicle accident. *Journal of Anxiety Disorders*, **9**, 503–514.

Malt, U.F. & Olafsen, O.M. (1992). Psychological appraisal and emotional response to physical injury: a clinical phenomenological study of 109 adults. *Psychiatric Medicine*, **10**, 117–134.

March, J.S. (1993). What constitutes a stressor? The "criterion A" issue. In J.T.R. Davidson & E.B. Foa (eds), *Post-traumatic Stress Disorder: DSM-IV and Beyond* (pp. 37–53). Washington, DC: American Psychiatric Press.

Mayou, R., Bryant, B. & Duthie, R. (1993). Psychiatric consequences of road traffic accidents. *British Medical Journal*, **307**, 647–651.

Mayou, R., Simkin, S. & Threlfall, J. (1991). The effects of road traffic accidents on driving behaviour. *British Journal of Accident Surgery*, **22**, 365–378.

McCaffrey R.J. & Fairbank, J.A. (1985). Behavioral assessment and treatment of accident-related post-traumatic stress disorder: two case studies. *Behavior Therapy*, **16**, 406–416.

McNally, R.J. & Saigh, P.A. (1993). On the distinction between traumatic simple phobia and post-traumatic stress disorder. In J.T.R. Davidson & E.B. Foa (eds), *Post-traumatic Stress Disorder: DSM-IV and Beyond* (pp. 207–212). Washington, DC: American Psychiatric Press.

Munjack, D.J. (1984). The onset of driving phobias. *Journal of Behavior Therapy & Experimental Psychiatry*, **15**, 305–308.

Norris, F.H. (1992). Epidemiology of trauma: frequency and impact of different potentially traumatic events on different demographic groups. *Journal of Consulting Clinical Psychology*, **60**, 409–419.

O'Brien, M. (1993). Loss of memory is protective. Letter to the Editor. *British Medical Journal*, **307**, 1283.

Pitman, R.K., Altman, B., Greenwald, E., Longre, R.E., Macklin, M.L., Poire, R.E. & Steketee, G.S. (1991). Psychiatric complications during flooding therapy for post-traumatic stress disorder. *Journal of Clinical Psychiatry*, **52**, 17–20.

Parker, N. (1977). Accident litigands with neurotic symptoms. *Medical Journal of Australia*, **2**, 318–322.

Pilowsky, I. (1992). Minor accidents and major psychological trauma: a clinical perspective. *Stress Medicine*, **8**, 77–78.

Slocum, R. (1981). Injury: *an Ontario Survey of the Societal and Personal Costs of Hospitalized Motor Vehicle Accident Victims*. Interministerial Task Force Report. Toronto: ON Government Press.

Swinson, R.P., Soulios, C., Cox, B.J. & Kuch, K. (1992). Brief treatment of emergency room patients with panic attacks. *American Journal of Psychiatry*, **149**, 944–946.

Thompson, K.J. & Adams, H.E. (1984). Psychophysiological characteristics of headache patients. *Pain*, **18**, 41–52.

Taylor, S. & Koch, J. (1986). Anxiety disorders due to motor vehicle accidents: nature and tretment. *Clinical Psychology Review* (in press).

Chapter 9

Claustrophobia

S.J. Rachman
*Department of Psychology, University of British Columbia,
Vancouver, BC, Canada*

Claustrophobia, the fear of enclosed spaces (*claustro* means closed), is common but seldom incapacitating. It can be unpleasant, even distressing, but most people who experience the fear find ways to cope, usually by the deliberate avoidance of enclosed spaces. It is for them an inconvenience and a puzzle, but seldom a cause for seeking professional help.

Small rooms, locked rooms, tunnels, cellars, elevators, subway trains and crowded areas are all capable of provoking the fear, and people who fear one of these situations tend to fear them all. Fears of restriction and entrapment, such as sitting in a barber's chair, or waiting in line at a supermarket, are associated with a fear of being enclosed and usually are regarded as signs of claustrophobia.

The prospect of entering a closed space causes anxiety, and affected people engage in extensive avoidance behavior. It is not uncommon to hear of people who walk up 10 or more flights of steps rather than use the elevator, or who follow extremely devious routes in order to avoid driving through tunnels. Before considering the distribution and associations of claustrophobia, it is worthwhile asking what precisely is frightening these people.

A person who has claustrophobic reactions is not frightened of an elevator, as elevator, but is frightened of what might happen to him or her while in it. We then go on to ask what exactly the person fears might happen in the enclosed space. For just as agoraphobia is increasingly being regarded as a fear of what might happen to one in a public place, rather than as a fear of the place itself, so too claustrophobia can be re-analyzed in this manner.

The subjective feeling of being trapped may be important and certainly features in the accounts given by many claustrophobic people. Most closed spaces entail a degree of entrapment, sometimes total entrapment. Enclosed places also

Phobias—A Handbook of Theory, Research and Treatment. Edited by G.C.L. Davey.
© 1997 John Wiley & Sons Ltd.

entail a restriction of movement. Some claustrophobics feel excessively vulnerable when their movements are restricted. The fear reaction resembles the one animals display when their flight is prevented, and it is possible that the human fear of enclosed spaces is a vestigial fear of being trapped in a way that prevents escape when threatened. It should be borne in mind that animals certainly, and people probably, are more vulnerable "in conditions of confined space"; experimental neuroses are more easily induced when the animal is confined (Wolpe, 1958).

The fear of suffocating is prominent in claustrophobia, and is also reported by many people who are not troubled by enclosed spaces (Kirkpatrick, 1984). This extremely intense but remarkably common fear has evaded the attention of psychologists for too long. At least three types of suffocation fear can be distinguished, but at present we have little information about these variations: a fear of suffocation may arise from the belief that there is insufficient air available, that adequate access to the air is blocked (for example, by a mask), or that there is adequate air but a psychophysiological dysfunction is impeding normal breathing (e.g. an airway is blocked).

Being confined in an enclosed space might well be interpreted as a threat to one's breathing, and it is therefore understandable that for those people who are especially frightened of suffocation, enclosed spaces present a serious threat. A large majority of claustrophobics express a fear of suffocating in the closed space, and in experimental investigations this fearful cognition was closely associated with the bodily sensation of shortness of breath (Rachman, 1988). Even though in the large majority of these fears the threat of suffocation is exaggerated, it is at least understandable in the sense that very many people, not only claustrophobics, overestimate how much oxygen is needed in order to survive. For example, a group of highly educated students greatly overestimated how much oxygen they would need in order to survive in a small, enclosed room that is not airtight; in fact, it is possible to survive indefinitely in such a room. Even in an airtight room, a person can survive for several days (Rachman, Levitt & Lopatka, 1987, 1988).

Claustrophobia is notable for the speed with which people obtain relief from particular episodes of fear. With the exception of traumatic or prolonged experiences, the fear subsides directly the person leaves the enclosure.

There are fears of enclosure in which suffocation plays no part. There is no danger of suffocation while sitting in a barber's chair and, other than the risk of losing a piece of one's ear, there is no rational basis for being frightened. The fear of crowds, which often is associated with claustrophobia, brings little risk of suffocation when the crowds are gathered in the open air.

Attempts to elicit from claustrophobic people the fundamental basis of their fear of closed spaces are seldom rewarding. Quite soon, the affected person runs out of explanations, and expresses puzzlement about quite what it is that he/she is frightened might happen: "I just feel trapped". The difficulty in finding an explanation and the persistence of the fear even in the face of credible and reassuring information are indications of a non-cognitive quality in claustrophobia. As mentioned earlier, it has even been suggested that claustrophobia might be, in part, a vestigial fear of being in danger if trapped (Rachman, 1990).

INCIDENCE

There is a notable discrepancy between the common occurrence of claustrophobia in the general population and the small number of people who seek professional help in overcoming their problem. Presumably, most people with claustrophobia manage to avoid enclosed spaces or have learned to endure them. In roughly three out of four cases the claustrophobia is not severe (Rachman, 1990) and there is no need for professional help, but the gap between the prevalence of claustrophobia in the population and the small number seeking help cannot be attributed entirely to low levels of fear. Survey data indicate that severe claustrophobia may affect as many as 2–5% of the population, but very few of this large total seek assistance. The incidence of claustrophobia in clinics is low (Marks, 1987). In part this reflects ignorance, for few people appear to know that in most instances claustrophobia declines smoothly with appropriate training.

Costello (1982; 1987, personal communication) found a high prevalence of mild fears and of phobias among women in Calgary. Of the 449 women who took part in his study, 66 (12%) reported that they had a fear of enclosed spaces, crowds or elevators. Of this group, 18 (4%) said that their fears were severe. The figures reported in a study carried out in Indiana are slightly higher (Kirkpatrick, 1984; 1987, personal communication). Among 342 women, 77 (22.5%) reported a fear of enclosed spaces and of these, 46 (13.4%) said that it was a severe fear (that is, very much fear or terror). Another 25 women reported a fear of elevators, and 16 of them said it reached severe intensity. The 200 men in the sample reported fewer and less intense fears. Fifteen of them said that they were frightened of enclosed spaces, but only six said the fear was intense. The highest frequency of fear was reported in the age groups 18–25, and least fear was reported by men between the ages of 25 and 45 years.

The related fear of suffocation was found to be even more common than the fear of enclosed spaces, especially in young females. No less than 17.6% of the 188 females below the age of 24 said that they had an intense fear or terror of suffocating. Nine per cent of the men below 24 expressed this degree of fear. These figures are remarkable and, because there is no explanation for them at present, it points to the need for attention to be directed toward this relatively unnoticed but serious fear. The peak period for the fear of suffocation was early adulthood, but people of all ages were affected to some extent.

The results of the large NIMH survey (Bourdon, 1988) of five communities are consistent with those of Costello and Kirkpatrick, given that the questions asked of the 18 572 respondents were more restricted. "Being in a closed place" was the eighth commonest fear, and "tunnels or bridges" the ninth commonest. Twice as many women as men endorsed these fears, but there were no gender differences in age of onset of any of the fears.

It is worth mentioning that in Kirkpatrick's study, the fear of suffocating was one of the most commonly reported of all fears. The incidence of the fear of suffocating was twice as common as the fear of enclosed spaces, and it is therefore evident that the fear can occur in a range of different circumstances and in response to different types of hazard.

THE STRUCTURE OF CLAUSTROPHOBIA

In order to test the hypothesis that claustrophobia consists of two components, a fear of restriction and a fear of suffocation, a three-pronged analysis was undertaken (Rachman & Taylor, 1993). One hundred and seventy-nine students completed a specially designed questionnaire, revised from an earlier version, and then completed a set of five behavior tests, followed by a structured interview.

To determine whether fears of suffocation and restriction constitute separate factors, two principal components analyses of the claustrophobia questionnaire were conducted. In the first analysis two scales were rationally derived by selecting items from the claustrophobia scale. The suffocation (S) scale consisted of six questionnaire items that appeared to be primarily measures of the fear of suffocation. These items are presented in the lower half of Table 9.1. The restriction (R) scale consisted of six questionnaire items that appeared to be primarily measures of the fear of physical restriction (upper half of Table 9.1).

The five behavioral tests were carried out in a balanced sequence and no order effects occurred—breathing through a straw, donning a gas mask, standing in a closet, tied in a canvas bag, lying on shelf resembling a bunk bed. The fear ratings

Table 9.1 Factor loadings for the rationally derived restriction and suffocation scales

Item	Factor I (restriction)	Factor II (suffocation)
Tied up with hands behind back for 15 min	0.90^a	−0.13
Handcuffed for 15 min	0.85^a	−0.09
Standing for 15 min in a straitjacket	0.81^a	0.04
Having your legs tied to an immovable chair	0.78^a	−0.02
Lying in a tight sleeping bag enclosing legs and arms, tied at the neck, unable to get out for 15 min	0.64^a	0.22
In a public washroom and the lock jams	0.45^a	0.24
Swimming with a noseplug	−0.05	0.80^a
Snorkelling in a safe practice tank for 15 min	−0.04	0.66^a
Trying to catch your breath during vigorous exercise	−0.09	0.65^a
Having a bad cold and finding it difficult to breathe through your nose	0.07	0.62^a
Lying in a sauna for 15 min	0.08	0.55^a
Having a pillow over your face	0.25	0.39^a

[a]Salient. From Rachman & Taylor (1993), with permission.

Table 9.2 Claustrophobia scale: loadings for the two-factor solution

Item	Factor I (restriction)	Factor II (suffocation)
Standing for 15 min in a straightjacket	0.87[a]R	−0.13
Having your legs tied to an immovable chair	0.84[a]R	−0.15
Tied up with hands behind back for 15 min	0.83[a]R	−0.13
Handcuffed for 15 min	0.79[a]R	−0.07
Locked in a small dark room without windows for 15 min	0.71[a]	−0.05
Lying in a tight sleeping bag enclosing legs and arms, tied at the neck, unable to get out for 15 min	0.70[a]R	0.05
Lying in the trunk of a car with air flowing through freely for 15 min	0.67[a]	−0.10
Caught in tight clothing and unable to remove it	0.61[a]	0.15
Head-first into a zipped-up sleeping bag, able to leave when you wish	0.53[a]	0.00
Locked in a small well-lit room without windows for 15 min	0.51[a]	0.04
In a crowded train which stops between stations	0.49[a]	0.10
In a public washroom and the lock jams	0.54[a]R	0.19
In an elevator at the time when there is a strong likelihood of a power cut	0.41[a]	0.25
Having a nylon stocking over your face for 15 min	0.40[a]	0.28
Sitting with a tight seat belt on for 15 min	0.40[a]	0.31[a]
Having a pillow over your face	0.36[a]	0.22
200 feet below the surface in a small submarine	0.36[a]	0.33[a]
In the middle of a long line at a supermarket	0.35[a]	0.16
Sleeping in a room without windows with the door closed but unlocked	0.31[a]	0.24
Back of a crowded bus	0.30[a]	0.297
Swimming with nose plug	−0.03	0.67[a]S
Working under a sink for 15 min	0.10	0.65[a]
Standing in an elevator on the ground floor with the doors closed	0.03	0.64[a]
Trying to catch your breath during vigorous exercise	−0.10	0.63[a]S
Having a bad cold and finding it difficult to breathe through your nose	0.00	0.62[a]S
Snorkelling in a safe practice tank for 15 min	−0.01	0.57[a]S
Using an oxygen mask	0.22	0.52[a]
Lying on a bottom bunk-bed	−0.13	0.48[a]
Standing in the middle of the third row at a packed concert realizing that you will be unable to leave until the end of the show	0.12	0.46[a]
In the center of a full row at a cinema	0.13	0.45[a]
Working under a car for 15 min	0.28	0.43[a]
At the furthest point from an exit on a tour of an underground mine shaft	0.22	0.41[a]
In back of a small two-door car with a person on either side of you, and all the windows fogged up	0.31[a]	0.39[a]
Lying in a sauna for 15 min	0.15	0.39[a]S
Waiting in a plane on the ground with the door closed for 15 min	0.28	0.34[a]
In a barber's/hairdresser's chair	−0.05	0.31[a]

R and S respectively indicate markers for the rationally derived restriction and suffocation scales.
[a]Salient. From Rachman & Taylor (1993), with permission.

were submitted to a principal components analysis with oblique rotation. The ratings for the straw test were predicted to define the suffocation factor, and the ratings for the shelf test were expected to define the restriction factor. Ratings for the closet test were expected to define both factors. The scree test (Cattell, 1966) indicated a two-factor solution, which accounted for 58% of the variance. The factors were moderately correlated, $r = 0.56$, $p < 0.001$, and the factor loadings are shown in Table 9.2. The results were largely as predicted, with ratings for the restriction and suffocation tests emerging on separate factors. Contrary to expectation, the ratings for the closet test loaded only on the restriction factor. It may have been that our test closet was too well ventilated to evoke fears of suffocation. Nevertheless, the results are very similar to those obtained from the claustrophobia questionnaire (Table 9.3), providing further support for the two-factor conceptualization of claustrophobia.

Interviews

From their responses in the interview, subjects were classified on the basis of whether or not they regarded themselves as having a fear of enclosed spaces (claustrophobia), and whether they regarded themselves as fearful of restriction or suffocation. The fears of suffocation and restriction were significantly associated in claustrophobic subjects, but not in non-claustrophobic subjects. That is, in claustrophobics the fears of restriction and suffocation tended to co-occur, whereas in non-claustrophobics the occurrence of restriction fear was independent of suffocation fear. This finding, too, is consistent with the hypothesized importance of the fears of restriction and suffocation in claustrophobia.

THE ONSET OF CLAUSTROPHOBIA

Notwithstanding the weaknesses of the method of collecting the information, with its reliance on the patients' recall of their experiences and their interpretation of that information, Öst's (1985) comparison of five different types of phobia is most enlightening. Just over two-thirds of the 31 claustrophobic people in Öst's (1985) sample of 167 phobic patients reported that their problem had been acquired as a result of a conditioning experience. A comparable percentage of children who reported "a lot of fear" of not being able to breathe reported a conditoning onset, but many of them said the onset came from information received (Ollendick & King, 1991). Relative to the two comparison phobias, social and animal, significantly fewer of the claustrophobic patients in the Öst sample said that they had acquired their problem vicariously (see Table 9.3).

In an extraordinary experiment, never to be repeated, Sanderson, Campbell & Laverty (1962) produced traumatic conditioned reactions in 10 alcoholic patients by subjecting them to a temporary respiratory paralysis. For a short period after the injection of a curarizing drug, the subjects were unable to move or breathe.

Table 9.3 Pathways to claustrophobia and other fears (based on Öst, 1985)

	Claustrophobia	Agoraphobia	Social-phobia	Animal	Dental
Sample (n =)	31	36	32	36	32
Age	37	36	34	30	35
Phobia duration (years)	17	8	18	23	23
Acquired by (%)					
Conditioning	67	89	56	50	66
Modeling	6	5	15	22	16
Instruction/ information	13	0	3	19	0
No recall	13	5	25	8	19

The experience was "harrowing to a degree" (p. 1235) and conditioned fears were induced. The incidence of specifically claustrophobic responses was not stated.

The presence of claustrophobia early in life, 37% by the age of 14 (Öst, 1987), is not incompatible with a conditioning explanation, but does raise the possibility of innate determination in a proportion of cases. The conditioning events that are generally thought to be responsible consist of aversive experiences in an enclosed space. This idea, drawn from clinical experience, is consistent with the conclusion from experiments on the induction of neuroses in animals, in which confinement can make an important contribution to the onset of fear (Wolpe, 1958). There is in addition some evidence from naturally occurring disasters, and the effects of medical diagnostic images.

Ploeger (1977) studied 10 miners who survived an underground disaster and remained trapped underground for 14 days. Of the 21 miners who had taken refuge at the time of the accident, six were suffocated. Ten of the survivors were studied for up to 10 years and, according to Ploeger, all but one of them experienced important personality changes. "Phobias were observed in six out of the 10 surviving miners. In particular, they feared darkness, loneliness, murmuring of water . . . and confining or limiting situations. In addition, most of them complained of intrusive memories and nightmares" (Ploeger, 1977, p. 25). Bearing in mind the wartime evidence of the fear-preventing effects of a responsible job and of required helpfulness (Rachman, 1990), it is noteworthy that the miner who functioned as leader both before and after the catastrophe developed no symptoms.

A new source of claustrophobia arises from the introduction of medical diagnostic imaging techniques. It is estimated that 4–10% of patients are unable to complete the procedure because of their fear (Friday & Kubal, 1990; McIsaac, 1995) and the genesis or exacerbation of claustrophobia as a result of undergoing a scan has been described by several writers (Melendez & McCrank, 1993). For example, Kilborn & Labbe (1990) reported that seven of 108 first-time scanners stopped the procedure "due to claustrophobia" (p. 396). The majority completed the scan, even in the presence of pain (42% of the sample), and whatever anxiety they had prior to the scan declined after the procedure. Among those who stopped the scan, a large increase in fear was recorded at 1-month follow-up. It is highly probable that people who are vulnerable to claustrophobia, especially if they have both the restriction and the suffocation components, which are of course likely to be provoked by being restrained in a supine position in a confining cylindrical tube for an hour or more, will experience significant fear during imaging. In a recently completed study McIsaac (1995) found that scores on the Claustrophobia scale sensitively predicted panic during the MRI exam. It is also probable that the experience will sensitize some people, and make it exceedingly difficult for them to endure second or subsequent scans. Fortunately, claustrophobia is modifiable and a therapeutic modeling procedure is likely to overcome the problem for most of the vulnerable patients.

A tragic example of the probable genesis of claustrophobia by *indirect* experiences was seen after the fire that destroyed a large section of King's Cross underground station in the London subway system. The intense heat and dense smoke trapped many travelers, and 31 people were killed and many injured. For some weeks after the tragedy, many people avoided the system and used other forms of transport. Many expressions of claustrophobia—new, revived and inflated—were reported in the newspapers and on radio and television (Thompson, 1989). On the available evidence of the extensive avoidance and expressions of fear, it is difficult to separate the instances of vicarious acquisition (especially the fear acquired by observing television pictures of frightened survivors) from the instances of fear acquired by the processing of non-visual information about the disaster. It is likely that both of these indirect pathways, vicarious and informational, were involved. Claustrophobia probably can be acquired indirectly.

In summary, it is probable that many people develop the fear as a consequence of enduring an aversive experience in an enclosed space. Others acquire the fear indirectly, vicariously or informationally. Also, the wide distribution of the fear, its relatively early onset and seemingly easy acquisition (one nasty experience usually is sufficient), and its non-cognitive features strengthen the possibility that it might be a prepared phobia. The fact that claustrophobia is easily reduced goes against the deduction from the theory of prepared phobias but is not fatal to the essential propositions of the theory. On the present evidence, it is not possible to be certain about the ease with which claustrophobia is acquired and, because this is a key feature of prepared phobias, it is necessary to await further information. Finally, the fact that 13% could not recall the onset of their phobia (Öst, 1985) introduces the possibility in some instances of what Menzies & Clarke (1995) describe as "non-associative" onset.

SYMBOLIC FEAR

We have also to consider whether anxiety that is not provoked by enclosed spaces can nevertheless give rise to a sense of *psychological* entrapment, symbolic entrapment. Such feelings often are associated with or arise out of unsatisfactory personal relationships. In a well known example, Dr Joseph Wolpe described "the spread of anxiety to new stimuli based upon 'symbolism'" in a 30-year-old claustrophobic patient:

> The onset . . . turned out to be related to a marriage in which she felt "caught like a rat in a trap." Many years earlier she had had a frightening experience in a confined space, and this had led to slight uneasiness in such places as elevators. Her marital situation now generated a chronic undertone of "shut-in" feeling with which the physical enclosure of elevators now summated to produce a substantial fear reaction (Wolpe, 1958, p. 99).

Incidentally, this is an interesting use of the concept of fear summation (Rachman & Lopatka, 1986). It also provides an example of the way in which an "unrelated" aversive event can generate a fear.

With respect to fear symbolism, at present we have little to work on other than case descriptions. Some of these are illuminating and even persuasive, but they do not provide a satisfactory basis for deciding on the validity and nature of symbolic forms of claustrophobia.

Physical Restriction

Having argued that in most cases claustrophobia is a combination of entrapment and a threat to the person's supply of fresh air, it is necessary to examine in more detail the concept of physical restriction. First, it is argued that physical restriction is often aversive. Second, physical restriction plus danger or the threat of harm is more often and more intensely aversive. Third, physical restriction plus a threat to the supply of fresh air provide the most common combination for the experience of claustrophobia.

It is argued further that feelings of suffocation are experienced only when the person feels unable to escape under conditions in which his/her supply of fresh air is impeded, with the exception of threats that have an internal source. These internal threats to normal breathing arise in people who have a history of respiratory ill-health (e.g. asthmatics).

If the first proposition, that physical restraint is intrinsically aversive, is correct, then it follows that people who are particularly sensitive to this type of aversive experience are likely to develop a significant fear of being trapped. The notion that physical restriction, even in the absence of some threat of harm, can be aversive is supported by the results of animal research, and is also consistent with the recent finding that a significant number of people who suffer from claustrophobic experiences report intense fear whenever they are placed under restraint, even in the absence of any threat to their air supply or indeed any other kind of detectable threat. Assuming, for the present purposes, that these people are able to identify sources of external or internal threat correctly, we can then take seriously the possibility that the restraint itself is aversive. It is even possible that it is this element of claustrophobia, a fear of physical restraint, that comes closest to providing the vestigial element in claustrophobia—bearing in mind that a significant number of claustrophobic people are unable to identify or report fearful cognitions regarding claustrophobia, even when they are actually in a frightening enclosed space.

In the course of his systematic investigations into the phenomenon of sudden death, Richter (1957) uncovered strong evidence of the adverse and potentially dangerous effects of extreme restraint. In a series of laboratory experiments on the induction of sudden death among various types of rats, he was able to conclude that two of the ten variables that were systematically investigated were paramount: "the restraint involved in holding the wild rats, thus suddenly and finally abolishing all hope of escape . . . and the confinement in the glass jar further eliminating all chance of escape and at the same time threatening them with immediate drowning. Some of the wild rats died simply while being held in the hand; some even died when put in the water directly from the living cages without ever being held" (Richter, 1957, p. 195). Contrary to his expectation, EKG records indicated that the rats that died promptly showed a slowing of the heartbeat rather than acceleration.

Richter remarked on the "remarkable speed of recovery of which these animals are capable", for once they were freed from "restraint in the hand or confinement in the glass jars, a rat that quite surely would have died in another minute or two becomes normally active and aggressive in only a few minutes" (Richter, 1957, pp. 196–197).

Immobilization

In their review of the effects of immobilization and restraint on pain reactions in animals, Porro & Carli (1988) noted that restraint is one of the most commonly used laboratory stressors, that it produces somatic and emotional reactions and, in a proportion of instances, analgesia.

> During the initial period of acute restraint, rats display behaviors associated with emotionality, i.e. vocalization, defecation, struggling in an attempt to escape, and teeth chattering. These reactions usually vanish with time, and the animals remain motionless after the first few minutes of struggling. Daily repeated sessions induce diminished food intake and growth rate in the rat as well as gastric lesions. Immediately following removal from a single episode of restraint, rats do not tend to escape and usually display a decreased motility (Porro & Carli, 1988, pp. 290–291).

Restraint regularly produces initial increases in heart-rate, blood pressure and endocrine responses.

Following repeated exposures to restraint, habituation takes place, and it appears to be psychological in nature rather than biochemical. Repeated episodes of restraint in a variety of stressful situations that produce comparable physiological changes do not transfer from one situation to the other. Despite the physiological similarities, the habituation is specific to the situation in which the restraint takes place. Tranquilizing drugs, such as diazepam, reduce restraint-produced emotional behavior.

Confinement

One of the major features of proposition one, that physical restriction is intrinsically aversive, is that it shares some of the qualities of prepared phobias, including an essentially non-cognitive basis. Hence, many people who display claustrophobia are unable to explain what precisely they fear will happen to them when they are in an enclosed space. They feel frightened and experience an intense and urgent need to escape. If this adaptive reaction is impeded, neurotic behavior may emerge.

Accordingly, "research on the production of experimental neuroses in animals has shown that the restriction of the subject's behavior plays an important part in the development of these disorders. A probable explanation . . . is that confinement reduces the animal's chances of making an adaptive response in the face of noxious stimulation" (Eysenck & Rachman, 1965). Wolpe (1958) considered that confinement has its effects by preventing an escape and by restricting fear conditioning to a limited number of cues (see also Metzner, 1961). "Psychological confinement is no less real than physical confinement. The barriers which prevent a child from carrying out a particular response may easily reside within himself as in an external object" (Eysenck & Rachman, 1965, p. 85). Social restrictions provide numerous examples of the aversive consequences of being confined in a situation by the fear of embarrassment or humiliation.

In this connection, it is interesting that the feeling of being trapped is exceedingly prominent in the list of situations that provoke anxiety among people with agoraphobia. For example, Thorpe & Burns (1983) reported that 96% of their sample of several hundred agoraphobics reported anxiety while waiting in line at a store, and 89% reported feeling trapped at the hairdresser or in similar circumstances. Other examples of the aversive consequences of physical restriction come from the literature on combat psychology, and from a variety of sources in which people have been accidentally trapped (Craske, Rachman & Tallman, 1986; Rachman, 1990).

Fear of Suffocation

It is not surprising that the fear of suffocation is widespread and can be intense. Potential or actual interference with access to useable air is a serious threat to one's survival, hence an early warning system capable of detecting such a threat is a biological necessity. The detection of such a threat produces attempts to gain access to useable air, and of course these are almost invariably successful. The fear of suffocation is unusual in the speed with which successful access to air (safety) produces immediate relief and the elimination of the fear reaction.

However, if the person's access to air is impeded, physically or otherwise, the fear persists and tends to intensify, hence the connection with restriction. When a fear of suffocation arises, when access to air is threatened, it is essential to have freedom of movement. So, physical restriction and/or a feeling of being trapped is dangerous when combined with a threat to one's air supply. Restriction and a perceived threat to one's air supply are the ingredients for claustrophobia.

When these conditions combine they tend to produce feelings of panic (see below). Under laboratory test conditions, a fear of suffocating was the most commonly reported cognition during studies of claustrophobic panic (Rachman, Levitt & Lopatka, 1988). Klein (1993, 1994), who introduced the original theory of panic, recently published an elaborate revision of the theory that rests on the assumption of a powerful physiological monitoring system for the detection of possible suffocation. "A carbon dioxide hypersensitivity theory of panic has been posited. We hypothesize more broadly that a physiological misinterpretation by a suffocation monitor misfires an evolved suffocation alarm system" (Klein, 1993, p. 306). It is this misfiring that produces a spontaneous panic. Given the biological importance of a sensitivity to potential interruptions of one's air supply, it is entirely plausible that "misfirings" by the monitoring system will have important psychological consequences—specifically panic and its consequences. Recent research by McNally, Hornig & Donnell (1995) provided partial support for Klein's theory, as did the analyses of Taylor & Rachman (1994). However, there are indications that Klein's theory suffers from a failure to incorporate the role of disturbing cognitions (e.g. McNally, Hornig & Donnell, 1995). In the long run, Klein's theory of panic, based on "misfirings" of the suffocation alarm, may prove to be more relevant for reaching an understanding of claustrophobia than of panic disorder.

The Underlying Fear

Under laboratory conditions, the most commonly endorsed fearful cognitions reported during an episode of panic were a fear of *suffocating*, passing out, panicking, running out of air, and losing control—in descending order of frequency (Rachman, Levitt & Lopatka, 1988). These cognitions were linked in understandable connections with bodily sensations that commonly occur during high levels of fear. The most common fearful cognition, suffocating, was positively correlated with shortness of breath, and the fear of passing out was highly correlated with faintness and with chest pain. It was also found that certain combinations of bodily sensations and cognitions had an increased probability of ending, in, or being associated with, panic. For example, a combination of two of the three sensations of choking, shortness of breath and dizziness, when associated with a cognition of suffocation, occurred frequently during episodes of panic. Very many more cognitions were reported on the 50 trials during which a panic occurred than on the 64 no-panic trials. On every episode of panic the subjects reported at least one fearful cognition. These findings on the frequency of fearful cognitions and their close association with particular sensations, especially during episodes of panic (Rachman, Levitt & Lopatka, 1988), can be interpreted as support for Clark's (1986, 1988) theory that panics are caused by the misinterpretation of bodily sensations.

Most of the claustrophobic panics were associated with shortness of breath and an exaggerated fear of suffocation—a catastrophic misinterpretation of bodily sensations. However, in many instances, the occurrence of a fearful cognition, even of suffocating, was not associated with an episode of panic. The occurrence of these cognitions does not inevitably lead to a panic, and the suggestion is that it is the combination of unpleasant bodily sensations and matching cognitions that is responsible for producing a panic.

However, the research suffers from two weaknesses. The list of cognitions used in the investigations was adapted from the list prepared by Chambless & Caputo (1984) for use with agoraphobic subjects, and the feelings of being trapped or restricted, which now seem to be important contributors to claustrophobia, were not included in that list. It is also necessary to exercise caution because these findings are associations, not causal relationships. The simple co-occurrence of bodily sensations and fearful cognitions with an episode of panic does not permit causal inferences. The absence of physiological measurements during the test trials is another weakness. We have little information about this aspect of claustrophobia.

A significant elevation of heart rate occurs when a claustrophobic subject enters a closed test room (Miller & Bernstein, 1972). In a study by Johansson & Öst, the heart-rate of subjects also increased significantly, from 73 to 79 beats/minute, when they were in the experimental test room. In both studies, the increases in heart rate did not vary in correspondence with subjective fear (Johansson & Öst, 1982; Miller & Bernstein, 1972). Apparently, claustrophobics experience a moderate increase in heart rate when they are in an enclosed space, but these changes are not concordant with self-rated fear or with escape behavior. Interestingly, even though the subjects who participated in the experiments on claustrophobic cognitions reported a higher incidence of palpitations and chest pain during episodes of panic, none of them endorsed the fearful cognition of having a heart attack (Rachman, Levitt & Lopatka, 1988). The enclosed test room presents no "cardiac threat" and the subjects were young and healthy.

The importance of a fear of suffocation is indicated by the very high frequency with which claustrophobic subjects endorse this fear in experimental conditions (Miller & Bernstein, 1972). Additionally, in 80% of the episodes of claustrophobic panic, a fear of suffocation was reported (Rachman, Levitt & Lopatka, 1988). We also know that a fear of suffocation is associated with the bodily sensations of shortness of breath and dizziness. Furthermore, evidence from the Indiana survey (Kirkpatrick, 1984) indicates that fears of enclosed spaces and of suffocation are correlated, and that the fear of suffocation is one of the most frequently reported fears in a general population.

Given that a fear of suffocation constitutes a fear of an "internal event", it is not surprising that the presence or absence of other people has little effect on claustrophobia. The only exception is the increase in fear that can be caused by the arrival of extra people; if the new people are thought to be competitors for the potentially insufficient quantity of air, then their presence adds to the threat (e.g. a crowded elevator). With the exceptions of social phobias and fears of contamination, there are no other fears in which the arrival of other people increases fear.

If the underlying fear is indeed one of possible suffocation, then the distance from home is irrelevant. The determining factor in the increase or decrease in fear is the availability of sufficient air and regular breathing. The quick relief that claustrophobic people experience when they leave the enclosed space is consistent with the idea that many of them are frightened of suffocation. Access to ample quantities of fresh air is sufficient to remove the danger speedily.

The effects of treatment are consistent with the idea that a fear of suffocation plays a part in most cases of claustrophobia. Certainly, the effectiveness of applied relaxation, in which practice in regulated breathing is included, should have a beneficial effect. The therapeutic effects of exposure are less easily accommodated, and one has to resort to speculating that the exposure trials consist of a series of disconfirmations of the threat of suffocation.

The evidence to support the importance of a fear of suffocating is substantial and well connected. However, there are reasons against accepting it as a comprehensive explanation. To begin with, a minority of claustrophobic people deny that they are frightened of suffocation. Second, Miller & Bernstein (1972) found no evidence of respiratory disturbance when claustrophobic subjects entered the enclosed test room. (This finding is surprising but not too damaging, because it is possible for people to feel short of breath even though their respiration is normal. It is a question of misinterpreting one's bodily sensations.) Third, the occurrence of claustrophobic fears in situations where there is no threat or actual shortage of fresh air suggests that other types of fear might underlie claustrophobia (here too, however, one could argue that people who are vulnerable might well misinterpret their bodily sensations of shortness of breath, even when fresh air is freely available, but this defense seems lame). Fourth, in some types of claustrophobia, the element of entrapment might be paramount. As mentioned earlier, it seems most unlikely that people who get frightened while waiting in a barber's chair or similar circumstances are fearful of suffocating. In these situations, the fear seems to be provoked by physical restriction or by a feeling of being trapped. A feeling of being trapped, even when fresh air is plentiful, can give rise to a claustrophobic reaction.

The fact that claustrophobic fear is so little responsive to the provision of reassurance about the availability of oxygen either may count against an interpretation based on suffocation or, preferably, can be regarded as another example of the resistance of intense fears to rational persuasion.

All of this leads to the conclusion that a fear of suffocation is a prominent feature of most instances of claustrophobia, but that in a minority of instances other types of fear underlie it (entrapment and physical restriction are likely alternatives).

We have, however, a more direct and preferable way to test this interpretation. Any information or action that significantly reduces or eliminates the identified fear of suffocation should be followed by a reduction in fear. On the same lines, any procedures that leave the fear of suffocation unchanged should not be followed by a reduction of fear. In tests of this kind, it will be essential to ensure that the subjects are selected for the presence of a significant fear of suffocating. The methods of producing the changes, whether they are cognitive or relaxation or exposure practice, are of secondary importance. Any intervention that significantly alters the fear of suffocation will do.

THE REDUCTION OF CLAUSTROPHOBIA

In a series of experiments, we attempted to modify claustrophobia by rational means and by repeated exposures in a small enclosed room (Rachman & Levitt, 1988). Having learned that a fear of suffocating is the most common cognition during claustrophobic panics, we informed our volunteers as fully and convincingly as we could that there was sufficient oxygen in the rest room and that they would be safe while inside it. The subjects were given written information and were told that the room was not airtight and that they could survive indefinitely. They were also told that even if the room were airtight, which it was not, they would have sufficient oxygen for 4–7 days. The provision of this accurate and reassuring information had little effect on the subjects' fear, even though they found the information to be credible. The provision of lighting in the test room failed to produce any consistent effects on fear; some of the subjects felt less frightened when a light was provided, but others felt more frightened.

We made three attempts to suppress or prevent claustrophobic panics by providing safety signals, either in the form of conditioned signals or by the provision of reassuring information, but had limited success. The safety signals did reduce the fears to a significant but only very small extent.

There was some habituation of fear over successive trials, regardless of safety signals or information. The subjects' reports of fear declined with scant respect for our experimental intentions. Although most of the subjects showed evidence of considerable habituation, between 15 and 30% showed an increase in fear.

In order to track down the causes of this sensitization, we re-analyzed the information from the four relevant experiments and found that there were significant differences between the fearful cognitions of those subjects who did and those who did not show habituation of fear (Rachman & Levitt, 1988). Of the non-habituators and those who showed no change, 86% endorsed the cognitive items "I am going to pass out" and "I am going to suffocate". The comparable figures for the habituators were 23 and 32%. The non-habituators also endorsed such bodily sensations as shortness of breath far more frequently than did the habituators. Certain cognitions might have impeded the habituation of fear, and that possibility was examined in subsequent experimental analyses.

The next step was a controlled, comparative evaluation of the effects of cognitive therapy vs. repeated exposures (Booth & Rachman, 1992). Forty-eight participants were recruited from the community through the local media, and randomly assigned to one of four groups: pure exposure, exposure to the sensations of anxiety (interoceptive exposure), modification of negative cognitions, or a control group. All interventions were given over three sessions. The exposure group proved superior to the control on a wide range of measures. In the cognitive group, scores of reported fear and panic declined significantly. The interoceptive group made some modest gains.

As can be seen from Figure 9.1, all three interventions successfully reduced claustrophobia, with pure exposure in the lead. The most puzzling and potentially most significant outcome of this reassuring attempt to fashion a treatment for this phobia was the decline in negative cognitions that appeared after (during?) therapy. As expected, the subjects who received a purely cognitive form of treatment reported significant declines in negative claustrophobic cognitions, in association with their reduced fear. What was not expected was an equally significant decline in the negative cognitions of the subjects who received the avowedly non-cognitive exposure treatment.

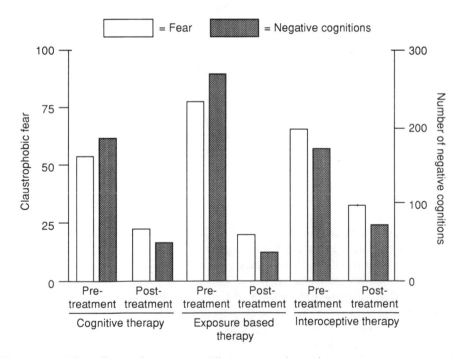

Figure 9.1 The effects of treatment. All 3 groups showed some improvement and a decline in negative cognitions (from Booth & Rachman, 1992, with permission)

The successful and stable reductions of claustrophobia achieved by Booth, and by Öst, Johansson & Jerremalm (1982) require interpretation. What are we to make of the relative ease with which claustrophobia can be reduced? In those instances in which the underlying fear is one of suffocation, presumably this cognition is amenable to modification. As mentioned earlier, the mere provision of accurate information is a weak method for achieving such modifications. As in other examples of fear modification, the disconfirmation might be most effective when the person repeatedly experiences the absence of any aversive outcome: "I did not suffocate". In the study by Öst, as in our experimental investigations, repeated exposures to the fear-provoking situation were part of the procedure, and they almost certainly facilitated the reduction of fear. The question to be decided is whether the exposures achieve their effects directly and independently, or through their influence on fearful cognitions.

In detailed analyses of the cognitive changes that occurred in the Booth and Rachman experiment on the reduction of claustrophobia, it emerged that high fear was always accompanied by believable negative cognitions (Shafran, Booth & Rachman, 1993). As can be seen in Figure 9.2, there were large differences in cognitions when fear was reduced vs. fear not reduced. A reduction in *believable* cognitions was accompanied by a large decline in fear, and the retention of believable negative cognitions was accompanied by persisting fear.

An absence of believable cognitions post-test was accompanied by an absence of claustrophobia in 10 of 13 subjects. Specifically, removal of belief in any of the cognitions, "I will be trapped", "I will suffocate" and/or "I will lose control" was associated with removal of belief in all the other cognitions and a dramatic reduction in claustrophobia. On the contrary, belief in one of these central cognitions was associated with the maintenance of fear. It was concluded that claustrophobia comprises a number of cognitions centered on the key thoughts of trappedness, suffocation and loss of control.

The results also suggest the possibility that removal of a central cognition can collapse the cognitive constellation and lead to the elimination of the claustrophobia.

SUMMARY

Claustrophobia is thought to comprise two components: a fear of restriction and a fear of suffocation. Either component can generate avoidance of enclosed spaces but the combination of both fears is virtually certain to do so.

Psychometric analyses indicate that the two components are moderately correlated and account for roughly 50% of the variance in tests of claustrophobia. This structure is consistent with the results of behavior tests and with data collected in structured interviews.

It has been suggested that there are three pathways to fear: conditioning, vicarious acquisition, instruction/information. It has also to be acknowledged that certain fears are readily acquired (e.g. fear of snakes) and others are acquired with difficulty and rarely (e.g. fear of electric sockets)—following the concept of prepared fears that was introduced by Seligman (1971). Claustrophobia may fall into this category—it has obvious survival value, is evident at an early age, is acquired readily and has clearly non-cognitive aspects—but there is no evidence that bears directly on this possibility (see also Menzies & Clarke, 1995).

It is argued that physical restriction is intrinsically aversive and provides the soil for claustrophobia. When a person is trapped and then experiences a threat to his/her air supply, a claustrophobic reaction is highly probable. The fear of suffocation is extremely common and of obvious biological value. It has been suggested that misfirings of a suffocation alarm system give rise to panic.

Claustrophobia is readily treatable by behavioral exposure—exercises and/ or cognitive behavior therapy. It is possible that removal of the central fear-cognition collapses the cognitive constellation and can lead to the elimination of the claustrophobia.

REFERENCES

Booth, R. & Rachman, S. (1992). The reduction of claustrophobia. I. *Behaviour Research and Therapy*, **30**, 207–221.

Bourdon, K. (1988). Gender differences in phobias: results of the ECA community study. *Journal of Anxiety Disorders*, **2**, 227–241.

Cattell, R.B. (1966). The scree test for the number of factors. *Multivariate Behavioral Research*, **1**, 245–276.

Chambless, D.L. & Caputo, G.C. (1984). Assessment of fear in agoraphobics: the Body Sensations Questionnaire and the Agoraphobic Cognitions Questionnaire. *Journal of Consulting and Clinical Psychology*, **52**, 1090–1097.

Clark, D.M. (1988). A cognitive model of panic attacks. In S. Rachman & J. Maser (eds), *Panic: Psychological Perspectives*. Hillsdale, NJ: Erlbaum.

Clark, D.M. (1986). A cognitive approach to panic. *Behaviour Research and Therapy*, **24**, 461–470.

Costello, C. (1982). Fears and phobias in women: a community study. *Journal of Abnormal Psychology*, **91**, 280–286.

Craske, M.G., Rachman, S. & Tallman, K. (1986). Mobility, cognitions, and panic. *Journal of Psychopathology and Behavioural Assessment*, **8**, 199–210.

Eysenck, H.J. & Rachman, S. (1965). *The Causes and Cures of Neurosis*. London: Routledge & Kegan Paul.

Friday, P.J. & Kubal, W.S. (1990). Magnetic resonance imaging: improved patient tolerance utilizing medical hypnosis. *American Journal of Clinical Hypnosis*, **33**, 80–84.

Johansson, J. & Öst, L.G. (1982). Perceptions of autonomic reactions and actual heart rate in phobic patients. *Journal of Behavioral Assessment*, **4**, 133–143.

Kilborn, L.C. & Labbe, E.E. (1990). Magnetic resonance imaging scanning procedures: development of phobic response during scan and at one-month follow-up. *Journal of Behavioral Medicine*, **13**, 391–401.

Kirkpatrick, D.R. (1984). Age, gender, and patterns of common intense fears among adults. *Behaviour Research and Therapy*, **22**, 141–150.

Klein, D.F. (1994). Testing the suffocation false alarm theory of panic disorder. *Anxiety*, **1**, 1–7.

Klein, D.F. (1993). False suffocation alarms, spontaneous panics, and related cognitions. *Archives of General Psychiatry*, **50**, 306–317.

Marks, I.M. (1987). *Fears, Phobias and Rituals*. Oxford: Oxford University Press.

McNally, R.J., Hornig, C.D. & Donnell, C.D. (1995). Clinical versus non-clinical panic: a test of suffocation false alarm theory. *Behaviour Research and Therapy*, **33**, 127–132.

McIsaac, H. (1995). Claustrophobia and the MRI procedure. Unpublished MA thesis, University of British Columbia.

Melendez, J. & McCrank, E. (1993). Anxiety-related reactions associated with magnetic resonance examinations. *Journal of the American Medical Association*, **270**, 745–747.

Menzies, R.G. & Clarke, J.C. (1995). The etiology of phobias: a non-associative account. *Clinical Psychology Review*, **15**, 23–48.

Metzner, R. (1961). Learning theory and the therapy of the neuroses. *British Journal of Psychology*, **33**, 62–86.

Miller, B. & Bernstein, D. (1972). Instructional demand in a behaviour avoidance test for claustrophic fears. *Journal of Abnormal Psychology*, **80**, 206–210.

Ollendick, T. & King, N. (1991). Origins of childhood fears: an evaluation of Rachman's theory of fear acquisition. *Behaviour Research and Therapy*, **29**, 117–123.

Öst, L.G. (1985). Ways of acquiring phobias and outcome of behavioural treatments. *Behaviour Research and Therapy*, **23**, 683–689.

Öst, L.G. (1987). Age of onset in different phobias. *Journal of Abnormal Psychology*, **96**, 223–229.

Öst, L.G., Johansson, J. & Jerremalm, A. (1982). Individual response patterns and the effects of behavioural methods in the treatment of claustrophobia. *Behaviour Research and Therapy*, **20**, 445–460.

Ploeger, A. (1977). A 10-year follow-up of miners trapped for two weeks under threatening circumstances. In C. Spielberger & I. Sarason (eds), *Stress and Anxiety*, Vol. 4. New York: Wiley.

Porro, C.A. & Carli, G. (1988). Immobilization and restraint effects on pain reactions in animals. *Pain*, **32**, 289–307.

Rachman, S. (1990). *Fear and Courage*, 2nd edn. New York: W.H. Freeman & Company.

Rachman, S. (1988). Biologically significant fears. *Behaviour Analysis and Modification*, **2**, 234–239.

Rachman, S. & Levitt, K. (1988). Panic, fear reduction and habituation. *Behaviour Research and Therapy*, **26**, 199–206.

Rachman, S., Levitt, K. & Lopatka, C. (1988). Experimental analysis of panic III—claustrophobic subjects. *Behaviour Research and Therapy*, **26**, 41–52.

Rachman, S., Levitt, K. & Lopatka, C. (1987). A simple method for distinguishing between expected and unexpected panics. *Behaviour Research and Therapy*, **25**, 149–154.

Rachman, S. & Lopatka, C. (1986). Do fears summate? *Behaviour Research and Therapy*, **24**, 653–660.

Rachman, S. & Taylor, S. (1993). Analyses of claustrophobia. *Journal of Anxiety Disorders*, **7**, 281–291.

Richter, C.P. (1957). On the phenomenon of sudden death in animals and man. *Psychosomatic Medicine*, **19**, 191–198.

Sanderson, R., Campbell, D. & Laverty, S. (1962). Traumatically conditioned responses acquired during respiratory paralysis. *Nature*, **196**, 1235–1236.

Seligman, M.E.P. (1971). Phobias and preparedness. *Behaviour Therapy*, **2**, 307–320.

Shafran, R., Booth, R. & Rachman, S. (1993). The reduction of claustrophobia. II. Cognitive analyses. *Behaviour Research and Therapy*, **30**, 75–85.

Taylor, S. & Rachman, S. (1994). Klein's suffocation theory of panic. *Archives of General Psychiatry*, **51**, 505–506.

Thompson, J. (1989). The King's Cross fire: psychological reactions. Paper presented at the British Psychological Society Conference, December.

Thorpe, G. & Burns, L. (1983). *The Agoraphobic Syndrome*. Chichester: Wiley.

Wolpe, J. (1958). *Psychotherapy by Reciprocal Inhibition*. Stanford: Stanford University Press.

Chapter 10

Atypical Phobias

Richard J. McNally
Department of Psychology, Harvard University,
Cambridge, MA, USA

Psychiatric nosologists are either "lumpers" or "splitters" who cope with symptomatic diversity in strikingly different ways. Lumpers see unity in diversity, and postulate a minimum of diagnostic entities. They interpret phenomenologic differences as variations on a few syndromal themes. Splitters, in contrast, interpret these differences as reflecting genuine nosological heterogeneity. They postulate more syndromes, more types and more subtypes than do their lumping counterparts.

There are lumpers and splitters throughout psychopathology, but no more dramatically than in the field of phobic disorders. At one extreme, the 2nd edn of the *Diagnostic and Statistical Manual of Mental Disorders* (DSM; American Psychiatric Association, 1968) lumped all phobias under the rubric of "phobic neurosis". All were seen as manifestations of the same psychodynamic process. At the other extreme, "unofficial" subtypes have proliferated in the literature. Indeed, Maser (1985) counted no less than 273 different kinds of phobic disorder! But perusal of Maser's list suggests that terminological proliferation has been driven more by etymology than by etiology. Different types often constitute little more than arcane labels for the same phobia. Thus, a person who dreads mice can be diagnosed with either *suriphobia* or *musophobia*; both denote a fear of mice. In fact, suffers of *hellenologophobia* (i.e. fear of "pseudoscientific terms") will surely tremble to contemplate many of entities uncovered by Maser in his search through the literature.

Subsequent to DSM-II, nosologists have steered an intermediate course between the extremes of lumping and splitting. Prompted by the seminal studies of Marks (1969), the architects of DSM-III (American Psychiatric Association, 1980) recognized three kinds of phobic disorder: agoraphobia, social phobia, and

Phobias—A Handbook of Theory, Research and Treatment. Edited by G.C.L. Davey.
© 1997 John Wiley & Sons Ltd.

simple phobia. DSM-III-R (American Psychiatric Association, 1987) retained these distinctions while specifying that agoraphobia is typically a consequence of panic disorder.

As part of the upsurge in research on anxiety disorders, behavioral scientists intensified their investigation of simple phobias throughout the 1980s (Norton et al., 1995). New studies on etiology, family history, age of onset, psychophysiology, treatment response and so forth prompted David H. Barlow, Chairman of the DSM-IV Simple Phobia Subgroup, to commission literature reviews addressing the issue of subtypes. The conclusions of this subgroup resulted in five specific phobia types in DSM-IV (American Psychiatric Association, 1994): (a) animal type; (b) natural environment type (e.g. storms, heights, water); (c) blood–injection–injury type; (d) situational type (e.g. enclosed places, airplanes, elevators); and (e) other type (e.g. fears of vomiting, choking, contracting an illness, costumed characters).

Common phobias recognized by DSM-IV are covered in other chapters in this volume. Therefore, the purpose of the present chapter is to review what is known about atypical phobias. Some of these phobic disorders were considered for recognition as formal subtypes (e.g. choking phobia; McNally, 1989), but were excluded primarily because of their relative rarity. Accordingly, most of the syndromes addressed in this chapter fall under the other type rubric.

CHOKING PHOBIA

People with choking phobia avoid swallowing food, pills, or fluids for fear of choking to death (McNally, 1994a). They typically eat only small amounts of "safe" foods (e.g. yogurt, noodles, ice cream), and consequently experience marked weight loss. Some can eat normally in the presence of other people, who presumably would provide first aid in the event of a choking emergency.

This phobia nearly always has a sudden onset, usually beginning after a frightening episode of choking on food. The disorder can emerge at any age. In published case studies, age of onset has ranged from 8 (Chatoor, Conley & Dickson, 1988) to 78 years of age (Brown et al., 1986). Published reports suggest a modest preponderance of female cases. Like most atypical phobias, its prevalence is unknown. While working on the DSM-IV Simple Phobia Subgroup, I located only 24 case reports of alleged choking phobia (McNally, 1989). Most fit the diagnosis, but a few seem best construed as cases of delusional disorder or obsessive–compulsive disorder (OCD). Four more clear-cut cases of choking phobia have subsequently appeared in the literature (Ball & Otto, 1994; Öst, 1992).

Although choking phobia can present as the sole disorder, it is often comorbid with panic disorder, depression or oppositional disorder. It is distinguishable from other general medical and psychiatric conditions. Choking phobia is distinct from dysphagia (i.e. difficulty in swallowing; Greenberg, Stern & Weilburg, 1988). Unlike dysphagia, choking phobia is characterized by fear, not discomfort or difficulty swallowing. Dysphagia can arise from a variety of non-psychiatric medical conditions, and warrants an assessment by an ear, nose and throat specialist.

"Feeling of choking" is a DSM-IV panic attack symptom, albeit an uncommon one, occurring in less than 20% of panic attacks (Krystal et al., 1991). Although choking phobia and panic disorder are not infrequently comorbid (e.g. Liebowitz, 1987), they are nevertheless easily distinguishable. Persons with choking phobia fear choking on food and so forth, whereas those with panic disorder experience choking sensations during panic attacks, not while eating. Nevertheless, there are two additional connections between choking phobia and panic disorder. Concerns about suffocation link panic disorder (Klein, 1993) and choking phobia, as do marked fears of bodily sensations. Unlike patients with most other specific phobias (Taylor, Koch & McNally, 1992), those with choking phobia are characterized by marked fears of bodily sensations (Ball & Otto, 1994; McNally, 1986), as indicated by high scores on the Anxiety Sensitivity Index (Reiss et al., 1986). Indeed, Ball & Otto noted that pre-existing exaggerated fears of death may predispose people to develop choking phobia.

OCD patients occasionally fear swallowing inedible objects, like thumbtacks, bits of glass and so forth. Concerns that they may have absentmindedly ingested these objects can provoking checking rituals. But fears about swallowing objects differ from fears about having food go down one's windpipe.

People with social phobia often fear dining in public, and sometimes report fears of choking on their food. But social phobics fear embarrassment, not death, should they choke.

Globus is the sensation of having a lump in one's throat. Although this symptom has often been viewed as indicative of conversion disorder (Wilson, Deary & Maran, 1988), as the label "globus hystericus" implies, it often has a treatable organic etiology (e.g. Puhakka & Kirveskari, 1988). Unlike choking phobics, patients complaining of globus do not report fears of choking.

Individuals with a hypersensitive gag reflex tolerate foreign objects in their mouths poorly, rendering dental work very difficult (Wilks & Marks, 1983). But these people do not report fears of choking, and choking phobics need not have a hypersensitive gag reflex.

Most choking phobias begin with a sudden, frightening event, and some authors have described such fears as "post-traumatic" (Chatoor, Conley & Dickson, 1988). But there is little evidence that choking on food is sufficient to initiate full-blown post-traumatic stress disorder (PTSD). Indeed, choking phobics are less preoccupied with past instances of choking than they are about the possibility of it happening again.

Finally, choking phobia is readily distinguishable from anorexia nervosa. People with the latter condition avoid eating for fear of becoming fat, not for fear of choking to death. With the exception, perhaps, of the obese, choking phobics express great distress at not being able to eat comfortably.

There are no controlled research trials on the treatment of choking phobia. Case studies, however, suggest that it is readily treatable through behavioral, cognitive–behavioral, or pharmacologic means. Using behavioral therapy methods, I treated a 30-year-old man whose phobia began after he had choked on a piece of fish at the age of 16 (McNally, 1986). His closest friend had died 2 years previously, choking to death on a hot dog. Although the patient was not present when his friend died, I suspect that his hearing about this tragedy sensitized him to choking sensations. Treatment involved graduated exposure *in vivo* to eating of feared foods, beginning with relatively non-threatening items (e.g. bread) and finishing with the most threatening items (e.g. bacon, lettuce, and tomato sandwich). Prompting, feedback and shaping of excessive chewing reduced the number of chews per bite from 90 to 20. Treatment reduced his fears and increased his consumption of previously avoided foods. He remained well at 6-month follow-up.

Initially using similar exposure methods, Öst (1992) encountered difficulties in treating a 68-year-old woman who had developed a fear of choking on fluids. He then conducted behavioral experiments (Salkovskis, 1991) designed not only to provide exposure to feared sensations, but also to refute her catastrophic beliefs about choking and suffocation. To counteract her belief that people cannot survive without oxygen for more than 30 seconds, he had her hold her breath for increasingly longer periods of time. To counteract her belief that coughing cannot expel water from the windpipe, Öst first had her cough into a paper cylinder to eject a pen from it; then he had her cough to expel water from her windpipe. By structuring exposure exercises as behavioral experiments that provide evidence against catastrophic beliefs, Öst abolished the patient's choking phobia, and she remained well at 1-year follow-up.

Combining behavioral and cognitive methods, Ball & Otto (1994) readily eliminated choking phobia in three patients. Their package comprised cognitive restructuring, interoceptive exposure to throat tightness (e.g. by rapid swallowing exercises) and graduated *in vivo* exposure to hierarchies of feared foods. Treatment abolished food avoidance, reduced choking fears and fostered weight regain.

Although behavioral and cognitive–behavioral methods appear to be the treatment of choice for choking phobia, psychopharmacologists have reported success with antipanic drugs such as alprazolam (e.g. Liebowitz, 1987) and imipramine (e.g. Kaplan, 1987). Given that selective serotonin re-uptake inhibitors (SSRIs) have surpassed high-potency benzodiazepines and tricyclic antidepressants as the pharmacologic treatments of choice for panic disorder (D.F. Klein, personal communication, September 6, 1995), it will be interesting to test their effectiveness against choking phobia.

VOMITING PHOBIA

Vomiting phobia comes in various guises. Some patients do not fear vomiting as such, but rather fear the embarrassment that might occur should they throw up in public. Thus, one of my patients would induce vomiting if she had to leave her home unexpectedly and before she had fully digested a meal. She preferred throwing up in the privacy of her home rather than in public. Such individuals are properly diagnosed as socially phobic. Thus, Lesage & Lamontagne (1985) treated two patients who complained of very frequent episodes of nausea coupled with fears of vomiting. Both engaged in extensive avoidance of situations that might provoke a nervous stomach. Much to the surprise of the authors, paradoxical instructions requiring patients to induce nausea backfired, and occasionally produced vomiting! *In vivo* exposure to avoided situations worked much better, and reduced episodes of nausea and fears of throwing up in public.

Other individuals dread vomiting in the midst of panic attacks. Herman, Rozensky & Mineka (1993) applied cognitive–behavioral antipanic methods to treat two panic patients whose chief concern was vomiting when anxious. Although their panic attacks and episodes of nausea diminished, their fears of vomiting remained.

Finally, other individuals present with vomiting phobia who qualify neither for social phobia nor panic disorder. McFadyen & Wyness (1983) treated a woman in her late 20s who feared being in the presence of a person who was vomiting, and accordingly avoided situations where she might encounter someone who might become sick (e.g. bars, parties, hospital, boats). She worried about having children and how she would cope with their intestinal viruses. She herself did not fear vomiting. *In vivo* exposure assignments involving avoided situations and activities did not alleviate her fear that someone might yet vomit under these circumstances while she was present. Accordingly, the authors themselves repeatedly simulated vomiting in the presence of the patient by using a mixture of rice pudding and minestrone soup. She acknowledged the realism of these simulations, and reported marked reductions in fear over the course of five sessions spread over a month's time. She remained phobia-free at 18-month follow-up.

Phillips (1985) treated five women and two men who presented with fears of seeing others vomit and fears of vomiting themselves. Their phobias were chronic and had persisted for an average of over 17 years. Two-thirds of these patients had secondary problems as well (e.g. agoraphobic symptoms, anorexia symptoms), but fear of vomiting was the most salient and disabling complaint. All could vividly recall a triggering incident, and the mean age of onset of their phobia was 8.5 years of age.

Rather than simulate vomiting herself, in the fashion of McFadyen & Wyness (1983), Phillips developed a videotape comprising several scenes in which a woman and then a man vomited. Sessions involved repeated viewing of this tape, first without and later with sound. Phillips found that repeated graduated exposure to simulated audiovideotaped vomiting reduced nausea and fear of vomiting. In four patients, fear and nausea diminished in synchrony, whereas in three patients nausea diminished but fear tended to return between sessions. Both groups eventually recovered from their phobia, but the group that tended to experience an intersession return of fear required more exposure than did the group whose fears remained low after a session. Audiovideotaped exposure to people vomiting was effective for both fears of witnessing vomiting and fears of vomiting oneself.

DISEASE PHOBIA

Individuals suffering from a specific phobia for disease exhibit unrealistic fear and avoidance of situations that might expose them to serious illness. They are aware that their fears excessive. In contrast, people with hypochondriasis believe that they may have already contracted a dreaded disease. If their disease conviction becomes impervious to contrary evidence, delusional disorder (somatic type) is diagnosed. Thus, individuals with disease phobia fear contracting a disease, whereas individuals with hypochondriasis believe they already have it.

Interpreting the literature on disease (or illness) phobia is difficult because researchers have often failed to distinguish between disease phobics and patients with hypochondriasis. Indeed, Kellner (1985) conceptualized both syndromes as subtypes of hypochondriasis rather than considering the former as a specific phobia. Moreover, despite attempts to clarify the nosological boundaries of disease phobia and hypochondriasis in DSM-IV (Salkovskis, Warwick & Clark, 1991), ambiguities remain. For example, the absence of compulsive rituals demarcates specific (disease) phobics from OCD patients who also fear diseases (American Psychiatric Association, 1994, p. 410), yet one can diagnose OCD in persons who have obsessions but no compulsions (American Psychiatric Association, 1994, p. 422). Accordingly, there is no principled basis for distinguishing disease phobics who avoid illness-related cues and OCD patients who avoid similar cues but who do not engage in compulsive rituals.

Behavioral treatment studies on disease phobia have apparently included patients with hypochondriasis. Treatments have been modelled on those for OCD. Patients are systematically exposed to illness-related cues (e.g. visiting hospitals) and are urged to refrain from compulsive checking of their bodies for signs of disease and from compulsive seeking of reassurance about their health from friends, physicians and medical textbooks (Marks, 1987, pp. 413–415). In contrast to traditional views (e.g. Kellner, 1985), continued provision of reassurance is viewed as counterproductive because it fosters continued compulsive checking. Indeed, based on their work with OCD patients, behavior therapists believe that disease fears persist *because of* the short-term anxiety reduction occurring after repeated reassurances about health, not *in spite of* it (Salkovskis & Warwick, 1986).

This exposure-plus-response-prevention strategy appears effective for many patients with disease phobia and hypochondriasis (Logsdail et al., 1991; Salkovskis & Warwick, 1986; Warwick & Marks, 1988). Some clinical researchers suspect, however, that patients with hypochondriasis may require additional cognitive therapy procedures designed to reduce their disease conviction (Warwick & Salkovskis, 1990; Salkovskis, Warwick & Clark, 1991), whereas those with disease phobia may need only exposure methods. However, in a cross-over design, Visser & Bouman (1992) found behavioral methods more effective than cognitive methods in alleviating hypochondriasis. Their data also suggested that behavior therapy followed by cognitive therapy was more effective than cognitive therapy followed by behavior therapy.

Finally, a recent case report showed that 40 mg/day of fluoxetine alleviated symptoms in a woman suffering from cancer phobia (Viswanathan & Paradis, 1991). She remained well as long as she was on this medication. Her symptoms returned whenever she stopped taking fluoxetine, and greatly reduced when this medication was reinstated. Desipramine and buspirone had negligible effects on her phobia. If replicated, this report suggests that further investigation of serotonin re-uptake blockers is warranted for people who fail to respond to behavior therapy.

TAIJIN-KYOFU-SHO

Taijin-kyofu-sho (TKS) is a Japanese syndrome characterized by "fear of other people" (*taijin*, in relation to other people; *kyofu*, fear; *sho*, symptom; Prince & Tcheng-Laroche, 1987; Russell, 1989). Unlike Westerners with social phobia whose avoidance rests on fears of public embarrassment, TKS patients fear that their behavior will embarrass or offend *other* people. Typical concerns include making others ill at ease by blushing in their presence or by glancing at their genital area, emitting foul odors, or making odd faces.

TKS was first described in the 1920s by the great Japanese psychiatrist, Shoma Morita, who believed that it developed in people characterized by *shinkeishitsu*, a constitutional disposition marked by nervous weakness and delicate sensitivity to other people (Kirmayer, 1991). Yamashita (1993), however, reported that only a minority of his 100 cases had a nervous temperament. The syndrome is more common in men than in women, usually develops during adolescence, and rarely begins after the age of 40. TKS is very common in Japan; between 7 and 36% of patients receive the diagnosis. TKS patients are most distressed when in the presence of acquaintances or co-workers, and much less so when with family, very close friends or strangers.

Many commentators have noted that TKS rarely occurs outside of Japan, and may therefore constitute a culture-bound syndrome (e.g. Prince & Tcheng-Laroche, 1987; Yamashita, 1993). Indeed, certain aspects of Japanese culture may increase the likelihood of TKS. In contrast to most Western (or at least American) people, Japanese people are less willfully individualistic and are more attentive to the feelings of others. At the same time, however, Japanese norms require that people not express their wishes and feelings directly, thereby requiring everyone to "read each other's minds". Thus, Japanese people are required to decode subtle forms of non-verbal behavior in an difficult attempt not to offend, embarrass or make others ill at ease, yet others are culturally debarred from providing any direct feedback.

Although Japanese culture may predispose people to develop TKS, it occasionally occurs elsewhere. For example, we treated a 34-year-old Black American teacher for TKS who had been referred to our Anxiety Disorders Clinic for OCD (McNally, Cassiday & Calamari, 1990). She did, indeed, have OCD symmetry obsessions and ordering compulsions, but these were mild relative to her severe, classic TKS. She had been troubled for years by the fear that she would embarrass others by glancing at their genital area. In addition to instituting standard *in vivo* exposure plus response prevention for her OCD symptoms, we had her systematically practice glancing at genital areas in a variety of settings. She enjoyed marked improvement in both OCD and TKS symptoms, but at 5-month follow-up her TKS relapsed, whereas her OCD remained in remission.

Kleinknecht and his colleagues have initiated cross-cultural studies on TKS (Kleinknecht et al., 1994, 1996). Studying Americans with and without Japanese ancestry on the west coast of the USA and in Hawaii, Kleinknecht et al. (1994) found that shared variance between TKS and social phobia questionnaires ranged only from 31 to 38%, depending on site. Neuroticism was positively correlated with both TKS symptoms and social phobia symptoms, but introversion was positively correlated only with social phobia, not TKS, symptoms. Scores on a measure of identification with Japanese culture were positively related to TKS scores, confirming empirically what Japanese clinicians have long suspected.

In their subsequent investigation, Kleinknecht et al. (1996) found that low scores on a measure of independent self-construal and high scores on a social phobia measure predicted high TKS scores in college students in Tokyo. Measures of social avoidance and social phobia predicted TKS scores among American students, whereas self-construal did not.

Unlike most American nosologists, Japanese psychiatrists tend to be diagnostic lumpers. Among the 100 TKS patients thoroughly described by Yamashita (1993), American clinicians would diagnose body dysmorphic disorder, delusional disorder, OCD and social phobia as well as TKS as described above. Despite their including a variety of other syndromes under this rubric, fear and avoidance of social situations for fear of embarrassing or offending others does seem to be a syndrome distinct from Western social phobia, and tied, if not to Japan *per se*, than at least to cultures where one has to be exquisitely sensitive to the feelings of people who nevertheless make every effort to conceal them.

FLIGHT PHOBIA

Inclusion of fear of flying in this chapter is justified solely by its failure to fit neatly into traditional phobia categories, not by its rarity. Thus, flight phobia is secondary to claustrophobia in only 37% of patients, and to height phobia in only 13% (Walder et al., 1987). Flight phobia is far from uncommon. One epidemiologic study revealed that approximately 10% of the population suffers from an intense fear of flying (Agras, Sylvester & Oliveau, 1969). Actuarial data underscore how unrealistic this fear is. For example, if people could only die in airplane crashes, the average person would live to be 1 million years old (Beck, Emery & Greenberg, 1985, p. 202).

Unfortunately, the Epidemiologic Catchment Area (ECA) study did little to advance knowledge about the prevalence of this disorder (for a critique of the ECA's assessment of anxiety disorders, see McNally, 1994b, pp. 30–40). The ECA protocol diagnosed all travel phobias as instances of agoraphobia, irrespective of the motivation for avoidance (Eaton, Dryman & Weissman, 1991), and therefore failed to distinguish individuals with specific phobia from those whose fear of flying was just another facet of their agoraphobia. This procedure resulted in the misclassification of specific phobics as "agoraphobics without panic" (Horwath et al., 1993).

Revising previous instruments (Craske, 1990; McNally & Steketee, 1985), Louro and I developed a structured interview to clarify the nosological status of flight phobia in 34 patients who sought behavior therapy for fear of flying (McNally & Louro, 1992). Seventeen patients had specific phobia, whereas the others had panic disorder with agoraphobia.

Our interview revealed several similarities between the groups. The sex ratio was similar; 82% of the agoraphobics and 71% of the specific phobics were women. Both groups had mean ages of onset for flight phobia in their late 20s. Reported symptom profiles and course of illness were very similar between the groups as well.

The groups tended to nominate different variables as important in the development of their flight phobias. More specific phobics (71%) than agoraphobics (18%) said that news reports about plane crashes figured in the development of their fear. Forty-one per cent of specific phobics cited frightening, turbulent flights as etiologically significant, whereas no agoraphobic did so. Twelve per cent of specific phobics said watching another become fearful during a flight worsened their own fear, whereas no agoraphobic said so. About the same number of agoraphobics (47%) as specific phobics (41%) nominated sudden panic attacks while aloft as etiologically important.

The groups differed dramatically in their motivation for flight avoidance (i.e. focus of apprehension). Using Likert scales, patients indicated the extent to which their flight avoidance was motivated by fear of harm from external sources (e.g. crashes) and from fear of panic and its possible consequences (e.g. loss of self-control). The results revealed that specific phobics were far more concerned about plane crashes than were agoraphobics, whereas agoraphobics were far more concern about panic and its consequences than were specific phobics. Moreover, agoraphobics indicated that their fear of flying would be drastically reduced if they knew they would not experience the physical sensations associated with fear while aloft, whereas specific phobics indicated that elimination of these sensations would have little impact on their flight avoidance.

In summary, although behavioral avoidance and most demographic and clinical features do not distinguish agoraphobics from specific phobics who fear flying, their focus of apprehension does. Agoraphobics avoid flying because they fear panic and its consequences; specific phobics avoid flying because they fear crashes.

Early treatments for flight phobia included imaginal systematic desensitization, implosive therapy, and imaginal flooding (e.g. Howard, Murphy & Clarke, 1983; Scrignar, Swanson & Bloom, 1973; Shaw, 1977). These reduced anticipatory anxiety about flying and increased the likelihood that patients would embark on a test flight at the end of treatment. It became apparent, however, that the test flight itself was at least as anxiolytic as the formal treatments (e.g. Walder et al., 1987). Accordingly, the goal of contemporary interventions is to provide patients with skills that enable them to engage in the therapeutic experience of flying itself (e.g. Beckham et al., 1990; Haug et al., 1987). For example, Beckham et al. randomly assigned flight phobics to either a no-treatment control condition or to a stress inoculation treatment. The latter required patients to master a manual that taught them relaxation and cognitive coping skills. During the 1-month treatment period, patients in the active treatment condition had brief, periodic phone contacts with the therapist that totalled no more than 45 minutes. The results indicated that patients in the active treatment condition reported less post-treatment fear, were more likely to embark on the post-treatment test flight, and were more likely to fly during the 2-month follow-up period than were patients in the no-treatment control group. During the test flight, the groups did not differ in either heart-rate or self-reported fear. However, those patients who flew during the follow-up period had higher heart-rates and greater reduction in heart-rate during the test flight than did patients who avoided flying during the follow-up period. Taken together, these results suggest that training in coping skills increases the likelihood that flight phobics will undertake flights that are themselves powerful means of reducing fear *in vivo*.

SPACE PHOBIA

Space phobia refers to a fear of absent visuospatial support and of falling (Marks & Bebbington, 1976). Unlike agoraphobia, it is genuinely characterized by a fear of open spaces. People with space phobia can walk easily if they grasp another's arm, use a walker, cling to fences and so forth. Some can walk unaided as long as support is nearby. Others resort to crawling at home. One of Marks's (1987, p. 319) patients could ride a bicycle normally, but could hardly walk; another could dance, but only on crowded floors. Only about one-third of the time does the phobia emerge following a fall. Only 17 cases have been described in the world literature (Jeans & Orrell, 1991; Marks, 1981; McCaffrey et al., 1990; McNally, 1990).

Space phobia is distinguishable from other phobias. It begins late in life, usually after the age of 50. Spontaneous panic, depression and personality disorders are uncommon. Most patients, however, have cardiovascular or neurological signs and symptoms indicative of organic pathology. Among these are diffuse non-focal electroencephalographic abnormalities, tinnitus, hypertension, cervical spondylosis and nystagmus. Vertigo is absent. Finally, unlike all other phobic disorders, space phobia rarely responds to exposure *in vivo* (cf. Jeans & Orrell, 1991).

Organic findings suggest that space phobia may result from aberrant integration of vestibulo-ocular reflexes that arise from varied lesions in the neck or in the central nervous system (Marks, 1987, p. 319). These findings, moreover, rule out conversion disorder. Indeed, people with space phobia are *afraid* to walk rather than unable to walk. Because the extent of organic disturbance is insufficient to impair ambulation, the fear of falling is excessive and, therefore, phobic.

Jeans & Orrell (1991) reported the only successful treatment of a case of space phobia. Their patient was a 50-year-old woman whose symptoms began 24 years earlier with attacks of giddiness and eventually resulted in her being bed-ridden in the hospital. Repeated medical assessments, however, revealed no neurologic or cardiac abnormalities (except recent mild hypertension). Unlike most space phobics, she developed agoraphobia and had panic attacks when she thought she was about to fall. A program of graduated exposure of walking progressively longer distances and fading of the presence of supportive relatives and staff enabled the patient to overcome her fear of falling and regain her ability to walk without anxiety. These encouraging findings suggest that space phobics may warrant a trial of exposure therapy, especially if they exhibit no signs of neurologic dysfunction.

NOISE PHOBIA

Fear of sudden noises provides the usual basis for fears of balloons, thunderstorms and so forth. Noise phobics do not merely startle at loud noises; rather they engage in extensive fear-motivated avoidance to decrease the chances they will hear loud noises.

Yule, Sacks & Hersov (1974) treated an 11-year-old boy's noise phobia by exposing him to the bursting of hundreds of balloons during two sessions over 2 days. While confined in a balloon-filled room with the therapist, the patient expressed much distress as the therapist burst balloons. But as his fear subsided, he began bursting them himself. He remained free of noise phobia at 25-month follow-up.

Wish, Hasazi & Jurgela (1973) treated another 11-year-old boy whose fear of loud noises developed years before when he became frightened during a 4th of July fireworks display. His fear spread to other sources of loud noises, such as thunder and jets. Wish et al. established a hierarchy of progressively more disturbing noises, and embedded them in tapes of the patient's favorite music. Over the course of 8 days, the patient's phobia dramatically diminished as he practiced this form of audiotaped self-exposure to feared cues.

Occasionally adults present with balloon (i.e. noise) phobia. Applying Yule et al.'s methods, Houlihan and his colleagues successfully treated a near-lifelong balloon phobia in a 21-year-old man (Houlihan et al., 1993). He had acquired the fear when frightened by a pop-gun at the age of 3, and became asymptomatic after several *in vivo* flooding sessions. AuBuchon (1993) used a variety of cognitive and social skills training methods to help a 21-year-old shy woman whose balloon phobia presumably prevented her from engaging in even more frightening social activities (e.g. attending parties where balloons might be present). Intensive flooding, however, was not tried, yet the patient overcame her fear through these indirect methods.

Öst (1978) treated six women, ranging in age from 23 to 77 years, who suffered from thunder and lightning phobia. All but one patient had acquired the phobia in early childhood. Three patients had apparently acquired their fears by watching the terrified behavior of their parents or grandparents during storms; two had been in houses that were struck by lightning; and the last case, who had acquired her fear in adulthood, was a very religious person who once mistook a bad storm for the End of the World, and had been frightened of storms ever since. Exposure to audiotapes of increasingly loud and violent thunderstorms eliminated the phobia in five women and greatly reduced it in the sixth.

MISCELLANEOUS PHOBIAS

The psychoanalyst Rangell (1952) treated a 38-year-old man with a near-lifelong fear of dolls. The patient experienced terror in the presence of manikins, statues and ceramic figurines as well. Rangell established that castration anxiety was the basis for the phobia: dolls, he discovered, were symbolic of the patient's detached penis. After 4 years of intensive psychoanalysis and over 700 hours on the couch, the patient began to approach and handle dolls with considerably diminished fear.

Not all doll phobias require 4 years of psychoanalysis for their resolution. Hatcher (1989) managed to abolish a lifelong doll phobia in an 11-year-old boy who exhibited no other psychopathology in twelve weekly 30-minute sessions of graduated exposure to dolls. Using five progressively more frightening dolls, Hatcher had the patient view, touch and then handle them until his fear had subsided. After mastering his fear of a doll, the patient took it home with him and practiced handling it until the next week's session. At 10-month follow-up, his fear remained negligible and he no longer avoided dolls.

Thomas & Rapp (1977) treated a 40-year-old woman who suffered from a lifelong fear of seeing eyepatches, especially those being worn by a person. She was subjected to a single 9-hour session comprising audiotaped flooding scenes concerning people wearing eyepatches, slide presentations of her family members wearing eyepatches, watching the therapist wearing an eyepatch, and finally her wearing one as well. Her heart-rate peaked at over 150 beats/minute (bpm), but it dropped to about 100 bpm after an hour, and eventually declined to under 90 bpm. Self-reported fear diminished as well, and the patient remained much improved at 2-year follow-up.

Finally, Goldberg & Weisenberg (1992) used token reinforcement procedures to ensure that a 9-year-old boy who had longstanding fear of newspapers engaged in graduated exposure *in vivo* to newspapers. The patient's fear had generalized from being a fear of eating in the presence of newspapers to merely seeing them on the street (e.g. he avoided walking near newspaper stands). He had no other psychopathology, including shyness, and he had an excellent response to treatment.

AVERSIONS

Aversions refer to profound dislike and avoidance of certain tactile, gustatory or auditory stimuli (Marks, 1987, pp. 396–399). People who have aversions experience shivers down the spine, nausea, shuddering, and feel their teeth set on edge and their hair stand on end when they encounter their aversive sensory stimulus. They do not experience fear or anxiety.

Common auditory aversions are the sound of chalk screeching on a blackboard and the sound of another person chewing. Tactile aversions are apparently the most common, and these often involve wool, peaches, tennis balls, velvet, cotton swabs, or rubber. Although the origins of auditory and tactile aversions are obscure, taste aversions usually develop after a person has become sick after eating a certain food (Garb & Stunkard, 1974). The food itself need not be the cause of sickness; merely developing a case of the stomach 'flu after eating a novel food may establish a lifelong conditioned nausea of the food.

There is no treatment research on aversions, chiefly because people rarely seek professional help for them. Clinical lore has it that they are not responsive to exposure therapy. Nevertheless, in his autobiography, written in the third person, the great Florentine architect and all-around Renaissance Man, Leon Battista Alberti, described how he overcame his aversions through self-exposure:

> By some defect in his nature he loathed garlic and also honey, and the mere sight of them, if by chance they were offered to him, brought on vomiting. But he conquered himself by force of looking at and handling the disagreeable objects, so that they came to offend him less, thus showing by example that men can do anything with themselves if they will (Alberti, 1460/1968, p. 491).

ACKNOWLEDGMENTS

Preparation of this manuscript was supported in part by NIMH grant MH51927, awarded to the author.

REFERENCES

Agras, S., Sylvester, D. & Oliveau, D. (1969). The epidemiology of common fears and phobias, *Comprehensive Psychiatry*, **10**, 151–156.

Alberti, L.B. (1460/1968). Self-portrait of a universal man. In J.B. Ross & M.M. McLaughlin (eds), *The Portable Renaissance Reader*. New York: Viking Press, pp. 480–492.

American Psychiatric Association (1968). *Diagnostic and Statistical Manual of Mental Disorders*, 2nd edn. Washington, DC: American Psychiatric Association.

American Psychiatric Association (1980). *Diagnostic and Statistical Manual of Mental Disorders*, 3rd edn. Washington, DC: American Psychiatric Association.

American Psychiatric Association (1987). *Diagnostic and Statistical Manual of Mental Disorders*, 3rd edn (revised). Washington, DC: American Psychiatric Association.

American Psychiatric Association (1994). *Diagnostic and Statistical Manual of Mental Disorders*, 4th edn. Washington, DC: American Psychiatric Association.

AuBuchon, P.G. (1993). Formulation-based treatment of a complex phobia. *Journal of Behavior Therapy and Experimental Psychiatry*, **24**, 63–71.

Ball, S.G. & Otto, M.W. (1994). Cognitive–behavioral treatment of choking phobia: three case studies. *Psychotherapy and Psychosomatics*, **62**, 207–211.

Beck, A.T., Emery, G. & Greenberg, R.L. (1985). *Anxiety Disorders and Phobias*. New York: Basic Books.

Beckham, J.C., Vrana, S.R., May, J.G., Gustafson, D.J. & Smith, G.R. (1990). Emotional processing and fear measurement synchrony as indicators of treatment outcome in fear of flying. *Journal of Behavior Therapy and Experimental Psychiatry*, **21**, 153–162.

Brown, S.R., Schwartz, J.M., Summergrad, P. & Jenike, M.A. (1986). Globus hystericus syndrome responsive to antidepressants. *American Journal of Psychiatry*, **143**, 917–918.

Chatoor, I., Conley, C. & Dickson, L. (1988). Food refusal after an incident of choking: a post-traumatic eating disorder. *Journal of the American Academy of Child and Adolescent Psychiatry*, **27**, 105–110.

Craske, M.G. (1990). The boundary between simple phobia and panic disorder with agoraphobia: a survey of clinical and nonclinical samples [Report prepared for the *DSM-IV* Simple Phobia Subgroup]. Washington, DC: American Psychiatric Association.

Eaton, W.W., Dryman, A. & Weissman, M.M. (1991). Panic and phobia. In L.N. Robins & D.A. Regier (eds), *Psychiatric Disorders in America*. New York: Free Press, pp. 155–179.

Garb, J.L. & Stunkard, A.J. (1974). Taste aversions in man. *American Journal of Psychiatry*, **131**, 1204–1207.

Goldberg, J. & Weisenberg, M. (1992). The case of a newspaper phobia in a 9-year-old child. *Journal of Behavior Therapy and Experimental Psychiatry*, **23**, 125–131.

Greenberg, D.B., Stern, T.A. & Weilburg, J.B. (1988). The fear of choking: three successfully treated cases. *Psychosomatics*, **29**, 126–129.

Hatcher, S. (1989). A case of doll phobia. *British Journal of Psychiatry*, **155**, 255–257.

Haug, T., Brenne, L., Johnsen, B.H., Berntzen, D., Götestam, K.-G. & Hugdahl, K. (1987). A three-systems analysis of fear of flying: a comparison of a consonant vs. a nonconsonant treatment method. *Behaviour Research and Therapy*, **25**, 187–194.

Herman, D.S., Rozensky, R.H. & Mineka, S. (1993). Cognitive–behavior therapy for panic disorder with a primary fear of vomiting: conceptual and treatment issues. Paper presented at the meeting of the Association for Advancement of Behavior Therapy, Atlanta, GA, USA, November.

Horwath, E., Lish, J.D., Johnson, J., Hornig, C.D. & Weissman, M.M. (1993). Agoraphobia without panic: clinical reappraisal of an epidemiologic finding. *American Journal of Psychiatry*, **150**, 1496–1501.

Houlihan, D., Schwartz, C., Miltenberger, R. & Heuton, D. (1993). The rapid treatment of a young man's balloon (noise) phobia using *in vivo* flooding. *Journal of Behavior Therapy and Experimental Psychiatry*, **24**, 233–240.

Howard, W.A., Murphy, S.M. & Clarke, J.C. (1983). The nature and treatment of fear of flying: a controlled investigation. *Behavior Therapy*, **14**, 557–567.

Jeans, V. & Orrell, M.W. (1991). Behavioural treatment of space phobia: a case report, *Behavioural Psychotherapy*, **19**, 285–288.

Kaplan, R.M. (1987). More on the globus hystericus syndrome. *American Journal of Psychiatry*, **144**, 528–529.

Kellner, R. (1985). Functional somatic symptoms and hypochondriasis: a survey of empirical issues. *Archives of General Psychiatry*, **42**, 821–833.

Kirmayer, L.J. (1991). The place of culture in psychiatric nosology: taijin Kyofusho and DSM-III-R. *Journal of Nervous and Mental Disease*, **179**, 19–28.

Klein, D.F. (1993). False suffocation alarms, spontaneous panics, and related conditions: an integrative hypothesis. *Archives of General Psychiatry*, **50**, 306–317.

Kleinknecht, R.A., Dinnel, D., Kleinknecht, E.E., Hiruma, N. & Hirada, N. (1996). *Cultural Factors in the Expression of Social Anxiety and Phobia: taijin Kyofusho and Social Phobia*. Manuscript submitted for publication.

Kleinknecht, R.A., Dinnel, D.L., Tanouye-Wilson, S. & Lonner, W.J. (1994). Cultural variation in social anxiety and phobia: a study of taijin kyofusho. *The Behavior Therapist*, **17**, 175–178.

Krystal, J.H., Woods, S.W., Hill, C.L. & Charney, D.S. (1991). Characteristics of panic attack subtypes: assessment of spontaneous panic, situational panic, sleep panic, and limited symptom attacks. *Comprehensive Psychiatry*, **32**, 474–480.

Lesage, A. & Lamontagne, Y. (1985). Paradoxical intention and exposure *in vivo* in the treatment of psychogenic nausea: report of two cases. *Behavioural Psychotherapy*, **13**, 69–75.

Liebowitz, M.R. (1987). Globus hystericus and panic attacks. *American Journal of Psychiatry*, **144**, 390–391.

Logsdail, S., Lovell, K., Warwick, H. & Marks, I. (1991). Behavioural treatment of AIDS-focused illness phobia, *British Journal of Psychiatry*, **159**, 422–425.

Marks, I.M. (1969). *Fears and Phobias*. New York: Academic Press.

Marks, I. (1981). Space "phobia": a pseudo-agoraphobic syndrome. *Journal of Neurology, Neurosurgery and Psychiatry*, **44**, 387–391.

Marks, I.M. (1987). *Fears, Phobias, and Rituals*. New York: Oxford University Press.

Marks, I. & Bebbington, P. (1976). Space phobia: syndrome or agoraphobic variant? *British Medical Journal*, **2**, 345–347.

Maser, J.D. (1985). List of phobias. In A.H. Tuma & J.D. Maser (eds), *Anxiety and the Anxiety Disorders*. Hillsdale, NJ: Erlbaum, pp. 805–813.

McCaffrey, R.J., Rapee, R.M., Gansler, D.A. & Barlow, D.H. (1990). Interaction of neuropsychological and psychological factors in two cases of "space phobia". *Journal of Behavior Therapy and Experimental Psychiatry*, **21**, 113–120.

McFadyen, M. & Wyness, J. (1983). You don't have to be sick to be a behaviour therapist but it can help! Treatment of a "vomit" phobia. *Behavioural Psychotherapy*, **11**, 173–176.

McNally, R.J. (1986). Behavioral treatment of a choking phobia. *Journal of Behavior Therapy and Experimental Psychiatry*, **17**, 185–188.

McNally, R.J. (1989). Fear of choking: a simple phobia subtype? [Report prepared for the *DSM-IV* Simple Phobia Subgroup.] Washington, DC: American Psychiatric Association.

McNally, R.J. (1990). Another case of "space phobia"? *Phobia Practice and Research Journal*, **3**, 79–80.

McNally, R.J. (1994a). Choking phobia: a review of the literature. *Comprehensive Psychiatry*, **35**, 83–89.

McNally, R.J. (1994b). *Panic Disorder: A Critical Analysis*. New York: Guilford.

McNally, R.J., Cassiday, K.L. & Calamari, J.E. (1990). Taijin-kyofu-sho in a Black American woman: behavioral treatment of a "culture-bound" anxiety disorder. *Journal of Anxiety Disorders*, **4**, 83–87.

McNally, R.J. & Louro, C.E. (1992). Fear of flying in agoraphobia and simple phobia: distinguishing features. *Journal of Anxiety Disorders*, **6**, 319–324.

McNally, R.J. & Steketee, G.S. (1985). The etiology and maintenance of severe animal phobias. *Behaviour Research and Therapy*, **23**, 431–435.

Norton, G.R., Cox, B.J., Asmundson, G.J.G. & Maser, J.D. (1995). The growth of research on anxiety disorders during the 1980s. *Journal of Anxiety Disorders*, **9**, 75–85.

Öst, L.-G. (1978). Behavioral treatment of thunder and lightning phobias. *Behaviour Research and Therapy*, **16**, 197–207.

Öst, L.-G. (1992). Cognitive therapy in a case of choking phobia. *Behavioural Psychotherapy*, **20**, 79–84.

Phillips, H.C. (1985). Return of fear in the treatment of a fear of vomiting. *Behaviour Research and Therapy*, **23**, 45–52.

Prince, R. & Tcheng-Laroche, F. (1987). Culture-bound syndromes and international disease classification. *Culture, Medicine and Psychiatry*, **11**, 3–19.

Puhakka, H.J. & Kirveskari, P. (1988). Globus hystericus: globus syndrome? *Journal Laryngology and Otology*, **90**, 1021–1026.

Rangell, L. (1952). The analysis of a doll phobia. *International Journal of Psychoanalysis*, **33**, 43–53.

Reiss, S., Peterson, R.A., Gursky, D.M. & McNally, R.J. (1986). Anxiety sensitivity, anxiety frequency and the prediction of fearfulness. *Behaviour Research and Therapy*, **24**, 1–8.

Russell, J.G. (1989). Anxiety disorders in Japan: a review of the Japanese literature on shinkeishitsu and taijinkyofusho. *Culture, Medicine and Psychiatry*, **13**, 391–403.

Salkovskis, P.M. (1991). The importance of behaviour in the maintenance of anxiety and panic: a cognitive account. *Behavioural Psychotherapy*, **19**, 6–19.

Salkovskis, P.M. & Warwick, H.M.C. (1986). Morbid preoccupations, health anxiety and reassurance: a cognitive–behavioural approach to hypochondriasis. *Behaviour Research and Therapy*, **24**, 597–602.

Salkovskis, P.M., Warwick, H.M.C. & Clark, D.M. (1991). Hypochondriasis, illness phobia and other anxiety disorders. [Report prepared for the *DSM-IV* Simple Phobia Subgroup.] Washington, DC: American Psychiatric Association.

Scrignar, C.B., Swanson, W.C. & Bloom, W.A. (1973). Use of systematic desensitization in the treatment of airplane phobic patients. *Behaviour Research and Therapy*, **11**, 129–131.

Shaw, H.L. (1977). A simple and effective treatment for flight phobia. *British Journal of Psychiatry*, **130**, 229–232.

Taylor, S., Koch, W.J. & McNally, R.J. (1992). How does anxiety sensitivity vary across the anxiety disorders? *Journal of Anxiety Disorders*, **6**, 249–259.

Thomas, M.R. & Rapp, M.S. (1977). Physiological, behavioural and cognitive changes resulting from flooding in a monosymptomatic phobia, *Behaviour Research and Therapy*, **15**, 304–306.

Visser, S. & Bouman, T.K. (1992). Cognitive–behavioural approaches in the treatment of hypochondriasis: six single case cross-over studies. *Behaviour Research and Therapy*, **30**, 301–306.

Viswanathan, R. & Paradis, C. (1991). Treatment of cancer phobia with fluoxetine. *American Journal of Psychiatry*, **148**, 1090.

Walder, C.P., McCracken, J.S., Herbert, M., James, P.T. & Brewitt, N. (1987). Psychological intervention in civilian flying phobia: evaluation and a 3-year follow-up. *British Journal of Psychiatry*, **151**, 494–498.

Warwick, H.M.C. & Marks, I.M. (1988). Behavioural treatment of illness phobia and hypochondriasis, *British Journal of Psychiatry*, **152**, 239–241.

Warwick, H.M.C. & Salkovskis, P.M. (1990). Hypochondriasis. *Behaviour Research and Therapy*, **28**, 105–117.

Wish, P.A., Hasazi, J.E. & Jurgela, A.R. (1973). Automated direct deconditioning of a childhood phobia. *Journal of Behavior Therapy and Experimental Psychiatry*, **4**, 279–283.

Wilks, C.G.W. & Marks, I.M. (1983). Reducing hypersensitive gagging. *British Dental Journal*, **155**, 263–265.

Wilson, J.A., Deary, I.J. & Maran, A.G.D. (1988). Is globus hystericus? *British Journal of Psychiatry*, **153**, 335–339.

Yamashita, I. (1993). *Taijin-Kyofu or Delusional Social Phobia*. Sapporo, Japan: Hokkaido University Press.

Yule, W., Sacks, B. & Hersov, L. (1974). Successful flooding treatment of a noise phobia in an 11-year-old. *Journal of Behavior Therapy and Experimental Psychiatry*, **5**, 209–211.

Chapter 11

Specific Phobias in Children

Thomas H. Ollendick
Department of Psychology, Virginia Polytechnic Institute and State University, Blacksburg, VA, USA
Louis P. Hagopian
The Kennedy Krieger Institute, Johns Hopkins University School of Medicine, Baltimore, MD, USA
and
Neville J. King
Faculty of Education, Monash University, Melbourne, Victoria, Australia

According to Marks (1969), "Fear is a normal response to active or imagined threat in higher animals, and comprises an outer behavioral expression, an inner feeling, and accompanying physiological changes" (p. 1). As we have noted elsewhere (Hagopian & Ollendick, 1993; King, Hamilton & Ollendick, 1988; Ollendick, King & Yule, 1994), nearly all children experience some degree of fear during their transition from infancy to childhood to adolescence. Further, while such fears vary in intensity and duration, they tend to be mild, age-specific and transitory. Typically, children evidence fear reactions to stimuli such as strangers, separation, loud noises, darkness, water, imaginary creatures and animals, as well as other circumscribed or specific events or objects. For the most part, these fears are adaptive; further, they appear to emanate from day-to-day experiences of growing children, and to reflect their emerging cognitive and representational capabilities. Moreover, most of these fears do not involve intense or persistent reactions, and they are short-lived.

In contrast, according to Marks (1969), a phobia:

1. Is out of proportion to the demands of the situation.
2. Cannot be explained or reasoned away.
3. Is beyond voluntary control.
4. Leads to avoidance of the feared situation.

Phobias—A Handbook of Theory, Research and Treatment. Edited by G.C.L. Davey.
© 1997 John Wiley & Sons Ltd.

Miller, Barrett & Hampe (1974) elaborated upon the definition of a phobia provided by Marks, with special reference to phobias of childhood. They suggested that a phobia also:

5. Persists over an extended period of time.
6. Is unadaptive.
7. Is not age- or stage-specific.

Because of its attention to the duration of fears and their developmental course, Miller, Barrett & Hampe's (1974) definition of a phobia has been accepted by most professionals working with children (see King, Hamilton & Ollendick, 1988; Morris & Kratochwill, 1983). In recent years, the two most widely accepted diagnostic classification systems for psychiatric disorders have also incorporated aspects of these criteria (American Psychiatric Association, 1994; World Health Organization, 1991). For example, the fourth edition of the Diagnostic and Statistical Manual of Mental Disorders (DSM-IV) specifies the following criteria for specific phobia (American Psychiatric Association, 1994, pp. 410–411):

1. Marked and persistent fear that is excessive or unreasonable, cued by the presence or anticipation of a specific object or situation (e.g. flying, heights, animals, receiving an injection, seeing blood).
2. Exposure to the phobic stimulus almost invariably provokes an immediate anxiety response, which may take the form of a situationally bound or situationally predisposed panic attack.
3. The person recognizes that the fear is excessive or unreasonable.
4. The phobic situation(s) is avoided, or else endured with intense anxiety or distress.
5. The avoidance, anxious anticipation or distress in the feared situation(s) interferes significantly with the person's normal routine, occupational (or academic) functioning, or social activities or relationships, or there is marked distress about having the phobia.
6. In individuals under 18 years, the duration is at least 6 months.
7. The anxiety, panic attacks or phobic avoidance associated with the specific object or situation are not better accounted for by another mental disorder such as: obsessive–compulsive disorder (e.g. fear of dirt in someone with an obsession about contamination); post-traumatic stress disorder (e.g. avoidance of stimuli associated with a severe stressor); separation anxiety disorder (e.g. avoidance of school); social phobia (e.g. avoidance of social situations because of fear of embarrassment); panic disorder with agoraphobia; or agoraphobia without history of panic disorder.

Of importance to this chapter on specific phobias in children, DSM-IV (American Psychiatric Association, 1994) acknowledges that children may not recognize their fears as excessive or unreasonable; further, DSM-IV allows that children's fears may be expressed in "childhood" ways such as crying, tantrums, freezing or clinging. These are important acknowledgements, since these criteria finally recognize the developmental nature of children and the developmental course of their fears (Ollendick & King, 1991a). In addition, DSM-IV (American Psychiatric Association, 1994) presents parameters for the duration of phobias in children (i.e. 6 months). In previous editions of the DSM, duration was not specified. This unfortunate situation resulted in many normal and short-lived fears being viewed as clinical fears or phobias. In partial response to this lack of clarity, Graziano, DeGiovanni & Garcia (1979) suggested that "clinical fears be defined as those with a duration of over 2 years" (p. 805). This conservative criterion was recommended since Hampe et al. (1973) had reported that even the most severe and intense "normal" fears of children seemed to dissipate within 2 years. However, as noted by Ollendick (1979), this criterion represented an unusually long duration and paid little attention to the discomfort and distress experienced by children during this extended period of time. The designation of fears which persist longer than 6 months and which meet DSM-IV or ICD-10 criteria as phobias makes good sense to us.

PREVALENCE OF SPECIFIC PHOBIAS IN CHILDREN

In the past 10 years, several well-controlled epidemiological studies have been conducted which estimate that the presence of any anxiety disorder (including specific phobia) in community samples of children ranges from 5.7 to 17.7% (see Costello & Angold, 1995, for a review). In general, anxiety disorders tend to be more prevalent in girls than boys and in older than younger children. However, different patterns have been found for different childhood anxiety disorders. For specific phobias, several studies report relatively low prevalence rates: Anderson et al. (1987) reported a 2.4% rate for 11-year-old children from New Zealand, whereas McGee et al. (1990) reported a rate of 3.6% for 15-year-old adolescents from that same country; Bird et al. (1988) reported a 2.6% rate for children and adolescents between 4 and 16 years of age from Puerto Rico; and Costello, Stouthamer-Loeber & DeRosier (1993) reported a 3.6% rate in 12–18-year-olds from the USA. In two other studies, both conducted in the USA, prevalence rates were somewhat higher and were found to be 9.1% in both communities and in two different age groups: 7–11-year-old children in the study by Costello et al. (1988) and 14–16-year-old adolescents in the Kashani et al. (1987) study. Differences in prevalence rates appear to be due to differences in ascertainment practices, methodological issues, and criterion definitions of diagnosis. These differences notwithstanding, it is evident that specific phobias range in prevalence from 2.6 to 9.1% of children, and that they average about 5% across studies. In their recent review of epidemiological studies, Costello & Angold (1995) conclude that "OAD/GAD (overanxious disorder/generalized anxiety disorder), separation anxiety, and simple (i.e. specific) phobia are nearly always the most commonly diagnosed anxiety disorders, occurring in around 5% of children, while social phobia, agoraphobia, panic disorder, avoidant disorder and obsessive–compulsive disorder are rare, with prevalence rates generally well below 2%" (p. 115). Thus, although specific phobias are not highly prevalent in children and adolescents, they do occur with considerable frequency.

Two other epidemiological findings are of potential interest. First, although findings are not conclusive, it appears that co-morbidity within the anxiety disorders is less frequent for phobic disorders than it is for other anxiety disorders in community samples of children and adolescents (Costello & Angold, 1995). That is, phobic disorders tend to be relatively "pure" in community samples, whereas other anxiety disorders, such as separation anxiety, social phobia, overanxious disorder and obsessive–compulsive disorder, tend to overlap and to be co-morbid with one another. Furthermore, these other anxiety disorders tend to co-occur with other internalizing (e.g. especially depression) and externalizing (e.g. conduct disorder, attention deficit disorder) disorders, whereas phobic disorders in community samples do not. Second, there appears to be a modest level of continuity for the anxiety disorders in general, as well as the specific phobias in particular across intervals varying from 2 to 5 years (20–40%). That is, about 30% of children with a phobic disorder at a later point in time also had one at an earlier point in time. This conclusion is based on studies conducted in New Zealand, Germany, Canada and the USA (for reviews, see Costello & Angold, 1995, Ollendick & King, 1994; Nottelmann & Jensen, 1995). These findings suggest that childhood phobias are moderately stable and relatively "pure" in community samples.

Somewhat different conclusions can be drawn from clinical samples, however. In their recent review of co-morbidity in clinical samples, Brady & Kendall (1992) reported that co-morbidity between anxiety disorders and other internalizing disorders (e.g. major depression/dysthymia) and externalizing disorders (e.g. conduct disorder, oppositional defiant disorder, attention deficit disorder) was as high as 61.9%. This very high rate was found in a group of children and adolescents referred to an outpatient clinic for school refusers (Bernstein, 1991), followed by rates of 55.2% in a sample of inpatients (mixed diagnoses), 36.4% in a sample of children with primary affective disorders, and 31.5% in a sample of 8–13-year-old outpatients (mixed diagnoses). Unfortunately, the studies reviewed by Brady & Kendall (1992) did not isolate co-morbidity effects for specific phobias vs. other anxiety disorders and, accordingly, we are unable to determine clearly the significance of these findings for our current purposes. Fortunately, at least one published study has done so (Last, Strauss & Francis, 1987), as has one study currently in progress (Silverman, personal communication, 1996). Last, Strauss & Francis (1987), in a sample of children and adolescents (between the ages of 5 and 18) referred to an anxiety disorder outpatient clinic, found that 15% of their referred sample met criteria for a primary diagnosis of simple (i.e. specific) phobia. Further, they reported that a majority of children and adolescents with a primary diagnosis of simple (i.e. specific) phobia presented with one or more additional diagnoses at the time of their initial evaluation (64%). Additional diagnoses included overanxious disorder, social phobia, obsessive–compulsive disorder, panic disorder, major depressive disorder, dysthymia, and oppositional defiant disorder. No clear-cut pattern was evident with these associated disorders. Similar results have recently been reported by Silverman (personal communication, 1996). She reports a co-morbidity rate of approximately 60% in children and adolescents referred specifically to an outpatient phobia assessment and treatment center. Secondary diagnoses for children with a primary diagnosis of specific phobia include both internalizing and externalizing disorders, with no apparent pattern evident. We have found similar results in our outpatient clinic for phobic and anxiety disorders in children.

Collectively, these findings indicate that clinically significant specific phobias are present in approximately 5% of children and adolescents in community samples and in about 15% of outpatient, clinic-referred samples. (The percentage of children and adolescents with a specific phobia presenting at less specialized clinics may be lower, although reliable data are not currently available to confirm this estimate.) Further, these findings suggest that clinic-referred children and adolescents who present with specific phobias to specialty clinics are more likely to be co-morbid with other anxiety disorders, affective disorders and disruptive disorders than are community samples. These findings may have important implications for the assessment and treatment of these phobic youths (Brady & Kendall, 1992; King, Ollendick & Gullone, 1991; Nottelmann & Jensen, 1995).

ETIOLOGY OF SPECIFIC PHOBIAS IN CHILDREN

The etiology of childhood phobias is not fully understood at this time. While childhood phobias may result from terrifying or frightening experiences, they may also be due to less direct and more subtle influences, such as observing a phobic reaction in another child or through reading about or hearing about phobias in others. Still, other childhood phobias apparently have no obvious environmental cause, direct or indirect, and reportedly "have always been present" in the child. In this latter instance, the child, according to parental report, has always been afraid of the phobic object, seemingly in the absence of direct or indirect conditioning experiences. For example, an intense fear and avoidance of carnival rides may develop in a child who has never been traumatized directly or indirectly. Yet the child is terrified of such rides and actively avoids going to the amusement park in dread of some frightening event occurring. To the parent's knowledge and the child's recollection, no terrifying event has ever occurred.

Menzies & Clarke (1993a) illustrated the extent of this etiological conundrum in a recent study with 50 water-phobic children (mean age 5.5 years). The parents of these children were administered a questionnaire consisting of a list of commonly reported origins of phobias, which included all three of Rachman's (1977) pathways to fear acquisition (i.e. direct classical conditioning, vicarious conditioning, and information/instruction). In addition, the parents were allowed to indicate that they did not know how the phobia developed or that their child had always been afraid of water (i.e. "fearful upon their very first contact with water"). Although 2% of parents attributed their child's phobia to a direct conditioning episode ("child was distressed by something while in or near the water") and another 26% reported vicarious conditioning episodes—"Witnessed someone else harmed while in or near the water" (4%); "Saw a distressing or water-related event on television or in a movie" (4%); "Witnessed other family members displaying distress towards water and water-related activities" (18%)— a majority of the parents (56%) believed that their child's phobic concern had been present from their very first contact with water. The remaining 16% of the parents were not able to offer any explanation of onset, recalling no traumatic experience but reporting nonetheless that their child had not always displayed a fear of water. Finally, none of the parents believed that information associated with adverse consequences (e.g. "told distressing stories about water and water-related activities" and "told by one or both parents that water and water-related activities may be dangerous") was the most influential factor in the development of their child's phobia (however, 14% of the parents believed that such information had been somewhat influential).

These findings obtained from the parents of water-phobic children are similar to those reported by McNally & Steketee (1985) for 22 adults (mean age 40.0 years) with severe animal phobias (snake, cat, bird, dog and spider). In this study, a structured interview was conducted to obtain information regarding the mode of onset, course of development and frequency of natural exposure to the phobic animal. Information was also obtained regarding the feared consequences that the phobic adults expected to occur following unavoidable encounters with the feared animal, as well as the specific stimulus characteristics of the feared animal that they found particularly distressing. As with the Menzies & Clark (1993a) study, a majority of the adults (68%) could not recall the onset of their phobia, reporting that they had the fear as long as they could remember. Of the remaining adults, 23% attributed their fear to a frightening encounter with the animal and thus were classified as conditioning cases (since in no instance did the animals inflict pain; however, they were interpreted as instances of S–R conditioning). The remaining 9% of phobic adults were classified as vicarious (4.5%) and instructional (4.5%) cases. In one instance, the patient reportedly acquired a bird phobia after her father teasingly told her that a bird "might swoop down and get her" (instructional onset), whereas in the other instance a patient attributed her snake phobia to watching frightening movies which depicted snakes as dangerous (vicarious conditioning). Interestingly, of those who could recall the origin of their phobia, all indicated that it began before the age of 10 and that the intensity of the phobia remained constant over the ensuing years (on average for 24 years). Moreover, nearly all patients (91%) reported that they expected to panic or at least experience very high levels of fear in an unavoidable encounter with the feared animal, while about half (46%) also expected that the animal would harm them or attack them. Finally, regarding stimulus characteristics of the feared animal, most patients (77%) reported that they found the way the animal moved to be most upsetting. Independent of movement, 64% of the patients cited the physical appearance of the animal as the second most distressing characteristic, followed by sounds made by the animal (27%) and specific tactile properties of the animal (23%).

Collectively, the findings by Menzies & Clarke (1993a) for young children and McNally & Steketee (1985) for adults stand in sharp contrast to those obtained by Öst and his colleagues for adult phobic patients (see Öst & Hugdahl, 1981, 1983, 1985). For example, in a study of 110 patients undergoing behavioral treatment of phobias (41 with small animal phobias such as snakes, spiders and rats, 34 with social phobias, and 35 with claustrophobia), Öst & Hugdahl (1981) reported that only 15.1% could not recall experiences of any kind regarding the onset of their phobias. In contrast, more than half (57.5%) ascribed their phobias to direct experiences of the conditioning type, with 17% attributing their phobias to vicarious conditioning experiences and 10.4% to informational or instructional experiences. Thus, in this sample, very few patients could not recall the origins of their phobias and twice as many patients recalled acquiring their phobias through direct conditioning experiences as through indirect experiences (vicarious or instructional). As in the McNally & Steketee study (1985), however, duration of the phobias was extended (average of 24 years), with most patients reporting childhood onset and unrelenting intensity over the intervening years. Inconsistencies in origins of phobias in these studies are difficult to reconcile but may be due, at least in part, to differences in questionnaires used, operational definitions of conditioning events as they illustrate Rachman's (1977) three pathways, and subject characteristics (for a recent review, see Menzies & Clarke, 1995).

In addition, these studies have not included a comparison group of non-fearful subjects. In order to establish the etiological significance of conditioning events or negative expected consequences in the development of specific phobias, such a control group is necessary. If painful or frightening experiences with the stimulus are equally prevalent among non-fearful controls, or if expectations of panic or harm are equally high among controls, then such experiences or expectations cannot be a sufficient explanation for the development of the phobia. Fortunately, at least two adult studies and one child study have included non-fearful groups and have made such comparisons. In the first such study, DiNardo et al. (1988) examined these issues in 16 dog-phobic young adults and 21 non-fearful matched controls. Similar to the Öst & Hugdahl (1981) findings, 56% of the phobic subjects reported direct conditioning events associated with the origin of their phobia; unexpectedly, however, 66% of the non-fearful subjects also reported direct conditioning events. Obviously, reliable differences between the two groups were not observed. In fact, direct conditioning experiences were reported by more of the non-fearful controls than the phobic group. Further, the majority of encounters for both phobic and non-fearful subjects were similar and consisted of painful events involving bites or scratches. Although the two groups had similar experiences with dogs, they had very different expectations about the consequences of an encounter with a dog. Not surprisingly, and consistent with the findings of McNally & Steketee (1985), 100% of phobic subjects expected to experience fear and harm upon an encounter with a dog, whereas only a small minority (14%) of non-fearful subjects expected similar outcomes. DiNardo and colleagues (1988) concluded that high expectations of fear and harm served to maintain phobic avoidance in the phobic group. Similar findings were reported recently by Menzies & Clarke (1993b) in a study of 50 height-phobic young adults and 50 non-fearful matched controls. Although percentages of subjects falling in the three acquisition categories differed from those obtained in the DiNardo et al. (1988) study (for example, only 18% of the subjects were classified as having had direct conditioning experiences, and more subjects were unable to recall specific conditioning events), there were no differences between the phobic and non-fearful groups in acquisition pathways. However, the groups did differ on expected consequences upon encounter with heights, as they did in the DiNardo et al. (1988) study on fear of dogs. A majority of the height-phobic young adults reported extreme fear and panic associated with heights.

Interestingly, even though many specific phobias are acquired in childhood and adolescence (Marks, 1987; Menzies & Clarke, 1993a, 1993b; Öst & Hugdahl, 1981, 1983, 1985; Rachman, 1976, 1977), efforts to explore the common pathways of acquisition have relied largely on retrospective reports of adults, frequently 20 years after onset of the phobias. As noted above, many adults report that they are simply unable to recall the onset of their phobias with sufficient specificity or, due to time and associated life experiences, recall events which afford them "meaning" and a rationale or justification for their fears or phobias. (See Hekmat, 1987, for a discussion of the latter point and McNally & Steketee, 1985, as well as Menzies & Clarke, 1993b, for an illustration of the former point.) To date, only one study has addressed these issues directly in a child adolescent sample. In this study, Ollendick & King (1991b) explored Rachman's (1977) three pathways of fear acquisition in 1092 Australian and American children between 9 and 14 years of age. In response to 10 commonly reported fears in children (Ollendick, 1983; Ollendick, King & Frary, 1989), the youths were asked to indicate their own levels of fear and then whether: (a) they remembered having a bad or frightening experience with the feared object (direct conditioning experience); (b) their parents, friends or other acquaintances ever showed fear or avoidance of the feared object (vicarious conditioning); and (c) they had been told, or heard stories about, frightening things regarding the feared object from either parents, teachers, friends or other acquaintances (instruction or information pathway). Responses to acquisition routes were highly dependent on specific fear stimuli. For example, 36% of the sample indicated a bad or frightening experience with snakes, whereas 70% indicated a similarly frightening experience with "not being able to breathe" (i.e. choking, gasping, not able to catch breath). Moreover, 65% indicated that someone they knew showed extreme fear of snakes, while 46% indicated that someone they knew showed extreme fear of "not being able to breathe". Finally, 89% of the youths indicated that they had heard or been told frightening stories about snakes, whereas 76% indicated similar instruction/information about "not being able to breathe". (Percentages do not add up to 100%, since youths could endorse more than one pathway.) These findings suggest that pathways may be phobia-specific and that the causes may be multiply determined, if not over-determined (Ollendick, 1979).

In this study, we also formed groups of high-fearful and low-fearful subjects based on endorsements to the 10 individual fear stimuli. Table 11.1 presents the findings for the two fear stimuli discussed above: snakes and not being able to breathe. As can be seen, the primary difference between high- and low-fearful snake-phobics was that the high-fearful subjects were more likely to endorse a combination of modeling plus information/instruction (30%) and direct conditioning plus modeling plus information/instruction (29.4%) than were their non-fearful counterparts (17.8% and 6.9%, respectively). The two groups did not differ on direct conditioning, modeling, or information/instruction as *sole* sources of influence, however. In a similar vein, the primary difference between high- and low- "not able to breathe" fearful subjects was that the high-fearful subjects were more likely to ascribe their fear to a combination of direct conditioning plus information/instruction (24.7%) and direct conditioning plus modeling plus instruction/information (28.9%) than their low-fearful counterparts (9.3% and 4.1%, respectively). As with snake fears, the two groups did not differ on direct conditioning, modeling or instruction/information as sole sources of influence. Thus, although direct conditioning sources were endorsed more frequently for subjects fearful of not being able to breathe, and indirect effects (modeling and information/instruction) were ascribed to more frequently for subjects fearful of snakes, high- and low-fearful subjects did not differ on these influences when viewed as the sole source of their level of fear. Rather, only when one of these sources was combined with another source (or multiple sources) were meaningful differences obtained. Direct conditioning alone *or* modeling alone *or* information/instruction alone did not result in fear acquisition for most of the youths. Finally, a significantly greater percentage of non-fearful youth indicated that they had not been exposed to any of the three primary pathways of fear acquisition compared with the fearful subjects (32.8% of those non-fearful of snakes and 34.0% of those non-fearful of "not being able to breathe").

Table 11.1 Percentage of subjects endorsing the various sources of fear, and their combinations, for two fears—snakes, and not being able to breathe

Sources of fear	Snakes		Not able to breathe	
	High fear (%)	Low fear (%)	High fear (%)	Low fear (%)
Direct conditioning only	1.0	1.0	10.8	12.4
Modeling only	4.5	6.9	1.0	6.2
Information/instruction only	26.1	29.9	12.9	17.5
Direct conditioning plus modeling	1.0	2.3	5.7	2.0
Direct conditioning plus information/instruction	2.6	2.9	24.7	14.4
Modeling plus information/ instruction	30.0	17.8	9.8	9.3
All three sources	29.4	6.9	28.9	4.1
None of the sources	5.9	32.8	6.2	34.0

Of course, it should be noted that these findings and those of others are based on retrospective analysis of self-reports and are therefore subject to the limitations of all self-report studies. Although the children and adolescents were "closer" in time to the onset of their fears than adults whose fears had a developmental onset and prolonged course, they still had to rely on their memories and recollections to posit the likely sources of onset. As such, these findings really speak to the causal attributions of the children and adolescents to account for the presence (or absence) of their fears. These attributions may or may not reflect actual causes and, accordingly, may or may not be accurate indices of acquisition. In future research, these self-reports should be examined further via intensive structured interviews, behavioral observations and the use of other informants (e.g. parents, teachers) to determine their accuracy.

Overall, these findings related to conditioning theory suggest that not all phobias are acquired through individual-specific learning histories and that other factors may need to be considered. Among these other factors are those related to the heritability of phobias, biological-constitutional factors of the child and, of course, influences of the family on the growing child. Early on, Darwin (1877, cited in Marks, 1987, p. 112) asked, "May we not suspect that . . . fears of children, which are quite independent of experience, are the inherited effects of real dangers . . . during savage times." Basically, Darwin suggested that aversive experiences with certain stimuli were not necessary for the acquisition of fear; rather, some fears were "independent of experience" and were innate (i.e. required no learning). Subsequently, Seligman (1971) adapted this theory and suggested that associations between certain stimuli and fear were more likely to be formed than others (i.e. "prepared" and constituting non-cognitive forms of associative learning). The status of these two related theories of "inherited phobia proneness" is certainly controversial and well beyond the scope of this chapter (for discussion of issues related to these theories, see Davey, 1992; Marks, 1987; McNally, 1987; Menzies & Clarke, 1995; Rescorla, 1988).

Nonetheless, the pursuit of heritability estimates over the years has continued to fuel this debate. Although no known studies of heritability exist for children with specific phobias, recent studies with adults suggest that specific phobias may be largely due to non-genetic factors (Carey, 1990; Fyer et al., 1990; Kendler et al., 1992). In discussing the role of genetics in specific phobias, social phobia and agoraphobia, Kendler et al. (1992) suggest that these subtypes of phobias can be placed along an etiologic continuum: at the one end of the continuum lies agoraphobia, which has the latest age of onset, the highest rates of co-morbidity, the highest heritability estimate, and the least specific environmental influences. At the other end of the continuum lie the specific phobias, which have the earliest age of onset, the lowest rates of co-morbidity, the lowest heritability estimates, and the highest specific environmental influences. Kendler and colleagues go on to suggest that social phobia lies intermediate between agoraphobia and specific phobias on nearly all of these measures. They conclude "The estimated heritability of liability of phobias . . . indicates that genetic factors play a significant but by no means overwhelming role in the etiology of phobias. Individual-specific envi-

ronment appears to account for approximately twice as much variance in liability
to phobias as do genetic factors" (Kendler et al., 1992, p. 279). Overall, genetic
factors appear to be associated with a general state or propensity toward "fearfulness", whereas the environment plays a stronger role in making an individual
afraid of, say, snakes rather than heights. Specificity is said to be afforded by the
environment.

Along with genetic factors, constitutional (i.e. temperament) characteristics of
the child may also play an important role in the onset and maintenance of specific
phobias in children. Temperament refers to stable response dispositions that are
evident early in life, observable in a variety of settings and relatively persistent
across time (Chess & Thomas, 1977, 1984). Two of the most important temperamental categories are based on responses or initial reactions to unfamiliar people
and novel situations, frequently referred to as "shyness vs. sociability", "introversion vs. extroversion", or "withdrawal vs. approach". In unfamiliar situations or
upon meeting new people, "shy" or "inhibited" children typically withhold responding or interrupt ongoing behavior, show vocal restraint and withdraw. In
contrast, "sociable" and "uninhibited" children typically seek out novelty, engage
in conversation, smile, and explore the environment around them. Data from
Chess & Thomas's New York Longitudinal Study (1977) show that these tendencies to approach or withdraw are relatively enduring dimensions of behavior.

In recent years, Kagan and his colleagues (Kagan, 1989; Kagan, Reznick &
Gibbons, 1989; Kagan, Reznick & Snidman, 1988) have demonstrated that approximately 10–15% of American Caucasian children are born predisposed to be
irritable as infants, shy and fearful as toddlers, and cautious, quiet and intro-
verted when they reach school age; in contrast, about 15% of the population
show the opposite profile, with the remainder of the population intermediate on
these dimensions. Kagan hypothesized that inhibited children, compared with
uninhibited children, have a low threshold for arousal in the amygdala and
hypothalamic circuits, especially to unfamiliar events, and that they react under
such conditions with sympathetic arousal (Kagan, Reznick & Snidman, 1987). In
general, sympathetic activation is indicated by high heart rate, low heart-rate
variability, and acceleration of heart rate under stressful conditions. Indeed,
inhibited children have been shown to have higher and more stable heart-rates
and to show greater heart-rate acceleration under stressful and novel conditions
than uninhibited children. Further, inhibited children have been shown to have a
greater increase in diastolic blood pressure when changing their posture from a
sitting to a standing position than uninhibited children, suggesting noradrenergic
tone (Biederman et al., 1995). Collectively, these findings indicate a more reactive sympathetic influence on cardiovascular functioning in inhibited children.
The behavioral response of withdrawal and avoidance shown by children with
behavioral inhibition, along with the considerable evidence of increased arousal
in the limbic–sympathetic axes, fits well with current hypotheses of the
neurophysiological underpinnings of anxiety disorders (for discussions, see Gray,
1982; Davis, 1992). Primate work by Suomi supports these findings (Suomi, 1984,
1986).

The sample of inhibited and uninhibited children studied by Kagan and colleagues has been described in detail elsewhere (see Kagan, Reznick & Snidman, 1987, 1988). Briefly, children were identified at 21 months of age for a study on the preservation of temperamental differences in normal children. The children were selected from a larger group of 305 Caucasian children born in the Boston area and whose mothers, in a 'phone interview, described them as displaying inhibited (manifesting withdrawal) or uninhibited behavior (displaying approach) across a range of situations. On the basis of the 'phone interviews, 117 children were invited to the Harvard Infant Study Laboratory and were studied more extensively. Initially, 28 children were identified as the most extremely inhibited and 30 as the most extremely uninhibited. Subsequent to identification, 22 inhibited and 19 uninhibited children were available for follow-up at ages 4, $5^{1}/_{2}$ and $7^{1}/_{2}$ years of age. Details of behavioral evidence of inhibition at the varying ages can be found in the original studies. Biederman and colleagues (1990) reasoned that the inhibited children identified by Kagan and colleagues would be at risk for the development of anxiety disorders. Their hypothesis was based on earlier work they had conducted with the offspring of parents with panic disorder and agoraphobia (PDAG). In this study, they reported a high prevalence of behavioral inhibition in the children born to adults with PDAG, compared with control children of parents without anxiety disorder (Rosenbaum et al., 1988). They then examined the Kagan et al. longitudinal sample of "normal" children when the children were 7–8 years of age. Mothers of the 22 inhibited and 19 uninhibited children were systematically interviewed using a well established structured diagnostic interview, the Diagnostic Interview for Children and Adolescents—Parent Version (Herjanic & Reich, 1982; Orvaschel, 1985). Although a variety of measures were obtained in this study, only the results of diagnosis for common childhood anxiety disorders (overanxious disorder, separation anxiety disorder, avoidant disorder and phobic disorders) will be presented here. Findings revealed that the rates of all anxiety disorders were higher in inhibited than in uninhibited children: overanxious disorder (13.6% vs. 10.5%), separation anxiety disorder (9.1% vs. 5.3%), avoidant disorder (9.2% vs. 0%) and phobic disorders (31.8% vs. 5.3%). Although all differences favored the inhibited group for presence of disorder, only differences for phobic disorders were statistically significant. Clearly, the inhibited group was found to be at risk for anxiety disorder, particularly phobic disorders. It should be recalled that designation of group status as inhibited vs. uninhibited occurred at 21 months of age and that assessment for psychopathology in the present study occurred when the children were approximately $7^{1}/_{2}$ years of age. In a subsequent study, Hirshfeld and colleagues (1992) re-examined these findings by contrasting children who remained inhibited or uninhibited throughout childhood with those who were less stable across the four assessment periods (21 months, 4 years, $5^{1}/_{2}$ years, and $7^{1}/_{2}$ years). Four groups of children were formed: stable inhibited ($n = 12$), unstable inhibited ($n = 10$), stable uninhibited ($n = 9$) and unstable uninhibited ($n = 10$). As is evident, 54.5% of the inhibited children and 47.4% of the uninhibited children maintained stable group status across the four assessment periods. Again, while a multitude of measures were obtained in this study, findings related to the rate of phobic disorders only will be highlighted here. Essentially, the researchers showed the following rates of phobic disorders at age $7^1/_2$: stable inhibited, 50%; unstable inhibited, 10%; stable uninhibited, 11.1%; and unstable uninhibited, 0%. (Rates for the other anxiety disorders were also higher for the stable inhibited group compared to the other groups.) Thus, children who remained consistently inhibited from 21 months through 4, $5^1/_2$ and $7^1/_2$ years of age accounted for the high rates of phobic disorders found to be associated with behavioral inhibition in the earlier study (Biederman et al., 1990). In this stability study, Hirshfeld et al. (1992) also obtained diagnostic interviews on the parents themselves, using modules of the National Institute of Mental Health Diagnostic Interview Schedule (NIMH-DIS) (Robins et al., 1981). Comparison between parents of the stable inhibited group and the other three groups indicated that the parents of the stable inhibited group themselves were also characterized by a greater prevalence of phobic disorders and related anxiety disorders. Again, it should be noted that these children and their parents in the Kagan, Reznick & Snidman (1987, 1988) longitudinal cohort were selected for a study on the preservation of temperamental differences in normal children. They were not selected because they were thought to be at risk or because they presented with anxious symptomatology.

The increased rates of anxiety disorders and phobic disorders in parents of stable inhibited children (as well as heightened levels of behavioral inhibition in children born from anxiety-disorder parents) raise the possibility that the association between stable behavioral inhibition and anxiety disorder is familial, perhaps genetic. If genetic, it is probable that the link is one that predisposes the child to a heightened level of general fearfulness or anxiety sensitivity, as suggested by Kendler et al. (1982). As noted by Hirshfeld et al. (1992, p. 108), "Whether behavioral inhibition is under genetic influence remains unresolved and can be elucidated ultimately only by carefully controlled twin or adoption studies and by genetic linkage studies".

Alternatively, stable behavioral inhibition in the child might be related to ongoing stressors associated with having a parent with an anxiety disorder. Continued exposure to a parent's anxious symptomatology might lead a child to remain cautious, uncertain and fearful in novel or unfamiliar situations. Further, phobic parents might model phobic avoidance on a regular basis and may have difficulty encouraging their youngsters to explore their surroundings and take risks (Hirshfeld et al., 1992). Parents of anxious children have long been described as "over-protective" and shielding their children from potential failure and misfortunes. Recent studies by Dadds and his colleagues, using direct behavioral observations of parent–child interactions in ambiguous and stressful situations, confirm such "protective" and "insulating" patterns (Dadds et al., in press; Barrett et al., in press/b). Finally, it is interesting to note that Kagan previously suggested that children who stopped being inhibited seemed to come from families in which children were encouraged to be more sociable and outgoing (Kagan, Reznick & Snidman, 1987). In the absence of such encouragement and modeling of avoidance, behavioral inhibition might be expected to persist and be refractory to change. In all probability, stability of behavioral inhibition may be related to a combination of genetic influences, parental psychopathology, and environmental factors that interact in a reciprocal manner.

In the final analysis, a host of factors converge to occasion the onset and maintenance of specific phobias in children. Genetic influences and temperamental tendencies may predispose the child to general fearfulness, behavioral inhibition and phobic disorder; however, particular forms of parental psychopathology and specific conditioning histories are seemingly necessary to set the stage for the development of a specific phobia such as fear of heights or fear of dogs.

TREATMENT OF SPECIFIC PHOBIAS

Inasmuch as specific phobias are acquired and maintained through a complex interactive process involving the principles of classical, operant, and vicarious conditioning, it is not surprising that behavioral therapy strategies based on each of these principles have been used in the treatment of phobias (Hagopian & Ollendick, 1993). The most effective and durable treatment effects occur when treatment involves multiple components drawing from all of these principles (Ollendick & Francis, 1988). The behavioral strategies used in the treatment of simple phobias in children include systematic desensitization, emotive imagery, flooding, contingency management, modeling, self-control training and behavioral family interventions. Although based on different conditioning principles, these various strategies can be considered to involve exposure to the feared stimulus (King, Hamilton & Ollendick, 1988; Marks, 1987).

Systematic Desensitization

Systematic desensitization (SD), the most frequently used behavioral treatment strategy to reduce fears and phobias in children, is derived from principles of classical conditioning. Wolpe (1958) understood SD as involving the process of reciprocal inhibition, whereby anxiety is suppressed by an incompatible response (relaxation) occurring in the presence of the feared stimulus. Although numerous case studies have supported the effectiveness of SD in the reduction of children's phobias, little well-controlled research has been reported (see Morris & Kratochwill, 1983; Ollendick, 1986). SD consists of three components: relaxation training; construction of an anxiety hierarchy; and systematic desensitization proper (for a detailed description of SD for phobic children, see King, Hamilton & Ollendick, 1988; Morris & Kratochwill, 1983). A critical issue in the use of SD with children is the child's ability to perform each of the steps.

Relaxation training scripts for adults may be appropriate with adolescents, but special considerations must be made in relaxation training with children. A relaxation readiness pretest may be used to assess the child's ability to comply with relaxation instructions (Cautela & Groden, 1978). Use of fantasy (e.g. "Pretend you have a whole lemon in your left hand. Now squeeze it hard") may also help maintain the child's interest (Koeppen, 1974). Finally, simplifying procedures and shortening the duration of training sessions may be useful (Ollendick & Cerny, 1981).

The anxiety hierarchy is a series of stimuli related to the feared stimulus and ranging from least to most anxiety-evoking. The development of the anxiety hierarchy typically involves the therapist and parent, with the child participating to the extent his/her abilities permit. For imaginal SD, assessment of the child's ability to image the hierarchy items can be conducted by showing a child a picture and then asking him/her to recall it, or asking the child to imagine an incongruous picture and then provide a description of it.

Systematic desensitization proper involves having the child attain a relaxed state and then instructing him/her to imagine the least anxiety-evoking hierarchy item. The therapist describes the situation and instructs the child to imagine being in the situation. The child is instructed to lift a finger if he or she experiences excessive anxiety; if this occurs, the hierarchy item is re-presented for a shorter duration. The child advances along the hierarchy when an item is imagined and anxiety is no longer evoked.

The use of *in vivo* exposure, which involves the actual presentation of the hierarchy items, is advocated when possible. *In vivo* exposure does not rely on the child's imagery abilities and may have more face validity than imaginal SD with children. If a child demonstrates inability to imagine the hierarchy items because he/she reports little anxiety when imaging, then the use of *in vivo* exposure to the hierarchy items may be required.

Emotive Imagery

Emotive imagery was designed by Lazarus & Abramovitz (1962) as an adaptation of SD for use with children. Like SD, emotive imagery involves the development of a fear hierarchy. Rather than relaxation, however, the child is instructed to imagine a positive and exciting story involving his/her favorite hero. The hierarchy items are then incorporated into the story so the child systematically encounters increasingly fearful stimuli in the company of the hero. No well-controlled group outcome studies have examined the effectives of this treatment, although some controlled single-case studies have supported its use (e.g. King, Cranstoun & Josephs, 1989).

Several procedural recommendations have been offered for the use of emotive imagery with children (King, Hamilton & Ollendick, 1988; Rosensteil & Scott, 1977). The complexity of the imagery should be adjusted to the individual child's level of understanding and imagery abilities. The child's existing fantasies and heroes should be used in treatment, and behavioral indicants of anxiety should be observed during the course of treatment. Finally, having children report and describe their images can facilitate their imagery.

Flooding

Unlike SD and emotive imagery, which involve graduated and brief exposure to the feared stimulus, flooding entails sudden and prolonged exposure to the feared stimulus. According to the principles of classical conditioning, the repeated and prolonged presentation of a feared stimulus—in the absence of an aversive unconditioned stimulus (e.g. pain)—can result in extinction of the anxiety response. Avoidance responses are prevented (response prevention) by the therapist so that they will not be reinforced by the relief experienced when the feared stimulus is avoided.

Although flooding can be imaginal, *in vivo* flooding is advocated with children (King, Hamilton & Ollendick, 1988). For children under 7 years of age, imaginal flooding has not been investigated, while *in vivo* flooding has been reported with children as young as 4 years old (Morris & Kratochwill, 1983). Although flooding procedures have been shown to be effective with adults, only a handful of case studies attest to the effectiveness of flooding with phobic children (Ollendick & Francis, 1988). Since flooding, by its very design, is an unpleasant and anxiety-evoking treatment, parents and children may be reluctant to participate.

Contingency Management

Contingency management procedures, which attempt to alter phobic behavior by manipulating its consequences, are derived from the principles of operant conditioning. Little attention is given to reducing the affective, cognitive and physiological aspects of the phobic response. Rather, acquisition of approach behavior toward the feared stimulus is the goal of contingency management procedures. These operant-based procedures require that a functional analysis of the phobic behavior has been conducted. The functional analysis will suggest the contingency management procedure to be used and the consequences to be altered. Positive reinforcement, shaping and extinction procedures are used separately or in combination.

Positive reinforcement procedures involve presentation of an event following a behavior that increases the probability that the behavior will recur. With phobic children, reinforcement is designed to increase the child's approach behavior toward the feared stimulus. Reinforcement procedures require the target behavior to be clearly identified, the reinforcers to be desirable to the child, the reinforcer to follow the target behavior immediately, the child to be aware of the positive consequences of engaging in the targeted behavior, and continuous reinforcement to be used initially, followed by partial reinforcement (King, Hamilton & Ollendick, 1988).

In cases in which the feared stimulus is rarely or never encountered because of extreme avoidance behavior, a shaping procedure may be useful. Shaping involves reinforcement of increasingly closer approximations to the desired approach behavior. Parents and children may find shaping appealing, given that the graduated approach may be easier for the child and involve little distress. Since shaping procedures are a variant of reinforcement, similar procedural guidelines should be followed. In addition, response requirements at each step should be easy enough to assure successful performance, and training sessions should be kept short so as to avoid fatigue and reinforcer satiation. When the child is performing the desired behavior for a step 80–90% of the time, the therapist should proceed to the next step (see Ollendick & Cerny, 1981, for details).

When the reinforcing consequences of the phobic behavior have been identified and can be eliminated, an extinction procedure may be appropriate. Extinction involves discontinuation of the reinforcement of a behavior. Whoever is providing reinforcement for the phobic behavior must be informed and alternative responses encouraged; and they should be warned that the child's behavior may worsen before it improves (extinction burst). Also, alternative sources of reinforcement for the phobic behavior must be identified and eliminated. Finally, the reinforcement of alternative, non-avoidant behaviors should be provided to the child during an extinction procedure.

The majority of support for contingency management procedures in the reduction of children's fears comes from uncontrolled clinical case studies or analog studies in which the subjects had subclinical levels of fear. As Ollendick & Francis (1988) speculate, these procedures, which do not directly attempt to alter the affective, cognitive and physiological aspects of the anxiety response, may be less effective than those that are designed to reduce anxiety and increase approach behavior, especially when the fear response is of phobic proportion.

Modeling

Modeling procedures, which involve learning by watching another engage in a behavior, are derived from the principles of vicarious conditioning (Bandura, 1969). In its use with phobic children, modeling entails demonstration of non-phobic approach behavior toward, and coping in the presence of, the feared stimulus. Thus, fear reduction and skill acquisition are the goals of modeling procedures. Several factors, that affect acquisition of the behavior (and factors that affect performance and generalization of the behavior) such as the characteristics of the model, observer and presentation, have been shown to be important and have been described elsewhere (Perry & Furukawa, 1980). Filmed, live and participant modeling procedures have been used with phobic children. These procedures typically involve reinforcement for the initiation of non-fearful imitative behavior.

Live modeling involves having the fearful child observe a model (with similar characteristics) and demonstrate successively greater interaction with the feared stimulus or participation in the feared situation. Filmed modeling is similar, in that the child watches a film of the model engaging in similar behaviors. Participant modeling entails live modeling and physical contact with the model (the therapist or fearless peer), who physically guides the child's interactions with the feared stimulus.

According to Ollendick (1979), participant modeling is the most effective modeling procedure in the reduction of fears in non-clinical children, followed by live and then filmed modeling. Although modeling procedures have received considerable empirical support for their utility in reducing subclinical levels of fear, few controlled studies have demonstrated their effectiveness in the treatment of severe phobias in children.

Cognitive–Behavioral Procedures

Cognitive–behavioral approaches include a variety of procedures designed to alter perceptions, thoughts, images and beliefs by manipulating and restructuring maladaptive cognitions. Since maladaptive cognitions are assumed to lead to maladaptive behavior, it is assumed that such cognitive changes will produce behavioral changes.

Verbal self-instructional training is the most frequently used cognitive–behavioral approach for reduction of fears in children. As developed by Meichenbaum & Goodman (1971), self-instructional training involves cognitive modeling and cognitive–behavioral rehearsal. Five training steps were designed to parallel the development of the verbal mediation of behavior as described by Luria (1961). For the treatment of simple phobias in children, the following training steps would be used: (a) the therapist encounters the feared stimulus while talking to himself aloud and coping with the fear (cognitive modeling); (b) the child performs the same behavior under the therapist's directions (overt, external guidance); (c) the child performs the same behavior while instructing him/herself aloud (overt self-guidance); (d) the child then whispers the instructions to him/herself (faded overt self-guidance); (e) and finally, the child performs the behavior while instructing him/herself covertly (covert self-instruction).

Relaxation training and operant-based procedures are often integrated into self-instructional approaches. Such treatment approaches have been shown to be effective in reducing fears and avoidance in night-time- and dog-phobic children (Graziano & Mooney, 1980; Graziano et al., 1979; Richards & Siegel, 1978). More recently it has been suggested that self-instructional training, in the absence of operant-based procedures, may not be sufficient to reduce fears in children (Hagopian, Weist & Ollendick, 1990; Ollendick, 1995; Ollendick, Hagopian & Huntzinger, 1991). Thus, use of self-instructional training or other cognitive–behavioral procedures when used alone cannot be advocated for the treatment of children's phobias at this time. However, as such approaches can be integrated readily into other treatments and may provide children a means of coping with exposure to the phobic stimulus (an element shared by all behavioral treatment approaches), their use as part of an integrated treatment package can be endorsed. This position, of course, is based on limited empirical findings and is in need of additional support (see Kendall, Howard & Epps, 1988, for an extended discussion of this issue).

Behavioral Family Interventions

While the treatment approaches described above may require intensive parental involvement, the "transfer of control" model (Ginsburg, Silverman & Kurtines, 1995) and Family Anxiety Management (FAM; Dadds, Heard & Rapee, 1992) emphasize the role of the parents to an even greater extent. The transfer of control model emphasizes the gradual fading of control from the therapist to the parent, and to the child. Both approaches involve training parents in contingency management strategies to deal with their child's anxiety and to facilitate the child's exposure to the phobic situation. Self-control strategies involving self-instruction and relaxation are taught to children so that they can control and manage their own anxiety and exposure to the feared situation. These approaches explicitly recognize and target parental anxiety, problematic family relationships, parent–child communication problems and parental problem-solving skills. In a recent controlled group study involving 79 anxious children, FAM was found to be superior to a waiting-list control group and a cognitive–behavioral therapy group after treatment and at 1 year post-treatment (Barrett et al., in press/a). Its utility to phobic disorders remains to be determined, however.

SUMMARY

Although childhood fears are a part of normal development, a significant minority of children evidence fears that interfere with their functioning. A specific phobia is said to exist when fear of a specific object or situation is exaggerated, cannot be reasoned away, results in avoidance of the feared object or situation, persists over time, and is not age-specific. Specific phobias occur in about 5% of the population and in approximately 15% of children referred for anxiety-related problems.

Specific phobias are multiply determined and over-determined (Ollendick, 1979). In the final analysis, genetic influences, temperamental tendencies, parental psychopathology, and individual conditioning histories probably converge to occasion the development and maintenance of specific phobias. Inasmuch as any one specific phobia is acquired and maintained through a complex interactive process involving the principles of classical, operant and vicarious conditioning, treatment approaches based on these learning principles have been used productively. Treatment packages that involve multiple components drawing from all these principles appear to be most effective.

Attention to developmental factors in the treatment of children's phobias is receiving continued support. The capabilities of children (cognitive, verbal, etc.)

appear critical in the assessment process and have implications for the design, implementation and evaluation of treatment. Finally, the importance of parental involvement throughout the assessment and treatment process is evident.

REFERENCES

American Psychiatric Association (1994). *Diagnostic and Statistical Manual of Mental Disorders*, 4th edn. Washington, DC: American Psychiatric Association.
Anderson, J.C., Williams, S., McGee, R. & Silva, P.A. (1987). DSM-III disorders in preadolescent children. *Archives of General Psychiatry*, **44**, 69–76.
Bandura, A. (1969). *Principles of Behavior Modification*. New York: Holt, Rinehart & Winston.
Barrett, P.M., Dadds, M.R., Rapee, R.M. & Ryan, S.M. (in press/a). Family intervention for childhood anxiety: a controlled trial. *Journal of Consulting and Clinical Psychology*.
Barrett, P.M., Rapee, R.M., Dadds, M.R. & Ryan, S.M. (in press/b). Family enhancement of cognitive style in anxious and aggressive children: threat bias and the FEAR effect. *Journal of Abnormal Child Psychology*.
Bernstein, G.A. (1991). Comorbidity and severity of anxiety and depressive disorders in a clinical sample. *Journal of the American Academy of Child and Adolescent Psychiatry*, **30**, 43–50.
Biederman, J., Rosenbaum, J.F., Chaloff, J. & Kagan, J. (1995). Behavioral inhibition as a risk factor. In J.S. March (ed.), *Anxiety Disorders in Children and Adolescents* (pp. 61–81). New York: Guilford.
Biederman, J., Rosenbaum, J.F., Hirshfeld, D.R., Faraone, V., Bolduc, E., Gersten, M., Meminger, S. & Reznick, S. (1990). Psychiatric correlates of behavioral inhibition in young children of parents with and without psychiatric disorders. *Archives of General Psychiatry*, **47**, 21–26.
Bird, H.R., Canion, G., Rubio-Stipes, M., Gould, M.S., Ribera, J., Sesman, M., Woodbury, M., Huertas-Goldman, S., Pagan, A., Sanches-Lacay, A. & Moscoso, M. (1988). Estimates of the prevalence of childhood maladjustment in a community survey in Puerto Rico. *Archives of General Psychiatry*, **45**, 1120–1126.
Brady, E.U. & Kendall, P.C. (1992). Comorbidity of anxiety and depression in children and adolescents. *Psychological Bulletin*, **111**, 244–255.
Carey, G. (1990). Genes, fears, phobias, and phobic disorders. *Journal of Counseling and Development*, **68**, 628–632.
Cautela, J.R. & Groden, J. (1978). *Relaxation: a Comprehensive Manual for Adults, Children, and Children with Special Needs*. Champaign, IL: Research Press.
Chess, S. & Thomas, A. (1977). Temperamental individuality from childhood to adolescence. *Journal of the American Academy of Child Psychiatry*, **16**, 218–226.
Chess, S. & Thomas, A. (1984). *Origins and Evolution of Behavior Disorders*. New York: Brunner/Mazel.
Costello, E.G. & Angold, A. (1995). Epidemiology. In J.S. March (ed.), *Anxiety Disorders in Children and Adolescents* (pp. 109–122). New York: Guilford.
Costello, E.J., Costello, A.J., Edelbrock, C.S., Burns, B.J., Dulcan, M.J., Brent, D. & Janiszewski, S. (1988). DSM-III disorders in pediatric primary care: prevalence and risk factors. *Archives of General Psychiatry*, **45**, 1107–1116.
Costello, E.J., Stouthamer-Loeber, M. & DeRosier, M. (1993). Continuity and change in psychopathology from childhood to adolescence. Paper presented at the Annual Meeting of the Society for Research in Child and Adolescent Psychopathology, Sante Fe.
Dadds, M.R., Barrett, P.M., Rapee, R.M. & Ryan, S.M. (in press). Family process and child psychopathology: an observational analysis of the FEAR effect. *Journal of Abnormal Child Psychology*.

Dadds, M.R., Heard, P.M. & Rapee, R.M. (1992). The role of family intervention in the treatment of child anxiety disorders: some preliminary findings. *Behaviour Change*, **9**, 171–177.

Davey, G.C.L. (1992). Classical conditioning and the acquisition of human fears and phobias: a review and synthesis of the literature. *Advances in Behaviour Research and Therapy*, **14**, 29–66.

Davis, M. (1992). The role of the amygdala in fear and anxiety. *Annual Review of Neuroscience*, **15**, 353–375.

DiNardo, P.A., Guzy, L.T., Jenkins, J.A., Bak, R.M., Tomasi, S.F. & Copland, M. (1988). Etiology and maintenance of dog fears. *Behaviour Research and Therapy*, **26**, 241–244.

Fyer, A.J., Mannuzza, S., Gallops, M.P., Martin, L.Y., Aaronson, C., Gorman, J.M., Liebowitz, M.R. & Klein, D.F. (1990). Familial transmission of simple phobias and fears. *Archives of General Psychiatry*, **47**, 252–256.

Ginsburg, G.S., Silverman, W.K. & Kurtines, W.K. (1995). Family involvement in treating children with phobic and anxiety disorders: a look ahead. *Clinical Psychology Review*, **15**, 457–473.

Gray, J.A. (1982). *The Neuropsychology of Anxiety*. New York: Oxford University Press.

Graziano, A., DeGiovanni, I.S. & Garcia, K. (1979). Behavioral treatment of children's fears: a review. *Psychological Bulletin*, **86**, 804–830.

Graziano, A.M. & Mooney, K.C. (1980). Family self-control instructions for children's night-time fear reduction. *Journal of Consulting and Clinical Psychology*, **48**, 206–213.

Graziano, A.M., Mooney, K.C., Huber, C. & Ignaziak, D. (1979). Self-control instructions for children's fear reduction. *Journal of Behavior Therapy and Experimental Psychiatry*, **10**, 221–227.

Hagopian, L.P. & Ollendick, T.H. (1993). Simple phobias. In R.T. Ammerman & M. Hersen (eds), *Handbook of Behavior Therapy with Children and Adults: a Developmental and Longitudinal Perspective* (pp. 123–136). Boston: Allyn & Bacon.

Hagopian, L.P., Weist, M.W. & Ollendick, T.H. (1990). Cognitive–behavior therapy with an 11-year-old girl fearful of AIDS and illness: a case study. *Journal of Anxiety Disorders*, **4**, 257–265.

Hampe, E., Noble, M., Miller, L.C. & Barrett, C.L. (1973). Phobic children at 2 years post-treatment. *Journal of Abnormal Psychology*, **82**, 446–453.

Hekmat, H. (1987). Origins and development of human fear reactions. *Journal of Anxiety Disorders*, **1**, 197–218.

Herjanic, B. & Reich, W. (1982). Development of a structured psychiatric interview for children: agreement between child and parent on individual symptoms. *Journal of Abnormal Child Psychiatry*, **10**, 307–324.

Hirshfeld, D.R., Rosenbaum, J.F., Biederman, J., Bolduc, E.A., Faraone, S.V., Snidman, N., Reznick, J.S. & Kagan, J. (1992). Stable behavioral inhibition and its association with anxiety disorder. *Journal of the American Academy of Child and Adolescent Psychiatry*, **31**, 103–111.

Kagan, J. (1989). Temperamental contributions to social behavior. *American Psychologist*, **44**, 668–674.

Kagan, J., Reznick, J.S. & Gibbons, J. (1989). Inhibited and uninhibited types of children. *Child Development*, **60**, 838–845.

Kagan, J., Reznick, J.S. & Snidman, N. (1987). The physiology and psychology of behavioral inhibition. *Child Development*, **58**, 1459–1473.

Kagan, J., Reznick, J.S. & Snidman, N. (1988). Biological bases of childhood shyness. *Science*, **240**, 167–171.

Kashani, J.H., Beck, N.C., Hoeper, E.W., Fallahi, C., Corcoran, C.M., McAllister, J.A., Rosenberg, T.K. & Reid, J.C. (1987). Psychiatric disorders in a community sample of adolescents. *American Journal of Psychiatry*, **144**, 584–549.

Kendall, P.C., Howard, B.L. & Epps, J. (1988). The anxious child: cognitive–behavioral treatment strategies. *Behavior Modification*, **12**, 281–310.

Kendler, K.S., Neale, M.C., Kessler, R.C., Heath, A.C. & Eaves, L.J. (1992). The genetic epidemiology of phobias in women: the interrelationship of agoraphobia, social phobia, situational phobia and simple phobia. *Archives of General Psychiatry*, **49**, 273–281.

King, N.J., Cranstoun, F. & Josephs, A. (1989). Emotive imagery and children's night-time fears: a multiple baseline design evaluation. *Journal of Behavior Therapy and Experimental Psychiatry*, **20**, 125–135.

King, N.J., Hamilton, D.I. & Ollendick, T.H. (1988). *Children's Phobias: a Behavioural Perspective*. Chichester: Wiley.

King, N.J., Ollendick, T.H. & Gullone, E. (1991). Negative affectivity in children and adolescents: relations between anxiety and depression. *Clinical Psychology Review*, **11**, 441–459.

Koeppen, A.S. (1974). Relaxation training for children. *Elementary School Guidance and Counseling*, **9**, 14–21.

Last, C.G., Strauss, C.C. & Francis, G. (1987). Co-morbidity among childhood anxiety disorders. *Journal of Nervous and Mental Disease*, **175**, 726–730.

Lazarus, A.A. & Abramovitz, A. (1962). The use of emotive imagery in the treatment of children's phobias. *Journal of Mental Science*, **108**, 191–195.

Luria, A.R. (1961). *The Role of Speech in the Regulation of Normal and Abnormal Behavior*. New York: Liveright.

Marks, I.M. (1969). *Fears and Phobias*. New York: Academic Press.

Marks, I.M. (1987). *Fears, Phobias and Rituals*. New York Oxford University Press.

McGee, R., Feehan, M., Williams, S., Partridge, F., Silva, P.A. & Kelly, J. (1990). DSM-III disorders in a large sample of adolescents. *Journal of the American Academy of Child and Adolescent Psychiatry*, **29**, 611–619.

McNally, R.J. (1987). Preparedness and phobias: a review. *Psychological Bulletin*, **101**, 283–303.

McNally, R.J. & Steketee, G.S. (1985). The etiology and maintenance of severe animal phobias. *Behaviour Research and Therapy*, **23**, 431–435.

Meichenbaum, D.H. & Goodman, J. (1971). Training impulsive children to talk to themselves: a means of developing self-control. *Journal of Abnormal Psychology*, **77**, 115–126.

Menzies, R.G. & Clark, J.C. (1993a). The etiology of childhood water phobia. *Behaviour Research and Therapy*, **31**, 499–501.

Menzies, R.G. & Clark, J.C. (1993b). The etiology of fear of heights and its relationship to severity and individual response patterns. *Behaviour Research and Therapy*, **31**, 355–365.

Menzies, R.G. & Clarke, J.C. (1995). The etiology of phobias: a non-associative account. *Clinical Psychology Review*, **15**, 23–48.

Miller, L.C., Barrett, C.L. & Hampe, E. (1974). Phobias of childhood in a prescientific era. In A. Davids (ed.), *Child Personality and Psychopathology: Current Topics* (pp. 89–134). New York: Wiley.

Morris, R.J. & Kratochwill, T.R. (1983). *Treating Children's Fears and Phobias*. Elmsford, NY: Pergamon.

Nottelmann, E.D. & Jensen, P.S. (1995). Co-morbidity of disorders in children and adolescents: developmental perspectives. In T.H. Ollendick & R.J. Prinz (eds), *Advances in Clinical Child Psychology*, Vol. 17 (pp. 109–155). New York: Plenum.

Ollendick, T.H. (1979). Fear reduction techniques with children. In M. Hersen, R.M. Eisler & P.M. Miller (eds), *Progress in Behavior Modification*, Vol. 8 (pp. 127–168). New York: Academic Press.

Ollendick, T.H. (1983). Reliability and validity of the revised Fear Survey Schedule for Children (FSSC-R). *Behaviour Research and Therapy*, **21**, 395–399.

Ollendick, T.H. (1986). Behavior therapy with children and adolescents. In S.L. Garfield & A.E. Bergin (eds), *Handbook of Psychotherapy and Behavior Change*, 3rd edn (pp. 525–564). New York: Wiley.

Ollendick, T.H. (1995). Cognitive–behavioral treatment of panic disorder with agoraphobia in adolescents: a multiple baseline design analysis. *Behavior Therapy*, **26**, 517–531.

Ollendick, T.H. & Cerny, J.A. (1981). *Clinical Behavior Therapy with Children*. New York: Plenum.

Ollendick, T.H. & Francis, G. (1988). Behavioral assessment and treatment of children's phobias. *Behavior Modification*, **12**, 165–204.

Ollendick, T.H., Hagopian, L.P. & Huntzinger, R. (1991). Cognitive–behavior therapy with night-time fearful children. *Journal of Behavior Therapy and Experimental Psychiatry*, **22**, 113–121.

Ollendick, T.H. & King, N.J. (1991a). Fears and phobias of childhood. In M. Herbert (ed.), *Clinical Child Psychology: Social Learning, Development and Behavior* (pp. 309–329). Chichester: Wiley.

Ollendick, T.H. & King, N.J. (1991b). Origins of childhood fears: an evaluation of Rachman's theory of fear acquisition. *Behaviour Research and Therapy*, **29**, 117–123.

Ollendick, T.H. & King, N.J. (1994). Diagnosis, assessment and treatment of internalizing problems in children: the role of longitudinal data. *Journal of Consulting and Clinical Psychology*, **62**, 918–927.

Ollendick, T.H., King, N.J. & Frary, R.B. (1989). Fears in children and adolescents: reliability and generalizability across gender, age, and nationality. *Behaviour Research and Therapy*, **27**, 19–26.

Ollendick, T.H., King, N.J. & Yule, W. (eds) (1994). *International Handbook of Phobic and Anxiety Disorders in Children and Adolescents*. New York: Plenum.

Orvaschel, H. (1985). Psychiatric interviews suitable for use in research with children and adolescents. *Psychopharamcological Bulletin*, **21**, 737–745.

Öst, L.-G. & Hugdahl, K. (1981). Acquisition of phobias and anxiety response patterns in clinical patients. *Behaviour Research and Therapy*, **19**, 439–447.

Öst, L.-G. & Hugdahl, K. (1983). Acquisition of agoraphobia, mode of onset and anxiety response patterns. *Behaviour Research and Therapy*, **21**, 623–631.

Ost, L.-G. & Hugdahl, K. (1985). Acquisition of blood and dental phobia and anxiety response patterns in clinical patients. *Behaviour Research and Therapy*, **23**, 27–34.

Perry, M.A. & Furukawa, M.J. (1980). Modeling methods. In F.H. Kanfer & A.P. Goldsten (eds), *Helping People Change*, 2nd edn (pp. 131–171). Elmsford, NY: Pergamon.

Rachman, S. (1976). The passing of the two-stage theory of fear and avoidance: fresh possibilities. *Behaviour Research and Therapy*, **14**, 125–134.

Rachman, S. (1977). The conditioning theory of fear acquisition: a critical examination. *Behaviour Research and Therapy*, **15**, 375–387.

Rescorla, R.A. (1988). Pavlovian conditioning: it's not what you think it is. *American Psychologist*, **43**, 151–160.

Richards, C.S. & Siegel, L.J. (1987). Behavioral treatment of anxiety states and avoidance behaviors in children. In D. Margolin (ed.), *Child Behavior Therapy* (pp. 274–338). New York: Gardner.

Robins, L.N., Helzer, J.E., Croughan, J. & Ratcliff, K.S. (1981). The National Institute of Mental Health Diagnostic Interview Schedule: its history, characteristics, and validity. *Archives of General Psychiatry*, **38**, 381–389.

Rosenbaum, J.F., Biederman, J., Gersten, M., Hirshfeld, D.R., Meminger, S.R., Herman, J.B., Kagan, J., Reznick, J.S. & Snidman, N. (1988). Behavioral inhibition in children of parents with panic disorder and agoraphobia: a controlled study. *Archives of General Psychiatry*, **45**, 463–470.

Rosensteil, A.K. & Scott, D.S. (1977). Four considerations in using imagery techniques with children. *Journal of Behavior Therapy and Experimental Psychiatry*, **8**, 287–290.

Seligman, M.E.P. (1971). Phobias and preparedness. *Behavior Therapy*, **2**, 307–320.

Suomi, S.J. (1984). The development of affect in rhesus monkeys. In N. Fox & R. Davidson (eds), *The Psychobiology of Affective Disorders* (pp. 119–159). Hillsdale, NJ: Erlbaum.

Suomi, S.J. (1986). Anxiety-like disorders in young non-human primates. In R. Gittelman (ed.), *Anxiety Disorders of Childhood* (pp. 1–23). New York: Guilford.

Wolpe, J. (1958). *Psychotherapy by Reciprocal Inhibition*. Stanford, CA: Stanford University Press.

World Health Organization (1991). *International Classification of Mental and Behavioral Disorders, Clinical Descriptions and Diagnostic Quidelines*, 10th edn. Geneva: World Health Organization.

Section II

The Treatment of Phobias

Chapter 12

Rapid Treatment of Specific Phobias

Lars-Göran Öst

Department of Psychology, University of Stockholm, Sweden

Treatment of specific phobias is one of the first areas in which behaviour therapy made a significant contribution. In the 1960s and 1970s a large number of so-called analog studies were published on college students with subclinical fears of various animals. However, there are some 60 randomized clinical trials with patients fulfilling the DSM-IV (Amercian Psychiatric Association, 1994) criteria for specific phobia. In the present chapter a subset of these studies is focused upon, namely those evaluating rapid treatments. Based on the author's development of the so-called one-session treatment, a tentative definition of rapid treatment is one that is carried out in a single session maximized to 3 hours, or a treatment containing more sessions but a total therapy time of 3 hours or less.

DESCRIPTION OF TREATMENT METHODS

One-Session Treatment

Öst (1989a) has developed a rapid treatment method, called one-session treatment, for specific phobias in general. The treatment consists of intensive exposure during a single session, which is maximized to 3 hours. Prior to this session the therapist has carried out a behaviour analysis, which for an experienced therapist usually takes 1 hour. In animal phobics the exposure is generally combined with modelling. Below follows a general description of the treatment, while more detailed descriptions are given under the different phobias to which it has been applied.

Phobias—A Handbook of Theory, Research and Treatment. Edited by G.C.L. Davey.
© 1997 John Wiley & Sons Ltd.

Exposure In Vivo

The guiding principle for exposure situations is a cognitive analysis of the pa-tient's catastrophic cognitions concerning the phobic object/situation, and the exposure is set up as a series of behavioural tests, instead of a straightforward exposure. My clinical impression is that there is a more rapid shift in avoidance behaviour and subjective anxiety by doing the exposure this way. Further, the general principles for exposure *in vivo* are followed; the patient makes a commit-ment to remain in the exposure situation until the anxiety fades away, he/she is encouraged to approach the phobic stimulus as much as possible and remain in contact with it until the anxiety has decreased, and the therapy session is not ended until the anxiety level has been reduced by at least 50% or has completely vanished.

Modelling

The principles developed by Bandura and his co-workers are followed, which means that the therapist first demonstrates how to interact with the phobic object. Then the therapist helps the patient gradually to approximate physical contact with the phobic object, e.g. by first holding the patient's hand, then the arm, and gradually reducing the physical assistance. Later the patient interacts with the animal on his/her own, with the help of the therapist's instructions only.

Rationale

As in all instances of working with behavioural treatments, it is necessary to give the patient a rationale for the treatment method. In doing this one should tailor the description of the treatment to the individual patient's problem behaviours so that he/she can understand more easily why the selected treatment method should work in his/her case. The purpose of the one-session treatment is to expose the patient to the phobic situation *in a controlled way* thus enabling him/ her to realize that the consequences one feared would happen do not occur. It is very important to emphasize the differences between therapeutic exposure dur-ing the one-session treatment and the ordinary confrontations that patients may have with the phobic stimuli in natural situations. In the therapy situation the exposure is planned. gradual and controlled, while in natural situations it is unplanned, ungraded and without control.

Finally, the one-session treatment should be seen as a *start* and the patient must continue exposing him/herself to phobic situations in everyday life after the therapy. It is not to be expected that a specific phobia of 20–30 years' duration will completely vanish after only one therapy session. However, the single session enables the patient to continue on his/her own with exposure in natural situa-tions, e.g. by following a voluntary maintenance program (Öst, 1989b), so that within a few months the remaining phobic behaviour will disappear.

Pre-treatment Instructions

At the end of the behavioural analysis interview the therapist gives the patient some instructions concerning what will happen during the treatment session. First of all, the patient is told that teamwork is important in carrying out the treatment, and that both the therapist and the patient have equal responsibility for achieving a good result. This kind of therapy is hard work and can only be successful if the patient fulfills his/her part in the teamwork.

Most patients fear that some kind of "shock treatment" may be applied, e.g. that the therapist will suddenly take out a spider and throw it in the patient's lap. Thus, it is important to inform the patient that the therapist will never do anything unplanned in the therapy room, but will describe to the patient what will happen, then demonstrate it, and finally will get the patient's permission to do it.

Another fear that many patients have is that they will be subjected to such a high level of anxiety and over such a long period (3 hours) that they will not be able to cope with it, mentally or physically. They believe, for example, that they may suffer a heart attack and die from anxiety. Here it is important that the patients think back on the most anxiety-arousing situation they have ever experienced in relation to the phobic stimulus, calling this 100 on the 0–100 Subjective Units of Disturbance (SUDs) scale. The therapist can inform the patient that even if the treatment means that he/she will be exposed to much more than they have ever experienced in natural situations, this will not "break their personal record" of anxiety in the phobic situation, owing to the planned, gradual and controlled way the exposure is carried out.

Finally, the patient is told that a high level of anxiety is not a goal in itself for the one-session treatment, but can be considered a side-effect. If the patient can achieve the treatment goal with a maximum anxiety level of 50, instead of 90–100, it is quite all right as long as no cognitive avoidance goes on and the necessary emotional processing can take place.

Immediately before the treatment session starts the patient's understanding of the rationale and the pre-treatment instructions is checked by letting him/her describe them to the therapist. Any misconceptions can easily be corrected and the patient is then better equipped to fulfil his/her part of the teamwork.

Goals

There are two types of goals in connection with one-session treatment. The first is what the patient should be able to manage in natural situations after completing the treatment. Examples of this goal are that a spider phobic should be able to catch a spider with a glass and a postcard and throw it out of the house, or an injection phobic should be able to have an injection or give a blood sample with no more discomfort that people in general.

The second goal is that the therapist wants the patient to achieve during the therapy session. For the spider phobic the therapist wants him/her to be able to have two spiders walking on his/her hands at the same time. Concerning the injection phobic, the therapist wants him/her to have his/her fingers pricked several times (10) and to undergo subcutaneous injections (5–10) and a few venipunctures (2–4). However, the therapist does not inform the patient about this goal because the knowledge would be detrimental when it comes to the patient's performance during the session. First of all, a large majority (90% of my patients) would never have presented for treatment had I told them about this goal during the screening interview. Furthermore, knowing what the therapist has planned as the final step will lead to the patient ruminating about this in a negative way, which will prevent him/her from focusing on the task at hand, i.e. carrying out the next immediate step. It may be considered unethical not to inform the patients about the second goal before starting the therapy, but so far, after eight outcome studies and numerous clinical patients, no single patient has complained about this. On the contrary, they are grateful that the therapist helped them to realize that they could achieve much more than they had ever imagined. Since withholding the second goal actually helps the patient I do not consider it unethical not to inform the patient about if beforehand.

Spider Phobia Treatment

The one-session treatment of animal phobias is illustrated by the procedure used for spider phobia. This is the most prevalent of the animal phobias, and the one having the most outcome studies. However, in my clinical work I have used the same treatment method for patients with phobias of snakes, rats, dogs, cats, birds, wasps, worms, frogs and hedgehogs.

In order to fulfil the aims of graduation and control, four spiders in increasing sizes from 0.5 to 3 cm are used, and the spider is placed in a large plastic bowl (50 × 30 × 15 cm) during the session. The first step is to teach the patient to catch the small spider with a glass and a piece of paper (e.g. a postcard) and throw it out of the house, which is the goal for natural situations. The glass is put upside down over the spider in the bowl and the postcard is slid under it. The postcard functions as a "lid" and, by putting one's fingers under the postcard, the glass can be turned upright and the postcard removed with caution, in case the spider has spun a thread on the card. After modelling the procedure the therapist helps the patient to carry out this task. Usually it is repeated 3–4 times and the last time the patient is instructed to hold the glass in the palm of her right hand and close to the body. At this point a brief role-play can be carried out in order to "force" the patient to look closely at the spider. The role-play consists of having the therapist play the part of a person born blind, and the patient has to describe what she is looking at in the glass by only using words that can convey meaning to a blind person. This procedure usually leads to a marked anxiety reduction.

The second step is touching the spider. Before starting this step the therapist should ask the patient what she believes will happen if she puts her hand in the bowl. Almost 100% of our patients say that the spider will crawl up on their hands, up the arm and underneath the clothes. This prediction can be tested out by the therapist putting his hand in the bowl, then touching the spider from behind with the right index finger. What happens, much to the surprise of the patient, is that the spider runs away. By repeating this 10 times the patient will realize that the spider gets tired quickly and runs gradually shorter distances. Then the same procedure is repeated form the left side, the right side, and from the spider's head. The conclusion is that the spider doesn't crawl up on the therapist's finger. This is then followed by the patient touching the spider in the same way, which usually takes physical guidance from the therapist. By letting the patient do this long enough, the assumption that the spider will react differently towards a phobic person can easily be corrected.

The third step is letting the spider walk on the patient's hands. This can be done by the therapist first taking the spider on his/her hand, letting it walk from one hand to the other. Then the patient is encouraged, with the therapist's help, to put his/her index finger on the therapist's hand so that the spider can walk across the finger and back on to the therapist's hand. This is repeated a number of times, and then the spider is gradually allowed to walk on all the patient's fingers, on the whole hand and across to the other hand. Gradually the therapist withdraws physical support, letting the patient manage on his/her own, just following the therapist's instructions. During this step the goal is to have the spider walk up to the elbow (on both arms), letting the patient realize that he/she can move his/her hands faster than the spider can run, to prevent it from crawling underneath the clothing.

The above three steps are then repeated with another three spiders of gradually larger size, the largest being about 3 cm (with legs). When this is accomplished the patient is encouraged to have two spiders (numbers 3 and 4 in size) walking on his/her hands simultaneously. This step is of course more difficult but, by being relaxed in his/her arms and hands, the patient can usually control the spiders.

Throughout the session the patient is taught that he/she can have indirect control over the spider by gradually being more correct in predicting what the spider is going to do. The patient will learn that the spider is not going to turn 180° and suddenly run in the opposite direction. Basically, it will crawl in the direction that its head is pointing.

The principle guiding how much time is spent on each step is the patient's SUDs rating and belief in the catastrophic cognitions. The goal is that the patient should be able to handle two spiders with low or no anxiety and no longer believe his/her catastrophic cognitions.

Snake Phobia Treatment

In an outstanding series of studies, Bandura and his co-workers have developed and evaluated a rapid treatment method called "participant modelling". In their first study (Bandura, Blanchard & Ritter, 1969) they describe that the treatment

starts with the patient observing the therapist through a one-way mirror performing a series of gradually more threatening activities with the snake, in order to
demonstrate to the patient that close interaction with the snake does not lead to
harmful consequences. During a 15 minute period the therapist handles the
snake, holds it close to his/her face, puts it in his/her lap, lets it loose on the floor,
and picks it up again. After observing this the patient is invited into the therapy
room and sits down on a chair. The therapist then removes the snake from its
glass cage and brings it gradually closer to the patient, who is instructed to touch,
stroke and hold the snake. If necessary the patient can use gloves initially, or put
his/her hand on the therapist's hand while the therapist strokes the snake. Gradually the therapist then withdraws his/her hand so that the patient touches and
strokes the snake with the therapist's physical support, and later completely
without that aid. In this way the patient is taught to perform the same activities
as the therapist had done initially; the therapist first modelling the step, then
helping the patient in various ways if necessary, and finally the patient carrying it
out on his/her own, following the therapist's verbal instructions only.

The maximum treatment time in this study was 5.25 hours, but the mean time
was 2 hours and 10 minutes. Later studies from Bandura and co-workers have
investigated different components of participant modelling (Bandura & Barab,
1973; Bandura, Jeffrey & Wright, 1974; Bandura, Jeffrey & Gajdos, 1975;
Bandura, Adams & Beyer, 1977).

Blood–Injury–Injection Phobia Treatment

In previous research I have developed and evaluated a specific treatment method
for blood phobia called "applied tension" (Öst & Sterner, 1987; Öst, Sterner &
Fellenius, 1989; Öst, Fellenius & Sterner, 1991). This is an intensive five-session
treatment having two aims: (a) teaching the patient to recognize the first signs of
a drop in blood pressure; and (b) teaching the patient to apply a rapid and
effective tension technique to reverse the blood pressure drop. After practising
the tension technique at home, the patient is exposed to 30 slides of wounded
people, blood donation at the hospital's blood donor centre, and watching a
thoracic operation, i.e. lung or open-heart surgery.

The above treatment has been reduced to a one-session format with a maximum time of 2 hours. The session starts with the rationale for applied tension, i.e.
by learning an effective way to counteract the drop in blood pressure which
occurs in the phobic situations, fainting is prevented. This is followed by a
description of the tension technique. The patient is taught to tense the gross body
muscles (arms, chest and legs) as much as possible and keep tensing for 15–20
seconds, then releasing the tension and returning to normal (without relaxing).
After a 30-second pause the patient tenses again, and then releases the tension,
etc. This practice goes on for 30 minutes with regular assessments of blood
pressure in order to show the patient that the tension technique actually leads to
an increase in blood pressure. After a brief pause, the application training with 10

slides of wounded people follows. The patient is instructed to watch a slide, scanning the body for the very first signs of a drop in blood pressure, and then applying the tension for as long as necessary. The goal is to be able to watch the slide without feeling faint. When this is achieved one continues with the next slide, etc. If there is time left in the session after the 10 slides have been worked through the patient can be exposed to other stimuli, e.g. pricking of a finger, examining blood in a test tube and blood-stained bandages, while applying the tension technique. The reason why 2 hours is used instead of 3, as in other specific phobias, is that the patients would get very sore muscles after practising tension for such a long period.

In injection phobia the one-session treatment consists of intense prolonged exposure to three procedures; pricking of fingers, subcutaneous injections and venipunctures. The goal is to prick 10 fingers, to do 10–12 subcutaneous injections (with saline) and 2–4 venipunctures. As in all one-session treatments, the team-work between therapist and patient is important and the therapist first describes and demonstrates each small step in the procedure before getting the patient's permission to perform the step. An important part of the treatment is educating the patient about the function of different utensils like lancets and vacutainer tubes, and the distribution of pain cells on the body. During one-session treatment exposure is carried out as a series of tests of the patient's idiosyncratic catastrophic cognitions.

Claustrophobia Treatment

The one-session treatment of claustrophobia consists of intensive exposure to the two to three most anxiety-arousing situations of the individual patient. Examples of situations covered are staying in small windowless rooms with the door locked, riding lifts, going by bus or underground train, etc. As in all one-session treatments it is important to emphasize the teamwork relationship and to involve the patient in decisions concerning the kind of exposure to be used. The patient should have a feeling the he/she can influence the exposure session by submitting suggestions concerning the content of the session. The communication between patient and therapist must be completely honest and an attitude of "let's test and see what happens to me when I am exposed to the worst phobic situations" should be conveyed to the patient. Since the patient usually has a high anticipatory anxiety when coming to the treatment session, it is very important to help the patient focus on the task at hand instead of ruminating about the last step.

The example of being in a small windowless closet or lavatory can be used. Before the start of exposure it is important to ask the patient to formulate what the focus of the treatment is, i.e. reducing the patient's anxiety reactions in the phobic situations. The patient's SUDs ratings at regular intervals is the information guiding the therapist. Initially the patient is instructed to open the door just to take a peek, but not to enter. Usually, he/she wants to check the lock to be sure about how it is opened from inside. Then the patient is encouraged to enter the room and close the door. If he/she wants to, the patient can exit without locking the door. The next step is to lock the door and stay there for a while. While the patient is inside the therapist prompts him/her to constantly talk aloud and verbalize what and how he/she is doing and feeling. In this way tendencies to cognitive avoidance are greatly reduced. After a while the patient may want to exit and talk face-to-face with the therapist about the experience. As soon as possible, however, he/she is instructed to enter the closet again and lock the door with the goal of staying longer than on the first attempt, the final goal being that the patient should be able to stay inside the locked room for 5 minutes with a maximum SUDs-rating of 20. If the patient finds that the therapist's presence outside the room has a calming effect, the therapist should remove him/herself some distance from the room. The exposure is usually ended with some generalization training, e.g. in a storage room and a public convenience with a coin-lock.

Booth & Rachman (1992) described the use of three different treatments carried out during three 1 hour sessions. *Exteroceptive exposure* was a graduated form of exposure *in vivo*, proceeding from less to more anxiety-arousing situations based on the individual patient's hierarchy. The exposure took place in a small ($7 \times 4 \times 2$ foot) "laboratory closet". *Interoceptive exposure* was based on a hierarchy of sensations related to fear. The exercises used in the treatment were those closely resembling what the patient experienced while being in the closet at pre-treatment assessment. Examples of exercises were overbreathing, underbreathing, spinning around on a chair, running on the spot, etc. Coping strategies or direct mention of cognitions were not used in the two exposure treatments. *Cognitive therapy* included teaching the patient to identify automatic negative thoughts and learning to identify and deal with logical errors in their way of thinking. Patients were also taught to rationally dispute thoughts related to physical sensations as well as those without such an association.

Dental Phobia Treatment

The only example of rapid treatment in dental phobia is described by Moses & Hollandsworth (1985). They used stress inoculation ($3\frac{1}{2}$ hours) and coping skills plus application ($2\frac{1}{2}$ hours). In the former method the patient first receives an educational component concerning the conceptualization of anxiety and pain. The second component contains the training of various coping skills, and the third requires the patient to practise these skills when confronted with various anxiety- or pain-eliciting stimuli. The latter method only contained the second and third components.

Flying Phobia Treatment

The one-session treatment of flying phobia is based on the same exposure *in vivo* principle as in the other specific phobias. However, it is of course not possible to arrange "behavioural experiments" during a flight, at least not with a regular airline. Instead, the testing of the patient's catastrophic cognitions must be done indirectly.

The description below is based on the procedure used in an outcome study on flying phobia (Öst, Brandberg & Alm, 1997), which was sponsored by the Scandinavian Airlines System in such a way that the project received free tickets for domestic flights with empty seats, leaving from Stockholm airport. The session starts at the bus terminal in the city, where the therapist and patient meet to take the bus to the airport. This bus trip, which takes 30–40 minutes, is used to elicit the patient's catastrophic cognitions concerning travelling by air, and tying these to the different phases of a flight. These can cover a number of steps from going to the airport to sitting in the plane during turbulence. The important factor is helping the patient to speak openly about what he/she fears and when during the flight these fears are elicited. When they reach the airport the therapist and patient go to the ticket office to collect their tickets and then they walk to the gate to check in. After a brief waiting period they board the plane and fly for 45–60 minutes. After disembarking they immediately check in again and take the same plane back to Stockholm. Then they take the bus back to the city.

From arriving at the airport to the second landing (coming back to Stockholm) there are a number of idiosyncratic situations that the individual patient will have pin-pointed as being connected to certain catastrophic thoughts. The therapist's role is to predict these circumstances before they occur and remind the patient about his/her thoughts concerning that situation. When the situation has passed the therapist asks the patient to draw conclusions about what really happened and contrast that to his/her belief. The session continues in this way and during the bus trip back to the city the patient is encouraged to summarize what he/she has learnt during the session and how these experiences can be built on to continue flying without the therapist's presence.

Height Phobia Treatment

The most well-developed rapid treatment method for height phobia is called "guided mastery" by Williams, Dooseman & Kleifeld (1984), and Williams, Turner & Peer (1985), and it is carried out in two $1\frac{1}{2}$-hour sessions. Guided mastery is a development from the early treatment method called "contact desensitization", which was used by Ritter (1969a,b) in two studies on acrophobia.

In guided mastery the therapist initially accompanies the patient in the phobic situation (a high building) and then gradually increases the distance between him/herself and the patient, so that at the end of the treatment period the therapist stands on the ground giving the patient instructions. The patient is instructed to expose him/herself to the phobic situation and to tackle difficult tasks as soon as possible. If the patient is experiencing difficulties, the therapist is there to help with various "performance induction aids". Examples of these are: (a) *modelling*, i.e. the therapist first performs the activity he/she wants the patient to attempt; (b) *physical support*, e.g. the patient holds the therapist under the arm while approaching the railing of the floor; (c) *mastery of subtasks*, e.g. if the patient could not look straight down when he/she was at the railing, the subtask could be to look at the ground far from the building and then gradually closer and closer; (d) *proximal goals*, i.e. instructing the patient to focus on intermediate goals if the given goal was found to be too difficult; (e) *eliminating defensive manoeuvres*, i.e. if the patient was performing a task in a "non-normal" way (e.g. gripping his/her clothes while standing at the railing), the therapist would give instructions to eliminate these defensive behaviours; (f) *varied performance*, e.g. if the patient was unable to look around while at the railing, he/she was instructed to perform the task in a variety of ways; (g) *graduated time*, i.e. the patient was instructed to perform a difficult task for gradually longer periods of time.

The other rapid treatment method that has been used in height phobia is exposure *in vivo* (Bourque & Ladouceur, 1980; Marshall, 1985). Emmelkamp & Felten (1985) used standard instructions for exposure, i.e. in order to overcome their phobia the patients had to do what they avoided, and try to confront the most difficult situation as soon as possible. The exposure session lasted a maximum of 1 hour and it was done on the fire escape of a six-storey building. Exposure "involved climbing the steps to reach the landing, going near the edge of the landing and looking down at the ground level. Each of these performance tasks was practised on each landing. The therapist gave standardized verbal guidance and social reinforcement to the S every 3 min" (Emmelkamp & Felten, 1985, p. 220).

OUTCOME OF RANDOMIZED CLINICAL TRIALS

The clinical trials with different rapid treatments for specific phobias are summarized in Table 12.1. First, for the different specific phobias, a review of the statistical significance between compared conditions is described. This is followed by the clinical significance obtained for the different treatments. There are different ways of measuring clinically significant change, but one of the soundest and best established is that proposed by Jacobson, Follette & Revenstorf (1984). According to these authors two criteria must be fulfilled: (a) the change from pre- to post-assessment achieved by the individual patient mush be statistically reliable; and (b) the post-treatment score must lie within the range of the normal population, or outside the range of the patient population, defined as the mean ± 2SD, in the direction of functionality. However, not all of the reviewed studies have used this method, so in the following a variety of measures will be described.

Snake Phobia

Statistical Significance

Bandura, Blanchard & Ritter (1969) showed that participant modelling (PM) was significantly better than systematic desensitization and symbolic modelling. In subsequent studies various components of participant modelling have been investigated. Bandura, Jeffery & Wright (1974) found that PM with a high degree of aid was equal to a moderate degree of aid, and both were better than a low degree of aid. Bandura, Jeffery & Gajdos (1975) showed that the addition of self-directed performance to PM was more effective than PM alone, and Bandura, Adams & Beyer (1977) found PM to be better than modelling alone (without the patient's active participation).

Clinical Significance

In research on snake phobia the proportion of patients *completing the terminal step of the behavioural test* has been reported in three studies. Bandura, Blanchard & Ritter (1969) found that participant modelling (PM) yielded 92% completers, compared to only 25% for systematic desensitization, and 33% for symbolic modelling. In the 1974 study, Bandura, Jeffery & Wright found that PM with high levels of response aid yielded 75%, compared to 58% for moderate aid, and 17% for low aid. PM with self-directed performance (Bandura, Jeffery & Gajdos, 1975) gave 100% completers, compared to 60% for PM alone.

Spider Phobia

Statistical Significance

In the first of a series of studies Öst, Salkovskis & Hellström (1991) found the one-session treatment to be much more effective than self-exposure with a specific manual for spider phobia. In a subsequent study Hellström & Öst (1995) replicated this finding and showed the therapist-directed one-session treatment to be significantly better than both a general manual for anxiety disorders (Marks, 1978) and the specific manual for spider phobia. Furthermore, this was irrespective of whether the self-exposure treatment was carried out in the patients' homes or at the clinic. An independent replication of these findings was reported by Arntz & Lavy (1993), showing no difference between the two compared conditions—stimulus elaboration and non-elaboration.

A further development of the one-session treatment was carried out by Öst (1996) by applying it in two group formats; a small group with 3–4 patients and a large group with 7–8 patients. There was a tendency for the small group format to yield better effects than the large format, but this was only significant on one measure—self-rating of anxiety during the behavioural test. In the latest study, Öst, Ferebee & Furmark (1997) compared three variations of the large group ($n = 8$) format. Direct treatment was found to be significantly better than indirect treatment (eight patients watching one getting treated) and indirect observation (eight patients watching the video tape of the treatment in the second condition).

Table 12.1 Outcome studies on rapid behavioral treatments in specific phobia

Study	Treatment methods	Times	Treatment (hours)	n	Drop-out
Animal phobia					
Bandura, Blanchard & Ritter (1969)	a. Systematic desensitization	1	4.5	12	0
(Snake)	b. Symbolic modeling	1	2.8	12	0
	c. Participant modeling (PM)	1	2.2	12	0
	d. Waiting list control group			12	0
Bandura & Barab (1973)	a. Symbolic modeling—child	1	0.2	22	0
(Snake)	b. Symbolic modeling—adult	1	0.2	22	0
	c. Irrelevant symbolic mod.	1	0.2	22	0
Bandura, Jeffery & Wright (1974)	a. PM with high aids	1	Mdn:	12	0
(Snake)	b. PM with moderate aids	1	1.4	12	0
	c. PM with low aids	1		12	0
Bandura, Jeffery & Gajdos (1975)	a. PM	1	1.0	10	0
(Snake)	b. PM + self-directed performance	1	2.1	10	0
	c. PM + varied self-directed performance	1	1.9	10	0
Bandura, Adams & Beyer (1977)	a. PM	1	Mdn:	11	0
(Snake)	b. Modeling	1	1.5	11	0
	c. Waiting list control group			11	0
Öst, Salkovskis & Hellström (1991)	a. Exposure + PM	1	2.1	17	0
(Spider)	b. Self-directed exposure	3.20	4.7	17	0
Arntz & Lavy (1993)	a. Exposure + PM with elaboration	1	2.50	19	0
(Spider)	b. Exposure + PM non-elaboration			22	0
Hellström & Öst (1995)	a. Exposure + PM	1	2.1	10	0
(Spider)	b. Specific manual—home	2.6	2.8	10	0
	c. Specific manual—clinic	1.7	3.3	11	27
	d. General manual—home	3.8	5.4	11	0
	e. General manual—clinic	1.9	3.4	10	10
Öst (1996)	a. Exposure + PM, small group	1	2.8	22	0
(Spider)	b. Exposure + PM, large group	1	3.0	20	0
Öst Ferebee & Furmark (1997)	a. Exposure + PM, large group	1	3.25	16	0
(Spider)	b. Direct observation, large group	1	2.11	14	0
	c. Indirect observation, large group	1	2.00	16	0
Blood–injury phobia					
Hellström, Fellenius & Öst (1996)	a. Applied tension—spaced	5	5	10	0
	b. Applied tension—massed	1	2	10	0
	c. Tension-only—massed	1	2	10	0
Injection phobia					
Öst, Hellström & Kåver (1992)	a. Massed exposure	1	2	20	0
	b. Spaced exposure	5	3.5	20	5
Claustrophobia					
Booth & Rachman (1992)	a. Exposure *in vivo*	3	3	12	8
	b. Interoceptive exposure			12	8
	c. Cognitive therapy			12	0
	d. Waiting list control group			12	0
Öst et al. (1997)	a. Exposure-massed	1	3	10	0
	b. Exposure-spaced	5	5	10	10
	c. Cognitive therapy	5	5	11	0
	d. Waiting-list controls			18	0
Dental phobia					
Moses & Hollandsworth (1985)	a. Education alone	1	1.5	6	17
	b. Stress inoculation training		3.5	6	0
	c. Coping skills + application		2.5	6	0
	d. Waiting list control group			6	0
Flying phobia					
Öst, Brandberg & Alm (1997)	a. Exposure, one session	1	3	15	7
	b. Exposure, five sessions	5	6	15	7

Measures	Results	Improvement (%)	Clinically significant improvement (%)
Behavioral test	c > a = b > d	a: 37, b: 47, c: 87, d: 1	a: 25, b: 33, c: 92, d: 0
Self-rating of anxiety	c = b > a > d	a: 48, b: 77, c: 86, d: 35	(completed last step)
Fear Inventory	c = b > a > d		
Behavioral test	a = b > c	No means	No data
Self-rating of anxiety	a = b > c		
GSR	a = b > c		
Behavioral test	a = b > c	a: 75, b: 69, c: 39	a: 75, b: 58, c: 17
Self-rating of anxiety	a = b = c	No means	(completed last step)
Fear Inventory	a = b = c	No means	
Behavioral test	b = c > a	No means	a: 60, b + c: 100
Self-rating of anxiety	b = c > a		(completed last step)
Fear Inventory	b = c > a		
Fear of snake encounters	b > c > a		
Behavioral test	a > b > c	No means	No data
Self-rating of anxiety	a > b > c		
Fear of snake encounters	a = b > c		
Behavioral test	a > b	a: 97, b: 26	a: 88, b: 18
Self-rating of anxiety	a > b	a: 70, b: 20	
Spider Questionnaire	a > b	a: 66, b: 26	
Behavioral test	a = b	a: 57, b:73	a + b: 63
Self-rating of anxiey	a = b	a: 48, b: 60	
Spider Questionnaire	a = b	a: 45, b: 52	
Behavioral test	a > b = c = d = e	a: 97, b: 49, c: 68, d: 53, e: 59	a: 90, b: 30, c: 55,
Self-rating of anxiety	a > b = d = e; c > b	a: 73, b: 8, c: 60, d: 30, e: 24	d: 27, e: 30
Spider Questionnaire	a > b = c = d = e	a: 65, b: 32, c: 34, d: 34, e: 31	
Behavioral test	a = b	a: 86, b: 72	a: 82, b: 70
Self-rating of anxiety	a > b	a: 64, b: 37	
Spider Questionnaire	a = b	a: 44, b: 40	
Behavioral test	a > b = c	a: 70, b: 30, c: 45	a: 75, b: 7, c: 31
Self-rating of anxiety	a = b = c	a: 37, b: 14, c: 21	
Spider Questionnaire	a > b; a = c; b = c	a: 44, b: 20, c: 28	
Behavioral test	a = b = c	a: 90, b: 95, c: 94	a: 80, b: 90, c: 90
Assessor rating of fainting	a = b = c	a: 71, b: 78, c: 71	
Self-rating of anxiety	a = b = c	a: 58, b: 67, c: 57	
Behavioral test	a = b	a: 97, b: 93	a: 80, b: 79
Self-rating of anxiety	a = b	a: 48, b: 67	
Injection Phobia Scale	a = b	a: 48, b: 65	
Reported fear	a = c > b > d	a: 80, b: 52, c: 72, d: 31	No data
Negative cognitions	a = b = c > d	a: 94, b: 57, c: 88, d: 8	
Anxiety Sensitivity Index	a = b = c = d	a: 19, b: 16, c: 12, d: 15	
Heart-rate	a > b = c = d		
Behavioral test	a = b = c > d	a: 85, b: 79, c: 73, d: −17	a: 80, b: 63, c: 56
Self-rating of anxiety	a = b = c > d	a: 70, b: 72, c: 69, d: 15	
Claustrophobia Scale—Anxiety	a = b = c > d	a: 51, b: 60, c. 48, d: 2	
Claustrophobia Scale—Avoidance	a = b = c > d	a: 62, b; 65, c: 57, d: 5	
Dental Anxiety Scale	a = b = c = d	a: 10, b: 7, c: 8, d: 0	a: 33, b: 83, c: 83, d: 0
STAI-S	a = b = c = d	a: 14, b: 38, c: 19, d: 11	(completed a dental appointment)
Behavioral test	a = b	a: 94, b: 82	a: 94, b: 79
Self-rating of anxiety	a = b	a: 40, b; 57	
Fear of Flying scale	a = b	a: 43, b: 54	

Table 12.1 *Continued*

Study		Treatment methods	Times	Treatment (hours)	n	Drop-out
Height phobia						
Ritter (1969a)	a.	Contact desensitization	1	0.40	4	0
	b.	No-contact desensitization			4	0
	c.	No-treatment control group			4	0
Ritter (1969b)	a.	Contact desensitization	1	0.60	5	0
	b.	Demonstration + participation			5	0
	c.	Live modelling			5	0
Morris & Magrath (1979)	a.	Contact desensitization warm therapist	3	1.30	8	0
	b.	Contact desensitization cold therapist			8	13
	c.	Waiting list control group			8	0
Bourque & Ladouceur (1980)	a.	Participant modelling	?	0.6–6.00	10	?
	b.	PM without therapist control			10	?
	c.	Modeling + resp. rehearsal			10	?
	d.	Therapist-controlled exposure			10	?
	e.	Client-controlled exposure			10	?
Williams, Dooseman & Kleifeld (1984)	a.	Exposure	2 weeks	3.0–4.5	13	23
(H + driving phobia)	b.	Guided mastery			14	7
	c.	Waiting list control group			9	0
Emmelkamp & Felten (1985)	a.	Exposure	1	1	10	10
	b.	Cognitive–exposure			10	0
Marshall (1985)	a.	No treatment control group	1	0	10	0
Study 1	b.	Brief 1–exposure		0.4	10	0
	c.	Brief 2–exposure		0.6	10	0
	d.	Standard exposure		1.2	10	0
	e.	Prolonged 1–exp.		1.6	10	0
	f.	Prolonged 2–exp.		1.5	10	0
Marshall (1985)	a.	Brief 1–exposure	1	?	10	0
Study 2	b.	Brief 2–exposure			10	0
	c.	Standard exposure			10	0
Williams, Turner & Peer (1985)	a.	Performance desensitization	1 week	3	12	0
	b.	Guided mastery			13	0
	c.	No treatment control group			13	0

Clinical Significance

All five studies on spider phobia used the method of Jacobson, Follette & Revenstorf (1984) to calculate clinically significant improvement. It was decided that a patient should display a significant change on three measures simultaneously (behaviour test, self-rating of anxiety and assessor rating of clinical severity) in order to be counted as clinically improved. In Öst, Salkovskis & Hellström (1991), one-session exposure treatment yielded 88% and manualized self-exposure 18% clinically improved patients. Hellström & Öst (1995) used the same criteria and found that 90% in the one-session group were clinically improved, compared to 33% across the four manualized self-exposure groups combined. Öst (1996) found that 82% of the patients in the small group condition compared to 70% in the large group fulfilled these criteria, a non-significant difference. Finally, Öst, Ferebee & Furmark (1997) reported that a significantly larger proportion of patients in the direct treatment condition (75%) were clinically improved, compared to only 7% in the direct observation and 31% in the indirect observation group. In the Arntz & Lavy (1993) study, 63% of the patients (across the two conditions) fulfilled the criteria on the behavioural test.

Measures	Results	Improvement (%)	Clinically significant improvement
Behavioral test	a > b = c	Only change-scores	No data
FSS-II	a = b = c		
Self-rating of fear	a > b = c		
Behavioral test	a > b > c	a: 37, b: 25, c: 9	No data
Self-rating of fear	a = b = c		
Behavioral test	a = b > c	a: 68, b: 78, c: 10	No data
Self-rating of fear	a = b = c		
FSS-III	b > a = c		
Behavioral test	a = b = c = d = e	a: 75, b: 100, c: 97, d: 100, e: 95	No data
Self-rating of fear	a = b = c = d = e		
Heart-rate	a = b = c = d = e		
Acrophobia Questionnaire	a = b = c = d = e		
Situation-specific Questionnaire	a = b = c = d = e		
Behavioral test	b > a = c	a: 35, b: 67, c: 9	a: 50, b: 87, c: 0
Level of self-efficacy	b > a > c	a: 39, b: 63, c: 8	(completed last step)
Self-rating of anxiety	b > a > c	a: 6, b: 42, c: −32	
Behavioral test	a = b	a: 55, b: 70	No data
Self-rating of anxiety	b > a	a: 31, b: 73	
HR	a = b		
Behavioral test	f = e = d > a = b = c	a: −4, b: 2, c; −3, d: 37, e: 52, f: 62	No data
Self-rating of anxiety	f = e = d > a = b = c	a: 27, b: 33, c: 24, d: 51, e: 51, f: 51	
Self-rating or height anxiety	f = e = d > a = b = c	a: 36, b: 30, c: 22, d: 49, e: 49, f: 52	
Behavioral test	c > a = b	a: 5, b: 19, c: 51	No data
Self-rating of anxiety	c > a = b	a: 4, b: 17, c: 47	
Self-rating of height anxiety	c > a = b	a: 6, b: 9, c: 63	
Behavioral test	b > a > c	a: 47, b: 80, c: 35	a: 17, b: 62, c: 0
Self-rating of anxiety	a = b > c	a: 39, b; 41, c: 11	(completed last step)
Self-efficacy strength	b > a > c	a: 18, b; 60, c: −17	

Blood–Injury–Injection Phobia

Statistical Significance

In a study on blood–injury phobia, Hellström, Fellenius & Öst (1996) found that one-session of applied tension as well as one-session of tension-only (without any exposure to phobic stimuli) were as effective as the full five-session format of applied tension. In a study on injection phobia, Öst, Hellström & Kåver (1992) reported that one session of massed exposure was equally effective as five sessions of spaced exposure, despite the fact that in the latter condition the subjects were exposed to twice the number of repetitions of the various anxiety-arousing procedures.

Clinical Significance

In my own research on blood phobia I have applied Jacobson's procedure to assess CSI. In order to be considered clinically improved, a patient has to watch the entire film of thoracic operations (30 minutes) without any fainting behaviour whatsoever, and a low anxiety rating. When these stringent criteria were applied in the Hellström, Fellenius & Öst (1996) study, 50% of the patients receiving applied tension for five sessions, compared to 0% in applied tension for one-session, and 30% in tension-only for one session, were clinically improved at post-treatment, while 60%, 70% and 60%, respectively, were clinically improved at 1-year follow-up. However, if only the behavioural measure (watching the entire film) is considered, the proportions were 80%, 90% and 90%, respectively.

The only study published about injection phobia (Öst, Hellström & Kåver, 1992) found that one session of exposure *in vivo* yielded 80% clinically improved at post-treatment and 90% at the 1-year follow-up. The corresponding figures for the five-session group were 79% and 84%, respectively.

Claustrophobia

Statistical Significance

Booth & Rachman (1992) found exteroceptive exposure (*in vivo*), interoceptive exposure (to anxiety sensations), and cognitive therapy to be about equally effective after a three-session treatment (3 hours). Öst et al. (1997) showed that one session of exposure was as effective as five sessions of exposure and five sessions of cognitive therapy (without exposure).

Clinical Significance

In our study of claustrophobia (Öst et al., 1997) 80% of the one-session exposure-treated patients, compared to 63% in the five-session exposure and 56% in the cognitive therapy group were considered clinically improved when applying the Jacobson, Follette & Revenstorf (1984) criteria. Unfortunately, Booth & Rachman (1992) failed to report any data on clinical improvement.

Dental Phobia

Statistical Significance

Moses & Hollandsworth (1985) found rather moderate effects and no significant differences on the main measure between education alone, stress inoculation training, and coping skills plus application training, However, they reported that more patients in the latter two conditions completed a dental appointment after therapy.

Clinical Significance

In dental phobia the obvious criterion is whether, after treatment, the patient can *visit a dentist and complete dental treatment*. Moses & Hollandsworth (1985) reported that SIT (83%) and coping skills plus application (83%) gave a significantly higher proportion that "completed a dental appointment" at the end of treatment than the waiting list control group (0%).

Flying Phobia

Statistical Significance

In the only study on rapid treatment of flying phobia, Öst, Brandberg & Alm (1997) found one-session treatment to be as effective as five sessions of exposure.

Clinical Significance

As with dental phobia, there is a natural criterion for flying phobia, i.e. whether the patient after treatment can *make ordinary flights on her/his own*. The only study of rapid treatment in this area (Öst, Brandberg & Alm, 1997) used flying at the pre-treatment behavioral test as an exclusive criterion, and reported that 94% after one session and 79% after five sessions of exposure too a domestic flight *unaccompanied*. These figures had dropped to 64% at the 1-year follow-up assessment, using the same behavioural test.

Height Phobia

Statistical Significance

Ritter (1969a) found contact desensitization (a method similar to PM) to be more effective than no-contact desensitization, and in a subsequent study (Ritter, 1969b) more effective than live modelling. Morris & Magrath (1979) found no difference between contact desensitization when the therapist acted in a warm and friendly way or in a cold way. Bourque & Ladouceur (1980) compared three forms of PM with two forms of exposure and found no difference on any of the outcome measures. However, Williams, Dooseman & Kleifeld (1984), in a study including both height-phobic and driving-phobic subjects, showed that guided mastery was significantly more effective than exposure *in vivo* on all the main measures. This was replicated in a subsequent study by Williams, Turner & Peer (1985) with only height phobics.

Different forms of exposure *in vivo* have been investigated in three studies. Emmelkamp & Felten (1985) found that exposure alone was as effective as the combination of cognitive therapy and exposure, with the exception of self-rating of anxiety where the combination was better. Marshall (1985) reported in his Study 1 that standard exposure and two forms of prolonged exposure were more effective than two forms of brief exposure. This was replicated in Study 2, where standard exposure was more effective than two forms of brief exposure.

Clinical Significance

Since no study has investigated the degree of approach behaviour displayed by
non-acrophobic individuals, a conservative measure of CSI in acrophobia would
be the proportion of patients that can *perform the maximum step* on the post- or
follow-up behavioural test. Data on his issue have been reported in only two out
of nine studies. Williams, Dooseman & Kleifeld (1984) found that significantly
more guided mastery patients (87%) than exposure patients (50%) completed all
treatment tasks. Williams, Turner & Peer (1985) also reported that a significantly
higher proportion of the guided mastery patients achieved maximal performance
during treatment (62%) compared to the exposure-treated patients (17%).

CONCLUSIONS

Are Rapid Treatments Effective?

The above review shows that rapid behavioural treatment methods for specific
phobias are *as effective as* the longer treatments with which they have been
compared, and in all but one study (Moses & Hollandsworth, 1985) significantly
better than the no-treatment or waiting-list control groups.

Treatments of Choice

It may seem presumptuous to conclude which treatments are the most effective
for the different types of specific phobia in view of the small number of studies on
most of them. However, I believe that suggestions can be made based on the
available studies. These are summarized in Table 12.2 together with the proportion of clinically significant improvement yielded in the studies reviewed. Across
the different specific phobias the rapid treatment methods yield 74–94% clinically improved patients after 2–3 hours of treatment.

Table 12.2 Rapid treatments of choice for specific phobias

Type of phobia	Treatment method	Mean CSI[1] (%)	Mean time (hours)
Snake phobia	Participant modeling	87	1.9
Spider phobia	One-session exposure: individual	89	2.1
	One-session exposure: group	74	3.0
Blood–injury phobia	One-session applied tension	90	2.0
Injection phobia	One-session exposure *in vivo*	80	2.0
Claustrophobia	One-session exposure *in vivo*	80	3.0
Dental phobia	Stress inoculation training	83	3.0
Flying phobia	One-session exposure *in vivo*	94	3.0
Height phobia	Guided mastery	77	3.5

[1] Proportion of patients achieving clinically significant improvement.

Further Research in this Area

Despite the impressive effectiveness of the rapid behavioural treatments described above there is still room for improvement in many areas. There are a number of specific phobias for which controlled outcome studies are lacking, e.g. phobias of choking, darkness, driving, illness, noise, storms, thunder and lightning, vomiting and water. At least some of these phobias are so common that it should not be any problem to recruit enough subjects for an outcome study. Furthermore, some phobias have been the subject of only a few studies (blood phobia, injection phobia, claustrophobia, dental phobia and flying phobia). All of these phobias should be investigated in new outcome studies. Also, assessment of clinically significant improvement should be included in new studies, e.g. employing the method described by Jacobson, Follette & Revenstorf (1984).

Moreover, new treatments and variations of current treatments should be developed to increase cost-effectiveness further. Examples include developing self-help treatment manuals (Öst, Salkovskis & Hellström, 1991; Hellström & Öst, 1995), and evaluating group formating of current treatments (Öst, 1996; Öst, Ferebee & Furmark, 1997). Finally, follow-up assessment is lacking in a number of studies, and only a few report long-term follow-up data (at least 1 year). Thus, there is a great need for further research on most types of specific phobias, both in order to evaluate current treatments for those phobias for which outcome studies are lacking and to develop new treatment methods.

REFERENCES

American Psychiatric Association (1994). *Diagnostic and Statistical Manual of Mental Disorders*, 4th edn. Washington, DC: American Psychiatric Association.

Arntz, A. & Lavy, E. (1993). Does stimulus elaboration potentiate exposure *in vivo* treatment? Two forms of one-session treatment of spider phobia. *Behavioral Psychotherapy*, **21**, 1–12.

Bandura, A., Adams, N.E. & Beyer, J. (1977). Cognitive processes mediating behavioral change. *Journal of Personality and Social Psychology*, **35**, 125–139.

Bandura, A. & Barab, P.G. (1973). Processes governing disinhibitory effects through symbolic modeling. *Journal of Abnormal Psychology*, **82**, 1–9.

Bandura, A., Blanchard, E.B. & Ritter, B. (1969). Relative efficacy of desensitization and modeling approaches for inducing behavioral, affective, and attitudinal changes. *Journal of Personality and Social Psychology*, **13**, 173–199.

Bandura, A., Jeffery, R.W. & Gajdos, E. (1975). Generalizing change through participant modeling with self-directed mastery. *Behaviour Research and Therapy*, **13**, 141–152.

Bandura, A., Jeffery, R.W. & Wright, C.L. (1974). Efficacy of participant modeling as a function of response aids. *Journal of Abnormal Psychology*, **83**, 56–64.

Booth, R. & Rachman, S. (1992). The reduction of claustrophobia—I. *Behaviour Research and Therapy*, **30**, 207–221.

Bourque, P. & Ladouceur, R. (1980). An investigation of various performance-based treatments with acrophobics. *Behaviour Research and Therapy*, **18**, 161–170.

Emmelkamp, P.M.G. & Felten, M. (1985). The process of exposure *in vivo*: cognitive and physiological changes during treatment of acrophobia. *Behaviour Research and Therapy*, **23**, 219–223.

Hellström, K. & Öst, L-G. (1995). One-session therapist-directed exposure vs. two forms or manual-directed self-exposure in the treatment of spider phobia. *Behaviour Research and Therapy*, **33**, 959–965.

Hellström, K., Fellenius, J. & Öst, L-G. (1996). One vs. five sessions of applied tension in the treatment of blood phobia. *Behaviour Research and Therapy*, **34**, 101–112.

Jacobson, N.S., Follette, W.C. & Revenstorf, D. (1984). Psychotherapy outcome research: methods for reporting variability and evaluating clinical significance. *Behavior Therapy*, **15**, 336–352.

Marks, I.M. (1978). *Living with Fear*. New York: McGraw-Hill.

Marshall, W.L. (1985). The effects of variable exposure in flooding therapy. *Behavior Therapy*, **16**, 117–135.

Morris, R.J. & Magrath, K.H. (1979). Contribution of therapist to the contact desensitization treatment of acrophobia. *Journal of Consulting and Clinical Psychology*, **47**, 786–788.

Moses, A.N. III & Hollandsworth, J.G. Jr (1985). Relative effectiveness of education alone vs. stress inoculation training in the treatment of dental phobia. *Behavior Therapy*, **16**, 531–537.

Öst, L-G. (1989a). One-session treatment for specific phobias. *Behaviour Research and Therapy*, **27**, 1–7.

Öst, L-G. (1989b). A maintenance program for behavioral treatment of anxiety disorders. *Behaviour Research and Therapy*, **27**, 123–130.

Öst, L-G. (1996). One-session group treatment for spider phobics. *Behaviour Research and Therapy*, **34**, 707–715.

Öst, L-G., Fellenius, J. & Sterner, U. (1991). Applied tension, exposure *in vivo*, and tension-only in the treatment of blood phobia. *Behaviour Research and Therapy*, **29**, 561–574.

Öst, L-G, Ferebee, I. & Furmark, T. (1997). Direct vs. indirect group treatment of spider phobia. Manuscript submitted for publication.

Öst, L-G., Alm, T., Brandberg, M. & Breitholtz, E. (1997). One vs. five sessions of exposure and cognitive therapy in the treatment of claustrophobia. Manuscript in preparation.

Öst, L-G., Brandberg, M. & Alm, T. (1997). One vs. five sessions of exposure in the treatment of flying phobia. Manuscript submitted for publication.

Öst, L-G., Hellström, K. & Kåver, A. (1992). One vs. five sessions of exposure in the treatment of injection phobia. *Behavior Therapy*, **23**, 263–282.

Öst, L-G., Salkovskis, P.M. & Hellström, K. (1991). One-session therapist-directed exposure vs. self-exposure in the treatment of spider phobia. *Behavior Therapy*, **22**, 407–422.

Öst, L-G. & Sterner, U. (1987). Applied tension. A specific behavioral method for treatment of blood phobia. *Behaviour Research and Therapy*, **25**, 25–29.

Öst, L-G., Sterner, U. & Fellenius, J. (1989). Applied tension, applied relaxation, and the combination in the treatment of blood phobia. *Behaviour Research and Therapy*, **27**, 109–121.

Ritter, B. (1969a). Treatment of acrophobia with contact desensitization. *Behaviour Research and Therapy*, **7**, 41–45.

Ritter, B. (1969b). The use of contact desensitization, demonstration-plus-participation and demonstration-alone in the treatment of acrophobia. *Behaviour Research and Therapy*, **7**, 157–164.

Williams, S.L., Dooseman, G. & Kleifeld, E. (1984). Comparative effectiveness of guided mastery and exposure treatments for intractable phobias. *Journal of Consulting and Clinical Psychology*, **52**, 505–518.

Williams, S.L., Turner, S.M. & Peer, D.F. (1985). Guided mastery and performance desensitization treatments for severe acrophobia. *Journal of Consulting and Clinical Psychology*, **53**, 237–247.

Chapter 13

A Comparison of Behavioral and Cognitive Treatments of Phobias

Michelle G. Craske
and
Melissa K. Rowe
Department of Psychology, University of California at Los Angeles, CA, USA

This chapter compares behavioral and cognitive approaches to the treatment of specific phobias, social phobia and agoraphobia. Comparisons are made in terms of theoretical bases, methods, mechanisms and treatment efficacy. The chapter concludes with methodological issues and directions for future research.

THEORETICAL BASIS OF TREATMENT

Behavioral

Behavioral treatments are based largely on classical conditioning theories of fear acquisition, which are reviewed by Davey in this series. In brief, classical conditioning is consistent with the clear association often made between phobia onset and a traumatic incident (e.g. Öst, 1985; Öst & Hugdahl, 1981, 1983)[1]. However, this model is inadequate for the many occasions when specific traumatic incidents are not recalled (e.g. Kleinknecht, 1982; Menzies & Clarke, 1995; Murray & Foote, 1979; Rimm et al., 1977), and traumatic experiences that do not lead to

---

[1] Barlow (1988) argues that unexpected fear in response to previously neutral stimuli serves as a traumatic unconditional stimulus.

Phobias—A Handbook of Theory, Research and Treatment. Edited by G.C.L. Davey.
© 1997 John Wiley & Sons Ltd.

phobias (e.g. DiNardo, Guzy & Bak, 1988). Furthermore, as summarized by Rachman (1990), the original conditioning model was unable to account for difficulty generating phobic fear via aversive laboratory procedures in humans, non-randomness of phobic stimuli, and fear of objects that were never experienced directly.

The revived behavioral theory (e.g. Mackintosh, 1983) relies less on contiguity and more on the provision of information about probable causes of events of significance (Rachman, 1990). Hence, effects such as latent inhibition and blocking help to explain differential patterns of phobia development following the same traumatic event. That is, impact of traumas is dependent on prior learning histories with relevant stimuli. Furthermore, current theorizing recognizes preparedness of stimuli (e.g. Seligman, 1971; Öhman, 1986) and individual differences (unrelated to learning histories with phobic stimuli) that predispose towards the development of phobias. The latter include Eysenck's (1987) biologically-based construct of neuroticism, and early experience with control over appetitive events as a buffer against the later expression of fear (Mineka, Gunnar & Champoux, 1986).

Nevertheless, phobias of objects that were never encountered remain problematic for classical condtioning theory. Hence, Rachman (1978) suggested three pathways of fear acquisition; direct trauma (i.e. classical conditioning), vicarious observation and informational transmission. Vicarious acquisition is supported by clinical observations and animal experimentation (e.g. Mineka et al., 1984).[2] Informational transmission is supported by effects of warnings from significant others and phobias that develop in the absence of direct or vicarious experience with the object (Rachman, 1990).

Another behavioral theory emphasizes skill deficiency, real or perceived. For example, Trower, Bryant & Argyle (1978) argued that social phobia emerged from deficits in socially skilled responses that lead to undesired outcomes and distress in social situations. Also, Bandura (1977) suggests that fears derive from low self-efficacy, or perceived inability to manage an encounter with the stimulus, although self-efficacy theory is more relevant to behavior change than etiology.

In summary, while behavioral theories of phobias recognize predisposing vulnerabilities, they are largely associative in nature, emphasizing specific learning experiences (e.g. classical conditioning) or response deficits in relation to specific stimuli. Consequently, behavioral treatments for phobias emphasize "unlearning of associations".

Cognitive

The cognitive approach stemmed from recognition of characteristic patterns of thinking in anxious patients that reflect perceptions of harm or danger. For example, patients with panic disorder and agoraphobia are more likely to per-

---

[2] Mineka (1987) views vicarious acquisition as a form of classical conditioning; observing others undergo trauma or fear serves as an unconditional stimulus.

ceive danger in relation to ambiguous physical symptoms than non-anxious controls, as are socially phobic patients in relation to ambiguous social cues (see review by Cameron, this volume). Basically, conscious and unconscious interpretations are assumed to generate anxiety. Only recently have cognitive theories been applied to specific phobias (e.g. Booth & Rachman, 1992; Thorpe & Salkovskis, 1995). In support, specific phobics tend to appraise phobic stimuli and responses as dangerous (DiNardo, Guzy & Bak, 1988; McNally & Steketee, 1985; Thorpe & Salkovskis, 1995).

Beck (1976) states that biases in information processing (i.e. decoding, encoding, retrieval, attention and interpretation) arise from specific beliefs incorporated into relatively stable structures (i.e. schemata or abstract organizational processes) and cause dysfunctional behavior and emotions. That is, three levels of cognition and identified. First are automatic, surface-level appraisals, sometimes arising spontaneously, that lead directly to emotional and behavioral reaction, are often fleeting and may not be recognized. Schemata refer to a set of underlying assumptions, or internal models of aspects of the self and the world, that guide interpretations and other aspects of information-processing. Schemata of danger and threat (i.e. anxiety) are universal because they are adaptive, but become more strongly developed in some individuals due to particular developmental experiences. Third are cognitive distortions that link schemata and automatic thoughts, such as over-generalizing, selective abstraction and so on (Robins & Hayes, 1993). Other cognitive approaches are proposed by Ellis (1962, 1993), who emphasizes irrational beliefs, and Meichenbaum (1977), who emphasizes internal self-dialogue about ongoing tasks.

Schema models contrast with associative network models. Bower (1981) posits that emotions are represented by nodes in memory space. Nodes related to similar concepts share associative connections. Associative networks account for phenomena such as mood-congruency in memory, attention and interpretation. Lang (1979) proposed an associative network theory of fear, called bioinformational theory. Fear is represented in a mental structure that consists of three major components; information about the feared stimulus, usual responses to the stimulus, and meanings attached to the stimulus and response. Structures are pathological to the extent that responses are excessive, structures are resistant to change, and/or the danger or valence associated with stimuli or responses is overestimated.

Macleod & Mathews (1991) point out that schema-based models reflect top-down processing, in which cognitive processing is organized by higher memory structures. In contrast, network models reflect bottom-up processing, that relies on activation by specific stimuli (e.g. stimuli, responses or cognitions that match elements of a fear structure). In addition, MacLeod & Mathews (1991) note that schema concepts are more consistent with long-term trait anxiety, whereas network concepts are more consistent with state anxiety effects. Also, schema concepts are more consistent with non-associative theories, whereas network concepts are more consistent with associative/behavioral theories of phobias.

With the exception of associative network models, cognitive accounts of phobias generally fail to explain the development of "danger" cognitions around certain objects and not others. That is, schema-based models refer to tendencies to perceive threat and danger, and do not elaborate on associations with specific phobic stimuli. Together, behavioral and cognitive models provide a comprehensive etiological account of phobias; that is, cognitive models account mostly for vulnerabilities, while behavioral models account best for which stimulus becomes the object of fear. Both approaches account for maintenance of phobias; safety signals and perceived inability to cope (from the behavioral perspective), and appraisals of danger (from the cognitive perspective) all predict continued fear and avoidance (Craske & Barlow, 1988).

METHODS OF TREATMENT

Behavioral

Following directly from behavioral theories, behavioral treatments for phobias emphasize (a) extinction of conditional responses, and (b) mastery development. Conditioning theory led to a set of procedures called exposure therapy, characterized by systematic and repeated confrontation with phobic stimuli until fear reduces. Extinction is enhanced by lengthy exposure and removal of safety signals.

There are several variations in the way exposure is conducted. These include: (a) imaginal vs. *in vivo* (in real life) and, most recently, virtual reality; (b) graded (progressing from the least to the most feared) vs. intense (sometimes referred to as flooding therapy, or exposure to most intensely feared stimuli for protracted lengths of time); (c) massed (e.g. once every day for several weeks) vs. spaced (e.g. once every week for several months); (d) with the aid of a therapist/other person (who may serve as an initial safety signal to promote more exposure, and whose presence is gradually withdrawn to facilitate independence) vs. self-directed (perhaps with manualized aid); and (e) continuation of each exposure trial until fear diminishes vs. termination of trials at the point of heightened anxiety, followed by re-exposure after anxiety has subsided.

Wolpe's (1958) systematic desensitization also involves exposure to feared stimuli. Individuals progress through increasingly more anxiety-provoking imagined encounters with phobic stimuli, while utilizing relaxation as a reciprocal inhibitor of rising anxiety. As relaxation is intended to compete with and inhibit the anxiety response, it is essential that anxiety remains weak, hence the value of a graded format.

While proponents of self-efficacy theory rely heavily on *in vivo* exposure to overcome phobias, their approach emphasizes skills and mastery acquisition vs. extinction of conditional fear. Hence, the term "guided mastery therapy" is used in place of exposure therapy (Williams, 1990). Performance accomplishment provides the most potent evidence of one's capabilities, in contrast to vicarious experience, imaginal practice or self-talk (Bandura, 1977). Therefore, the therapist's role is to promote performance success. Duration or level of anxiety during exposure are relatively unemphasized. Williams (1990) lists the following mastery induction methods during exposure: therapists perform tasks jointly with patients, model approach to tasks, set subtasks to be accomplished sequentially, graduate tasks and treatment settings, and provide physical and mechanical support. Proficiency and flexibility of performance are enhanced by helping patients to abandon defensive rituals (e.g. holding the rail of a balcony) and varying performance (e.g. walking over a bridge in a variety of different ways). Independence of performance is fostered by using the least assistance needed, withdrawing assistance as soon as possible, and training patients to be their own therapists.

Other behavioral treatments include social skills and assertiveness training for social anxiety and agoraphobia. Skills such as giving and receiving compliments, requesting information and refusing requests are taught through instruction, modelling, roleplay and feedback. Whereas Wolpe (1990) construes these skills as reciprocal inhibitors of fear, others propose a response deficit correction model (e.g. McFall & Marston, 1970). Finally, relaxation techniques, such as applied relaxation training and breathing retraining, constitute additional behavioral methods. Relaxation is rarely used for phobias without being incorporated as a coping technique or reciprocal inhibitor for exposure.

Cognitive

Following directly from cognitive theory, cognitive therapy assumes that emotions are based on cognitive processes that can be corrected or manipulated via conscious reasoning. For example, Ellis" (1993) rational–emotive therapy assumes that actively and directly disputing negative self-statements (or core irrational beliefs) is effective, especially when patients are taught ways of disputing their own statements. In self-instruction training, Meichenbaum (1975) modifies internal dialogues to include coping, task-oriented (i.e. preparing, confronting, coping and reinforcing) self-statements. Beck (1993) targets dysfunctional beliefs and faulty information-processing in what is generally referred to as cognitive therapy. Beck's treatment follows a course of collaborative empiricism, in which patient and therapist work together to identify and label errors in thinking, evaluate the evidence, and generate alternative, more realistic hypotheses. Through hypothesis testing and socratic questioning, patients are helped to make guided discoveries and design behavioral experiments to test the validity of automatic thoughts and assumptions. Various strategies are used to evaluate hypotheses, such as questioning of probabilities. Also, therapists assume the role of educator.

Paradoxical intention is a less frequently utilized cognitive approach. Patients are instructed to exaggerate and magnify their fears, so that, paradoxically, their fears lose strength and meaning. The exaggeration is intended to bring humor to the situation (Frankl, 1960).

Most cognitive therapies employ behavioral techniques, including exposure to feared situations, as a vehicle for testing and modifying beliefs. Recognition of behavioral experience as possibly the most powerful means of modifying cognitions leads to an inevitable overlap between cognitive and behavioral treatment methods (although with different intents). Chambless & Gillis (1993) note that it is rare for cognitive therapies to omit exposure in the treatment of anxiety disorders.

MECHANISMS OF TREATMENT

Behavioral Treatments

Although behavioral treatments developed from conditioning and mastery models, various theories of fear reduction exist. Some theories incorporate cognitive mediation but they are described in this section because they pertain to behavioral treatment methods.

Habituation

Habituation was first applied to fear reduction through exposure therapy by Lader & Wing (1966). The term "habituation" refers simply to reduction in response strength with repeated stimulus presentations. Theories of underlying processes include Groves & Thompsons" (1970) dual-process theory. They suggest that observed behavior reflects the summation of habituation and sensitization (or increased responding to repeated stimulation). Habituation is located in the S–R pathway, whereas sensitization is related to the state or general responsiveness of the organism. Wagner (1976) proposed an information-processing model of habituation. Mackintosh (1987) concluded that comparator theories, such as Wagner's, have not been empirically supported and are best considered as metaphors. Instead, the evidence supports habituation as residing in S–R pathways.

Support for the role of habituation in exposure therapy includes the finding that specific phobics who show more physiological habituation during exposure achieve a better outcome overall than non-habituators (Lang, Melamed & Hart, 1970; Marshall, 1988). Also, a number of independent variables effect habituation and fear reduction during exposure in the same way; depressant drugs, level of arousal, rate of stimulation, attenuation of stimuli, regularity of presentation, and complexity of stimuli (Rachman, 1990). Finally, dishabituation provides a good account for return of fear (i.e. partial increase of fear following successful fear reduction). However, there are a number of limitations. Rachman (1990) summarized these concerns as: persistence of some fears despite repeated stimulus presentation, and efficacy of flooding therapy (given that habituation is impeded by intense stimuli). Also habituation is generally regarded as a transient process that naturally dishabituates after an interval without stimulus exposure;

dishabituation contrasts with long-term effects of exposure. Although, Mackintosh (1987) argues that long-term habituation occurs via conditioning of habituated reactions to contextual stimuli. Barlow (1988) and Rachman (1990) note that habituation does not account well for desynchrony, or weak correlations, between verbal reports and physiological responding in fear reduction and return of fear. Finally, fear reduction is context-specific (see below), whereas habituation is not (Marks & Tobena, 1990).

Extinction

Extinction refers to decrements in responding through repetition of unreinforced responding. That is, a non-fearful pairing is generated through repeated encounters with feared stimuli without aversive consequences. Extinction accounts are supported by the finding that a single lengthy exposure session is generally more effective than a series of short exposures for the same total duration (e.g. Marshall, 1985).

However, the nature of the non-fearful pairing is unclear (i.e. what is learned?) as are the reinforcers (i.e. external threat or fear itself?). Also, sometimes fear does not reduce with repeated unreinforced exposure. Furthermore, the efficacy of exposure treatment in which subjects escape when fear becomes unduly high (i.e. controlled escape; Rachman et al., 1986) is not consistent with extinction.

Bouton and colleagues (Bouton & Swartzentruber, 1991; Bouton, 1993) proposed an interesting reconceptualization of "what is learned" during extinction. The original *excitatory meaning* of the conditional stimulus is not erased during extinction, but rather an additional *inhibitory meaning* is learned. The consequent dual meaning of the conditional stimulus creates an ambiguity which is resolved only by the current context of the conditional stimulus (e.g. a snake may mean danger in the wild and non-danger in the clinic). This conceptual development recognizes the context dependency of extinction, and is supported by extensive animal experimentation, although it awaits empirical investigation in human samples. Contexts include environmental factors (e.g. presence of therapist, location of exposure), internal sensations and mood states, drug states, and time. Thus, instead of viewing return of fear as simple spontaneous recovery from extinction, Bouton and colleagues postulate that return of fear represents contextual retrieval of fearful learning. Treatment implications include lengthy exposure to the full variety of contexts in which fear has been experienced, including that in which fear acquisition occurred, and exposure in a wide variety of naturalistic settings.

Endogenous Opioids

Release of endogenous opioids in response to fear may reinforce approach behavior and thereby promote extinction, or reduce the aversiveness of exposure, or directly increase approach behavior because endorphins have been shown to increase exploratory behavior (Merluzzi et al., 1991). In support, Egan et al. (1988) found that pharmacological blockade of endogenous opioids, via naloxone, impeded imaginal exposure relative to saline, in a group of six specific phobics. However, Merluzzi et al.'s (1991) larger study only partially replicated these findings. They found that naltrexone, another opioid antagonist, resulted in higher maximum heart-rate and more time to complete the tenth approach task in spider phobics, in comparison to placebo. However, there were no differences in average heart-rate or blood pressure. The paucity of evidence in this area precludes definitive conclusions regarding the function of endogenous opioids during exposure.

Emotional Processing

Foa & Kozak (1986) extended the notion of emotional processing initially pro-posed by Rachman (1980). They refer to habituation and cognitive change to explain "what is learned" during exposure. Using Lang's (1979) bioinformational model, Foa & Kozak (1986) hypothesized two necessary conditions for fear reduction: full activation of the fear structure, and incorporation of new material that is incompatible with the old structure. The most effective method for activat-ing fear structures is direct exposure to feared stimuli. With repeated exposure, incompatible information is derived from short-term physiological habituation that dissociates stimulus and response (i.e. recognition that the stimulus can occur in the absence of arousal). With multiple exposures, between-session ha-bituation occurs as well, due to changes in the meaning of the stimulus and response (i.e. risk of harm is lowered and affective valence becomes less nega-tive). That is, outcome expectancies are altered. Consequently, procedures that interfere with access to fear structures or integration of new information may mitigate exposure effects. Foa & Kozak (1986) suggest that such interference would arise from distraction, excessively high or very low levels of anxious arousal, or overly brief exposure durations, each of which have received some support. However, the data are contradictory. For example, Rodriguez & Craske (1995) found that distraction interfered with fear reduction during high-intensity exposures only, and earlier studies on the effects of distraction are contradictory and methodologically confusing (Rodriguez & Craske, 1993).

Most support for emotional processing derives from analogue research with specific fears, although recent studies with obsessive–compulsive disorder provide additional evidence (e.g. Kozak, Foa & Steketee, 1988). The model faces several difficulties, such as return of fear; it is unclear why fear structures, once modified, would return to their original state. Relatedly, the notion that fear structures are dismantled contrasts with evidence for the permanence of long-term memory (e.g. Klatsky, 1980). Generation of an additional non-fear structure is, perhaps, more likely than modification of an original fear structure. Also, emotional processing suffers the criticisms levelled at habituation earlier, and does not account for controlled escape exposure (e.g. Rachman et al., 1986), in which physiological habituation and information about the harmlessness of high anxiety are mini-mized. Moreover, Barlow (1988) notes that emotional processing does not fully account for significant improvements in behavioral and self-reported functioning, despite unaffected levels of physiological arousal. On the other hand, the cognitive changes proposed by emotional processing theory regarding dangerousness of the stimulus and likelihood of anxiety, have received empirical support (see below).

Self-efficacy

According to self-efficacy theory, therapeutic gains are dependent on the degree to which self-efficacy, or confidence to perform a certain task, is generated (Bandura, 1977). Note that self-efficacy is theoretically distinct from outcome expectancies. Extinction models are criticized for failing to explain why individuals respond differently to the same amount of exposure. It is noteworthy that self-efficacy is the only theory in this section that provides a mechanism for behavioral treatments other than exposure, such as skills and mastery training.

Several studies have shown that self-efficacy predicts treatment outcome (e.g. Williams, Dooseman & Kleifeld, 1984—height and driving phobics; Williams, Turner & Peer, 1985—height phobics; Williams, Kinney & Falbo, 1989—agoraphobics; Borden, Clum & Salmon, 1991—agoraphobics). Moreover, Williams and colleagues have shown that self-efficacy is predictive of treatment outcome regardless of treatment method, even after controlling outcome expectations of danger or anxiety, across targeted and non-targeted phobic stimuli.

Self-efficacy theory can account for the success of controlled escape exposure which minimizes the experience of high anxiety (e.g. Rachman et al., 1986). However, the theory has been criticized for being tautological and epiphenomenal (Borkovec, 1978; Teasdale, 1978). In addition, self-efficacy has not been well separated from other influences such as skills and incentives (Kazdin, 1978). Furthermore, Rachman (1990) describes an example of fearfulness accompanied by confidence and courage in war situations, or simultaneous self-efficacy and fear, thus contradicting the tenets of self-efficacy theory. Finally, Barlow (1988) notes that self-efficacy is more predictive of performance than anxiety, and has difficulty accounting for response desynchrony.

Predictive Accuracy

Recently, Rachman and colleagues emphasized cognitive mediation of exposure via accuracy of fear estimations (Rachman & Levitt, 1985; Rachman, Levitt & Lopatka, 1988; Rachman & Lopatka, 1986). That is, anxiety expectancies are altered. They and others (e.g. Telch et al., 1994) have found that phobics typically overestimate fear or likelihood of panicking in specific situations. These estimates in turn predict avoidance, and avoidance reduces disconfirmatory opportunities (Rachman, 1994). Furthermore, one trial of unexpected fear/panic tends to increase the expectancy that fear/panic will occur in subsequent exposures. Therefore, overpredictions of fear are believed to maintain phobic fear and avoidance (Rachman & Bichard, 1988). Therapeutic effects are believed to be due to disconfirmation of overpredictions, because predictions become more accurate with repeated exposures (Rachman & Lopatka, 1986). Relatedly, Kirsch (1985) proposed that anticipation of one's own reactions is self-fulfilling, and that exposure functions by providing experiential feedback that confirms expectancies of fear reduction.

However, van Hout & Emmelkamp (1994) failed to confirm increased accuracy of predictions with exposure, and actual fear reduced regardless of matches or mismatches between predicted and actual fear levels. Therefore, while it is clear that fearful individuals overpredict and that overpredictions may increase fear and avoidance, it is not clear that increased accuracy of predictions explains the effects of exposure therapy.

Cognitive Treatments

Cognitive theorists hypothesize that treatment is effective to the degree that information-processing distortions and underlying tacit beliefs and assumptions are altered (the overlap with aspects of emotional processing, self-efficacy and predictive accuracy accounts of behavioral treatments is noteworth). In addition, some have argued that behavioral treatments may be insufficient to alter cognitions (Butler et al., 1984). Therefore, we reviewed (a) the degree to which treatment outcome is a function of cognitive modification, and (b) the degree to which cognitive therapy leads to more cognitive modification than behavior therapy.

Cognitive Mediation of Treatment Effects

Evidence to suggest that cognitive modification predicts outcome from treatment is accruing. For example, measures of catastrophic thinking about panic predict outcome in terms of panic attacks and agoraphobic avoidance, regardless of treatment modality (Chambless & Gracely, 1988; Clark et al., 1994; Margraf & Schneider, 1991; Michelson, Marchione & Greenwarld, 1989). Also, Clark et al. (1994) found that cognitive status at post-treatment was more predictive of follow-up status than other post-treatment measures.

In terms of social phobia, Mattia, Heimberg & Hope (1993) showed that responders to either cognitive–behavioral treatment, medications or placebo had significant reductions in Stroop response latencies for threat words, whereas treatment non-responders did not. Notably, this effect was limited to social-threat words, showing specificity of treatment effects. Also, several studies show that changes in Fear of Negative Evaluation and/or Irrational Beliefs Test scores predict outcome for social phobics treated with either cognitive therapy, behavioral therapy or their combination (Hope, Heimberg & Bruch, 1989; Mattick & Peters, 1988; Mattick, Peters & Clarke, 1989). Indeed, changes in Fear of Negative Evaluation account for most outcome variance. On the other hand, Mattick, Peters & Clarke (1989) note that approximately 65% of outcome variance was unexplained, suggesting that factors other than cognitive modification are important also.

In terms of specific phobias, Shafran, Booth & Rachman (1993) found that reductions in negative cognitions correlated with claustrophobic fear reduction, and return of fear correlated with increases in negative cognitions (collapsing across cognitive therapy, *in vivo* exposure and interoceptive exposure). Furthermore, Shafran, Booth & Rachman (1993) suggest that certain key cognitions exist (e.g. "suffocation"). Similarly, Rachman (1993) proposed that critical cognitions must be modified for treatment success.

Rachman & Whittal (1989) noted instances of very abrupt changes in fearfulness during treatment (10 of 60 patients). They proposed that these are more characteristic of insight learning than the usual gradual progression of trial-and-error learning. Insight learning may occur as a result of a cognitive shift. That is, cognitive modification does not have to occur gradually, as would be predicted from extinction theory or emotional processing theory.

Despite evidence for cognitive mediation of treatment effects, Rachman (1993) notes the difficulty of establishing a causal role for cognitions. That is, do cognitions precede or follow fear reduction? This is especially difficult because change is often slow, and may occur between treatment sessions, rendering observation of the sequence of events problematic. Furthermore, measures of cognitive change are mostly limited to self-reports that are subject to responder bias and may confound cognitions with anxiety in general. For example, Feske & Chambless (1995) suggest that Fear of Negative Evaluation is more a measure of anxiety than cognitions.

Nevertheless, Rachman (1993) concludes that there is no plausible alternative to the cognitive explanation for cognitive therapy. Others (e.g. Boyd & Levis, 1983; Marks, 1987) argue that by discussing and imagining feared stimuli, cognitive therapy represents a degraded form of exposure, that allows processes of habituation, extinction and mastery to occur. Even degraded forms of exposure are capable of activating cohesive fear structures, according to bioinformational and emotional-processing theories (Foa & Kozak, 1986; Lang, 1979). Furthermore, cognitive therapy can be couched within conditioning terms of unconditioned stimulies (UCS) revaluation (Davey, 1992). That is, conditioned responses (CSs) are reduced when UCSs are devalued by socially or verbally transmitted information about the UCS (e.g. information to suggest that the UCS is unlikely to recur, or altered outcome expectancies) or through re-evaluating reactions to the UCS or CS (e.g. strengthening of self-efficacy) (Cracknell & Davey, 1988; White & Davey, 1989). The overlap between conditioning and cognitive models is very apparent from this perspective.

Finally, Robins & Hayes" (1993) question "if cognitions are responsible for treatment outcome, what exactly has changed?" For example, does the schema alter (as suggested by emotional processing theory and cognitive theory)? Is a new schema generated (as suggested indirectly by Bouton's context specificity model)? Or are compensatory skills taught to deal with the schema (as suggested by self-efficacy theory)?

Cognitive Change through Cognitive vs. Behavioral Therapy

Most evidence suggests that cognitions are changed to the same degree by behavioral and cognitive treatments. For example, Emmelkamp et al. (1986), Michelson, Marchione & Greenwald (1989) and Williams & Rappoport (1983) found that cognitive therapy vs. exposure or relaxation for agoraphobia did not differ in terms of cognitive outcome measures. However, the effects may have been mitigated by poorly implemented cognitive treatments, and sometimes the cognitive change was very small (e.g. Emmelkamp et al., 1986).

In terms of social phobia, several studies found no cognitive differences at post-treatment between cognitive and behavioral treatments (Mattick & Peters, 1988; Mattick, Peters & Clarke, 1989; Shahar & Merbaum, 1981), although, Mattick, Peters & Clarke (1989) found more within-group change and more improvement on cognitive measures at follow-up from cognitive treatment. On the other hand, Emmelkamp et al. (1985) and Butler et al. (1984) found that exposure therapy did not produce cognitive changes. From their review of 15 social phobia studies, Feske & Chambless (1995) concluded that there was generally no difference in cognitive outcome between cognitive–behavioral therapy vs. exposure alone. However, they note that cognitive therapy may require more therapist training than exposure therapy, and studies to date have not assessed treatment adherence or competency sufficiently to know whether more competent cognitive therapists achieve more cognitive change than equally competent exposure therapists.

With respect to specific phobias, Booth & Rachman (1992) found that *in vivo* exposure, interoceptive exposure, and cognitive therapy for claustrophobia were equally effective at post-treatment and follow-up in terms of cognitive change (note that the treatment was three sessions only). In contrast, Emmelkamp & Felten (1985) compared one session of exposure alone with exposure plus self-instruction training for acrophobics. While both treatments reduced heart rate and increased performance, exposure alone did not change cognitions, whereas the combination treatment did. However, one-session treatment limits the value of these data.

Booth & Rachman (1992) note that the challenge for cognitive theorists is to explain the success of exposure therapy that is conducted without cognitive therapy. Rachman (1993) provides an explanation: ". . . with each exposure, the patient acquires fresh, disconfirmatory evidence (e.g. no heart attack, did not lose control). The accumulation of this personal, direct, disconfirmatory evidence weakens the catastrophic cognitions" (p. 282). The overlap with emotional processing and self-efficacy theories is obvious; that is, cognitive change occurs as a result of experience, without the need for direct cognitive intervention strategies. However, it remains to be shown whether the exposure experience changes cognitions and thereby lessens anxiety, or whether lessened anxiety renders such cognitions less likely to arise (Rachman, 1993).

A final difficulty for cognitive theories is desynchrony; how can changes in behavioral or physiological reactions be explained if unaccompanied by changes in cognitions, as was found by Emmelkamp & Felten (1985)? Conversely, how can relative absence of behavioral change be explained when cognitive shifts have occurred, as was found by Emmelkamp et al. (1985) and Mattick, Peters & Clarke (1989)? It is probably unlikely that a single construct explains fear reduction. Different responses may be effected by different processes. For example, Rachman (1978) suggested that behavioral responses are most influenced by extinction, as are physiological responses by habituation, and self-report/cognitive responses by both mechanisms. The relevance of cognitive modification for behavioral vs. physiological vs. self-report response domains awaits further investigation.

SUMMARY OF THEORETICAL BASES, METHODS, AND MECHANISMS

The clearest difference between behavioral and cognitive approaches to the treatment of phobias lies in the theoretical basis, with the former emphasizing associative experiences and (perceived or real) response deficits in relation to specific stimuli, and the latter emphasizing general tendencies to perceive threat. Methods and proposed mechanims underlying each treatment approach overlap considerably. Behavioral methods aim to weaken specific associations by repeated exposure to feared stimuli and/or development of skills for managing phobic stimuli, whereas cognitive methods aim to change appraisals about phobic stimuli and responses. The methods overlap because cognitive therapy makes use of direct experience with phobic stimuli to garner disconfirming evidence, and behavioral therapy provides information about phobic stimuli via direct experience. The proliferation of theories for fear reduction through exposure therapy indicates lack of satisfaction with the original extinction and response-deficit correction models. Recent theories of exposure effects incorporate cognitive mediation in the form of outcome expectancies regarding dangerousness of phobic stimuli (emotional processing theory), expectancies of anxiety (emotional processing and predictive accuracy), and self-efficacy. These clearly overlap with cognitive theories of fear reduction. Evidence supports the role of cognitive mediation in fear reduction, regardless of whether treatment is primarily behaviorally or cognitively oriented. Remaining issues include: (a) does cognitive modification precede or follow anxiety reduction?; (b) how to account for response desynchrony?; and (c) what exactly is modified (i.e. a schema?, a network of associations?).

TREATMENT EFFICACY

In this section, we review controlled treatment outcome studies (i.e. random assignment and comparisons to wait-list, placebo, or alternative treatments) for clinically diagnosed samples (unless otherwise specified) of specific phobia, social phobia and agoraphobia. Regardless of whether samples included patients with agoraphobia or not, investigations that targeted treatment of panic disorder were not included in this review. For each type of phobia, we review treatment efficacy for: (a) behavioral and cognitive treatments; (b) combination of behavioral and cognitive treatment; and (c) matching of behavioral or cognitive treatment to individual response profiles. Efficacy is examined in terms of statistical change on individual measures and, when available, percentages of improvement and/or achievement of high end-state functioning (i.e. within normal range of functioning).

Treatment Efficacy: Specific Phobias

Specific phobias are rarely the primary reason why individuals seek treatment, although they often accompany diagnoses of other anxiety disorders and depression (Emmelkamp, 1986). Because very few investigations have been conducted with diagnosed populations, this review includes some well-conducted investigations of analog samples. Nevertheless, because of the evidence that analog and diagnosed samples differ considerably in terms of severity of complaints, concomitant psychopathology (Emmelkamp, 1986) and cognitions (Last & Blanchard, 1982), the generalizability of some of these investigations must be carefully considered.

Efficacy of Behavioral and Cognitive Treatments

Much of the research compares different types of behavioral treatments. Although systematic desensitization and flooding in imagery demonstrated efficacy in early treatment studies of specific phobias (e.g. Marks, Boulougouris & Marset, 1971), imaginal procedures were consistently less effective (e.g. Barlow et al., 1969; Crowe et al., 1972; Dyckman & Cowan, 1978; McReynolds & Grizzard, 1971). Matthews (1978) concluded that direct exposure is always superior in the treatment of specific phobias. However, Hecker (1990) demonstrated equivalent effectiveness for imaginal and *in vivo* exposure in an analogue sample of snake phobics. At post-treatment, groups were equivalent on three of four self-report measures of fear and avoidance, and did not differ on behavioral approach performance.

Williams, Turner & Peer (1985) compared *in vivo* desensitization to *in vivo* guided mastery. Both groups of acrophobics were accompanied by a therapist and practiced confronting a series of increasing heights in which they were instructed to look over a railing for brief intervals. The desensitization group were instructed to approach the railing slowly while remaining calm. Guided mastery subjects were given a variety of therapist aids, such as a more structured approach, encouraging attempts at portions of the task or intermediate goals, physical support when needed, varying the task, and modeling. Not surprisingly, individuals receiving guided mastery demonstrated more fear reduction and more enhancement of self-efficacy. At 1-month follow-up, 54% of mastery subjects performed maximally on behavioral tasks compared to 17% of desensitization subjects. Also, mastery subjects remained significantly less phobic on all five behavioral measures compared to desensitization subjects.

Two types of physiological treatments and their combination were compared for the treatment of blood phobia (Öst, Sterner & Fellenius, 1989). Thirty patients with blood phobia were randomly assigned to either applied tension, applied relaxation (i.e. application of tension or relaxation as coping skills for *in vivo* exposure assignments), or their combination, for five, nine, and 10 sessions respectively. All groups improved significantly on 11 of 12 self-report, behavioral and physiological measures, and there were no differences between groups. At the end of treatment, 73% were clinically improved, as were 77% at follow-up. Öst et al. (1984) had previously compared the combination treatment to exposure *in vivo*. Both treatments produced clinically significant improvements which were maintained at 6-month follow-up, and there were no differences between treatments. Considering the results of both investigations (the only controlled treatment studies of blood phobia), Öst, Sterner & Fellenius (1989) concluded that applied tension should be the treatment of choice for blood phobia, because therapeutic effects were achieved with only five sessions compared to 9–10 sessions required for applied relaxation and combination treatments.

Although some researchers concluded that specific phobias are not treatable via cognitive therapy (Last, 1987; Marks, 1987), evidence now exists to suggest efficacy for cognitive interventions. Booth & Rachman (1992) randomly assigned claustrophobic individuals to *in vivo* exposure, interoceptive exposure, cognitive restructuring or a control group. *In vivo* exposure treatment produced reductions across a variety of measures of fear of the target situation (i.e. a laboratory closet). Although cognitive treatment did not generate as pervasive reductions in fear, this group demonstrated significant reductions in reports of panic and fear, and number and severity of negative cognitions and physical sensations. Interoceptive exposure treatment demonstrated reductions only on measures of negative cognitions and physical sensations. Surprisingly, none of the treatments reduced anxiety sensitivity relative to wait-list control (although this was perhaps due to the brevity of the treatment).

In a recently published investigation of dental phobia (De Jongh et al., 1995), 1 hour of cognitive restructuring and 1 hour of information about oral health and treatment were compared to each other and to a wait-list control. By the end of treatment, cognitive restructuring had led to significant reductions in frequency and believability of negative cognitions, and a drastic reduction in dental trait anxiety. Using dental trait anxiety as the clinical improvement index, 33% of the cognitive group were significantly improved at post-treatment, as were 36% at a 1-month follow-up, and 93% at a 1-year follow-up. Although percentages were not provided for the information and wait-list conditions, the authors stated that the cognitive therapy group was significantly more improved than the other groups post-treatment. Interestingly, by 1-year-follow-up, information and cognitive groups were equivalent on measures of dental anxiety and avoidance. These studies (Booth & Rachman, 1992; De Jonhg et al., 1995) support the efficacy of cognitive therapy for specific phobias.

Efficacy of Combination Treatments

As for other anxiety disorders, recent treatment comparisons focus on potentiating effects of cognitive therapy; that is, to what degree does cognitive therapy enhance outcome from behavioral treatments? Emmelkamp & Felten (1985) found some superiority for a cognitive–behavioral treatment relative to a pure exposure condition. In the combined treatment, acrophobics were supplied with a list of positive self-statements to use every 3 minutes while engaged in an *in vivo* task. Subjects in the exposure-alone condition were not given these statements. The groups improved equally in terms of behavioral approach performance. The combination treatment improved on cognitive measures of positive and negative thoughts and self-reported anxiety, whereas the exposure-alone treatment did not. However, brevity of treatment may have accounted for these results; the exposure-alone group may have achieved equivalent cognitive changes with more time.

In a study of dental phobics, no differences were detected between a combined treatment and a pure behavioral treatment (Getka & Glass, 1992), although both were superior to a wait-list condition. The behavioral treatment consisted of applied relaxation, exposure to videos of dental procedures, and *in vivo* practices. The combination procedure was similar except individuals were instructed in cognitive techniques that were practiced during video-tape viewing. The authors attributed the similar outcomes to the shared treatment components of relaxation, graduated exposure and *in vivo* practice. That is, cognitive techniques did not potentiate the effects derived from exposure and/or relaxation. In a fourth group, patients were assigned to a dentist whom other dentists rated as particularly gentle and understanding of dental anxiety. Although this group was not as improved overall as the two active conditions, it achieved equivalent reductions in pain and negative anticipatory thoughts, and increases in self-efficacy.

Matching

There has been a strong interest in matching individual response profiles to seemingly complementary treatments. Rachman (1978) suggested that the ways in which fears are acquired may predict treatment outcome. Similarly, Wolpe (1981) suggested that fear acquired via classical conditioning responds best to desensitization, flooding, etc., whereas fear based on cognitive learning (observation and information) responds best to cognitive treatment. Wolpe et al. (1985) noted that fear origins can be inferred from response profiles, with classical conditioning leading to more prominent behavioral and physiological responding than cognitive learning, which leads to more subjective responding. Fear origins aside, however, predominance of behavioral, physiological or verbal responding may predict treatment outcome from different treatment approaches.

Öst, Johansson & Jerremalm (1982) divided claustrophobics into behavioral and physiological reactors according to responses to a test situation. Individuals were randomly assigned to either *in vivo* exposure, applied relaxation or a wait-list control condition. Both interventions produced significant improvements compared to the wait-list condition. Furthermore, treatment "matches" led to superior outcomes; behavioral reactors progressed more with exposure treatment and physiological reactors progressed more with applied relaxation. For behavioral reactors, 100% who received exposure, 50% who received applied relaxation and 0% who were wait-listed, were "clinically" improved. Corresponding figures for physiological reactors were 50%, 100% and 0%.

Jerremalm, Jansson & Öst (1986a) attempted to replicate the superiority of matching in a group of dental phobics. Subjects were divided into cognitive reactors and physiological reactors and randomly assigned to either self-instruction training or applied relaxation. Both treatments demonstrated significant reductions in dental anxiety and avoidance across self-report, behavioral and physiological measures. Unfortunately, percentages of clinical improvement were not reported. Unlike the previous investigation (Öst, Johansson & Jerremalm, 1982), results did not support the treatment-matching hypothesis. Jerremalm, Jansson & Öst (1986a) attributed the negative results to an inadequately developed measure of cognitions and the test situation used to categorize individuals as cognitive or physiological reactors. This does not explain the failure to replicate the superior effects found in the physiological reactors/applied relaxation group in the first study (Öst, Johansson & Jerremalm, 1982). Consequently, the authors suggested that cognitive and relaxation techniques both function primarily to distract and calm patients who are receiving dental work, hence leading to undifferentiated effectiveness. A third explanation is that there is no reliable benefit of treatment matching. It is noteworthy that this study also demonstrated the efficacy of a cognitive therapy for specific phobias.

Summary

Despite the potential of other approaches, *in vivo* exposure has been the treatment of choice for specific phobias (Emmelkamp, 1992). A series of investigations in the 1970s clearly demonstrated the superiority of *in vivo* exposure over imaginal procedures, although recent work suggests that they may be equivalent. Cognitive interventions alone have demonstrated some utility, although, according to one study, the effects may be limited to cognitive outcome measures. Results regarding the degree to which cognitive approaches potentiate behavioral approaches are contradictory. Similarly, matching of treatment to individual response profiles has received mixed support, although this area of research may be hindered by cognitive interventions of limited scope.

Treatment Efficacy: Social Phobia

The majority of investigations reviewed in the following section were conducted with individuals diagnosed with generalized social phobia. Studies of behavioral treatments, and systematic desensitization in particular, for public speaking anxiety were not included because the samples did not represent clinically diagnosed individuals. Most studies included self-report measures and behavioral measures of social anxiety and avoidance. Occasionally, physiological measures and clinican ratings are included.

Efficacy of Behavioral and Cognitive Treatments

Although social skills training was at one time a popular treatment for social phobia, the majority of studies did not include clinically diagnosed subjects and/ or did not include a control condition or comparison group. The few controlled investigations of social skills training concerned the effects of treatment matching. Details of these investigations are presented later but to summarize, social skills training has been shown to be as effective as cognitive therapy, exposure therapy and applied relaxation (Mersch et al., 1989; Öst, Jerremalm & Johansson, 1981; Trower et al., 1978). Nevertheless, the current treatment literature reflects a distinct move away from conceptualizing social phobia as a social skills deficit for which social skills training is the treatment of choice (e.g. Rapee, 1993). Some researchers suggest that the efficacy of social skills training is due to the inherent *in vivo* exposure component vs. the acquisition of skills (Heimberg, 1989; Stravynski, Grey & Elie, 1987). Others suggest that it is more useful in the treatment of avoidant personality disorder which, until recently, has not been adequately distinguished from social phobia in treatment outcome literature (Heimberg, 1989).

Emmelkamp et al. (1985) published the first controlled investigation comparing a behavioral treatment (*in vivo* exposure) to two types of cognitive treatment: rational–emotive therapy and self-instruction training. Only the two cognitive approaches produced significant improvement on the Irrational Belief Test. Only the exposure treatment reduced pulse rate during a 5-minute conversation with two confederates. Other than these differences, the groups produced equivalent decreases on various self-report measures of social anxiety and avoidance.

Applied relaxation is rarely studied as a treatment for social phobia, although it has demonstrated some efficacy in the context of treatment-matching investigations detailed later (e.g. Jerremalm, Jansson & Öst, 1986b; Öst, Jerremalm & Johansson, 1981). Heimberg (1989) suggested that applied relaxation may be a valuable tool in the treatment of social phobia that deserves additional development. While it would seem an unlikely candidate as a sole-treatment approach, it may be a useful adjunct given the clear physiological component of social phobia (e.g. Butler et al., 1984).

Although not a controlled investigation, a recent behavioral treatment, social effectiveness therapy (Turner, 1994), demonstrated exceptionally strong efficacy. Social effectiveness therapy is a multicomponent treatment designed to affect various aspects of social phobia via four interrelated components: education, social skills training, *in vivo* and/or imaginal exposure and programmed practice. A particularly interesting feature of the treatment is the combination of individual and group treatment. Education and social skills training are conducted in small groups with two therapists, whereas exposure sessions and programmed practices are conducted individually. Employing a new composite index (Turner, Beidel & Wolff, 1994), 84% of patients showed moderate to high end-state functioning. Two years later (Turner, Beidel & Cooley-Quille, 1995), eight of 13 original completers demonstrated continued improvement on several self-report and clinician-rated measures. End-state functioning was not reported, most likely due to the lack of behavioral data.

Efficacy of Combination Treatments

In 1993, Scholing & Emmelkamp published two investigations that compared the relative efficacy of *in vivo* exposure, rational–emotive therapy, and their combination. In the first study (Scholing & Emmelkamp, 1993a) social phobics with primary fears of blushing, sweating or trembling were randomly assigned to one of three treatment conditions. Half were additionally assigned to a 4-week wait period. The treatment conditions were: (a) *in vivo* exposure followed by cognitive therapy; (b) cognitive therapy followed by *in vivo* exposure; and (c) a cognitive–behavioral treatment that integrated both approaches throughout. At post-treatment and 3-month follow-up, all groups were significantly improved compared to the wait-list condition. None of the treatments demonstrated superior efficacy on target problems, avoidance of social situations, cognitions or somatic complaints.

In the second study, Scholing & Emmelkamp (1993b) compared: (a) 16 sessions of *in vivo* exposure therapy; (b) eight sessions of cognitive therapy followed by eight sessions of *in vivo* exposure; and (c) a 16-session integrated format. Additionally, subjects were randomly assigned to individual or group modality. No significant differences were detected between treatments at post-treatment on subjective, behavioral or cognitive measures of social phobia. At 3-month follow-up, greatest progress was found on cognitive measures in the group treatment with cognitive therapy followed by exposure. Surprisingly, the combination group treatment demonstrated the poorest efficacy. No other differences were detected between groups at follow-up.

Most recently, Mersch (1995) compared *in vivo* exposure therapy to a combination of rational–emotive therapy, social skills training and *in vivo* exposure. Mersch hypothesized that the combined treatment would produce greater and more durable improvements in social cognitions and self-reported anxiety and avoidance. Both treatments demonstrated significant improvement on all variables and were superior to a wait-list condition. Contrary to expectations, the treatments were equally effective in the short term and 18 months later.

Contrary to the above studies, other researchers have found superior results from combined treatments compared to pure behavioral or pure cognitive approaches. Butler et al. (1984) published the first investigation testing the efficacy of *in vivo* exposure treatment for social phobia. The combined treatment group received exposure with anxiety management training (distraction, relaxation and rational self-talk), and the other received exposure with a non-specific treatment filler. Both groups demonstrated significant improvement compared to a wait-list control. The combination treatment demonstrated some superiority over the exposure group at post. At 6-month follow-up, these differences appeared across several measures. Although these results suggested superior efficacy for a combined treatment approach, the comparison was biased in that the exposure group received only half of an "active" treatment. Essentially, this comparison demonstrated that anxiety management was superior to placebo; it did not demonstrate that a combination treatment was superior to a pure exposure treatment.

Mattick & Peters (1988) presented a partial replication of Butler et al. (1984). They compared exposure to a combination of exposure plus cognitive techniques, but their design did not include a placebo filler in place of the cognitive aspect of the combined treatment, allowing individuals in the exposure-alone treatment equal time receiving an active treatment. Utilizing a composite measure of end-state functioning that included self-report, behavioral and cognitive measures of social anxiety and avoidance, Mattick & Peters (1988) concluded that the combination treatment was superior to the exposure treatment. Eighty-one per cent of the combination group, compared to 43% of the exposure group, were functioning in the moderate to very high range 3 months after treatment.

These results were not replicated in an investigation comparing *in vivo* exposure therapy, cognitive therapy and their combination to a wait-list control (Mattick, Peters & Clarke, 1989). In terms of end-state functioning, only 27% of the combination group demonstrated moderate to very high functioning, in contrast to 45% of the cognitive and exposure groups. Interestingly, efficacy of the exposure group appeared to be delayed: improvement occurred only on the behavioral approach test by post-treatment, but improvements were apparent on several other measures by follow-up, with the exception of cognitive self-report scales. The authors concluded that exposure therapy was inferior, given the lack of cognitive shift in comparison to the combination and cognitive therapy groups, thus rendering the results in agreement with their previous study (Mattick & Peters, 1988). Although they recognized the discrepancy between this conclusion and the end-state functioning results, this discrepancy was ultimately dismissed by arguing that the criteria composing end-state were overly stringent.

Heimberg et al. (1990) developed and tested a combination treatment for social phobia against a credible placebo control. Cognitive–behavioral group treatment consisted of exposure to simulated phobic events, cognitive restructuring and self-directed exposure and cognitive restructuring between sessions. The credible placebo condition consisted of lecture-discussion and group support, shown to be comparable to the cognitive–behavioral group treatment on measures of treatment credibility and expectations of treatment outcome. Both groups improved significantly on subjective measures of anxiety and avoidance, a cognitive thought-listing measure, and a behavioral-approach test. Cognitive–behavioral group treatment patients were significantly more improved than the placebo group on the behavioral approach test and reported fewer negative and more positive self-statements on the thought-listing task. Seventy-five per cent of the cognitive–behavioral group were judged to manifest clinically significant improvement, compared to only 40% of the placebo control group.

A 5-year follow-up (Heimberg et al., 1993) demonstrated slightly better maintenance of treatment gains for the cognitive–behavioral group on self-report measures of social phobia and judges' rating of speech performance. However, the groups did not differ in terms of anxiety during the behavioral-approach test or on the thought-listing cognitive measure. Eight of nine cognitive–behavioral group patients were classified as significantly improved, compared to four of nine placebo patients.

In a dismantling study (Hope, Heimberg & Bruch, 1995), the cognitive–behavioral group treatment was compared to exposure-alone and a wait-list condition. As expected, both treatments demonstrated superior efficacy compared to the wait-list group. Unexpectedly, cognitive–behavioral group treatment was not superior to exposure alone. Both produced significant gains across all measures of social phobia. At 6-month follow-up, only 37.5% of cognitive–behavioral group individuals were classified as responders compared to 62.5% of exposure-alone individuals, although this difference was not statistically different. The authors attribute the superiority of the behavioral treatment to an odd lack of effectiveness for cognitive–behavioral group treatment. Considered as a whole, these investigations provide a mixed picture of the efficacy of cognitive–behavioral group treatment. To their credit, Heimberg, Hope and colleagues have tested their treatment against two critical comparison groups: placebo and exposure. The failure of other investigators to include these critical comparisons (i.e. placebo, wait-list and active treatment) within a single study may distort the apparent efficacy of combination treatments.

Matching

Attempts to match individuals to treatments has been investigated in the area of social phobia. Trower (1978) categorized individuals as either "socially phobic" or "socially inadequate". As hypothesized, socially inadequate individuals improved significantly more on self-report measures of social anxiety when treated with social skills training vs. exposure therapy. Socially phobic individuals benefited equally from both treatment approaches.

Öst, Jerremalm & Johansson (1981) divided subjects into "behavioral reactors" and "physiological reactors". Behavioral reactors demonstrated inadequate social skills but little physiological arousal during a simulated social interaction, whereas physiological reactors demonstrated the reverse. Although social skills training and applied relaxation were equally effective overall, social skills training produced greater change for behavioral reactors, whereas applied relaxation produced greater change for physiological reactors. That is, the treatments were more effective when "matched" to patients. Utilizing a similar design, Jerremalm, Jansson & Öst (1986b) compared "physiological" reactors with "cognitive reactors", randomly assigned to either applied relaxation or self-instruction training. Matching did not improve treatment outcome, and the treatments were equally effective overall. They attributed negative treatment-matching results to poorly developed cognitive measures and the possibility that self-instruction training may not be a sufficiently potent cognitive treatment.

Mersch et al. (1989) categorized individuals on the basis of a behavioral test and a cognitive measure of social phobia. Individuals scoring at the extreme ends on each of these measures were randomly assigned to social skills training or rational–emotive therapy. Within-group differences demonstrated significant improvement for all groups, regardless of classification as "behavioral" or "cognitive reactor". There were no significant differences between treatments and no support garnered for superior efficacy via matching individual characteristics to treatment approach.

Summary

Cognitive and behavioral approaches for the treatment of social phobia have demonstrated clear and consistent efficacy compared to placebo or wait-list conditions. These treatments include social skills training, *in vivo* exposure, applied relaxation, various cognitive treatments and their combinations. However, research aimed at demonstrating differential efficacy has met with little reward. Combinations of behavioral and cognitive approaches do not clearly potentiate treatment effects. That is, several studies show the superiority of combination treatments and others demonstrate no superiority or even inferiority compared to pure exposure or cognitive therapy. A recent meta-analysis that included all of the above listed studies found that effect sizes did not differ between combination and pure exposure treatments on measures of social anxiety and avoidance, cognitions, depression or general anxiety (Feske & Chambless, 1995). No such analysis has compared purely cognitive treatments to exposure and combination treatments. However, several studies reviewed above showed that pure cognitive therapy was as effective as pure exposure or combination treatments. Some investigations suggest a benefit from matching treatments to individual response profiles, while more recent studies have failed to do so. This may be due to imprecise determinations of individual characteristics.

Treatment Efficacy: Agoraphobia

Efficacy of Behavioral and Cognitive Treatments

Michelson, Mavissakalian & Marchione (1985) published their first of a series of investigations comparing different behavioral treatments to various cognitively-oriented treatments for agoraphobia. Individuals diagnosed with agoraphobia with panic attacks were randomly assigned to one of three treatments: paradoxical intention, graduated exposure or progressive deep muscle relaxation. All received instructions to conduct self-directed, prolonged, graduated exposure between sessions. At post-treatment, paradoxical intention demonstrated equivalent rates of improvement but inferior end-state functioning compared to graduated exposure and relaxation. At 3-month follow-up, 73% of graduated exposure subjects and 70% of relaxation subjects were classified as high end-state functioning in contrast to only 30% of paradoxical intention subjects.

Michelson, Mavissakalian & Marchione (1988) replicated this design with almost twice as many subjects. Contrary to the first study, few significant differences were detected between treatments. Percentages of improvement and end-state functioning did not differ between groups at post-treatment or follow-up. High end-state functioning rates at 3-month follow-up were 60% for paradoxical intention, 58.8% for graduated exposure and 52.6% for relaxation. These results were replicated in a third study (Michelson et al., 1990): there were no main effects for treatment and no statistical differences in improvement or end-state functioning.

Several investigators report limited or no efficacy of cognitive therapy for agoraphobia. In a series of investigations, Emmelkamp and colleagues compared cognitive therapy to prolonged *in vivo* exposure. The form of cognitive therapy tested was a combination of rational–emotive therapy and self-instruction training. *In vivo* exposure was superior to cognitive therapy on an array of behavioral and self-report measures of anxiety and avoidance (Emmelkamp et al., 1986; Emmelkamp, Kuiper & Eggeraat, 1978; Emmelkamp & Mersch, 1982).

A recently published study by Hoffart (1995) contrasted cognitive therapy (developed by Clark, 1986) and guided mastery (Williams, 1990) for individuals diagnosed with panic disorder with moderate to severe agoraphobia. Individuals considered agoraphobia to be their main problem. Fifty-seven per cent of cognitive therapy patients were treatment responders, as defined by at least 50% reduction on core agoraphobic fears compared to only 35% of guided mastery patients, although this difference was not statistically significant. In terms of high end-state functioning, 39% of cognitive patients were so classified compared to only 13% of guided mastery patients (which was significantly different). However, individual measures of outcome did not differ significantly between groups.

Efficacy of Combination Treatments

Marchione et al. (1987) found a clear superiority of combination treatments. Agoraphobics were assigned to either cognitive therapy plus graduated exposure, relaxation training plus graduated exposure, or graduated exposure alone. Cognitive therapy was based on Clark's (1986) model which emphasizes catastrophic thinking and hypothesis testing. At post-treatment, 100% of individuals in the combination treatments were classified as high end-state functioners in contrast to only 25% of individuals treated with graduated exposure alone.

Other researchers have failed to find superior efficacy for combination treatments. Following the Emmelkamp, Kuipers & Eggeraat (1978) investigation discussed above, Emmelkamp & Mersch (1982) replicated the cognitive and exposure treatment comparison and added a third combination comparison group. They reported no superiority of the combination treatment on measures of anxiety and avoidance. In a follow-up analysis, it was determined that the exposure component of the combination treatment was responsible for treatment effects (Emmelkamp et al., 1986).

Williams & Rappoport (1983) compared guided exposure to guided exposure combined with self-statement training for agoraphobics with severe driving phobias. Although the combination treatment resulted in the use of more coping thoughts while driving, the groups improved equally across all outcome measures. van den Hout, Arntz & Hoekstra (1994) similarly found that cognitive therapy did not potentiate the effects of exposure in terms of self-rated agoraphobia or behavioral avoidance.

Some researchers have examined the effectiveness of brief cognitive–behavioral treatments for agoraphobia. Evans, Holt & Oei (1991) compared a 2-day group cognitive–behavioral treatment to a wait-list condition. Eighty-five per cent of treated patients were reported to be either symptom-free or symptomatically improved, and these results were maintained by 1-year follow-up. In contrast, the wait-list group did not demonstrate any significant changes in self-reported symptoms of panic or agoraphobia after 4 months. Rijken et al. (1992) compared short-term treatments consisting of either breathing retraining plus cognitive therapy, graded *in vivo* self-exposure, or their combination. The treatments were equally effective. These results suggest that exposure therapy alone was as effective as combination treatments and was not improved by the addition of cognitive techniques.

Matching

Öst, Jerremalm & Jansson (1984) tested the treatment matching hypothesis for agoraphobia. Based on reactions in a naturalistic agoraphobic situation, subjects were classified as either behavioral (i.e. high self-rated anxiety) or physiological (i.e. high heart-rate) reactors. Subjects were randomly assigned to either 12 sessions of *in vivo* exposure therapy or 12 sessions of applied relaxation. Both treatments produced significant gains: 60% of the *in vivo* exposure group and 70% of the applied relaxation group were considered clinically improved after treatment. However, improvement was not related to an individual's match to treatment; thus, no support was garnered for the treatment-matching hypothesis.

Mackay & Liddell (1986) classified agoraphobics as cognitive responders or non-cognitive responders based on a self-report symptom questionnaire. Individuals were assigned to either cognitive therapy plus *in vivo* exposure or relaxation training plus *in vivo* exposure. Of the four groups created by crossing response type with treatment mode, three demonstrated significant treatment gains; the non-cognitive responders who received cognitive therapy failed to improve. These results are not clearly supportive of the treatment-matching hypothesis, although they do suggest a possible individual trait (i.e. non-cognitive responder) which may suppress the efficacy of cognitive therapy.

Summary

Behavioral treatments are clearly effective for agoraphobia. Combination treatments seem to provide little or no added benefit compared to pure exposure therapy. Only one study demonstrated superiority of a combination cognitive–behavioral approach compared to exposure therapy alone. Pure cognitive treatments for agoraphobia have received little support. While some studies show the value of paradoxical intention and cognitive therapy, the majority show that cognitive treatments are inferior to exposure alone. This may be due to differences among cognitive therapies. Until further research is conducted to determine which of the cognitive approaches is most effective, it appears that exposure treatments are the recommended standard for the treatment of agoraphobia. Matching of treatments to individual response profiles produces mixed results. Note that cognitive and behavioural therapies have been shown to be very effecture for panic disorder.

Treatment Efficacy Summary

Treatment outcome data can be summarized in five areas. First, are behavioral treatments effective for phobias? Clearly, the answer is yes. Behavior therapies are effective for specific phobias (*in vivo* and imaginal exposure, guided mastery, and applied relaxation and tension), social phobias (social skills training, applied relaxation, *in vivo* and imaginal exposure, and programmed practice), and agoraphobia (relaxation, guided mastery, and *in vivo* exposure).

Second, are cognitive treatments effective for phobias? While the number of studies is limited evidence is accruing for each type of phobia. There is some evidence for cognitive treatments for specific phobias, although range of effectiveness may be limited relative to *in vivo* exposure, perhaps due to brevity of treatment. The research clearly shows the efficacy of cognitive treatments for social phobia. However, the majority of studies suggest cognitive therapy is of limited value for agoraphobia. Notably, the one study that supported the efficacy of cognitive therapy implemented the most recent, and perhaps most sophisticated, version of cognitive therapy for panic disorder and agoraphobia. Thus, more sophisticated cognitive therapies may prove to be more effective.

Third, how well do cognitive therapies compare to behavior therapies for phobias? Cognitive therapy was inferior or equivalent to behavior therapy for specific phobias, and mostly inferior to behavior therapy for agoraphobia. In contrast, cognitive therapy consistently was as effective as behavior therapy for social phobia.

Fourth, does cognitive therapy enhance the effects of behavior therapy for phobias? The results generally do not show a potentiation effect. The two studies of specific phobias provided contradictory results. For social phobia, where research is more prolific, the results show no clear pattern. The majority of agoraphobia studies demonstrated no added benefit to a combination treatment, with the exception of a study that incorporated more recently developed cognitive strategies for panic disorder with agoraphobia. Again, therefore, results may differ with more sophisticated cognitive treatments.

Finally, is treatment outcome improved by matching treatment modality to individual response profiles? A benefit was observed from matching behavioral and physiological treatments to corresponding response profiles. However, results from matching were less promising with regard to cognitive vs. behavioral treatments and response styles. Only one study addressed this issue for specific phobias, and reported no benefit. The same was true for social phobia, and very limited support for cognitive vs. behavioral matching was found for agoraphobia.

METHODOLOGICAL ISSUES FOR FUTURE RESEARCH

Posing the comparison of behavioral vs. cognitive treatment approaches forces an artifical dichotomy, given the considerable overlap in their methods and mechanisms. On the other hand, recognizing differences between the approaches generates a multimodal orientation that may facilitate treatment research and outcome. The following methodological issues are relevant to continued efforts to research behavioral vs. cognitive methods and mechanisms.

The first is the competency with which treatments are delivered. This is particularly relevant to cognitive therapy research, given that early studies relied on limited cognitive strategies, often restricted to one or a few sessions. This may account in part for the lack of support for matching of cognitive and behavioral treatments to cognitive vs. behavioral response profiles, and the generally poor outcome from cognitive therapy for agoraphobia. More recent and well developed cognitive therapies, combined with measurement of the competency with which treatment is delivered, would improve outcome research in this area.

A related issue concerns the various forms of cognitive therapy (paradoxical intention, rational–emotive therapy, self-instruction training and cognitive therapy) and the possibility of their differential effectiveness overall, or for different types of phobias. For example, more recently developed cognitive therapies (e.g. Clark, 1986) seem more effective than earlier cognitive approaches for panic disorder and agoraphobia. Thus, comparisons with behavior therapy are confounded by the different types of cognitive therapy implemented across studies.

A third issue concerns research design for combinations of behavioral and cognitive approaches. Attempts to examine the benefits of combining these approaches are thwarted by dilution of each approach when combined with the other approach over the same duration as each approach presented alone. Furthermore, combinations may detrimentally affect therapists' competency to execute treatment. The alternative, to expand combination treatments over longer durations than pure treatments, obviously confounds treatment efficacy with time. Nevertheless, further research might examine the benefits of combination approaches under conditions of matched as well as expanded duration. Related is the need for more research concerning optimal combinations; for example, should behavioral strategies precede, follow or begin simultaneously with cognitive strategies?

Our review of treatment efficacy was impeded by the lack of standardized measures across studies. This includes individual outcome measures and composite indices of improvement and end-state functioning. A related issue pertains to treatment-matching research, where methods for categorizing individuals as behavioral, cognitive or physiological responders vary across studies and warrant further development.

Finally, many methodological issues arise in the area of treatment mechanisms. For example, assessment of cognitive mediation has relied mostly upon self-report instruments, which are subject to response bias. These scales could be supplemented by cognitive paradigms, such as dichotic listening, modified Stroop, or dot probe detection tasks. A problematic issue concerns differential sensitivity of measures of different response domains; that is, cognitive, behavioral and physiological measures may not be equally sensitive, resulting in false attribution of outcome patterns to underlying mechanisms. A related question is when measurements should occur. Frequent measurement would facilitate detection of the sequence of changes across cognitive, behavioral and physiological responses, but increases the likelihood of reactivity and regression to the mean.

Obviously, the area of cognitive and behavioral treatments for phobias deserves further research attention, with standardized therapies, assured competency of therapists and standardized procedures and instruments for measurement of outcome and mediation of therapeutic efficacy.

REFERENCES

Bandura, A. (1977). Self-efficacy: toward a unifying theory of behavioral change. *Psychological Review*, **84**, 191–215.

Barlow, D.H. (1988). *Anxiety and its Disorders: the Nature and Treatment of Anxiety and Panic*. New York: Guilford.

Barlow, D.H., Leitenberg, H., Agras, W.S. & Wincze, J.P. (1969). The transfer gap in systematic desensitization: an analogue study. *Behaviour Research and Therapy*, **7**, 191–196.

Beck, A.T. (1976). *Cognitive Therapy and the Emotional Disorders*. New York: International Universities Press.

Beck, A.T. (1993). Cognitive therapy: past, present and future. *Journal of Consulting and Clinical Psychology*, **61**, 194–198.

Booth R. & Rachman, S.J. (1992). The reduction of claustrophobia—I. *Behaviour Research and Therapy*, **30**, 207–221.

Borden, J.W., Clum, G.A. & Salmon, P.G. (1991). Mechanisms of change in the treatment of panic. *Cognitive Therapy and Research*, **15**, 257–272.

Borkovec, T.D. (1978). Self-efficacy: cause or reflection of behavioral change? *Advances in Behaviour Research and Therapy*, **1**, 163–170.

Bouton, M.E. (1993). Context, time, and memory retrieval in the interference paradigms of Pavlovian learning. *Psychological Bulletin*, **114**, 80–99.

Bouton, M.E. & Swartzentruber, D. (1991). Sources of relapse after extinction in Pavlvian and instrumental learning. *Clinical Psychology Review*, **11**, 123–140.

Bower, G.H. (1981). Mood and memory. *American Psychologist*, **36**, 129–148.

Boyd, T.L. & Levis, D.J. (1983). Exposure is a necessary condition for fear reduction: a reply to de Silva and Rachman. *Behaviour Research and Therapy*, **21**, 143–149.

Butler, G., Cullington, A., Munby, M., Amies, P. & Gelder, M. (1984). Exposure and anxiety management in the treatment of social phobia. *Journal of Consulting and Clinical Psychology*, **52**, 642–650.

Chambless, D.L. & Gillis, M.M. (1993). Cognitive therapy of anxiety disorders. *Journal of Consulting and Clinical Psychology*, **61**, 248–260.

Chambless, D.L. & Gracely, E.J. (1988). Prediction of outcome following *in vivo* exposure treatment of agoraphobia. In I. Hand & H-U. Wittchen (eds), *Panic and Phobias*, Vol. II (pp. 209–220). Berlin: Springer-Verlag.

Clark. D.M. (1986). A cognitive approach to panic. *Behaviour Research and Therapy*, **24**, 461–470.

Clark, D.M., Salkovskis, P.M., Hackmann, A., Middleton, H., Anastasiades, P. & Gelder, M. (1994). A comparision of cognitive therapy, applied relaxation and imipramine in the treatment of panic disorder. *British Journal of Psychiatry*, **164**, 759–769.

Cracknell, S. & Davey, G.C.L. (1988). The effect of perceived unconditioned response strength on conditioned responding inhumans. *Medical Science Research*, **16**, 169–170.

Craske, M.G. & Barlow, D.H. (1988). A review of the relationship between panic and avoidance. *Clinical Psychology Review*, **8**, 667–685.

Crowe, M.J., Marks, I.M., Agras, W.S. & Leitenberg, H. (1972). Time-limited desensitization, implosion, and shaping for phobic patients: a cross-over study. *Behaviour Research and Therapy*, **10**, 319–328.

Davey, G.C.L. (1992). Classical conditioning and the acquisition of human fears and phobias: a review and synthesis of the literature. *Advances in Behaviour Research and Therapy*, **14**, 29–66.

De Jongh, A., Muris, P., Ter Horst, G., Van Zuuren, F., Schoenmakers, N. & Makkes, P. (1995). One-session cognitive treatment of dental phobia: preparing dental phobics for treatment by restructuring negative cognitions. *Behaviour Research and Therapy*, **33**, 947–954.

DiNardo, P.A., Guzy, J.A. & Bak, R.M. (1988). Anxiety response patterns and etiological factors in dog-fearful and non-fearful subjects. *Behaviour Research and Therapy*, **26**, 245–252.

Dyckman, J.M. & Cowan, P.A. (1978). Imagining vividness and the outcome of *in vivo* and imagined scene desensitization. *Journal of Consulting and Clinical Psychology*, **48**, 1155–1156.

Egan, K.J., Carr, J.E., Hunt, D.D. & Adamson, R. (1988). Endogenous opiate system and systematic desensitization. *Journal of Consulting and Clinical Psychology*, **56**, 287–291.

Ellis, A. (1962). *Reason and Emotion in Psychotherapy*. New York: Lyle Stuart.

Ellis, A. (1993). Reflections on rational–emotive therapy. *Journal of Consulting and Clinical Psychology*, **61**, 199–201.

Emmelkamp, P.M.G. (1986). Behaviour therapy with adults. In S.L. Garfield & A.E. Bergin (eds), *Handbook of Psychotherapy and Behaviour Change*. New York: Wiley.

Emmelkamp, P.M.G. (1992). Obsessive–compulsive disorder: the contributions of an experimental-clinical approach. In A. Ehlers, W. Feigeubaum, I. Florin & J. Margraf (eds), *Perspectives and Promises of Clinical Psychology* (pp. 149–156). New York: Plenum.

Emmelkamp. P.M.G., Brilman, E., Kuiper, H. & Mersch, P.P. (1986). The treatment of agoraphobia: a comparison of self instruction training, rational–emotive therapy and exposure *in vivo*. *Behavior Modification*, **10**, 37–53.

Emmelkamp, P.M.G. & Felten, M. (1985). The process of exposure *in vivo*: cognitive and physiological changes during treatment of acrophobia. *Behaviour Research and Therapy*, **23**, 219–223.

Emmelkamp, P.M.G., Kuipers, A.C.M. & Eggeraat, J.B. (1978). Cognitive modification versus prolonged exposure *in vivo*: a comparison with agoraphobics as subjects. *Behaviour Research and Therapy*, **16**, 33–41.

Emmelkamp, P.M.G. & Mersch, P.P. (1982). Cognition and exposure *in vivo* in the treatment of agoraphobia: short-term and delayed effects. *Cognitive Therapy and Research*, **6**, 77–90.

Emmelkamp, P.M.G., Mersch, P.P., Vissia, E. & van der Helm, M. (1985). Social phobia: a comparative evaluation of cognitive and behavioural interventions. *Behaviour Research and Therapy*, **23**, 365–369.

Evans, L., Holt, C. & Oei, T.P.S. (1991). Long-term follow-up of agoraphobics treated by brief intensive group cognitive–behavioural therapy. *Australian and New Zealand Journal of Psychiatry*, **25**, 343–349.

Eysenck, H.J. (1987). The role of heredity, environment, and "preparedness" in the genesis of neurosis. In H.J. Eysenck & I. Martin (eds), *Theoretical Foundations of Behavior Therapy* (pp. 379–402). New York: Plenum.

Feske, U. & Chambless, D.L. (1995). Cognitive–behavioural versus exposure only treatment for social phobia: a meta-analysis. *Behavior Therapy*, **26**, 695–720.

Foa, E.B. & Kozak, M.J. (1986). Emotional processing of fear: exposure to corrective information. *Psychological Bulletin*, **99**, 20–35.

Frankl, V.E. (1960). Paradoxical intention: a logotherapeutic technique. *American Journal of Psychotherapy*, **14**, 520–535.

Getka, E.J. & Glass, C.R. (1992). Behavioral and cognitive–behavioral approaches to the reduction of dental anxiety. *Behavior Therapy*, **23**, 433–448.

Groves, P.M. & Thompson, R.F. (1970). Habituation: a dual-process theory. *Psychological Review*, **77**, 419–450.

Hecker, J.E. (1990). Emotional processing in the treatment of simple phobia: a comparison of imaginal and *in vivo* exposure. *Behavioural Psychotherapy*, **18**, 21–34.

Heimberg, R.G. (1989). Cognitive and behavioral treatments for social phobia: a critical analysis. *Clinical Psychology Review*, **9**, 197–128.

Heimberg, R.G., Dodge, C.S., Hope, D.A., Kennedy, C.R., Zollo, L.J. & Becker, R.E. (1990). Cognitive–behavioural group treatment for social phobia: comparison with a credible placebo control. *Cognitive Therapy and Research*, **14**, 1–23.

Heimberg, R.G., Salzman, D.G., Holt, C.S. & Blendell, K.A. (1993). Cognitive–behavioral group treatment for social phobia: effectiveness at five-year follow-up. *Cognitive Therapy and Research*, **17**, 1993.

Hoffart, A. (1995). A comparison of cognitive and guided mastery therapy of agoraphobia. *Behaviour Research and Therapy*, **33**, 423–434.

Hope, D.A., Heimberg, R.G. & Bruch, M.A. (1989). Treatment of social phobia with and without cognitive restructuring. Poster presented at 23rd Annual Meeting of the Association for the Advancement of Behavior Therapy. Washington, DC, November.

Hope, D.A., Heimberg, R.G. & Bruch, M.A. (1995). Dismantling cognitive–behavioral group therapy for social phobia. *Behaviour Research and Therapy*, **33**, 637–650.

Jerremalm, A., Jansson, L. & Öst, L.-G. (1986a). Individual response patterns and the effects of different behavioral methods in the treatment of dental phobia. *Behaviour Research and Therapy*, **24**, 587–596.

Jerremalm, A., Jansson, L. & Öst, L.-G. (1986b). Cognitive and physiological reactivity and the effects of different behavioural methods in the treatment of social phobia. *Behaviour Research and Therapy*, **24**, 171–180.

Kazdin, A.E. (1978). Conceptual and assessment issues raised by self-efficacy theory. *Advances in Behaviour Research and Therapy*, **1**, 177–185.

Kirsch, I. (1985). Response expectancy as a determinant of experience and behaviour. *American Psychologist*, **40**, 1189–1202.

Klatsky, R.L. (1980). *Human Memory: Structures and Processes*. San Francisco, CA: Freeman.

Kozak, M.J., Foa, E.B. & Steketee, G. (1988). Process and outcome of exposure treatment with obsessive–compulsives: psychophysiological indicators of emotional processing. *Behavior Therapy*, **19**, 157–169.

Kleinknecht, R.A. (1982). The origins and remission of fear in a group of tarantula enthusiasts. *Behaviour Research and Therapy*, **20**, 437–443.

Lader, M. & Wing, L. (1966). *Physiological Measures, Sedative Drugs, and Morbid Anxiety*. London: Oxford University Press.

Lang, P.J. (1979). A bio-informational theory of emotional imagery. *Psychophysiology*, **16**, 495–512.

Lang, P.J., Melamed, B. & Hart, J. (1970). A psychophysiological analysis of fear modification using an automated desensitization technique. *Journal of Abnormal Psychology*, **76**, 220–234.

Last, C. (1987). Simple phobias. In L. Michelson & M. Ascher (eds), *Anxiety and Stress Disorders: Cognitive–Behavioral Assessment and Treatment* (pp. 176–190). New York: Guilford.

Last, C.G. & Blanchard, E.B. (1982). Classification of phobic versus fearful non-phobics: procedural and theoretical issues. *Behavioral Assessment*, **4**, 195–210.

Mackay, W. & Liddell, A. (1986). An investigation into the matching of specific agoraphobic anxiety response characteristics with specific types of treatment. *Behaviour Research and Therapy*, **24**, 361–364.

Mackintosh, N.J. (1983). *Conditioning and Associative Learning*. New York: Oxford University Press.

Mackintosh, N.J. (1987). Neurobiology, psychology and habituation. *Behaviour Research and Therapy*, **25**, 81–98.

Macleod, C. & Mathews, A. (1991). Cognitive-experimental approaches to emotional disorders. In P.R. Martin (ed.), *Handbook of Behaviour Therapy and Experimental Science* (pp. 116–150). New York: Pergamon.

Marchione, K.E., Michelson, L., Greenwald, M. & Dancu, C. (1987). Cognitive–behavioral treatment of agoraphobia. *Behaviour Research and Therapy*, **25**, 319–328.

Margraf, J. & Schneider, S. (1991). Outcome and active ingredients of cognitive-behavioural treatments for panic disorder. Paper presented at 25th Annual Meeting of the Association for Advancement of Behaviour Therapy, New York, November.

Marks, I.M. (1987). *Fears, Phobias and Rituals*. Oxford: Oxford University Press.

Marks, I.M., Boulougouris, J. & Marset, P. (1971). Flooding versus desensitization in the treatment of phobic patients. *British Journal of Psychiatry*, **119**, 353–375.

Marks, I.M. & Tobena, A. (1990). Learning and unlearning of ear: a clinical evolutionary perspective. *Neuroscience and Biobehavioural Reviews*, **14**, 365–384.

Marshall, W.L. (1985). The effects of variable exposure in flooding therapy. *Behavior Therapy*, **16**, 117–135.

Marshall, W.L. (1988). Behavioural indices of habituation and sensitization during exposure to phobic stimuli. *Behaviour Research and Therapy*, **23**, 167–175.

Mathews, A. (1978). Fear reduction research and clinical phobias. *Psychological Bulletin*, **85**, 390–404.

Mattia, J.I., Heimberg, R.G. & Hope, D.A. (1993). The revised Stroop color-naming task in social phobics. *Behaviour Research and Therapy*, **31**, 305–313.

Mattick, P.R. & Peters, L. (1988). Treatment of severe social phobia: effects of guided exposure with and without cognitive restructuring. *Journal of Consulting and Clinical Psychology*, **56**, 251–260.

Mattick, R.P., Peters, L. & Clarke, J.C. (1989). Exposure and cognitive restructuring for social phobia: a controlld study. *Behavior Therapy*, **20**, 3–23.

McFall, R.M. & Marston, A.R. (1970). An experimental investigation of behaviour rehearsal in assertive training. *Journal of Abnormal Psychology*, **76**, 295–305.

McNally, R.J. & Steketee, G.S. (1985). The etiology and maintenance of severe animal phobias. *Behaviour Research and Therapy*, **23**, 431–435.

McReynolds, W.T. & Grizzard, R.H. (1971). A comparison of three fear reduction procedures. *Psychotherapy: Theory, Research and Practice*, **8**, 264–268.

Meichenbaum, D.H. (1975). Self-instruction methods. In F.H. Kanfer & A.P. Goldstein (eds), *Helping People Change*. Elmsford, NY: Pergamon.

Meichenbaum, D.H. (1977). *Cognitive–Behavior Modification: an Integrative Approach*. New York: Plenum.

Menzies, R.G. & Clarke, J.C. (1995). The etiology of acrophobia and its relationship to severity and individual response patterns. *Behaviour Research and Therapy*, **33**, 795–804.

Merluzzi, T.V., Taylor, C.B., Boltwood, M. & Gotestam, K.G. (1991). Opioid antagonist impedes exposure. *Journal of Consulting and Clinical Psychology*, **59**, 425–430.

Mersch, P.P.A. (1995). The treatment of social phobia: the differential effectiveness of exposure *in vivo* and an integration of exposure *in vivo*, rational–emotive therapy and social skills training. *Behaviour Research and Therapy*, **33**, 259–269.

Mersch, P.P.A., Emmelkamp, P.M.G., Bogels, S.M. & van der Sleen, J. (1989). Social phobia: individual response patterns and the effects of behavioral and cognitive interventions. *Behaviour Research and Therapy*, **27**, 421–434.

Michelson, L., Marchione, K. & Greenwald, M. (1989). Cognitive and behavioural treatments of agoraphobia. Paper presented at 23rd Annual Meeting of the Association for the Advancement of Behaviour Therapy, Washington, DC, November.

Michelson, L., Mavissakalian, M. & Marchione, K. (1985). Cognitive and behavioral treatments of agoraphobia: clinical, behavioral, and psychophysiological outcomes. *Journal of Consulting and Clinical Psychology*, **53**, 913–925.

Michelson, L., Mavissakalian, M. & Marchione, K. (1988). Cognitive, behavioral, and psychophysiological treatments of agoraphobia: a comparative outcome. *Behaviour Therapy*, **19**, 97–120.

Michelson, L., Mavissakalian, M., Marchione, K., Ulrich, R.F., Marchione, N. & Testa, S. (1990). Psychophysiological outcome of cognitive, behavioural and psychophysiologically-based treatments of agoraphobia. *Behaviour Research and Therapy*, **28**, 127–139.

Mineka, S. (1987). A primate model of phobic fears. In H.J. Eysenck & I. Martin (eds), *Theoretical Foundations of Behaviour Therapy* (pp. 81–112). New York: Plenum.

Mineka, S., Davidson, M., Cook, M. & Keir, R. (1984). Observational conditioning of snake fear in rhesus monkeys. *Journal of Abnormal Psychology*, **93**, 355–372.

Mineka, S., Gunnar, M. & Champoux, M. (1986). Control and early socioemotional development: infant rhesus monkeys reared in controllable versus uncontrollable environments. *Child Development*, **57**, 1241–1256.

Murray, E.J. & Foote, F. (1979). The origins of fears of snakes. *Behaviour Research and Therapy*, **17**, 489–493.

Öhman, A. (1986). Face the beast and fear the face: animal and social fears as prototypes for evolutionary analyses of emotion. *Psychophysiology*, **23**, 123–145.

Öst, L.-G. (1985). Ways of acquiring phobias and outcome of behavioural treatments. *Behaviour Research and Therapy*, **23**, 683–689.

Öst, L.-G. & Hugdahl, K. (1981). Acquisition of phobias and anxiety response patterns in clinical patients. *Behaviour Research and Therapy*, **19**, 439–447.

Öst, L.-G. & Hugdahl, K. (1983). Acquisition of agoraphobia, mode of onset and anxiety response patterns. *Behaviour Research and Therapy*, **21**, 623–631.

Öst, L.-G., Jerremalm, A. & Jansson, L. (1984). Individual response patterns and the effects of different behavioral methods in the treatment of agoraphobia. *Behaviour Research and Therapy*, **22**, 697–707.

Öst, L.-G., Jerremalm, A. & Johansson, J. (1981). Individual response patterns and the effects of different behavioural methods in the treatment of social phobia. *Behaviour Research and Therapy*, **19**, 1–16.

Öst, L.-G., Johansson, J. & Jerremalm, A. (1982). Individual response patterns and the effects of different behavioural methods in the treatment of claustrophobia. *Behaviour Research and Therapy*, **20**, 445–460.

Öst, L.-G., Lindahl, I.-L., Sterner, U. & Jerremalm, A. (1984). Physiological responses in blood phobics. *Behaviour Research and Therapy*, **22**, 109–127.

Öst, L.-G., Sterner, U. & Fellenius, J. (1989). Applied tension, applied relaxation, and the combination in the treatment of blood phobia. *Behaviour Research and Therapy*, **27**, 109–121.

Rachman, S.J. (1978). *Fear and Courage*. New York: W.H. Freeman.

Rachman, S.J. (1980). Emotional processing. *Behaviour Research and Therapy*, **18**, 51–60.

Rachman, S.J. (1990). *Fear and Courage*, 2nd edn. New York: W.H. Freeman.

Rachman, S.J. (1993). A critique of cognitive therapy for anxiety disorders. *Journal of Behaviour Therapy and Experimental Psychiatry*, **24**, 279–288.

Rachman, S.J. (1994). The overprediction of fear: a review. *Behaviour Research and Therapy*, **32**, 683–690.

Rachman, S.J. & Bichard, S. (1988). The overprediction of fear. *Clinical Psychology Review*, **8**, 303–313.

Rachman, S.J., Craske, M.G., Tallman, K. & Solyom, C. (1986). Does escape behaviour strengthen agoraphobic avoidance? A replication. *Behaviour Therapy*, **17**, 366–384.

Rachman, S.J. & Levitt, K. (1985). Panic, fear reduction and habituation. *Behaviour Research and Therapy*, **26**, 169–206.

Rachman, S.J., Levitt, K. & Lopatka, C. (1988). III. Experimental analyses of panic: claustrophobic subjects. *Behaviour Research and Therapy*, **26**, 41–52.

Rachman, S.J. & Lopatka, C. (1986). Match and mismatch in the prediction of fear-1. *Behaviour Research and Therapy*, **24**, 387–393.

Rachman, S.J. & Whittal, M. (1989). Fast, slow and sudden reductions in fear. *Behaviour Research and Therapy*, **27**, 613–620.

Rapee, R. (1993). Recent advances in the treatment of social phobia. *Australian Psychologist*, **28**, 168–171.

Rijken, H., Kraaimaat, F., De Ruiter, C. & Garssen, B. (1992). A follow-up study on short-term treatment of agoraphobia. *Behaviour Research and Therapy*, **30**, 63–66.

Rimm, D.C., Janda, L.H., Lancaster, D.W., Nahl, M. & Dittmar, K. (1977). An exploratory investigation of the origin and maintenance of phobias. *Behaviour Research and Therapy*, **15**, 231–238.

Robins, C.J. & Hayes, A.M. (1993). An appraisal of cognitive therapy. *Journal of Consulting and Clinical Psychology*, **61**, 205–214.

Rodriguez, B. & Craske, M.G. (1993). The effects of distraction during exposure to phobic stimuli. *Behaviour Research and Therapy*, **31**, 549–558.

Rodriguez, B. & Craske, M.G. (1995). Does distraction interfere with fear reduction during exposure: a test with animal-fearful subjects. *Behaviour Therapy*, **26**, 337–350.

Scholing, A. & Emmelkamp, P.M.G. (1993a). Cognitive and behavioural treatments of fear of blushing, sweating, or trembling. *Behaviour Research and Therapy*, **31**, 155–170.

Scholing, A. & Emmelkamp, P.M.G. (1993b). Exposure with and without cognitive therapy for generalized social phobia: effects of individual and group treatment. *Behaviour Research and Therapy*, **31**, 667–681.

Seligman, M.E.P. (1971). Phobias and preparendness. *Behaviour Therapy*, **2**, 307–320.

Shafran, R., Booth, R. & Rachman, S.J. (1993). The reduction of claustrophobia II: cognitive analyses. *Behaviour Research and Therapy*, **31**, 75–86.

Shahar, A. & Merbaum, M. (1981). The interaction between subject characteristics and self-control procedures in the treatment of interpersonal anxiety. *Cognitive Therapy and Research*, **5**, 221–224.

Stravynski, A., Grey, S. & Elie, R. (1987). Outline of the therapeutic process in social skills training with socially dysfunctional patients. *Journal of Consulting and Clinical Psychology*, **55**, 224–228.

Teasdale, J.D. (1988). Self-efficacy: toward a unifying theory of behavioral change? *Advances in Behaviour Research and Therapy*, **1**, 211–215.

Telch, M.J., Ilai, D., Valentiner, D. & Craske, M.G. (1994). Match-mismatch of fear, panic, performance. *Behaviour Research and Therapy*, **32**, 697–700.

Thorpe, S.J. & Salkovskis, P.M. (1995). Phobic beliefs: do cognitive factors play a role in specific phobias? *Behaviour Research and Therapy*, **33**, 805–816.

Trower, P., Yardley, K., Bryant, B. & Shaw, P. (1978). The treatment of social failure: a comparison of anxiety-reduction and skills-acquisition procedures on two social problems. *Behaviour Modification*, **2**, 41–60.

Trower, P., Bryant, B.M. & Argyle, M. (1978). *Social Skills and Mental Health*. London: Methuen.

Trower, P., Yardley, K., Bryant, B. & Shaw, P. (1978) The treatment of social failure: a comparison of anxiety reduction and skills-acquisition procedures on two social problems. *Behaviour Modification*, **2**, 41–60.

Turner, S.M., Beidel, D.C. & Cooley-Quille, M.R. (1995). Two-year follow-up of social phobics treated with Social Effectiveness Therapy. *Behaviour Research and Therapy*, **33**, 553–555.

Turner, S.M., Beidel, D.C., Cooley, M.R., Woody, S.R. & Messer, S.C. (1994). A multicomponent behavioral treatment for social phobia: social effectiveness therapy. *Behaviour Research and Therapy*, **32**, 381–390.

Turner, S.M., Beidel, D.C. & Wolff, P.L. (1994). A composite measure to determine improvement following treatment for social phobia: the index of social phobia improvement. *Behaviour Research and Therapy*, **32**, 471–476.

van Hout, W.J.P.J. & Emmelkamp, P.M.G. (1994). Overprediction of fear in panic disorder patients with agorpahobia: does the (mis)match model generalize to exposure *in vivo* therapy. *Behaviour Research and Therapy*, **32**, 723–734.

Wagner, A.R. (1976). Priming in STM: an information processing mechanism for self-generated or retrieval-generated depression in performance. In T.J. Tighe & R.N. Leaton (eds), *Habituation: Perspectives from child development, animal behaviour and neuropsychology* (pp. 95–128). Hillsdale. NJ: Erlbaum.

White, K. & Davey, G.C.L. (1989). Sensory preconditioning and UCS inflation in human "fear" conditioning. *Behaviour Research and Therapy*, **27**, 161–166.

Williams, S.L. (1990). Guided mastery treatment of agoraphobia: beyond stimulus exposure. *Progress in Behavior Modification*, **26**, 89–121.

Williams, S.L., Dooseman, G. & Kleifield, E. (1984). Comparative effectiveness of guided mastery and exposure treatments for intractable phobics. *Journal of Consulting and Clinical Psychology*, **52**, 505–518.

Williams, S.L., Kinney, P.J. & Falbo, J. (1989). Generalization of therapeutic changes in agoraphobia: the role of perceived self efficacy. *Journal of Consulting and Clinical Psychology*, **57**, 436–442.

Williams, S.L. & Rappoport, A. (1983). Cognitive treatment in the natural environment for agoraphobia. *Behavior Therapy*, **14**, 299–313.

Williams, S.L., Turner, S.M. & Peer, D.F. (1985). Guided mastery and performance desensitization treatments for severe acrophobia. *Journal of Consulting and Clinical Psychology*, **53**, 237–247.

Wolpe, J. (1958). *Psychotherapy by Reciprocal Inhibition*. Stanford, CA: Stanford University Press.

Wolpe, J. (1981). The dichotomy between classically conditioned and cognitively learned anxiety. *Journal of Behaviour Therapy and Experimental Psychiatry*, **12**, 35–42.

Wolpe. J. (1990). *The Practice of Behavior Therapy*. 4th edn. New York: Pergamon.

Wolpe, J., Lande, S.D., McNally, R.M. & Schotte, D. (1985). Differentiation between classically conditioned and cognitively based neurotic fears: two pilot studies. *Journal of Behaviour Therapy and Experimental Psychiatry*, **16**, 287–293.

Chapter 14

The Use of Medication in the Treatment of Phobias

Peter Hayward
and
Jane Wardle
Department of Psychology, Institute of Psychiatry, London, UK

Writers and thinkers have long been aware that many fear reactions are irrational (e.g. Montaigne, 1592/1993). The use of anxiolytic medication is also not new; soldiers, for example, have often used alcohol before battle to boost their courage (Keegan, 1993). But the idea that phobias could be appropriate objects of medical treatment is of more recent origin. This should not surprise us, in that two early models of phobia, the psychodynamic and the behavioural models, would seem to contraindicate such treatment. Psychodynamic models suggest that the appropriate treatment of phobia would be analysis of unconscious motivations, while the behavioural model proposes conditioning processes as a basis for treatment (Watson & Rayner, 1920; Jones, 1924). Nonetheless, a literature has grown up suggesting that pharmacological treatments could offer a real prospect for efficient and effective management of some of the more disabling phobic conditions. There is also a body of opinion suggesting that combining drug treatment with psychological treatment could provide the optimal conditions for therapeutic benefit. However, this position has attracted considerable controversy, with many authorities arguing that pharmacotherapy is ineffective, and may even be contra-indicated, in the management of phobias. Unfortunately, examination of the limited evidence on the efficacy of either pharmacological or combined treatment of phobias does not allow a definitive resolution of the controversy, but in this chapter we provide a summary of the current state of knowledge and thinking. The discussion is largely restricted to the management of the more severe and complex phobias, agoraphobia and social anxiety, since pharmacological treatments have rarely been applied to simple phobias.

Phobias—A Handbook of Theory, Research and Treatment. Edited by G.C.L. Davey.
© 1997 John Wiley & Sons Ltd.

THE EFFICACY OF PHARMACOLOGICAL TREATMENT OF PHOBIAS

Panic Disorder and Agoraphobia

One psychiatrist, Donald Klein, has probably done more than any other researcher to offer a theoretically-based argument for the use of medication in the treatment of a large class of phobias. Starting in the 1960s, he published a series of papers arguing that responses to psychotropic medication could be used to distinguish two types of anxiety, anticipatory anxiety and panic, which were hypothesized to originate in different areas of the brain (Klein, 1964; Klein, 1980). Dealing specifically with the case of agoraphobia, he suggested that agoraphobics suffered not from a fear of open spaces and public places *per se*, but from a propensity to sudden, inexplicable panic attacks. The fear of such attacks then caused them to avoid situations in which an attack would be particularly embarrassing or distressing, such as public places, places from which escape would be difficult, or situations in which they did not have ready access to trusted carers. Repeated panics would lead to a secondary, anticipatory anxiety, based on fear of the panic attacks. Klein argued that these two psychologically distinct forms of anxiety had different physiological bases. Panic, like depression, was a development from a set of responses seen in both humans and animals and triggered in the first instance by separation from the mother. Anticipatory anxiety, on the other hand, was a learned response to threat cues. He hypothesized that panic, like depression, would be most effectively treated with antidepressants, while anticipatory anxiety, part of a different set of anxiety responses, would be best treated with anxiolytics (Klein, 1980). Klein's views on panic and agoraphobia have proved to be highly influential. Certainly they led to a revision of diagnostic practice, in that the newer versions of the American diagnostic system DSM-III (DSM-IIIR and DSM-IV) classify agoraphobia as a form of panic disorder.

There have now been a number of clinical trials of antidepressant medication as a treatment for panic disorder (Mavissakalian, Michelson & Dealy, 1983), or of a treatment combination consisting of anti-depressants and exposure therapy (Zitrin, Klein & Woerner, 1980; Telch et al., 1985). On the whole, the outcome has been favourable, with most antidepressant studies showing that at least some panic patients respond well to anti-depressants, and that treatment can lead to a drop in panic frequency.

The idea that anti-depressants represent a unique drug therapy for panic was soon challenged by results of trials of drugs from other pharmacological "families". For example, the atypical benzodiazepine, alprazolam, was also identified as a specific treatment for panic, with the suggestion that its unusual biochemical structure explained its success in this area (Chouinard et al., 1982; Ballenger et al., 1988). However, to complicate the matter, there then followed trials of more conventional benzodiazepines which suggested that, in high doses, these drugs also seemed to be effective against panic (Sheehan, 1987). Such findings would seems to cast doubt on Klein's specific physiological model, but in the meantime the antipanic efficacy of both antidepressants and benzodiazepines appeared to be an established finding.

Another class of drugs which has had some popularity for the treatment of anxiety is the beta-blockers. These drugs have a variety of uses, principally for the treatment of high blood pressure, but they also block many of the physical symptoms of anxiety. Newer models of panic have suggested that fear of the physical symptoms of fear plays a role in the aetiology and maintenance of panic—the so-called "fear of fear" effect (Chambless et al., 1984). On the basis of this model, beta-blockers should offer an effective treatment of panic, and some early results were encouraging (Kathol et al., 1980). However, more extensive assessments have failed to demonstrate a strong therapeutic effect in double-blind trials (Hayes & Schulz, 1987; Noyes et al., 1984), and it has been suggested that beta-blockers may intensify depression in some patients (Hayes & Schulz, 1987). It is our impression that beta-blockers continue to be prescribed in spite of these equivocal findings, perhaps because they are reasonably well tolerated by many patients (Lader, 1988; Wheatley, 1990).

One other drug, the 5-HT$_{1a}$ antagonist buspirone, has also been used in the treatment of panic disorder. However, controlled trials have failed to demonstrate superiority to placebo (Sheehan et al., 1990, 1993). Sheehan et al. (1993) commented on buspirone's advantages in terms of its low level of side-effects and potential for abuse: "In the final analysis, what would be most desirable in treating panic disorder is a medicine with the anxiolytic power and speed of onset of action of benzodiazepines but with the safety profile of 5-HT$_{1a}$ antagonists" (p. 10). This probably accurately characterizes the situation for pharmacological treatment of phobias and anxiety; nothing works either very well or without costs. Indeed, a similar pattern can be seen with a number of different pharmacotherapies: a medication is introduced as a useful treatment, and initial uncontrolled trials and clinical case-series give promising results. Controlled, double-blind studies then follow, with more mixed results, some seemingly favouring the use of the drug, but others suggesting that its benefits are limited and the adverse effects more profound than had been initially realized. Meanwhile, the search for a better drug treatment for anxiety continues (e.g. Schneier et al., 1993a).

Performance Anxiety and Social Phobia

As noted above, beta-blockers are thought to block physical symptoms of anxiety and, as such, they have attracted some attention as treatments for performance anxiety. The rationale for their use is that anxiety symptoms can interfere with motor tasks which require a steady hand or voice. Furthermore, awareness of anxiety symptoms can lead to further increases in anxiety, as the sufferer begins to worry about how anxiety will affect his/her performance. The same effect might be observed in sporting activities, such as darts or snooker, but is usually studied in performing activities, such as acting or playing the violin. Early results of clinical trials with beta-blockers were promising (Brewer, 1972; James et al., 1977). There is now a significant body of results showing that beta-blockers can be helpful for performance anxiety, where their lack of a sedative effect and ability to "steady the hand" and mask external symptoms seems to be reassuring (Hartley et al., 1983; James & Savage, 1984; Lader, 1988). However, one recent study of performance anxiety found that many subjects had tried beta-blockers with little benefit (Clark & Agras, 1991).

Worry that anxiety will hamper performance is not restricted to manual tasks, but is also seen in that most ubiquitous of performances, social interaction. Social phobics often fear that those they interact with will identify their anxiety, and will judge them negatively as a result. By this logic, beta-blockers should also be useful in the treatment of social anxiety, and they seem to have some efficacy in this area (Gorman & Gorman, 1987; Gorman et al., 1985; Liebowitz et al., 1987). However, the results of controlled trials have proved to be more equivocal (Hayes & Schulz, 1987). With regard to social phobia, the balance of evidence suggests that beta-blockers can result in improvement in some cases, but that this effect is not robustly demonstrated in a double-blind situation (Falloon, Lloyd & Harpin, 1981; Liebowitz et al., 1991). Unlike anti-depressants for panic disorder or beta-blockers for performance anxiety, the use of benzodiazepines and antidepressants for the treatment of social phobia does not seem to have a clear theoretical rationale. Nevertheless, a variety of different drugs have been used to treat social phobia, and successful outcomes are reported using several of them. These include monoamine oxidase inhibitors (Liebowitz et al., 1993), alprazolam (Lydiard et al., 1988), other benzodiazepines (Davidson et al., 1991), fluoxetine (Van Ameringen, Mancini & Streiner, 1993) and buspirone (Schneier et al., 1993b).

Mechanisms Underlying the Success of Drug Treatments

Although the results have been mixed, few would now argue that drug treatments are entirely ineffective. However, the observed success of at least some forms of pharmacological treatment, for at least some forms of phobia, is not yet underpinned by any widely agreed understanding of the therapeutic mechanisms. Unlike depression, phobias are not usually episodic, so unless the pharmacological treatment effects a permanent change, then the phobic symptoms could be expected to return when the medication is withdrawn. In most cases there is at least an implicit assumption of an indirect effect, operating through psychological processes, i.e. the drug causes a neurochemical/physiological change, which modifies the patient's experience, and this in turn allows phobic behaviour to be modified through either exposure or cognitive changes. Some of the ideas about mechanisms depend on specific processes identified with maintenance of particular aspects of the phobic response. The hypothesized specificity of the effect of antidepressants on panic disorder (Klein, 1980) is one example, although it has been undermined by the success of other pharmacological treatments. Nevertheless, the general model is that the pharmacological management of the panic "allows" the phobic ptaient freedom from anticipatory anxiety. It has also been suggested that antidepressants may work by "toughening" the person, making him/her less sensitive to unfavourable social reactions and other forms of aversive stimuli (Kramer, 1994). Again, this may allow the individual to tolerate exposure to the phobic situation and to learn new approach behaviours. The control of performance anxiety by the action of beta-blockers on peripheral symptoms of anxiety may work through similar indirect mechanisms. In the short term the troublesome symptoms are suppressed; this permits the performer to develop renewed confidence. When the medication is withdrawn, the sympathetic activation and the associated symptoms do not return to the previous high levels. The implication of these models is that treatment efficacy would depend on both the direct drug effect and the indirect effect on phobic behaviour patterns. It would therefore seem logical to try to enhance the efficacy of pharmacological treatment by giving concurrent psychological treatment, or at least giving advice which would tend to encourage the patient to engage in self-directed exposure to the phobic stimuli.

ADVERSE EFFECTS OF PHARMACOLOGICAL TREATMENTS

Withdrawal Effects and Side-effects

The benefits of pharmacological treatments for phobias must of course be balanced against risks and side-effects. Of all the drugs discussed in this chapter, none has come in for so much criticism as the benzodiazepines (Kraupl Taylor, 1989). The main criticism levelled at benzodiazepines is that they create dependency. There is evidence that a substantial percentage of patients will experience withdrawal symptoms, especially if they have taken high doses of high-potency benzodiazepines for a prolonged period of time (Burrows et al., 1990; Noyes et al., 1988). The newer benzodiazepines, such as alprazolam and clonazepam, seem to be as likely to produce withdrawal symptoms as the older drugs like diazepam (Fyer et al., 1987). However, withdrawal is by no means a universal finding (Bowden & Fisher, 1980; Laughren et al., 1982), and our own clinical experience suggests that, at least with low-dose benzodiazepines, the symptoms are not usually protracted or unduly distressing (Hayward et al., 1996). Nevertheless, the possibility of dependence frightens many patients and makes them reluctant to take medications of this sort.

Unlike benzodiazepines, anti-depressants are not generally associated with a withdrawal syndrome. Unfortunately, they have two other significant drawbacks: a period of several weeks before they become effective, and a number of unde-

sirable side-effects (Arana & Hyman, 1991). Use of monoamine oxidase inhibitors required the patient to stay on a special diet or risk high blood pressure,
while the tricyclic antidepressants have a number of unpleasant side-effects,
including sedation, dry mouth, weight gain and urinary and sexual problems. In
a study by Noyes et al. (1989), 35% of patients who were treated for panic with
antidepressants discontinued treatment because of side-effects, the two main
reasons for termination being overstimulation (i.e. excessive arousal and insomnia) and weight gain. The tricyclics are also very dangerous in overdose, with a
risk of both suicide and accidental self-harm (Arana & Hyman, 1991). The newer
antidepressants (e.g. the serotonin re-uptake inhibitors) are better tolerated by
some patients, but they are not free from side-effects and still require a period of
weeks before they become effective. Antidepressant efficacy also requires the
patient to follow a strict routine, taking medication regularly and in a sufficient
dose, and some patients find this difficult. Overall, antidepressants are not pleasant drugs to take, and while this reduces the risk of recreational use and abuse, it
also may reduce compliance.

Risk of Relapse

The principal drawback of pharmacological treatments for phobias is the risk of
relapse when the drug is withdrawn, and a number of studies have documented
the return of symptoms (Burrows et al., 1990; Noyes et al., 1989). The problem is
especially worrying in the case of the benzodiazepines where, even if relapse
were not inevitable, withdrawal effects might trigger the return of fear (Pecknold
et al., 1988; Noyes et al., 1991). Antidepressants have not been associated with a
withdrawal syndrome, but there is evidence that many patients may have to
remain on them indefinitely if they are to derive continued benefit. A follow-up
study by Noyes, Garvey & Cook (1989) found that over half of a group of patients
treated for panic and agoraphobia with antidepressants were still on medication
1–4 years afterwards.

   The existence of relapse may be taken to imply that the indirect processes
referred to above either have not happened or at least have not happened to an
adequate extent. However, there is another possible explanation for relapse
following drug withdrawal, based on an attributional model derived from social
psychology: if patients attribute a change in their behaviour to medication, this
change is less likely to be maintained after drug withdrawal than if they attribute
the change to their own efforts. Two studies, (Davison & Valins, 1969; Davison,
Tsujimoto & Glaros, 1973), are generally cited in support of this argument. In the
first of these experiments, subjects were subjected to an electric shock, while in
the second they suffered from insomnia. The experimental manipulation involved giving them tablets and convincing them that the tablets had helped them,
respectively, to endure the shocks or to fall asleep. Half the group therefore
attributed their "success" to the drug, but the other half were later told that the
tablets were in fact ineffective, so that any improvement must have been due to

their own efforts, The results showed that the self-attribution group coped better than the drug-attribution groups at drug-free follow-up assessments. Grimm (1980) has criticized these studies for poor statistical analysis, misinterpretation of data, and uncertainties of interpretation induced by the use of such a complex series of deceptions. His critique is a cogent one, but nevertheless, the argument posed in the original articles seems to have considerable face validity: if phobic patients attribute their decreased fear of the phobic stimulus to a drug, they would expect the fear to return if the drug were discontinued, and this expectation might well influence their self-efficacy and their behaviour. As far as we know, the attributional interpretation of relapse has only been tested once, in a treatment study combining drugs and behaviour therapy (see Basoglu et al., 1994); this study will be discussed below.

Is Long-term Use an Answer?

A point relatively little discussed is that long-term maintenance treatment might be an alternative to short-term treatment followed by risk of withdrawal symptoms or relapse. However, the issues around long-term treatment with benzodiazepines and antidepressants are rarely discussed (DuPont, 1990; Noyes & Perry, 1990). Noyes, Garvey & Cook (1989) reported follow-up data collected 1– 4 years after patients had been treated for panic disorder with antidepressants, and found that 63% of the patients were still on some kind of medication at follow-up. They also reported that the patients in the study showed an improvement in their symptoms, and that there was no difference in outcome between those on and off medication. As Noyes & Perry (1990) note, there may be both risks and benefits to the long-term use of medications. Kraupl Taylor (1989) also points out that if the long-term use of a medication, either an antidepressant or a benzodiazepine, results in improved functioning for the patient, then such "dependence" is not necessarily to be condemned. However, both patients and health professionals are wary of long-term medication use and fearful both of the processes of dependence and the possibility that there may be more serious long-term adverse effects, which have not yet been fully documented.

COMBINING DRUG TREATMENT WITH PSYCHOLOGICAL TREATMENT

One alternative to relying on haphazard self-exposure or the uncertainties of long-term medication is to use a combination of medication and psychological treatment. The question then is whether this would be more effective than either treatment alone. On the assumption that drug treatments are "permissive" of behavioural treatment, then drug effects should be augmented by behavioural treatment. It has even been suggested that the relief from anxiety provided by medication could make behavioural treatments easier and less aversive, and hence dropout rates might be lower and treatment compliance higher (Mavissakalian & Jones, 1990). On the basis of these arguments, the outcome of combined treatment would be expected to be better than either drug treatment or behavioural treatment alone. However, there have also been a number of suggestions that the outcome of behavioural treatment would be disadvantaged by concurrent drug use because of drug effects on the processing of either anxiety stimuli, state dependency, amnesic effects or attributional processes. It is to these issues that we now turn.

Objections to Combined Treatment

A strong case has been made on the basis of animal research that the action of benzodiazepines could increase resistance to extinction. Insofar as exposure treatment can be identified with unreinforced exposure to conditioned aversive stimuli, then treatment outcome would be poorer. Feldon & Gray (1981) showed that animals which are "pre-exposed" to an aversive stimulus have a greater tolerance for the stimulus on subsequent presentations, but this increased resistance is reduced or eliminated in animals that are given benzodiazepines at the same time. Gray (1987) has argued that the pre-exposure to aversive stimuli is analogous to *in vivo* exposure treatment for phobics, hence taking benzodiazepines during treatment might block the beneficial effects of exposure. Kamano (1972) and Gorman, Dyak & Reid (1979) describe experiments in which animals undergo procedures closely modelled on exposure therapy for phobias, and find that the extinction produced by such exposure is indeed blocked by concurrent benzodiazepines, offering some support for Gray's position.

It has also been suggested that reducing anxiety during exposure therapy may be counterproductive, on the grounds that the experience of anxiety is necessary for such treatment to work effectively (Sanderson & Wetzler, 1993). This objection is based on the hypothesis that exposure therapy works, at least in part, by exposing the patient to the symptoms of anxiety and increasing his/her ability to tolerate such symptoms. Certainly many cognitive theories of panic suggest that panic sufferers react with exaggerated, and even catastrophic, fear to such sensations (Clark, 1986). A cognitive therapy perspective has also been used to suggest that exposure therapy works by teaching patients that such sensations are not followed by catastrophe (Clark, 1989).

Two other processes whereby medication could interfere with behavioural treatment have been suggested. One is state dependency; it has been shown that material learned while the subject is in one particular physiological state can be more difficult to retrieve when the subject is in a different state (Eich, 1980). Thus, in the case of behavioural treatment, approach behaviours learned under the influence of a drug might not be so effectively recalled or reproduced in the absence of the drug. This hypothesis has been most commonly stated with respect to the benzodiazepines, but could presumably apply equally with antidepressants or any other drug which produced changes in state. Finally, benzodiazepines in particular have been shown to have an amnesic effect, and it has been suggested that patients who use such medications during therapy might, in effect, forget the approach skills that they learned through such therapy (Curran, 1986; Lister et al., 1988). We are not aware of empirical evidence that directly addresses these ideas.

The attributional argument discussed above is particularly salient in relation to combined treatment. Furthermore, it would not matter if the drug had any real effect on anxiety or not, since if the patients attributed their improvement to medication, then relapse on withdrawal could be predicted, even if the "drug" were in fact placebo. It would be ironic if gains made principally through the agency of the psychological element of combined treatments were likely to be lost because patients (incorrectly) attributed their successes to medication.

The Efficacy of Combined Treatment

There are now many studies in which, in the treatment of phobias, medication is combined with some form of behaviourally-orientated approach. One observation emerges very clearly from all these studies, and that is that behavioural treatment, alone or in combination, is an efficacious treatment (Mattick et al., 1990; Mavissakalian & Jones, 1990). This finding is not surprising, in that behavioural approaches have clearly become the treatment of choice for phobias (see Chapter ••, this volume). A second finding also appears to be robust: that outcomes tend to be better when medication is combined with formal or informal exposure to phobic stimuli during the period of drug treatment than with medication alone (Mavissakalian & Jones, 1990; Telch et al., 1985).

The controversial issue is whether drugs improve or impair the efficacy of behavioural treatment. In this area there seem to be some investigators who favour concurrent drug therapy and some who do not; as Mattick et al. (1990) comment, ". . . it is difficult for a clinician to develop a reasoned view that is independent of the polemics" (p. 567). The class of drug whose use has been most often supported is antidepressants, in keeping with Klein's model of panic aetiology. A number of placebo controlled trials have evaluated the efficacy of antidepressant and behavioural therapy for the treatment of agoraphobia and panic. In many cases the antidepressant used was imipramine, but others have been used: trials include Sheehan, Ballenger & Jacobsen's (1980) work on imipramine and phenelzine, Solyom et al.'s (1981) study, which used phenelzine, and Oehrberg et al.'s (1995) work with paroxetine. The majority of these studies (e.g. Mavissakalian & Michelson, 1986a; Oehrberg et al., 1995; Sheehan, Ballenger & Jacobsen, 1980; Telch et al., 1985; Zitrin, Klein & Woerner, 1980; Zitrin et al., 1983) follow a similar pattern of findings: the placebo-plus-behaviour group shows considerable therapeutic improvement, but the antidepressant-plus-behaviour therapy group shows significantly better results on at least some outcome measures. In general, these authors conclude that combined treatment is therefore superior to psychological treatment alone. Two studies (Marks et al., 1983; Solyom et al., 1981) find that the two groups do equally well, and that there is therefore no advantage in the use of medication, but the fact that there are some non-significant results does not mean that the positive effects observed in the previous studies can be discounted. Marks et al. (1983) suggest that one explanation for the discrepancies could be variability in levels of depression in the different samples. According to this reasoning, depression might decrease motivation and make exposure more difficult, and therefore without any special antiphobic properties, the antidepressant would still improve treatment motivation. However, Mavissakalian (1987) showed that, among the patients in his study, initial depression had no relationship with treatment success or drug effect, and Marks later conceded that antidepressants might have some antipanic and antiphobic effects (Marks & O'Sullivan, 1988). The pattern of good results for combined treatment has led some authorities to argue that the combination of antidepressant and behavioural therapy is the treatment of choice for panic and agoraphobia (Mavissakalian & Jones, 1990).

On the basis of these results, one might indeed infer that combined treatment is to be preferred, but there is an important caveat, and that is that the final assessment of functioning is commonly made while the patients are still taking medication, or shortly after they have stopped. Only two of the favourable studies report any long-term follow-up data. Zitrin, Klein & Woerner (1980) report 6-month follow-up data and show a disturbingly higher rate of relapse among patients taking drug as opposed to placebo (27 vs. 6%), although this effect does not reach statistical significance. In a 2-year follow-up report, Mavissakalian & Michelson (1986b) reported continued superior results for antidepressants at 1 month follow-up, but this superiority disappears thereafter, suggesting somewhat greater loss of therapeutic gains by the group on active medication, although their results remain comparable to those in the placebo group. Finally, Cohen, Monteiro & Marks (1984) report no difference in their treatment groups after 2 years, but this is not surprising as they did not find any original group differences, a finding that is confirmed in a 5-year follow-up reported by Lelliott et al. (1987). These results suggest that even if antidepressants increase the effectiveness of behavioural therapy in the short term, this advantage may not prove to be long-lasting, especially if the patient is no longer taking the medication. A similar result is reported in a study by Clark et al. (1994), in which one-fifth of patients receiving imipramine plus behavioural therapy, and functioning at a high level at the end of treatment, relapsed within a few months of stopping their medication. In general, the evidence does *not* support the view that drug therapy interferes with treatment, only that, in the longer term, those on drug may do *no better* than those on placebo. The alternative is long-term drug treatment; Nagy et al. (1993) report a 2.9-year follow-up of panic patients treated with imipramine and behavioural group treatment, which suggests that treatment gains are maintained, but that half the patients continued on some form of antipanic medication.

The other class of drugs that has been studied using a combined treatment is the benzodiazepines, and it is of course in relation to concurrent benzodiazepine treatment that there has been the strongest case for interference. One study (Wardle et al., 1994) compared a low dose of diazepam with placebo, each combined with exposure treatment in the treatment of agoraphobia. The other (Marks et al., 1993a), used a high dose of alprazolam or placebo, combined with self-exposure instructions. Wardle et al. (1994) found no significant differences in functioning between the drug and placebo groups, either immediately after treatment or during a 1-year follow-up. Marks et al. (1993a), on the other hand, found a tendency for those receiving alprazolam to relapse after the end of drug treatment, losing many of the gains accomplished through the combined treatment. These results, with their strikingly anti-benzodiazepine outcome, seem to have provoked a heated controversy concerning the place of benzodiazepines in the management of phobias (see Spiegel et al., 1993, and the reply by Marks et al., 1993b).

As well as the treatment outcome, the authors also carried out an investigation of patients' attributions for success following treatment, and showed that attributing success to medication predicted relapse (Basoglu et al., 1994). In this study, the use of a large dose of benzodiazepine led to 80% of patients being able to identify correctly whether they were on benzodiazepine or placebo, so the result is confounded to some extent with actual medication status. However, a questionnaire concerning beliefs about the importance of tablets vs. personal effort in improvement also proved to be a powerful predictor of relapse. As part of our combined treatment trial (Wardle et al., 1994), we have also collected data on patients' attributions for success in completing their homework assignments, and in an unpublished analysis found that very few patients attributed their success to medication, but those that did fared just as well as those who did not. The differences may be due to the much lower level of drug used in this study. These are the only studies that we know of to evaluate the attributional effect discussed above.

Although these two studies differ in their results, they both suggest that benzodiazepines fail to increase the effectiveness fo behavioural treatment. The implication would seem to be that taking a low dose of benzodiazepine may not undermine the effectiveness of behavioural treatment, but high doses may have leave the patient vulnerable to relapse when medication is withdrawn. Nagy et al. (1989) report a naturalistic follow-up of patients who received a combination of alprazolam and behavioural group treatment, with a dosage of alprazolam around half of that given in the Marks et al. (1993a) trial. They found that most of their subjects had maintained their gains for 2.5 years. However, more than half of their subjects were still taking medication, albeit at a lower dose than they had received in the study. Once more, the suggestion is that gains made with the help of medication may need continued medication if they are to be maintained.

One other drug, buspirone, has been evaluated in combination with cognitive therapy in a treatment study with panic disorder patients. Cottraux et al. (1995) found that after 16 weeks, buspirone plus cognitive–behavioural therapy was more effective that buspirone alone on two out of 18 outcome measures. There were no significant differences on the 16 other measures, and no significant differences at all on long-term follow-up (68 weeks). This finding would suggest that adding buspirone to cognitive–behavioural therapy offers little practical benefit.

In the light of the variable results from outcome studies, two recent meta-analyses have been carried out to clarify the situation, and it is interesting that they reach opposite conclusions. Mattick et al. (1990) concluded that exposure therapy combined with imipramine is probably the best treatment for panic and agoraphobia, while Cox et al. (1992) concluded that there is little evidence that imipramine is effective, while alprazolam shows the strongest effects in controlling panic. If nothing else, these conclusions indicate continuing controversy in the field.

On the subject of social phobia, three studies are worth mentioning. Falloon, Lloyd & Harpin (1981) treated social phobics with a programme of social skills training and real-life practice, plus either a beta-blocker or placebo. No difference was found between the two groups, and the authors concluded that beta-blockers did not offer any benefit over and above that of behavioural treatment. In a study by Gelernter et al. (1991), patients received instructions on exposure to phobic situations plus either phenelzine, alprazolam or placebo. All groups improved, with the phenelzine group being significantly better than the other two groups on only one of seven measures, i.e. medication added marginally to the effectiveness of exposure treatment. Finally, Clark & Agras (1991) describe treating a group of musicians for performance anxiety, but note that all their subjects also fulfilled the diagnostic criteria for social phobia. Buspirone was found to be ineffective by itself and to offer no additional benefit when combined with cognitive–behavioural therapy. So, in the field of social phobia, there is little to commend the use of pharmacological treatment.

The controversy concerning the benefits and risk of combined treatment is likely to continue. Much current research is funded by the pharmaceutical industry, and therefore money will continue to be available to study the effects of new drugs on phobias. Some authors (e.g. Marks et al., 1993c) have suggested that this can impair scientific objectivity: we must hope that all investigators, whatever their source of funding, will strive to evaluate the benefits and drawbacks of medication in an even-handed way.

CONCLUSIONS

As with many review papers, this one may remind some of the fable by Aesop about the mountains labouring to bring forth a mouse. A few clear ideas stand out, a good deal of data is reviewed, and very little can finally be concluded with any certainty. In relation to the efficacy of pharmacotherapy for phobias, some drug treatments do seem to be effective, at least in the shorter term. Of the three classes of drugs reviewed, each has certain advantages: the antidepressants seem to have the most robust effect on long-term functioning, the benzodiazepines to offer the quickest relief, and the beta-blockers to have the fewest side-effects. There is little evidence, however, that any of these drugs can alter phobic behaviour in the long term, and such limited evidence as is available points to relapse when medication is withdrawn. Adding behavioural treatment to drug treatment provides a novel approach to boosting the efficacy of drug treatment, and all lines of argument would appear to point to beneficial effects—in fact, it could be argued that the very efficacy of drug treatment depends on the patients using at least self-exposure, so there would be every reason to suppose that good behavioural therapy could only be an efficacious addition. However, the other question is whether the combination treatment is better that behavioural therapy alone— since if it is not, there would be little point in adding the drug to the behavioural therapy. From the perspective of psychological theory, adding drug treatment to behavioural therapy could give a better outcome if the drug promoted exposure, and a worse outcome if either the drug blocked the effectiveness of exposure or the use of concurrent medication caused the patient to attribute his/her improvement (incorrectly) to the drug. There is little sign that treatment outcomes are worse with combined treatment in the short term, but little sign either that they are better. In the longer term, after drug withdrawal, relapse is common, as is return to medication. At the present time, therefore, the combination treatment would appear to have little advantage over behavioural therapy alone, so there would be no point in starting drug treatment unless a very rapid treatment response was essential. However, if the patient was already on medication, this should not oppose the efficacy of behavioural treatment, but great care would need to taken over the withdrawal regimen. Surprisingly little attention has been paid to the effect of drug treatment on the *process* of behaviour change. If the real goal is to maximize treatment effectiveness, then the appropriate intermediate target of investigation should be the *effects* of treatment. An understanding of how the effects of drug treatment might impact upon the processes of behaviour change would be a better basis for progress than the sterile terrain of comparative research.

REFERENCES

Arana, G.W. & Hyman, S.E. (1991). *Handbook of Psychiatric Drug Therapy*. Boston: Little, Brown.

Ballenger, J.C., Burrows, G.D., DuPont, R.L., Lesser, I.M., Noyes, R., Pecknold, J.C., Rifkin, A. & Swinson, R.P. (1988). Alprazolam in panic disorder and agoraphobia: results from a multicenter trial. I. Efficacy in short-term treatment. *Archives of General Psychiatry*, **45**, 413–422.

Basoglu, M., Marks, I.M., Kilic, C., Brewin, C.R. & Swinson, R.P. (1994). Alprazolam and exposure for panic disorder with agoraphobia: attribution of improvement to medication predicts subsequent relapse. *British Journal of Psychiatry*, **164**, 652–659.

Bowden, C.L. & Fisher, J.G. (1980). Safety and efficacy of long-term diazepam therapy. *Southern Medical Journal*, **73**, 1581–1584.

Brewer, C. (1972). Beneficial effect of beta-adrenergic blockade on "examnerves". *Lancet*, **2**, 435.

Burrows, G.D., Norman, T.R., Judd, F.K. & Marriott, P.F. (1990). Short-acting versus long-acting benzodiazepines: discontinuation effects in panic disorders. *Journal of Psychiatric Research*, **24**(suppl. 2), 65–72.

Chambless, D.L., Caputo, G.C., Bright, P. & Gallagher, R. (1984). Assessment of fear of fear in agoraphobics: the Body Sensations Questionnaire and the Agoraphobic Cognitions Questionnaire. *Journal of Consulting and Clinical Psychology*, **52**, 1090–1097.

Chouinard, G., Annable, L., Fontaine, R. & Solyom, L. (1982). Alprazolam in tbe treatment of generalized anxiety and panic disorders: a double-blind placebo-controlled study. *Psychopharmacology*, **77**, 229–233.

Clark, D.B. & Agras, W.S. (1991). The assessment and treatment of performance anxiety in musicians. *American Journal of Psychiatry*, **148**, 598–605.

Clark, D.M. (1986). A cognitive approach to panic. *Behaviour Research and Therapy*, **24**, 461–470.

Clark, D.M. (1989). Anxiety states: panic and generalized anxiety. In K. Hawton, P.M. Salkovskis, J. Kirk & D. Clark (eds), *Cognitive Behaviour Therapy for Psychiatric Problems: A Practical Guide* (pp. 52–96). Oxford: Oxford University Press.

Clark, D.M., Salkovskis, P.M., Hackmann, A., Middleton, H., Anastasiades, P. & Gelder, M. (1994). A comparison of cognitive therapy, applied relaxation, and imipramine in the treatment of panic disorder. *British Journal of Psychiatry*, **164**, 759–769.

Cohen, S.D., Monteiro, W. & Marks, I.M. (1984). Two-year follow-up of agoraphobics after exposure and imipramine. *British Journal of Psychiatry*, **144**, 276–281.

Cottraux, J., Note, I.-D., Cungi, C., Legeron, P., Heim, F., Chneiweiss, L., Bernard, G. & Bouvard, M. (1995). A controlled study of cognitive–behavioural therapy with buspirone or placebo in panic disorder with agoraphobia. *British Journal of Psychiatry*, **167**, 635–641.

Cox, B.J., Endler, N.S., Lee, P.S. & Swinson, R.P. (1992). A meta-analysis of treatments for panic disorder with agoraphobia: imipramine, alprazolam, and *in vivo* exposure. *Journal of Behavior Therapy and Experimental Psychiatry*, **23**, 175–182.

Curran, H.V. (1986). Tranquillising memories: a review of the effects of benzodiazepines on human memory. *Biological Psychology*, **23**, 179–213.

Davidson, J.R.T., Ford, S.M., Smith, R.D. & Potts, N.L.S. (1991). Long-term treatment of social phobia with clonazepam. *Journal of Clinical Psychiatry*, **52**(suppl. 11), 16–20.

Davison, G.C., Tsujimoto, R.N. & Glaros, A.G. (1973). Attribution and the maintenance of behavior change in falling asleep. *Journal of Abnormal Psychology*, **82**, 124–133.

Davison, G.C. & Valins, S. (1969). Maintenance of self-attributed and drug-attributed behavior change. *Journal of Personality and Social Psychology*, **11**, 25–33.

DuPont, R.L. (1990). Thinking about stopping treatment for panic disorder. *Journal of Clinical Psychiatry*, **51**(12, suppl. A), 38–45.

Eich, J.E. (1980). The cue-dependent nature of state-dependent retrieval. *Memory and Cognition*, **8**, 157–173.

Falloon, I.R.H., Lloyd, G.G. & Harpin, R.E. (1981). The treatment of social phobia: real-life rehearsal with non-professional therapists. *Journal of Nervous and Mental Disease*, **169**, 180–184.

Feldon, J. & Gray, J.A. (1981). The partial reinforcement extinction effect after treatment with chlordiazepoxide. *Psychopharmacology*, **73**, 269–275.

Fyer, A.J., Liebowitz, M.R., Gorman, J.M., Campeas, R., Levin, A., Davies, S.O., Goetz, D. & Klein, D.F. (1987). Discontinuation of alprazolam treatment in panic patients. *American Journal of Psychiatry*, **144**, 303–308.

Gelernter, C.S., Uhde, T.W., Cimbolic, P., Arnkoff, D.B., Vittone, B.J., Tancer, M.E. & Bartko, J.J. (1991). Cognitive–behavioral and pharmacological treatments of social phobia. *Archives of General Psychiatry*, **48**, 938–945.

Gorman, J.E., Dyak, J.D. & Reid, L.D. (1979). Methods of deconditioning persisting avoidance: diazepam as an adjunct to response prevention. *Bulletin of the Psychonomic Society*, **14**, 46–48.

Gorman, J.M. & Gorman, L.K. (1987). Drug treatment of social phobia. *Journal of Affective Disorders*, **13**, 183–192.

Gorman, J.M., Liebowitz, M.R., Fyer, A.J., Campeas, R. & Klein, D.F. (1985). Treatment of social phobia with atenolol. *Journal of Clinical Psychopharmacology*, **5**, 298–301.

Gray, J.A. (1987). Interactions between drugs and behavior therapy. In H.J. Eysenck & I. Martin (eds), *Theoretical Foundations of Behavior Therapy* (pp. 433–447). New York: Plenum.

Grimm, L.G. (1980). The maintenance of self- and drug-attributed behavior change: a critique. *Journal of Abnormal Psychology*, **89**, 282–285.

Hartley, L.R., Ungapen, S., Davie, I. & Spencer, D.J. (1983). The effect of beta-adrenergic blocking drugs on speakers' performance and memory. *British Journal of Psychiatry*, **142**, 512–517.

Hayes, P.E. & Schulz, S.C. (1987). Beta-blockers in anxiety disorders. *Journal of Affective Disorders*, **13**, 119–130.

Hayward, P., Wardle, J., Higgitt, A. & Gray, J. (1996). Changes in "withdrawal symptoms" following discontinuation of low-dose diazepam. *Psychopharmacology*, **125**, 392–397.

James, I.M., Pearson, P.M., Griffith, D.N.W. & Newbury, P. (1977). Effect of oxprenolol on stage-fright in musicians. *Lancet*, **2**, 952–954.

James, I. & Savage, I. (1984). Beneficial effect of nadolol on anxiety-induced disturbances of performance in musicians: a comparison with diazepam and placebo. *American Heart Journal*, **108**, 1150–1155.

Jones, M.C. (1924). The elimination of children's fears. *Journal of Experimental Psychology*, **7**, 382–390.

Kamano, D.K. (1972). Using drugs to modify the effect of response prevention on avoidance extinction. *Behaviour Research and Therapy*, **10**, 367–370.

Kathol, R.G., Noyes, R., Slymen, D.J., Crowe, R.R., Clancy, J. & Kerber, R.E. (1980). Propranolol in chronic anxiety disorders: a controlled study. *Archives of General Psychiatry*, **37**, 1361–1365.

Keegan, J. (1993). *The Face of Battle*. London: Pimlico.

Klein, D.F. (1964). Delineation of two drug-responsive anxiety syndromes. *Psychopharmacologia*, **5**, 397–408.

Klein, D.F. (1980). Anxiety reconceptualized: early experience with imipramine and anxiety. *Comprehensive Psychiatry*, **21**, 411–427.

Kramer, P.D. (1994). *Listening to Prozac*. London: Fourth Estate.

Kraupl Taylor, F. (1989). The damnation of benzodiazepines. *British Journal of Psychiatry*, **154**, 697–704.

Lader, M. (1988). Beta-adrenoceptor antagonists in neuropsychiatry: an update. *Journal of Clinical Psychiatry*, **49**, 213–223.

Laughren, T.P., Battey, Y., Greenblatt, D.J. & Harrop, D.S. (1982). A controlled trial of diazepam withdrawal in chronically anxious outpatients. *Acta Psychiatrica Scandinavica*, **65**, 171–179.

Lelliott, P.T., Marks, I.M., Monteiro, W.O., Tsakiris, F. & Noshirvani, H. (1987). Agoraphobics 5 years after imipramine and exposure: outcome and predictors. *Journal of Nervous and Mental Disease*, **175**, 599–605.

Liebowitz, M.R., Campeas, R., Levin, A., Sandberg, D., Hollander, E. & Papp, L. (1987). Pharmacotherapy of social phobia: a condition distinct from panic attacks. *Psychosomatics*, **28**, 305–308.

Liebowitz, M.R., Schneier, F., Gitow, A. & Feerick, J. (1993) Reversible monoamine oxidase-a inhibitors in social phobia. *Clinical Neuropharmacology*, **16**(suppl. 2), S83–88.

Liebowitz, M.R., Schneier, F.R., Hollander, E., Welkowitz, L.A., Saoud, J.B., Feerick, J.,

Campeas, R., Fallon, B.A., Street, L. & Gitow, A. (1991). Treatment of social phobia with drugs other than benzodiazepines. *Journal of Clinical Psychiatry*, **52**(11, suppl.), 10–15.

Lister, R.G., Weingartner, H., Eckardt, M.J. & Linnoila, M. (1988). Clinical relevance of effects of benzodiazepines on learning and memory. *Psychopharmacology Series*, **6**, 117–127.

Lydiard, R.B., Laraia, M.T., Howell, E.F. & Ballenger, J.C. (1988). Alprazolam in the treatment of social phobia. *Journal of Clinical Psychiatry*, **49**, 17–19.

Marks, I.M., Basoglu, M., Noshirvani, H., Greist, J., Swinson, R.P. & O'Sullivan, G. (1993c). Drug treatment of panic disorder: further comment. *British Journal of Psychiatry*, **162**, 795–796.

Marks, I.M., Grey, S., Cohen, D., Hill, R., Mawson, D., Ramm, E. & Stern, R.S. (1983). Imipramine and brief therapist-aided exposure in agoraphobics having self-exposure homework. *Archives of General Psychiatry*, **40**, 153–162.

Marks, I. & O'Sullivan, G. (1988). Drugs and psychological treatments for agoraphobia/panic and obsessive–compulsive disorders: a review. *British Journal of Psychiatry*, **153**, 650–658.

Marks, I.M., Swinson, R.P., Basoglu, M., Kuch, K., Noshirvani, H., O'Sullivan, G., Lelliott, P.T., Kirby, M., McNamee, G., Sengun, S. & Wickwire, K. (1993a). Alprazolam and exposure alone and combined in panic disorder with agoraphobia: a controlled study in London and Toronto. *British Journal of Psychiatry*, **162**, 776–787.

Marks, I.M., Swinson, R.P., Basoglu, M., Noshirvani, H., Kuch, K., O'Sullivan, G. & Lelliott, P.T. (1993b). Reply to comment on the London/Toronto study. *British Journal of Psychiatry*, **162**, 790–794.

Mattick, R.P., Andrews, G., Hadzi-Pavlovic, D. & Christensen, H. (1990). Treatment of panic and agoraphobia: an integrative review. *Journal of Nervous and Mental Disease*, **178**, 567–576.

Mavissakalian, M. (1987). Initial depression and response to imipramine in agoraphobia. *Journal of Nervous and Mental Disease*, **175**, 358–361.

Mavissakalian, M. & Jones, B. (1990). Comparative efficacy and interaction between drug and behavioral therapies for panic/agoraphobia. In R. Noyes, M. Roth & G.D. Burrows (eds), *Handbook of Anxiety, Vol. 4: The Treatment of Anxiety* (pp. 73–86). Amsterdam: Elsevier.

Mavissakalian, M. & Michelson, L. (1986a). Agoraphobia: relative and combined effectiveness of therapist-assisted *in vivo* exposure and imipramine. *Journal of Clinical Psychiatry*, **47**, 117–122.

Mavissakalian, M. & Michelson, L. (1986b). Two-year follow-up of exposure and imipramine treatment of agoraphobia. *American Journal of Psychiatry*, **143**, 1106–1112.

Mavissakalian, M., Michelson, L. & Dealy, R.S. (1983). Pharmacological treatment of agoraphobia: imipramine versus imipramine with programmed practice. *British Journal of Psychiatry*, **143**, 348–355.

Montaigne, M. de (1592/1993). Of fear. In M.A. Screech (ed.), *The Essays: a Selection* (pp. 13–16). Harmondsworth: Penguin.

Nagy, L.M., Krystal, J.H., Charney, D.S., Merikangas, K.R. & Woods, S.W. (1993). Long-term outcome of panic disorder after short-term imipramine and behavioral group treatment: 2.9-year naturalistic follow-up. *Journal of Clinical Psychopharmacology*, **13**, 16–24.

Nagy, L.M., Krystal, J.H., Woods, S.W. & Charney, D.S. (1989). Clinical and medication outcome after short-term alprazolam and behavioral group treatment in panic disorder: 2.5-year naturalistic follow-up study. *Archives of General Psychiatry*, **46**, 993–999.

Noyes, R., Anderson, D.J., Clancy, J., Crowe, R.R., Slymen, D.J., Ghoneim, M.M. & Hinrichs, J.V. (1984). Diazepam and propranolol in panic disorder and agoraphobia. *Archives of General Psychiatry*, **41**, 287–292.

Noyes, R., Garvey, M.J. & Cook, B.L. (1989). Follow-up study of patients with panic disorder and agoraphobia with panic attacks treated with tricyclic antidepressants. *Journal of Affective Disorders*, **16**, 249–257.

Noyes, R., Garvey, M.J., Cook, B.L. & Perry, P.J. (1988). Benzodiazepine withdrawal: a review of the evidence. *Journal of Clinical Psychiatry*, **49**, 382–389.

Noyes, R., Garvey, M.J., Cook, B.L. & Samuelson, L. (1989). Problems with tricyclic antidepressant use in patients with panic disorder or agoraphobia: results of a naturalistic follow-up study. *Journal of Clinical Psychiatry*, **50**, 163–169.

Noyes, R., Garvey, M.J., Cook, B. & Suelzer, M. (1991). Controlled discontinuation of benzodiazepine treatment for patients with panic disorder. *American Journal of Psychiatry*, **148**, 517–523.

Noyes, R. & Perry, P. (1990). Maintenance treatment with antidepressants in panic disorder. *Journal of Clinical Psychiatry*, **51**(12, suppl. A), 24–30.

Oehrberg, S., Christiansen, P.E., Behnke, K., Borup, A.L., Severin, B., Soegaard, J., Calberg, H., Judge, R., Ohrstrom, J.K. & Manniche, P.M. (1995). Paroxetine in the treatment of panic disorder: a randomised, double-blind, placebo-controlled study. *British Journal of Psychiatry*, **167**, 374–379.

Pecknold, J.C., Swinson, R.P., Kuch, K. & Lewis, C.P. (1988). Alprazolam in panic disorder and agoraphobia: results from a multicenter trial. III. Discontinuation effects. *Archives of General Psychiatry*, **45**, 429–436.

Sanderson, W.C. & Wetzler, S. (1993). Observations on the cognitive behavioral treatment of panic disorder: impact of benzodiazepines. *Psychotherapy*, **30**, 125–132.

Schneier, F.R., Carrasco, J.L., Hollander, E., Campeas, R., Fallon, B., Saoud, J.B., Feerick, J. & Liebowitz, M.R. (1993a). Alpidem in the treatment of panic disorder. *Journal of Clinical Psychiatry*, **13**, 150–153.

Schneier, F.R., Saoud, J.B., Campeas, R., Fallon, B.A., Hollander, E., Coplan, J. & Liebowitz, M.R. (1993b). Buspirone in social phobia. *Journal of Clinical Psychopharmacology*, **13**, 251–256.

Sheehan, D.V. (1987). Benzodiazepines in panic disorder and agoraphobia. *Journal of Affective Disorders*, **13**, 169–181.

Sheehan, D.V., Ballenger, J. & Jacobsen, G. (1980). Treatment of endogenous anxiety with phobic, hysterical, and hypochondriacal symptoms. *Archives of General Psychiatry*, **37**, 51–59.

Sheehan, D.V., Raj, A.B., Sheehan, K.H. & Soto, S. (1990). Is buspirone effective for panic disorder? *Journal of Clinical Psychopharmacology*, **10**, 3–11.

Sheehan, D.V., Raj, A.B., Harnett-Sheehan, K., Soto, S. & Knapp, E. (1993). The relative efficacy of high-dose buspirone and alprazolam in the treatment of panic disorder: a double-blind placebo-controlled study. *Acta Psychiatrica Scandinavica*, **88**, 1–11.

Solyom, C., Solyom, L., LaPierre, Y., Pecknold, J. & Morton, L. (1981). Phenelzine and exposure in the treatment of phobias. *Biological Psychiatry*, **16**, 239–247.

Spiegel, D.A., Roth, M., Weissman, M., Lavori, P., Gorman, J., Rush, J. & Ballenger, J. (1993). Comment on the London/Toronto study of alprazolam and exposure in panic disorder with agoraphobia. *British Journal of Psychiatry*, **162**, 788–789.

Telch, M.J., Agras, W.S., Taylor, C.B., Roth, W.T. & Gallen, C.G. (1985). Combined pharmacological and behavioral treatment for agoraphobia. *Behaviour Research and Therapy*, **23**, 325–335.

Van Ameringen, M., Mancini, C. & Streiner, D.L. (1993). Fluoxetine efficacy in social phobia. *Journal of Clinical Psychiatry*, **54**, 27–32.

Wardle, J., Hayward, P., Higgitt, A., Stabl, M., Blizard, R. & Gray, J. (1994). Effects of concurrent diazepam treatment on the outcome of exposure therapy in agoraphobia. *Behaviour Research and Therapy*, **32**, 203–215.

Watson, J.B. & Rayner, R. (1920). Conditioned emotional reactions. *Journal of Experimental Psychology*, **3**, 1–14.

Wheatley, D. (1990). Beta-blockers in anxiety: the stress connection. In D. Wheatley (ed.), *The Anxiolytic Jungle: Where Next?* (pp. 137–162). Chichester: Wiley.

Zitrin, C.M., Klein, D.F. & Woerner, M.G. (1980). Treatmant of agoraphobia with group exposure *in vivo* and imipramine. *Archives of General Psychiatry*, **37**, 63–72.
Zitrin, C.M., Klein, D.F., Woerner, M.G. & Ross, D.C. (1983). Treatment of phobias: I. Comparison of imipramine hydrochloride and placebo. *Archives of General Psychiatry*, **40**, 125–138.

General Theoretical Perspectives on Aetiology and Maintenance

Chapter 15

A Conditioning Model of Phobias

Graham C.L. Davey
*School of Cognitive & Computing Sciences,
University of Sussex, Brighton, UK*

Conditioning models of phobias have certainly suffered a chequered history. A reading of most clinical psychology text books from the 1970s and 1980s will show conditioning models of phobias being given brief consideration and then usually dismissed as inadequate. The grounds cited for this dismissal are often numerous. However, what is paradoxical about this attitude to conditioning models is that, if they are so inadequate, why continue to discuss them at all? The reason is probably that, while the models at the time were inadequate as predictive models of phobias, there was a general intuitive feeling that conditioning ought to be widely involved in the aetiology of phobias.

This chapter will attempt to provide a broad insight into how contemporary conditioning models can contribute to an understanding of the aetiology and maintenance of phobias. The emphasis will be on how the rules which govern associative learning can contribute to a predictive conditioning model of phobias, and also how conditioning processes can be extended to help explain phobic responding, even in situations where the individual may not have experienced a conditioning episode at the onset of the phobia. This approach will look not only at the influence of associative factors in the generation and maintenance of phobias, but also at non-associative performance processes which may result in fluctuations in phobic responding (cf. Davey, 1989, 1992a). In this sense, the conditioning view espoused in this chapter is one which extends beyond simple contiguity learning to include information-processing factors and biases which affect the formation and strength of associations, and non-associative cognitive processes which affect the perception and evaluation of events in the associative episode. It will be argued that this broad-based conditioning approach provides

Phobias—A Handbook of Theory, Research and Treatment. Edited by G.C.L. Davey.
© 1997 John Wiley & Sons Ltd.

the best conceptual framework in which to organize our knowledge of the aetiology and maintenance of phobic responding in general.

THE TRADITIONAL CONDITIONING PARADIGM AND ITS MAIN CRITICISMS

Attempts to explain human fears and phobias in terms of conditioning date back to the "Little Albert" study reported by Watson & Rayner (1920). Watson & Rayner attempted to condition in 11-month-old Albert a fear of his pet white rat. They did this by pairing the pet rat (the conditioned stimulus, CS) with a loud noise produced by striking an iron bar (the unconditioned stimulus, UCS). After several pairings of CS and UCS, Albert would begin to cry when the rat was introduced into the room (the conditioned response, CR). In the subsequent 70 years, this study has drifted into psychological folklore, being quoted in nearly all psychology textbooks (frequently with inaccurate details) as the prototypical example of phobia learning through classical conditioning (Harris, 1979). This simple type of model highlights temporal contiguity between CS and UCS as being important (rather than the predictive significance of the CS), and also ignores previous experiences with CS and UCS that might influence the acquisition of fear. Watson did not formulate a coherent conditioning model of phobias from this, but merely left critics to examine his poorly reported procedural details. A subsequent series of failures to replicate the "Little Albert" study also led to scepticism about the utility of conditioning models (English, 1929; Bergman, in Thorndike, 1935; Valentine, 1930; but see Delprato, 1980, for a critique of these failures).

The major criticisms thus levelled at conditioning models of phobias are ones which address a simple contiguity-based model. It is worth detailing these criticisms here so that they can be assessed in the context of broader contemporary conditioning models.

First, many phobics appear unable to recall any trauma or aversive conditioning experience at the time of the onset of their phobia (Rachman, 1977; Marks, 1969; Emmelkamp, 1982). This appears to be particularly true of some animal phobics such as snake and spider phobics (Davey, 1992b; Murray & Foote, 1979), and also height and water phobics (Menzies & Clarke, 1993a,b). This does not necessarily seem to be because traumatic memories by their very nature are repressed, since other types of phobics can readily recall traumatic experiences in the aetiology of their fear (e.g. dental phobics, Davey, 1988a; dog phobics, DiNardo et al., 1988; Doogan & Thomas, 1992).

Second, not all people who have pain or trauma paired with a situation develop a phobia. For example, not everyone who has a traumatic experience undergoing dental treatment acquires a dental phobia (Lautch, 1971); not everyone who experiences a violent thunderstorm acquires a thunderstorm phobia (Liddell & Lyons, 1978); and not all fliers who experience a traumatic flying accident express a subsequent anxiety of flying (Aitken, Lister & Main, 1981; Goorney, 1970). A simple contiguity-based conditioning model does not appear to have the power to predict when an individual will acquire a phobia and when he/she will not.

Third, a simple incremental–decremental conditioning model (where pairing a CS with an aversive UCS produces an increment in fear to the CS, and an unreinforced presentation of the CS produces a decrement in fear) does not appear to account for the common clinical phenomenon of incubation. Incubation is where fear increases in magnitude over successive non-reinforced presentations of the CS (Eysenck, 1979; Sandin & Chorot, 1989; Campbell, Sanderson & Laverty, 1964), and is a phenomenon that is frequently observed clinically (Eysenck, 1979), but is rarely found in laboratory analogue studies (cf. Richards & Martin, 1990). Incremental–decremental conditioning models of phobia would predict a successive decrease in fear with successive non-reinforced CS presentations (extinction).

Fourth, simple conditioning models treat all stimuli as equally likely to enter into association with aversive consequences, yet fears and phobias are not evenly distributed across stimuli and experiences. People appear to develop phobias of animals (e.g. snakes, spiders), heights, water, death, thunder and fire more readily than fears of hammers, electric outlets, knives, guns, etc., even though the latter group of stimuli seem to have a high likelihood of being associated with pain or trauma (Seligman, 1971; Kirkpatrick, 1984; Agras, Sylvester & Oliveau, 1969). This uneven distribution of fear violates the traditional Pavlovian concept of the equipotentiality of stimuli.

Fifth, many surveys suggest that a substantial percentage of phobics appear to acquire their fear through observational learning rather than direct experience with trauma (Öst & Hugdahl, 1981; Menzies & Clarke, 1993a; Rachman, 1977). This has been generally conceived of as an alternative learning route to direct conditioning (but see below).

It will be argued that none of these criticisms are damaging for contemporary models of human conditioning which have evolved from their simplistic Watsonian ancestors.

A CONTEMPORARY COGNITIVE MODEL OF HUMAN CLASSICAL CONDITIONING

Contemporary models of human classical conditioning differ from their contiguity-based predecessors in a number of important ways. First, unlike their behaviourist forefathers, modern learning theorists are quite happy to talk about processes that cannot be directly observed, and have to be inferred. Examples of such processes are the kinds of associations that are formed during conditioning. Inferential techniques have established that both animals and humans tend to learn associations between the CS and UCS during classical conditioning, and that it is this learnt association that mediates the CR (Rescorla, 1980; Davey & McKenna, 1983). For example, once it has been established that a CS–UCS associative link mediates learnt phobic response, then it can also be concluded that any processes that influence the strength of that association will also influence the magnitude of the fear reaction.

Second, it is now well accepted that many factors other than the experienced pairings of CS and UCS can affect the strength of the association between these events. In the case of humans, these include verbally and culturally transmitted information about the CS–UCS contingency (e.g. Dawson & Grings, 1968; Wilson, 1968), existing beliefs and expectancies about the possible consequence associated with a particular CS (Davey, 1992c; Honeybourne, Matchett & Davey, 1993) and emotional reactions currently associated with the CS (Davey & Dixon, 1996; Diamond, Matchett & Davey, 1995).

Third, and arguably of most importance in this context, is the finding that the strength of a CR can be radically influenced, not just by the strength of the CS–UCS association, but also by the way in which the individual evaluates the UCS (Davey, 1989; 1992a). In humans there are a variety of processes that can influence the evaluation of a traumatic UCS, and some of these are discussed below.

Figure 15.1 provides a schematic representation of a contemporary model of human classical conditioning. This illustrates the kinds of factors that may influence the strength of an association between a CS and the UCS representation (expectancy evaluations), and also how the UCS representation's evocation of a CR will be influenced by how the UCS has been evaluated or revalued (UCS revaluation processes). The next section will discuss these expectancy evaluation and UCS revaluation processes in more detail.

Expectancy Evaluation

Traditional incremental–decremental models of conditioning claim that the strength of an association between CS and UCS is dependent on the number of experienced pairings of the CS and UCS. It is now clear that many more factors than this can influence the strength of the learnt association.

Situational Contingency Information

While the number of experienced pairings of CS and UCS does contribute to the strength of the CR, of greater importance is the predictive significance of the CS as measured by the correlation between CS and UCS (Alloy & Tabachnik, 1984; Prokasy & Williams, 1979; Prokasy & Kumpfer, 1969). For example, although they might be paired with traumatic UCSs on some occasions, some stimuli may have previously been paired with other UCSs (or nothing at all), and in this sense the correlation between the CS and the new UCS is still quite weak. An extreme example of this is when the CS has been presented alone on many occasions, and is then subsequently paired with a UCS. In these circumstances it is much harder

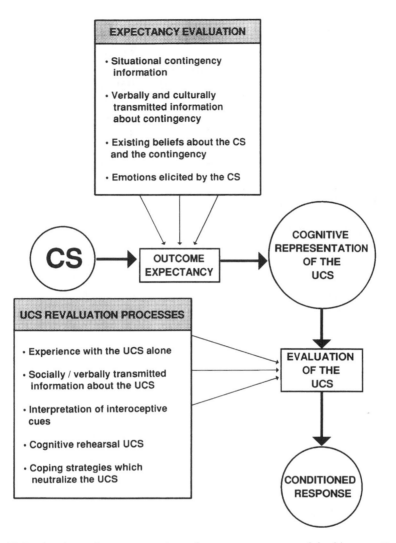

Figure 15.1 A schematic representation of a contemporary model of human Pavlovian conditioning (see text for further explanation)

to learn to associate the CS with the new UCS than if there had been no previous CS-alone trials. This is known as latent inhibition, and is an established feature of human classical conditioning (Siddle, Remington & Churchill, 1985; Siddle & Remington, 1987). The implication of this for phobia acquisition is that, if the individual has had many trauma-free experiences with a stimulus, it will then be much harder to subsequently associate that stimulus with a trauma (cf. Davey, 1988a; Doogan & Thomas, 1992; De Jongh et al., 1995).

Verbally and Culturally Transmitted Information about the Contingency

People do not have to experience pairings of CS and UCS in order to learn the association, they can simply be told what the relationship is between these stimuli. In laboratory conditioning experiments, merely informing the subjects of the CS–UCS contingency can generate a CR prior to any pairings of CS and UCS (e.g. Dawson & Grings, 1968; Katz, Webb & Stotland, 1971; McComb, 1969; Wilson, 1968). Often, even when subjects are given false information about the contingencies, their conditioned responding complies with this false information rather than the situational contingencies (Deane, 1969; Epstein & Clarke, 1970). An implication of this is that an association between a stimulus and a traumatic outcome can be learned as a result of information about the contingency, or through observing someone else experiencing the contingency (vicarious learning). In terms of the current model, this is still conditioning. What is lacking at present, however, is any information on the strength and persistence of associations that are learned in these vicarious manners. They may be weaker and less resistant to extinction than situationally acquired associations (cf. Rachman, 1977; Öst & Hugdahl, 1985), but they appear to be mediated by the same mechanism that mediates situational learning (Mineka & Cook, 1993). The evidence that is available suggests that direct conditioning experiences are more memorable than vicarious learning experiences, and that a majority of strong fears are attributed by subjects to direct conditioning, rather than to vicarious conditioning experiences (Merckelbach et al., 1989; Withers & Deane, 1995).

Existing Beliefs about the CS and the Contingency

When individuals enter a conditioning episode they are not *tabula rasa* but hold existing beliefs and expectancies about what is likely to happen in that episode. Often these prior expectancies are based on previous experiences with the events in the episode, or they are based on *ad hoc* judgements about those events.

An example of the associative biases that influence the formation of learned associations can be found in co-variation assessment studies. Studies of co-variation have pointed out that assessing the relationship or co-variation between events appears to be influenced by both situational information (i.e. current information about the contingency) and prior expectations or beliefs about the co-variation (e.g. Crocker, 1981; Nisbett & Ross, 1980; Alloy & Tabachnik, 1984). For example, in circumstances where situational information is unambiguous and prior expectations are low, human subjects can detect event contingencies fairly accurately (e.g. Beach & Scopp, 1966; Erlick & Mills, 1967; Peterson, 1980). However, there are a variety of circumstances in which the combination of situational information and prior expectancies give rise to what is called a *co-variation bias*, which generates a distorted perception of the co-variation— usually in the direction of the prior expectation (Crocker, 1981; Nisbett & Ross, 1980).

Co-variation biases can be found in exactly those circumstances which might generate CS–UCS associations. For instance, Tomarken, Mineka & Cook (1989) exposed subjects to slides of fear-relevant (snakes, spiders) and fear-irrelevant (flowers, houses) stimuli that were followed by electric shock, a tone or nothing. Although the relationship between the slides and outcomes was completely random, subjects consistently overestimated the contingency between slides of fear-relevant stimuli and shock.

A series of experiments by Davey (1992c) showed that this tendency to over-estimate the association between fear-relevant stimuli and aversive consequences is probably the result of a pre-experimental expectancy bias, rather than a computational bias that occurs during exposure to the stimuli. In a "threat" conditioning procedure (where subjects are warned that they might receive shocks following some CSs, but in fact receive none) subjects began the experiment with a significantly higher expectancy of aversive UCSs following fear-relevant stimuli than fear-irrelevant stimuli. This UCS expectancy bias dissipated with continued non-reinforcement, but could be reinstated by a single CS–UCS pairing. These studies indicate that individuals enter a conditioning episode believing that fear-relevant stimuli are more likely to have aversive consequences than fear-relevant stimuli. This speeds up the learning of associations between fear-relevant CSs and aversive UCSs, and also makes them more resistant to extinction. This expectancy bias can be found with both phylogenetic (e.g. snakes, spiders) and ontogenetic (e.g. guns, electricity outlets) fear-relevant stimuli (Honeybourne, Matchett & Davey, 1993; McNally & Heatherton, 1993), and may well provide an explanation of many of the rapid learning effects previously ascribed to biological preparedness (see Davey, 1995a; Chapter 16, this volume).

While it is now clear that expectancy biases do exist and can influence the rate at which a CS–UCS association is learned, it is less clear how these biases originate. Davey (1995a) has argued that they originate in a number of judgements that the individual makes about the nature of the stimuli in the episode. The initial UCS expectancy bias is one which can be found with fear-relevant CSs in general, whether they are phylogenetic or ontogenetic (Honeybourne, Matchett & Davey, 1993; McNally & Heatherton, 1993) and whether or not prior fear has already accrued to them (de Jong, 1993; Diamond, Matchett & Davey, 1995). This suggests that the expectancy bias to fear-relevant stimuli reflects some initial general assessment of the danger or threat-potential of the stimulus. A co-variation assessment study by Davey & Dixon (1996) indicated that a number of judgements about the CS and UCS are correlated with ratings of UCS expectancy. These include estimates of how dangerous the CS is, and judgements about the semiotic similarity between CS and UCS (see also Hamm, Viatl & Lang, 1989; Hugdahl & Johnsen, 1989). The Davey & Dixon (1996) study also indicated that CS–UCS similarity on a number of dimensions is also associated with increased UCS expectancy. These are ratings of CS–UCS similarity on the dimensions of valence, arousal and anxiety (see also Lang, 1985; Tomarken, Sutton & Mineka, 1995).

What studies such as these show is that prior outcome expectancies can influence the speed with which a CS–UCS association is learnt. These expectancy biases tend to be associated especially with fear-relevant stimuli and appear to be based on judgements about the nature of the CS and the features that the CS shares in common with the potential UCS. The kinds of judgements that are important also suggest that there will be cultural differences in expectancy biases to fear-relevant stimuli, since different cultures will value stimuli differently, and differ in the extent to which they consider stimuli to be dangerous (cf. Davey, 1995a).

Emotions Elicited by the CS

One other important factor that influences UCS expectancy is the degree to which the CS already elicits prior fear or anxiety. Tomarken, Mineka & Cook (1989) found that initial fear of a stimulus was an important determinant of co-variation bias with phylogenetic fear-relevant stimuli when the number of stimulus-shock pairings was relatively small (33%), but not when it was increased to 50% (see also de Jong & Merckelbach, 1991; de Jong et al., 1992). There is more direct evidence linking prior fear with a UCS expectancy bias. In a factorial design, Diamond, Matchett & Davey (1995) presented spider phobics and non-phobics with slides of either spiders or kittens. UCS expectancy was measured using the "threat" conditioning procedure employed by Davey (1992b). Although there was a main effect for spiders at the outset of the procedure (i.e. subjects shown slides of spiders gave higher UCS expectancy ratings regardless of whether they were phobic), there was also a significant picture–phobia interaction in which phobic subjects receiving spider slides gave higher UCS expectancy ratings than non-phobics receiving spider slides. The co-variation bias study of Davey & Dixon (1996) also demonstrated that prior fear to both ontogenetic and phylogenetic fear-relevant stimuli was directly correlated with UCS expectancy ratings, and that prior fear predicted variance in UCS expectancy ratings independently of other factors such as CS–UCS similarity.

One implication of this role of prior fear, of course, is that prior fear to a CS will hasten its association with an aversive UCS, and is also likely to retard extinction of the association (cf. Diamond, Matchett & Davey, 1995).

UCS Revaluation Processes

Davey (1989, 1992a) has argued that contemporary human conditioning models are basically incomplete without a performance factor which describes processes by which the subject's evaluation of the UCS may be changed. Figure 15.1 shows that the learned fear CR is mediated through a representation of the UCS which is activated through the CS–UCS association; this implies that changes in the strength or nature of the fear CR will be affected by any factor which changes knowledge about the UCS contained in the UCS representation. For example, if the subject acquires information which suggests that the UCS is now less noxious or aversive than they had previously conceived, then this will result in the UCS representation mediating a significantly weaker fear CR when the CS is next encountered.

There are two important points to make about UCS revaluation processes in relation to conditioning models of phobias. First, UCS revaluation can occur independently of any changes in the strength of the association between CS and UCS. Thus, changes in the strength of the fear CR can be caused without the subject having any experiences which might affect the strength of the CS–UCS association (e.g. without any further CS–UCS pairings). Second, although the animal conditioning literature has identified a few processes by which a UCS can be revalued (see Davey, 1992a), the ability to symbolically represent information and to communicate complex information between individuals opens up the possibility for many more modes of UCS revaluation in humans than in animals. Some of these modes are represented under UCS Revaluation Processes in Figure 15.1.

Experience with the UCS Alone

Post-conditioning experiences with the UCS alone (i.e. in the absence of the CS) can lead to revaluation of the UCS—especially if these experiences lead to the individual perceiving the UCS as either more or less aversive than it was during the conditioning episode. For example, an individual may reassess a UCS more favourably if they experience a number of UCS-alone trials that allow their fear to the UCS to habituate (Davey & McKenna, 1983). The next presentation of the CS then evokes a much weaker fear CR. Similarly, the perceived aversiveness of the UCS may be inflated by experiences with a similar UCS of greater intensity (e.g. White & Davey, 1989). In this latter example, an individual may learn to associate a CS and UCS while the UCS is perceived as being relatively unaversive (i.e. there will be little or no conditioned fear to the CS). Some time later that individual may have an experience with the UCS which inflates the aversive evaluation of it. Subsequent encounters with the CS will then evoke a much stronger and perceivable fear response (for examples, cf. White & Davey, 1989; Davey, de Jong & Tallis, 1993). This type of UCS inflation scenario means that a contemporary conditioning model of phobias is not bound by the need to discover contiguous stimulus (CS)–trauma (UCS) experiences in the histories of clinical phobias in order to verify the conditioning account.

Socially/Verbally Transmitted Information about the UCS

A second method of UCS revaluation involves socially or verbally transmitted information about the UCS. For example, in a laboratory conditioning experiment subjects can simply be told that on future presentations the UCS will be more or less intense than before. If the subject believes this information, then the evaluation of the UCS is changed, and this affects the strength of the CR on subsequent CS presentations (Davey, 1983; Davey & McKenna, 1983).

However, UCS revaluation through verbally transmitted information appears to be a particularly asymmetric process. It appears to be relatively easy to produce large increases in fear as a result of verbal information, leading to the inflation of the aversiveness of the UCS, but significantly less easy to produce UCS devaluation effects as a result of verbal information about the UCS. For example, Davey, de Jong & Tallis (1993) report the case history of M.F., a 29-year-old male bank employee. M.F. was present when the bank in which he worked was robbed, and he was threatened with a gun. He showed no signs of residual fear caused by this experience and returned to work the next day. However, 10 days after the robbery he was interviewed by the police. During the interview he was told that he was lucky to be alive because the bank robber was considered to be a dangerous man who had already killed several people. From this point on, M.F. did not return to work and developed severe post-traumatic stress symptoms. A second example, describes how, at the age of 10 years, H.B. woke at night to find a large tropical spider on her face. At the time she reported not being particularly frightened, but when she told her parents about this the next morning, they were extremely concerned and expressed their alarm at the incident. From that moment H.B. exhibited severe spider phobia, which eventually required treatment. These two examples are representative of the way in which post-conditioning verbally transmitted information about a consequential UCS can severely inflate the aversive evaluation of the UCS, and result in subsequent phobic responding.

Nevertheless, attempting to devalue an already aversively valued UCS through verbal information appears to be extremely difficult—as any therapist who has attempted to explain the irrationality of a phobic response to a phobic client will appreciate. The source of this asymmetry in the effects of verbally transmitted information about the UCS is unclear, although the relative ineffectiveness of verbal information in *devaluing* a UCS may be due to the fact that phobics give priority to contradictory forms of information which appear to confirm the aversive nature of the UCS. Such contradictory information might include the phobic's perception of his/her own anxiety and fear to the CS or the UCS, leading him/her to believe that the UCS is still aversive and threatening (Arntz, Rauner & van den Hout, 1995; see below). Alternatively, because of the potentially dangerous consequence of interacting with their phobic stimulus, most phobics may require more direct evidence that the stimulus is no longer threatening than that conveyed in verbal say-so; such evidence would presumably involve actual experiences which disconfirm the phobic's beliefs about the threatening and aversive nature of the UCS.

Interpretation of Interoceptive Cues

Many anxious people attend to their own bodily sensations and use these stimuli as information about possible threatening events or as a means of assessing the aversive nature of potentially threatening consequences (cf. Valins, 1966; Parkinson, 1985; Davey, 1988b). As a result, the subject's reaction to either the

CS or UCS can act as an important source of information for evaluating the UCS. Studies of the effects of interoception in aversive conditioning studies have revealed that: (a) when the CR is made more discriminable (by providing auditory feedback for changes in skin conductance CRs), subjects usually emit a greater magnitude CR and show a relative resistance to extinction, compared with subjects who have poor CR discrimination (Davey, 1987); (b) when subjects believe they are emitting a strong fear CR even when they are not (e.g. in a false feedback study), they emit a stronger differential CR and exhibit a resistance to extinction compared with attentional control subjects, and subjects who believe they are emitting only a weak CR (Davey, 1987; Russell & Davey, 1991); and (c) subjects who believe they are emitting a strong UCR emit a greater magnitude CR and show a greater resistance to extinction than subjects who believe they are emitting only a weak UCR (Cracknell & Davey, 1988).

Davey (1988b, 1992a, 1995b) has argued that CR and UCR interoception influences CR magnitude by influencing the subject's evaluation of the UCS. That is, a subject may perceive what they believe to be a strong CR and attribute this to the fact that they must still be anxious or frightened at the forthcoming UCS; this inflates the aversive evaluation of the UCS, which in turn activates a higher magnitude CR on subsequent trials. Two experiments by Davey & Matchett (1996) support this interpretation. The first experiment found that subjects receiving false feedback indicating high levels of responding gave significantly higher UCS aversiveness ratings than other subjects. The second experiment indicated that response feedback influenced CRs by changing the subject's evaluation of the UCS rather than the CS.

More direct evidence that phobics use information from emotional responding to evaluate potentially threatening consequences (UCSs) comes from a study by Arntz, Rauner & van den Hout (1995). They asked anxiety patients and normal controls to rate the danger they perceived in a hypothetical scenario when information about objective safety–danger or anxious–non-anxious responding was systematically varied. The results showed that anxiety patients inferred danger on the basis of information regarding anxious responding significantly more than non-anxious controls. Such findings suggest that phobics use interoceptive cues as an important source of information in inferring and defining the threatening or aversive nature of a consequence.

Cognitive Rehearsal of the UCS

It is clear that individuals who suffer anxiety disorders do have a tendency to focus on and rehearse the possible aversive outcomes of phobic encounters (Marks, 1987), and this ruminative tendency may act to inflate their aversive evaluation of the aversive outcome (UCS).

In a laboratory-based study using normal subjects, Jones & Davey (1990) found that subjects asked to cognitively rehearse the UCS after conditioning produced larger magnitude CRs to subsequent test presentations of the CS than did subjects who did not rehearse the UCS. Davey (1992a) argued that, while

UCS rehearsal appeared to maintain differential fear CRs, there may be circum-stances in which persistent UCS rehearsal might enhance fear responding to the aversive CS in a way that is characteristic of incubation. One such factor that might facilitate the effects of UCS rehearsal is a high level of trait anxiety. High levels of anxiety have been shown to be associated with the selective processing of threatening information (Mathews & MacLeod, 1994), and this might elabo-rate and define the threatening features of the UCS during UCS rehearsal—thus inflating the aversive evaluation of the UCS. To test this possible facilitative effect of anxiety on the UCS-rehearsal phenomenon, Davey & Matchett (1994) conducted two experiments using the same cued-UCS rehearsal procedure de-vised by Jones & Davey (1990). The first experiment compared the effects of UCS rehearsal in high- and low-trait anxious subjects. This study found that subjects with high levels of trait anxiety exhibited significantly greater CRs fol-lowing UCS rehearsal than did subjects who were low in trait anxiety, and these higher magnitude CRs were associated with significantly higher levels of self-reported aversiveness of the rehearsal process. High-trait anxious subjects also exhibited a significant *increase* in CR strength following UCS rehearsal. In the second experiment, Davey & Matchett found that post-rehearsal enhancement of the CR could be found in normal subjects who, just prior to UCS rehearsal, had experienced an anxious mood induction procedure. Thus, CR enhancement fol-lowing UCS rehearsal is not confined to subjects who report high levels of trait anxiety, but can also be found in subjects who report experimentally induced increases in levels of state anxiety. A subsequent study by Matchett & Davey (1995) found that increases in CR magnitude as a result of UCS rehearsal during anxious mood were also accompanied by increases in self-reported aversiveness of the UCS. These results are consistent with the hypothesis that increases in CR magnitude following UCS rehearsal are a result of the rehearsal process inflating the aversive evaluation of the UCS.

While this evidence suggests that UCS rehearsal during anxious mood may cause the enhancement of phobic responding as a result of inflation of the aversive evaluation of the UCS, it is still unclear whether this type of process contributes significantly to instances of clinical incubation (cf. Davey, 1995b). There is at present still no evidence that UCS rehearsal produces successive enhancements of fear responding over a series of exposures to the phobic stimu-lus. Such evidence would be required to provide a faithful analogue of clinical incubation.

Coping Strategies which Neutralize the UCS

It was pointed out earlier that many individuals who have traumatic experiences fail to develop phobic reactions. One reason for this failure may be the ability of some individuals to devalue the trauma immediately following the experience, and they may do this by adopting coping strategies which allow them to effectively devalue the stressful meaning of the trauma. In an early survey of methods of coping with marriage, parenting, household economics and occupation, Pearlin &

Schooler (1978) described three major types of coping with stressors. The first two types closely resembled the problem- and emotion-focused coping outlined in most traditional accounts of coping (cf. Lazarus & Folkman, 1984). However, the third type of coping dealt with strategies that functioned to control the meaning of the stressor or trauma. Pearlin & Schooler reported that this could be achieved in at least three ways: by positive comparisons (e.g. "Lots of people experience similar stressful experiences"), by selective ignoring (e.g. "I'll try and forget this problem and look at the good things in life"), or by devaluing the importance of the stressful event (e.g. "This problem isn't worth getting upset about").

In a preliminary investigation of the kinds of stressor-devaluing strategies described by Pearlin & Schooler, Davey (1993) used a factor analysis procedure to identify a coherent neutralizing strategy labelled *threat devaluation*. This construct was derived from the coping strategies categorized by Pearlin & Schooler as ones which functioned to control the traumatic meaning of the stressor. Clearly, the use of such threat devaluation strategies has implications for the development of phobic responding following traumatic experiences: if individuals are able actively to devalue the impact of trauma by deploying threat devaluation strategies, then they should be significantly less likely to develop phobic reactions to stimuli associated with the trauma. There is some evidence that this is the case. Davey, Burgess & Rashes (1995) compared the coping strategies of simple phobics, panic disorder patients and normal controls (DSM-III-R). They found that both simple phobics and panic disorder patients differed from normal controls by reporting greater use of avoidance coping strategies and reduced use of threat devaluation strategies in dealing with stressors. In a second study, they also found that use of threat devaluation strategies was inversely related to levels of some specific fears as measured by the Fear Survey Schedule (Wolpe & Lang, 1964). Both studies imply that the use of threat devaluation strategies is associated with a significantly reduced incidence of phobic responding.

In a more recent study, Davey et al. (1997) have refined the threat devaluation construct and identified seven factorially independent constructs, all of which contribute to trauma or UCS devaluation. These are downward comparison (e.g. "Other people are worse off than me") (Wills, 1981); positive reappraisal (e.g. "In every problem there is something good") (Davey, 1993); cognitive disengagement (e.g. "The problems involved in this situation simply aren't important enough to get upset about"); optimism (e.g. "Everything will work itself out in the end") (Scheier & Carver, 1992); faith in social support (e.g. "I have others who can help me through this"); denial (e.g. "I refuse to believe this is happening") (Breznitz, 1983); and life perspective (e.g. "I can put up with these problems as long as everything else in my life is okay"). Davey et al. (1995) found that use of all of these strategies (except for denial) was positively correlated with measures of psychological health and inversely correlated with a variety of measures of psychopathology. In addition, a prospective study discovered that the use of these devaluing strategies was not simply an inverse function of existing psychopathology, but predicted future psychological health even when existing levels of psychological health were controlled for.

Studies such as these imply that the use of coping strategies which effectively devalue the aversive meaning of a trauma will have a beneficial effect across a broad range of psychological health measures. From the point of view of a conditioning model of phobias, they also imply that use of such strategies will help to insulate the individual against the development of phobias following traumatic experiences, and may help to explain at least some of the instances when experienced trauma does not result in phobia.

SOME IMPLICATIONS OF A CONTEMPORARY CONDITIONING MODEL OF PHOBIAS

Apart from some more specific implications which are outlined below, contemporary conditioning models have two rather broad implications for our conceptions of the aetiology and maintenance of phobias. First, changes in the strength or probability of phobic responding are not solely dependent on changes in the strength of the associative link between CS and UCS. Performance factors—especially those related to the evaluation of the UCS—can also cause dramatic and immediate changes in the strength of phobic responding. Second, associations between a neutral CS and an aversive UCS can often be formed in the absence of a direct conditioning episode in which the individual experiences the CS paired with a traumatic UCS. This may be because the association has been formed through vicarious experiences (the subject being told about the CS–UCS relationship, or viewing some other person experiencing that relationship). Alternatively, the individual may learn the CS–UCS association when the UCS is relatively innocuous, and this learned association may not immediately give rise to conditioned phobic responding (cf. White & Davey, 1989). However, subsequent experiences may inflate the aversive evaluation of the UCS and, as a result, a phobic reaction to the CS may evolve over time. In such circumstances, a failure to find a direct conditioning experience in the aetiology of the phobia (i.e. an experienced contiguous association between the phobic stimulus and trauma) is not in any way contrary to a conditioning explanation (cf. Menzies & Clarke, 1995a).

Direct Conditioning Experiences in the Aetiology of Different Specific Phobias

Direct conditioning experiences are found more readily in the aetiology of some specific phobias rather than others. For example, Davey (1988a) found that over 90% of individuals reporting anxiety of dental treatment recalled having at least one painful or traumatic experience at the dentist's (see also De Jongh et al., 1995). Similarly, a majority of dog phobics report having been attacked or bitten by a dog (DiNardo, Guzy & Bak, 1988; DiNardo et al., 1988; Doogan & Thomas,

1992). However, direct conditioning experiences appear to be significantly rarer in the aetiology of some other phobias. For example, Murray & Foote (1979) reported that only three out of a total of 35 highly snake-fearful individuals had been bitten by a snake, and the majority had had little or no direct experiences with snakes at all. In a study of spider-fearful individuals, Davey (1992b) found that only eight out of 118 subjects reported a traumatic experience associated with spiders, and only one of these reported a truly arbitrary experience of the kind proposed by traditional conditioning theory ("A spider appeared while I was being sexually harassed by my boss"). Similarly, in a study of childhood water phobia, Menzies & Clarke (1993a) found only one out of 50 phobic children where the onset of the phobia could be ascribed to a direct conditioning experience. In the case of height phobia, Menzies & Clarke (1993b) found direct conditioning experiences reported in only 18% of the aetiologies that they investigated.

Such striking discrepancies between specific phobias in the degree to which direct conditioning experiences can be held causally responsible for the onset have raised a number of questions. First, these discrepancies have led some writers to query the validity of many of the instruments which have been used to determine the origin of phobias (e.g. the Phobic Origin Questionnaire, Öst & Hugdahl, 1981), and suggest that they may overestimate the involvement of direct conditioning experiences in the aetiology of phobias (e.g. Menzies & Clarke, 1995a). Second, the failure to find a majority of direct conditioning experiences in the aetiology of phobias such as height and water phobia has led some authors to postulate a Darwinian account of their origins in which, given normal maturational processes and normal background experiences, most members of a species will show fear to a set of evolution-relevant stimuli on their first encounter. This initial fearful response will then habituate across non-traumatic exposures, except for those who are either poor habituators or who do not get the opportunity for safe exposure (Clarke & Jackson, 1983).

However, the present conditioning model suggests that the apparent absence of direct conditioning experiences in the aetiology of a phobia should be interpreted with some caution. It does not imply the absence of conditioning processes in the development of the phobia, and does not lend anything other than circumstantial support to explanations of phobias which imply some form of biological pre-wiring (cf. Davey, 1995a).

As an example, the present model predicts that phobic responding can be established through a combination of sensory preconditioning and UCS inflation (White & Davey, 1989; Davey, de Jong & Tallis, 1993). In this scenario, the phobic stimulus (CS) may become associated with a potential UCS when the UCS is not perceived as aversive (sensory preconditioning). At this point the CS does not elicit a fear response because the UCS is perceived as benign. However, at some later date, experiences with the UCS alone may cause the individual to inflate the aversive evaluation of the UCS. This in turn then causes phobic reactions to the stimulus with which it had previously been associated. Thus, a phobic response has been established without any *direct* pairing of the phobic stimulus (CS) with an aversive experience (UCS). Examples of how this may occur in clinical practice are described by Davey, de Jong & Tallis (1993) (see also p. 310 above). Furthermore, there is no reason to suppose that UCS inflation should occur only through traumatic experiences with the UCS. An individual may gradually inflate the aversive evaluation of a UCS over a period of time as either new information about the UCS is processed, or biases develop in how the UCS is perceived. For example, if interoceptive cues are important in helping an individual to evaluate a particular outcome (UCS), then the development of biases in how these cues are interpreted may (through the development of catastrophic misinterpretations of bodily sensations) inflate the aversive evaluation of the outcome of certain potentially phobic encounters. One possible example of such a process may exist in some height phobics, where biases in the perception of bodily cues when in high places may be interpreted as indicating dizziness and the possibility of falling. In support of this hypothesis is the finding that height phobia is correlated with a tendency to attend to bodily sensations (as measured by the Body Sensations Questionnaire) and to interpret these sensations as threatening (Davey, Menzies & Gallards, unpublished manuscript).

Thus, the failure to find direct conditioning processes in the aetiology of phobias does not mean that conditioning processes are not involved, and are not the major source of such phobias. The present model predicts that the consequences of interaction with a stimulus or event may be inflated over time, thus giving the impression that no single traumatic event has ever been paired with that stimulus—even though it has come to elicit phobic reactions.

The Overestimation of Fear

The present conditioning model also predicts that phobic responding will be maintained by a significant bias towards expecting fearful or traumatic consequences following encounters with the phobic stimulus. There is now considerable evidence that indicates that, compared with nonphobics, phobics do indeed overestimate the level of consequential danger associated with the phobic stimulus. This has been shown to be true of spider phobics (Arntz et al., 1993), snake phobics (Taylor & Rachman, 1994), height phobics (Menzies & Clarke, 1995b), claustrophobics (Telch, Valentiner & Bolte, 1994), social phobics (Lucock & Salkovskis, 1988) and agoraphobics (van Hout & Emmelkamp, 1994). Furthermore, path models and structural equation modelling have indicated that the overprediction of aversive consequences in phobics arises from the overprediction of danger elements of the phobic stimulus and the underprediction of available safety resources (e.g. escape routes) (Taylor & Rachman, 1994; Arntz, Hildebrand & van den Hout, 1994).

These findings are predicted by and consistent with the present conditioning model, which assumes that phobic responding will be maintained by a bias towards expecting the phobic stimulus (CS) to be followed by an aversive outcome (UCS) (Davey, 1992b, 1995a). Furthermore, they are consistent with laboratory-based conditioning studies which have indicated that judgements about the dangerousness of the CS contribute to this UCS expectancy bias (Davey & Dixon, 1995; Davey, 1995a).

These findings also raise questions about the degree of insight that phobics have concerning their fear, and also the degree to which strategic cognitive processes are involved in the aetiology and maintenance of phobias. First, what do phobics exactly mean when they say that they know their fear is "senseless" (Nesse & Abelson, 1995)? One thing is certain: although they may describe their fear as senseless, they still expect frightening or aversive outcomes to follow contact with their phobic stimulus. Furthermore, these estimations of the aversiveness of the outcome appear to arise out of strategic judgements concerning the nature and status of the phobic stimulus (e.g. how dangerous it is, how much fear it evokes, what features it shares in common with the potential consequence) (Davey, 1995a; Taylor & Rachman, 1994). Thus, when clinically anxious phobics describe their fear as being "senseless", it does not mean that they believe there will be no aversive or dangerous outcome.

Other studies indicate that, far from being "non-cognitive" (Seligman, 1971), phobias appear to be maintained by conscious cognitions relating to the potential aversive outcomes associated with contact with the phobic stimulus (e.g. Thorpe & Salkovskis, 1995; Menzies & Clarke, 1995b; Arntz et al., 1993; Riskind, Moore & Bowley, 1995). This network of cognitions contains information not only about potential external dangers associated with the phobic stimulus, but also about individual concerns about the aversiveness of their own reactions to the phobic stimulus (e.g. panic, going mad) (Thorpe & Salkovskis, 1995; McNally & Steketee, 1985).

The maintenance of phobic responding as a result of the overestimation of fear (see Chapter 18) or a UCS expectancy bias is strongly indicated by the available evidence. What is not so clear, however, is how these biases originate to create the phobic responding in the first place. The conditioning model outlined in the present chapter does provide some possibilities, however. These biases could arise from: (a) the traumatic direct and vicarious conditioning experiences that are often experienced in the aetiology of phobic responding (e.g. Davey, 1989; Öst & Hugdahl, 1981; Merckelbach et al., 1989; Merckelbach, Arntz & de Jong, 1991); (b) culturally-determined beliefs and values which favour the association of certain stimuli with fear and danger (e.g. the association of spiders with fear and danger in many Western cultures, cf. Davey, 1994); and (c) UCS revaluation experiences, which could inflate conceptions of the aversive outcome of contact with a particular stimulus (cf. Davey, de Jong & Tallis, 1993).

SUMMARY AND CONCLUSIONS

This chapter has described a contemporary conditioning model of phobias. This model differs from more traditional conditioning accounts in that it explicitly contains both an associative element and an element which allows the CR to be modulated through revaluation of the UCS. A number of different processes have been described which contribute to both the associative and UCS revaluation elements.

It has been argued that this contemporary conditioning model can now account for most, if not all, of the traditional criticisms of conditioning accounts of phobias, and it also provides a systematic framework for the understanding of many of the features of phobic responding.

ACKNOWLEDGEMENTS

The author is grateful to Andy Field for the preparation of Figure 15.1 and to both the Wellcome Trust and the Economic & Social Research Council of the UK for financially supporting much of the author's own research reported in this chapter.

REFERENCES

Agras, S., Sylvester, D. & Oliveau, D. (1969). The epidemiology of common fears and phobias. *Comprehensive Psychiatry*, **10**, 151–156.
Aitken, R.C.B., Lister, J.A. & Main, C.J. (1981). Identification of features associated with flying phobias in aircrew. *British Journal of Psychiatry*, **139**, 38–42.
Alloy, L.B. & Tabachnik, N. (1984). Assessment of variation by humans and animals: the joint influence of prior expectations and current situational information. *Psychological Review*, **91**, 441–485.
Arntz, A., Hildebrand, M. & van den Hout, M. (1994). Overprediction of anxiety and disconfirmatory processes in anxiety disorders. *Behaviour Research & Therapy*, **32**, 709–722.
Arntz, A., Lavy, E., van den Berg, G. & van Rijsoort, S. (1993). Negative beliefs of spider phobics: a psychometric evaluation of the Spider Phobia Beliefs Questionnaire. *Advances in Behaviour Research & Therapy*, **15**, 257–277.
Arntz, A., Rauner, M. & van den Hout, M. (1995). "If I feel anxious, there must be danger": *ex consequentia* reasoning in inferring danger in anxiety disorders. *Behaviour Research & Therapy*, **33**, 917–925.
Beach, L.R. & Scopp, T.S. (1966). Inferences about correlations. *Psychonomic Science*, **6**, 253–254.
Breznitz, S. (ed.) (1983). *The Denial of Stress*. New York: International Universities Press.
Campbell, D., Sanderson, R.E. & Laverty, S.G. (1964). Characteristics of a conditioned response in human subjects during extinction trials following a simple traumatic conditioning trial. *Journal of Abnormal & Social Psychology*, **68**, 627–639.
Clarke, J.C. & Jackson, J.A. (1983). *Hypnosis and Behavior Therapy: the Treatment of Anxiety and Phobias*. New York: Springer.
Cracknell, S. & Davey, G.C.L. (1988). The effect of perceived unconditioned response strength on conditioned responding in humans. *Medical Science Research*, **16**, 169–170.
Crocker, J. (1981). Judgements of co-variation by social perceivers. *Psychological Bulletin*, **90**, 272–292.
Davey, G.C.L. (1983). An associative view of human classical conditioning. In G.C.L. Davey (ed.), *Animal Models of Human Behaviour*. Chichester: Wiley.
Davey, G.C.L. (1987). An integration of human and animal models of Pavlovian conditioning: associations, cognitions and attributions. In G.C.L. Davey (ed.), *Cognitive Processes and Pavlovian Conditioning in Humans*. Chichester: Wiley.

Davey, G.C.L. (1988a). Dental phobias and anxieties: evidence for conditioning processes in the acquisition and modulation of a learned fear. *Behaviour Research & Therapy*, **27**, 51–58.

Davey, G.C.L. (1988b). Pavlovian conditioning in humans: UCS revaluation and self-observation of conditioned responding. *Medical Science Research*, **16**, 957–961.

Davey, G.C.L. (1989). UCS revaluation and conditioning models of acquired fears. *Behaviour Research & Therapy*, **27**, 521–528.

Davey, G.C.L. (1992a). Classical conditioning and the acquisition of human fears and phobias: a review and synthesis of the literature. *Advances in Behaviour Research & Therapy*, **14**, 29–66.

Davey, G.C.L. (1992b). Characteristics of individuals with fear of spiders. *Anxiety Research*, **4**, 299–314.

Davey, G.C.L. (1992c). An expectancy model of laboratory preparedness effects. *Journal of Experimental Psychology: General*, **121**, 24–40.

Davey, G.C.L. (1993). A comparison of three cognitive appraisal strategies: the role of threat devaluation in problem-focused coping. *Personality & Individual Differences*, **14**, 535–546.

Davey, G.C.L. (1994). The "disgusting" spider: the role of disease and illness in the perpetuation of fear of spiders. *Society & Animals*, **2**, 17–24.

Davey, G.C.L. (1995a). Preparedness and phobias: specific evolved associations or a generalized expectancy bias. *Behvioral & Brain Sciences*, **18**, 289–325.

Davey, G.C.L. (1995b). Rumination and the enhancement of fear: some laboratory findings. *Behavioural & Cognitive Psychotherapy*, **23**, 203–215.

Davey, G.C.L. & Dixon, A. (1996). The expectancy bias model of selective associations: the relationship of judgements of CS dangerousness, CS–UCS similarity and prior fear to *a priori* and *a posteriori* co-variation assessments. *Behaviour Research & Therapy*, **34**, 235–252.

Davey, G.C.L. & Matchett, G. (1994). UCS rehearsal and the retention and enhancement of differential 'fear' conditioning: effects of trait and state anxiety. *Journal of Abnormal Psychology*, **103**, 708–718.

Davey, G.C.L. & Matchett, G. (1996). The effcts of response feedback on conditioned responding during extinction: implications for the role of interoception in anxiety-based disorders. *Journal of Psychophysiology*, **10**, 291–302.

Davey, G.C.L. & McKenna, I. (1983). The effects of postconditioning revaluation of CS1 and UCS following Pavlovian second-order electrodermal conditioning in humans. *Quarterly Journal of Experimental Psychology*, **35B**, 125–133.

Davey, G.C.L., Burgess, I. & Rashes, R. (1995). Coping strategies and phobias: the relationship between fears, phobias and methods of coping with stressors. *British Journal of Clinical Psychology*, **34**, 423–434.

Davey, G.C.L., De Jong, P.J. & Tallis, F. (1993). UCS inflation in the aetiology of a variety of anxiety disorders: some case histories. *Behaviour Research & Therapy*, **31**, 495–498.

Davey, G.C.L., McDonald, A.S., Ferguson, C.E., O'Neill, A.-M., Shepherd, J. & Band, D. (1997). Cognitive neutralizing strategies, coping and psychological health. Submitted.

Dawson, M.E. & Grings, W.W. (1968). Comparison of classical conditioning and relational learning. *Journal of Experimental Psychology*, **76**, 227–231.

De Jong, P.J. (1993). Covariation bias in phobia: mere resistance to pre-experimental expectancies? *Behavior Therapy*, **24**, 447–454.

De Jong, P. & Merckelbach, H. (1991). Co-variation bias and electrodermal responding in spider phobics before and after behavioral treatment. *Behaviour Research & Therapy*, **29**, 307–314.

De Jong, P., Merckelbach, H., Arntz, A. & Nijman, H. (1992). Co-variation detection in treated and untreated spider phobics. *Journal of Abnormal Psychology*, **101**, 724–727.

De Jongh, A., Muris, P., Ter Horst, G. & Duyx, M.P.M.A. (1995). Acquisition and maintenance of dental anxiety: the role of conditioning experiences and cognitive factors. *Behaviour Research & Therapy*, **33**, 205–210.

Deane, G.E. (1969). Cardiac activity during experimentally induced anxiety. *Psychophysiology*, **6**, 17–30.

Delprato, D.J. (1980). Hereditary determinants of fears and phobias: a critical review. *Behavior Therapy*, **11**, 79–103.

Diamond, D., Matchett, G. & Davey, G.C.L. (1995). The effect of prior fear levels on UCS-expectancy ratings to a fear-relevant stimulus. *Quarterly Journal of Experimental Psychology*, **48A**, 237–247.

DiNardo, P.A., Guzy, L.T. & Bak, R.M. (1988). Anxiety response patterns and etiological factors in dog-fearful and non-fearful subjects. *Behaviour Research & Therapy*, **26**, 245–251.

DiNardo, P.A., Guzy, L.T., Jenkins, J.A., Bak, R.M., Tomasi, S.F. & Copland, M. (1988). Etiology and maintenance of dog fears. *Behaviour Research & Therapy*, **26**, 241–244.

Doogan, S. & Thomas, G.V. (1992). Origins of fear of dogs in adults and children: the role of conditioning processes and prior familiarity with dogs. *Behaviour Research & Therapy*, **30**, 387–394.

Emmelkamp, P.M.G. (1982). *Phobic and Obsessive–Compulsive Disorders*. New York: Plenum.

English, H.B. (1929). Three cases of the "conditioned fear response". *Journal of Abnormal & Social Psychology*, **34**, 221–225.

Epstein, S. & Clarke, S. (1970). Heart rate and skin conductance during experimentally induced anxiety: effect of anticipated intensity of noxious stimulation and experience. *Journal of Experimental Psychology*, **73**, 9–14.

Erlick, D.E. & Mills, R.G. (1967). Perceptual quantification of conditional dependency. *Journal of Experimental Psychology*, **73**, 9–14.

Eysenck, H.J. (1979). The conditioning model of neurosis. *Behavioral & Brain Sciences*, **2**, 155–199.

Goorney, A.B. (1970). Treatment of aviation phobias by behaviour therapy. *British Journal of Psychiatry*, **117**, 535–544.

Hamm, A.O., Viatl, D. & Lang, P.J. (1989). Fear conditioning, meaning and belongingness: a selective analysis. *Journal of Abnormal Psychology*, **98**, 395–406.

Harris, B. (1979). Whatever happened to Little Albert? *American Psychologist*, **34**, 151–160.

Honeybourne, C., Matchett, G. & Davey, G.C.L. (1993). An expectancy model of preparedness effects: a UCS-expectancy bias in phylogenetic and ontogenetic fear-relevant stimuli. *Behavior Therapy*, **24**, 253–264.

Hugdahl, K. & Johnsen, B.H. (1989). Preparedness and electrodermal fear conditioning: ontogenetic vs. phylogenetic explanations. *Behaviour Research & Therapy*, **27**, 345–353.

Jones, T. & Davey, G.C.L. (1990). The effects of cued UCS rehearsal on the retention of differential "fear" conditioning: an experimental analogue of the worry process. *Behaviour Research & Therapy*, **28**, 159–164.

Katz, A., Webb, L. & Stotland, E. (1971). Cognitive influences on the rate of GSR extinction. *Journal of Experimental Research in Personality*, **5**, 208–215.

Kirkpatrick, D.R. (1984). Age, gender and patterns of common intense fears among adults. *Behaviour Research & Therapy*, **22**, 141–150.

Lang, P.J. (1985). The cognitive psychophysiology of emotion: fear and anxiety. In A.H. Tuma & D. Maser (eds), *Anxiety and the Anxiety Disorders*. Hillsdale, NJ: Erlbaum.

Lautch, H. (1971). Dental phobia. *British Journal of Psychiatry*, **119**, 151–158.

Lazarus, R.S. & Folkman, S. (1984). *Stress, Appraisal and Coping*. New York: Springer.

Liddell, A. & Lyons, M. (1978). Thunderstorm phobias. *Behaviour Research & Therapy*, **16**, 306–308.

Lucock, M.P. & Salkovskis, P.M. (1988). Cognitive factors in social anxiety and its treatment. *Behaviour Research & Therapy*, **26**, 297–302.

Marks, I.M. (1969). *Fears and Phobias.* New York: Academic Press.

Marks, I.M. (1987). *Fears, Phobias and Rituals.* New York: Academic Press.

Matchett, G. & Davey, G.C.L. (1995). UCS rehearsal during anxious mood: enhancement but not incubation of "fear" responding. Submitted.

Mathews, A. & MacLeod, C. (1994). Emotional processing biases. *Annual Review of Psychology*, **45**, 25–50.

McComb, D. (1969). Cognitive and learning effects in the production of GSR conditioning data. *Psychonomic Science*, **16**, 96–96.

McNally, R.J. & Heatherton, T.F. (1993). Are co-variation biases attributable to *a priori* expectancy biases? *Behaviour Research & Therapy*, **31**, 653–658.

McNally, R.J. & Steketee, G.S. (1985). The etiology and maintenance of severe animal phobias. *Behaviour Research & Therapy*, **23**, 431–435.

Menzies, R.G. & Clarke, J.C. (1993a). The aetiology of childhood water phobia. *Behaviour Research & Therapy*, **31**, 499–501.

Menzies, R.G. & Clarke, J.C. (1993b). The etiology of fear of heights and its relationship to severity and individual response patterns. *Behaviour Research & Therapy*, **31**, 355–365.

Menzies, R.G. & Clarke, J.C. (1995a). The etiology of phobias: a non-associative account. *Clinical Psychology Review*, **15**, 23–48.

Menzies, R.G. & Clarke, J.C. (1995b). Danger expectancies and insight in acrophobia. *Behaviour Research & Therapy*, **33**, 215–221.

Merckelbach, H., Arntz, A. & De Jong, P. (1991). Conditioning experiences in spider phobics. *Behaviour Research & Therapy*, **29**, 333–335.

Merckelbach, H., de Ruiter, C., van den Hout, M.A. & Hoekstra, R. (1989). Conditioning experiences and phobias. *Behaviour Research & Therapy*, **27**, 657–662.

Mineka, S. & Cook, M. (1993). Mechanisms involved in the observational conditioning of fear. *Journal of Experimental Psychology: General*, **122**, 23–38.

Murray, E. & Foote, F. (1979). The origins of fear of snakes. *Behaviour Research & Therapy*, **17**, 489–493.

Nesse, R.M. & Abelson, J.L.(1995). Natural selection and fear regulation mechanisms. *Behavioral & Brain Sciences*, **18**, 309–310.

Nisbett, R.E. & Ross, L. (1980). *Human Inference: Strategies and Shortcomings of Social Judgement.* Englewood Cliffs, NJ: Prentice-Hall.

Öst, L.G. & Hugdahl, K. (1981). Acquisition of phobias and anxiety response patterns in clinical patients. *Behaviour Research & Therapy*, **19**, 439–447.

Öst, L.G. & Hugdahl, K. (1985). Acquisition of blood and dental phobia and anxiety response patterns in clinical patients. *Behaviour Research & Therapy*, **23**, 27–34.

Parkinson, B. (1985). Emotional effects of false autonomic feedback. *Psychological Bulletin*, **98**, 471–494.

Pearlin, L.I. & Schooler, C. (1978). The structure of coping. *Journal of Health & Social Behevior*, **19**, 2–21.

Peterson, C.R. (1980). Recognition of non-contingency. *Journal of Personality & Social Psychology*, **38**, 727–734.

Prokasy, W.F. & Kumpfer, K.A. (1969). Conditioning, probability of reinforcement and sequential behavior in human conditioning with intermittent schedules. *Psychonomic Science*, **10**, 49–50.

Prokasy, W.F. & Williams, W.C. (1979). Information processing and the decremental effect of intermittent reinforcement schedules in human conditioning. *Bulletin of the Psychonomic Society*, **14**, 57–60.

Rachman, S. (1977). The conditioning theory of fear acquisition: an critical examination. *Behaviour Research & Therapy*, **15**, 375–387.

Rescorla, R.A. (1980). *Pavlovian Second-order Conditioning.* Hillsdale, NJ: Erlbaum.

Richards, M. & Martin, I. (1990). Eysenck's incubation of fear hypothesis: an experimental test. *Behaviour Research & Therapy*, **28**, 373–384.

Riskind, J.H., Moore, R. & Bowley, L. (1995). The looming of spiders: the fearful perceptual distortion of movement and menace. *Behaviour Research & Therapy*, **33**, 171–178.

Russell, C. & Davey, G.C.L. (1991). The effects of false response feedback on human "fear" conditioning. *Behaviour Research & Therapy*, **29**, 191–196.

Sandin, B. & Chorot, P. (1989). The incubation theory of fear/anxiety: experimental investigation in a human laboratory model of Pavlovian conditioning. *Behaviour Research & Therapy*, **27**, 9–18.

Scheier, M.F. & Carver, C.S. (1992). Effects of optimism on psychological and physical well-being: theoretical overview and empirical update. *Cognitive Therapy & Research*, **16**, 201–228.

Seligman, M.E.P. (1971). Phobias and preparedness. *Behavior Therapy*, **2**, 307–320.

Siddle, D.A.T. & Remington, B. (1987). Latent inhibition and human Pavlovian conditioning: research and relevance. In G.C.L. Davey (ed.), *Cognitive Processes and Pavlovian Conditioning in Humans*. Chichester: Wiley.

Siddle, D.A.T., Remington, B. & Churchill, M. (1985). Effects of conditioned stimulus pre-exposure on human electrodermal conditioning. *Biological Psychology*, **20**, 113–127.

Taylor, S. & Rachman, S.J. (1994). Stimulus estimation and the overprediction of fear. *British Journal of Clinical Psychology*, **33**, 173–181.

Telch, M.J., Valentiner, D. & Bolte, M. (1994). Proximity to safety and its effects on fear prediction bias. *Behaviour Research & Therapy*, **32**, 747–751.

Thorndike, E.L. (1935). *The Psychology of Wants, Interests and Attitudes*. London: Appleton-Century-Crofts.

Thorpe, S.J. & Salkovskis, P.M. (1995). Phobic beliefs: do cognitive factors play a role in specific phobias? *Behaviour Research & Therapy*, **33**, 805–816.

Tomarken, A.J., Mineka, S. & Cook, M. (1989). Fear-relevant selective associations and co-variation bias. *Journal of Abnormal Psychology*, **98**, 381–394.

Tomarken, A.J., Sutton, S.K. & Mineka, S. (1995). Fear-relevant illusory correlations: what types of associations promote judgmental bias? *Journal of Abnormal Psychology*, **104**, 312–326.

Valentine, C.W. (1930). The innate bases of fear. *Journal of Genetical Psychology*, **37**, 394–419.

Valins, S. (1966). Cognitive effects of false heart-rate feedback. *Journal of Personality & Social Psychology*, **4**, 400–408.

van Hout, W.J.P.J. & Emmelkamp, P.M.G. (1994). Overprediction of fear in panic disorder patients with agoraphobia: does the (mis)match model generalize to exposure *in vivo* therapy? *Behaviour Research & Therapy*, **32**, 723–734.

Watson, J.B. & Rayner, R. (1920). Conditioned emotional reactions. *Journal of Experimental Psychology*, **3**, 1–14.

White, K. & Davey, G.C.L. (1989). Sensory preconditioning and UCS inflation in human "fear" conditioning. *Behaviour Research & Therapy*, **27**, 161–166.

Wills, T.A. (1981). Downward comparison principles in social psychology. *Psychological Bulletin*, **90**, 245–271.

Wilson, G.D. (1968). Reversal of differential GSR conditioning by instructions. *Journal of Experimental Psychology*, **76**, 491–493.

Withers, R.D. & Deane, F.P. (1995). Origins of common fears: effects on severity, anxiety responses and memories of onset. *Behaviour Research & Therapy*, **33**, 903–915.

Wolpe, J. & Lang, P.J. (1964). A fear survey schedule for use in behavior therapy. *Behaviour Research & Therapy*, **2**, 27.

Chapter 16

Evolutionary Models of Phobias

Harald Merckelbach
and
Peter J. de Jong
*Department of Psychology, University of Limburg,
Maastricht, The Netherlands*

At first sight, it seems odd to invoke evolutionary notions to account for psycho-pathological syndromes. After all, psychopathological syndromes are defined by chronic dysfunctions in a number of domains (e.g. emotional, cognitive, social, etc.) and these are difficult to connect to notions such as "natural selection" and "adaptive advantage" (e.g. McGuire, 1988). However, other branches of medicine offer clear examples of dysfunctions that are likely to have some adaptive value. The genetics behind sickle-cell anemia are a case in point: the allele for sickle-cell anemia is maintained in some African environments because if protects against malaria (Kitcher, 1985). Another good example is fever. An evolutionary analysis strongly suggests that fever has a protective function in that it inhibits the spread of bacteria (Williams & Nesse, 1991). Indeed, in their thought-provoking review, Williams & Nesse (1991) demonstrate that the Darwinian approach may explain and predict interesting features of various bodily dysfunctions, ranging from nausea in pregnancy to symptoms of the sprained ankle. If this is true for the traditional branches of medicine, why wouldn't a similar line of reasoning apply to psychological dysfunctions?

The present chapter evaluates Darwinian interpretations of phobias. It is structured as follows. First, we briefly consider several types of Darwinian explanation that have been advanced for psychopathological conditions. Next, we summarize the most important evolutionary models that have been proposed with regard to phobias. We then turn to an extensive discussion of these models. We conclude with a critical reflection on evolutionary accounts of phobias.

Phobias—A Handbook of Theory, Research and Treatment. Edited by G.C.L. Davey.
© 1997 John Wiley & Sons Ltd.

THE ADAPTATIONIST APPROACH TO PSYCHOPATHOLOGY

Referring to the role of Darwinian notions in psychology, Ghiselin writes, as late as 1973: "The history of the assimilation of Darwin is the history of the failure to assimilate Darwinism. But Darwin's contribution to psychology was neither understood nor accepted, and only now are we beginning to realize what that contribution was" (p. 968). The 1970s were, indeed, characterized by a downfall of extreme environmentalism and an influx of evolutionary concepts into academic psychology (Delprato, 1980). For example, in 1971, Razran published his *Mind in Evolution*, which sought to reconcile Pavlovian and Darwinian notions. At about the same time, students of emotions (e.g. Ekman, 1973; Izard, 1971) began to rediscover the relevance of Darwin's *Expression of the Emotions in Man and Animals* (Darwin, 1872/1965). The role of evolutionary mechanisms in social behavior was underlined in programmatic texts, such as Wilson's *Sociobiology: the New Synthesis* (1975) and Eibl-Eibesfeld's "Human ethology: concepts and implications for the sciences of Man" (1979). Even human reasoning became the object of evolutionary analysis (Tooby & Cosmides, 1989).

The rising tide of Darwinian considerations within psychology also encouraged speculations about the evolutionary origins of abnormal behavior. In this context, some evolutionary theorists have tried to elucidate isolated deviancies. For instance, a number of authors (e.g. Erickson, 1993) have advocated an evolutionary perspective on incest, claiming that such a perspective brings to light several features of this phenomenon that are not easily recognized by traditional approaches. In their view, incest avoidance is a cross-cultural universal that evolved to give a selective advantage. Incestuous mating is known to have detrimental effects, i.e. it increases the expression of deleterious recessive genes. A biologically-based incest taboo would inhibit close inbreeding, thereby promoting genetic fitness (Erickson, 1993). According to some theorists, the incest taboo is likely to break down in societies where paternity is not guaranteed. Under such circumstances, incestuous intercourse would serve the need to assure paternity (Welham, 1990).

Certainly, evolutionary models might offer alternative ways of describing and explaining phenomena like incest (Welham, 1990) or homicide (Kenrick & Sheets, 1993; Daly & Wilson, 1994). For example, the cross-cultural incest avoidance emphasized by evolutionary theorists clearly casts doubts on one of the central tenets of Freudian psychology, namely the assumption that humans are innately incestuous and, therefore, prone to develop an Oedipus complex that, in turn, underlies neurotic symptoms (Erickson, 1993). However, one major problem with the evolutionary approach is that its hypotheses cannot be subjected to direct tests. This is inherent to the evolutionary analyses of human behavior, precisely because it is impossible to reconstruct natural selection processes in the psychological laboratory. In the case of isolated aberrations (e.g. incest, homicide), researchers may use epidemiological and anthropological data to provide an indirect test of evolutionary hypotheses (e.g. Welham, 1990; Daly & Wilson, 1994). Yet in the case of broad psychopathological disorders, such a research strategy is more difficult to implement because of the large number of dysfunctions involved, the unreliability of psychiatric diagnoses and the like. Nevertheless, there have been many attempts to explain complex psychopathological conditions in evolutionary terms. More specifically, three types of evolutionary explanations have been advanced (McGuire, 1988).

The first type proposes that some dysfunctions confer a selective advantage and, therefore, are not eliminated by selective pressure. Lewis's (1934) suggestion that depression may be adaptive in the sense that it elicits empathy and caretaking behavior is an early example of this "dysfunction as selective advantage" approach. While more recent evolutionary models have sketched alternative scenarios for depression, they maintain that it may confer an advantage. Thus, Sloman & Price (1987; p. 100) argue that "depression could be advantageous and therefore possibly adaptive to the individual by making him or her avoid competitive interaction when social factors are unfavorable". Another illustration of this approach is provided by the suggestion that anorexia nervosa might be an adaptive tactic since it suppresses reproductive activity, which is advisable when offspring have poor chances for survival (Voland & Voland, 1989).

The second type of explanation stresses that a dysfunction may reflect "archaic" behavior that once was adaptive. This type of explanation holds that human biology and behavior were designed for Stone Age conditions. The inertia of the gene pool, combined with the rapid ecological changes that brought the human race into an industrial environment, would explain the emergence of "atavistic" behavior. An example is the nocturnal theory of schizophrenia (Feierman, 1994). According to this theory, nocturnalism was an adaptive trait during a certain phase of human evolution. As a result, there are still persons who "could be thought of as trying to process information while awake with a brain that is processing information, at least in part, as though they were asleep" (Feierman, 1994; p. 265). These individuals would suffer from a severe deregulation of behavioral and cognitive functions that eventually results in schizophrenia.

The third type of explanation assumes that some dysfunctions represent an exaggeration of a trait that might be adaptive. For example, cheating can be interpreted as a successful strategy when social networks rapidly change and repeated encounters with the same actor are not very likely. Harpending & Sobus (1987; p. 69) have speculated that psychopaths are skilled cheaters: "The best current model is that there is some underlying quantitative trait that predisposes the bearer to sociopathy. Beyond a threshold value of the trait the individual becomes a sociopath".

The types of evolutionary explanations summarized above have one thing in common: they examine psychopathology from an adaptationist perspective. Williams & Nesse (1991; p. 3) summarize the adaptationist program as follows: "Adherents of this program, when confronted with a biological phenomenon, try to envision it as an aspect of an adaptation. An adaptation is some sort of biological machinery or process shaped by natural selection to help solve one or more problems faced by the organism". Therefore, the adaptationist perspective deals with ultimate causes (e.g. evolutionary scenarios) rather than proximal causes (e.g. neurotransmitters, learning processes, etc.) of phenomena (e.g. psychopathological behavior). There are three major problems when the adaptationist program is applied to psychopathology. The first is that evolutionary accounts of psychopathology run the risk of being "imaginative reconstructions" (Lewontin, 1979) or "adaptive stories" (McNally, 1995) that rely entirely on plausibility. As was already noted, evolutionary models of human behavior are difficult to evaluate because it is impossible to reconstruct and manipulate selective pressure in the laboratory. Admittedly, some evolutionary models come up with fairly specific predictions about the proximal mechanisms shaped by natural selection. For example, from his nocturnal theory of schizophrenia, Feierman (1994) deduces that schizophrenic patients should exhibit a peculiar circadian rhythm of the neurohormone melatonin. This prediction is open to empirical examination and, if corroborated, would provide indirect support for this particular model.

The second problem is that evolutionary models of psychopathology can easily be taken to mean that natural selection acts on single behavioral characteristics (e.g. cheating, nocturnalism, etc.). If it were reasonable to assume that a characteristic affected survival to a great extent, this position might have some credit (for an example from the animal literature, see Kettlewell, 1973). In all other instances, this view would be incorrect because selection pressures act on the total organism rather than on an isolated trait (Hailman, 1979).

The third point that can be raised is that evolutionary models often allude to genetically-based predispositions that would mediate certain behaviors. In fact, an adaptationist argument must assume that the behavioral dysfunction it intends to explain is, at least to some extent, under genetic control: by definition, natural selection operates through genes. However, in some cases, there is little or no evidence that the behavioral phenomenon to be explained is genetically transmitted. Cheating is a case in point (Harpending & Sobus, 1987). But even when it can be shown that a particular phenomenon is under genetic control, there is still a problem. As Miller (1995; p. 307) points out, "the fact remains that genes code for proteins, not for structures, behaviors, or predispositions for behaviors". Indeed, most evolutionary models of human behavior are characterized by a low degree of specification with regard to the more proximal mechanisms involved.

A consequence of these problems is the impossibility of an *experimentum crucis* for testing adaptationist models of psychopathology. Does that mean that we have to abandon these models? Not necessarily. It does imply, however, that one has to examine the indirect support for such models very carefully. A hypothesis that relies on an empirically inaccessible assumption can only be accepted if it generates a set of predictions that meet two criteria. For one thing, these predictions must be corroborated by research. And in the second place, these predictions should not flow from alternative hypotheses (Merckelbach, 1989).

With this in mind, let us turn to adaptationist models of phobia and examine whether or not they meet these two requirements.

EVOLUTION AND PHOBIAS

The Non-random Distribution of Fears

A curious and consistent finding is that specific fears and phobias are non-randomly distributed. Fear survey studies (Agras, Sylvester & Oliveau, 1969; Costello, 1982) have shown that in the general population, some fears (e.g. of snakes or spiders) are far more prevalent than others (e.g. of electricity). Like-wise, factor analyses of normal subjects' responses to fear questionnaires indicate that the most prevalent fears can be grouped together in a relatively small number of distinct categories (e.g. fear of animals, fear of death, injury, and illness; see Arrindell et al., 1991). In other words, specific fears and phobias typically pertain to a relatively limited set of stimuli. This fact is acknowledged in the official nomenclature of the DSM-IV (American Psychiatric Association, 1994). DSM-IV differentiates between four highly prevalent types of specific phobias: animal type (e.g. spider phobia), natural environment type (e.g. phobia of heights), blood–injection–injury type (e.g. dental phobia), and situational type (e.g. claustrophobia). In addition, DSM-IV introduces a miscellaneous category ("other type") that encompasses, for example, chocking phobia.

It is self-evident that fear and anxiety play a crucial role in the survival of organisms. As Marks & Nesse (1994; p. 254) state: "Too little anxiety leads to behavior that makes us more likely to fall off a cliff, be attacked by a wild beast, hurt by other humans, or to act in ways that lead to social exclusion". Further-more, there is some evidence that fearfulness is, at least partially, under genetic control. For example, examining a large sample of dizygotic and monozygotic twin pairs aged 8–18, Stevenson, Batten & Cherner (1992) found significant heritabilies for fearfulness, especially for those fears "concerned with risk of life" (p. 983), i.e. fear of the unknown, fear of injury and of small animals, and fear of danger.

The non-random distribution of fears, their apparent survival value, and their possible genetic basis invite adaptationist explanations. In what follows, three evolutionary models are briefly summarized. The first is limited in its scope (and ambitions) in that it focuses on one particular fear, namely, blood–injection–injury phobia. This phobia is known to have a number of peculiar features that are not shared by other specific phobias. The second evolutionary model aims at explaining the full range of specific phobias. It assumes that many phobias repre-sent innate fears that require no learning (e.g. conditioning). This approach strongly emphasizes the spontaneous developmental fears found in children (e.g. the visual cliff phenomenon). The third and most sophisticated evolutionary model holds that humans are prepared to fear those stimuli that once threatened prehistoric man. It assumes that a genetically-based tendency to fear "archaic"

...igers interacts with learning processes (e.g. conditioning) to produce specific and social phobias. The evolutionary prepared tendency to fear stimuli that once posed a threat to our ancestors would explain the non-random distribution of fears.

Blood–Injection–Injury Phobia

In general, patients suffering from specific phobias react with sympathetic hyperarousal (e.g. tachycardia, hypertension) when exposed to their feared object (e.g. small animals, heights, etc.). At the subjective level, feelings of fear and apprehension dominate. Blood–injection–injury phobia is an atypical fear because it has a rather different symptom profile (see Page, 1994; Marks, 1988; Thyer, Himle & Curtis, 1985). Unlike other phobias, it is dominated by a parasympathetic response (e.g. bradycardia, hypotension) to the feared stimulus. Furthermore, exposure to blood or related items elicits not only subjective feelings of fear, but also disgust and sometimes nausea.

The parasympathetic hyperarousal in blood–injection–injury phobia often results in "emotional fainting" or vasovagal syncope. Connolly, Halam & Marks (1976) found that 100% of their sample of blood phobics reported fainting when exposed to blood or related stimuli. There are two evolutionary hypotheses about emotional fainting in blood–injection–injury phobias. The first assumes that emotional fainting is related to tonic immobility, freezing, and death-feigning in animals (Marks, 1988; Marks & Nesse, 1994). These animal defenses are adaptive because predators usually attack prey that is moving. A second evolutionary hypothesis about emotional fainting holds that it slows down blood circulation, which might be adaptive when the organism is hurt and loses blood (Thyer, Himle & Curtis, 1985; Barlow, 1988). Of course, these two interpretations are not mutually exclusive and it may well be that emotional fainting has several adaptive functions.

There is circumstantial evidence that appears to support evolutionary interpretations of emotional fainting. For example, researchers have found a relatively strong familial aggregation (e.g. parent–child correspondence) of blood–injection–injury phobias (Kozak & Montgomery, 1981). Likewise, twin studies have reported elevated heritability estimates for blood–injection–injury phobias as compared to other specific fears (for a review, see Page, 1994). Furthermore, blood–injection–injury fears are common in the normal adult population (Agras, Sylvester & Oliveau, 1969). This is also true for children. In fact, 44% of children aged 6–8 report a mild fear of blood (Lapouse & Monk, 1959). Finally, blood–injection–injury phobia is characterized by an early onset, with onset ages ranging between 7 and 9 years (Öst, 1991). Taken together, these findings suggest that aversion and fainting in the presence of blood is not a unique psychopathological syndrome, but rather a reflex-like phenomenon with a relatively high prevalence in the normal population (Thyer, Himle & Curtis, 1985). Thus, one could argue that "patients with blood–injury phobia are at the extreme end of a normal continuum of genetically influenced heart-rate slowing in response to blood–injury stimuli . . ." (Marks, 1988; p. 1211).

Developmental Fears, "Prepotency" and Specific Phobias

By and large, a substantial proportion of specific phobias begin in childhood (Öst, 1987). Interestingly, surveys have consistently found that mild fears are commonplace among young children (e.g. MacFarlane, Allen & Honzik, 1954). Moreover, the mild fears seen in children often seem to appear and disappear spontaneously. They represent transient developmental phenomena with a predictable course (for an extensive discussion, see Marks, 1987). For example, Bauer (1976) found that fear of animals is common in younger children, whereas fear of injury is more characteristic of older children. It is plausible to argue that in a subgroup of these children, specific fears do not wane with the passage of time, but instead become chronic phobias that persist into adulthood (for a review, see Merckelbach et al., 1996).

Several authors have argued that the stimuli that elicit developmental fears (e.g. fear of strangers, fear of heights, fear of separation, etc.) represent "prepotent" cues (Gray, 1982; Menzies & Clarke, 1995). In their view, these cues posed a challenge to the survival of prehistoric man and "innate" fear reactions to them would have increased fitness. Therefore, the developmental fears are spontaneous in the sense that they are not dependent on aversive associative learning (e.g. conditioning). Supporters of this non-associative view do not deny that background experiences may contribute in a subtle way to developmental fears. For example, it is well known that self-produced locomotion precedes visual-cliff fear seen in young infants: prelocomotive infants do not display this fear and it is only after the infant has mastered certain motor abilities that this particular fear begins to emerge (Berthental & Campos, 1984).

The important point that adherents of the non-associative account make is that developmental fears do not rely on aversive learning experiences. They further claim that specific phobias seen in adult patients echo these early, innate fears (Menzies & Clarke, 1995). But if this is the case, one might ask why all adults do not suffer from specific phobias. Menzies & Clarke (1993a, 1995) propose that poor habituators may remain fearful of innate fear cues. In these individuals, developmental fears become chronic and take the form of a specific phobia. Alternatively, non-specific stressors (e.g. interpersonal conflicts, depression) may produce dishabituation and the reinstatement of developmental fears (for a similar analysis, see Jacobs & Nadel, 1985). In either case, specific phobias would reflect developmental fears which, in turn, would derive from innate fear reactions to prepotent stimuli. This, then, would offer a comprehensive account of the non-random distribution of fears and phobias. It would also explain why patients with specific phobias frequently report that they have always been afraid and that aversive conditioning or modeling experiences played no role in the onset of their complaints (Menzies & Clarke, 1993a, 1994, 1995).

Preparedness Theory

In the early 1970s, Seligman (1971) introduced his preparedness hypothesis, According to this hypothesis, the non-random distribution of fears is caused by an evolutionary predisposition (i.e. preparedness) operating in fear conditioning. Briefly, the hypothesis states that, as a result of genetic transmission, modern man tends to react fearfully to stimuli that once were threatening to prehistoric man (e.g. snakes, spiders, high places, etc.). Even a mild, aversive event (unconditioned stimulus; UCS) that accompanies these stimuli would activate this tendency and would consequently produce a highly resistant conditioned fear. It should be noted that preparedness does not refer to an inborn fear of snakes, heights, strangers and the like, but rather to the ease of acquiring such fears by Pavlovian conditioning. In other words, in explaining the origins of phobias and their non-random distribution, the preparedness hypothesis combines an adaptationist perspective with a Pavlovian conditioning interpretation. This would explain why some highly aversive experiences (e.g. air raids, Rachman, 1977; motor car accidents, Marks & Nesse, 1994) fail to produce phobias. In Rachman's (1977; p. 384) words: "These modern artifacts do not feature in our biological heritance". In a similar vein, Marks & Nesse (1994: p. 255) argue that "stimuli that come to be feared are mostly ancient threats . . . Most phobias are exaggerations of these natural fears".

Öhman and co-workers (Öhman, 1986; Öhman & Dimberg, 1984; Öhman, Dimberg & Öst, 1985) have proposed a more detailed version of the preparedness hypothesis. These authors postulated the existence of two evolutionarily-based fear systems: a predator-defense system that mobilizes fear of snakes, spiders, and the like and a social-submissiveness system that initiates fear of conspecifics. These systems differ with regard to their adaptive function, the way in which they are triggered, their developmental course, and the types of phobias to which they give rise. Thus, whereas the predator-defense system would be in charge of defense strategies against predators, the social-submissiveness system would help to establish a social hierarchy. Similarly, while the predator-defense system would be activated when predatory features (e.g. pictures of spiders, snakes, etc.) coincide with aversive conditioning (i.e. UCS), the social-submissiveness system would be activated when social stimuli (e.g. angry faces, threatening posture) occur along with an aversive UCS. Furthermore, a predator-defense system is urgently needed as soon as a young child is able to move away from its parents. In contrast, the social-submissiveness system becomes necessary during adolescence, when social hierarchies are important. Finally, animal phobias would originate from the predator-defense system, while social phobias would be related to the social-submissiveness system. Note that the finding that animal phobias have an earlier onset than social phobia is consistent with this analysis (Öst, 1987).

Four important predictions can be derived from the preparedness hypothesis (Seligman, 1971). The first is that most phobias are directed at stimuli that were probably dangerous to pretechnological man (i.e. "phylogenetically-relevant stimuli"). The second prediction is that fear of these stimuli is easily acquired because humans tend to associate these stimuli with aversive experiences. Furthermore, it is predicated that, due to their biological significance, phobic fears are non-cognitive (third prediction) and resist extinction (fourth prediction).

The central assumption of the preparedness hypothesis, i.e. phobias are the product of Darwinian and conditioning processes operating in concert, is, of course, hard to test. Seligman and colleagues admit that Darwinian arguments "are rather slippery and can be glibly made. The only way of validating the view that, say, avoiding going out in the dark has been selected for in evolution to a greater extent than avoiding eating in public places, would be to recreate past evolutionary pressures and see which phobia is more amplified over generations. Such an experiment verges on the impossible and is unlikely to be funded" (de Silva, Rachman & Seligman, 1977; p. 74). Nevertheless, studies using a variety of research methods have found evidence to support the predictions that flow from the preparedness hypothesis, thereby providing indirect evidence for the central assumption of the preparedness hypothesis.

Retrospective clinical studies in which records of phobic patients were examined have reported that a majority of phobias involve stimuli that can be interpreted as dangerous to pretechnological man (de Silva, Rachman & Seligman, 1977; Zafiropoulou & McPherson, 1986; de Silva, 1988). This appears to confirm the first prediction.

Anecdotal evidence suggests that fear of phylogenetically relevant stimuli develops quickly. For example, Marks (1977) described a case of a woman who happened to be looking at a photograph of a snake when the car in which she was travelling became involved in an accident. Afterwards, the woman developed a phobia of snakes, not of cars. The illusory correlation paradigm introduced by Tomarken, Mineka & Cook (1989) has been employed to investigate such phenomena under laboratory conditions. In these experiments, subjects are shown slides of phylogenetically relevant stimuli (i.e. spider or snake) and phylogenetically irrelevant stimuli (i.e. flower and mushroom), followed by either an electric shock (aversive outcome), a neutral tone, or nothing at all (neutral outcomes). The contingency between cue and outcome is such that all cue–outcome combinations occur equally often. After subjects have been exposed to all cue–outcome trials, they have to estimate the contingency between different cues and different outcomes. In general, people tend to overestimate the connection between phylogenetically relevant cues and aversive outcomes (Tomarken, Mineka & Cook, 1989; de Jong & Merckelbach, 1991). Illusory correlation experiments thus seem to support the prediction that subjects readily associate phylogenetically relevant stimuli with aversive outcomes.

A similar conclusion can be drawn from studies examining the acquisition of fears in rhesus monkeys. In what seems to be the best controlled studies on prepared learning, Mineka and co-workers (e.g. Mineka, 1987; Cook & Mineka, 1989; Mineka & Cook, 1993) exposed laboratory-reared monkeys ("observers") with no prior fear of snakes to videotapes of wild-reared monkeys ("models") reacting fearfully in the presence of a snake or a flower. Using editing techniques,

Mineka and associates were able to design the videotapes in such a way that model monkeys displayed identical fear behaviors toward phylogenetically relevant (i.e. snakes) and phylogenetically irrelevant (i.e. flowers) stimuli. With this paradigm, Mineka and associates found that observer monkeys acquired an extremely persistent fear of snakes after they had watched models reacting fearfully to snakes. In contrast, observer monkeys failed to acquire a fear of flowers after they had seen models exhibiting identical fears of flowers.

Human conditioning studies by Öhman and co-workers have provided support for the resistance to extinction of phylogenetical fears and their non-cognitive nature (for reviews, see Öhman, Fredrikson & Hugdahl, 1978; Öhman, Dimberg & Öst, 1985; Öhman, 1986). In most of their studies, autonomic reactions (e.g. skin conductance, heart-rate, etc.) of non-phobic subjects were conditioned to phylogenetically relevant (e.g. slides of spiders or angry faces) or phylogenetically irrelevant (e.g. slides of flowers or happy faces) cues by pairing these cues with aversive electric shock UCSs. Employing this classical conditioning set-up, Öhman and co-workers reported in more than a dozen studies that once acquired, conditioned responses to phylogenetically relevant cues are slower to extinguish than conditioned responses to phylogenetically irrelevant cues. These researchers also found some support for the alleged non-cognitive nature of prepared learning. That is, Öhman and associates demonstrated that once acquired, conditioned responses to phylogenetically relevant cues are not abolished by "no more shock" instructions and removal of the shock electrodes. In contrast, extinction of conditioned responses to phylogenetically irrelevant cues is speeded up by such interventions (see review of Öhman & Hugdahl, 1979).

In their recent experiments, Öhman and associates investigated the non-cognitive nature of phobias with still another research technique. These studies examined whether phylogenetically relevant stimuli that were presented outside phobics' awareness (i.e. subliminally presented) elicited a fear response (e.g. skin conductance response). In general, Öhman & Soares (1993; 1994) found that this was, indeed, the case. For example, Öhman & Soares (1994) exposed subjects with fear of snakes, with fear of spiders, and control subjects with neither fear to short presentations of slides showing a spider, snake, flower or mushroom. Slide duration was 30 ms and exactly at slide offset a mask appeared with a duration of 100 ms. The authors claim that under these conditions, subjects are not able to recognize the slides above chance level. Nonetheless, subjects with fear of snakes were found to react with a skin conductance response to backwardly masked snake pictures, and subjects with fear of spiders were found to react with a skin conductance response to masked spider slides, whereas control subjects failed to react to the slides. In another study (Öhman & Soares, 1993) it was shown that non-phobic subjects reacted with a skin conductance response to backwardly masked pictures of snakes or spiders when these pictures were previously paired with an aversive shock UCS in a conditioning procedure. In contrast, phylogenetically irrelevant stimuli presented subliminally failed to elicit conditioned responses, even when they had been previously paired with an aversive shock UCS. Taken together, these findings seem to indicate that a rough and pre-attentive (i.e. non-cognitive) analysis of phylogenetically relevant stimuli may be sufficient for a fear response to occur.

In summary, the predictions that flow from the preparedness hypothesis have received support from various sources. However, before concluding that the preparedness hypothesis rests on a sound empirical basis, it may be wise to ask how robust these empirical findings are and whether there are alternative explanations that do not invoke Darwinian notions.

A CRITICAL EVALUATION

The Non-random Distribution of Fears

Community studies have clearly shown that some stimuli are more frightening than others (Agras, Sylvester & Oliveau, 1969). It was this selectivity of fears that led some theorists to propose evolutionary interpretations of specific phobias and fears. The way in which they describe the selectivity of specific fears almost automatically points in an adaptationist direction. For example, Lumsden & Wilson (1982; p. 3) stated:

> It is a remarkable fact that phobias are easily evoked by many of the greatest dangers of mankind's ancient environment, including closed spaces, heights, thunderstorms, running water, snakes, and spiders. Of equal significance, phobias are rarely evoked by the greatest dangers of modern technological society, such as guns, knives, automobiles, and electric sockets.

It is beyond doubt that fears and phobias are unevenly distributed across stimuli. However, supporters of an adaptationist interpretation of this fact often ignore the following points. To begin with, it must be recognized that the number and type of stimulus items that are included in fear surveys are likely to affect the results of these surveys. The often cited study of Agras, Sylvester & Oliveau (1969) employed only 40 items derived from traditional fear scales. In contrast, a fear survey study by Kirkpatrick (1984) was based on 133 items. In addition, the latter study inquired about fears other than those listed by the items. Thus, it is not surprising to find that the results of the two surveys were quite different. Agras, Sylvester & Oliveau found fear of snakes to be the most prevalent fear among men and women, yet in Kirkpatrick's survey, fear of snakes ranked 6th and 21st for women and men, respectively. This researcher found that fear of roller coasters and fear of untimely death were the top intense fears for women. For men, the fear of being punished by God ranked highest. Obviously, when the fear rank order found by Agras, Sylvester & Oliveau has to be explained, an adaptationist interpretation might provide a useful starting point. However, unless it is plausible to assume that the fear of, say, God can be traced back to some phylogenetically relevant preoccupation, an adaptationist interpretation of the fear rank order described by Kirkpatrick is not very convincing.

A second critique has to do with the suggestion that humans do not easily develop fear of evolutionarily recent objects. Thus, Marks & Nesse (1994; p. 255) claim that "few fear motor cars". This claim is problematic. A substantial proportion (38%) of survivors of road vehicle accidents develop a phobia related to driving a car (accident phobia; Kuch et al., 1994). Thus, phobias directed at evolutionarily recent objects do occur and it is far from clear whether they are rare. Perhaps it is important to differentiate between the distribution of common fears and that of clinical phobias. It might well be that different etiological factors shape the distribution of both categories. Unfortunately, no data are available with regard to the distribution of common and clinical fears across the stimuli that figure in the DSM-IV category of specific phobias.

Thirdly, it is one thing to say that most specific fears are evolutionary prepared, but quite another to determine the amount of phylogenetic relevance of the various stimuli. Consider this example. In their conditioning studies on prepared learning, Öhman and co-workers employed slides of mushrooms as phylogenetically irrelevant stimuli. But, as Delprato (1980; p. 89) pointed out, "considering the fact that approximately 100 species of poisonous mushrooms have been identified in the USA alone . . ., it is reasonable to suspect that mushrooms have posed a greater threat to the survival of the human species than have spiders and snakes combined" (see also Merckelbach, et al. 1988). As another example, in a conditioning study by Eifert & Schermelleh (1985; p. 102), a rabbit served as a phylogenetically irrelevant stimulus because "rabbits are usually considered cuddly, cute pets". However, Seligman (1971) emphasized that Watson's classical conditioning experiment with Little Albert succeeded because phylogenetically relevant stimuli were involved, namely "furry things, like rats and rabbits" (p. 315). Similarly, in a recent study by Regan & Howard (1995), slides of dogs and cats served as phylogenetically relevant stimuli. Yet, in a study by Dawson, Schell & Banis (1986), pictures of dogs and cats served as *neutral* filler stimuli. Obviously, then, researchers have rather idiosyncratic views on what constitutes a phylogenetically relevant stimulus. There is no easy solution to this problem because inferring the phylogenetic relevance of stimuli from the prevalence of fears and phobias would be tautological.

Emotional Fainting and Blushing

While patients with a blood–injury–injection phobia often report that they faint in the presence of blood or related stimuli, the phenomenon of emotional fainting is by no means limited to this category of individuals. Emotional fainting is relatively common in blood donors and only a subgroup of these persons will qualify for a diagnosis of blood–injury–injection phobia (Page, 1994). By implication, adaptationists' interpretations of emotional fainting do not offer a complete account of blood–injury–injection phobia.

The connection between emotional fainting and blood–injury–injection phobias can be compared to that between blushing and social phobia. Social phobics are often preoccupied with blushing (Edelmann, 1990). Furthermore, there are several speculations about the adaptive value of this reflex-like phenomenon (for a review, see Leary et al., 1992). For example, some authors have argued that social blushing serves as a non-verbal apology that indicates that the person accepts a certain social hierarchy. While such speculations might have some *prima facie* plausibility, they do not elucidate the etiology of social phobia, simply because most people will blush now and then and only a small minority of them can be considered to be social phobics.

The idea that emotional fainting and tonic immobility or death-feigning are evolutionary communalities comes close to the second type of adaptationist explanation that was discussed earlier. In this view, the inactivity produced by emotional fainting once had an adaptive value during confrontations with potential predators. However, as Fridlund (1991; p. 11) stresses, "Expressive communalities across species are not always clear, and they are often in the eye of the observer". Indeed, the parallel between emotional fainting, on the one hand, and tonic immobility and death-feigning, on the other hand, is more apparent than real. Whereas emotional fainting results in loss of consciousness, tonic immobility in animals is accompanied by high arousal and readiness for action (Page, 1994; Barlow, 1988).

The second adaptationist hypothesis about emotional fainting is more related to the first type of adaptationist explanation that was described earlier. It proposes that emotional fainting slows down blood circulation, thereby reducing blood loss. However, this proposal is difficult to reconcile with hemodynamic principles. For example, tissue damage and blood loss usually produce an increase in heart-rate and blood pressure, i.e. the opposite reaction pattern of that found in emotional fainting (Page, 1994).

Marks (1988) has argued that blood–injury–injection phobics are at the extreme end of a normal adaptive continuum. His explanation capitalizes on both the alleged adaptive significance of emotional fainting (type 1 explanation) and individual differences in this adaptive behavior (type 3 explanation). A discussion about adaptive genetic variation in psychology is beyond the scope of this chapter. Suffice it to say that there is no consensus among specialists in this area, with some of them arguing that behavioral variations stem from phenotypic plasticity (e.g. Tooby & Cosmides, 1989) and others believing that behavioral diversity might originate from adaptive genetic variation (e.g. Wilson, 1994).

To sum up, emotional fainting is an isolated, reflex-like phenomenon. Consequently, it is suitable for an adaptationist explanation. Unfortunately, the evolutionary interpretations that have been advanced thus far are inconsistent with proximal data (i.e. hemodynamics, comparative findings). In his review article, Page (1994; p. 451) rightly concluded that "the adaptive advantage of vasovagal syncope remains obscure. Indeed, vasovagal syncope may serve no adaptive advantage".

The Non-associative Account

Like the preparedness position, the non-associative account holds that specific fears reflect the dangers that our ancestors faced in their Pleistocene savannah environment. Thus, the non-associative account is related to the second type of evolutionary approach, which assumes that some behavioral phenomena are archaic manifestations.

The non-associative account is flawed on several counts. First, its claim that developmental fears and specific phobias involve innate fear stimuli assumes that researchers can reconstruct the challenges of the Pleistocene savannah. Again, this is difficult to accomplish. Obviously, it is reasonable to assume that fear of heights and fear of strangers are relevant to fitness. However, an adaptive argument for fear of spiders is less persuasive. In fact, only a tiny percentage (i.e. 0.1%) of the 35 000 spider varieties are dangerous (Renner, 1990), and pretechnological man must have had more urgent problems than dealing with spiders.

Second, and most importantly, the non-associative account leaves unexplained why not all people suffer from specific phobias. Menzies & Clarke (1995) argue that developmental fears take a chronic course in poor habituators, but this is begging the question. Why, exactly, do some individuals habituate rapidly and others poorly to prepotent fear stimuli? The non-associative account provides no direct answer to this question. Of course, one could assume that genetic variation is responsible for these individual differences in fearfulness. Still, there is no convincing evidence that a selective genetic factor contributes to the etiology of specific phobias (Kendler et al., 1992).

Menzies & Clarke further suggest that non-specific stress may provoke a reinstatement of developmental fears. But again, this argument leads to an overprediction of the prevalence of phobias in adults. Most individuals will now and then experience aversive life events, but only a small minority of them actually develop a specific phobia.

Third, the non-associative account is difficult to reconcile with the results from genetic epidemiological research. More specifically, in their large-scale study on phobias in twins, Kendler and colleagues (1992) found that specific phobias are the joint product of a modest common genetic factor and traumatic events that are highly specific to these phobias (i.e. conditioning experiences). Thus, although the non-associative account may explain developmental fears in children, the findings of Kendler et al. (1992) suggest that a preparedness approach might provide a better alternative for understanding the origins of clinical phobias in adults.

Preparedness

Since its introduction in the early 1970s, the preparedness hypothesis has been extremely influential and remains to this day a dominant view of how the non-random distribution of fears can be understood. Numerous studies have sought to test the predictions that flow from the preparedness account. This has brought to light some weaknesses of this approach. They are reviewed in depth by Delprato (1980), McNally (1987) and Davey (1995). Their detailed comments will not be repeated here. Instead, the present discussion will emphasize two points: empirical evidence for the preparedness of specific phobias is either weak or is subject to contrary interpretations.

As the earlier discussion indicated, indirect support for the preparedness hypothesis has come from various sources. For example, advocates of the preparedness hypothesis have referred to clinical studies in which it was found that a majority of phobias and obsessive–compulsive disorders are directed at phylogenetically relevant cues (Zafiropoulou & McPherson, 1986). A potential problem with these studies is that *a priori* beliefs of the researchers may have affected judgments about the phylogenetic relevance of phobias. In addition, not all studies were able to replicate the basic findings (Merckelbach et al., 1988). Furthermore, a number of studies have come up with results that are difficult to reconcile with Öhman's speculations about the predator-defense system and the social-submissiveness system. For instance, Matchett & Davey (1991) provided evidence to suggest that fear of small animals is related to disgust and contamination sensitivity, rather than to a fear of being attacked. In line with this, Mulkens, de Jong & Merckelbach (1996) showed that clinical spider phobia is associated with a relatively strong disgust sensitivity. They also found that spider-phobic women but not non-fearful controls consider spiders *per se* to be disgusting. This feature of spider phobia fits better with a disease-avoidance interpretation than with a predator-defense model, a point to which we will return.

Evidence for the idea that social phobia is intimately linked to a fear of angry facial expressions is also far from encouraging: compared to control subjects, social phobic patients do not react with stronger subjective or physiological fear responses to slides of angry faces (Merckelbach et al., 1989; van den Horne, 1995). These data cast doubts on the characteristics that Öhman (1986) ascribes to the social-submissiveness system.

Case reports have been presented to illustrate the prepared learning that would characterize specific phobias (Marks, 1977), yet some specific phobias are hard to interpret in evolutionary terms. For instance, it is not easy to design an adaptive story for choking phobias.

The basic findings of the illusory correlation studies of Tomarken, Mineka & Cook (1989) have been replicated time and again (De Jong & Merckelbach, 1991). Yet, the fact that high-fear subjects in particular tend to overestimate the association between phylogenetically relevant stimuli and aversive outcomes suggests that prior fear, rather than an evolutionarily-based predisposition, is the most important antecedent of the selective associations found in illusory correlation studies (e.g. de Jong et al., 1992). In addition, studies by McNally & Heatherton (1993) and de Jong (1993) underline the importance of prior expectations and cast doubts on the idea that selective associations gradually develop during illusory correlation experiments. Moreover, de Jong, Merckelbach &

Arntz (1995) recently showed that phylogenetically relevant illusory correlations arise from initial expectations that survive extinction or from expectations that are reinstated by incidental slide-shock pairings. Obviously, such an expectation bias does not imply a biologically prewired schema; prior fear and cultural connotations seem to be more credible candidates for the sources of pre-experimental expectations.

The impressive results of studies on observational learning in rhesus monkeys (Cook & Mineka, 1989) have been cited by many authors as strong evidence in favor of the preparedness concept (see e.g. Rachman, 1990; Davey, 1995). However, an alternative interpretation of these results is possible. More specifically, Davey (1995) has suggested that in the observational conditioning set-up, model monkeys communicate not only their fear to naïve observer monkeys, but also fairly specific information about the source of that fear, namely, snakes. If true, one would expect that edited video fragments displaying models' snake-related fear responses to flowers would not be very effective in eliciting observers' fear of these flowers. Mineka & Cook (1995) have countered that there is no evidence that laboratory-reared rhesus monkeys use and understand such a specific signal system. Clearly, this point warrants further examination. Whatever the outcome, one should keep in mind that the observational conditioning studies of Mineka and colleagues are about snake fear in monkeys, while the preparedness hypothesis of human phobias is about a different species living in a different ecological niche. In Schwartz's (1974; p. 195) words, "The capacity for and frequency of arbitrary learning may increase with increasing species complexity and developmental progression. It seems clear that most of the learning done by human adults is arbitrary, or at least largely independent of evolutionary constraints".

A consistent finding in the psychophysiological conditioning studies of Öhman and co-workers was that skin conductance responses conditioned to phylogenetically relevant stimuli (e.g. spiders, angry faces) are more resistant to extinction than skin conductance responses conditioned to phylogenetically neutral stimuli (e.g. mushrooms, happy faces). While some studies were able to replicate this phenomenon (Foa et al., 1991), others failed to document the critical effect (McNally & Foa, 1986; Packer et al., 1991; Kirsch & Boucsein, 1994). Moreover, there are indications that a resistance to extinction can also be obtained by pairing ontogenetically fear-relevant stimuli with aversive UCSs. Thus, Hugdahl & Johnsen (1989) found that responses conditioned to slides of a gun pointing towards the subject are slow to extinguish. This implies that the resistance to extinction phenomenon is not uniquely tied to phylogenetically relevant stimuli.

It is still not clear what parameters are important for the resistance to extinction effect to be observed. It may well be the case that this phenomenon critically depends on subjects' expectations rather than the phylogenetic relevance of the stimuli. Germane to this issue is the point raised by Davey (1992; 1995). He suggested that subjects enter psychophysiological conditioning experiments with more or less articulated expectations about the dangerousness of stimuli such as spiders, angry faces and the like. A conditioning procedure in which these stimuli are paired with an aversive shock may promote these expectations, that is, may result in a stronger UCS expectation bias with regard to these stimuli. This, in turn, would contribute to a resistance to extinction. There is much evidence to support the UCS expectation model of laboratory preparedness effects (Davey, 1992; Honeybourne, Matchett & Davey, 1993; Lovibond, Siddle & Bond, 1993). However, some authors have questioned the explanatory power of this concept (Fantino & Goldshmidt, 1995). They argue that the concept is silent about the origins of subjects' *a priori* expectation bias with regard to spiders, snakes, etc. That is to say, the concept does not exclude the possibility that evolutionary processes underlie the UCS expectation bias. This criticism is only partially justified because the UCS expectation interpretation can easily be linked to the influence of culturally transmitted ideas about phobogenic stimuli (e.g. Davey, 1995). A good example of the cultural dimension of specific fears is provided by Bartholomew (1994). His analysis of the widespread fear of harmless tarantula spiders in seventeenth century Italy makes plain that myths and false beliefs may be a powerful source of danger expectations (for similar examples, see Davey, 1994a).

According to the original preparedness hypothesis, aversive learning that involves phylogenetically relevant stimuli is non-cognitive. Several studies have examined this issue with sophisticated conditioning set-ups. By and large, the results of these studies are confusing, with some authors obtaining evidence for the non-cognitive nature of responses conditioned to phylogenetically relevant stimuli (Schell, Dawson & Marinkovic, 1991) and others failing to find such evidence (Dawson, Schell & Banis, 1986). The most convincing evidence for the non-cognitive nature of prepared learning comes from Öhman et al.'s recent studies (Öhman & Soares, 1994). Using subliminal stimulation techniques, these studies seem to indicate that a pre-attentive analysis of phylogenetically relevant stimuli is sufficient for a fear response to occur. However, a problem with these studies is that the below-threshold quality of the stimuli and their ability to evoke responses were established in different samples. Thus, it is not clear to what extent the stimuli were genuinely subliminal. Subliminal stimulation techniques are notoriously difficult (Holender, 1986) and, consequently, it remains to be seen whether below-threshold presentations of phylogenetically relevant stimuli produce robust effects.

Studies regarding phobics' beliefs further challenge the idea that specific phobias are typically non-cognitive phenomena. For instance, Arntz, Lavy, van den Berg & van Rijsoort (1993) showed that spider phobia is accompanied by elaborated irrational beliefs about spiders (e.g. "They will make me ill"). Irrational beliefs have also been found in other types of specific phobias (Thorpe & Salkovskis, 1995). The importance of such beliefs in the maintenance of fear is substantiated by a recent study by de Jong & Arntz (1995). They reported that strong negative beliefs about spiders predict poor effects of exposure *in vivo* treatment.

CONCLUDING COMMENTS

The adaptationist approach to phobias is not new. A quotation from Freud's *Introductory Lectures on Psychoanalysis* (1917/1974; p. 460) may illustrate this point: "It must be admitted, subject to the necessary qualifications, that among the contents of phobias there are a number which, as Stanley Hall insists, are adopted to serve as objects of anxiety owing to phylogenetic inheritance". Behaviorism has long ignored Darwinian theory and genetics (Eysenck, 1987). However, in the past two decades, neo-Darwinism and the rising tide of sociobiology have contributed to a renewed interest in the evolutionary origins of phobias.

Evolutionary scenarios about the biological advantage of phobias are difficult to test. Therefore, such scenarios can only be accepted if there is strong evidence to sustain the predictions that flow from such scenarios. Moreover, concurrent interpretations of the accumulated evidence should be ruled out. As Kitcher (1985; p. 66) expressed it, "Darwinian histories win their way to the top through the elimination of rivals". In the case of phobias, there are no Darwinian histories that fulfill these two criteria. As it stands, the evidence is either equivocal (e.g. failed replications) or open to alternative interpretations (e.g. expectation bias).

This is not to say that Darwinian considerations of fear are doomed to fail. Evolutionary analyses of the reflex-like defense behavior have yielded important insights. A good example is provided by theories about the adaptive significance of the diving reflex (Gooden, 1993). Similarly, a Darwinian approach to the developmental fears found in young children may provide the only clue for understanding the origins of these fears (Marks, 1987). However, it is a huge step from defensive reflexes and isolated, developmental fears to phobic disorders in adults.

It is premature to invoke Darwinian accounts for the non-random distribution of phobias as long as ontogenetic determinants of the non-random distribution have not been exhaustively analyzed. Of particular interest in this context is the role of disgust and disgust sensitivity. In a series of studies, Davey and co-workers (Matchett & Davey, 1991; Davey, 1994b) demonstrated that normal subjects tend to evaluate small animals such as spiders, snakes and rats as disgusting rather than dangerous. This is consistent with a study by Bennett-Levy & Marteau (1984), who showed that there is a positive correlation between fear of these animals and the extent to which they are perceived as ugly and slimy. Accordingly, one could speculate that when such evaluations are transmitted through modelling and negative information (Rachman, 1977), especially people with a high disgust sensitivity will come to fear these small animals. Disgust sensitivity is a trait that can be measured with a questionnaire that focuses on food rejection. There is now abundant evidence that at least spider phobics display a heightened disgust sensitivity (Merckelbach et al., 1993; Mulkens, de Jong & Merckelbach, 1996).

Thus far, most studies concerned with disgust and phobia have relied on a correlational approach. However, an experiment by Webb & Davey (1992) clearly indicated that fear is causally affected by disgust. In that study, it was found that prior exposure to repulsive material (i.e. video scenes of a medical operation) leads to an increase in fear of spiders, snakes, etc. Of further relevance to the causality issue is a study by Davey, Forster & Mayhew (1993). These authors found that parents' disgust sensitivity predicts fear of small animals in their offspring.

The role of disgust and disgust sensitivity is not restricted to the domain of small animal fears. For example, Page (1994) suggested that disgust sensitivity is an important vulnerability factor for emotional fainting in blood–injection–injury phobia. In line with this suggestion are the results of Matchett & Davey (1991), who found a positive correlation between disgust sensitivity and blood–injection–injury fear.

The findings on disgust and disgust sensitivity fit well with a cultural interpretation of the non-random distribution of phobias. Of course, one could argue that disgust sensitivity is a genetically transmitted trait that confers an adaptive advantage. Yet, there is no obvious reason to postulate such an assumption. At the very least, the findings on the disgust-evoking status of small animals cast doubts on the evolutionary predator-defense system hypothesized by Öhman (1986). Small animal phobias can better be understood in terms of a disease-avoidance model than in terms of a predator-defense system (Matchett & Davey, 1991).

The clinical significance of discussions about the evolutionary origins of specific phobia is limited. There are no reasons to believe that phobias directed at phylogenetically relevant stimuli are more severe, have an earlier age of onset, or are more difficult to treat than phobias directed at modern artifacts (de Silva, Rachman & Seligman, 1977; Zafiropoulou & McPherson, 1986). By and large, specific phobias respond extremely well to behavioral interventions. This is true for small animal phobias (Öst, 1989), blood–injury–injection phobias (Öst, Fellenius & Sterner, 1991), situational fears (e.g. claustrophobia; Craske et al., 1995), and natural environment phobias (e.g. water phobia; Menzies & Clarke, 1993b). Admittedly, in approximately 10–20% of patients with specific phobias, behavioral interventions fail to produce adequate results, but it is questionable whether adaptationist theories will help to reduce this percentage. More is to be expected from studies concerned with the proximal mechanisms involved in the etiology and maintenance of phobias.

As for the proximal mechanisms involved in specific phobias, one promising line of research is focused on a highly cognitive phenomenon, namely, phobics' style of reasoning. For example, Arntz, Rauner & van den Hout (1995) showed that phobic subjects are prone to the fallacy of *ex consequentia* reasoning: "If I feel anxious, there must be danger". Unlike non-phobic control subjects, phobic people seem to believe that anxiety symptoms imply the presence of danger. Interestingly, Arntz et al. found that this reasoning error was not restricted to situations relevant to phobics' anxiety complaints. The lack of situational specificity suggests that this bias is a premorbid characteristic that predisposes one to pathological anxiety. Another cognitive vulnerability factor for the etiology of phobic fear may be a strong belief bias. That is, phobic subjects exhibit a general tendency to confirm rather than falsify prior beliefs (de Jong et al., 1995). Whereas the absence of such a bias would allow subjects to give up phobogenic beliefs in the face of incompatible experiences, the presence of an enhanced belief bias is likely to immunize against refutation of phobogenic beliefs. One could argue that treatment strategies that do not tackle such fear-confirming reasoning biases are likely to produce less than optimal results. Obviously, this point is far removed from the adaptationist approach to specific phobias.

REFERENCES

American Psychiatric Association (1994). *Diagnostic and Statistical Manual of Mental Disorders*, 4th edn. Washington, DC: American Psychiatric Association.

Agras, S., Sylvester, D. & Oliveau, D. (1969). The epidemiology of common fears and phobias. *Comprehensive Psychiatry*, **10**, 151–156.

Arntz, A., Lavy, E., van den Berg, G. & van Rijsoort, S. (1993). Negative beliefs in spider phobics: a psychometric evaluation of the spider phobia beliefs questionnaire. *Advances in Behaviour Research and Therapy*, **15**, 257–277.

Arntz, A., Rauner, M. & van den Hout, M.A. (1995). "If I feel anxious, there must be danger": *ex consequentia* reasoning in inferring danger in anxiety disorders. *Behaviour Research and Therapy*, **33**, 917–926.

Arrindell, W.A., Pickersgill, M.J., Merckelbach, H., Ardon, A.M. & Cornet, F.C. (1991). Phobic dimensions: III. Factor analytic approaches to the study of common phobic fears: an updated review of findings with adult subjects. *Advances in Behaviour Research and Therapy*, **13**, 73–130.

Barlow, D.H. (1988). *Anxiety and its Disorders: the Nature and Treatment of Anxiety and Panic*. New York: Guilford.

Bartholomew, R.E. (1994). Tarantism, dancing mania, and demonopathy: the anthropolitical aspects of "mass psychogenic illness". *Psychological Medicine*, **24**, 281–306.

Bauer, D.H. (1976). An exploratory study of developmental changes in children's fears. *Journal of Child Psychology and Psychiatry*, **17**, 69–74.

Bennett-Levy, J & Marteau, T. (1984). Fear of animals: what is prepared? *British Journal of Psychology*, **75**, 37–42.

Bertenthal, B.L. & Campos, J.J. (1984). A re-examination of fear and its determinants on the visual cliff. *Psychophysiology*, **21**, 413–417.

Connolly, J.C., Hallam, R.S. & Marks, I.M. (1976). Selective association of fainting with blood–injury–illness. *Behavior Therapy*, **7**, 8–13.

Cook, M. & Mineka, S. (1989). Observational conditioning of fear to fear-relevant versus fear-irrelevant stimuli in rhesus monkeys. *Journal of Abnormal Psychology*, **98**, 448–459.

Costello, C.G. (1982). Fears and phobias in women: a community study. *Journal of Abnormal Psychology*, **91**, 280–286.

Craske, M.G., Mohlman, J., Yi, J., Glover, D. & Valeri, S. (1995). Treatment of claustrophobia and snake/spider phobias: fear of arousal and fear of context. *Behaviour Research and Therapy*, **33**, 197–203.

Daly, M. & Wilson, M.I. (1994). Some differential attributes of lethal assaults on small children by stepfathers versus genetic fathers. *Ethology and Sociobiology*, **15**, 207–217.

Darwin, C. (1872/1965). *The Expression of the Emotions in Man and Animals*. Chicago: University of Chicago Press.

Davey, G.C.L. (1992). An expectancy model of laboratory preparedness effects. *Journal of Experimental Psychology: General*, **121**, 24–40.

Davey, G.C.L. (1994a). The disgusting spider: the role of disease and illness in the perpetuation of fear of spiders. *Society and Animals*, **2**, 17–25.

Davey, G.C.L. (1994b). Self-reported fears to common indigenous animals in an adult UK population: the role of disgust sensitivity. *British Journal of Psychology*, **85**, 541–554.

Davey, G.C.L. (1995). Preparedness and phobias: specific evolved associations or a generalized expectancy bias? *Behavioral and Brain Sciences*, **18**, 289–325.

Davey, G.C.L., Forster, L. & Mayhew, G. (1993). Familial resemblances in disgust sensitivity and animal phobias. *Behaviour Research and Therapy*, **31**, 41–50.

Dawson, M.E., Schell, A.M. & Banis, H.T. (1986). Greater resistance to extinction of electrodermal responses conditioned to potentially phobic CSs: a non-cognitive process? *Psychophysiology*, **23**, 552–561.

Delprato, D.J. (1980). Hereditary determinants of fears and phobias: a critical review. *Behavior Therapy*, **11**, 79–103.

de Jong, P.J. (1993). Covariation bias in phobia: mere resistance to pre-experimental expectancies? *Behavior Therapy*, **24**, 447–454.

de Jong, P.J. & Arntz, A. (1995). Negative beliefs concerning spiders predict poor treatment outcome for one-session exposure treatment of spider phobic women. Submitted.

de Jong, P.J. & Merckelbach, H. (1991). Covariation bias and electrodermal responding in spider phobics before and after behavioural treatment. *Behaviour Research and Therapy*, **29**, 307–314.

de Jong, P.J., Merckelbach, H. & Arntz, A. (1995). Covariation bias in phobic women: the relationship between *a priori* expectancy, on-line expectancy, autonomic responding, and *a posteriori* contingency judgement. *Journal of Abnormal Psychology*, **104**, 55–62.

de Jong, P.J., Merckelbach, H., Arntz, A. & Nijman, H. (1992). Covariation detection in treated and untreated spider phobics. *Journal of Abnormal Psychology*, **101**, 724–727.

de Jong, P.J., Weertman, A., Horselenberg, R. & van den Hout, M.A. (1995). Deductive reasoning and pathological anxiety: evidence for a relatively strong belief bias in phobic subjects. Submitted.

de Silva, P. (1988). Phobias and preparedness: replication and extension. *Behaviour Research and Therapy*, **26**, 97–98.

de Silva, P., Rachman, S. & Seligman, M.E.P. (1977). Prepared phobias and obsessions: therapeutic outcome. *Behaviour Research and Therapy*, **15**, 65–77.

Edelmann, R.J. (1990). *Coping with Blushing*. London: Sheldon.

Eibl-Eibesfeld, I. (1979). Human ethology: concepts and implications for the sciences of man. *Behavioral and Brain Sciences*, **2**, 1–57.

Eifert, G.H. & Schermelleh, K. (1985). Language conditioning, emotional instructions, and cognitions in conditioned responses to fear-relevant and fear-irrelevant stimuli. *Journal of Behavior Therapy and Experimental Psychiatry*, **16**, 101–109.

Ekman, P. (1973). *Darwin and Facial Expressions*. New York: Academic Press.

Erickson, M.T. (1993). Rethinking Oedipus: an evolutionary perspective of incest avoidance. *American Journal of Psychiatry*, **150**, 411–416.

Eysenck, H.J. (1987). The role of heredity, environment, and "preparedness" in the genesis of neurosis. In H.J. Eysenck & I. Martin (eds), *Theoretical Foundations of Behavior Therapy*. New York: Plenum.

Fantino, E. & Goldshmidt, J. (1995). Rule-governed and contingency-governed fears. *Behavioral and Brain Sciences*, **18**, 299–300.

Feierman, J.R. (1994). A testable hypothesis about schizophrenia generated by evolutionary theory. *Ethology and Sociobiology*, **15**, 263–282.

Foa, E.B., McNally, R.J., Steketee, G.S. & McCarthy, P.R. (1991). A test of preparedness theory in anxiety-disordered patients using an avoidance paradigm. *Journal of Psychophysiology*, **5**, 159–163.

Freud, S. (1917/1974). *Introductory Lectures on Psychoanalysis.* Harmondsworth: Penguin.

Fridlund, A.J. (1991). Evolution and facial action in reflex, social motive, and paralanguage. *Biological Psychology*, **32**, 3–100.

Gooden, B.A. (1993). The evolution of the asphyxial defense. *Integrative Physiological and Behavioral Science*, **28**, 317–330.

Gray, J.A. (1982). *The Neuropsychology of Anxiety: an Enquiry into the Functions of the Septo-hippocampal System.* Oxford: Clarendon.

Hailman, J.P. (1979). The ethology behind human ethology. *Behavioral and Brain Sciences*, **2**, 35–36.

Harpending, H.C. & Sobus, J. (1987). Sociopathy as an adaptation. *Ethology and Sociobiology*, **8**, 63–72s.

Holender, D. (1986). Semantic activation without conscious identification in dichotic listening, parafoveal vision, and visual masking: a survey and appraisal. *Behavioral and Brain Sciences*, **9**, 1–66.

Honeybourne, C., Matchett, G. & Davey, G.C.L. (1993). Expectancy models of laboratory preparedness effects: a UCS-expectancy bias in phylogenetic and ontogenetic fear-relevant stimuli. *Behavior Therapy*, **24**, 253–264.

Hugdahl, K. & Johnsen, B. (1989). Preparedness and electrodermal fear conditioning: ontogenetic vs. phylogenetic explanations. *Behaviour Research and Therapy*, **27**, 269–278.

Izard, C. (1971). *The Face of Emotion.* New York: Appleton-Century-Crofts.

Jacobs, W.J. & Nadel, L. (1985). On stress-induced recovery of fears and phobias. *Psychological Review*, **92**, 512–531.

Kendler, K.S., Neale, M.C., Kessler, R.C., Heath, A.C. & Eaves, L.J. (1992). The genetic epidemiology of phobias in women: the interrelationship of agoraphobia, situational phobia, and simple phobia. *Archives of General Psychiatry*, **49**, 273–281.

Kenrick, D.T. & Sheets, V. (1993). Homicidal fantasies. *Ethology and Sociobiology*, **14**, 231–246.

Kettlewell, H. (1973). *The Evolution of Melanism.* Oxford: Oxford University Press.

Kirkpatrick, D.R. (1984). Age, gender, and patterns of common intense fears among adults. *Behaviour Research and Therapy*, **22**, 141–150.

Kirsch, P. & Boucsein, W. (1994). Electrodermal conditioning with prepared and unprepared stimuli. *Integrative Physiological and Behavioral Science*, **29**, 134–140.

Kitcher, P. (1985). *Vaulting Ambitions: Sociobiology and the Quest of Human Nature.* Cambridge, MA: MIT Press.

Kozak, M.J. & Montgomery, G.K. (1981). Multimodal behavioral treatment of recurrent injury-scene-elicited fainting (vasodepressor syncope). *Behavioural Psychotherapy*, **9**, 316–321.

Kuch, K., Cox, B.J., Evans, R.E. & Shulman, I. (1994). Phobias, panic, and pain in 55 survivors of road vehicle accidents. *Journal of Anxiety Disorders*, **8**, 181–187.

Lapouse, R. & Monk, M.A. (1959). Fears and worries in a representative sample of children. *American Journal of Orthopsychiatry*, **29**, 803.

Leary, M.R., Britt, T.W., Cutlip, W.D. & Templeton, J.L. (1992). Social blushing. *Psychological Bulletin*, **112**, 446–460.

Lewis, A.J. (1934). Melancholia: a clinical survey of depressive states. *Journal of Mental Science*, **80**, 277–378.

Lewontin, R.C. (1979). Sociobiology as an adaptationist program. *Behavioral Science*, **24**, 5–14.

Lovibond, P.F., Siddle, D.A.T. & Bond, N.W. (1993). Resistance to extinction of fear-relevant stimuli: preparedness or selective association? *Journal of Experimental Psychology: General*, **122**, 449–461.

Lumsden, L.J. & Wilson, E.O. (1982). Precis of genes, mind, and culture. *Behavioral and Brain Sciences*, **5**, 1–7.

MacFarlane, J.W., Allen, L. & Honzik, M.P. (1954). *A Developmental Study of the Behavior Problems of Normal Children between 21 Months and 14 Years*. Berkeley: University of California Press.

Marks, I. (1977). Phobias and obsessions. Clinical phenomena in search of laboratory models. In J.D. Maser & M.E.P. Seligman (eds), *Psychopathology: Experimental Models*. San Francisco: Freeman.

Marks, I. (1987). *Fears, Phobias, and Rituals: Panic, Anxiety, and their Disorders*. Oxford: Oxford University Press.

Marks, I. (1988). Blood–injury phobia: a review. *American Journal of Psychiatry*, **145**, 1207–1213.

Marks, I. & Nesse, R.M. (1994). Fear and fitness: an evolutionary analysis of anxiety disorders. *Ethology and Sociobiology*, **15**, 247–261.

Matchett, G. & Davey, G.C.L. (1991). A test of a disease avoidance model of animal phobias. *Behaviour Research and Therapy*, **29**, 91–94.

McGuire, M.T. (1988). On the possibility of ethological explanations of psychiatric disorders. *Acta Psychiatrica Scandinavica*, **77**, 7–22.

McNally, R.J. (1987). Preparedness and phobias: a review. *Psychological Bulletin*, **101**, 283–303.

McNally, R.J. (1995). Preparedness, phobias, and the Panglossian paradigm. *Behavioral and Brain Sciences*, **18**, 303–304.

McNally, R.J. & Foa, E.B. (1986). Preparedness and resistance to extinction to fear-relevant stimuli: a failure to replicate. *Behaviour Research and Therapy*, **24**, 529–535.

McNally, R.J. & Heatherton, T.F. (1993). Are covariation biases attributable to *a priori* expectancy biases? *Behaviour Research and Therapy*, **31**, 653–658.

Menzies, R.G. & Clarke, J.C. (1993a). The etiology of fear of heights and its relationship to severity and individual response patterns. *Behaviour Research and Therapy*, **31**, 355–366.

Menzies, R.G. & Clarke, J.C. (1993b). A comparison of *in vivo* and vicarious exposure in the treatment of childhood water phobia. *Behaviour Research and Therapy*, **31**, 9–15.

Menzies, R.G. & Clarke, J.C. (1994). Retrospective studies of the origins of phobias: a review. *Anxiety, Stress, and Coping*, **7**, 305–318.

Menzies, R.G. & Clarke, J.C. (1995). The etiology of phobias: a non-associative account. *Clinical Psychology Review*, **15**, 23–48.

Merckelbach, H. (1989). Preparedness and classical conditioning of fear: a critical inquiry. Unpublished PhD thesis, Limburg University, Maastricht.

Merckelbach, H., de Jong, P.J., Arntz, A. & Schouten, E. (1993). The role of evaluative learning and disgust sensitivity in the etiology and treatment of spider phobia. *Advances in Behaviour Research and Therapy*, **15**, 243–255.

Merckelbach, H., de Jong, P.J., Muris, P. & van den Hout, M.A. (1996). The etiology of specific phobias: a review. *Clinical Psychology Review*, **16**, 337–361.

Merckelbach, H., van den Hout, M.A., Hoekstra, R. & van Oppen, P. (1988). Are prepared fears less severe, but more resistant to treatment? *Behaviour Research and Therapy*, **26**, 527–530.

Merckelbach, H., van den Hout, M.A., Jansen, A. & van der Molen, G.M. (1988). Many stimuli are frightening, but some are more frightening than others: the contributions of preparedness, dangerousness, and unpredictability to making a stimulus fearful. *Journal of Psychopathology and Behavioral Assessment*, **10**, 355–366.

Merckelbach, H., van Hout, W., van den Hout, M.A. & Mersch, P.P. (1989). Psychophysiological and subjective reactions of social phobics and normals to facial stimuli. *Behaviour Research and Therapy*, **27**, 289–294.

Miller, D.B. (1995). Nonlinear experiential influence on the development of fear reactions. *Behavioral and Brain Sciences*, **18**, 306–307.

Mineka, S. (1987). A primate model of phobic fears. In H.J. Eysenck & I. Martin (eds), *Theoretical Foundations of Behavior Therapy*. New York: Plenum.

Mineka, S. & Cook, M. (1993). Mechanisms involved in the observational conditioning of fear. *Journal of Experimental Psychology: General*, **122**, 23–38.

Mineka, S. & Cook, M. (1995). Expectancy bias as sole or partial account of selective associations? *Behavioral and Brain Sciences*, **18**, 307–309.

Mulkens, A.A,N., de Jong, P.J. & Merckelbach, H. (1996). Disgust sensitivity and spider phobia. *Journal of Abnormal Psychology*, in press.

Öhman, A. (1986). Face the beast and fear the face: animal and social fears as the prototypes for evolutionary analyses of emotion. *Psychophysiology*, **23**, 123–145.

Öhman, A. & Dimberg, U. (1984). An evolutionary perspective on human social behavior. In W.M. Waid (ed.), *Sociophysiology*. New York: Springer.

Öhman, A., Dimberg, U. & Öst, L.G. (1985). Animal and social phobias: biological constraints on learned fear responses. In S. Reiss & R.R. Bootzin (eds), *Theoretical Issues in Behavior Therapy*. Orlando, FL: Academic Press.

Öhman, A., Fredrikson, M. & Hugdahl, K. (1978). Towards an experimental model for simple phobic reactions. *Behavioural Analysis and Modification*, **2**, 97–114.

Öhman, A. & Hugdahl, K. (1979). Instructional control of autonomic responses: fear relevance as a critical factor. In N. Birbaumer & H.D. Kimmel (eds), *Biofeedback and Self-regulation*. New York: Wiley.

Öhman, A. & Soares, J.J.F. (1993). On the automatic nature of phobic fear: conditioned electrodermal responses to masked fear-relevant stimuli. *Journal of Abnormal Psychology*, **102**, 121–132.

Öhman, A. & Soares, J.J.F. (1994). "Unconscious anxiety": phobic responses to masked stimuli. *Journal of Abnormal Psychology*, **103**, 231–240.

Öst, L.G. (1987). Age of onset in different phobias. *Journal of Abnormal Psychology*, **96**, 223–229.

Öst, L.G. (1989). One-session treatment for specific phobias. *Behaviour Research and Therapy*, **27**, 1–8.

Öst, L.G. (1991). Acquisition of blood and injection phobia and anxiety response patterns in clinical patients. *Behaviour Research and Therapy*, **29**, 323–332.

Öst, L.G., Fellenius, J. & Sterner, U. (1991). Applied tension, exposure *in vivo*, and tension-only in the treatment of blood phobia. *Behaviour Research and Therapy*, **29**, 561–575.

Packer, J.S., Clark, B.M., Bond, N.W. & Siddle, D.A.T. (1991). Conditioning with facial expression of emotion: a comparison of aversive and non-aversive unconditioned stimuli. *Journal of Psychophysiology*, **5**, 79–88.

Page, A.C. (1994). Blood–injury phobia. *Clinical Psychology Review*, **14**, 443–461.

Rachman, S. (1977). The conditioning theory of fear acquisition: a critical examination. *Behaviour Research and Therapy*, **15**, 375–387.

Rachman, S. (1990). The determinants and treatment of simple phobias. *Advances in Behaviour Research and Therapy*, **12**, 1–30.

Razran, G. (1971). *Mind in Evolution*. Boston: Houghton-Mifflin.

Regan, M. & Howard, R. (1995). Fear conditioning, preparedness, and the contingent negative variation. *Psychophysiology*, **32**, 208–214.

Renner, F. (1990). *Spinnen: Ungeheuer-sympathisch*. Kaiserslautern: Verlag.

Schell, A.M., Dawson, M.E. & Marinkovic, K. (1991). Effects of potentially phobic conditioned stimuli on retention, reconditioning, and extinction of the conditioned skin conductance response. *Psychophysiology*, **28**, 140–152.

Schwartz, B. (1974). On going back to nature: a review of Seligman and Hager's Biological Boundaries of Learning. *Journal of the Experimental Analysis of Learning*, **21**, 183–198.

Seligman, M.E.P. (1971). phobias and preparedness. *Behavior Therapy*, **2**, 307–320.

Sloman, L. & Price, J.S. (1987). Losing behavior (yielding subroutine) and human depression: proximate and selective mechanisms. *Ethology and Sociobiology*, **8**, 99–109s.

Stevenson, J., Batten, N. & Cherner, M. (1992). Fears and fearfulness in children and adolescents: a genetic analysis of twin data. *Journal of Child Psychology and Psychiatry*, **33**, 977–985.

Thorpe, S.J. & Salkovskis, P.M. (1995). Phobic beliefs: do cognitive factors play a role in specific phobias? *Behaviour Research and Therapy*, **33**, 805–816.

Thyer, B.A., Himle, J. & Curtis, G.C. (1985). Blood–injury–illness phobia: a review. *Journal of Clinical Psychology*, **41**, 451–459.

Tomarken, A.J., Mineka, S. & Cook, M. (1989). Fear relevant selective associations and covariation bias. *Journal of Abnormal Psychology*, **98**, 381–394.

Tooby, J. & Cosmides, L. (1989). Evolutionary psychology and the generation of culture. *Ethology and Sociobiology*, **10**, 29–49.

van den Horne, W. (1995). Central and peripheral psychophysiological characteristics of social phobics. Unpublished Master's thesis, Limburg University, Maastricht.

Voland, E. & Voland, R. (1989). Evolutionary biology and psychiatry: the case of anorexia nervosa. *Ethology and Sociobiology*, **10**, 223–240.

Webb, K. & Davey, G.C.L. (1992). Disgust sensitivity and fear of animals: effect of exposure to violent or revulsive material. *Anxiety, Stress, and Coping*, **5**, 329–335.

Welham, C.V.J. (1990). Incest: an evolutionary model. *Ethology and Sociobiology*, **11**, 97–111.

Williams, G.C. & Nesse, R.M. (1991). The dawn of Darwinian medicine. *Quarterly Review of Biology*, **66**, 1–22.

Wilson, E.O. (1975). *Sociobiology: the New Synthesis*. Cambridge MA: Harvard University Press.

Wilson, D.S. (1994). Adaptive genetic variation and human evolutionary psychology. *Ethology and Sociobiology*, **15**, 219–235.

Zafiropoulou, M. & McPherson, F.M. (1986). Preparedness and the severity and outcome of clinical phobias. *Behaviour Research and Therapy*, **24**, 221–222.

Chapter 17

Unconscious Pre-attentive Mechanisms in the Activation of Phobic Fear

Arne Öhman
Department of Clinical Neuroscience, Karolinska Institute,
Stockholm, Sweden

THE IRRATIONALITY OF PHOBIAS

To the onlooker, phobias appears strikingly irrational. Even phobics themselves may acknowledge their fear as irrational and uncontrollable. For example, traces of spider web in the doorway may make a nice summer house completely inaccessible to a spider phobic, who rather goes for a walk than joins the party that is going on inside. Indeed, the criteria for a specific phobia according to DSM-IV include that "the person recognizes that the fear is excessive or unreasonable" (American Psychiatric Association, 1994, p. 410).

In a sense, therefore, phobias are dissociated from the rational insight that we take for granted as a governing factor in the control of human behaviour. For some observers this breakdown of rationality is what qualifies phobias as instances of psychopathology. Others feel invited to interpret phobias as the outflow of unconscious mental mechanisms that salvage the conscious ego from dangerous instinctual energies. Yet others take the dissociation as a basis for suggesting that phobias result from a learning principle, Pavlovian conditioning, which (in fact erroneously, see e.g. Öhman, 1983; Rescorla, 1988) is taken to be non-conscious and irrational. Not surprisingly, to some, the commonly held principle that causal factors determining behaviour converge in conscious cognition is so important that they are pressed to challenge the premise and argue that phobics, indeed, view their fear as rationally justifiable (Menzies & Clarke, 1995; Thorpe & Salkovskis, 1995).

Phobias—A Handbook of Theory, Research and Treatment. Edited by G.C.L. Davey.
© 1997 John Wiley & Sons Ltd.

The notion of phobias as dissociated from rational thought suggests a dichotomy according to which psychological events are either consciously and unconsciously controlled. In the perspective of current cognitive psychology, however, such a dichotomy appears ill-founded. Regardless of whether one adheres to an information-processing or a connectionistic model (see Greenwald, 1992), more or less consciously accessible mechanisms interact in the control of virtually all behaviour. In general, the over-emphasis on conscious control that scientific psychology has shared with its commonsense counterpart appears to be on the decline, as a results of a series of influential challenges (e.g. Bornstein & Pittman, 1992; Greenwald, 1992, with commentaries; Zajonc, 1980). Even though often of crucial importance, consciousness comes in late in the information-processing chain, and its scope is restricted (e.g. Posner, 1978). In an emotional context, conscious factors are important in the interpretation and elaboration of events in the surrounding world in relation to responses of the individual that are set in motion by automatic, unconscious mechanisms (e.g. Öhman, 1987, 1993a, 1996). What eventually becomes accessible to conscious awareness, therefore, is determined by a series of preconscious or pre-attentive processes. In contrast to the slow, effortful, serial and voluntary information-processing of consciousness, this pre-attentive processing is fast, parallel, automatic and unconscious (e.g. Schneider, Dumais & Shiffrin, 1984). And contrary to the notion of linear processing from perception, to decision, to action of intuitive psychology, pre-attentive processing has immediate effects at the efferent level by eliciting a series of reflexes, such as orienting (e.g. Öhman, 1979) and startle (e.g. Lang, Bradley & Cuthbert, 1990) reflexes, that may affect subsequent processing. In the case of phobias, we shall see shortly that the fear component originates in automatic, unconscious mechanisms that are consciously inaccessible, but that the eventual outcome is also affected by the cognitive interpretation of the situation.

EVOLUTIONARY PERSPECTIVES ON PHOBIAS

The fact that phobic fears appear better correlated with threats in the hunter-gatherer ecology of early humans than with the distribution of dangers in modern life, has stimulated interpretations that phobias originate from an evolutionarily-derived readiness to fear situations that threatened the survival of our distant ancestors (e.g. Marks, 1969, 1987; Öhman, Dimberg & Öst, 1985; Seligman, 1971; see Chapter ••). This evolutionary perspective is easy to combine with a perspective that stresses automatic, pre-attentive mechanisms in the control of phobias.

It takes time consciously to perceive, attend, memorize, remember, think, decide and act. The natural environment in which humans evolved could select for the complex behavioural control system we call consciousness only after systems able to deal with contingencies at a much more compressed time-scale were already at hand. For example, an attacking predator strikes hard and fast, and conscious deliberation before defensive action is likely to leave the genes of the prey unrepresented in the next generation. Immediately and automatically activated flight, on the other hand, is likely to keep the reactive distance (Russell, 1979) between predator and potential prey at a level which allows the prey's successful escape. Thus, the evolution of human consciousness is predicated on a more basic level of mental functioning, the automaticity and speed of which sets it apart from the slow conscious activity. Rather than waiting for consciousness to decide where the focus of attention should be placed, evolution is likely to have equipped humans with parallel processing sensory systems that automatically and continuously scan the environment for potential danger. It took a snake to distract Adam and Eve from their awe of the Father's creation.

As soon as a potential threat is located, defence should be activated. In this perspective, "false negatives", i.e. fleeing a situation that actually turns out to be harmless, is less evolutionarily costly than "false positives", i.e. failing to initiate flight in the face of a threatening stimulus (LeDoux, 1990). The latter situation may result in death, whereas the former only leads to wasted energy (and the experience of aversive emotion). Mineka (1992) has used the term "evolutionary conservatism" to capture the cautiousness of evolution when it comes to handling potential threats.

In an evolutionary perspective, parts of the pre-attentive mechanism are likely to be hard-wired. Pervasive threats should be possible to identify and react to with only minimal training. Contrary to mainstream psychology, which seeks to establish general, domain-independent laws, evolutionary considerations promote the postulation of domain-specific psychological mechanisms (Seligman, 1970; Tooby & Cosmides, 1992). Thus, it could be argued that the pre-attentive mechanisms should be tuned to specific features of recurrent threats to the well-being of the hominids and their forerunners. From this postulate it follows that stimulus configurations reliably associated with phobias should be particularly effective in activating fear. Indeed, a strong prediction would be that phobic fear should be possible to activate when the critical stimulus features are present, even if the phobics themselves were not able consciously to identify them.

PREATTENTIVE ACTIVATION OF PHOBIC FEAR

The hypothesis that phobic fear does not require conscious perception of the phobic stimulus for its elicitation was tested by Öhman & Soares (1994). They made use of the consistent finding that snake- and spider-phobic subjects show elevated psychophysiological responses to visual representations of their feared object (e.g. Fredrikson, 1981; Hare & Blevings, 1975; for a review, see Sartory, 1983) to measure fear by means of skin conductance responses (SCRs).

Backward Masking as a Method to Assure Preattentive Processing

In normal perception, pre-attentive and conscious information-processing inter-act to determine what is eventually perceived. These levels are intimately inter-woven, and therefore special methods are needed to tease them apart. One such method is backward masking. With this procedure, the conscious recognition of a target stimulus is impeded by an immediately following masking stimulus. The extent to which the target stimulus is perceived is primarily dependent on the interval between the onsets of the target and the masking stimuli, the stimulus-onset-asynchrony (SOA) (Esteves & Öhman, 1993). When this interval is short (say, less than 50 ms), the masking stimulus tends completely to block recognition of the target stimulus. However, it can be demonstrated that the target stimulus, even thought it remains completely blocked from awareness, influences the per-son's behaviour (for a review, see Holender, 1986). For example, Marcel (1983) demonstrated that reaction times to identify the colour of patches presented to subjects were affected by preceding colour-words, even when the words were impossible to recognize because of backward masking.

Esteves & Öhman (1993) and Öhman & Soares (1993; 1994) adapted the backward masking technique for use with emotional stimuli. As masks for com-mon phobic objects, such as pictures of snakes and spiders, Öhman & Soares (1993; 1994) used pictures of similar objects that were cut in pieces and then randomly reassembled and re-photographed so that no central object could be discerned (see Figure 17.1 for examples of target and masking stimuli). Esteves & Öhman (1993) examined the effectiveness of facial pictures with a neutral emo-tional expression as masks for facial pictures portraying affects of anger of happiness.

A forced-choice procedure was used to determine masking effects as a func-tion of the SOA. The subjects were exposed to long series of stimulus pairs, in which the first stimulus served as target and the second as mask. They were required to guess the nature of the target stimulus, and then to state their confidence in the guess. Öhman & Soares (1993; 1994) studied four different, targets: snakes, spiders, flowers and mushrooms. The subject's task was to guess which of these four classes of stimuli was present as the target. There were also control trials without any target. The target stimuli were presented for 30 ms (except when the SOA was 20 ms, when the target duration was also 20 ms). The results (see Figures 17.2 and 17.3) showed that the subjects required a SOA of about 100 ms for confident correct recognition of the target stimulus, and there was no difference between the stimulus categories. When the SOA was 30 ms or less, the subjects both performed and felt that they performed randomly. These results were stable irrespective of whether the subjects were randomly selected non-fearful university students (Figure 17.2) or classified as highly fearful or non-fearful on the basis of questionnaire data (Figure 17.3).

Esteves & Öhman (1993) reported similar findings for faces expressing emo-

Figure 17.1   Black-and-white versions of colour slides used as targets and masks in the backward masking studies

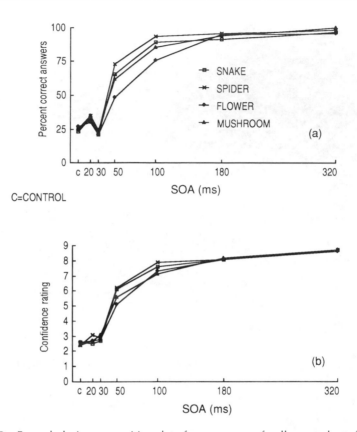

C=CONTROL

Figure 17.2   Forced-choice recognition data from a group of college students for masked pictures of snakes, spiders, flowers and mushrooms as a function of the stimulus-onset-asynchrony (SOA) between the target and the mask. "C" stands for control trials where no target was presented. (a) Mean percentage of correct responses. (b) The rated confidence in the decisions. With SOAs of 20 and 30 ms, recognition was at chance level, and the confidence in the ratings was low. There were no reliable differences between stimulus categories (from Öhman & Soares, 1993, reprinted by permission, copyright © 1993 American Psychological Association)

tions of anger and happiness. In addition they showed that the relation between SOA and recognition performance was independent of physical characteristics of the stimuli, such as intensity relations between target and masks, and whether the target was on for the whole SOA.

Phobic Responses to Masked Stimuli

Armed with the backward masking technique, Öhman & Soares (1994) set out to test the hypothesis that phobic fear can be pre-attentively activated. From a large pool of university students, they selected subjects who were either highly fearful

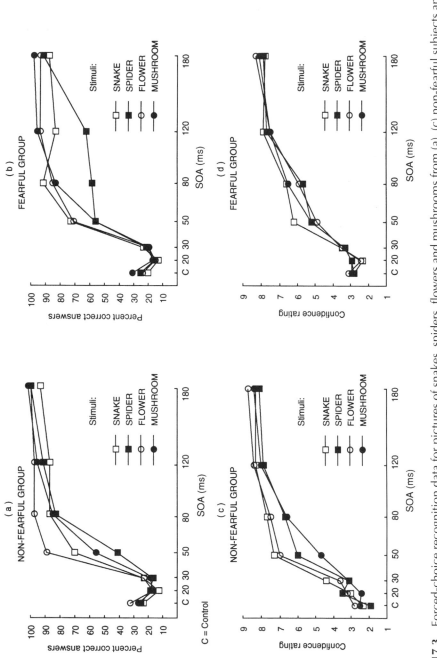

Figure 17.3 Forced-choice recognition data for pictures of snakes, spiders, flowers and mushrooms from (a), (c) non-fearful subjects and (b), (d) subjects fearing either snakes or spiders. The upper panels (a), (b) show percentage of correct answers and the lower panels (c), (d) show decision confidence as a function of the stimulus-onset-asynchrony between target and masks. Control trials without the target stimulus are indicated by "C". SOAs of 20 and 30ms gave chance level performance with low confidence. There were no reliable differences between groups and target stimulus categories (from Öhman & Soares, 1994, reprinted by permission, copyright © 1994 American Psychological Association)

(>90 percentile in the distribution) of snakes or of spiders (but not of both), as well as non-fearful controls.

These subjects were exposed to two stimulus series consisting of repeated presentations of pictures of snakes, spiders, flowers and mushrooms. In the first series, these target pictures were masked by immediately following non-recognizable pictures (cut and randomly reassembled, see Figure 17.1) at a SOA producing effective masking (30 ms). In the second series, the targets were presented without masks.

Skin conductance responses were recorded as an index of the physiological response component of fear. In addition, the subjects were exposed to an extra series of pictures in which they were asked to rate their subjective response in terms of valence (like/dislike), activation, and control.

The skin conductance results were very clear and are presented in Figure 17.4. As can be seen in the left panel of the figure, the subjects who were afraid of snakes showed elevated responding to snakes compared to spiders and neutral stimuli, the spider-fearful subjects showed specifically elevated responses to spiders, and the non-fearful subjects did not differentiate between the categories. This interpretation of the results was supported by a highly significant interaction between groups and stimulus categories, with subsequent Tukey follow-up tests. The results from the masked series (panel a), indeed, were very similar to those from the non-masked series (panel b), which suggests that most of the response was pre-attentively recruited. The apparent decrease in general response magnitude from the first to the second series most probably can be attributed to habituation from the first to the second series, as the order between the conditions was fixed.

Interestingly, the psychophysiological findings were paralleled in the ratings of the subjective response to the pictures. Thus, the snake-fearful subjects rated themselves as more disliking, more activated and less in control when exposed to the masked snake pictures than to any other pictures. Similar results were obtained for spiders pictures among the spider-fearful subjects, whereas the non-fearful controls did not differentiate between the stimulus categories. Thus, some aspect of the stimulus content became available to the cognitive system even though conscious recognition can be ruled out as a factor behind these findings. Perhaps the subjects were able to use their pre-attentively activated bodily response to guide their ratings.

Conclusion

These results show quite conclusively that conscious perception of the phobic stimulus is not necessary to activate fear in phobics. Masked presentation of the phobic stimulus appeared as effective as non-masked presentation in inducing enhanced SCRs to feared pictures. Thus, pre-attentive processing of a phobic stimulus is sufficient to recruit at least part of the phobic response. This means that fear and anxiety can be activated from stimuli in the environment that are

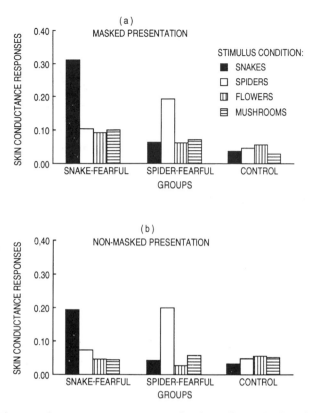

Figure 17.4 Skin conductance responses to (a) backwardly masked and (b) non-masked presentations of pictures of snakes, spiders, flowers and mushrooms in snake-fearful, spider-fearful, and non-fearful control subjects. Note the specifically enhanced responding to the feared stimulus in fearful subjects, even under backward masking conditions that effectively prevented recognition of the masked stimulus (from Öhman & Soares, 1994, reprinted by permission, copyright © 1994 American Psychological Association)

too weak or too peripheral in the perceptual field to enter the focus of conscious attention. Thus, apparently stimulus-independent anxiety floating around in the consciousness of an individual may in fact be elicited from stimuli (both external and internal) that in themselves remain inaccessible to consciousness.

These data also show conclusively that phobic fear is essentially stimulus-driven. It is very hard to see how the fear responses that were observed could reflect top-down, expectancy processes, because there was no way that the subjects could identify which mask hid his/her feared stimuli and which hid an innocuous stimulus. To the extent that expectancies are important in phobias, therefore, they must operate on a response that is automatically recruited by pre-attentive processes. Indeed, our ratings data seem to indicate that some aspects of phobic response (other than explicit recognition) became available to the cognitive system of the subjects. For example, they may have experienced stronger albeit still diffuse bodily feelings when exposed to the masked feared stimuli as compared to masked non-feared stimuli, and then used these feelings to inform their ratings.

THE ORIGIN OF PHOBIC RESPONSES: PAVLOVIAN CONDITIONING

Preattentive Elicitation of Conditioned Responses to Small Animal Stimuli

Evolutionary constraints on behaviour can be mediated more or less directly through genes. Mayr (1974) made a distinction between closed and open genetic programs in the evolutionary control of behaviour. In closed genetic programs, a genetic program can be directly transcribed into a neural program controlling behaviour with no need for specific environmental input. With an open genetic program, on the other hand, specific environmental inputs are necessary in the transcription from genetic to neural program. In this latter case, one could talk about evolutionarily constrained learning, for which language acquisition could serve as a convenient example (e.g. Pinker, 1994). Phobias are likely to result from open genetic programs. For example, behavioural genetics data suggest that specific phobias result from the interaction of a general genetic predisposition for phobias and specific individual experiences (Kendler et al., 1992). According to the preparedness theory of phobias (Öhman, Dimberg & Öst, 1985; Seligman, 1971), phobias are acquired through biologically prepared Pavlovian conditioning. Because most phobias involve potentially dangerous situations such as snakes, dogs, heights or enclosed spaces, Seligman (1971) argued that evolution has put a survival premium on genes promoting rapid fear learning and subsequent avoidance of such stimuli. This theory has received a fair amount of experimental support in human conditioning studies (McNally, 1987; Öhman, 1993b). If this theory is correct, it should be possible to produce effects similar to those observed in fearful subjects in normals conditioned to potentially phobic stimuli. Thus, one would expect that SCRs conditioned to pictures of snakes or spiders should be elicited even when the conditioned stimuli (CSs) are presented during masking conditions preventing their recognition. This hypothesis was tested by Öhman & Soares (1993) and Esteves, Dimberg & Öhman (1994).

Öhman & Soares (1993) used a differential conditioning paradigm to condition different groups of subjects to either fear-relevant (snakes or spiders) or fear-irrelevant (flowers or mushrooms) stimuli. Subjects in the fear-relevant groups were shown two pictures portraying snakes and spiders, respectively. Subjects in the fear-irrelevant groups were shown pictures of flowers and mushrooms. After some initial habituation trials, there was an acquisition phase in which one of the stimuli was followed by an electric shock unconditioned stimulus (UCS), with a 0.5 s interstimulus interval. This picture was designated the CS+. The other picture (e.g. a spider if the CS+ was a snake) was designated the

CS–. With this paradigm, the difference in SCR to the CS+ and the CS– reflects pure conditioning effects uncontaminated by sensitization, initial responding, etc. (see Öhman, 1983). In the extinction phase that terminated the experiment, the CS+ and the CS– were presented without any UCSs. Half of the subjects conditioned to fear-relevant and fear-irrelevant stimuli, respectively, were extinguished with masked stimuli and the other half without any masks. Thus, subjects in the masked groups had both the CS+ and the CS– masked by a randomly cut and reassembled picture with a 30 ms SOA, exactly as in the experiment on fearful subjects reported by Öhman & Soares (1994).

The results demonstrated reliable differential skin conductance responding to the CS+ and the CS– in both the groups extinguished without masks, suggesting robust conditioning effects to both types of stimuli. In fact, these groups did not differ from each other. This failure to obtain the standard preparedness effect (see e.g. Öhman, Dimberg & Öst, 1985) may perhaps be attributed to the short interstimulus interval used during training. For the groups extinguished with masked CSs, however, fear relevance of the CS made a dramatic difference. Whereas masking completely abolished differential responding in the groups conditioned to fear-irrelevant stimuli, differential responding to the CS+ and the Cs– remained reliable in the group conditioned to snakes or spiders. The result for this group therefore paralleled those obtained with fearful subjects in the previous experiment (cf. Figure 17.4).

Soares & Öhman (1993b) took this analysis one step further. On the basis of a development of preparedness theory by Öhman, Dimberg & Öst (1985), they argued that subjects fearful of, for example, snakes, should have an enhanced readiness to associated fear to any animal stimuli, such as, for example, spiders. This hypothesis derives from the proposition that all animal fear goes back to a common predatory-defence system, which has evolved to help animals survive predation pressure (Öhman, Dimberg & Öst, 1985). To test this hypothesis, Soares & Öhman recruited fearful and non-fearful subjects by criteria similar to those used by Öhman & Soares (1994). Then half of the subjects fearing snakes were conditioned to pictures of spiders, with pictures of rats as control stimuli, whereas half of the spider-fearful subjects were conditioned to snakes, again with rats as control stimuli. Thus the fearful subjects were conditioned to a non-feared but still fear-relevant animal stimulus. The remaining halves of the fearful groups were conditioned to fear-irrelevant stimuli (flowers and mushrooms). Half of the normal controls were conditioned to fear-relevant stimuli (snakes or spiders) and half to fear-irrelevant stimuli. Then all subjects were extinguished with masked CSs.

The results were straightforward but devastating to the specific hypothesis: the fear-relevance of the CS turned out to be the only important factor in promoting differential response to masked stimuli. Both fearful and non-fearful subjects showed remaining differential response to the CS+ and the CS– during masked extinction if the CSs were fear-relevant, but no differential response if they were fear-irrelevant, with no effect whatsoever of prior fearfulness. Thus, fearing one animal was not associated with any increased readiness to acquire fear of other animals. In other words, preparedness appeared to be specific to the type of animal.

In the final experiment of this series, Soares & Öhman (1993a) examined the interaction between fear-relevance, masking and instructed extinction (i.e. the effects of instructions explicitly informing the subject that no more shocks would be presented). Lack of voluntary control is considered a hallmark of phobias (Marks, 1969). Accordingly, information about the actual innocuousness of the phobic situation has little effect in alleviating phobic fear. In agreement with this notion, Hugdahl & Öhman (1997) reported that instructed extinction had no effect on skin conductance responses conditioned to fear-relevant stimuli (snakes or spiders), but removed differential response completely to fear-irrelevant stimuli (flowers or mushrooms). In the present experiment, half of the subjects were conditioned to fear-relevant and the other half to fear-irrelevant stimuli in a differential conditioning paradigm with a shock UCS presented 0.5 s after the CS+ during acquisition. These two main groups were subdivided into halves and extinguished with or without masks. Finally, these four groups were further subdivided according to whether they were informed about shock omission during extinction or not, leaving 8 groups with 16 subjects each. For the informed subjects, the experimenter entered the cubicle where the subject was seated before extinction started, told the subject that no more shocks would be presented, and removed the shock electrodes. For non-informed subjects, he entered the cubicle allegedly to check the skin conductance electrodes, but did not mention anything about the shocks. The results showed that instructions and masking, independently and additively, removed differential response to fear-irrelevant stimuli, but left reliable differential response to fear-relevant stimuli. Thus, even the fear-relevant group exposed to both masking and instruction showed reliable differential response during extinction.

This series of studies shows quite convincingly that SCRs which have been conditioned to fear-relevant stimuli reliably survive backward masking, whereas differential responses conditioned to fear-irrelevant stimuli are abolished by this procedure. This surviving response is automatic in the sense that it is unaffected by instruction, and the effect appears specific to particular stimulus categories, such as snakes and spiders.

Preattentive Elicitation of Conditioned Responses to Facial Stimuli

Even though animal phobias differ in several important respects from social phobias, the two syndromes share fear and avoidance of a specific stimulus situation as their core. Öhman, Dimberg & Öst (1985) postulated that evolutionarily prepared Pavlovian contingencies were important in both. In particular, they argued that the fear of being looked at that is shared by many social phobics (Marks, 1969) may result from conditioned aversion to facial stimuli. This assertion was supported by conditioned SCR data reported by

Öhman & Dimberg (1978). Similar to findings with conditioning to animal stimuli (e.g. Öhman et al., 1976) they found that subjects conditioned to fear-relevant stimuli, in this case angry faces, showed enhanced resistance to extinction compared to subjects conditioned to fear-irrelevant happy or neutral faces (see Dimberg & Öhman, 1996, for a review of subsequent findings). From these data one may ask whether SCRs conditioned to angry faces, similar to those conditioned to snakes or spiders (Öhman & Soares, 1993), would survive backward masking.

Esteves, Dimberg & Öhman (1994) reported three experiments in which subjects were conditioned to angry faces by a shock UCS in paradigms similar to those used with animal stimuli by Öhman & Soares. The subjects were exposed to a conditioning procedure in which one facial expression was reliably followed by a shock UCS during an acquisition phase, whereas another facial expression expressed by another person was not followed by shock. After conditioning had been established (documented by enhanced SCRs to the CS+), the subjects were tested by masked presentations of the CS+ and the CS–. In spite of the fact that the masking conditions prevented conscious perception of the stimuli (Esteves & Öhman, 1993), SCR data consistently showed larger responses to the CS+ than to the CS– if the CS+ was an angry face, but not if it was a happy face.

A second series of experiments was reported by Parra et al. (1997). Two of these experiments used a more complex conditioning paradigm in which several exemplars of angry and happy faces were presented to the subjects. Some of the angry faces were followed by shock during an acquisition phase. In a subsequent extinction phase, the previously shocked faces were either presented as targets and masked by neutral faces, or as masks (and thus recognizable) for neutral faces. Regardless of whether the presentation was non-conscious or conscious (i.e. the CSs+ were presented as targets or masks) the subject showed reliable differential SCRs that did not differ between conditions. However, whereas the verbal recognition of previously presented faces was good when they occurred in the mask position, it was very poor when they occurred as targets. Thus, there was a clear and instantaneous dissociation between the SCRs that showed a strong conditioning effect and no effect of masking, and the verbal recognition ratings which showed no conditioning effect and a very strong effect of masking.

In a third experiment, Parra et al. (1997) compared masked and non-masked extinction after conditioning to (non-masked) angry CSs+ and happy CSs– while the subjects rated their shock expectancy in the interval between the CS and the UCS, which was extended to 3.5 s for this purpose. Again, a dramatic dissociation between the conscious and the non-conscious measures was observed in the extinction data. Skin conductance responses showed equal and reliable differential response to the CS+ and the CS– with no effect of masking (see Figure 17.5a). The ratings, on the other hand, showed a highly significant interaction between conditioning and masking, to the effect that the differentiation between CS+ and CS– was much larger in the non-masked than in the masked condition (Figure

A. ÖHMAN

17.5b). However, closer analysis revealed a small but consistent and reliable differentiation between the CS+ and the CS– in ratings performed during the masked condition, suggesting that some information about the targets was consciously accessible.

A related finding was reported by Wong, Shevrin & Williams (1994). They used schematic faces selected to be either negatively and positively evaluated in pilot experiments. In addition to the SCR, they included measurement of slow cortical potentials as a dependent variable. After conditioning with the negative stimulus serving as the CS+ and the positive stimulus serving as the CS–, subject were exposed to masked presentations of the stimuli below rigorously defined individual thresholds for recognition. Their SCR data replicated those of Esteves, Dimberg & Öhman (1994) in demonstrating reliable differential response to masked presentations of the CS+ and the CS– during extinction. The electrocortical data showed a distinct slow negative potential that uniquely preceded the point of previous UCS presentations after the CS+ during the masked extinction trials. This waveform was identified with a previously described expectancy wave occurring before an expected emotionally or motivationally relevant stimulus (e.g. Simons, Öhman & Lang, 1979). Wong, Shevrin & Williams (1994) concluded that they had demonstrated the unconscious activation of an anticipatory process. The small but consistent expectancy rating differentiation

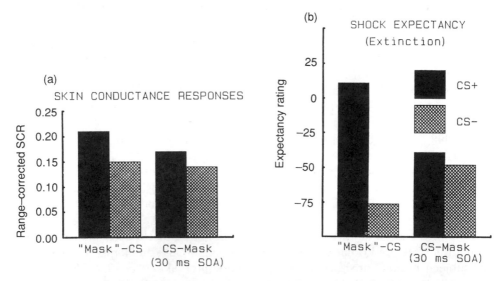

Figure 17.5 (a) Skin conductance responses and (b) ratings of shock expectancy to an angry face previously associated with an electric shock unconditioned stimulus (CS+), and a happy face not associated with the shock (CS–). Half of the subjects had the CSs followed by an effective masking stimulus (CS-mask), whereas the other half had an ineffective masking arrangement with the CS as the second stimulus ("mask"-CS). The anchor points for shock expectancy ratings were +100 ("sure of shock") and –100 ("sure of no shock") (reprinted from Öhman, 1992, with permission, copyright © 1992, Lawrence Erlbaum Associates)

between masked CSs+ and CSs− reported by Parra et al. (1996) may indicate that this anticipatory process could indeed be accessible to subjects to influence their ratings of shock probabilities.

PRE-ATTENTIVE ASSOCIATION BETWEEN AVERSIVE AND FEAR-RELEVANT STIMULI

The results on masked elicitation of phobic and conditioned fear demonstrate that previously conditioned responses to fear-relevant stimuli can be *performed* without the involvement of conscious awareness. A completely independent issue is whether such responses could also be *learned* outside of awareness. This is a possibility that typically is denied by theorists on Pavlovian conditioning directed both at human (Dawson & Schell, 1985; Öhman, 1979, 1983) and animal (Wagner, 1976) experimentation. If such learning could be demonstrated, it could be used to address what has often been regarded a crucial shortcoming of conditioning interpretation of phobias, namely that many phobics are unable to recall a conditioning episode (e.g. Murray & Foote, 1979). Thus, the to-become phobic stimulus may not have been present in the awareness of the potential phobic, yet have been pre-attentively activated, when he/she encountered a traumatic event. As a result, the stimulus could have acquired power later to elicit a fear response without the person making a conscious connection between the stimulus and the trauma.

To test the hypothesis that fear responses can be conditioned to masked stimuli, it is, in a sense, necessary to reverse the method used to study pre-attentive elicitation of fear responses. Thus, what is required here is an acquisition series with masked CSs, followed by tests fro conditioning with non-masked stimuli.

Conditioning to Masked Facial Stimuli

Such a series of studies was reported by Esteves et al. (1994). They exposed subjects to an angry face CS+ and a happy face CS−, where the former stimulus was followed by a shock UCS after a 0.5 s interstimulus interval. The CSs were followed by a neutral face masking stimulus after either an effective (30 ms) or an ineffective (330 ms) masking interval. The purpose of including a conditioning group with an ineffective masking interval was to make sure that occurrence of the masking stimulus *per se* in the CS–UCS interval would not block conditioning unless it effectively prevented recognition of the CS. For control subjects, the UCS was presented after one of the neutral masking stimuli with no preceding target stimulus. In a subsequent extinction session subjects in all groups were presented with unmasked presentations of the angry and happy faces. Both conditioning groups showed larger responses to the angry than to the happy face, whereas the control groups did not differentiate between the two facial categories. Thus, regardless of whether the masking interval resulted in effective masking or not, subjects were able to associate the CS+ with the UCS. In other words, conditioning proved possible even in the absence of conscious perception of the CSs. These results are illustrated in Figure 17.6.

In a second experiment, Esteves et al. (1994) again conditioned subjects to facial stimuli using effective or ineffective masking intervals to prevent or allow conscious perception of the CSs. However, in this experiment some subjects were conditioned with an angry CS+ and some with a happy CS+. Control groups were given effectively and ineffectively masked CSs with random, non-paired UCSs to control for sensitization effects. In the subsequent non-masked extinction series, reliably larger responses were observed to angry than to happy faces among subjects who had been exposed to an angry CS+, even with the effective masking interval. Subjects conditioned to a happy CS+, however, showed no evidence of conditioning. Rather, like the sensitization control groups, they showed equal SCRs to happy and angry faces.

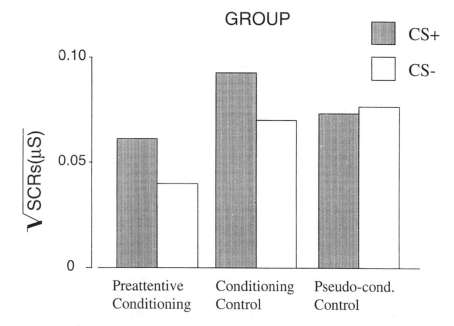

Figure 17.6 Skin conductance responses during extinction to non-masked angry (CS+) and non-masked happy (CS–) faces after a conditioning procedure with the masked angry face followed by shock and the masked happy face not followed by shock. The preattentive conditioning group had an effective masking interval that completely masked the target stimulus, the conditoning control group had a long ineffective masking interval, and the pseudo-conditioning control group had no targets and only masks during conditioning. Note that conditioning effects were present in both the conditioning groups but not in the control group (reprinted from Esteves et al., 1994b, with permission, copyright © 1994, Cambridge University Press)

These results show quite conclusively that conscious perception of a facial CS is not necessary for conditioning, provided that the CS is a threatening angry display. With a non-threatening happy display, such conditioning effects were not observed. Thus, again, it is demonstrated that angry facial displays have a special affinity with aversive outcomes, exactly as posited by the preparedness hypothesis. Indeed, conditioning to masked stimuli could be taken as a prototype of conditioning with "degraded input", a condition that was used by Seligman & Hager (1972) in defining the preparedness continuum.

Conditioning to Masked Animal Stimuli

Similar results to those reported for conditioning to masked facial stimuli were reported by Öhman & Soares (1996) using snakes and spiders as fear-relevant, and flowers and mushrooms as fear-irrelevant, stimuli. One group of subjects was conditioned to masked snakes or spiders CSs+ with masked spiders or snakes, respectively, serving as CSs−, not associated with shock. Another group of subjects was conditioned to masked flowers or mushrooms in a similar differential conditioning paradigm. In this experiment, the effect of the conditioning contingency was not only assessed during non-masked extinction but also in a series of acquisition test-trials where the masked CS was presented without the shock US. Such test-trials are necessary to assess conditioning when the CS–US interval (0.5 s in this case) is shorter than the latency of the response (approximately 1–2 s in case of SCRs) (see Öhman, 1983, for a discussion of interpretational problems raised by this procedure). The results showed clearly larger responses to the masked CS+ than to adjacent masked non-shocked CSs− during the test trials, provided that the stimuli were fear-relevant. Furthermore, as in the study by Esteves et al. (1994), subjects conditioned to masked fear-relevant stimuli showed reliable differential response to conditioning and control stimuli when they were presented non-masked during extinction. Such differential responding was not observed in subjects conditioned to fear-irrelevant stimuli.

Further experimental work by Öhman & Soares (1996) documented that subjects were unable to distinguish verbally between snakes and spiders as assessed in a concurrent forced-choice recognition test. Thus, the differential conditioning effects could not be attributed to conscious recognition of the stimuli, e.g. as a result of conditioning training. However, some aspect of the CS–US contingency obviously became available to the conscious cognitive system, because a group of subjects required to rate their shock expectancy in the CS–US interval (extended to 4 s) demonstrated a reliably larger (albeit still small) shock expectancy to the CS+ than to the CS−, even though they were both effectively masked. Thus, in spite of the fact that they could not consciously identify the stimuli (i.e. tell which was a snake and which was a spider), they obviously had some vague feeling of when a shock was more or less likely. This suggests that the subjects were able to use fragments of information either from the stimulus or from their own (conditioned ?) response to the stimulus to govern their shock expectancies. The possibility that feedback from autonomic responses may be critical for the observed effect is, of course, of considerable theoretical interest and clearly deserves further investigation. For example, it is consistent with Damasio's (1994) hypothesis that feedback from the autonomic component of the emotional response governs subsequent cognitive activity.

However, in the present context the most important result from the masked conditioning studies is the quite conclusive demonstration that conditioned association can be developed to stimuli that are only pre-attentively processed, but only provided that they are fear-relevant.

PRE-ATTENTIVE CAPTURE OF ATTENTION BY FEAR-RELEVANT STIMULI

From the data reviewed so far, it appears that phobic fear can be activated by unconscious, pre-attentive mechanisms that automatically pick out aversively conditioned fear-relevant stimuli in the surrounding world. These mechanisms not only activate already conditioned fear responses, but also appear sufficient for unconsciously establishing associative couplings between previously non-feared evolutionarily fear-relevant threats and aversive UCSs. However, the more exact nature of these mechanisms remains obscure. An attractive possibility is that they are related to attentional processes, and more specifically to the capture of attention.

Such an assumption would connect the set of data reviewed in this chapter with the by now large literature on attentional bias in anxiety disorder (e.g. MacLeod, 1991; Mathews, 1990; Wells & Matthews, 1994). Watts et al. (1986) provided such a conceptual bridge by demonstrating retarded colour-naming latencies of spider-related words in a Stroop task. One interpretation of this finding is that performing the primary task, colour naming, was disrupted by the attention automatically recruited by spider-related words. Thus, the pre-attentive mechanisms that activate fear responses may exert their effect through the automatic capture of attention by fear-associated stimuli. Indeed, the fact that our masking studies used an index, the SCR, that is closely related to orienting and thus to attention (e.g. Öhman, 1979, 1987) is completely consistent with such a hypothesis.

The attention that is invested in stimuli through this mechanism may be sufficient to result in some learning (Öhman, 1992). If this hunch is correct, it should be possible to demonstrate that attention is invested preferentially in fear-relevant stimuli at a pre-attentive level. The data that have been reviewed so far have relied on experimental paradigms where there is only one stimulus input. Thus, there is no competition for attention from different inputs and processing is limited to the pre-attentive level by means of backward masking. However, if attention is the critical process, threatening stimuli should be automatically detected independently of the current direction of attention. Thus, with multiple stimulus inputs, attention should be drawn selectively to inputs related to biologically relevant threat. This possibility has been confirmed in an independent experimental context provided by visual search studies.

In an often quoted study, Hansen & Hansen (1988) developed an experimental paradigm in which subjects were required to detect faces with a deviant emotional expression in an array of faces. They reported that normal subjects were quicker to identify a threatening angry face against a background of happy faces, than a happy face against a background of angry faces, and that this effect appeared to have a pre-attentive origin. Even though these conclusions were later retracted by the authors (Hampton et al., 1989; Hansen & Hansen, 1994), it inspired Byrne & Eysenck (1995) to use a similar paradigm to examine whether subjects high in trait anxiety would be particularly prone to pick out threatening information from visual displays. In agreement with their hypothesis, they reported that high-anxious subjects were significantly faster than low-anxious subjects in finding an angry face against a background of neutral faces, whereas the two groups did not differ with regard to happy faces in a "neutral crowd". The preoccupation with threat in high-anxious subjects was further documented by their slowness in discovering a deviant neutral face in an angry crowd.

We have used a similar visual search paradigm with snakes and spiders as fear-relevant stimuli in my laboratory in studies on normal, non-fearful subjects (Öhman, Flykt & Esteves, 1996). Subjects were exposed to matrices of pictures of either snakes, spiders, flowers or mushrooms, where in half of the cases all stimuli in the matrix were of the same category, whereas the other half had a stimulus from a deviant category. The subjects were quicker to find a deviant snake or spider among flowers and mushrooms than *vice versa*. This increase in speed of detection was not accompanied by more errors. The time to identify a deviant stimulus was generally longer for a large (3×3) than for a small (2×2) matrix but this effect, as indicated by a reliable interaction between fear relevance and size of matrix, was more obvious when the subject's task was to locate a fear-irrelevant than a fear-relevant target. In fact, separate tests showed a reliable size-of-matrix effect only for fear-irrelevant targets. This failure of matrix size reliably to affect the detection of deviant fear-relevant stimuli among fear-irrelevant background stimuli suggests that attention was automatically drawn to deviant snakes and spiders, whereas a more sequential search strategy was used to locate deviant flowers and mushrooms. Thus, these results indicate that fear-relevant stimuli were picked up independent of their position in the perceptual field in a process reminiscent of a "pop-out" effect of pre-attentive origin.

There are at least two important differences between our experiments and their results and those of Hansen & Hansen (1988). First, in their critical experiment, they used the same angry face against a background of several identical happy faces. This experimental strategy risks confounding effects that one hopes to attribute to facial expression with accidental features of the stimulus, such as, for example, a particular shadow in the face (see Hansen & Hansen, 1994). Because we used categories of stimuli with several exemplars in each, this type of confounding is less likely in our study, Second, Hansen & Hansen (1988) reported that subjects were quicker to decide that no deviant stimulus was present in a matrix of happy than in a matrix of angry faces. This result was used by Hampton et al. (1989) to argue that the faster discovery of deviant angry faces actually could be due to generally faster identifications of happy faces. To identify a deviant angry face, the subjects had to pass through and discard a number of background happy faces. To identify a deviant happy face, on the other hand, they had to identify and discard a series of angry background faces. Because they were quicker to identify happy than angry faces, the time to identify deviant angry background faces could be confounded by the generally quicker identification of the background happy faces. On the basis of such data as well as on data indicating that the position of the deviant stimulus in the matrix was important, Hampton et al. (1989) questioned the pop-out interpretation advanced by Hansen & Hansen (1988). In our data, however, the subjects were overall faster to identify fear-relevant (snakes, spiders) than fear-irrelevant (flowers, mushrooms) background stimuli. Thus, they were quicker to decide that a deviant mushroom or flower was *not* present among snake and spider background stimuli than to decide that deviant snakes or spiders were *not* present among background flowers or mushrooms. In spite of the shorter time to identify background fear-relevant stimuli, therefore, they nevertheless were quicker to identify a deviant fear-relevant stimuli among background fear-irrelevant stimuli than *vice versa*. This finding, then, supports our interpretation that the subjects' attention was automatically drawn to deviant snakes and spiders.

The visual search studies show that biological fear-relevant stimuli such as angry faces, snakes and spiders can be automatically picked up from a complex visual display. It is noteworthy that this effect is not predicated on prior fear. Even though Byrne & Eysenck (1995) showed that the "face in the crowd effect" for angry faces was enhanced by high trait anxiety, other studies have reported faster discovery of deviant fear-relevant stimuli in normal, non-fearful subject. This finding indicates that early mechanisms of perceptual processing may be tuned to respond to threatening features in perceptual displays (Öhman, 1992). However, this tuning may, of course, be enhanced for stimuli that, in the history of the individual, have been turned into strong fear signals, such as in phobias.

CONCLUDING COMMENTS

The data reviewed in this chapter show quite conclusively that autonomic responses related to fear activation can be elicited from phobic stimuli (real or laboratory conditioned) that are not consciously recognized. Thus, conscious appraisal of a fear stimulus appears not to be necessary for the activation of fear responses. This is an instance where content counts. As pointed out by Tooby & Cosmides (1992), psychologists have typically tried to organize their science in terms of content-independent laws. From an evolutionary perspective, however, domain-specific rather than generally applicable psychological processes should be expected. The handling of threat is one such evolutionarily likely domain (Tooby & Cosmides, 1992). In agreement with this notion, in the data presented so far pre-attentive effects were restricted to threatening stimuli (snakes, spiders, angry faces) for which an evolutionary basis for the threat appears likely (see e.g., Öhman, Dimberg & Öst, 1985). However, recently collected data indicate that similar results may be obtained with severe ontogenetic threat, such as close-up pictures of a pointed gun.

A second series of studies (Esteves et al., 1994; Öhman & Soares, 1996) showed that conditioning of autonomic responses to fear-relevant stimuli can occur even in situations where the subjects remain unaware of the CSs that become associated with the aversive UCSs. These data imply that a phobic may have been conditioned to fear a specific situation, yet may have failed consciously to register the coupling between situation and trauma because the critical stimulus feature was not in the focus of attention at the time of learning.

The evidence of enhanced autonomic responses to stimuli that subjects have failed to recognize indicates a dramatic dissociation between cognitions and autonomic indices of fear. The fact that the evidence of recognition failures and enhanced autonomic responding was obtained in different experiments, often with different subjects, provides one limitation of the claimed dissociation. How can we be sure that the subjects did not consciously perceive the stimuli on some of the trials? Such partial awareness is an unlikely basis of the results for several reasons. First, Wong, Shevrin & Williams (1994) used a much more elaborated procedure than that used in my laboratory to determine individual thresholds for every subject that took part in their experiment. Nevertheless, their SCR data were similar to ours (Esteves, Dimberg & Öhman, 1994), and their slow cortical potential data gave clear evidence of differential response to non-recognized stimuli. Similarly, when different aspects of recognition and expectancy were assessed simultaneously with SCRs, dramatic dissociations emerged to the extent that verbal measures were very sensitive to masking, whereas SCRs were not (Parra et al., 1997; Öhman & Soares, 1996). Finally, automatic processing appears to be the dominant mode of processing stimuli of much longer duration than those used in our experiments (e.g. Neely, 1977). Furthermore, extending the masking interval well beyond the range where complete masking is produced does not make any clear difference for the results (Esteves, Dimberg & Öhman, 1994; Esteves et al., 1994). Thus, more than occasional glimpses of masked targets appears to be necessary for the stimulus to be genuinely processed in the conscious mode.

Nevertheless, there was evidence of some "leakage" between the unconscious and conscious levels. Even though the fearful subjects studied by Öhman & Soares (1994) remained unaware of the content of the masked stimuli, they nevertheless rated themselves as more disliking, more aroused, and less in control when the masks hid their fearful stimulus than some other stimulus. Parra et al. (1997) reported a small but consistent differential effect in expectancy ratings to masked stimuli. After conditioning to non-masked stimuli, the subjects rated shock as less likely after the CS− than after the CS+ during masked extinction (see Figure 17.5). Similarly, even though they appeared completely unable to recognize whether masked pictures depicted snakes or spiders, subjects were able (albeit weakly) to pick up the contingency between the CS+ and the UCS in expectancy ratings in the masked conditioning experiment reported by Öhman & Soares (1996). Thus, some aspect of the masked stimuli appeared to become available to the cognitive systems of the subjects. One appealing possibility is that this leakage occurred through feedback from physiological responses that had been conditioned to the stimuli. Thus, the subjects may have felt vague hunches from their bodies that shock was more or less likely and then used these hunches to guide their ratings. This leakage does not detract from the clear dissociation between cognition and autonomic responses that we have reported with regard to stimulus recognition. However, it provides a caveat that the border between unconscious and conscious psychological mechanisms may not be absolute, but at least partly permeable. For example, the cognitions that are regarded as critical in panic disorder interact closely with more or less consciously perceived feedback from bodily processes (e.g. Rapee, 1993). It is important to keep in mind that pre-attentive processes under normal conditions interact with psychological processes such as biased expectancies (Davey, 1995) that are located in focal attention. Indeed, it could be argued that such interactions provide one of the keys to anxiety and the anxiety disorders (Öhman, 1993a).

The dissociation between cognition and autonomic fear arousal seen in the masking studies shows that the activation of fear is a stimulus-driven process. Stimuli that are not registered in awareness can not in any reasonable way be seen as the targets of top-down, conceptually-driven processes. Cognitive theories claiming that conceptually-driven processes such as biased expectancies of harm are the central element of phobia (e.g. Beck & Emory, 1985; Davey, 1995) are difficult to reconcile with these findings unless they retreat to obscure notions of unconscious expectancy. As shown by Tomarken, Mineka & Cook (1989) and Davey (1992), biased expectancies for negative outcomes are important determinants of fear responding to fear-relevant stimuli. However, even though they may be sufficient to elicit fear responses, the masking studies show that they are not necessary. Thus, expectancy biases may be more important for the maintenance than for the acquisition of fear. The data reviewed in this chapter show that there are pre-attentive mechanisms that are activated by specific stimuli to set fear in motion. Once a fear response is moving, however, the surrounding circumstances, including the automatically triggered bodily response, can be accessed by conscious cognition, and at this stage, expectancy mechanisms become important for the further development of the response. An interactional scheme for this type of panic disorder was proposed by Rapee (1993).

Phobics do indeed believe that the feared object may be harmful to them, physically or socially (e.g. "making a fool of oneself") (Thorpe & Salkovskis, 1995), and they rate the phobic situation as more risky and reasonable to fear, particularly during exposure (Menzies & Clarke, 1995). Questionnaire and rating data, however, do not allow strong conclusions as to whether these cognitions are driven by, or drive, fear responses. These measures are so open to "the pressure to make sense" that characterizes our culture that they are uniquely unsuitable to test any hypothesis of an irrational or unconscious origin of a psychological phenomenon. Masking and visual search, on the other hand, provide strong methodologies that can be used to further investigate the interplay between stimulus- and expectancy-driven processes in phobias.

ACKNOWLEDGEMENTS

Preparation of this chapter was facilitated by a series of grants from the Swedish Council for Research in the Humanities and Social Sciences. The author is indebted to Ulf Dimberg, Francisco Esteves, Anders Flykt, Cristina Parra and Joaquim Soares for assistance in the research that forms the basis for the chapter.

REFERENCES

American Psychiatric Association (1994). *Diagnostic and Statistical Manual of Mental Disorders*, 4th edn. Washington, DC: American Psychiatric Association.

Beck, A.T. & Emory, G. (1985). *Anxiety Disorders and Phobias: a Cognitive Perspective*. New York: Basic Books.

Bornstein, R.F. & Pittman, T.S. (eds) (1992). *Perception Without Awareness*. New York: Guilford.

Byrne, A. & Eysenck, M.W. (1995). Trait anxiety, anxious mood, and threat detection. *Cognition and Emotion*, **6**, 549–562.

Damasio, A.R. (1994). *Descartes' Error. Emotion, Reason, and the Human Brain*. New York: G.P. Putnam's Sons.

Davey, G.C.L. (1992). An expectancy model of laboratory preparedness effects. *Journal of Experimental Psychology: General*, **121**, 24–40.

Davey, G.C.L. (1995). Preparedness and phobias: specific evolved assocaitions or a generalized expectancy bias. *Behavioral and Brain Sciences*, **18**, 289–325.

Dawson, M.E. & Schell, A.M. (1985). Information processing and human autonomic classical conditioning. *Advances in Psychophysiology*, **1**, 89–165.

Dimberg, U. & Öhman, A. (1996). Behold the wrath: psychophysiological responses to facial stimuli. *Motivation and Emotion*, **20**, 149–182.

Esteves, F. & Öhman, A. (1993). Masking the face: recognition of emotional facial expressions as a function of the parameters of backward masking. *Scandinavian Journal of Psychology*, **34**, 1–18.

Esteves, F., Dimberg, U. & Öhman, A. (1994) Automatically elicited fear: conditioned skin conductance responses to masked facial expressions. *Cognition and Emotion*, **8**, 393–413.

Esteves, F., Parra, C., Dimberg, U. & Öhman, A. (1994). Non-conscious associative learning: Pavlovian conditioning of skin conductance responses to masked fear-relevant facial stimuli. *Psychophysiology*, **31**, 375–385.

Fredrikson, M. (1981). Orienting and defensive responses to phobic and conditioned stimuli in phobics and normals. *Psychophysiology*, **18**, 456–465.

Greenwald, A.G. (1992). Unconscious cognition reclaimed. *American Psychologist*, **47**, 766–779.

Hampton, C., Purcell, D.G., Bersine, L., Hansen, C.H. & Hansen, R.D. (1989). Probing "pop-out": another look at the face-in-the-crowd effect. *Bulletin of the Psychonomic Society*, **27**, 563–566.

Hansen, C.H. & Hansen, R.D. (1988). Finding the face in the crowd: an anger superiority effect. *Journal of Personality and Social Psychology*, **54**, 917–924.

Hansen, C.H. & Hansen, R.D. (1994). Automatic emotion: attention and facial efference. In P.M. Niedertahl & S. Kitayama (eds), *The Heart's Eye: Emotional Influences in Perception and Attention* (pp. 217–243). San Diego, CA: Academic Press.

Hare, R.D. & Blevings, G. (1975). Defensive responses to phobic stimuli. *Biological Psychology*, **3**, 1–13.

Holender, D. (1986). Semantic activation without conscious identification in dichotic listening, parafoveal vision, and visual masking: a survey and appraisal. *Behavioral & Brain Sciences*, **9**, 1–66.

Hugdahl, K. & Öhman, A. (1977). Effects of instruction on acquisition and extinction of electrodermal responses to fear-relevant stimuli. *Journal of Experimental Psychology: Human Learning and Memory*, **3**, 608–618.

Kendler, K.S., Neale, M. C., Kessler, R.C., Heath, A.C. & Eaves, L.J. (1992). The genetic epidemiology of phobias in women: the interrelationship of agoraphobia, social phobia, situational phobia and simple phobia. *Archives of General Psychiatry*, **49**, 273–281.

Lang, P.J., Bradley, M.M. & Cuthbert, B.N. (1990). Emotion, attention, and the startle reflex. *Psychological Review*, **97**, 377–395.

LeDoux, J.E. (1990). Information flow from sensation to emotion: plasticity in the neural computation of stimulus value. In M. Gabriel & John Moore (eds), *Learning and Computational Neuroscience. Foundations of adaptive networks*. Cambridge, MA: MIT Press.

MacLeod, C. (1991). Clinical anxiety and the selective encoding of threatening information. *International Review of Psychiatry*, **3**, 279–292.

Marcel, A. (1983). Conscious and unconscious perception: an approach to the relations between phenomenal experience and perceptual processes. *Cognitive Psychology*, **15**, 238–300.

Marks, I.M. (1969). *Fears and Phobias*. London: Heinemann Medical Books.

Marks, I.M. (1987). *Fears, Phobias, and Rituals: Panic, Anxiety and their Disorders*. New York: Oxford University Press.

Mathews, A. (1990). Why worry? The cognitive function of anxiety. *Behaviour Research and Therapy*, **28**, 455–468.

Mayr, E. (1974). Behavior programs and evolutionary strategies. *American Scientist*, **62**, 650–659.

McNally, R.J. (1987). Preparedness and phobias: a review. *Psychological Bulletin*, **101**, 283–303.

Menzies, R.E.G. & Clarke, C. (1995). Danger expectancies and insight in acrophobia. *Behaviour Research and Therapy*, **33**, 215–221.

Mineka, S. (1992). Evolutionary memories, emotional processing, and the emotional disorders. In D. Medin (ed.), *The Psychology of Learning and Motivation*, Vol. 28. New York: Academic Press.

Murray E.J. & Foote, F. (1979). The origin of fear of snakes. *Behaviour Research and Therapy*, **17**, 489–493.

Neely, J.H. (1977). Semantic priming and retrieval from lexical memory: the role of inhibitionless spreading activation and limited capacity attention. *Journal of Experimental Psychology: General*, **106**, 226–254.

Öhman, A. (1979). The orienting response, attention, and learning: an information processing perspective. In H.D. Kimmel, E.H. van Olst & J.F. Orlebeke (eds), *The Orienting Reflex in Humans* (pp. 443–472). Hillsdale, NJ: Erlbaum.

Öhman, A. (1983). The orienting response during Pavlovian conditioning. In D.A.T. Siddle (ed.), *Orienting and Habituation: Perspectives in Human Research* (pp. 315–369). Chichester: Wiley.

Öhman, A. (1987). The psychophysiology of emotion: an evolutionary–cognitive perspective. *Advances in Psychophysiology*, **2**, 79–127.

Öhman, A. (1992). Orienting and attention: preferred pre-attentive processing of potentially phobic stimuli. In B.A. Campbell, H. Haynes & R. Richardson (eds), *Attention and Information Processing in Infants and Adults. Perspectives from Human and Animal Research.* Hillsdale, NJ: Erlbaum.

Öhman, A. (1993a). Fear and anxiety as emotional phenomena: clinical phenomenology, evolutionary perspectives, and information processing mechanisms. In M. Lewis & J.M. Haviland (eds), *Handbook of Emotions* (pp. 511–536). New York: Guilford.

Öhman, A. (1993b). Stimulus prepotency and fear: data and theory. In N. Birbaumer & A. Öhman (eds), *The Organization of Emotion: Cognitive, Clinical and Psychophysiological Perspectives.* Toronto: Hogrefe.

Öhman, A. (1996). Preferential pre-attentive processing of threat in anxiety: preparedness and attentional biases. In R.M. Rapee (ed.), *Current Controversies in the Anxiety Disorders* (pp. 253–290). New York: Guilford.

Öhman, A. & Dimberg, U. (1978). Facial expressions as conditioned stimuli for electrodermal responses: a case of "preparedness"? *Journal of Personality and Social Psychology,* **36**, 1251–1258.

Öhman, A., Dimberg, U. & Öst, L.-G. (1985). Animal and social phobias: biological constraints on learned fear responses. In S. Reiss & R.R. Bootzin (eds), *Theoretical Issues in Behavior Therapy* (pp. 123–178). New York: Academic Press.

Öhman, A., Flykt, A. & Esteves, F. (1996). "The snake in the grass effect": visual search for fear-relevant stimuli in a complex display. Manuscript submitted for publication.

Öhman, A., Fredrikson, M., Hugdahl, K. & Rimmö. P.-A. (1976). The premise of equipotentiality in human classical conditioning: conditioned electrodermal responses to potentially phobic stimuli. *Journal of Experimental Psychology: General,* **105**, 313–337.

Öhman, A. & Soares, J.J.F. (1993). On the automaticity of phobic fear: conditioned skin conductance responses to masked phobic stimuli. *Journal of Abnormal Psychology,* **102**, 121–132.

Öhman, A. & Soares, J.J.F. (1994). "Unconscious anxiety": phobic responses to masked stimuli. *Journal of Abnormal Psychology,* **103**, 231–240.

Öhman, A. & Soares, J.J.F. (1996). Emotional conditioning to masked stimuli: unconsciously originated expectancies for aversive outcomes following non-recognized fear-relevant stimuli. Manuscript submitted for publication.

Parra, C., Esteves, F., Flykt, A. & Öhman, A. (1997). Pavlovian conditioning to social stimuli: backward masking and the dissociation of implicit and explicit cognitive processes. *European Psychologist,* in press.

Pinker, S. (1994). *The Language Instinct.* Boston: W. Morrow & Co.

Posner, M.I. (1978). *Chronometric Explorations of Mind.* Hillsdale, NJ: Erlbaum.

Rapee, R.M. (1993). Psychological factors in panic disorder. *Advances in Behaviour Research and Therapy,* **15**, 85–102.

Rescorla, R.A. (1988). Pavlovian conditioning: it's not what you think it is. *American Psychologist,* **43**, 151–160.

Russell, P.A. (1979). Fear-evoking stimuli. In W. Sluckin (ed.), *Fear in Animals and Man.* New York: Van Nostrand Reinhold.

Sartory, G. (1983). The orienting response and psychopathology: anxiety and phobias. In D. Siddle (ed.), *Orienting and Habituation: Perspectives in Human Research* (pp. 449–474). Chichester: Wiley.

Schneider, W., Dumais, S.T. & Shiffrin, R.M. (1984). Automatic and control processing and attention. In R. Parasuraman & D.R. Davies (eds), *Varieties of Attention* (pp. 1–28). Orlando, FL: Academic Press.

Seligman, M.E.P. (1970). On the generality of the laws of learning. *Psychological Review,* **77**, 406–418.

Seligman, M.E.P. (1971). Phobias and preparedness. *Behavior Therapy,* **2**, 307–320.

Seligman, M.E.P. & Hager, J.E. (eds) (1972). *Biological Boundaries of Learning.* New York: Appleton-Century-Crofts.

Simons, R.F., Öhman, A. & Lang, P.J. (1979). Anticipation and response set: Cortical, cardiac and electrodermal correlates. *Psychophysiology*, **16**, 222–233.

Soares, J.J.F. & Öhman, A. (1993a). Backward masking and skin conductance responses after conditioning to non-feared but fear-relevant stimuli in fearful subjects. *Psychophysiology*, **30**, 460–466.

Soares, J.J.F. & Öhman, A. (1993b). Pre-attentive processing, preparedness, and phobias: effects of instruction on conditioned electrodermal responses to masked and non-masked fear-relevant stimuli. *Behaviour Research and Therapy*, **31**, 87–95.

Thorpe, S.J. & Salkovskis, P.M. (1995). Phobic beliefs: do cognitive factors play a role in specific phobias. *Behaviour Research and Therapy*, **33**, 805–816.

Tomarken, A.J., Mineka, S. & Cook, M. (1989). Fear-relevant selective associations and co-variation bias. *Journal of Abnormal Psychology*, **98**, 381–394.

Tooby, J. & Cosmides, L. (1992). The psychological foundation of culture. In J.H. Barkow, L. Cosmides & J. Toody (eds), *The Adapted Mind: Evolutionary Psychology and the Generation of Culture* (pp. 20–136). New York: Oxford University Press.

Wagner, A.R. (1976). Priming in STM: an information-processing mechanism for self-generated or retrieval-generated depression in performance. In T.J. Tighe & R.N. Leaton (eds), *Habituation: Perspectives from Child Development, Animal Behavior, and Neurophysiology* (pp. 95–128). Hillsdale, NJ: Erlbaum.

Watts, F.N., McKenna, F.P., Sharrock, R. & Trezise, L. (1986). Colour naming of phobia-related words. *British Journal of Psychology*, **77**, 97–108.

Wells, A. & Matthews, G. (1994). *Attention and Emotion. A Clinical Perspective.* Hove, UK: Erlbaum.

Wong, P.S., Shevrin, H. & Williams, W.J. (1994). Conscious and non-conscious processes: an ERP index of an anticipatory response in a conditioning paradigm using visually masked stimuli. *Psychophysiology*, **31**, 87–101.

Zajonc, R.B. (1980). Feeling and thinking: preferences need no inferences. *American Psychologist*, **35**, 151–175.

Chapter 18

The Match–Mismatch Model of Phobia Acquisition

Arnoud Arntz
Department of Psychology, Maastricht University,
Maastricht, The Netherlands

Cognitive models of anxiety disorders have acquired a prominent position in the last years. Most of these models have ascribed a central role to danger perceptions (Beck & Emery, 1985; Clark, 1986; Clark & Beck, 1988). People with anxiety disorders would have incorrect ideas about the dangerous nature of the stimuli they fear: they incorrectly assume that catastrophic things might happen when they are confronted with the feared stimulus, they overestimate the dangerousness of the stimulus. Beck and co-workers have also suggested that anxiety patients tend to underestimate their capabilities to deal successfully with the situations they fear.

In 1985, Rachman drew attention to the idea that, in addition to biased danger expectations, expectations about the level of fear (and the probability to panic) may play a prominent role in phobias. He formulated a set of hypotheses, stressing the anticipatory-fear-increasing effects of an unexpectedly anxious experience. The model also states that people in general, and phobic people in particular, tend to overestimate how fearful they will be when entering a feared situation. In other words, overestimation of fear would, in addition to overestimation of danger and underestimation of successful coping, be a central factor in phobic fear. This theory has become known as *the match–mismatch model of fear*, with one of its central hypotheses now often referred to as if it were an established phenomenon, *the overprediction of fear* (Rachman & Levitt, 1985; Rachman & Lopatka, 1986a,b; Rachman & Bichard, 1988).

One might argue that if a subject overpredicts the dangerousness of a situation, he/she will expect to be more fearful during confrontation than should actually be the case. If the feared catastrophe does not happen, experienced anxiety will probably be less than when the catastrophe actually occurred. Thus, experienced

Phobias—A Handbook of Theory, Research and Treatment. Edited by G.C.L. Davey.
© 1997 John Wiley & Sons Ltd.

anxiety will probably be lower than expected. In this case, the role of fear expectations in phobias can be entirely explained by other cognitive biases, especially danger and safety expectation biases. It will be argued that this is probably not the case. Expectations of fear seem to play their own unique role in the generation and maintenance of phobic fear. Phobic people do not only seem to fear the stimuli they are afraid of because of the danger they expect, but also because of the fear or panic they expect. The emotional experience during confrontation, and especially its deviation from expectation, is probably an important basis on which people base inferences about how dangerous the situation is.

One of the most important and intriguing aspects of the processing of fearful experiences that deviate from the expected fear level is the asymmetry between the effects of underpredicted and overpredicted fear. An underpredicted fearful experience (experience is more fearful than expected) is far more influential than an overpredicted experience. Several explanations for this phenomenon have been put forward, and several have received some attention in empirical work. The evidence will be discussed, and it will be concluded that the asymmetry probably results from differential processing built-in in the organism, with good survival reasons.

Before discussing these issues, the match–mismatch model will be outlined and the empirical evidence will be discussed. Following discussion of explanations for the asymmetrical processing of under- and overpredicted fear, and the related phenomenon of overprediction of fear by phobic people, the relationships between the match–mismatch model and other cognitive models of phobias will be discussed. Lastly, clinical implications will be treated.

THE MATCH–MISMATCH MODEL

The model is concerned with effects and causes of inaccurate expectations of subjective fear (or anxiety). It is important to realize that expectations and experiences are measured by subjective reports, generally by asking subjects to rate predicted and experienced anxiety on Visual Analogue Scales (VAS). The model is therefore applicable to expectations that people càn report upon, and not necessarily to expectations as theoretical constructs, as in modern learning theories (Gray, 1975, 1976, 1982, 1985; Rescorla & Wagner, 1972; Wagner, 1976, 1978, 1979, 1981).

Compared to the fear experienced, predicted fear might have been too low (*underprediction*), too high (*overprediction*), or accurate (*match*). The match–mismatch model of fear states that the three types of prediction-experience contrasts have different effects. The model can be summarized in the following set of statements:

1.   An underprediction tends to be followed by an increase in predicted fear and increases in related anticipatory variables, such as anticipatory

anxiety, uncertainty, physiological responses, hesitations and avoidance behaviour.

2. A match tends to be followed by unchanged fear predictions and unchanged other anticipatory parameters.

3. An overprediction tends to be followed by a decrease in predicted fear and decreases in related anticipatory parameters.

4. The effects of an underprediction are stronger and longer-lasting than the effects of an overprediction (asymmetry).

5. Reports of fear tend to decrease with repeated exposures, regardless of the accuracy of the earlier predictions (mismatches do not influence habituation/extinction processes).

6. Predictions of fear tend to become more accurate with practice.

7. Fearful people tend to overpredict how much fear they will experience. (Rachman & Lopatka, 1986a,b; Rachman & Bichard, 1988).

Thus, the model states that, in general, inaccurate fear expectations are followed by adjustments of expectation. This rather trivial statement is complemented by a set of hypotheses important for understanding pathological fear. First, the model states that other variables, like avoidance behaviour and anticipatory fear, are influenced by mismatches. Underpredictions are hypothesized to be followed by increases in these fear parameters, overpredictions by decreases. Second, the model states that underpredictions and overpredictions are asymmetrically processed: an underprediction is assumed to have intrinsically alarming effects, causing immediate and long-lasting increases in fear expectations, anticipatory fear and avoidance tendencies. An overprediction, on the other hand, is hypothesized to have only moderate effects on reduction of fear expectation, anticipatory fear and avoidance. If there is a tendency to overpredict fear, people generally need several disconfirmatory experiences before becoming accurate in their expectations; whereas one instance of underpredicted fear is enough to lead to a sharp raise in expectations. Third, the model assumes that processes involved in habituation/extinction of fear responses *during* confrontation are not influenced by inaccurate fear expectations. In other words, a second process is assumed to control fear habituation/extinction, dissociated from the process controlling anticipatory responses. Fourth, it is assumed that people generally learn to predict their fear response more accurately with practice. Lastly, it is assumed that fearful people tend to overpredict the fear they will experience during confrontation.

Various studies have tested this model. Most of them have studied spontaneously occurring mismatches in subclinically phobic subjects. A smaller number have studied clinical subjects. There is a disturbing lack of studies that have experimentally manipulated inaccurate predictions of fear. This limits the possibility of drawing firm conclusions as to the causal status of mismatches in the origin and maintenance of phobic fear. Fortunately, there are a number of studies on pain that have experimentally manipulated mismatches. They largely support the model, and most of their findings are probably applicable to fear.

EMPIRICAL STATUS

The empirical status of the match-mismatch model will now be reviewed. Other reviews are provided by Rachman (1994), and by Marks & de Silva (1994).

Effects of Mismatches on Subsequent Predictions

Following Rachman & Lopatka (1986a), most studies have defined mismatches by a 2 mm discrepancy between fear prediction and fear report on a 100 mm VAS. Underpredictions are defined by differences between prediction and report ≤2 mm; overpredications by differences ≥2 mm, and matches by differences smaller than 2 mm. Increases, decreases and no change in fear predictions are generally defined by the same criterion. Other studies have used parametric methods (regression analysis) to test the relationship between *the amount* of overprediction or underprediction, and *the amount* of change in fear prediction (e.g. Arntz, Hildebrand & van den Hout, 1994; Schmidt, Jacquin & Telch, 1994).

Most studies report strong associations between mismatches and changes in fear prediction, in various samples: subclinical animal phobics (Rachman & Lopatka, 1986a); subclinical claustrophobics (Rachman, Levitt & Lopatka, 1988; Telch et al., 1994); people with fear of dental treatment (Arntz, van Eck & Heijmans, 1990); and various groups of anxiety patients, mainly panic patients (Arntz, Hildebrand & van den Hout, 1994; van Hout & Emmelkamp, 1994; Schmidt, Jacquin & Telch, 1994). Studies that tested whether the size of prediction inaccuracy was related to the size of change in prediction report strong evidence for this hypothesis. With pain predictions and experiences, the same relationships were demonstrated with experimental and clinical pain (Arntz & van den Hout, 1988; Arntz, van Eck & Heijmans, 1990; Arntz et al., 1990b; Rachman & Lopatka, 1988; McCracken et al., 1993).

Effects of Mismatches: True Psychological Influences or Artifacts?

Despite the apparently self-evident character of the relationship between inaccuracy of prediction and changes in subsequent predictions, concerns have been raised about whether the findings truly reflect psychological processes. It has been demonstrated that if random processes are assumed to underlie fear predictions and reports, and no relationship between fear experience and subsequent fear prediction is assumed, associations between mismatches and changes in prediction are found that are strikingly similar to the empirically found effects (Arntz et al., 1990b). How is this possible?

The "random model" assumes that fear predictions and fear reports are independent, that random processes determine their value, and that both are generated from the same distribution. For the sake of simplicity, it is further assumed that 1 in 3 of the predictions can be classified as high (H), 1 in 3 as medium (M), and 1 in 3 as low (L), which therefore also holds for the fear reports (generated from the same distribution). It then follows that three random combinations of fear prediction and fear report can be classified as overpredictions—(H,M), (H,L) and (M,L)—three as matches—(H,H), (M,M) and (L,L)—and three as underpredictions—(M,H) (L,M) and (L,H). The frequencies of all combinations are identical (1 in 9), as are the frequencies of the (mis)matches (1 in 3). Since we assumed that fear predictions are randomly generated, 1 in 3 of the predictions will be "H", 1 in 3 "M" and 1 in 3 "L" after each type of (mis)match . This implies that after an overprediction there are 9 prediction–experience–prediction sequences, equally probable. Five of them reflect decreases in prediction level— (H,M,M), (H,M,L), (H,L,M), (H,L,L) and (M,L,L); three no change in prediction—(H,M,H), (H,L,H) and (M,L,M); and one an increase in prediction— (M,L,H). Thus, after an overprediction 5 in 9 of the predictions decrease, 3 in 9 remain stable, and 1 in 9 increase. By the same logic, following an under-

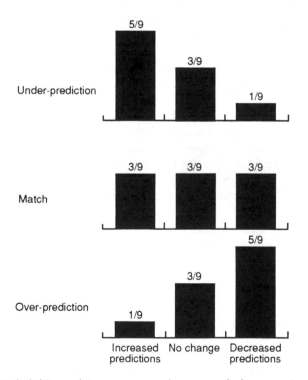

Figure 18.1 Probabilities of increase, no change, and decrease in prediction after underprediction, match and overprediction in random data (H0 model). The distribution closely resembles the empirically found distributions (from Arntz et al., 1990c, copyright © 1990 by kind permission from Elsevier Science Ltd, The Boulevard, Langford Lane, Kidlington OX5 1GB, UK)

prediction, 5 in 9 of the predictions increase, 3 in 9 do not change, and 1 in 9 decrease; and after a match, 3 in 9 of the predictions increase, 3 in 9 do not change, and 3 in 9 decrease. Figure 18.1 illustrates the relationships generated by the random model between mismatches and changes in fear prediction. The distribution resembles empirical findings to a remarkable degree.

Another way to understand the strong effects of the "random model" is to view the relationships as resulting from regression to the mean: to the degree that measurement is random error, extreme observations will probably be less extreme on the next occasion. Applied to the random model, where each observation is 100% error, extreme fear predictions have a higher chance to regress to the mean than to remain stable. Since the definition of an overprediction implies that extremely high fear predictions are over-represented, and extremely low predictions are underrepresented, there is a good chance that the next prediction will be lower. Analogously, regression to the mean predicts a higher probability of an increase in prediction after an underprediction than a stable or a decreased prediction.

If a random model can generate effects that strongly resemble the empirical data, it should be used as the H0 model to test the mismatch model. Early tests of the model have employed invalid H0 model. Consequently, Arntz et al. (1990b) used the random model to test mismatches and their effects observed in agoraphobic patients during a series of exposure exercises. To obtain a data set with random relations between mismatch and changes in prediction, all possible combinations of two predictions and one fear report of the set of predictions and reports of each individual were made (complete randomization). This data set served as an (approximate) H0 distribution. The empirically observed data were compared to the random data set, and found to reflect slightly stronger relationships between mismatch and change in prediction than the random model, ($p <$ 0.05; Figure 18.2). Thus, despite the fact that random processes may account for a large proportion of the change in predictions after a mismatch, there is clear evidence that the mismatch model's hypothesis that psychological processes cause these effects is true.

More refined statistical techniques to control for the random effects are possible with multiple regression analysis. Arntz et al. (1990b) have suggested controlling for these effects by forcing the discrepancy between prediction and the individual subject's prediction level in a regression analysis. The amount of change in prediction level is then expressed as follows:

$$Pi + 1 - Pi = B0 + B1(Pi - M) + B2(Pi - Ei),$$

where Pi = fear prediction at trial i; M = mean prediction level of the subject; Ei = experienced fear at trial i; $B0,1,2$ = regression coefficients. The term $B1(Pi - M)$ represents the regression to the mean effect: the change in prediction is assumed to be a function of the discrepancy of the old prediction with the mean prediction level. The other discrepancy term, $B2(Pi - Ei)$, represents the mismatch effect. Tested in a sample of 37 anxiety patients, Arntz, Hildebrand & van den Hout (1994) found that although there was a significant regression to the

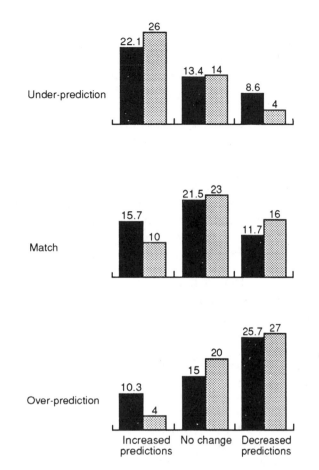

Figure 18.2 Distributions of changes in prediction of fear after (mis)-matches (1) as found after individually randomizing the predictions of agoraphobic patients (solid bars) and (2) as empirically found in the sample (dotted bars). The numbers of underpredictions, overpredictions and matches in the randomized data were held equal to the empirical numbers. Although the randomization produced a distribution much alike the empirical distribution, the empirical findings differ significantly from the random distribution, supporting the match/mismatch model [$\chi^2(4) = 12.60$, $p = 0.013$] (from Arntz et al., 1990c, copyright © 1990 by kind permission from Elsevier Science Ltd, The Boulevard, Langford Lane, Kidlington OX5 1GB, UK)

mean effect, the effect of the second discrepancy term, $B2(Pi - Ei)$, was much larger. Thus, again there was strong evidence for the model's hypothesis that changes in prediction are related to the discrepancy between predicted and experienced fear, and not a result of a simple random process. This conclusion is further strengthened by pain studies where mismatches were experimentally manipulated: experimentally induced mismatches were followed by changes in predictions hypothesized by the model (e.g. Arntz et al., 1991). Regretfully, there have been no report of experimentally manipulated mismatches of fear predictions so far.

Taken together, there is strong evidence that mismatches are followed by corrected predictions. Although random processes may partially explain these observations, there is ample evidence that the influence of mismatches on subsequent predictions is based on true psychological processes.

Problems with the Criteria of a Mismatch

The reasons for the 2 mm criterion for defining mismatches have always remained unclear. It may be that in some experiments this criterion produces more or less equal numbers of underpredictions, matches and overpredictions, but in other studies investigators have used other criteria for this reason (e.g. Arntz et al., 1990b). A more justifiable criterion would be based on measurement theory. For instance, a prediction-experience difference exceeding two measurement errors could be defined as a mismatch. In that case, there is reasonable certainty that the observed difference represents a true mismatch. However, since people probably differ in the reliability of their ratings on a VAS, individual criteria based on individual measurement errors might be preferable. The development of a useful methodology would be welcome.

Effects of Mismatches on Anticipatory Anxiety and Avoidance

The evidence strongly suggests that the amount of fear subjects expect has a greater effect upon anticipatory anxiety and avoidance than the fear they actually experience (Cox & Swinson, 1994; Marks & de Silva, 1994). Several studies have found strong relationships between fear and panic expectancies, and avoidance (Craske, Rapee & Barlow, 1988; Telch et al., 1989; Valentiner et al., 1993; Kirsh et al., 1983; Warren, Zgourides & Jones, 1989: but see Williams, Kinney & Falbo, 1989; Adler et al., 1989). Arntz et al. (1994) demonstrated that anticipatory anxiety of a behavioural test was strongly related to both predicted fear and strength of dysfunctional belief. Following behavioural tests, changes in anticipatory anxiety were strongly related to changes in anxiety prediction. Taken together, there is clear evidence that fear prediction is one of the best predictors of anticipatory anxiety and avoidance in phobias (Rachman, 1990).

Whereas these findings are highly suggestive as to the influence of mismatches on anticipatory anxiety and avoidance, they mainly address the role of fear expectancies, and not of mismatches as such. Pain studies experimentally manipulating mismatches have directly demonstrated that anticipatory anxiety, anticipatory physiological responding, avoidance and escape are increased by underpredictions of pain; whereas overpredictions have only modest anxiety-reducing effects (Arntz & van den Hout, 1988; Arntz & Lousberg, 1990; Arntz et al., 1990a, 1991; Arntz, van Eck & de Jong, 1991, 1992). There is, therefore, indirect evidence from laboratory models that underpredictions as such increase anticipatory anxiety and avoidance.

Asymmetry between Under- and Over-predictions

From the moment the model was introduced, it has been suggested that there are important asymmetries between the effects of under- and over-predictions. Rachman & Lopatka (1986a) have suggested that "after mismatches of fear, people are quick to inflate their predictions of future fear but slow to reduce their predictions of fear" (p. 391). This has been an explanation for the tendency of anxious people to overpredict fear. In panic patients, Schmidt, Jacquin & Telch (1994) have indeed demonstrated that following an underprediction, the association between prediction inaccuracy and change in prediction level is stronger than following an overprediction. However, in a sample of subclinical claustrophobics, Telch et al. (1994) found only a marginal difference between the two types of mismatch. Moreover, in a sample of agoraphobics, van Hout & Emmelkamp (1994) observed a predominance of no change in prediction after an underprediction. In addition to the small number of observations, their use of slightly different instruments and procedures may have been related to the anomalous finding.

Most importantly, the key difference between the two types of mismatch probably is not their different influence on immediate changes in prediction, but their long-term effects on predictions (and related variables) and their immediate effects during confrontation. The non-experimental design of most studies precludes the possibility of properly investigating these issues. Moreover, in studies using prolonged exposure to feared stimuli as confrontation, subjects probably learn (and are instructed) that fear will reduce with practice, so that a superordinate prediction pattern (Rachman & Eyrl, 1989) can obscure the effects of underprediction on later predictions. Nevertheless, some evidence for asymmetrical processing has been found. Rachman & Lopatka (1986b) observed important differences between under- and overpredictions on *immediate* fear responses. Underpredictions were strongly associated with hesitations and withdrawals, whereas overpredictions (and matches) were not.

As already stated, the use of correlational data severely reduces the possibility of investigating the differential effects of under- and overpredictions. Studies which have manipulated predicted pain level have demonstrated that following an underprediction, prediction levels are raised and only slowly reduced despite disconfirmatory experiences (Arntz et al., 1991). Following an overprediction, there is usually a reduction in prediction level, but subjects quickly correct the new level if it turns out to be over-optimistic. Thus, after an overprediction there is no evidence for a resistance to disconfirmation. Pain studies have also yielded clear evidence for the causal role of underprediction in increasing subjective fear and uncertainty, anticipatory physiological fear responses (SCR, HRR) and increased physiological responding to the pain stimulus. Overpredictions do not have such dramatic effects. Since studies experimentally manipulating under- and overpredictions of fear are still lacking, there is only indirect evidence for the asymmetrical effects of under- and overpredictions of fear.

To summarize, most studies on mismatches of fear predictions have not investigated asymmetrical processing of under- and overpredictions. Moreover, the correlational design of these studies precludes a sound investigation of the hypothesis. Nevertheless, there is some evidence from fear studies that underpredictions have more influence in the short and long term than overpredictions. Experimental pain research has yielded strong support for the hypothesis that underpredictions are more influential than overpredictions. However, it is still unclear whether these results can be generalized to (clinical) fear.

Effects of Mismatches on Habituation/Extinction

Another somewhat controversial issue is whether or not mismatches influence habituation and extinction processes. In the paper preluding the formal formulation of the mismatch model, Rachman & Levitt (1985) report how unexpected panic is related to a slower increase in reported safety at the next trial, compared to an expected panic. Similarly, unexpected non-occurrence of panic was related to a steeper increase in safety at the next trial, rather than expected non-occurrence of panic. A similar effect was not found on fear reports. Thus, this study suggested that mismatches do not influence reduction of fear, but may influence the growth of experienced safety. Regretfully, later studies concentrated on fear, and did not study effects of mismatches on safety.

In accordance with the model, most studies report that whereas mismatches influence later fear predictions, they do not influence fear reports on later trials (Rachman & Lopatka, 1986a,b; Telch et al., 1994). In other words, mismatches do not seem to influence the reduction of experienced fear during confrontation.

There are several problems with the evidence so far. As stated before, the lack of experimental control over mismatches in the fear studies makes it hazardous to conclude that mismatches do not influence habituation/extinction. Moreover, there are good theoretical reasons to expect that mismatches might somehow influence habituation/extinction processes. Most modern habituation theories assume that the organism develops a model of the stimulus, and inhibits the responses to the stimulus relative to the degree by which the internal model matches with the stimulus (Arntz et al., 1991). A mismatch between consciously reported prediction and experience, although not necessarily directly reflecting the automatic processes hypothesized by these models, might be related to it, or influence them. In addition, there might be an important difference between short- and long-term effects of mismatches on fear responses. Mismatches might influence short-term habituation/extinction processes but not long-term ones. Most fear studies have employed relatively long-lasting confrontations with the phobic stimulus (minutes to hours)

Laboratory pain research of the mismatch model has combined experimental control over mismatches with short-duration painful experiences, and measured both subjective and physiological responses. This research has demonstrated that underpredictions cause dishabituation of physiological pain responses, but not of subjective pain responses. Subjective fear is generally also increased. Overpredictions have some fear-reducing effects (Arntz et al., 1991). Combined with the finding by Rachman & Lopatka (1986b) that underpredictions are related to more hesitations and withdrawals, compared to matches and overpredications, these findings suggest that underpredictions have fear-dishabituating effects, at least at the short-term, possibly more evident from sympathetic and behavioural responses than from subjective reports.

To summarize, it is still unclear whether or not mismatches influence fear habituation/extinction. Several studies report zero correlations between mismatch and subsequent changes in fear reports, but the correlational nature of the studies and the double role fear reports of the mismatch trial play (namely, in defining a mismatch and as baseline for defining change in fear report in the next trial) makes it impossible to draw conclusions. Research on laboratory pain and one study on short-term processes suggest that underpredictions might especially influence habituation/extinction of fear experiences during confrontation. Studies experimentally manipulating mismatches of fear predictions are needed to clarify this issue.

Increased Accuracy with Practice

Studies in which subjects were repeatedly confronted with the same stimulus generally report that subjects became more accurate in their fear predictions (Rachman & Lopatka, 1986a,b; Rachman & Bichard, 1988). Others have studied fear predictions of confrontations with different stimuli, and these studies generally find no increase or only modest increase in accuracy of fear prediction (Arntz et al., 1994; van Hout & Emmelkamp, 1994; Schmidt, Jacquin & Telch, 1994). It seems obvious that only when people can repeatedly practise with the same stimulus does prediction accuracy increase. Otherwise, predictions will be fairly inaccurate, clinical subjects generally showing an overprediction bias.

Overprediction of Fear in Phobic People

Most studies in subclinical and clinical subjects have found a robust tendency for anxious people to overpredict the amount of fear they will experience during confrontation (Rachman & Lopatka, 1986a; Rachman & Bichard, 1988; Arntz et al., 1994; van Hout & Emmelkamp, 1994; Schmidt, Jacquin & Telch, 1994; Taylor, 1994; Taylor & Rachman, 1994a). Similarly, anxious people tend to overpredict the probability of a panic attack, to underpredict experienced safety, to underpredict their approach behaviour, etc. (Rachman & Levitt, 1985; Rachman & Bichard, 1988; Telch et al., 1994).

Taylor (1994) has argued and demonstrated that the fear overprediction bias is *not* the result of regression to the mean, caused by selecting highly anxious people who first rate high levels of prediction and subsequently give lower responses (at confrontation). Arntz et al. (1994) similarly found no evidence for this explanation.

Some exceptions to the rule have been reported. The data of agoraphobic patients analysed by Arntz et al. (1990b) do not show the overprediction bias. This may be explained by the fact that patients did not make their predictions immediately before the exposure exercise. Fear prediction probably rises, as does belief in catastrophic outcomes and anticipatory anxiety, as the confrontation comes nearer (Marks & de Silva, 1994). Thus, the overprediction bias might be more prominent immediately before confrontation.

A long interval between prediction and confrontation cannot explain the anomalous findings by Telch et al. (1994). An over-representation of under-predictions in subclinical claustrophobics was observed. This study differs from most other studies on several factors. First, the claustrophobic subjects made fear predictions before they got the exact information about the task. Second, the claustrophobic stimulus was of an exceptional type (a corridor of 11.40 m in length; subjects had to go to the other end), whose difficulty subjects probably underestimated. Third, subjects were left in complete uncertainty about the duration of the task, whereas in most other experiments duration is more predict-able (i.e. by information from the experimenter) or controllable by the subject. It may be that with predictable/controllable duration, overprediction of fear domi-nates, whereas with free duration, underprediction of approach (courageous) behaviour dominates; both being manifestations of a general overcautious and pessimistic bias. It may also be that with less exceptional stimuli, general predic-tion biases dominate, whereas with exceptional stimuli, subjects rely more on current information (cf. Alloy & Tabachnik, 1984).

In search of an explanation, Telch, Valentiner & Bolte (1994) have argued that fearful people tend to underutilize safety information in making fear predictions. Most situations phobic people fear are safe, and if they do not use safety informa-tion in forming expectations, they will experience less fear than expected. In the Telch et al. (1994) experiment the room was exceptionally long (11.40 m), thus safety (the exit) was less than would generally be the case. Therefore, Telch et al. reason, subjects have experienced more fear than they expected. To test this explanation further, Telch, Valentiner & Bolte (1994) replicated their previous study but with manipulation of safety (distance subjects had to walk from the door—escape). Subjects were now exactly told where they were expected to stay in the room before making predictions: one group near the exit, the other group at the other end. As expected, safety (proximity from escape) influenced fear reports more strongly than fear predictions. Thus, it seems that phobic people tend to underutilize safety information in making predictions, whereas these safety factors do influence the experience of fear. However, in contradiction to their hypothesis, Telch et al. failed to demonstrate the fear overprediction bias in the high-safety condition. It remains, therefore, to be demonstrated whether this is the essential factor in their divergent findings.

ASYMMETRIC PROCESSING OF UNDERPREDICTIONS AND OVERPREDICTIONS

Although direct experimental evidence from fear studies is still lacking, it is generally assumed that underpredictions are far more influential than overpredictions. What are the reasons for this processing bias? Various explanations have been put forward:

1. Underpredictions are more significant events than overpredictions, which have a "non-event" impact (Rachman & Bichard, 1988).
2. Overpredictions reduce the impact of an aversive event, underpredictions increase it (Rachman & Arntz, 1991).
3. The stimulus-comparator function (part of many learning and habituation theories) processes asymmetrically, in that it is especially sensitive for detecting deviation into the more dangerous (aversive) direction, and is relatively insensitive for detecting deviation below the expected level (Rachman & Lopatka, 1986b; Arntz et al., 1991; Arntz, 1996).

On closer inspection, the first explanation does not clarify *why* overpredictions are relatively ignored (considered as "non-events"), and can be considered as a redescription of the problem. It is true that cognitive psychology has demonstrated that events are generally more deeply processed than non-occurrences of events (Alloy & Tabachnik, 1984). But research (especially pain research) of the mismatch model has demonstrated that with the same level of the inaccurately predicted experience, underpredictions have more profound effects than overpredictions. Thus, it remains to be explained why an underprediction is more an "event" than an overprediction.

The second explanation assumes that overpredictions have a functional value, in dampening the impact of an aversive event, whereas underpredictions would intensify the response. Pain research has, however, demonstrated that overpredicted pain does not hurt less than underpredicted pain (Arntz et al., 1991; Arntz, 1996; but see Crombez, Baeyens & Eelen, 1994). Although experimental research on fear mismatches is missing, the evidence so far does not point in the direction that overprediction of fear (usually associated with increased anticipatory anxiety) dampens the experience of fear during confrontation. If there is any influence, a self-fulfilling prophecy influence seems more probable (e.g. Arntz, 1996).

The third explanation therefore remains. It expands earlier theories on learning and habituation (e.g. Gray, 1975, 1976, 1982, 1985; Rescorla & Wagner, 1972; Wagner, 1976, 1978, 1979, 1981). These theories assume symmetrical processing of both kinds of deviation from expectancy. In contrast, the present explanation assumes that learning depends not only on the intensity of the experience, but also on the degree that the experience exceeds expectancy in a dangerous direction. It seems that our organism has a comparator function that gives an alarm if an experience unpredictably exceeds expectation. It is as if an unexpected deviation in a more fearful direction has an intrinsic meaning that potentially the confrontation might the next time exceed bearable limits, and may therefore become life-threatening (Arntz et al., 1991; Arntz, 1996). Underpredictions are therefore followed by relatively longstanding pessimistic expectations, increased fear, cautiousness and avoidance, all serving survival.

Empirical evidence so far indeed suggests that underprediction, but not overprediction, is related to hesitations and withdrawal, manifestations of the Behavioural Inhibition System hypothesized by Gray (1975, 1976, 1982, 1985) to function in case of a mismatch. Also, as discussed above, pain research has shown that underprediction causes increases in anticipatory anxiety, predictions, escape, avoidance, etc. Asymmetrical processing seems to help the organism better predict and avoid (or prepare to fight) potentially unpredictably dangerous stimuli. As such, underprediction of fear might be an important route to the development of a phobia. This also implies that people make (implicit) inferences about the dangerousness of a stimulus on the basis of the experienced fear level, and the degree to which it exceeded expectation. In other words, the (inner) emotional experience forms an important database for making inferences about the dangerousness of the outside world, a process also known as "emotional reasoning" (cf. Beck & Emery, 1985; Arntz, Rauner & van den Hout, 1995).

WHY DO PHOBIC PEOPLE TEND TO OVERPREDICT?

A phenomenon not entirely understood is the tendency of phobic people to overpredict fear. What are the causes of this bias? One explanation follows directly from the observed asymmetry between the processing of under-predictions and overpredictions. As explained above, one underprediction is often followed by a series of overpredictions, needing various disconfirmations before an accurate level is reached. However, although underprediction might be an important cause of overprediction bias, it is probably not the only cause (Rachman, 1994). Non-phobic people also occasionally make underpredictions, but they usually do not develop the longstanding fear-overprediction bias phobic people have.

Taylor & Rachman (1994a) have hypothesized that the fear prediction bias results from two other biases, known from cognitive theories of anxiety disorders: the overprediction of danger and the underprediction of safety. If fear expectation is based on expected danger and expected safety, and danger is overpredicted while safety is underpredicted, it follows that fear will be overpredicted. In other words, the overprediction of fear could be entirely explained by the other two prediction biases. Taylor & Rachman (1994a) tested this hypothesis by asking non-clinical snake-fearful students to rate expected fear, expected danger (through a number of indices) and expected safety before confrontation with a harmless snake, and afterwards to report experienced fear and perceived danger and safety. As hypothesized, subjects overpredicted fear and danger, and underpredicted safety. Structural equation modelling (LISREL) demonstrated that the danger and safety biases (combined in one stimulus-prediction bias variable) were strongly related to the overprediction of fear. Nevertheless, the relationship was far from perfect (standardized regression coefficient 0.49), indicating that a considerable amount of variance of the fear overprediction was unique. Comparable findings have been reported by Arntz et al. (1994). Anxiety disorder patients rated believability of dysfunctional (cata-strophic) beliefs before and after a behavioural experiment designed to test their catastrophic beliefs. Predictions and reports of fear were also obtained. Overprediction of fear was strongly related to decrease in believability of the dysfunctional belief. In sum, overprediction of fear is strongly related to overprediction of danger and underprediction of safety, but it is highly unlikely that it can be entirely explained by these biases (cf. Arntz, 1995).

As discussed above, Telch, Valentiner & Bolte (1994) have proposed a slightly different explanation for the overprediction of fear. They argue that fearful people underutilize safety information in making fear predictions. Most situa-tions phobic people fear are safe, and if they do not use this information in forming expectations, they will experience less fear than expected. Therefore, phobics generally overpredict fear. But, if a situation has low safety features (e.g. difficult escape routes), fearful people will underpredict fear, because they tend to underutilize safety information. Although this hypothesis can explain the divergent finding by Telch et al. (1994) that phobics underpredicted fear, and Telch, Valentiner & Bolte (1994) report some experimental evidence for this explanation, the evidence is still too weak to draw firm conclusions. For instance, Telch, Valentiner & Bolte failed to induce an fear-overprediction bias in their high safety condition, although their model predicted it.

Both Taylor & Rachman and Telch et al. have speculated about the possible role of attentional factors in the genesis of fear-overprediction bias. During anticipation, attentional resources might be (automatically) drawn towards dan-ger cues (attentional bias), at the expense of safety cues. Thus, fear expectations might be biased by the relative neglect of safety information. During confronta-tion, safety cues might draw attention, thus reducing fear below the expected level. Such processes might facilitate avoidance and escape. Future research should be directed to this explanation.

Still another explanation is that in anticipation of feared stimuli, threat-relevant memories might be more easily accessible than threat-irrelevant memo-ries (Taylor & Rachman, 1994b). In general, vivid (emotional) memories are better available than pallid memories (Tversky & Kahneman, 1974; Nisbett & Ross, 1980), and the emotional congruency between fear-related memories and fearful anticipation might further increase this memory bias. Taylor & Rachman (1994b) tested this hypothesis. Spider-fearful students either underwent a fear-relevant memory priming task, or a fear-irrelevant memory priming task. Con-trary to the hypothesis, fear-relevant priming did not lead to increased overprediction of fear, but to accurate fear predictions. Further analyses sug-gested that fear-relevant priming increased state anxiety, which was transferred to the confrontation phase, thus increasing fear during confrontation. Thus, fear reports were higher in the fear-relevant priming group than in the fear-irrelevant priming group, but fear predictions were not influenced. Taken together, the findings suggest that if fear-relevant memories are primed during anticipation, it is more likely that they reduce the overprediction bias (by increasing fear during confrontation), than that they cause an increase in fear overprediction. This finding also suggests that anxious people tend to underutilize fear-relevant memories: otherwise, their fear predictions would be more accurate.

To summarize, overprediction of fear by phobic people is still poorly understood. It can party result from asymmetrical processing of underpredictions and overpredications, it is probably partly related to danger/safety prediction biases, but it is unlikely that it can be entirely explained by these factors. A potential fruitful direction for further research is the investigation of attentional processes. Possibly, pessimistic biases during anticipation affect both stimulus and experience predictions. There is no *a priori* reason why stimulus prediction should be primary to experience prediction.

RELATIONSHIP OF MATCH–MISMATCH MODEL WITH OTHER COGNITIVE MODELS

Some investigations have shed further light on the relationship between the match–mismatch model and other cognitive models of phobias. According to Reiss & McNally's (1985) model, phobic fear is determined by (a) the expectation of danger, and (b) the interaction between the expectation of anxiety and anxiety sensitivity. Thus, people highly sensitive for (afraid of) the experience of anxiety react with stronger phobic responses to the expectation of anxiety than people low in anxiety sensitivity. Valentiner et al. (1993) tested the model in subclinical claustrophobics, and demonstrated that behavioural approach was related to expectations of both danger and anxiety and, to a lesser extent, to the interaction between anxiety sensitivity and anxiety expectation. Subjective fear and heart-rate response during confrontation were, however, only related to anxiety expectations. Thus, in contrast to the model, the interaction between anxiety sensitivity and anxiety expectation did not play an important role, and danger expectations only in the behavioural component. Anxiety expectations as such were clearly related to all phobic facets.

Comparable findings have been reported in anxiety patients (Arntz et al., 1994). Anticipatory fear of a behavioural experiment designed to test idiosyncratic catastrophic beliefs was strongly related to fear predictions and, to a lesser extent, to a rating of the catastrophic belief. The latter study also investigated changes due to behavioural experiments in anticipaory fear, dysfunctional beliefs and fear predictions. Relationships between these variables and their determinants were tested with structural equation modelling (LISREL). The resulting model is depicted in Figure 18.3. Changes in anticipatory fear were strongly related to changes in anxiety prediction. Change in dysfunctional belief was not directly, but only indirectly via fear prediction, related to change in fear of the

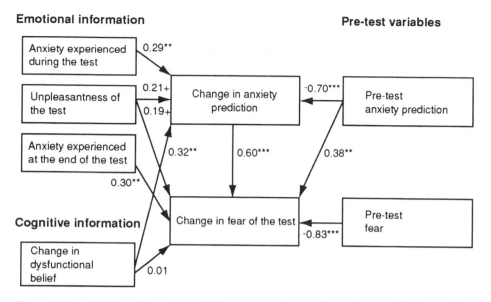

Figure 18.3 LISREL path-model of influences on changes in anxiety prediction and fear. +$p < 0.10$, **$p < 0.01$, ***$p < 0.005$ (from Arntz, Hildebrand & van den Hout, 1994, copyright © 1994 by kind permission from Elsevier Science Ltd, The Boulevard, Langford Lane, Kidlington OX5 1GB, UK)

behavioural experiment. In addition to changes in dysfunctional beliefs (cognitive information), emotional factors influenced the change in phobic fear: the levels of anxiety experienced during and at the end of the test, and the general evaluation (unpleasantness) of the test.

Taken together, these findings strongly suggest that fear expectations play an important and unique role in determining phobic responses. There are even indications that fear expectations are more proximate determinants of phobic responses than danger expectations. In terms of Davey's (1989) UCS-revaluation model (see Chapter 15), not only the UCS representation and its current evaluation, but also (or especially) the CR representation, and its evaluation, determine the phobic responses. Whereas most cognitive models have highlighted the role of danger and safety expectations, the match–mismatch model suggests that expectations about emotional reactions are at least as important in determining phobic fear.

CLINICAL IMPLICATIONS

Because fear predictions are so strongly related to phobic avoidance and anticipatory anxiety, several suggestions have been made about the use of therapeutic strategies to help phobic patients reduce overpredictions of fear to more accurate levels. Rachman has suggested that feedback about the inaccuracy might be corrective. This hypothesis has been tested in an analogue experiment with normal subjects (van den Hout et al., 1990). Half of the subjects were confonted with the inaccuracy of their predictions of experienced distress of a loud cry (on tape), while the other half received no any feedback. Whereas distress reports in the control group reduced, there was no reduction in the experimental group. Thus, confrontation with inaccuracies of predictions might lead people to report the same level as predicted, instead of to correct their prediction, and may therefore be counterproductive.

Based on the speculation that underutilization of safety information, and overutilization of danger information, plays a role in the formation of biased fear expectations, Taylor & Rachman (1994a,b) have speculated that it may be thera-peutic to let phobic patients direct attention to safety factors in anticipation of feared confrontations. This is somewhat similar to cognitive procedures, in which the patient challenges catastrophic beliefs and investigates alternative ideas about a feared situation. It would be interesting to study experimentally the influence of such therapeutic strategies on fear prediction biases.

Although reducing the tendency to overpredict fear might be helpful in reduc-ing other phobic parameters, especially avoidance and anticipatory suffering, there is an increased risk that the experience will be underpredicted. As clarified above, underpredicted fear (panic) can have strongly negative effects. Thus, paradoxically, it may be dangerous to reduce fear prediction levels during treat-ment. If the explanation of the asymmetrical effects of mismatches is correct, people fear unpredictable deviations above expectation, because this signals possible increases above bearable levels. Any therapeutic strategy, whether cog-nitive, experiential or behavioural, should therefore help the patient understand that fear and danger will remain within safe (although sometimes unpleasant) limits. Exposure exercises and behavioural tests should preferably be designed in a manner that emotional experiences remain below predicted levels. Given clini-cal findings that (peak) anxiety experienced during, as well as at the end of, a fearful confrontation is important for changes in anticipatory fear and avoidance tendencies (e.g. Figure 18.3), it might be helpful if strategies could be developed to reduce the level of fear during confrontation, without reducing the validity of the experimental test that each confrontation constitutes. The same holds for general evaluations of confrontations: the less negative, the larger the reduction of fear predictions and anticipatory fear will be. The development of therapeutic strategies to help patients view their fearful experiences in less negative ways might be very helpful.

CONCLUSION

The match–mismatch theory constitutes a useful completion of other cognitive theories. Whereas other theories mainly address the role of stimulus (UCS) representations, the match–mismatch theory has stressed the role of the repre-sentation of the emotional experience (CR). It has been suggested that the expection of the emotion of fear plays an important role in phobias. Phobic problems may originate from, or increase through, underpredicted fearful experiences. Once originated, phobias are characterized by a fear-overprediction bias. There is a disturbing lack of direct experimental evidence for the effects of mismatches of fear, although indirect experimental evidence from pain studies is encouraging. Further research is needed to strengthen the empirical base of the model, and to clarify which processes underly the various phenomena observed in studies on matches and mismatches of fear.

REFERENCES

Adler, C.M., Craske, M.G., Kirshenbaum, S. & Barlow, D.H. (1989). Fear of panic: an investigation of its role in panic occurrence, phobic avoidance, and treatment outcome. *Behaviour Research and Therapy*, **27**, 391–396.

Alloy, L.B. & Tabachnik, N. (1984). Assessment of covariation by humans and animals: the joint influence of prior expectations and current situational information. *Psychological Review*, **91**, 112–149.

Arntz, A. (1995). Stimulus estimation and the overestimation of fear: a reply to Taylor. *Behaviour Research and Therapy*, **33**, 817–818.

Arntz, A. (1996). Why do people tend to overpredict pain? On the asymmetries between underpredictions and overpredictions of pain. *Behaviour Research and Therapy*, **34**, 545–554.

Arntz, A. & van den Hout, M. (1988). Generalizability of the match/mismatch model of fear. *Behaviour Research and Therapy*, **26**, 207–223.

Arntz, A., van Eck, M. & Heijmans, M. (1990). Predictions of dental pain: the fear of any expected evil is worse than the evil itself. *Behaviour Research and Therapy*, **28**, 29–41.

Arntz, A., van Eck, M., de Jong, P. & van den Hout, M.A. (1990a). The relationship between underpredicted pain and escape. *Behaviour Research and Therapy*, **28**, 87–90.

Arntz, A., van den Hout, M.A., Lousberg, R. & Schouten, E. (1990b). Is the match/mismatch model based on a statistical artefact? *Behaviour Research and Therapy*, **28**, 249–253.

Arntz, A. & Lousberg, R. (1990). The effects of underestimated pain and their relationship to habituation. *Behaviour Research and Therapy*, **28**, 15–28.

Arntz, A., van den Hout, M.A., van den Berg, G. & Meijboom, A. (1991). The effects of incorrect pain expectations on acquired fear and pain responses. *Behaviour Research and Therapy*, **29**, 547–560.

Arntz, A., van Eck, M. & de Jong, P. (1991). Avoidance of pain of unpredictable intensity. *Behaviour Research and Therapy*, **29**, 197–201.

Arntz, A., van Eck, M., de Jong, P. (1992). Unpredictable sudden increases in intensity of pain and acquired fear. *Journal of Psychophysiology*, **6**, 54–64.

Arntz, A., Hildebrand, M. & van den Hout, M. (1994). Overprediction of anxiety and disconfirmatory processes in anxiety disorders. *Behaviour Research and Therapy*, **32**, 709–722.

Arntz, A., Rauner, M. & van den Hout, M. (1995). "If I feel anxious, there must be danger": *ex-consequentia* reasoning in inferring danger in anxiety disorders. *Behaviour Research and Therapy*, **33**, 917–925.

Beck, A.T. & Emery, G. (1985). *Anxiety Disorders and Phobias*. New York: Basic Books.

Clark, D.M. (1986). A cognitive approach to panic. *Behaviour Research and Therapy*, **24**, 461–470.

Clark, D.M. & Beck, A.T. (1988). Cognitive approaches. In C.G. Last & M. Hersen (eds), *Handbook of Anxiety Disorders*. Oxford: Pergamon.

Cox, B.J. & Swinson, R.P. (1994). Overprediction of fear in panic disorder with agoraphobia. *Behaviour Research and Therapy*, **32**, 735–739.

Craske, M.G., Rapee, R.M. & Barlow, D.H. (1988). The significance of panic expectancy for individual patterns of avoidance. *Behaviour Therapy*, **19**, 577–592.

Crombez, G., Baeyens, F. & Eelen, P. (1994). Sensory and temporal information about impending pain: the influence of predictability on pain. *Behaviour Research and Therapy*, **32**, 611–622.

Davey, G.C.L. (1989). UCS revaluation and conditioning models of acquired fears. *Behaviour Research and Therapy*, **27**, 521–528.

Gray, J.A. (1975). *Elements of a Two-process Theory of Learning*. London: Academic Press.

Gray, J.A. (1976). The behavioural inhibition system: a possible substratum for anxiety. In M.P. Feldman & A. Broadhurst (eds), *Theoretical and Experimental Bases of the Behaviour Therapies* (pp. 3–41). Chichester: Wiley.

Gray, J.A. (1982). *The Neuropsychology of Anxiety*. Oxford: Oxford University Press.

Gray, J.A. (1985). Issues in the neuropsychology of anxiety. In A. Tuma & J. Maser (eds), *Anxiety and the Anxiety Disorders*. Hillsdale, NJ: Erlbaum.

Kirsch, I., Tennen, H., Wickless, C., Saccone, A.J. & Cody, S. (1983). The role of expectancy in fear reduction. *Behaviour Therapy*, **14**, 520–533.

Marks, M. & de Silva, P. (1994). The "match/mismatch" model of fear: empirical status and clinical implications. *Behaviour Research and Therapy*, **32**, 759–770.

McCracken, L.M., Gross, R.T., Sorg, P.J. & Edmunds, T.A. (1993). Prediction of pain in patients with chronic low back pain: effects of inaccurate prediction and pain-related anxiety. *Behaviour Research and Therapy*, **31**, 647–652.

Nisbett, R.E. & Ross, L. (1980). *Human Inference: Strategies and Shortcomings of Social Judgements*. Englewood Cliffs, NJ: Prentice Hall.

Rachman, S. (1990). *Fear and Courage*, 2nd edn. New York: Freeman.

Rachman, S. (1994). The overprediction of fear: a review. *Behaviour Research and Therapy*, **32**, 683–690.

Rachman, S. & Bichard, S. (1988). The overprediction of fear. *Clinical Psychology Review*, **8**, 303–313.

Rachman, S. & Eyrl, K. (1989). Predicting and remembering recurrent pain. *Behaviour Research and Therapy*, **27**, 621–636.

Rachman, S. & Levitt, K. (1985). Panics and their consequences. *Behaviour Research and Therapy*, **23**, 585–600.

Rachman, S. & Lopatka, K. (1986a). Match and mismatch in the prediction of fear—I. *Behaviour Research and Therapy*, **24**, 387–393.

Rachman, S. & Lopatka, K. (1986b). Match and mismatch of fear in Gray's theory—II. *Behaviour Research and Therapy*, **24**, 395–401.

Rachman, S., Levitt, K. & Lopatka, C. (1988). Experimental analyses of panic—III. Claustrophobic subjects. *Behaviour Research and Therapy*, **26**, 41–52.

Rachman, S. & Lopatka, K. (1988). Accurate and inaccurate predictions of pain. *Behaviour Research and Therapy*, **26**, 291–296.

Rachman, S. & Arntz, A. (1991). The overprediction and underprediction of pain. *Clinical Psychology Review*, **11**, 339–355.

Reiss, S. & McNally, R.J. (1985). Expectancy model of fear. In S. Reiss, & R.R. Bootzin (eds), *Theoretical Issues in Behaviour Therapy* (pp. 107–122). New York: Academic Press.

Rescorla, R.A. & Wagner, A.R. (1972). A theory of Pavlovian conditioning: variations in the effectiveness of reinforcement and nonreinforcement. In A.H. Black & W.F. Prokasy (eds), *Classical Conditioning*, Vol. 2. New York: Appleton-Century-Crofts, 64–99.

Schmidt, N.B., Jacquin, K. & Telch, M.J. (1994). The overprediction of fear and panic in panic disorder. *Behaviour Research and Therapy*, **32**, 701–707.

Taylor, S. (1994). The overprediction of fear: is it a form of regression toward the mean? *Behaviour Research and Therapy*, **32**, 753–757.

Taylor, S. & Rachman, S.J. (1994a). Stimulus estimation and the overprediction of fear. *British Journal of Clinical Psychology*, **33**, 173–181.

Taylor, S. & Rachman, S.J. (1994b). Role of selective recall in the overprediction of fear. *Behaviour Research and Therapy*, **32**, 741–746.

Telch, M.J., Brouillard, M., Telch, C.F., Agras, W.S. & Taylor, C.B. (1989). Role of cognitive appraisal in panic-related avoidance. *Behaviour Research and Therapy*, **27**, 373–383.

Telch, M.J., Ilai, D., Valontiner, D. & Craske, M.G. (1994). Match–mismatch of fear, panic and performance. *Behaviour Research and Therapy*, **32**, 691–700.

Telch, M.J., Valentiner, D. & Bolte, M. (1994). Proximity to safety and its effects on fear prediction bias. *Behaviour Research and Therapy*, **32**, 747–751.

Tversky, A. & Kahneman, D. (1974). Judgement under uncertainty: heuristics and biases. *Science*, **185**, 1124–1131.

Valentiner, D.P., Telch, M.J., Ilai, D. & Hehmsoth, M.M. (1993). Claustrophobic fear behaviour: a test for expectancy model of fear. *Behaviour Research and Therapy*, **31**, 395–402.

van Hout, W.J.P.J. & Emmelkamp, P.M.G. (1994). Overprediction of fear in panic disorder patients with agoraphobia: does the (mis)match model generalize to exposure *in vivo* therapy? *Behaviour Research and Therapy*, **32**, 723–734.

van den Hout, M.A., Lavy, I., Franse, A. & Arntz, A. (1990). Over het lijden dat men vreest (On the suffering one fears). *Gedragstherapie*, **23**, 110–122.

Wagner, A.R. (1976). Priming in STM: an information-processing mechanism for self-generated or retrieval-generated depression in performance. In T.J. Tighe & R.N. Leaton (eds), *Habituation, Perspectives from Child Development, Animal Behavior, and Neurophysiology*, (pp. 95–128). Hillsdale NJ: Erlbaum.

Wagner, A.R. (1978). Expectancies and the priming of the STM. In S.H. Hulse, H. Fowler & W.K. Honig (eds), *Cognitive Processes in Animal Behavior* (pp. 177–209). Hillsdale, NJ: Erlbaum.

Wagner, A.R. (1979). Habituation and memory. In A. Dickinson & R.A. Boakes (eds), *Mechanisms of Learning and Motivation*. Hillsdale, NJ: Erlbaum.

Wagner, A.R. (1981). SOP: a model of automatic memory processing in animal behavior. In N.E. Spear & R.R. Miller (eds), *Information Processing in Animals: Memory Mechanisms* (pp. 5–47). Hillsdale, NJ: Erlbaum.

Warren, R., Zgourides, G. & Jones, A. (1989). Cognitive bias in irrational beliefs as predictors of avoidance. *Behaviour Research and Therapy*, **27**, 181–188.

Williams, S.L., Kinney, P.J. & Falbo, J. (1989). Generalization of therapeutic changes in agoraphobia: the role of perceived self-efficacy. *Journal of Consulting and Clinical Psychology*, **57**, 436–442.

Chapter 19

Information-processing Approaches to Phobias

Catherine M. Cameron
School of Cognitive & Computing Sciences,
University of Sussex, Brighton, UK

Over the last 15 years, psychological research into the emotional disorders has increasingly involved experimental studies of cognition. This trend reflects the predominance of cognitive approaches to such disorders, both in treatment and theory, with their emphasis on the need to understand cognitive processes in psychopathology. Initial research on cognition, which looked at thinking in depression, often relied on self-report data, with all its inherent problems in terms of both measurement (Clark, 1988) and interpretation (Nisbett & Wilson, 1977). Behavioural data from information-processing paradigms overcomes such problems (Macleod, 1995), offering a promising means of studying cognition in clinical disorders such as the phobias.

While behavioural treatments of phobias have been very successful, the associated theories of phobias have been less successful (Foa & Kozak, 1986). In addition, it is clear from some of the more complex phobias that behavioural avoidance, a core element in behavioural theories of phobias, is not necessary for the maintenance of phobic anxiety (e.g. Butler, 1985). Thus, the possible role of cognition in the onset and maintenance of phobias needs to be studied and outlined. This chapter will review work on cognitive processing in specific phobics. It will be argued that results from experimental studies highlight continuities with patterns of information-processing biases for material that is personally threatening in the anxiety disorders, as well as factors that may be specific to phobias and warrant further work to help outline the role of cognition in these disorders.

However, before considering the work on information processing in phobias, experimental findings relating to anxiety generally will be reviewed briefly (for a fuller review, see Mathews & Macleod, 1994; Eysenck, 1992). Research has

Phobias—A Handbook of Theory, Research and Treatment. Edited by G.C.L. Davey.
© 1997 John Wiley & Sons Ltd.

produced evidence of anxiety biases in attentional paradigms, such that individuals suffering from generalized anxiety disorder (GAD) and individuals high in trait anxiety appear to attend preferentially to threatening material (Williams et al., 1988; Watts & Dalgleish, 1991). Clear biases have not been found in tasks involving presentations of single stimuli alone, such as lexical decision and word recognition threshold (e.g. Eysenck, 1992). Effects of anxiety on attention appear to be limited to those paradigms involving two stimuli competing for attention (Mathews & Macleod, 1994). This pattern of results supports the idea that rather than increasing the speed or efficiency for processing of emotionally negative information, anxiety may prioritize such stimuli for encoding (Mathews & Macleod, 1994).

Work on judgements and expectancies has also shown clear evidence of biases in anxious groups. For example, anxious individuals overestimate the likelihood of negative outcomes, an effect that is not limited to outcomes related to their primary worries (Butler & Mathews, 1983, 1987). Thus, in a group about to undergo examinations, effects of anxiety were found on judgements concerning events unrelated to their exams. However, there are problems in interpreting such results. This partly relates to the problems of self-report data noted earlier. Another problem is that of response bias—the tendency of anxious individuals to preferentially endorse threat-related responses. For example, in one study, anxious individuals tended to report the threatening meaning of a series of homophones presented on tape (words having two meanings—one threatening, the other non-threatening, e.g. Pane vs. Pain) (Eysenck, Macleod & Mathews, 1987). It is difficult to know whether only one meaning was activated, or whether both meanings came to mind, but anxious individuals chose to report the threatening meaning—hence showing a response bias. In general, though, the work in this area has been interpreted as supporting the effects of anxiety on judgements and expectancies (e.g. Williams et al., 1988).

In contrast to findings in attention and judgements, results from studies of anxiety effects on memory for threatening material have been less consistent (Watts & Coyle, 1992). Generally the pattern of results has been seen as indicating a lack of memory biases for threat-related material in those who are anxious (e.g. Mathews & Macleod, 1994). The pattern in anxiety thus differs from findings in depression, where memory biases are found. For example, mood-congruent memory (the tendency to show a relative memory advantage for material that is in line with one's mood) is an established effect in depressives (Blaney, 1986; Williams et al., 1988), with this group recalling a greater proportion of negative autobiographical memories than non-depressed individuals, and more negative self-descriptive adjectives. Thus the pattern of findings for the emotional disorders appears to show clear attentional biases relating to anxiety but not depression, while for memory the converse pattern holds (biases relating to depression but not anxiety) (e.g. Williams et al., 1988; Dalgleish & Watts, 1990; Mathews & Macleod, 1994).

Mathews & Macleod (1994) have proposed that the distinction between automatic and controlled processing (Shiffrin & Schneider, 1977) may provide a framework for understanding this empirical pattern. Controlled and automatic processing were originally seen as different forms of processing which varied on three main factors—extent of awareness, resource dependence and degree of voluntary control involved (Wells & Matthews, 1994). Automatic processes are triggered by set patterns of external or internal input with no need for effort or attention; they appear to be resource-independent and have limited flexibility (Bargh, 1992). Controlled or strategic processing, on the other hand, involves serial sequences of operations under the control of the individual's attention (Bargh, 1992). It is modifiable, but is also constrained by capacity limitations (Bargh, 1992). While the distinction was originally put forward as a dichotomy, it is evident that there is not always a correlation between these different defining attributes (Wells & Matthews, 1994); thus, for example, a task which is "automatic" in terms of the degree to which it comes under voluntary control may vary in the degree to which it "takes up" cognitive capacity (i.e. is resource independent). In terms of the emotional disorders, then, it is proposed that anxiety predominantly leads to biases for threatening material at automatic stages of processing, leading to automatic attentional biases rather than biases in controlled processed (hence the lack of memory biases) (Mathews & Macleod, 1994). Depression, on the other hand, affects controlled processing operations leading to memory biases but has no parallel effects on attention (Mathews & Macleod, 1994).

Wells & Matthews (1994), however, have noted a number of methodological problems in the area which they feel limit interpretation of results to date:

1. The high co-morbidity of anxiety and depression.
2. The lack of differentiation in type of stimuli used (e.g. negative vs. threat).
3. Small sample sizes (especially where clinical groups have been used), leading to possibilities of type II errors.
4. Uneven use of a limited number of experimental paradigms.

Such procedural problems, they argue, make it difficult to conclude that the results to date provide unequivocal support for automatic attentional biases towards threatening stimuli in anxious subjects.

This does not preclude the possibility of such biases existing; rather, they have not been demonstrated satisfactorily given the paradigms used to date. This last problem ties in with the final point noted by Wells & Matthews. Where consistent results are found using a limited number of paradigms, there is the possibility that these findings reflect procedural aspects of the tasks used and not more general phenomena. Converging evidence is needed from a number of tasks in which the processes underlying performance on the tasks are established.

Not all of the above factors are immediately relevant to the work with phobics. However, they need to be noted, since the pattern of findings from anxiety and other clinical anxiety disorders has generally guided work on cognition in phobias, shaping the areas studied and the particular paradigms used.

RESULTS OF STUDIES INVOLVING PHOBIC SUBJECTS

The areas of empirical study can be broadly categorized as attention, judgements and memory; each of these areas will be considered in turn.

Attention

Emotional Stroop Findings

One paradigm which has been studied in a number of different disorders is the Emotional Stroop or colour-naming interference task (e.g. suicide attempters—Williams & Broadbent, 1986; eating disorders—Cooper & Fairburn, 1992). This consists of a modified version of the original Stroop. Subjects are presented with words printed in coloured inks; the content of some of the words presented relates to the relevant clinical disorder, e.g. "cobweb" in the case of a spider phobic. Subjects are required to name the colour of the ink in which the words are printed. Clinical groups are generally slower to name the colour of words related to their disorder (e.g. threat words in generalized anxiety—Mogg, Mathews & Weinman, 1989) and this interference effect is generally presumed to reflect some form of attentional bias towards threatening material.

Such interference has been found for phobics for stimuli relevant to their specific phobia, e.g. spider phobics (Watts et al., 1986; Lavy, van den Hout & Arntz, 1993); snake phobics (Mathews & Sebastian, 1993); social phobics (Hope et al., 1990). The effect does not appear to be restricted to word stimuli; pictorial stimuli also produce interference effects (Lavy & van den Hout, 1993). The stimulus used by these authors consisted of a coloured disc on which a spider stimulus was superimposed. However, the interference effects they found for visual stimuli, while still significant, were smaller than for words. They explained this pattern in terms of the number and nature of associations activated by the two types of stimuli. Noting that the spider pictures were more constrained than the words which related to aspects of spiders other than the actual insect (e.g. cobwebs), they proposed that the linguistic stimuli may trigger both more threatening and larger numbers of associations, leading to greater interference effects. The non-integration of colour and meaning within a single stimulus may also be a factor underlying the differences, since such separation can affect the size of interference effects (Macleod, 1991). While the authors' explanation seems plausible, further work is needed to clarify the basis of the difference between verbal and pictorial stimuli.

Pictorial stimuli also showed a similar pattern to that found for words following an exposure-based treatment session, with slowing effects for both types of stimuli becoming non-significant following exposure (Lavy & van den Hout, 1993a). This loss of interference following exposure appears to be a reliable effect (e.g. Watts et al., 1986; Mattia, Heimberg & Hope, 1993). While initial work with spider phobics did not rule out the possibility of practice effects underlying loss of interference (e.g. Watts et al., 1986), results from control subjects who completed the Stroop task twice, with no intervening exposure session, support changes in interference being due to the exposure sessions themselves (Lavy, van den Hout & Arnst, 1993).

Such a change following exposure treatment challenges alternative explanations of the Emotional Stroop effect relating to the procedures and stimuli used. For example, Mogg & Marden (1990) and Dalgleish (1995) highlight the possibility that stimulus familiarity and not an "emotionally-based" bias causes the interference. In their respective studies, control stimuli relating to the interest of a non-clinical control group were used (rowers—Mogg & Marden, 1990; ornithologists—Dalgleish, 1995). The former study found no effects of rowing expertise on Stroop performance for rowing-related words, while in the latter study there was a clear effect of interest in ornithology on colour-naming of bird-related words. Dalgleish (1995) argues that his control groups may represent a more valid "expertise" control. Thus, he argues, potential effects of stimulus familiarity need to be allowed for in interpreting effects with phobics. However, the change in Stroop effects following exposure treatment argues against such an expertise/stimulus familiarity interpretation of the effect, as one might expect accessibility of spider constructs to be higher following exposure.

Martin and her colleagues have put forward the pattern of Emotional Stroop effects they found in phobic children of different ages as evidence that the effect is inherently related to phobic anxiety, rather than being learnt through the association of emotional states with particular situations (Martin, Horder & Jones, 1992). In a study looking at Stroop effects in 6–7-, 9–10- and 11–12-year-old spider phobics, they found that the size of the interference effect did not appear to vary with age. In addition, the average interference found for the three age groups was similar to that found by Watts and his colleagues in their earlier study of spider phobia using adults, a pattern implying a similar magnitude of interference in child and adult phobics and providing indirect support for the proposals of Martin and her colleagues about the basis of Stroop interference found in phobics.

The pattern of Stroop results in phobics also appears to differ from that found in GAD. A recent study looking at Stroop effects in snake phobics found that the interference effect also vanished when the task was completed in the presence of the phobic object (a snake) or another threatening stimulus (in this case a spider) (Mathews & Sebastian, 1993). As the authors note, this finding does not fit with previous results for Stroop effects in anxious groups following state manipulations of anxiety, where the interference effect was found to be increased (e.g. Mogg, Mathews & Weinman, 1989). They propose that their paradoxical results do not reflect some form of distraction, which would lead to a general performance decrement. Rather, they may be due to either a narrowing of attentional focus related to threat-induced arousal, or a change in processing priorities in the context of a threatening situation. Further work clearly needs to be done to determine what exactly underlies this effect.

Stroop effects in phobic groups also differ from those in GAD subjects in that the effects appear to be specific, occurring only for phobia-related words (e.g. Watts et al., 1986; Mathews & Sebastian, 1993). In GAD, interference has been found to occur for positive as well as threatening stimuli (e.g. Martin, Williams & Clark, 1991). There is some evidence that, for generalized anxiety, positive words being antonyms of words related to current concerns, may thus produce interference (an idea that is supported by findings of Mathews & Klug, 1993). However, this effect may also relate to stimulus presentation, occurring only for blocked and not for single stimuli (Dalgleish, 1995). Both stimulus presentation forms have been used with phobic groups, with some studies using "blocked" stimulus presentation and including other emotional or threatening control words (e.g. Watts et al., 1986, blocked presentation with failure-related words; Mattia, Heimberg & Hope, 1993), blocked stimulus presentation with physical threat-related words). In these studies, the interference found in the phobic groups related to the phobia-relevant words only.

While the Emotional Stroop has been used extensively in work on information processing in clinical disorders, understanding of the cognitive processes underlying this task is limited. The standard Stroop interference (i.e. effects of words denoting a colour on naming the ink colour) has itself been the focus of an enormous amount of empirical research (>700 studies) (Macleod, 1991), but the mechanisms underlying the effect are not fully known (Macleod, 1991, 1992). Also, as Wells & Matthews (1994) note, it cannot be assumed that the same mechanisms are at work in the Emotional Stroop, and there may be a number of factors producing Emotional Stroop effects. It thus becomes important to identify and outline the role of such possible factors. Thus, at present, it is not clear how useful current evidence of Emotional Stroop effects is in specifying the nature of and explaining the role of biases in clinical disorders.

Other Attention Paradigms

Dichotic listening and the visual dot probe or attention deployment paradigm are two other tasks which have shown biases in work on anxiety and attention. Both of these paradigms involve presenting two competing stimuli, and generally involve responses to non-threatening stimuli, thus eliminating response bias accounts of slowing in anxious groups. Results from GAD groups indicate that anxious subjects, at the very least, do not avoid negative material, appearing to attend to threat stimuli in preference to neutral stimuli (Mathews & Macleod, 1986).

Dichotic listening tasks generally involve "shadowing" (or repeating) the material presented in one ear (the "attended" ear), while ignoring material that is presented at the same time to the other ear. Shadowing errors (e.g. Trandel & McNally, 1987) or reaction times on a separate target detection task (e.g. Mathews & Macleod, 1986) are used to monitor the effects of threat material presented in the non-attended ear. The task has been used to study attentional effects in agoraphobics (Burgess et al., 1981). In this version of the task, subjects had to indicate when a target word/probe appeared in either channel (i.e. attended or non-attended). Phobic groups were more likely than non-phobics to detect the probe in the unattended ear when it followed phobia-related material. However, as the instructions were liable to encourage attempts to attend to both channels, it cannot be assumed that subjects really "ignored" the material coming to the "unattended" ear (Wells & Matthews, 1994). Thus, the finding of higher target recognition in the rejected message when the message on that channel was phobia-related is interesting, but cannot be assumed to represent an automatic attentional bias towards threatening material.

The visual dot probe or attention deployment task is an interesting task which has also been used to study automatic attentional biases. In this paradigm, subjects are presented with a word pair (one in an upper and one in a lower position) with one word being threat-related and the other neutral. Subjects have to read the upper word. Following this, on a number of the trials, a dot probe appears in the location of one of the previously shown words, and subjects are required to indicate the probe's position as quickly as possible.

In a study using this task, Asmundson & Stein (1994) found that social phobics responded more quickly to dot probes which followed social threat words than those following neutral or physical threat, when the social threat words were in the upper position of the word pair. As subjects were required to read the upper of the two words, however, it is not clear that this result is due to an attentional shift. Rather, it may represent maintenance of attention to threatening stimuli which subjects are already actively reading.

This result differs from initial findings with GAD patients, which found slowing for probes which followed anxiety-relevant words in both upper and lower positions (Macleod, Mathews & Tata, 1986). Later studies, however, have found effects more similar to those found by Asmundson & Stein, with speeding of response to the dot probe being limited to threat words in the upper position, both for GAD (e.g. Mogg, Mathews & Eysenck, 1992) and for panic patients (Asmundson et al., 1992). Thus, while the initial results supported the idea that anxiety produces attentional shifts towards threatening stimuli, later studies have put this interpretation in question (Wells & Mathews, 1994). The results from social phobics presented above certainly only support the more conservative interpretation that phobic groups continue to attend to threatening stimuli, and not necessarily that they shift attention towards such stimuli (Wells & Matthews, 1994).

Given the problems of interpretation for the Emotional Stroop, the instructions and task format used for the dichotic listening, and the restriction of slowing to the upper probe position for the dot probe, it is not clear that current findings with phobics support the ideas of Mathews & Macleod about automatic attentional biases related to anxiety. Further work is thus needed to replicate and clarify factors relating to the pattern of findings presented above. To summarize, there appears to be consistent evidence of attentional effects in phobics. However, results to date have not indicated whether such effects are automatic; thus the exact nature of these effects remains to be established.

Judgements

There are a number of studies of judgements in phobias using questionnaire or rating measures (e.g. McNally & Foa, 1987) with results indicating negative biases in judgements concerning phobia-related stimuli/events. For example, there is accumulating evidence that socially anxious individuals show a bias towards interpreting others' evaluations of themselves as negative (Rapee & Lim, 1992; Stopa & Clark, 1993) and identifying others' emotional expressions as negative (Winton, Clark & Edelmann, 1995). Winton and her colleagues found that students high in fear of negative evaluation were more likely to identify an expression as negative than neutral in a forced-choice response paradigm. When analysed using a signal detection analysis, this pattern was shown to be due to response bias—social phobics were not better at identifying negative emotions in others, rather they tended to interpret more stimuli as showing negative emotion. As well as response bias problems, self-report measures are subject to a number of factors such as demand (reporting the pattern that the subject feels the experimenter expects), problems of accuracy (items endorsement may not reflect exact thought content—Glass & Arnkoff, 1982) and validity (cf. Clark, 1988, for a fuller discussion of these issues). While the results indicate that there are biases in judgement in phobias, such studies will not be considered further here.

Problems of response bias were overcome in two studies looking at anxiety effects in individuals who were afraid of interviews (Hirsch & Mathews, 1994). In the first task, subjects were primed with ambiguous phrases concerning interview situations and were then required to state whether a probe (either threatening or non-threatening) gave a grammatically correct ending to the preceding phrase. The second task was similar and involved the same sentences, but subjects had to decide whether the probe presented following the sentence was a word or a non-word string. A control task was run for each study in which similar threat probes were used out of context within the sentences—no differences related to anxiety were found in speed of response to the probe in this task. Thus, the group differences appear to be due to activation of negative constructs associated with upcoming events/outcomes in the text, and are not just a function of response bias. Obviously this study needs to be replicated with clinical groups, but provides initial evidence that previous findings with self-report measures are not artefactual.

Another area which supports the idea of biases in phobics' processing of phobia-related material is the work on illusory correlation of co-variation bias. The typical procedure used to study this effect involves the presentation of different types of stimulus slides (neutral/phobia-related, e.g. flowers, snakes), followed by a number of varying outcomes (aversive/neutral, e.g. shock/nothing). The stimulus–outcome pairings are arranged so that each of the stimulus types (e.g. flowers, snakes) is followed by an aversive outcome in an equal proportion of trials. Although the shock occurs equally following all stimulus types, phobic subjects overestimate the proportion of times that the shock occurs followed phobic stimuli (e.g. de Jong et al., 1992; Tomarken, Mineka & Cook, 1989).

Work on co-variation bias has focused mainly on differences in reports of stimulus/aversive outcome pairings relating to stimulus "preparedness" (i.e. the proposed biological predisposition which has evolved to favour the acquisition of phobic reaction to particular stimuli). McNally & Heatherton (1993) found biases prior to the presentation of stimulus/outcome pairings among subjects who fear snakes or faulty electrical outlets, with biases both for the "prepared" and non-prepared stimuli. However, such subjects appear to learn the correct contingen-cies for the non-prepared stimuli (Sutton et al., 1991), but do not change their ratings after the pairing procedure for the "prepared" stimuli. Like the Stroop interference, the biases appear to disappear post-treatment (de Jong et al., 1992).

More recently, work has begun to look at the nature of the cognitive processes underlying the effect, with studies such as that by de Jong, Merckelbach & Arntz (1995) looking at expectancies in treated and untreated spider phobics on the initial trial, on-line and after the presentation of the pairings. Their results indi-cate that, in untreated subjects, initial expectancies may not change during the pairings (de Jong, Merckelbach & Arntz, 1995), thus leading to biases in reported expectancies after the procedure, supporting the findings of McNally & Heatherton. The data from the treated group differed from earlier findings (de Jong et al., 1992), with some evidence of a co-variation bias in this group in *a posteriori* ratings. The type of the measure used (e.g. *a posteriori* ratings vs. on-line expectancies) may affect the results found, or this result may represent a re-instantiation of the expectancy bias. Thus, further work is needed to replicate de Jong et al.'s results and to establish how expectancies vary with use of on-line ratings. Potentially, though, the analysis of co-variation bias may help in under-standing how biases in the processing of phobic stimuli may maintain phobic anxiety.

Memory

The earliest work in this area looked at memory in agoraphobics (Nunn, Stevenson & Whalan, 1984). These researchers found that agoraphobics showed enhanced recall of agoraphobia-related material for both text and word stimuli when compared to a non-anxious control group. In the words study, though, the neutral words used were not semantically related. This makes it difficult to interpret the effects found for words, as clinical groups may have been able to use the relatedness of the phobic words to cluster that material (Wells & Matthews, 1994).

An attempt was made to replicate these findings by Pickles & Van den Broek (1987), using the same phobia-related stimuli but with a counterbalanced design and larger, better-specified subject groups. Their analysis of the text recall experi-ment was also more sophisticated, but failed to find any interaction of groups with passage content (phobic/neutral). No group by word type effects were found for word stimuli either. Thus, the results of Nunn and her colleagues for both words and text need to be regarded with caution and may be due to the stimulus sets used.

Other work on memory in phobias has tended to focus on two phobic groups—spider phobics and social phobics. These two lines of research are interesting both because they involve a simple and a complex phobia respectively and because, where there is evidence of biases, the results appear to differ for the different types of phobia.

Studies Involving Spider Phobics

In a number of studies, Watts and his colleagues have looked at both recall and recognition for spider-related material in spider phobics (Watts, Trezise & Sharrock, 1986; Watts & Dalgleish, 1991; Watts & Coyle, 1992, 1993). They initially studied recognition of previously presented dead spiders, when re-presented with a paired unseen spider (Watts et al., 1986). They found little evidence of differences in recognition rates between phobic and non-phobic subjects. Post hoc analyses, however, indicated that recognition varied with the spider size, with phobics showing poorer recognition of big spiders but better recognition of small spiders than non-phobics, an effect that the authors proposed related to the degree of emotion elicited by the different sizes of spiders. Following a desensitization session, recognition for the big spiders improved. However, improvement also occurred to a lesser degree in the untreated group, indicating possible practice effects.

To investigate recognition effects relating to spider size, size was specifically studied in a further study (Watts et al., 1986; study 2). A forced elaboration condition, in which phobics were asked to focus on specific aspects of the stimuli, was also included to try and see if encouraging phobic subjects to attend to such attributes improved recognition rates.

Recognition was tested both immediately and after delay. In a signal detection analysis, no significant effects were found relating to the group and thus the study failed to replicate the results from the first study. Arithmetically, however, there appeared to be variability in the results relating to the severity of the phobia. Thus post hoc correlations of reported fear of spiders with d' were studied within the different conditions (big/small spiders; elaboration/no elaboration; immediate/delayed recognition); in the forced elaboration condition, where the stimuli were big spiders, there was a negative correlation between d' and the spider phobia questionnaire score. While the authors themselves cannot explain the difference in results from the two studies, they state that the findings are generally "consistent with the view that the capacity for detailed attention is modified by levels of emotional processing" [p. 259].

The results from these studies were generally not clear-cut; also, non-phobic controls were not used in all of the studies, and many of the significant findings were from post hoc analyses. The inconsistent pattern of results may relate to the use of recognition as a dependent variable—it is likely that recall of personally threatening stimuli may show stronger memory biases, as has been shown in mood-related memory biases (Singer & Salovey, 1988).

More recent work, therefore, has looked at recall of spider-related words in spider phobics (Watts & Dalgleish, 1991). Following unclear results in an initial study, which the authors attributed to methodological problems, a second study was run comparing recall of matched phobic and neutral (baby-related) words in phobic and non-phobic groups. The study also manipulated presentation factors—stimuli were presented in the presence of a dead or a live spider. They found that spider phobics who had learnt the words in the presence of a live spider showed lower recall of spider words but not neutral words, with no such group differences being found for those phobics in the dead spider condition. A similar pattern of results was found for recognition. Overall then, the results from this study support the idea that spider phobics show poorer recall of spider-related stimuli than non-phobics under conditions of threat (i.e. under conditions of exposure to a live spider or when spider stimuli used are large).

However, two recent studies by Watts & Coyle (1992, 1993) have added to the varying picture of results in this area. Initially, they failed to replicate the results of Watts & Dalgleish, with spider phobics showing lowered recall for baby-related, but not for spider-related, words. In a later study, words relevant to phobic responses were also studied along with the spider-stimulus words. A near significant group × word type (response/stimulus) interaction was found, such that phobics showed impaired recall of response words at both immediate and delayed recall. However, no group effects were found for the spider-stimulus words.

Thus, to date studies of spider phobics' memory for spider-related words have produced varying results, with findings of lowered recall and recognition in phobics, no group-related differences in recall, or evidence of enhanced recognition for non-threatening (small) spiders.

The work of Nunn, Stevenson & Whalan (1984) though is not the only study to show enhanced recall of phobia-related elements of text. Using groups of spider-phobic students (categorized using the criteria of Watts, Trezise & Sharrock, 1986), Rusted & Dighton (1991) looked at recall of material from a story about a house, either in an undirected free recall task or specifically from the perspective of a burglar. In the free recall condition, they found that phobics recalled more spider-relevant units than burglar-related units, while this pattern did not hold for non-phobics (between-groups analyses were not reported). Text recall is generally subject to less in the way of mood effects (e.g. Hasher et al., 1985), and given the results reported above for word stimuli, the enhanced recall is interesting. As the authors themselves note, the spider units were not highly threatening (no direct reference was made to spiders) and no state anxiety manipulation was used. Thus memory effects may vary with the degree to which the stimuli are phobia-related and subjects' level of anxiety. Unfortunately, the study did not fully to control for encoding times for the different story units (material was written and reading time was not set); it is thus difficult to interpret these results definitively. While needing a controlled replication, nonetheless these results are potentially of interest, as they highlight the possibility of enhanced recall under certain limited conditions relating to threat of stimuli and anxiety state of subjects.

To summarize, the results from studies of spider phobics' recall and recognition of spider-relevant material are contradictory, with evidence of no effects, or of lowered and enhanced memory for spider-related material in spider phobics. Thus, the pattern follows that of memory biases in anxiety generally. The results, though, highlight a number of factors that may be important in recall effects (e.g. presence/absence of phobic stimuli during encoding, type of stimuli and degree of threat in stimuli used) and warrant further systematic work.

Studies Involving Social Phobics

Work looking at memory in social phobias has studied the effects of associated anxiety on general memory performance, with consistent evidence for deficits related to social anxiety (e.g. Hope et al., 1990), with studies of memory biases accounting for less of the research. Only the latter type of research will be considered here.

Memory biases in clinically defined social phobics have been examined in a series of studies by Rapee et al. (1994), who studied word recall, implicit and explicit memory, memory for positive and negative performance feedback, and autobiographical recall. In none of these studies were any effects of social phobia found. These results then do not support the existence of memory biases in phobias.

There are two points of interest in the findings reported by Rapee et al. when compared to other work in the area. First, these results may highlight differences between findings for phobias and for GAD. While autobiographical memory appears to be biased in GAD (Burke & Mathews, 1992), no such bias was found for social phobics. Also, in GAD groups, there is some evidence pointing towards an implicit memory bias—a tendency to show greater accessibility of previously encountered material in the absence of ability to necessarily recall such material; for example, if given a word stem to complete, e.g. pan——, the subject is more likely to produce the previously encountered threat-relevant word (panic), rather than other equally frequent and likely alternatives. While evidence for an implicit memory bias in GAD is inconsistent (Eysenck & Byrne, 1994), the failure of social phobics to show such a bias may highlight another difference between memory biases in GAD and in social phobia. Second, the form of encoding used by Rapee et al. may have been an important factor in his results. The studies by Rapee et al. do not fit with results from other studies of memory in socially anxious groups (e.g. Breck & Smith, 1983). Mood-congruent memory effects may be limited to material that is "personally relevant" (Blaney, 1986). Thus, reliable effects are more commonly found for autobiographical material (e.g. Teasdale & Fogarty, 1979) and for material encoded for self-reference (e.g. Derry & Kuiper, 1981). Only two of the studies by Rapee et al. involved any form of personally relevant encoding. As the authors themselves noted, the encoding manipulation in study 3, in which subjects were asked to imagine how they would feel if the feedback performance they heard related to their performance, may not have been equivalent to self-referent encoding manipulations. Thus, in their studies, the only finding involving personally relevant encoding is that relating to autobiographical memory.

In contrast to the negative findings of Rapee et al., work looking at recall of semantic material encoded for self-references in socially anxious students has reported evidence of memory biases (e.g. Breck & Smith, 1983; Claeys, 1989; Mansell & Clark, 1995). In each of these studies, differences relating to social anxiety were found in recall of self-referent adjectives, with two of the studies finding such effects only where subjects' anxiety was experimentally manipulated (e.g. being told that they would have to make a speech later). It is too early to say as yet that there is solid and consistent evidence for a memory bias—available details of the Mansell & Clark study are limited and the other two studies both have methodological limitations [Breck & Smith failed to control for depression]; while the Claeys study does not appear to have used matched stimuli; and both studies based their results on comparisons of proportional data corrected for initial adjective endorsement, an approach that does not allow for differences in absolute endorsement or recall ([Bradley & Matthews, 1988]). These accumulating positive findings are of interest, though, given findings in spider phobics and in other anxiety disorders. Clearly, then, studies such as these need replicating with clinical groups to see if differences from the findings of Rapee and his colleagues relate to the clinical status of the groups or to the type of stimuli and encoding task involved.

At present, research into memory in phobias has produced results that are as inconsistent and difficult to interpret as those from other anxiety disorders. In spider phobics, general evidence points to a possible lowering of recall of spider-related material, especially when the material itself is highly threatening and presented in the presence of a spider, or when the material relates to phobic responses to spiders. In contrast, the results from studies of socially anxious individuals appear to indicate that, where any biases are found, they show *enhanced* recall. Such effects may be limited to encoding under conditions of threat and for personally relevant material only. It is not clear whether such a pattern reflects the nature of the paradigms used—intentional vs. incidental learning; personal relevance of stimuli; the clinical status of subjects; or differences concerning the social nature of the phobic stimulus/situation. Again further work is needed to address these points and to relate this pattern of results to the picture of anxiety as a whole.

CONCLUSION

In general, results from studies of information processing in phobias show evidence of biases in attention and judgements, with a more equivocal pattern of results for memory. This pattern is, in general, consistent with findings for other anxiety disorders. As in clinical anxiety generally, it is not clear as yet what underlies such effects and further work is needed to outline the role of such biases in the onset and maintenance of phobias.

While the overall pattern is similar, there are a number of specific areas in which the pattern of findings for phobias diverges from that found, for example, in GAD. (e.g. effects of presenting threatening (phobic) stimuli during experimental tasks such as the Stroop and effects of the disorder on autobiographical recall). These areas warrant further investigation, as they may indicate differences in the way that threatening stimuli are represented in phobias when compared to other anxiety disorders.

This area potentially has a valuable contribution to make to the understanding of specific phobias. For example, the study of biases in phobics may prove useful as a means of investigating cognitive change during both treatment or exposure. While Wells & Matthews (1994) highlight the possibility that group differences in strategic processing may underlie such biases, this does not imply that patients are aware of the role of such processing in their fear. Thus, continued work on information processing may help, both in adding to our understanding of how phobic stimuli are represented and processed in phobic individuals, and in highlighting aspects of information processing that need to be changed in order to facilitate treatment of these disorders.

REFERENCES

Asmundson, G.J.G. & Stein, M.B. (1994). Selective processing of social threat in patients with generalized social phobia: evaluation using a dot probe paradigm. *Journal of Anxiety Disorders*, **8**, 107–117.

Asmundson, G.J., Sandler, L.S., Wilson, K.G. & Walker, J.R. (1992). Selective attention toward physical threat in patients with panic disorder. *Journal of Anxiety Disorders*, **6**, 295–303.

Bargh, J.A. (1992). The ecology of automaticity: toward establishing the conditions needed to produce automatic processing effects (Special issue: Views and varieties of automaticity). *American Journal of Psychology*, **105**, 181–199.

Blaney, P.H. (1986). Affect and memory: a review. *Psychological Bulletin*, **99**, 229–246.

Bradley, B.P. & Mathews, A. (1988). Memory bias in recovered clinical depressives (Special issue: Information processing and the emotional disorders). *Cognition and Emotion*, **2**, 235–245.

Breck, B.E. & Smith, S.H. (1983). Selective recall of self-descriptive traits by socially anxious and non-anxious females. *Social Behaviour and Personality*, **11**, 71–76.

Burgess, I.S., Jones, L.M., Robertson, S.A., Radcliffe, W.N. & Emerson, E. (1981). The degree of control exerted by phobic and non-phobic verbal stimuli over the recognition behaviour of phobic and non-phobic subjects. *Behaviour Research and Therapy*, **19**, 233–243.

Burke, M. & Mathews, A. (1992). Autobiographical memory and clinicial anxiety. *Cognition and Emotion*, **6**, 23–25.

Butler, G. (1985). Exposure as a treatment for social phobia: some instructuve diffculties. *Behaviour Research and Therapy*, **23**, 651–657.

Butler, G. & Mathews, A. (1987). Anticipatory anxiety and risk perception. *Cognitive Therapy and Research*, **11**, 551–565.

Butler, G. & Mathews, A. (1983). Cognitive processes in anxiety. *Advances in Behaviour Research and Therapy*, **5**, 51–62.

Claeys, W. (1989). Social anxiety, evaluative threat and incidental recall of trait words. *Anxiety Research*, **2**, 27–43.

Clark, D.A. (1988). The validity measures of cognition: a review of the literature. *Cognitive Therapy and Research*, **12**, 1–20.

Cooper, M.J. & Fairburn, C.G. (1992). Selective processing of eating, weight and shape related words in patients with eating disorders and dieters. *British Journal of Clinical Psychology*, **31**, 363–365.

Dalgleish, T. (1995). Performance on the emotional Stroop task in groups of anxious, expert, and control subjects: a comparison of computer and card presentation formats. *Cognition and Emotion*, **9**, 341–362.

Dalgleish, T. & Watts, F.N. (1990). Biases of attention and memory in disorders of anxiety and depression. *Clinical Psychology Review*, **10**, 589–604.

de Jong, P.J., Merckelbach, H. & Arntz, A. (1995). Covariation bias in phobic women: the relationship between *a priori* expectancy, on-line expectancy, autonomic responding, and *a posteriori* contingency judgment. *Journal of Abnormal Psychology*, **104**, 55–62.

de Jong, P.J., Merckelbach, H., Arntz, A. & Nijman, H. (1992). Covariation detection in treated and untreated spider phobics. *Journal of Abnormal Psychology*, **101**, 724–727.

Derry, P.A. & Kuiper, N.A. (1981). Schematic processing and self-reference in clinical depression. *Journal of Abnormal Psychology*, **90**, 286–297.

Eysenck, M.W. (1992). Anxiety: the Cognitive Perspective. Hillsdale, NJ: Erlbaum.

Eysenck, M.W. & Byrne, A. (1994). Implicit memory bias, explicit memory bias, and anxiety. *Cognition and Emotion*, **8**, 415–431.

Eysenck, M.W., Macleod, C. & Mathews, A. (1987). Cognitive functioning and anxiety. *Psychological Research*, **49**, 189–195.

Foa, E.B. & Kozak, M.J. (1986). Emotional processing: exposure to corrective information. *Psychological Bulletin*, **99**, 20–35.

Glass, C.R. & Arnkoff, D.B. (1982). Think cognitively: selected issues in cognitive assessment and therapy. In P.C. Kendall (ed.), *Advances in Cognitive–Behavioral Research and Therapy*, Vol. 1. London: Academic Press.

Hasher, L., Rose, K.C., Zacks, R.T., Sanft, H. & Doren, B. (1985). Mood, recall and selectivity effects in normal college students. *Journal of Experimental Psychology: General*, **114**, 104–118.

Hirsch, C. & Mathews, A. (1994). Does anxiety affect the inferences people make? In N.H. Frijda (ed.), *Proceedings of the VIIIth Conference of the International Society for Research on Emotions*. Storrs, CT: ISRE.

Hope, A., Rapee, R.M., Heimberg, R.G. & Dombeck, M.J. (1990). Representations of the self in social phobia: vulnerability to social threat (Special issue: Selfhood processes and emotional disorders). *Cognitive Therapy and Research*, **14**, 177–189.

Lavy, E. & van den Hout, M. (1993). Selective attention evidenced by pictorial and linguistic Stroop tasks. *Behavior Therapy*, **24**, 645–657.

Lavy, E.H., van den Hout, M. & Arntz, A. (1993). Attentional bias and spider phobia: conceptual and clinical issues. *Behaviour Research and Therapy*, **31**, 17–24.

Macleod, C. (1995). The information-processing approach to emotional pathology: adding a cognitive core to the best of behaviourism. Paper presented at the World Congress of Behavioural and Cognitive Therapies, Copenhagen, Denmark.

MacLeod, C., Mathews, A. & Tata, P. (1986). Attentional bias in emotional disorders. *Journal of Abnormal Psychology*, **95**, 15–20.

MacLeod, C.M. (1992). The Stroop task: the "gold standard" of attentional measures. *Journal of Experimental Psychology: General*, **121**, 12–14.

MacLeod, C.M. (1991). Half a century of research on the Stroop effect: an integrative review. *Psychological Bulletin*, **109**, 163–203.

Mansell, W. & Clark, D.M. (1995). Social anxiety: an investigation of memory bias, autonomic awareness and self–other differences in anxiety visibility. Poster presented at the World Congress of Behavioural and Cognitive Therapy, Copenhagen.

Martin, M., Horder, P. & Jones, G.V. (1992). Integral bias in naming of phobia-related words. *Cognition and Emotion*, **6**, 479–486.

Martin, M., Williams, R.M. & Clark, D.M. (1991). Does anxiety lead to selective process-ing of threat-related information? *Behaviour Research and Therapy*, **29**, 147–160.

Mathews, A. & Klug, F. (1993). Emotionality and interference with color naming in anxiety. *Behaviour Research and Therapy*, **31**, 57–62.

Mathews, A. & MacLeod, C. (1994). Cognitive approaches to emotion and emotional disorders. *Annual Review of Psychology*, **45**, 25–50.

Mathews, A. & MacLeod, C. (1986). Discrimination of threat cues without awareness in anxiety states. *Journal of Abnormal Psychology*, **95**, 131–138.

Mathews, A.M. & Sebastian, S. (1993). Suppression of emotional Stroop effects by fear-arousal. *Cognition and Emotion*, **7**, 517–530.

Mattia, J.I., Heimberg, R.G. & Hope, D.A. (1993). The revised Stroop color-naming task in social phobics. *Behaviour Research and Therapy*, **31**, 305–313.

McNally, R.J. & Foa, E.B. (1987). Cognition and agoraphobia: bias in the interpretation of threat. *Cognitive Therapy and Research*, **11**, 567–581.

McNally, R.J. & Heatherton, T.F. (1993). Preparedness, phobias & covariation bias: the role of pre-experimental expectations. *Behaviour Research and Therapy*, **31**, 653–658.

Mogg, K. & Marden, B. (1990). Processing of emotional information in anxious subjects. *British Journal of Clinical Psychology*, **29**, 227–229.

Mogg, K., Mathews, A. & Weinman, J. (1989). Selective processing of threat cuse in anxiety states: a replication. *Behaviour Research & Therapy*, **27**, 317–323.

Mogg, K., Mathews, A. & Eysenck, M. (1992). Attentional bias to threat in clinical anxiety states. *Cognition and Emotion*, **6**, 149–159.

Nisbett, R.E. & Wilson, T.D. (1977). Telling more than we can know: verbal reports on mental processes. *Psychological Review*, **84**, 231–259.

Nunn, J.D., Stevenson, R. & Whalan, G. (1984). Selective memory effects in agoraphobic patients. *British Journal of Clinical Psychology*, **23**, 195–201.

Pickles, A.J. & van den Broek, M.D. (1987). Failure to replicate evidence for phobic schemata in agoraphobic patients. *British Journal of Clinical Psychology*, **27**, 271–272.

Rapee, R.M. & Lim, L. (1992). Discrepancy between self and observer ratings of perform-ance in social phobics. *Journal of Abnormal Psychology*, **101**, 728–731.

Rapee, R.M., McCallum, S.L., Melville, L.F., Ravenscroft, H. & Rodney, J.M. (1994). Memory bias in social phobia. *Behaviour Research and Therapy*, **32**, 89–99.

Rusted, J.M. & Dighton, K. (1991). Selective processing of threat-related material by spider phobics in a prose recall task. *Cognition and Emotion*, **5**, 123–132.

Shiffrin, R.M. & Schneider, W. (1977). Controlled and automatic human information processing: II. Perceptual learning, automatic attending and a general theory. *Psychological Review*, **84**, 127–190.

Singer, J.L. & Salovey, P. (1988). Mood & memory: evaluating the network theory of affect. *Clinical Psychology Review*, **8**, 211–251.

Stopa, L. & Clark, D.M. (1993). Cognitive processes in social phobia. *Behaviour Research and Therapy*, **31**, 255–267.

Sutton S.K., Mineka S. & Tomarken A.J. (1991). Affective versus semantic determinant of covariation bias between fear relevant stimuli and aversive outcome. *Paper Presented at Midwest Psychological Association, Chicago, Illinois*.

Teasdale, J.D. & Fogarty, S.J. (1979). Differential effects of induced mood on retrieval of pleasant and unpleasant events form episodic memory. *Journal of Abnormal Psychology*, **88**, 248–257.

Tomarken, A.J., Mineka, S. & Cook, M. (1989). Fear-relevant selective associations and covariation bias. *Journal of Abnormal Psychology*, **98**, 381–394.

Trandel, D.V. & McNally, R.J. (1987). Perception of threat cues in posttraumatic stress disorder: semantic processing without awareness? *Behaviour Research and Therapy*, **25**, 469–476.

Watts, F.N. & Coyle, K. (1992). Recall bias for stimulus and response anxiety words in spider phobics. *Anxiety Research*, **4**, 315–323.

Watts, F.N. & Coyle, K. (1993). Phobics show poor recall of anxiety words. *British Journal of Medical Psychology*, **66**, 373–382.

Watts, F.N. & Dalgleish, T. (1991). Memory for phobia-related words in spider phobics. *Cognition and Emotion*, **5**, 313–329.

Watts, F.N., McKenna, F.P., Sharrock, R. & Trezise, L. (1986). Colour-naming of phobia-related words. *British Journal of Psychology*, **77**, 97–108.

Watts, F.N., Sharrock, R. & Trezise, L. (1986). Processing of phobic stimuli. *British Journal of Clinical Psychology*, **25**, 253–261.

Wells, A. & Matthews, G. (1994). *Attention and Emotion: a Clinical Perspective*. Hove: Erlbaum.

Williams, J.M. & Broadbent, K. (1986). Distraction by emotional stimuli: use of a Stroop task with suicide attempters. *British Journal of Clinical Psychology*, **25**, 101–110.

Williams, J.M.G., Watts, F.N., Macleod, G. & Mathews, A. (1988). *Cognitive Psychology and the Emotional Disorders*. Chichester; Wiley.

Winton, E.C., Clark, D.M. & Edelmann, R.J. (1995). Social anxiety, fear of negative evaluation and the detection of negative emotion in others. *Behaviour Research and Therapy*, **33**, 193–196.

Chapter 20

The Epidemiology of Fears and Phobias

Tim F. Chapman
Rutgers University, New Brunswick, NJ, USA

Our goal in this chapter is to review the epidemiology of phobias and fears and to present summaries of the findings of the more important studies in an easily accessible format. We divide our analysis into three major sections. In the introduction, we briefly survey the place of phobias in general in contemporary psychiatric and clinical psychological research. We include a discussion of some significant diagnostic and methodological issues of particular relevance to the sorts of epidemiologic studies we will be examining. In the Findings section, we review epidemiological studies that have attempted specifically to evaluate fears and phobias. We provide an extended discussion of the most important of these results, from the Epidemiologic Catchment Area (ECA) studies, which were conducted in the USA in the early 1980s. In the Summary and Future Directions section, we provide a brief synopsis.

PHOBIAS: CURRENT VIEWS

Phobias were among Freud's enduring interests as he constructed the grand edifice of psychoanalytic theory, lying at the heart of some of his most memorable case studies. They have provided rich sources of dramatic as well as comic inspiration for movie directors ranging from Alfred Hitchcock to Mel Brooks. They are among the most familiar aspects of the psychopathology of everyday life. Few of us know anyone who suffers from paranoid schizophrenia, but most of us can tell phobia stories—the cousin who refuses to fly because he is overcome with fear whenever the plane takes off or lands; the friend who is panic-stricken

Phobias—A Handbook of Theory, Research and Treatment. Edited by G.C.L. Davey.
© 1997 John Wiley & Sons Ltd.

whenever she sees a mouse; the child who faints whenever a hypodermic syringe is wielded in his vicinity.

These observations point to the fact that phobias are seemingly familiar, prevalent phenomena. Yet despite their familiarity, prominence and rather weighty historical credentials, it is only recently that these disorders have begun to be incorporated into the mainstream of psychiatric epidemiology.

This neglect has perhaps affected certain categories of phobia more than others. Barely 10 years ago, in a now widely cited article published in the *Archives of General Psychiatry*, Michael Liebowitz and his colleagues (Liebowitz et al., 1985) were writing of social phobia as "the neglected anxiety disorder". The neglect Liebowitz identified extended across a wide range of different clinical concerns, not just in the field of epidemiology, and it is worth briefly reviewing some of the factors that may have contributed to this comparative neglect. Two problem areas are particularly apparent.

Problem 1. Severity

There is an enduring perception that phobias are among the "less serious" forms of mental disorder. Awareness of this problem prompted Marks (1987) to observe that one reason why the label "specific phobia" is inherently preferable to the established notion of "simple phobia" in psychiatric nomenclature is because the word "simple implies a (misleading) sense of "mildness".

Few individuals who suffer from simple or social phobias ever end up in treatment for their problems (e.g. Agras, Syvester & Oliveau, 1969; Boyd et al., 1990). This finding has also been used as an index of severity, the implication being that if few seek treatment, the disorders are unlikely to be significantly impairing.

However, the question of whether treatment-seeking is indeed a valid indicator of severity is open to some question, since the same finding appears to be true for the majority of psychiatric disorders in the population (e.g. Kessler et al., 1994, Table 4), and significant new research (e.g. Schneier et al., 1994) indicates that untreated phobias may often be associated with striking social and occupational impairment.

Problem 2. Reliability Issues

Another factor that may have hindered epidemiological research into phobias is arguably problematic diagnostic reliability. Psychiatric epidemiology began its striking period of expansion in the early 1980s, in part because the statistical reliability of many of its important diagnostic constructs had been shown, more or less for the first time, to be within the acceptable-to-good range (Eaton & Kessler, 1985). This in turn occurred largely because of the adoption by researchers in the mental health field of the highly structured diagnostic criteria for identifying disorders introduced in DSM-III (American Psychiatric Association, 1980; Wilson, 1993).

Unfortunately, while disorders ranging from major depression to antisocial personality were showing moderate-to-good test–retest and inter-rater reliability in the late 1970s and early in the DSM-III era (Grove, 1987)—thereby encouraging epidemiologists to go out and search for them—the diagnostic reliability of some types of phobias and subdisorder fears tended to remain only fair-to-poor. This was so even in research studies undertaken by trained clinicians applying DSM criteria strictly. In one of the first systematic series of reliability studies of DSM-III anxiety disorders undertaken, for example, Fyer, Mannuzza and colleagues (Mannuzza et al., 1989; Fyer et al., 1989), found that even trained PhD-level clinical psychologists using a semi-structured clinical interview were often unable to reliably identify simple phobias using DSM-III and DSM-III-R (American Psychiatric Association, 1987) phobia criteria. (Reliabilities for most simple phobia categories, including general disorder categories, were consistently under 0.50, often a good deal lower.)

These results were not apparent, however, for social phobia, which was more reliable in the same studies. Indeed, not only has social phobia been shown to be a reliable diagnosis, recent research has indicated that the newly-introduced DSM-IV distinction between generalized and non-generalized social phobia is a reliably identifiable one (Mannuzza et al., 1995).

Nonetheless, since epidemiological studies are crucially dependent for their validity on the basic reliability of the constructs they examine, and since published data continue to suggest that some important phobia categories, particularly simple phobias, remain statistically unreliable, this has undoubtedly had at least some impact in the field.

Sources of Unreliability

Why have phobias remained arguably somewhat unreliable diagnoses? Among the reasons why may be that phobias have, in general, been defined in less algorithmic terms than other disorders.

DSM-IV (American Psychiatric Association, 1994) defines Specific (formerly Simple) Phobia using core concepts outlined in Table 20.1. These five basic ideas are similar in key respects to the central elements of a phobia diagnosis introduced in DSM-III. However, a close analysis reveals problematic aspects to these criteria. One is a lack of explicit attention to the question of when the *threshold* for "caseness" has been crossed; i.e. with exactly *when* fears of an object or situation become "marked, persistent, excessive, or unreasonable".

For Criterion A in Table 20.1 to be easily applicable to real-life cases, it must be assumed that there exist intersubjectively valid external "gold standards" of fear severity, which can be applied somehow to differentiating fears from phobias. If such standards do exist, however, DSM says little about them, and it certainly provides no explicit guidelines regarding how one would go about

Table 20.1   Core phobia criteria: DSM-IV

Concept A	*Persistent excessive/unreasonable fear* Marked or persistent fear that is excessive or unreasonable, cued by the presence of anticipation of a specific object or situation
Concept B	*An associated anxiety response* Exposure to the phobic stimulus almost invariably provokes an immediate anxiety response, which may take the form of a situationally bound or situationally predisposed panic attack
Concept C	*Subjective awareness of the problem* The person recognizes that the fear is excessive or unreasonable
Concept D	*Avoidance or endurance with dread* The phobic situation is avoided or else is endured with intense anxiety
Concept E	*Significant interference or distress* The avoidance, anxious anticipation, or distress in the feared situations interferes significantly with the person's normal routine, occupational/academic functioning, or social activities or relationships, or there is marked distress about having the phobia

applying them to particular cases. This issue is of particular relevance for epidemiology, of course, since ambiguity about when a threshold is crossed and when "symptoms" turn into "illness" has the potential to affect estimates of prevalence (see, for example, the recent study of social phobia by Stein, Walker & Forde, 1994).

EPIDEMIOLOGY: BACKGROUND INFORMATION

As a field, epidemiology broadly defined encompasses the study of factors affecting the distribution of health and illness in a population—over time and across space (Last, 1983). *Prevalence* is one of the discipline's most important concepts:

> The first objective of epidemiological studies is a community diagnosis to estimate the rates of illness in a population. This estimate provides a baseline for understanding the mix of disorders present and the extent to which untreated cases exist in the population. Basic prevalence rates are important for health planners, who must provide for the types of treatment services that will be needed if currently untreated cases are to be brought into the health system (Regier & Robins, 1991, p. 2).

Prevalence and Retrospective Recall

Despite its importance, prevalence is a methodologically complex notion in psychiatric epidemiology. Implicit in the concept itself is a time period—the most commonly used being 1-month, 6-month, 1-year and lifetime prevalence estimates (see, for example, Weissman et al., 1991). To gauge such estimates accurately in psychiatric research, however, requires some method of evaluating the over-time status of individuals. Determining a 1-month prevalence figure requires a cross-sectional survey (or equivalent) to determine *point prevalence* (i.e.

the number of affected individuals present in the population at a particular time), combined with a 1-month estimate of *incidence* (i.e. the number of new cases occurring over a 1-month period). The sum of the two numbers (i.e. point prevalence plus 1-month incidence) represents 1-month prevalence. (An alternative way of conceptualizing the figure is as the total number of individuals who were affected at any point during the 1-month period in question.)

Psychiatric epidemiology has typically tried to measure prevalence retrospectively. This has meant using retrospectively-oriented interview schedules, designed to evaluate either an individual's entire life-history or a portion thereof (Eaton & Kessler, 1985). Prevalence figures have thus been derived from reconstructed life-histories (as provided by the subjects during cross-sectional interviews), not from direct longitudinal observation of these individuals across time. This technique is, of course, dependent for its validity upon subjective recall. If individuals are not able accurately to recall episodes of illness, prevalence estimates will inevitably be incorrect to some extent (Ruben, 1986; Cohen, 1988).

Whom to Study? The Importance of Generalizability

Attempts to evaluate prevalence of psychiatric disorders in different groups in the population can be of limited value if their results are hard to generalize to populations beyond the one sampled. Phobia prevalence studies have been no exception to this rule. These disorders have been evaluated, for example, in patients with alcoholism (Weiss & Rosenberg, 1985; Smail et al., 1984), in patients with type 1 diabetes mellitus (Popkin et al., 1988), in women attending family physicians (Costello, Devins & Ward, 1988), and in broadly defined general practice settings (Burns, 1980). In each case, the studies are of value in regard to their specific populations, but their generalizability is limited.

Ideally, to be as representative as possible, epidemiological studies should sample target either populations that are directly representative of the population as a whole (e.g. because they rely on random probability samples of that population), or populations that are known to have predictable profiles relative to the larger population, thus permitting statistical controls to extrapolate beyond the constraints of the particular sample to the larger population (see the discussion in Leaf, Myers & McEvoy, 1991, pp. 16ff.).

FINDINGS

Epidemiological Studies of Fears and Phobias

There have been few large-scale epidemiological studies that have focused solely on phobia prevalence. Indeed, most of the information available about phobia epidemiology derives from studies whose main aims were to evaluate a variety of different disorders, of which phobias represented just one component.

Agras and colleagues (Agras, Sylvester & Oliveau, 1969) conducted what is still regarded as one of the most important population studies focusing specifically on the epidemiology of fears and phobias. The study involved a random probability sample of the household population of Burlington, Vermont, totalling 325 individuals. Forty commonly feared situations were investigated, and an overall 1-year prevalence estimate of 7.7% was reported. Most of these phobias, however, were deemed only mildly disabling. When phobias were classified as "severe", the prevalence rate was much lower, at only 0.2%.

Comparable 1-year prevalence rates from the pre-DSM-III era include a variety of results: Angst & Dobler-Mikola's (1985) 1-year prevalence estimate of 1.2% for non-agoraphobic phobias in 456 young adults identified as part of the Zurich Study; and Uhlenhuth et al.'s (1984) 1-year prevalence estimate of 2.3%. A much higher prevalence was found by Costello (1982), who examined fears and phobias in a female sample, reporting a 19.4% 1-year prevalence rate for "mild" phobias.

These observations highlight a finding that has often been made in phobia epidemiology: i.e., that wide variations in prevalence rates have been found across different studies (often to the extent that rates vary by entire orders of magnitude). One possible reason for this finding is the definitional problem discussed earlier. Numerous studies have shown that variations in the way cases are defined do indeed have the potential to significantly alter estimations of prevalence (e.g. Stein, Walker & Forde, 1994; Davidson et al., 1993; Pollard & Henderson, 1988; Bryant & Trower, 1974; Wacker et al., 1992).

Findings from the ECA Study

The Epidemiologic Catchment Area (ECA) Study is the single largest psychiatric epidemiology survey undertaken to date, with upwards of 20 000 subjects receiving detailed diagnostic interviews at five US sites (New Haven, Connecticut; Baltimore, Maryland; St. Louis, Missouri; Los Angeles, California; and Durham/Piedmont, North Carolina: see Eaton et al., 1984; Robins & Regier, 1991).

The ECA surveys were conducted in the early 1980s, and were begun in conjunction with the publication of DSM-III. They attempted to apply DSM-III diagnostic criteria as much as possible in a highly structured retrospective diagnostic interview, the Diagnostic Interview Schedule (DIS) (Robins et al., 1981). A major advantage of the DIS was that it was possible for trained lay persons to administer it, rather than clinicians (Leaf, Myers & McEvoy, 1991; Kessler et al., 1994).

The phobia data from the ECA study have been subject to detailed analysis and, although there are some problematic aspects in the data, they represent the single most useful source of information regarding phobia prevalence and distribution in the general population available to date. For this reason, these results will be described in some detail here. For more detailed information, the reader is encouraged to consult Eaton, Dryman & Weissman's (1991) summary chapter on panic and phobias in the ECA. Schneier et al. (1992) also represents a useful source for social phobias.

Phobias were defined in the ECA study in terms of "unreasonable fears of [a] particular situation". These fears had to be deemed "severe" in order for the computerized diagnostic algorithm to assign the diagnosis (Eaton, Dryman & Weissman, 1991). Typically, severity was determined by asking questions about whether the subject had engaged in help-seeking behavior for their fears (if the answer was yes, the severity criterion was automatically scored); or (b) whether the subject's fears had "interfere[d] with your life or activities a lot" (again, if yes, the fear was deemed severe). If subjects responded that they avoided the feared situation, so the fear thus caused relatively little interference, they were then asked whether the avoidance itself had "interfered with their life a lot".

In each case, the two central criteria utilized by the ECA were broadly similar to the central elements of the phobia diagnosis that were first introduced in DSM-III, and which remain current in DSM-IV. (However, note that the study relied upon the subjects' *own* evaluations of (a) whether or not the fears they experienced were "unreasonable", and (b) whether they caused "a lot" of interference.)

In terms of fears, interviewed subjects in the ECA were asked about whether they had ever experienced unreasonable fears in 15 distinct situations (see Table 20.3 for a complete listing).

Table 20.2 DIS/DSM-III life-time prevalence estimates for simple and social phobias: results from seven cross-national studies

Site	Sample size (n)	Simple phobia, L/t (%)			Social phobia, L/t (%)		
		All	M	F	All	M	F
1. ECA (4 Sites)	14429	11.3	7.8	14.5	2.7	2.5	2.9
2. Edmonton	3258	7.2	4.6	9.8	1.7	1.4	2.0
3. Christchurch, NZ	1498	n/a	n/a	n/a	3.0	4.3	3.5
4. Florence	1110	0.6	0.2	1.1	1.0	1.4	0.5
5. Puerto Rico	1513	8.6	7.6	9.6	1.6	1.5	1.6
6. Taiwan							
Metropolitan Taipei	5005	3.6	2.2	5.0	0.6	0.2	1.0
Small Town	3004	4.9	2.1	7.9	0.5	0.6	0.5
Rural	2995	2.7	1.7	3.8	0.4	0.4	0.5
7. South Korea (Rural)	1966	4.7	1.8	8.1	0.7	0.2	1.1

References for the studies reported in this table, respectively, are: ECA, Eaton, Dryman & Weissman, 1991; Edmonton, Bland, Orn & Newman, 1988; Christchurch, NZ, Wells et al., 1989; Florence, Faravelli, Innoceati & Giardindli, 1989; Puerto Rico, Canino et al., 1987; Taiwan, Hwu, Yeh & Chang, 1989; South Korea, Lee et al., 1990. ECA data do not include data from the New Haven site, since the phobia questions were different. Published Christchurch, NZ, data do not differentiate simple phobia from agoraphobia. Data from Korea do not include figures on 3134 subjects interviewed in metropolitan Seoul, since these data are not broken down by gender.

Potential Problems with ECA Phobia Data

Site Differences in Questions Asked

Although five sites were studied, not all phobia-related questions were asked at all sites, resulting in missing data. The version of the DIS used in New Haven (the first site to be evaluated in the study) did not, for example, include any questions about social phobias at all. In the definitive ECA publication on phobias (Eaton Dryman & Weissman, 1991), data from the New Haven site are not presented at all, ostensibly because of this problem. This results in an overall sample size of just over 14 000 interviewed individuals for the phobia dataset, compared to about 20 000 for the ECA data as a whole. However, data on simple phobias was collected at New Haven, and are available in other publications (e.g. Boyd et al., 1990).

Differentiation of Simple Phobias from Agoraphobia

A more significant problem is that disaggregating the data on simple phobias from those on agoraphobia is frequently impossible with the published ECA study data, since the two disorders were defined in the study with a degree of potential overlap. An example of this is that Eaton, Dryman & Weissman (1991, Table 7.5a, p. 166) lump fears of "tunnels or bridges", "crowds" and "public transport" into their "agoraphobia" category only. Yet, fears of such situations may, clinically speaking, be indicative of simple phobias rather than agoraphobia (Fyer & Klein, 1992). Applying a hierarchical rule that always assigned such fears to the agoraphobia category ignores this possibility. One consequence is that the ECA's agoraphobia category may include mixtures of individuals who do suffer from what would today be termed genuine panic-related agoraphobia (i.e. avoidance stemming from fears of having panic attacks in situations where help might not be available, or where escape might be difficult or embarrassing), and other individuals who suffer from simple phobias or social phobia, where the fear is of the situation itself and is not ultimately panic-related (Mannuzza et al., 1990). Overall, the rates of simple, and possibly social, phobias reported in ECA-related publications may thus underestimate the true prevalence of these disorders.

Overall Number of Phobic Situations Evaluated

Although the ECA study did ask about no less than 15 distinct situations, certain important categories were never explicitly covered. For example, fears of visiting dentists are known to be relatively common in the general population (Marks, 1987, p. 381 ff; Hallstrom & Halling, 1984; Francis & Stanley, 1990), but the ECA study never explicitly questioned subjects about such fears. Neither did it include any other questions about potentially common medical-related fears of blood–injury, injections, needles, or visits to doctors and/or hospitals.

Although these types of phobias may be uncommon in clinically derived (i.e. treated) samples of phobia sufferers, recent evidence suggests that they may, relatively speaking, be much more common in ill individuals in the population as a whole—most of whom remain untreated (e.g. Chapman et al., 1993). The ECA provided only a single general-purpose question about "any other unreasonable fears" to cover all these possibilities, suggesting that diagnoses may have been missed.

Questions relating to fears of social situations were also few in the ECA study, perhaps because social phobia itself was a late addition to the ECA's roster of evaluated diagnoses. Only three relevant situations were asked about in the DIS (speaking in public, eating in public, and speaking to new acquaintances). Other potential social phobic situations, such as fears of performing (not necessarily speaking) before an audience, fears of writing in public, fear of test-taking, fears of using public lavatories, or fears of authority figures, were not directly addressed. It is also unclear whether the "Other Fears" category in published ECA reports is restricted to other *simple* phobias, or if it potentially includes other fears that may have been related to social interactions (Eaton, Dryman & Weissman, 1991).

In any case, these observations suggest that the ECA study may have underestimated the true prevalence of fears of social situations as a whole, simply because the questions asked of interviewed subjects were not sufficiently specific. For a more detailed discussion of this problem, see Chapman, Mannuzza & Fyer (1995).

Results from the ECA Study

Phobic disorders as a whole in the ECA study were more prevalent than any other group of psychiatric disorders studied, a result that strongly confirms popular perceptions that these disorders are widespread (Robins et al., 1984; Eaton, Dryman & Weissman, 1991). More than 14% of all interviewed individuals met DIS/DSM-III criteria for at least one diagnosable episode of a phobic disorder during their lifetimes.

However, recall that this figure includes data from a heterogeneous agoraphobia category, which included individuals who had what today would be termed panic disorder with agoraphobia. Hence this overall 14% figure for phobias in general should probably be reduced somewhat to more accurately reflect combined rates of specific phobia and social phobia only.

As noted above, some simple phobias were almost certainly included in the aforementioned agoraphobia category. Nonetheless, simple phobias themselves still represented the single most prevalent type of disorder in the ECA, with 11.25% of 14436 subjects receiving a life-time simple phobia diagnosis. An agoraphobia diagnosis was made in 5.6% of subjects. Social phobias were less common, with 2.73% receiving a life-time diagnosis.

Site Differences

Among the most striking and curious of the phobia findings from the ECA study are strongly statistically significant differences in simple phobia prevalence rates among the five sites studied (Boyd et al., 1990). Relatively few major cross-site differences in other disorder rates were found in the ECA study as a whole, and site differences in social phobia and agoraphobia were not particularly marked. But two sites, Baltimore and Durham/Piedmont, showed prevalence rates of simple phobia that were well over twice those of two other sites—St. Louis and Los Angeles (Boyd et al., 1990: actual 1-month prevalence figures for simple phobia for the five ECA sites were, for example: Baltimore, 9.7%; Durham, 9.3%; New Haven, 4.3%; St. Louis, 3.3%; Los Angeles, 3.8%). The pattern is duplicated for lifetime prevalence, since full-blown phobias as a whole affected almost one-quarter of the entire Baltimore sample (23.7%), and over one-fifth of the Durham sample (21.8%), but less than one-in-ten individuals in St. Louis (9.5%).

These cross-site differences are marked, and perplexing. The sites in question (while obviously located in different parts of the USA) do not differ particularly strongly in terms of age structure or socio-economic profiles, and the differences remain strongly statistically significant even after controlling for these potential underlying socio-economic and age-structural site differences (Boyd et al., 1990). Eaton, Dryman & Weissman (1991) speculated that "cultural differences related to living along the East Coast" may perhaps in part explain the difference.

ECA Risk Factors for Phobic Disorders

Age

Eaton, Dryman & Weissman (1991) reported no clear overall relationship between age-at-interview and prevalence rates for phobias as a whole in the ECA data. However, Schneier et al.'s (1994) re-analysis of the ECA's social phobia data shows a distinct *inverse* age relationship for this disorder, with the highest rates of illness occurring in the youngest age groups. Whether this occurs because of a cohort effect or because older subjects tended systematically to forget earlier episodes of social phobia, or both, remains unclear. Evidence for post-World War II cohort effects for major depression has been documented by Weissman and her colleagues (e.g. Wickramaratne et al., 1989). Since major depression and social phobia are often comorbid in the general population (Schneier et al., 1992), such a cohort-rate-based explanation may well also be plausible in the case of social phobia.

Gender

Differences between men and women in phobia prevalence have been found in the ECA study for phobias of all types, particularly in the simple phobia and agoraphobia categories, both of which were typically twice as common in female subjects as they were in males. Bourdon et al. (1988) analysed these gender differences in detail, finding that higher rates of phobia were apparent in females in each of the 15 ECA phobia categories—including all three social phobia categories (although the latter differences were not statistically significant). Schneier et al.'s (1992) re-analysis of the same data found that there was in fact a statistically significant aggregate-level 3:2 tendency for ECA social phobia diagnoses to disproportionately affect women.

Taken as a whole, these findings strongly confirm the notion that phobias, including social phobia, disproportionately affect women in the general population.

Ethnicity

Clear ethnic differences were found for simple phobia rates in the ECA study (Eaton, Dryman & Weissman, 1991), but not for social phobia (Schneier et al., 1992). Prevalence rates for simple phobias were consistently almost twice as high in Black individuals, both males and females, than in Whites or Hispanics. Almost 20% of all Black individuals in the sample met criteria for a lifetime diagnosis of simple phobia vs. only 10% for both Whites and Hispanics.

The differences in Black v. White/Hispanic simple phobia rates are approximately of similar magnitude to the gender differences described above, and are thus clearly far from trivial (Brown, Eaton & Sussman, 1990). There do not appear to be any ethnicity–gender interaction effects in the data, however (Eaton, Dryman & Weissman, 1991, Table 7.2c). For example, Black women show the highest lifetime rates of simple phobia of any group (24.4%), and White and Hispanic men show the lowest rates (7.1% and 6.3%, respectively). Both these results would be predicted from a simple additive model in which gender and ethnicity represent factors that contribute independently to risks for developing disorder. Interestingly, despite the overall finding that simple phobia was more likely to affect women, the lifetime prevalence of simple phobia in Black men in the ECA study (14.1%) was a little higher than the equivalent rates in either White or Hispanic women (13.3% and 12.8%, respectively).

Marital Status

This factor is correlated with phobia diagnoses in the ECA data only in the case of social phobia (Schneier et al., 1992). Single (never married) individuals were significantly more likely to be affected by social phobia than their married counterparts. It is unclear whether this happens because pervasive fears of meeting new people, attending social gatherings, and so on, tend to handicap individuals active in the marriage market (resulting in reduced probabilities of marriage), or because remaining single is associated with increased risks for subsequently developing social phobia.

Socio-economic Factors

Socio-economic status (SES) seems to be clearly inversely associated with overall risk for developing a phobic disorder in the ECA data. Schneier et al.'s (1992) analysis of the ECA's social phobia data revealed particularly strong inverse correlations between SES and risk for developing disorder. Boyd et al. (1990) also found higher rates of phobias as a whole in groups with low SES. These findings are consistent with a wide range of previous studies in the literature that have identified inverse correlations between SES and risk for developing mental disorders of various different types (e.g. Dohrenwend, 1990).

In general, two distinct types of explanations exist for this finding (Regier & Robins, 1991; Dohrenwend et al., 1992). The first, "selection", posits that individuals who manifest symptoms of disorder are systematically selected "downwards" into low-SES occupations or settings, as a direct consequence of the impairment that the symptoms of disorder cause (e.g. an inability to finish school or college because of a social phobia of test-taking). The second explanation, "causation", posits that illness itself is actually somehow etiologically precipitated by exposure to risk factors that are characteristic of low-SES environments (Schwartz & Link, 1991). Whether selection or causation represent the best explanations for the phobia–SES findings remains unclear. The typically early age-at-first-onset that is characteristic of many phobias (e.g. Thyer et al., 1985; Schneier et al., 1992) suggests that either type of explanation may be plausible.

Sub-threshold Fears in the ECA

Detailed information regarding fear prevalence for the 15 categories evaluated in the ECA study are also available. Table 20.3 summarizes these results. These data adapt and expand upon numbers presented in Eaton, Dryman & Weissman (1991); the numbers differ somewhat from these already discussed above, because unweighted rates are used.

According to this Table, phobic symptoms (i.e. fears) in general are extraordinarily common: in fact, a clear majority of the general population (60.2%) experience "unreasonable fears" of at least one situation or stimulus at some point in their lives.

By far the most common category of fears relate to simple phobic situations: more than 50% of all subjects interviewed reported at least one such unreasonable fear. Almost one-quarter (23.3%) of all subjects report at least one agoraphobic fear. A good deal fewer (11.7%) report fears of social phobic situations.

Bugs/Mice/Snakes/Bats

Of the large number of individuals who report any fears of simple phobic situations, the category "bugs, mice, snakes or bats" is the most frequently cited. Indeed, individuals who report fears of this stimulus category comprise almost

Table 20.3 Symptoms (fears) and disorders (phobias) in the ECA Study, sorted by fear prevalence (unweighted life-time prevalence figures)

Stimulus	With any fears (symptoms) (%)	Meeting DIS/DSM-III "severe" criterion (phobias) (%)	Proportion of symptoms diagnosed (%)
Bugs, mice, snakes, bats	22.4	6.1	27
Heights	18.2	4.7	26
Water	12.5	3.3	26
Public transport	10.5	3.2	31
Storms	9.3	2.8	30
Closed spaces	8.0	2.4	30
Tunnels, bridges	7.0	2.1	30
Crowds	6.8	2.6	38
Speaking in public	6.5	1.8	28
"Other fears"	6.3	2.1	33
Talking to new acquaintances	4.7	1.4	30
Animals	3.9	1.1	28
Being alone	3.8	1.4	37
Going out by oneself	3.3	1.4	42
Eating in public	2.7	0.9	33
Any simple phobia	50.2	15.1	30
Any social phobia	11.7	3.2	27
Any agoraphobia	23.3	7.6	33
Any phobia	60.2	18.5	31

The first column of numbers represents the proportion (%) of all subjects who responded positively to the stem questions about fears ("unreasonable fear"). The middle column indicates the proportion of all subjects who also met severity criteria, and therefore received a formal DIS/DSM-III phobia diagnosis. The right hand column indicates the proportion (%) of symptomatic individuals who met severity criteria and were also eventually diagnosed as ill. "Agoraphobia" in the summary row is defined as any of the following stimuli: "being alone"; "tunnels or bridges"; "crowds"; "public transport"; and "going out by oneself". "Social phobia" in the summary row is defined as any of the following: "eating in public"; "speaking in public"; or "speaking to new acquaintances". The remaining categories refer to "simple phobia".

one-half (46%) of the total group of individuals who reported *any* simple phobic fears. The pattern for full-blown diagnoses is approximately similar. Over 6% of all individuals receive a "bugs/mice/snakes/bats" diagnosis, which comprises no less than 40% of the total group of individuals who meet full criteria for any simple phobia diagnosis. One reason why phobias in general are so common, in other words, may simply be because phobias relating to this particular stimulus category are so widespread.

Heights

Fear of heights is the second most widely-cited category of fear in the ECA data. This symptom is reported by almost 20% of all subjects, representing about 40% of the individuals who report any simple fears at all. Almost 5% of all subjects receive a full-blown diagnosis of heights phobia, which in turn represents about one-third of the total group of individuals who receive any simple phobia diagnosis.

These observations highlight a fact that is particularly apparent from Table 20.3, but which is nonetheless worth emphasizing, i.e., that a relatively small number of fear stimuli seem to contribute disproportionately to the high overall prevalence rates for both fears and disorders.

Proportion Diagnosed

Table 20.3 also indicates that, for all fear categories, a clear majority of all individuals who report fear symptoms never actually go on to meet the full-blown severity criterion, and therefore never receive a full diagnosis (Eaton, Dryman & Weissman, 1991). The percentage of symptomatic individuals who do eventually meet criteria for disorder ranges from lows of 26–27% for fears of heights, water and bugs/mice/snakes/bats, to 37–42% for fears of going out by oneself, crowds, and being alone (all of which were included in the ECA's agoraphobia category).

It is apparent that the three commonest fears (bugs/etc., heights and water) are also the three categories in which the lowest proportion of symptomatic individuals is actually ultimately diagnosed as having full-blown phobia. However, overall differences across fear categories in the proportion diagnosed are not actually very marked. In general (and with few exceptions) the pattern seems to be that only about one-quarter to one-third of all individuals who report fears of any particular stimulus will ultimately receive a full-blown diagnosis, meaning that 60–70% of all symptomatic individuals experience only mild symptoms.

Cross-national DIS/DSM-III Findings

The ECA Study provided a model for a range of similar psychiatric epidemiology surveys conducted in other parts of the world in the 1980s. These include two major studies undertaken in South-East Asia: Taiwan (Hwu, Yeh & Chang, 1989) and South Korea (Lee et al., 1990); a Canadian study undertaken in Edmonton, Alberta (Bland, Orn & Newman, 1988); a study in Christchurch, New Zealand (Wells et al., 1989); a study in Puerto Rico (Canino et al., 1987); and a smaller Italian study (Faravelli, Innocenti & Giardinelli, 1989).

All these studies used comparable versions of the DIS, translated where appropriate, and their results are therefore broadly comparable with the findings from the ECA. In general, the phobia results from these studies have typically not been subjected to the sorts of detailed analyses that the ECA data have received (a recent exception is Dick et al., 1994). But overall prevalence estimates for phobic disorders have been published for most of these studies. These are summarized, where available, in Table 20.2. The Table provides summary life-time prevalence results for social and simple phobias, broken down by gender.

The following patterns emerge particularly strongly from these data. First, simple phobias seem consistently to be widespread, and are more common across all sites than social phobias (the exception is Faravelli, Innocenti & Giardinelli, 1989, who reported very low rates of simple phobias in Florence). Second, the gender discrepancies in susceptibility to simple phobia reported in the ECA data are strongly validated across all these studies, i.e. the disorder is always more prevalent in females, often markedly so.

The results for social phobia are less consistent. Considerable cross-site variation in social phobia prevalence seems to be present, with some evidence indicating that the disorder may be less prevalent overall in South-East Asia. Although space considerations prevent this finding being examined in detail here, a more detailed discussion is available in Chapman, Mannuzza & Fyer (1995).

Findings from the National Co-morbidity Survey (NCS)

The NCS is a recent, large-scale, psychiatric epidemiologic survey of the USA population (Kessler et al., 1994). The survey differs from the earlier ECA surveys in several important respects. First, unlike the ECA data, the NCS consisted of a stratified random probability sample of the entire population of the USA, totalling more than 8000 interviewed subjects. Second, the NCS used an updated version of the DIS, the Composite International Diagnostic Interview (CIDI) (Robins et al., 1988), which evaluated not DSM-III but DSM-III-R (American Psychiatric Association, 1987) criteria.

Detailed analyses of NCS phobia data are yet to be published. However, summary lifetime prevalence figures on DSM-III-R simple and social phobias were available (Kessler et al., 1994, Table 2). A number of important similarities and differences are apparent between the ECA and NCS data.

Simple Phobia

First, the simple phobia results appear to be strikingly consistent across the two studies. As noted above, the ECA study reported an overall life-time prevalence for simple phobia of 11.25%, which is almost exactly matched by the life-time rate in the NCS (11.3%). The NCS figures for simple phobia broken down by gender are also similar to the approximately 2:1 ratio obtained by the ECA study: 15.7% of female subjects in the NCS reported a lifetime simple phobia diagnosis and 6.7% of males; compared to 14.5% of ECA females and 7.8% of ECA males.

However, the findings for social phobia in the NCS differ dramatically from those of the ECA study. In the ECA data, for example, social phobia diagnoses were, overall, only about one-quarter as common as simple phobia diagnoses in the general population (2.73% life-time for social vs. 11.25% life-time for simple phobias). By contrast, social phobias are actually *more* prevalent in the NCS data than simple phobias (13.3% social vs. 11.3% simple, life-time, respectively). This approximately *five-fold discrepancy* between the overall social phobia rates across the ECA and NCS studies calls for some explanation. This issue has recently been addressed elsewhere by the authors (Chapman, Mannuzza & Fyer, 1995). However, to summarize, several possible explanations seem to be apparent.

First, the social phobia criteria were expanded in several respects between DSM-III and DSM-III-R, which perhaps resulted in an increased scope for the social phobia diagnosis. For example, avoidant personality disorder was considered an hierarchical exclusion for receiving a social phobia diagnosis in DSM-III, but this convention was dropped in DSM-III-R. Second, DSM-III tended to conceive of social phobia in terms of a single feared situation (Liebowitz et al., 1985). DSM-III-R, by contrast, explicitly recognized that social phobia may extend across a range of different social situations (Schneier et al., 1992). Relatedly, as noted above, the DIS only asked explicitly about a limited range of potential social phobic situations, which perhaps led to an overall underestimation of the true prevalence of the disorder.

Whatever the explanations for these findings, the striking differences between the ECA and NCS figures regarding the overall prevalence of social phobia in the general population—in particular the NCS's finding that social phobia may be one of the commonest of all psychiatric disorders—has helped to focus renewed research attention on this disorder (e.g. Heimberg et al., 1995). This trend has been further encouraged by findings (e.g. Schneier et al., 1994) indicating that social phobia may in general be markedly impairing.

SUMMARY AND FUTURE DIRECTIONS

The purpose of this chapter has been to review findings from epidemiologic studies of social and simple/specific phobias. Epidemiology contributes very basic information to health-related research, in that it provides key information on the frequency with which disorders occur in populations. To date, however, studies involving phobias have been relatively few.

When they have been undertaken, overall prevalence rates have often been widely variable. This finding may be due to the continuing difficulty psychiatric classification systems have experienced regarding the problem of how to define "caseness" in phobic disorders, i.e. with providing unambiguous, reliable ways to identify the threshold of fear severity above which symptomatic individuals should be diagnosed. This problem is not trivial, and may account at least in part for why phobia prevalence rates obtained in previous studies have varied by upwards of two orders of magnitude, i.e. from 0.2% to more than 20%.

The phobia findings from the ECA represents the largest single source of information on phobia prevalence available to date. These results, combined with more recent results from other studies both in the USA and elsewhere, suggest the following basic conclusions:

1.   Fears in general are extremely prevalent phenomena in the general population. They probably affect more than 50% of all individuals at some point in

their lives. Phobias too are remarkably common; simple/specific phobia alone appears consistently to affect more than 10% of the population during their lifetimes. This result appears to have considerable validity (at least in the USA), having been replicated independently by the two most important large-scale studies done to date. (Cross-national findings also generally point to prevalence rates with similar orders of magnitude, with overall rates typically between 3 and 10%.)

Social phobia estimates are more variable, but recent studies consistently seem to indicate that early evaluations of social phobia prevalence markedly underestimated the frequency with which this disorder occurs. The most recent findings indicate that more than 10% of the population probably suffers from social phobia also at some point in their lives. But again, ongoing debates about case definition and thresholds mean that these results may be subject to change in the future.

2. Striking gender discrepancies exist regarding overall prevalence of phobias. Women seem to be at twice the overall life-time risk for developing simple phobia than men. Such gender differences are less marked for social phobia, although women do still seem to be most at risk. This elevation in risk for females seems to be apparent across a wide range of phobic situations.

3. A variety of other socio-economic and demographic factors correlate, often strongly, with phobia prevalence. Among the most important are: age (social phobia; young persons at greatest risk); ethnicity (simple/specific phobias; Blacks in the US at greatest risk); marital status (social phobias; unmarried individuals at greatest risk); and socio-economic status (phobias in general; low-SES groups at highest risk).

In the past phobias have arguably been neglected in epidemiologic research. This is so despite the fact they are among the commonest of all psychiatric conditions, often causing striking impairment in untreated individuals in the general population, and resulting in a large overall cumulative impact on society as a whole. Bearing all this in mind, future epidemiologic research must begin from the observation that phobias lie not at the periphery, but at the very center, of the study of mental health and illness.

REFERENCES

Agras, W.S., Sylvester D. & Oliveau, DC. (1969). The Epidemiology of common fears and phobias, *Compr. Psychiatry*, **10**, 151–156.

American Psychiatric Association (1980). *Diagnostic and Statistical Manual of Mental Disorders* 3rd edn. (DSM-III). Washington, DC: American Psychiatric Association.

American Psychiatric Association (1987). *Diagnostic and Statistical Manual of Mental Disorders*, 3rd edn. Revised (DSM-III-R). Washington, DC: American Psychiatric Association.

American Psychiatric Association (1994). *Diagnostic and Statistical Manual of Mental Disorders*, 4th edn. (DSM-IV). Washington, DC: American Psychiatric Association.

Angst J. & Dobler-Mikola, A. (1985). The Zurich Study VI. A continuum from depression to anxiety disorders? *Eur. Arch. Psychiatr. Neurol. Sci.*, **235**, 179–186.

Bland, R.C., Orn, H. & Newman, S.C. (1988). Lifetime prevalence of psychiatric disorders in Edmonton. *Acta Psychiatrica Scandinavica*, **77**(suppl. 338), 24–32.

Bourdon, K.H., Boyd, J.H., Rae, D.S., Burns, B.J., Thompson, J.W. & Locke, B.Z. (1988). Gender differences in phobias: results from the ECA community survey. *Journal of Anxiety Disorders*, **2**, 227–241.

Boyd, J.H., Rae, D.S., Thompson, J.W., Burns, B.J., Bourdon, K., Locke, B.Z. & Regier, D.A. (1990). Phobia: prevalence and risk factors. *Social Psychiatrica and Psychiatric Epidemiology*, **25**(6), 314–323.

Brown, D.R., Eaton, W.W. & Sussman, L. (1990). Racial differences in prevalence of phobic disorders. *Journal Nervous and Mental Disease*, **178**, 434–441.

Bryant, B. & Trower, P.E. (1974). Social difficulty in a student sample. *British Journal of Educational Psychology*, **44**, 13–21.

Burns, L.E. (1980). The epidemiology of fears and phobias in general practice. *J. Int. Med. Res.*, **8**(suppl. 3), 1–7.

Canino, G.J., Bird, H.R., Shrout, P.E., Rubio-Stipec, M., Bravo, M., Martinez, R, Sesman, M. & Guevara, L.M. (1987). The prevalence of specific psychiatric disorders in Puerto Rico. *Archives of General Psychiatry*, **44**, 727–735.

Chapman, T.F., Fyer, A.J., Mannuzza, S. & Klein, D.F. (1993). A comparison of treated and untreated simple phobia. *American Journal of Psychiatry*, **150** (May), 816–818.

Chapman, T.F., Mannuzza, S. & Fyer, A.J. (1995). Epidemiologic and family studies of social phobia. In R. Heimberg, M.R. Liebowitz, D. Hope & F. Schneier (eds), *Social Phobia: Diagnosis, Assessment, and Treatment*. New York: Guilford.

Cohen, P. (1988). The effects of instruments and informants on ascertainment. In D.L. Dunner, E.S. Gershon & J.E. Barrett (eds), *Relatives at Risk for Mental Disorder*. New York: Raven.

Costello, C.G., Devins, G.M. & Ward, K.W. (1988). The prevalence of fears, phobias and anxiety disorders and their relationship with depression in women attending family physicians. *Behaviour Research and Therapy*, **26**, 311–320.

Costello, C.G. (1982). Fears and phobias in women: a community study. *Journal of Abnormal Psychology*, **91**, 280–286.

Davidson, J.R.T., Hughes, D.L., George, L,K. & Blazer D.G. (1993). The epidemiology of social phobia: findings from the Duke Epidemiologic Catchment Area study. *Psychological Medicine*, **23**, 709–718.

Dick, C.L., Sowa, B., Bland, R.C. & Newman, S.C. (1994). Epidemiology of psychiatric disorders in Edmonton. Phobic disorders. *Acta Psychiatrica Scandinavica*, suppl. **376**, 36–44.

Dohrenwend, B.P. (1990). Socioeconomic status (SES) and psychiatric disorders: are the issues still compelling? *Social Psychiatry and Psychiatric Epidemiology*, **25**, 41–47.

Dohrenwend, B.P., Levav, I., Shrout, P.E., Schwartz, S., Naveh, G., Link, B.G., Skodol, A.E. & Stueve, A. (1992). Socioeconomic status and psychiatric disorders: the causation–selection issue. *Science*, **255**, 946–951.

Eaton, W.W. & Kessler, L.G. (eds) (1985). *Epidemiologic Field Methods in Psychiatry: the NIMH Epidemiologic Catchment Area Program*. Orlando, FL: Academic Press.

Eaton, W.W., Dryman, A. & Weissman, M.M. (1991). Panic and Phobia. In L.N. Robins & D.A. Regier (eds), *Psychiatric Disorders in America: the Epidemiologic Catchment Area Study* (pp. 155–179). New York: Free Press.

Eaton, W.W., Holzer C.E. III, von Korff, M., Anthony, J.C., Helzer, J.E., George, L., Burman, M.A., Boyd, J.H., Kessler, L.G. & Locke, B.Z. (1984). The design of the Epidemiologic Catchment Area surveys: the control and measurement of error. *Archives of General Psychiatry*, **41**, 942–948.

Faravelli, C.B., Innocenti, G.D. & Giardinelli, L. (1989). Epidemiology of anxiety disorders in Florence. *Acta Psychiatrica Scandinavica*, **79**, 308–312.

Francis, R.D. & Stanley, G.V. (1990). Estimating the prevalence of dental phobias. *Australian Dental Journal*, **35**, 449–453.

Fyer, A.J. & Klein, D.F. (1992). Agoraphobia, social phobia, and simple phobia. In R. Michels, A.M. Cooper & S.B. Guze (eds), *Psychiatry*, Vol 1. Philadelphia: J.B. Lippincott.

Fyer, A.J., Mannuzza, S., Martin, L.Y., Gallops, M.S., Endicott, J., Schleyer, B., Gorman, J., Liebowitz, M. & Klein, D.F. (1989). Reliability of anxiety assessment. II. Symptom agreement. *Archives of General Psychiatry*, **46**, 1102–1110.

Grove, W.M. (1987). The reliability of psychiatric diagnosis. In C.G. Last & M. Hersen (eds), *Issues in Diagnostic Research* (pp. 99–119). New York: Plenum.

Hallstrom, T. & Halling, A. (1984). Prevalence of dentistry phobia and its relation to missing teeth, alveolar bone loss and dental care habits in an urban community sample. *Acta Psychiatrica Scandinavica*, **70**, 438–446.

Heimberg, R., Liebowitz, M., Hope, D. & Schneier, F. (eds) (1995). *Social Phobia: Diagnosis, Assessment, and Treatment*. New York: Guilford.

Hwu, H., Yeh, E.K. & Chang, L.Y. (1989). Prevalence of psychiatric disorders in Taiwan defined by the Chinese Diagnostic Interview Schedule. *Acta Psychiatrica Scandinavica*, **79**, 136–147.

Kessler, R.C., McGonagle, K., Zhao, S., Nelson, C., Hughes, M., Eschlemann, S., Wittchen, H.-U. & Kendler, K.S. (1994). Lifetime and 12-month prevalence of DSM-III-R psychiatric disorders in the United States: results from the National Comorbidity Survey. *Archives of General Psychiatry*, **51**, 8–19.

Last, J.M. (1983). *A Dictionary of Epidemiology*. New York: Oxford University Press.

Leaf, P.J., Myers, J.K. & McEvoy, L.T. (1991). Procedures used in the Epidemiologic Catchment Area Study. In L.N. Robins & D.A. Regier (eds), *Psychiatric Disorders in America: the epidemiologic Catchment Area Study* (pp. 11–32). New York: Free Press.

Lee, C.-K., Kwak, Y.-S., Yamamoto, J., Rhee, H., Kim, Y.S., Han, J.H., Choi, J.O. & Lee, Y.H. (1990). Psychiatric epidemiology in Korea: I. Gender and age differences in Seoul. *Journal of Nervous and Mental Disease*, **178**, 242–246.

Liebowitz, M.R., Gorman, J.M., Fyer, A.J. & Klein, D.F. (1985). Social phobia: review of a neglected anxiety disorder. *Archives of General Psychiatry*, **42**, 729–735.

Mannuzza, S., Fyer, A.J., Martin, L.Y., Gallops, M.S., Endicott, J., Schleyer, B., Gorman, J., Liebowitz, M. & Klein, D.F. (1989). Reliability of anxiety assessment. I. Diagnostic agreement. *Archives of General Psychiatry*, **46**, 1093–1101.

Mannuzza, S., Fyer, A.J., Liebowitz, M. & Klein, D.F. (1990). Delineating the boundaries of social phobia: its relationship to panic disorder and agoraphobia. *Journal of Anxiety Disorders*, **4**, 41–59.

Mannuzza, S., Schneier, F.R., Chapman, T.F., Liebowitz, M.R., Klein, D.F. & Fyer, A.J. (1995). Generalized social phobia: reliability and validity. *Archives of General Psychiatry*, **52**, 230–237.

Marks, I.M. (1987). *Fears, Phobias, and Rituals: Panic, Anxiety, and their Disorders*. New York: Oxford University Press.

Pollard, C.A. & Henderson, J.G. (1988). Four types of social phobia ·in a community sample. *Journal of Nervous and Mental Disease*, **176**, 440–445.

Popkin, M.K., Callies, A.L., Lentz, R.D., Colon, E.A. & Sutherland, D.E. (1988). Prevalence of major depression, simple phobia and other psychiatric disorders in patients with long-standing type I diabetes mellitus. *Archives of General Psychiatry*, **45**, 64–68.

Regier, D.A. & Robins, L.N. (1991). Introduction. In L.N. Robins & D.A. Regier (eds), *Psychiatric Disorders in America: the Epidemiologic Catchment Area Study* (pp. 1–10). New York: Free Press.

Robins, L.N., Helzer, J.E., Croughan, J. & Ratcliff, K.S. (1981). National Institute of Mental Health Diagnostic Interview Schedule: its history, characteristics and validity. *Archives of General Psychiatry*, **38**, 381–389.

Robins, L.N., Helzer, J.E., Weissman, M.M., Orvaschel, H., Gruenberg, E., Burke, J.D. & Regier, D.A. (1984). Lifetime prevalence of specific psychiatric disorders in three sites. *Archives of General Psychiatry*, **41**, 949–958.

Robins, L.N. & Regier, D.A. (eds) (1991). *Psychiatric Disorders in America: the Epidemiologic Catchment Area Study*. New York: Free Press.

Robins, L.N., Wing, J., Wittchen, H.-U. & Helzer, J.E. (1988). The Composite International Diagnostic Interview: an epidemiologic instrument suitable for use in conjunction with different diagnostic systems and in different cultures. *Archives of General Psychiatry*, **45**, 1069–1077.

Ruben D.C. (ed.) (1986). *Autobiographical Memory*. New York: Cambridge University Press.

Schneier, F.R., Heckelman, L.R., Garfinkel, R., Campeas, R., Fallon, B.A., Gitow, A., Street., L., Del Bene, D. & Liebowitz, M. (1994). Functional impairment in social phobia. *Journal of Clinical Psychiatry*, **55**, 322–331.

Schneier, F.R., Johnson, J., Hornig, C.D., Liebowitz, M.R. & Weissman, M.M. (1992). Social phobia: comorbidity and morbidity in an epidemiologic sample. *Archives of General Psychiatry*, **49**, 282–288.

Schwartz, S. & Link, B.G. (1991). Sociological perspectives on mental health: an integrative approach. In D. Offer & M. Sabshin (eds), *The Diversity of Normal Behavior* (pp. 239–274). New York: Basic Books.

Smail, P., Stockwell, T., Canter, S. & Hodgson, R. (1984). Alcohol dependence and phobic anxiety states. I. A prevalence study. *British Journal of Psychiatry*, **144**, 53–57.

Stein, M.B., Walker, J.R. & Forde, D.R. (1994). Setting diagnostic thresholds for social phobia: considerations from a community survey of social anxiety. *American Journal of Psychiatry*, **151**, 408–412.

Thyer, B.A., Parrish, R.T., Curtis, G.C., Nesse, R.M. & Cameron, O.G (1985). Ages of onset of DSM-III anxiety disorders. *Compr. Psychiatry*, **26**, 113–122.

Uhlenhuth, E.H., Balter, M.B., Mellinger, G.D., Cisin, I.H. & Clinthorne, J. (1984). Anxiety disorders: prevalence and treatment. *Curr. Med. Res. Opin.*, **8**(suppl. 4), 37–47.

Wacker, H.R., Müllejans, R., Klein, K.H. & Battegay, R. (1992). Identification of cases of anxiety disorders and affective disorders in the community according to ICD 10 and DSM-III-R by using the Composite International Diagnostic Interview (CIDI). *International Journal of Methods in Psychiatric Research*, **2**, 91–100.

Weiss, K.J. & Rosenberg, D.J. (1985). Prevalence of anxiety disorder among alcoholics. *Journal of Clinical Psychiatry*, **46**, 3–5.

Weissman, M.M., Bruce, M.L., Leaf, P.J., Florio, L.P. & Holzer, C. III (1991). Affective disorders. In L.N. Robins & D.A. Regier (eds), *Psychiatric Disorders in America: the Epidemiologic Catchment Area Study* (pp. 53–80). New York: Free Press.

Wells J.E., Bushnell, J.A., Hornblow, A.R., Joyce P.R. & Oakley-Browne, M.A. (1989). Christchurch Psychiatric Epidemiology Study: methodology and lifetime prevalence for specific psychiatric disorders. *Australian and New Zealand Journal of Psychiatry*, **23**, 315–326.

Wickramaratne, P.J., Weissman, M.M., Leaf, P.J. & Holford, T.R. (1989). Age, period and cohort effects on the risk of major depression: results from five United States communities. *Journal of Clinical Epidemiology*, **42**, 333–343.

Wilson, M. (1993). DSM-III and the transformation of American psychiatry. *American Journal of Psychiatry*, **150**(3), 399–410.

Author Index

Index compiled by Liz Granger

Subject Index

Related titles of interest from Wiley...

Handbook of Memory Disorders
Edited by Alan Baddeley, Barbara A. Wilson and Fraser Watts

An international and authoritative team of leading scientists and clinicians present a critical and thorough account of memory disorders.

0-471-95078-5   668pp   1995   Hardback
0-471-96704-1   668pp   1996   Paperback

Worrying
Perspectives on Theory, Assessment and Treatment
Edited by Graham C.L. Davey and Frank Tallis

Outlines how worry may be assessed and how it may affect people throughout the lifespan. The authors then place this in the context of the latest developments in cognitive and behavioural therapy.

0-471-94114-X   328pp   1994   Hardback
0-471-96803-X   328pp   1995   Paperback

Handbook of Eating Disorders
Theory, Treatment and Research
Edited by George Szmukler, Christopher Dare and Janet Treasure

Provides an up-to-date review of the eating disorders anorexia nervosa and bulimia nervosa.

0-471-96307-0   438pp   1995   Paperback

Psychology in Counselling and Therapeutic Practice
Jill D. Wilkinson and Elizabeth A. Campbell

Offers a concise and selective account of psychological concepts and processes, illustrated by examples and cases that relate to problems and processes of counselling.

0-471-95562-0   300pp   1997   Paperback

Visit the Wiley Home Page at http://www.wiley.co.uk